Affirmative Counseling
with
LGBTQI+
People

edited by
Misty M. Ginicola • Cheri Smith • Joel M. Filmore

AMERICAN COUNSELING
ASSOCIATION
2461 Eisenhower Avenue • Suite 300
Alexandria, VA 22331
www.counseling.org

Affirmative Counseling with LGBTQI+ People

American Counseling Association
2461 Eisenhower Avenue • Suite 300
Alexandria, VA 22331

Associate Publisher   Carolyn C. Baker

Digital and Print Development Editor   Nancy Driver

Senior Production Manager   Bonny E. Gaston

Production Coordinator   Karen Thompson

Copy Editor   Beth Ciha

Cover and text design by Bonny E. Gaston

Library of Congress Cataloging-in-Publication Data
Names: Ginicola, Misty M., author. | Smith, Cheri, author. | Filmore, Joel M., author.
Title: Affirmative counseling with LGBTQI+ people / Misty M. Ginicola, Cheri Smith,
    Joel M. Filmore.
Description: Alexandria, VA : American Counseling Association, 2017. | Includes
    bibliographical references and index.
Identifiers: LCCN 2016048753 | ISBN 9781556203558 (pbk. : alk. paper)
Subjects: LCSH: Sexual minorities—Counseling of. | Sexual minorities—Psychology.
Classification: LCC RC451.4.G39 G56 2017 | DDC 616.890086/64—dc23 LC record
    available at https://lccn.loc.gov/2016048753

With ignorance comes fear—from fear comes bigotry.
Education is the key to acceptance.

—Kathleen Patel

• • •

We would like to dedicate this book to all of those who are brave enough to live and love authentically as well as those who are looking for hope that it does indeed get better. We would also like to honor those counselors and helping professionals who commit their lives to learning about and helping lesbian, gay, bisexual, transgender, queer, questioning, intersex, asexual, ally, pansexual/polysexual, and two-spirited people find their way, their joy, and their value.

Table of Contents

Section I
Foundations

Section II
Counseling Considerations and Counseling Strategies

Developmental Issues for LGBTQI+ People

Counseling Treatment Issues With LGBTQI+ Clients

Section III
Specialized Populations

Section IV
Emerging Issues

The Role of Ethnicity

The Role of Religion

Counselor Advocacy

Preface

We should indeed keep calm in the face of difference
and live our lives in a state of inclusion and
wonder at the diversity of humanity.

—George Takei

• • •

Possessing counseling competence in serving the lesbian, gay, bisexual, transgender, queer, questioning, intersex, asexual, ally, pansexual/polysexual, and two-spirited (LGBTQQIAAP-2S, henceforth referred to as LGBTQI+) communities is important, particularly because previous research has shown that large numbers of this population seek therapy (Garnets, Hancock, Cochran, Goodchilds, & Peplau, 1991). If counselors are unprepared for work with this population, they could potentially do harm to these clients. Many counselors have not received adequate training to work with affectional orientation and gender minority clients; LGBTQI+ clients are aware of this deficit in the field and prescreen therapists for safety and competence in issues of affectional orientation and gender orientation (Kaufman et al., 1997; Liddle, 1997). Although many standard counseling interventions will be appropriate for work with the LGBTQI+ population, counselors need an awareness and knowledge of this population and its cultures and subcultures that extend beyond typical client concerns (Bieschke, Perez, & DeBord, 2007; Dworkin & Pope, 2012).

The needs of LGBTQI+ individuals are different from those of clients who identify as heterosexual because of variant affectional and developmental experiences that occur as well as the increased stigma and oppression that they may face in their current cultural context. A theme throughout this book is the high level of minority stress that LGBTQI+ persons experience. Without a doubt, common issues of oppression, abuse and neglect, and discrimination are threaded throughout the subgroups of the LGBTQI+ communities; however, it is both the common struggles and the unique ones that are addressed in this text.

Members of the LGBTQI+ population have frequently been lumped together as if their individual needs were exactly the same and they formed one singular community. However, there is a rich history of development, strengths, and needs in this population, both as a collective group and also in its singular subgroups (Bérubé, 1990; Faderman, 1991) that bears acknowledgment and understanding. For example, issues specific to the development of lesbian identity and culture are different from those of other subgroups (Chapman & Brannock, 1987; McCarn & Fassinger, 1996); the same can be said for identity development for gay men, bisexuals, and transgender individuals.

Another theme that is addressed in this book and is crucial for counselors to understand is that of intersectionality; stressors and difficulties are compounded for LGBTQI+ individuals when other minority statuses, such as race and ethnicity, are also present (Chung & Katayama, 1998). Racial identity development and affectional orientation identity development are complex processes, with research suggesting that they occur concurrently (Jamil, Harper, & Fernandez, 2009). Although some assume that in LGBTQI+ communities there is more acceptance of differences, including race, there is not; in fact, there is just as much racism and prejudice in the queer community as the heterosexual community (Goode-Cross & Tager, 2011). Queer people of color (QPOC) often feel as if they are unable to identify with the predominantly White gay culture (Balsam, Molina, Beadnell, Simoni, & Walters, 2011). They also have difficulty identifying with their racial/ethnic culture, from which they risk rejection and the loss of their only social support and cultural ties because of their affectional orientation (Diamond & Savin-Williams, 2003). The research that has focused on the intersection of race/ethnicity and affectional orientation has suggested that individuals who have to negotiate multiple identities, such as QPOC, are at an increased risk for psychosocial distress because of heterosexism and racism, which is beyond what White LGBTQI+ individuals experience (Smith, Foley, & Chaney, 2008). The discrimination suffered by QPOC is also unique based on various cultural/religious traditions and can contribute to isolation among QPOC, exacerbating psychosocial distress (Lewis, 2009). Along with these factors, one must also consider socioeconomic variables and geography, as well as other -isms that can impact a client's development, such as sexism, ageism, ableism, and the like (Smith et al., 2008).

Given these complex and specialized needs, it is imperative that counselors and other helping professionals obtain specific training on working with members of the LGBTQI+ communities; a brief class session in a multicultural course will not prepare practitioners for understanding the needs and interventions that the entirety of this population requires. As use of the LGBT acronym has increased, so too has the need to understand these complex, varied, and sometimes overlapping identities. A competent counselor needs to have an awareness of the LGBTQI+ experience and knowledge of this population and its specialized needs, as well as the skills required to work with various subcultures in the LGBTQI+ population.

This book seeks to aid in filling the gap in counselor training by providing a current and inclusive reference for developing the awareness, knowledge, and skills needed to work with the LGBTQI+ population. The intended audience is counselor educators, all counselors-in-training, and practicing counselors. This book is also appropriate for other helping professionals, such as psychologists and social workers.

By seeking out the most recent literature and including chapters by authors who serve as experts on LGBTQI+ populations in the counseling field, we have focused on making this book current and of practical importance for the clinician, student, and educator. The book is divided into four main sections: (a) Foundations, (b) Counseling Considerations and Counseling Strategies, (c) Specialized Populations, and (d) Emerging Issues.

Section I: Foundations

In Chapter 1, "Developing Competence in Working With LGBTQI+ Communities: Awareness, Knowledge, Skills, and Action," the authors review the multicultural counseling framework and multiple American Counseling Association–based competencies as well as aspects of basic competencies, including terminology and a history of oppression among the LGBTQI+ population. In Chapter 2, the author reviews the science of gender and affectional orientation.

Section II: Counseling Considerations and Counseling Strategies

In this section developmental issues for LGBTQI+ people are explored. The authors of Chapter 3 provide a conceptualization of growing up LGBTQI+ and how being an affectional orientation and gender minority may result in additional challenges to development. In Chapter 4, the authors review what is known about LGBTQI+ youth development. Chapter 5 discusses LGBTQI+ persons in adulthood. In Chapter 6, issues surrounding identity development, coming out, and family adjustment are reviewed. It is crucial to understand the process of coming to terms with having a minority gender and/or affectional orientation as well as how the coming out process impacts both individuals and their families. Finally, in Chapter 7, the authors review issues that, because of excessive minority stress, may bring those in the LGBTQI+ population in for medical care and mental health counseling. This chapter, "Physical and Mental Health Challenges Found in the LGBTQI+ Population," provides counselors with an understanding of normative symptoms in the population due to the oppression, marginalization, and trauma surrounding being a minority. Special attention is paid to how stress may be expressed differently in the subgroups of the queer community.

In addition, counseling treatment issues with LGBTQI+ clients are explored. In Chapter 8, the empirical basis of treatment strategies for these clients is reviewed in "Disaffirming Therapy: The Ascent and Descent of Sexual Orientation Change Efforts," in which the authors explore the traumatizing role that past mental health professionals and faith-based leaders played in treating affectional orientation as a curable disease. Chapter 9, "Evidence-Based Practice for Counseling the LGBTQI+ Population," provides a review of the literature as well as an introduction to the importance of using an affirmative approach with clients who are gender and affectional orientation minorities. Finally, in Chapter 10, the authors focus specifically on the affirmative approach in "Affirmative, Strengths-Based Counseling With LGBTQI+ People." The elements of an affirmative approach, as well as specific methods that can be utilized, are discussed.

Section III: Specialized Populations

In this section, the individual populations that make up the LGBTQI+ community are reviewed in order to provide the crucial counseling competence required to meet each population's specialized needs. In each chapter, authors address (a) an awareness of differences in the population, (b) knowledge of issues and problems faced by the specific population, and (c) the counseling skills and techniques appropriate for use with each specialized population.

Chapters 11 through 19 discuss issues relevant to counseling lesbian clients, gay male clients, bisexual/pansexual/polysexual clients (individuals whose relationships and bonding are not based on gender), transgender clients (individuals whose designated sex at birth and gender identity do not match), queer and genderqueer clients (individuals whose gender and affectional orientation do not fit into distinct categories), clients questioning their affectional orientation, intersex clients (those born with ambiguous or both male and female genitalia), asexual clients (those who have little or no sexual attraction to others), and two-spirit clients (individuals who are both indigenous peoples to the Americas and LGBTQI+ persons).

Section IV: Emerging Issues

The last section includes emerging issues in the field: ethnicity, religion, and advocacy needs.

The Role of Ethnicity

In Chapter 20, "Counseling an LGBTQI+ Person of Color," the intersectional issues of ethnicity and LGBTQI+ identity are discussed. In Chapter 21, "Counseling LGBTQI+ Immigrants," intersectional issues surrounding immigration and naturalization as a member of the queer community are delineated.

The Role of Religion

In Chapter 22, "The Role of Religion and Spirituality in Counseling the LGBTQI+ Client," the impact of religion on clients' identity development, numerous affirmative religions, and issues involving counselors' religious beliefs are discussed. In Chapter 23, "The GRACE Model of Counseling: Navigating Intersections of Affectional Orientation and Christian Spirituality," an established counseling model for working with religious LGBTQI+ clients is delineated. In Chapter 24, "Working With LGBTQI+ Clients Who Have Experienced Religious and Spiritual Abuse Using a Trauma-Informed Approach," the authors discuss the impact of religious trauma.

Counselor Advocacy

In Chapter 25, "Becoming an Ally: Personal, Clinical, and School-Based Social Justice Interventions," the authors discuss why it is important for counselors to identify as allies as well as how counselors can do so in their specific setting.

Glossary of Terms

The book concludes with an extensive glossary of terms that counselors working with this community should know. Problematic terms to avoid are also covered in the glossary.

Conclusion

Each chapter in this book focuses not only on the knowledge base important for practice but also on specific counseling strategies important for treatment planning. The goal of this book is to provide information that is widely needed in practice as well as in counselor training programs. Each chapter additionally has several elements to help counselors understand how to apply this knowledge as well as how to gain resources in the field. First, the "Awareness of Attitudes and Beliefs Self-Check" has three questions designed to increase counselors' cultural competence, particularly their self-awareness of marginalization and privilege. Second, each chapter contains a brief narrative and case study of a client who represents the content covered. These narratives provide a context that personalizes the information and helps the reader envision a potential client. This context is important, as it helps in the development of a practical framework of counseling strategies for a client who could present in a counselor's practice or agency. It also provides a transition into each chapter, where authors provide the essential information for counseling practice via theoretical knowledge and established research. At the end of each chapter is a list of five questions related to the original case that represents content for further discussion, which is especially useful for practicing counselors and counselor educators. Finally, online resources are provided to guide readers to more information on each topic.

When counselors have the awareness, knowledge, and skills required to work with the LGBTQI+ population, they will be much more competent providers. The key to being an effective counselor for members of these communities is truly being able to work with each client using an authentic, ethical, and affirmative approach tailored to that client's individual needs and identity. This book provides a deeper understanding of the theory and process behind counseling LGBTQI+ clients, what these clients' lives and cultures may entail, and trends in serving this population. We believe that with this information, counselors will enhance their aptitude for serving the needs of this population, which often faces misunderstanding and rejection from others in their lives. Counselors who work with this population can then provide the understanding, acceptance, affirmation, and healing that LGBTQI+ clients so very often seek in counseling.

References

Balsam, K. F., Molina, Y., Beadnell, B., Simoni, J., & Walters, K. (2011). Measuring multiple minority stress: The LGBT People of Color Microaggressions Scale. *Cultural Diversity and Ethnic Minority Psychology, 17*(2), 163–174.

Bérubé, A. (1990). *Coming out under fire: The history of gay men and women in WWII.* New York, NY: Free Press.

Bieschke, K. J., Perez, R. M., & DeBord, K. A. (Eds.). (2007). *Handbook of counseling and psychotherapy with lesbian, gay, bisexual and transgender clients* (2nd ed.). Washington, DC: American Psychological Association.

Chapman, B. E., & Brannock, J. C. (1987). Proposed model of lesbian identity development. *Journal of Homosexuality, 14*(3–4), 69–80.

Chung, Y. B., & Katayama, M. (1998). Ethnic and sexual identity development of Asian American lesbian and gay adolescents. *Professional School Counseling, 1,* 21–25.

Diamond, L. D., & Savin-Williams, R. C. (2003). Gender and sexual identity. In R. M. Lerner, F. Jacobs, & D. Wertlieb (Eds.), *Handbook of applied developmental science: Promoting positive child, adolescent, and family development through research, policies, and programs: Applying developmental science for youth and families* (Vol. 1, pp. 101–121). Thousand Oaks, CA: Sage.

Dworkin, S. H., & Pope, M. (2012). *Casebook for counseling lesbian, gay, bisexual and transgender persons and their families.* Alexandria, VA: American Counseling Association.

Faderman, L. (1991). *Odd girls and twilight lovers: A history of lesbian life in twentieth-century America.* New York, NY: Columbia University Press.

Garnets, L., Hancock, K. A., Cochran, S. D., Goodchilds, J., & Peplau, L. (1991). Issues in psychotherapy with lesbians and gay men: A survey of psychologists. *American Psychologist, 46,* 964–972. doi:10.1037/0003-066X.46.9.964

Goode-Cross, D. T., & Tager, D. (2011). Negotiating multiple identities: How African American gay and bisexual men persist at a predominantly White institution. *Journal of Homosexuality, 58,* 1235–1254.

Jamil, O. B., Harper, G. W., & Fernandez, M. I. (2009). Sexual and ethnic identity development among gay/bisexual/questioning (GBQ) male ethnic minority adolescents. *Cultural Diversity & Ethnic Minority Psychology, 15*(3), 203–214.

Kaufman, J. S., Carlozzi, A. F., Boswell, D. L., Barnes, L. B., Wheeler-Scruggs, K., & Levy, P. A. (1997). Factors influencing therapist selection among gays, lesbians and bisexuals. *Counselling Psychology Quarterly, 10*(3), 287–297. doi:10.1080/09515079708254180

Lewis, N. M. (2009). Mental health in sexual minorities: Recent indicators, trends, and their relationships to place in North America and Europe. *Health & Place, 15,* 1029–1045.

Liddle, B. J. (1997). Gay and lesbian clients' selection of therapists and utilization of therapy. *Psychotherapy: Theory, Research, Practice, Training, 34*(1), 11–18. doi:10.1037/h0087742

McCarn, S. R., & Fassinger, R. E. (1996). Revisioning sexual minority identity formation: A new model of lesbian identity and its implications for counseling and research. *The Counseling Psychologist, 24,* 508–534.

Smith, L., Foley, P. F., & Chaney, M. P. (2008). Addressing classism, ableism, and heterosexism in counselor education. *Journal of Counseling & Development, 86,* 303–309.

About the Editors

Misty M. Ginicola, PhD, is a professor in the clinical mental health counseling program in the Counseling and School Psychology Department at Southern Connecticut State University.

Dr. Ginicola earned a bachelor's degree in psychology from State University of New York at Cortland. She earned a master's in psychology from State University of New York at New Paltz, where she received training in counseling psychology. She received two additional master's degrees (MS, MPh) from Yale University and graduated with a Doctor of Philosophy from Yale in 2006, where she completed her postdoctoral fellowship focusing on school-based mental health programming and social-emotional skills in youth.

Dr. Ginicola is of Cherokee and Celtic descent and identifies as two-spirited. Her personal experiences and professional interests have developed into specific research areas: working with diverse clients, including the lesbian, gay, bisexual, transgender, queer, questioning, intersex, asexual, ally, pansexual/polysexual, and two-spirited (LGBTQI+) population; teaching multicultural competence; and teaching creative counseling strategies. Her previous and ongoing research studies address the broad definition of multicultural issues, including ethnicity, disability, women's issues, affectional orientation and gender orientation, and religion and spirituality, among others.

She additionally serves as her department's liaison for the Council for Accreditation of Counseling and Related Educational Programs and chair of the Diversity Committee. She also is currently the chair of the President's Commission of Campus Climate and Inclusion LGBTQI+ Subcommittee. In the Connecticut Counseling Association, Dr. Ginicola is a past-president of the Connecticut Association for Counseling Education and Supervision; chair of the Special Interest Group Connecticut-Association for Lesbian, Gay, Bisexual, and Transgender Issues in Counseling (CT-ALGBTIC); and chair of the Multicultural Counseling and Development Committee. Dr. Ginicola has served on national task forces for the American Counseling Association's ALGBTIC and is currently an editorial review board member for the *Journal of LGBT Issues in Counseling*.

In addition, she is a licensed professional counselor in the state of Connecticut and operates a private counseling practice called Walk in Balance Counseling. The name has a specific meaning attached to her cultural identity of Cherokee. Reflecting the Native saying "Walk in balance and beauty," she works with clients on a holistic level to ensure that physically, emotionally, psychologically, cognitively, and spiritually (if desired) they are caring for themselves. She also uses a person-centered existential approach to therapy, thereby helping individuals see and maintain the beauty in their lives, even in times of trauma and stress.

Her most challenging and fulfilling role has been as a mother to two sons, Wilson and Waylon. Raising her children has taught her more about teaching and modeling compassion and acceptance than she has ever learned in any textbook.

• • •

Cheri Smith, PhD, is a professor at Southern Connecticut State University. She earned her bachelor's degree at the University of West Florida and her master's in education in school counseling and Doctor of Philosophy in educational psychology/counseling at Mississippi State University. She worked in student affairs at Mississippi State University and Florida Atlantic University. Her teaching career began at the University of Montevallo. She has also taught at St. John's University, the University of West Georgia, the New York Institute of Technology, and Troy University. In 1995, while serving as president of the Association for Spiritual, Ethical, and Religious Values in Counseling (ASERVIC), she participated in the first Summit on Spirituality, where the initial ASERVIC competencies were developed. In the late 1980s and 1990s, her research also included HIV/AIDS education. This connection led her to combine her research in the area of spirituality with the LGBTQ+ community.

Dr. Smith is a member of the American Counseling Association, the Connecticut and Alabama Counseling Associations, ASERVIC, ALGBTIC, the Association for Specialists in Group Work, the Association for Counselor Education and Supervision, and Chi Sigma Iota. She has served on the editorial review board for the *Alabama Counseling Association Journal*. Also, she has served as president of the Montevallo chapter of the American Association of University Women and president of the Alabama Counseling Association. In addition, for 5 years she served on the Alabama Board of Examiners in Counseling. She has served on the editorial review board for the journal *Counseling and Values*, and currently she is a site visitor for the Council for Accreditation of Counseling and Related Educational Programs.

She is a licensed professional counselor and supervising counselor in Alabama as well as a National Board Certified Counselor. Her proudest role has been as a parent. Along with her husband, she is raising two daughters with open hearts and open minds.

• • •

Joel M. Filmore, EdD, is the founder, co-owner, and director of clinical services for the Lighthouse Professional Counseling Center; he is also lead faculty and program coordinator for Springfield College in Milwaukee. Dr. Filmore earned his bachelor's degree in psychology from the University of Illinois at Chicago. He earned his master's in clinical psychology from Roosevelt University in Chicago. He earned his Doctor of Education in counselor education and supervision from Northern Illinois University in DeKalb, Illinois, where he also earned a graduate certificate in quantitative research methods.

Prior to becoming a counselor educator, Dr. Filmore worked as an academic advisor in the university setting as well as a counselor in the community college setting. He also worked for more than 8 years in social services, predominantly with homeless, HIV-positive, drug-addicted, chronically mentally ill, lesbian, gay, bisexual, transgender, and other disenfranchised populations. Dr. Filmore is a biracial (African American and German/Norwegian) gay man. His personal and professional interests are in the areas of LGBTQI+ populations, multicultural issues, substance abuse/addiction, sex offender issues, sex trafficking, and trauma, as well as counselor competency.

Dr. Filmore currently serves as President-Elect for the national ALGBTIC. He also served as the cochair of the LGBTQQIA Affirmative Counseling and Social Justice

Committee 2 years running for ALGBTIC. He is past-president of the South Dakota Association for Counselor Education and Supervision as well as the cofounder and past-president of the Illinois ALGBTIC.

• • •

About the Contributors

Jahaan Abdullah, MA, Governors State University

Cindy Anderton, PhD, LPC, NCC, University of Wisconsin–Whitewater

Eric R. Baltrinic, PhD, Winona State University

David Barreto, MA, LPC, NCC, Waubonsee Community College

Jamie Bower, PhD, Old Dominion University

R. Lewis Bozard, Jr., PhD, MDiv, NCC, ACS, LPC, Care & Counseling Center of Georgia; Adjunct Faculty, Mercer University–Atlanta

Robyn Brammer, PhD, LMHC, Golden West College

Madeline Clark, PhD, LPC, University of Toledo

Michael DeVoll, MEd, LPC-S, Private practice, Houston, Texas

Diane Estrada, PhD, LMFT, University of Colorado Denver

Peter Finnerty, MS, PCC-S, Ursuline College

Brett H. Furth, PhD, Texas A&M University at Galveston; Houston Community College

Kristopher M. Goodrich, PhD, LPCC, The University of New Mexico

Amney J. Harper, PhD, University of Wisconsin–Oshkosh

Melanie Kautzman-East, PhD, LPC, Carlow University

Michael M. Kocet, PhD, LMHC, Chicago School of Professional Psychology

Ryan Liberati, PhD, LPC, PSC, ACS, Webster University

Melissa Luke, PhD, LMHC, NCC, ACS, Syracuse University

Jeff Lutes, MS, LPC, Private practice, Austin, Texas

Jeffry Moe, PhD, LPC, Old Dominion University

Amy Moore-Ramirez, MAEd, LPC/CR, LSW, The University of Akron

Jared S. Rose, PhD, LPCC, NCC, Bowling Green State University

Angela Ruggiero, MS, Southern Connecticut State University

Samuel Sanabria, PhD, LMHC, Rollins College

The Rev. Cody J. Sanders, PhD, Pastor; Old Cambridge Baptist Church, Adjunct Faculty, Andover Newton Theological School

Anneliese A. Singh, PhD, LPC, University of Georgia

Michael Stokes, MS, LPC, ACS, Stokes Counseling, private practice, Naugatuck, Connecticut

Lindsay Woodbridge, MS, University of Wisconsin–Madison

Chad Yates, PhD, Idaho State University

Acknowledgments

We would like to thank the American Counseling Association for its unwavering support of the lesbian, gay, bisexual, transgender, queer, questioning, intersex, asexual, ally, pansexual/polysexual, and two-spirited (LGBTQI+) community. We are proud to be members of an organization that always advocates for and works toward social justice for the most vulnerable populations among us.

We would also like to thank all of the authors who contributed to this book for their continual work to help those in the LGBTQI+ communities. The impact they make in education, research, and practice truly makes an immeasurable difference in the lives of the clients we serve.

Misty would like to acknowledge her brother, Steve, who taught her that being different was something to be celebrated; growing up with him as a big brother has been an honor and a blessing. She would also like to thank her husband, Mike, who loved and valued her differences from the moment he met her. She would also like to thank her sons, Wilson and Waylon, for opening up a whole new chapter of her life and identity; she works every day to make the world a more accepting place that will value their differences.

Cheri would like to thank Misty, whose hard work and desire to make a difference in the world and in the counseling profession are inspirational. She would also like to thank her fellow coeditor, Joel, and the contributing authors who helped to make this book a reality. She is also thankful to her mentors and colleagues in the Association for Spiritual, Ethical, and Religious Values in Counseling who, for the past 20+ years, have shown her the importance of religion and spirituality in the counseling profession. She would like to acknowledge her parents, who taught her to treat everyone with respect and that social justice is not optional. Cheri would also like to acknowledge Billy R. Cox, an HIV/AIDS activist whose life taught her by example how to fight for a cause with grace and whose death underscored the importance of not waiting for someone else to speak up. Mark Fitzhugh, her favorite Episcopal priest, has supported her with unconditional love and acceptance. Her children, Emma and Ella, both already activists in their own right, give her joy and hope for the future.

Joel would like to thank all of the people who, along the journey of his life, were able to see beyond his brash persona to recognize that underneath was a broken little boy who simply wanted to be loved and accepted. He acknowledges the one woman who helped forge him into the strong, determined firebrand that he is today: his grandmother, Anna Chatfield. He would especially like to thank the one person who can say he truly knows him: his husband and true love, Angel (Chino). Over the past 12 years, Angel has taught him that there really is such a thing as unconditional love.

Section I

FOUNDATIONS

• • •

Counselors working with lesbian, gay, bisexual, transgender, queer, questioning, intersex, asexual, ally, pansexual/polysexual, and two-spirited (LGBTQI+) people need a tremendous amount of information in order to serve their clients effectively. Using the framework of American Counseling Association competencies, the authors explore awareness, knowledge, and skills relevant to working with affectional orientation and gender minorities. In this section, the foundation for developing LGBTQI+ competence is addressed through an exploration of American Counseling Association competencies, terminology, history, current civil rights and social struggles, the need for advocacy, and the scientific research surrounding gender and affectional orientation variance.

Chapter 1

Developing Competence in Working With LGBTQI+ Communities: Awareness, Knowledge, Skills, and Action

Misty M. Ginicola, Joel M. Filmore, and Cheri Smith

*We struggled against apartheid because we were being blamed
and made to suffer for something we could do nothing about.
It is the same with homosexuality.
The orientation is a given, not a matter of choice.
It would be crazy for someone to choose to be gay,
given the homophobia that is present.*

—Desmond Tutu

• • •

Awareness of Attitudes and Beliefs Self-Check

1. When did you first learn what being gay meant? Was it a positive or negative message?
2. What assumptions do you make about the sexual or affectional orientation of your clients? How might these assumptions emerge in your behavior?
3. What is your knowledge of the history of oppression for lesbian, gay, bisexual, transgender, queer, questioning, intersex, asexual, ally, pansexual/polysexual, and two-spirited (LGBTQI+) persons?

Case Study

Martin is a 35-year-old Jamaican American gay male who has come to counseling. Martin was born in Jamaica and then moved with his family at age 10 to New York City. One of his first memories from Jamaica was watching a man be beaten to death for being gay. His father died when he was 20, and he has been responsible for caring for his family ever since. He has always known that he is gay but kept it a secret because of the extreme prejudice in his culture and family. Martin has been in a 2-year relationship with Angel, a Puerto Rican man. They have recently talked about moving forward in their relationship and moving in together. However, Martin is afraid because that will mean coming out to his deeply religious mother, who is affiliated with the Church of God.

His family lives with him in his house, so there is no way that he could keep it a secret. He has been depressed and, although not overtly suicidal, has some suicidal ideation.

• • •

Multicultural Competence

The main purpose of this book is to assist counselors and other mental health professionals in gaining competence in working with LGBTQI+ clients such as Martin. In Martin's case, there are multiple issues that a counselor without cultural competency may miss. Martin has multiple identities: Jamaican, American, gay, male, caretaker, son, brother, and partner. These roles and identities are conflicting; they may also be something with which a counselor is unable to identify. If a counselor has never had the experience of being an ethnic minority, being an immigrant, being a gay man, growing up in a disaffirming religion and culture, or being the sole provider and caretaker for the family, the way the counselor views the world will be incredibly different from Martin's schema. This is the essential reason why counselors must enhance their cultural competency skills when working with diverse populations.

The American Counseling Association (ACA) *Code of Ethics* has established several standards that apply to counseling LGBTQI+ people (ACA, 2014). ACA ethical standards require counselors to be developmentally and culturally sensitive in all stages of counseling with all clients as well as in counselor education and supervision (Standards A.2.c., B.1.a., E.5.b., E.8., F.2.b., F.7.c., F.11.c., H.5.d.). The *ACA Code of Ethics* also requires counselors to be aware of historical prejudices in diagnosis (Standard E.5.c.); this directly applies to work with LGBTQI+ persons, as they were pathologized as mentally ill through much of history. Standard A.4.b. requires counselors to be aware of personal values; counselors working with LGBTQI+ clients must be aware of their own values related to gender and affectional orientation in order not to impose these attitudes in their work with clients. This is very important, as Standard A.11.b. maintains that counselors cannot refer clients based on value conflicts. Standard C.2.a. specifically requires counselors to develop multicultural counseling competence in order to work appropriately with diverse clients; counselors should also receive continuing education to improve their multicultural competence (Standard C.2.f.).

Several sets of specific competencies developed by groups in ACA can be helpful in guiding counselor learning. The Association for Lesbian, Gay, Bisexual, and Transgender Issues in Counseling (ALGBTIC) competencies for counseling with lesbian, gay, bisexual, transgender, queer, questioning, intersex, and ally individuals (Harper et al., 2013) is the quintessential standard for counselors who serve LGBTQI+ clients (see http://www.algbtic.org/competencies.html). Organized along Council for Accreditation of Counseling and Related Educational Programs areas, it provides a framework for understanding all that is needed to be a positive influence in a counseling environment with this minority population. ALGBTIC (2010) also has a set of competencies for working with transgender clients (also available at http://www.algbtic.org/competencies.html).

Beyond the specific ALGBTIC competencies, another important framework to utilize is the Association for Multicultural Counseling and Development competencies. The *Multicultural and Social Justice Counseling Competencies* (Ratts, Singh, Nassar-McMillan, Butler, & McCullough, 2015) model addresses a variety of cultures through counselor self-awareness, client worldview, counseling relationship, as well as counseling and advocacy interventions (see Figure 1.1). An important focus in achieving multicultural competence is understanding the perspectives of a privileged or marginalized counselor as well as a privileged or marginalized client. The dynamics between marginalization and privilege impact a counselor's perspective and behavior. Each minority status carries marginaliza-

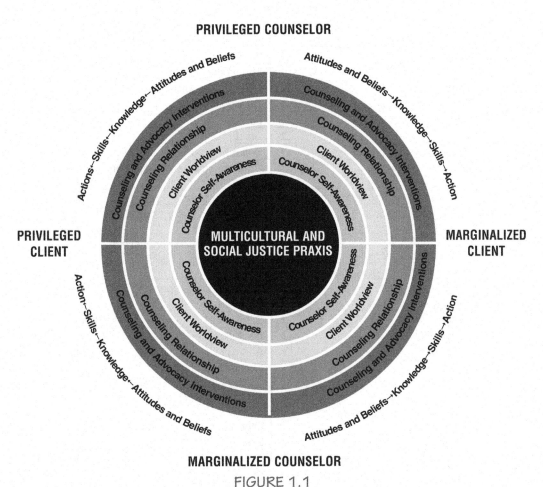

FIGURE 1.1

Multicultural and Social Justice Counseling Competencies

Note. From *Multicultural and Social Justice Counseling Competencies* (p. 4), by M. J. Ratts, A. A. Singh, S. Nassar-McMillan, S. K. Butler, and J. R. McCullough, 2015. Retrieved from https://www.counseling.org/docs/default-source/competencies/multicultural-and-social-justice-counseling-competencies.pdf?sfvrsn=20. Copyright 2015 by M. J. Ratts, A. A. Singh, S. Nassar-McMillan, S. K. Butler, and J. R. McCullough. Reprinted with permission.

tion; each majority status carries privilege. However, every person carries a series of complex identities and backgrounds (age, gender, ability status, religion/spirituality, socio-economic level, race/ethnicity, affectional orientation and gender orientation, immigrant status, indigenous heritage, mental health status, etc.) that form multiple perspectives of both privilege and marginalization, as one person can be a minority in some statuses and in the majority in others. This complex interconnection of social identities is called *intersectionality* (Harper et al., 2013). For counselors, understanding the impact of discrimination, power, stereotypes, privilege, and oppression is central to serving any population but is particularly important with the LGBTQI+ population.

In considering their own privilege and marginalization, counselors must consider their intersectional identities, as they will very likely experience privilege in some areas and marginalization in others. Kocet (2008) adapted a checklist from Operation Concern to represent an activity to fully explore power and privilege (see Figure 1.2). In this activity, counselors can identify where they have more power, enjoy less stigma, and have an

NORM (Have Privilege)		OTHER (Less Privileged)	
Men	❏	Women	❏
White	❏	People of color	❏
Heterosexual	❏	Lesbian, gay, bisexual	❏
Non-transgender	❏	Transgender	❏
Wealthy	❏	Poor	❏
Adult	❏	Child	❏
Traditionally educated	❏	Self-educated	❏
Society's definition of sane	❏	Other than society's definition of sane	❏
Temporarily able bodied	❏	Differently abled	❏
Society's definition of attractive	❏	Other than society's definition of attractive	❏
Society's definition of emotionally stable	❏	Other than society's definition of emotionally stable	❏
Young adult or middle aged	❏	Older	❏
English speaking	❏	Other language speaking	❏
Average size	❏	Other sized	❏
White collar	❏	Blue collar	❏
Noninstitutionalized	❏	Institutionalized	❏
Nonvictim	❏	Survivor	❏
Christian	❏	Those with other religious/spiritual beliefs	❏
North American	❏	The rest of the world	❏
Two heterosexual parents per family	❏	Other family compositions	❏
Healthy	❏	Less healthy	❏
Land owners	❏	Tenants	❏

FIGURE 1.2

Kocet's (2008) Adapted Power and Privilege Checklist

Note. Adapted from "My Personal Privileges Handout," by M. Kocet, 2008, at http://vc.bridgew.edu/cgi/viewcontent.cgi?filename=2&article=1003&context=change&type=additional. Originally adapted from National Centers of Excellence in Women's Health Cultural Competence Curriculum, originally from Operation Concern, Department of Social Work Education, San Francisco State University, San Francisco, CA. Copyright 1993 by B. G. Gordon and H. B. Hogue. Adapted with permission.

opportunity to serve as allies for the less privileged or marginalized group. Both privilege and marginalization will shape a counselor's attitudes and beliefs, which can potentially interfere with counseling clients, if one is unaware of them.

The multicultural competence model also requires counselors to develop an awareness of attitudes and beliefs, requisite knowledge, skills, and actions to take in the areas of counselor self-awareness, client worldview, and the counseling relationship. These areas culminate in establishing competency with counseling and advocacy interventions with and on behalf of clients at multiple levels.

Two other sets of competencies can be valuable for counselors who work with LGBTQI+ clients: the Association for Specialists in Group Work *Multicultural and Social Justice Competence Principles for Group Workers* (Singh, Merchant, Skudrzyk, & Ingene, 2012) and the Spiritual Competencies of the Association for Spiritual, Ethical, and Religious Values in

Counseling (2009). Each of these sets of competencies can help counselors develop skills for working on the wide variety of issues that may present in counseling with clients in LGBTQI+ communities.

Awareness of Attitudes and Beliefs

When working with an LGBTQI+ client, it is crucial that counselors be aware of their own attitudes and beliefs to ensure that they maintain an awareness of their own privilege, marginalization, and potential biases, which could negatively impact the client. These include issues surrounding gender, affectional orientation, and sexuality. Counselors should understand the attitudes and beliefs of their LGBTQI+ clients as well as how these clients' identity development and experiences of oppression, privilege, and marginalization impact their worldviews, attitudes, beliefs, behavior, and physical and mental health. Counselors should be aware of how external cultures, stereotypes, marginalization, power, and privilege will impact the counseling relationship. For example, Martin may be reluctant to seek counseling because of a mistrust of the mental health field resulting from previous experiences of oppression and discrimination. He may be reticent to connect with the counselor for fear that the counselor will be rejecting or might not understand his Jamaican culture. If the counselor is heterosexual and Caucasian, this mistrust may be compounded and Martin may present as resistant. The goal for both heterosexual and LGBTQI+ counselors is to become *allies,* which are people who are supportive of individuals in the LGBTQI+ communities who may also face discrimination themselves (Harper et al., 2013).

There are several constructs to be aware of in understanding attitudes and beliefs surrounding this population. The overarching acronym that represents this community varies depending on the focus (e.g., LGBQQ is typical for work on affectional orientation), organization (e.g., many use LGBT or LGBTQ as their main acronym), or inclusiveness (ALGBTIC uses LGBQQIA in its competencies). However, there are currently 11 recognized identities under the affectional orientation and gender minority umbrella, including allies. The entire population is referred to (in several iterations with different orders) as *LGBTQQIAAP-2S* (lesbian, gay, bisexual, transgender, queer, questioning, intersex, asexual, ally, pansexual/polysexual, and two-spirited). As the complete acronym is quite unwieldy, two umbrella terms are commonly used to refer to this population without compromising inclusiveness: *queer community* (which refers to queer theory and includes both affectional orientation and gender minorities) and *LGBTQI+* populations or communities. Although *queer* was once, and sometimes still is, utilized as a pejorative term, many in the LGBTQI+ community have reclaimed the term as an indicator of strength and unity (Harper et al., 2013). It is important to note that in this book, the acronym may be LGBTQ or LGBQQ when discussing research studies of limited populations.

In relation to specific terminology, there are several terms to be aware of in the LGBTQI+ population. One is *affectional orientation,* which refers to "the direction an individual is predisposed to bond with and share affection emotionally, physically, spiritually, and/or mentally" (Harper et al., 2013, p. 38). It is meant to replace *sexual orientation* as an outdated term; these constructs are similar, in that they refer to both the nature of an individual's romantic attractions and the identity surrounding those attractions (VandenBos, 2015). However, *affectional orientation* highlights the full spectrum of relationships rather than just the sexuality aspect (Harper et al., 2013). Although these concepts are similar, shifting to using the term *affectional orientation* rather than *sexual orientation* can purposely broaden the focus of discussion of LGBTQI+ people to their relationships rather than just their sexual behavior (Crethar & Vargas, 2007; Klein, 1993). In the realm of affectional identity, there are *lesbians,* or women who bond romantically with other women, and *gay men,* or men who bond romantically with other men (Harper et al., 2013). *Bisexual, pansexual,* and *polysexual* individuals bond based on a wider range of gender identities, which may include male, female, genderqueer, and transgender. *Queer* refers to individuals who specifically identify as such because the other categories do not capture the complexity of their identity; this could be because of their identified nonbinary gender identity, relationship status (e.g., polyamory), or political reasons (Harper et al., 2013). *Questioning* individuals are those who identify with the LGBTQI+ communities but are unsure of the nature of their emotional, physical, mental, and/or spiritual attractions (Harper et al., 2013). *Asexual* individuals are those who may experience a romantic bonding attraction but not sexual or physical attractions; when present, their romantic attractions can vary from none to heterosexual or gay, lesbian, or bisexual (Bogaert, 2004).

Another characteristic in these communities is *gender identity,* or the personal identity surrounding masculinity or femininity (Harper et al., 2013; VandenBos, 2015). Gender identity and affectional orientation are not *binary,* or two separate concepts: male/female, gay/heterosexual. Rather, they both appear to be on a continuum. Gender and affectional orientation are not finite, fixed concepts; they are *fluid,* meaning that they develop, shift, and evolve throughout the life span. These developmental issues are further delineated in Chapters 3 through 6. In terms of gender identity, persons may identify as *genderqueer,* or someone who experiences a blending of genders, or as a gender minority. Gender minorities, who may also identify as *transgender,* experience a mismatch between their physical assigned sex and their gender identity. These individuals present as *gender nonconforming,* an umbrella term that indicates a child who at a young age does not exhibit gender-stereotyped play or interests. Some gender-conforming individuals may certainly be LGBTQI+; however, heterosexual individuals can also be gender nonconforming. Transgender persons who experience significant distress and/or impairment may be diagnosed as having *gender dysphoria* according to the *Diagnostic and Statistical Manual of Mental Disorders, Fifth Edition* (American Psychiatric Association, 2013). Another related term in the gender identity category is *cisgender,* which describes someone whose sex and gender identity align: in other words, non-transgender. Some individuals are also born *intersex,* with male and female or ambiguous genitalia; such individuals were formerly known as *hermaphrodites,* but the new term is less pejorative and not associated with the negative aspects with which *hermaphrodite* was once associated (Harper et al., 2013). *Two-spirit* individuals are those who have an indigenous heritage and who identify with traditional Native concepts of variant gender and affectional orientation as having spiritual and social value (Jacobs, Thomas, & Lang, 1997).

Some confuse affectional orientation with *relationship systems.* For example, one might believe that bisexuals have multiple romantic partners at one time. However, this is not the case; relationship systems include monogamy (romantic involvement with one partner) and polyamory (multiple partners). These relationship systems are discussed and are consensual in nature, whether it is to only be involved with each other as romantic partners or to have multiple partners in some constellation or formation (i.e., an open relationship to date anyone, three partners, a partner who bonds with only one individual in a couple, etc.). These relationship systems are present in all affectional orientation identities, most commonly heterosexual partnerships. However, even in a heterosexual context, consensually non-monogamous relationships are severely stigmatized in society and seen as negative or doomed to fail, despite evidence to the contrary (Conley, Moors, Matsick, & Ziegler, 2013).

A key component of being multiculturally aware is understanding how a personal experience may be different from a minority experience in terms of both marginalization and privilege. The majority culture experiences a privilege that those in the LGBTQI+ communities do not, and that is having a gender and affectional orientation that is the norm for and reinforced by society. There are several constructs to be aware of in this regard.

Heteronormativity is the view that people's assigned sex, gender identity, gender roles, and affectional identity are immutable, binary (male vs. female), and heterosexual in nature (VandenBos, 2015). This norm or standard is expressed in human societies, leading those who do not meet this norm to feel abnormal or in violation of society's standards.

Heterosexism is a prejudice against any individuals who do not meet heteronormative expectations, which include binary male versus female gender expression and identity, as well as heterosexual attractions (VandenBos, 2015). These prejudices can lead to *homophobia,* which is fear associated with same-sex relationships, which can also be internalized into one's own self, or *internalized homophobia.* Sometimes termed *homoprejudice,* these prejudices can result in acts of violence and discrimination in employment, housing, and personal relationships.

Knowledge

Having advanced knowledge related to multicultural counseling is important not only to understanding behavior in the counseling process but also to increasing positive outcomes in a multicultural context (LeBeauf, Smaby, & Maddux, 2009). Although counseling programs accredited by the Council for Accreditation of Counseling and Related Educational Programs (2015) are required to infuse multicultural counseling across the eight domains into their curricula, there are no required methods for how to do so. As long as a counseling program discusses multicultural issues and assesses student learning in social and cultural diversity, that can suffice as having met the requirements.

Unfortunately, the truth is that even if counselors were to take a semester-long course on multicultural counseling, they would not necessarily be considered competent or knowledgeable, as such classes are most often introductory. Regardless, the onus is on individual counselors to increase and maintain their knowledge after graduating and engage in a process of learning that continues throughout their professional development.

Counselors who work with LGBTQI+ clients should have knowledge of history and cultural events that have shaped their own privileges and marginalized statuses as well as their clients' intersectional backgrounds and identity development. Counselors should also be knowledgeable about international and global affairs. For example, the counselor working with Martin should understand his Jamaican culture, how his experience of trauma in his childhood impacts his own identity development, and what he is risking by coming out to his family and community.

Multicultural counseling has been called the *fourth force* in the helping professions (Pedersen, 2001) and as such connotes the importance of having a strong knowledge base from which to draw when working with clients who are *other than* the majority population. Providing counseling services to minority populations has become increasingly commonplace in professional counseling. Although the United States has never been so diverse, when it comes to racial, gender, and affectional orientation differences, the populace struggles with divisiveness brought on by incendiary rhetoric, both political and social.

A History of Oppression and Bias

Throughout ancient history, there were records of same-sex relations, both monogamous and polyamorous bisexual and gay or lesbian relationships, just as there were heterosexual ones (Greenberg, 1988; Hubbard, 2003; Mussi, 2002; Talalay, 2005; Wilhelm, 2008). There is also evidence of transgender and third-gender persons in virtually every civilization across recorded history (Greenberg, 1988). This evidence can be found in Africa, the Americas, Assyria, China, Egypt, Europe, India, Israel, Japan, the Middle East, Persia, and the South

Pacific. Although the cultural beliefs and practices differed in each context, the existence of gender and affectional orientation variance was seen as normative, often valued in the civilization (Greenberg, 1988; Hubbard, 2003; Mussi, 2002; Talalay, 2005; Wilhelm, 2008). There is also some evidence that many great leaders, notably Alexander the Great, had same-sex relationships and were highly valued in their time (Green, 2007).

Starting in the fourth century, these previously sanctioned relationships began to be seen as immoral (Fone, 2000). The apparent precedent for the massive change in attitude against acceptance of gender and affectional orientation variance was the advent of Westernized religion, specifically the Roman Catholic Church. Although there is some evidence that the Roman Catholic Church originally accepted same-sex relationships, at some point gender roles associated with natural law (e.g., intercourse for purposes of procreation) became standard teaching, and "homosexuality" and sodomy were condemned in Europe. In 390, sodomy was made illegal by Christian emperors and became punishable by death. From the fifth to the 17th centuries, these laws began to spread to virtually every government around the world where Europeans emigrated and the Catholic Church spread. During the Spanish Inquisition, more than 1,600 individuals were stoned, castrated, and burned at the stake for being sodomites. As the religion spread, so did the negative attitudes regarding sexuality in general as well as affectional orientation and gender variance in particular. During the Renaissance, same-sex acts were punished by assault (e.g., flogging), genital mutilation, and/or death.

In the 18th and 19th centuries, civil rights groups began forming in Europe and countries began to decriminalize "homosexuality" (Fone, 2000). France became the first to decriminalize sodomy between consenting adults, and several other countries followed, including Prussia, The Netherlands, Indonesia, Brazil, and Japan. However, this viewpoint was not accepted globally; during the same period of time, sodomy laws were enacted in the United States, Poland, Guatemala, and Mexico. Subsequently, several countries, including Russia, Panama, Paraguay, Peru, Iceland, Switzerland, Sweden, Portugal, Greece, England, Wales, and Thailand, to name a few, repealed sodomy laws. Although LGBTQI+ individuals were gaining more acceptance, many people around the world were still commonly arrested and detained for same-sex sexual activity; during World War II, gay men, along with other minorities, were persecuted and executed in Nazi concentration camps, with the pink triangle being used to label them in the camps.

The field of psychiatry was partially responsible for the movement to decriminalize same-sex sexual activity; theorists and psychiatrists coined the term *homosexual* and argued that it was a clinical disorder (Bayer, 1987; Drescher & Merlino, 2007; Krajeski, 1996). The origin of *homosexuality* as a pathological term is one reason why it is no longer used in the LGBTQI+ community. With the advent of seeing "homosexuality" as a disorder, psychiatrists advocated for the removal of criminal penalties while simultaneously pathologizing those in LGBTQI+ communities. Psychiatric theories regarding the origin of affectional orientation variance at the time ranged from a congenital disorder to degenerative neurological conditions to serious mental illness. Some theorists argued that "homosexuality" was a sexual inversion, which was a variation, not a disease. However, even some of these theorists believed that it could be reversed or cured. One theorist who agreed with the ideas surrounding sexual inversion but disagreed with the idea of a cure was Sigmund Freud. Freud theorized about the role of the oedipal conflict in creating affectional orientation variance but also stipulated that sexual inversion could be completely natural; he particularly believed that bisexuality was universal but sublimated in heterosexuals. Unfortunately, most psychiatrists who practiced after Freud supported the belief that "homosexuality" was pathological and needed to be cured.

In America, the history of LGBTQI+ treatment can be split into pre-Stonewall and post-Stonewall, which refers to the revolt in New York City that began the American LGBTQI+

civil rights movement (Edsall, 2003; Fone, 2000; Foster, 2007; Godbeer, 2002). Before Stonewall, Europeans interpreted the Native gender and affectional orientation variance (now known as *two-spirit*) as sinful and derogatory. Derived from the laws from the English versions of buggery, sodomy remained a taboo and illegal act that would result in genital mutilation and death. Although in the late 1700s states began removing the death penalty for sodomy, it remained an illegal act. The Federal Bureau of Investigation and local police departments kept lists of gay and lesbian persons, the bars and bathhouses they patronized, as well as their friends; sweeps on cities, parks, bars, and beaches were regularly performed to rid cities of LGBTQI+ persons. The mafia, which sometimes blackmailed the wealthier customers, commonly ran the bars that served LGBTQI+ persons in New York City; some historians theorize that local police were receiving kickbacks from this blackmail that kept the bars open. Wearing opposite-gender clothing had been outlawed in some states; educational organizations fired teachers and professors who were suspected of being lesbian, gay, or bisexual. As a result, a multitude of LGBTQI+ persons were exposed, were harassed, lost their jobs, were placed in mental institutions, and/or were jailed. Therefore, it was necessary to be closeted during this time. There had been some LGBTQI+ civil rights organizations and social justice activism in the 1950s and 1960s, but little had changed. A small riot in response to police harassment occurred in Los Angeles in 1959; another occurred in San Francisco in 1966 at Compton's Cafeteria, when police attempted to arrest transgender women and drag queens for dressing in women's clothing.

The landscape of American culture changed with one major event: the Stonewall riots (Carter, 2004; Duberman, 1993; Edsall, 2003). In the 20th century, police raids on bathhouses and bars were common; the police would commonly arrest gay men, lesbians, transgender persons, and drag queens for simply being present in such an establishment. On June 28, 1969, a police raid occurred at the Stonewall Inn in Greenwich Village, New York City. Greenwich Village was known to have a large LGBTQI+ population, making it a frequent target for police harassment. At 1:20 a.m., four plainclothes police officers attempted to arrest any men dressed as women (all individuals dressed as women were asked to go with female police officers to the bathroom to verify their sex) from among the approximately 200 persons in the bar. Patrons refused to comply, and a crowd began to form outside. The crowd became irate as police became aggressive with a male dressed as a woman, and a lesbian was hit on the head with a police baton. The crowd began to overturn the police vehicles, yell, and throw things at the now 10 police officers, who retreated into the bar for safety. The impact of the oppression and discrimination from every angle reached its boiling point in the crowd that night; the anger and outrage were palpable. The Tactical Police Force eventually arrived and cleared the street, but it took close to 3 hours, with injuries to police as well as those in the crowd. Standing up to the oppression empowered the community, which reported the riot to several media outlets. The next night, another riot broke out, indicating a shift in the community's willingness to actively confront oppression as well as in the number of allies who were on board with joining the fight. Following this, several LGBTQI+ advocacy groups formed and became active in protesting and mobilizing the community. The first gay pride parades were held in three cities across America on the 1-year anniversary of the Stonewall riot, which came to represent the LGBTQI+ civil rights movement, empowerment, pride, and the communities' willingness to fight for equal rights.

Following Stonewall, major political movements fighting for LGBTQI+ rights sprang up across the globe, with the repeal of sodomy laws in many countries (Deitcher, 1995; Marcus, 2002). As a result of LGBTQI+ activism, the Kinsey sexuality studies (Kinsey, Pomeroy, & Martin, 1948; Kinsey, Pomeroy, Martin, & Gebhard, 1953), and Evelyn Hooker's (1956) research showing no differences between heterosexual and "homosexual" men, the American Psychiatric Association voted to remove "homosexuality" from the *Diagnostic and Statistical*

Manual of Mental Disorders (*DSM*) in 1973 (Bayer, 1987; Drescher & Merlino, 2007; Krajeski, 1996). However, the *DSM* included sexual orientation disturbance to represent clients who were unhappy with their affectional orientation variance, which continued to legitimize sexual orientation change efforts (Drescher & Merlino, 2007). The mental health field continued to have a strained relationship with the LGBTQI+ community, as reparative and curative therapies were still espoused (Bayer, 1987; Drescher & Merlino, 2007; Krajeski, 1996). Also in 1973, Gerry Eastman Studds became the first openly gay individual to serve as a congressperson (Deitcher, 1995; Marcus, 2002). Another noteworthy event occurred when Harvey Milk, a well-admired and openly gay politician in San Francisco, was assassinated (Deitcher, 1995; Marcus, 2002). In 1987, the *DSM* removed all references to "homosexuality" as a mental illness; the World Health Organization followed suit in 1992, as did the American Medical Association in 1994 (Deitcher, 1995; Marcus, 2002).

Another formidable historical event in the LGBTQI+ communities was the HIV and AIDS epidemic in the 1980s (Cohen, 2012; Shilts, 1987). When the illness was first noted in 1981, it was thought to be a rare form of cancer. Although the virus impacted intravenous drug users and those with hemophilia as well, it predominantly spread in the gay male community; in 1992, it was termed *gay-related immune deficiency*. In 1985, more than 20,000 cases of HIV/AIDS were reported globally. By 1989, there were more than 100,000 cases in the United States alone, with approximately 10 million people living with HIV globally. The impact of this epidemic on the queer community was devastating. The number of gay males who died caused a panic among the LGBTQI+ community; immense grief as many watched all of their friends die; and outrage at the lack of support from the government, which saw this as an isolated gay problem. Because LGBTQI+ persons, particularly gay males, were so devalued, there was a very long delay in any type of attention or public health response. In addition, many heterosexual persons became fearful of LGBTQI+ people, who began to carry the stigma of being diseased. Discrimination against gay men and those living with HIV/AIDS was palpable throughout these decades. Although these tragic events decimated the LGBTQI+ communities in many ways, they also mobilized LGBTQI+ persons and allies to engage in activism. In 1999, it was estimated that 14 million people had died from AIDS around the globe. Because of the tremendous public health initiatives promoting safe sex, the activism of the LGBTQI+ communities and allies, and programs to eliminate the sharing of needles by drug users, the spread of the virus began to slow. With the advent of medication used to treat HIV, the diagnosis was no longer a death sentence. The prevalence of HIV/AIDS peaked in 2005 but then began to decrease; in 2013, it was estimated that 35 million people currently had a diagnosis of HIV. The activism in response to the AIDS crisis became a template for later social justice work, including the development of allies. It also brought about the beginnings of the LGBTQI+ community by building solidarity between gay men and lesbians surrounding HIV/AIDS.

Although civil unions were being accepted in many countries globally, in the mid-1990s America passed the Defense of Marriage Act of 1996 defining marriage as between a man and a woman. LGBTQI+ civil rights issues began to be addressed at a fast pace under the Barack Obama administration. In 2009, definitions of federal hate crime regulations were expanded to include affectional and gender orientation as a minority group. In 2010, Don't Ask, Don't Tell, which required members of the military to be closeted about their minority affectional orientation status or face discharge, was repealed (Don't Ask, Don't Tell Repeal Act of 2010). In 2013, the Defense of Marriage Act was repealed (*United States v. Windsor et al.*, 2013), and the Supreme Court granted marriage equality in 2015 (*Obergefell et al. v. Hodges et al.*, 2015). In 2016, state bans on same-sex couple adoptions were ruled to be unconstitutional (*Campaign for Southern Equality et al. v. Mississippi Department of Human Services et al.*, 2016). In 2016, the Pentagon also ended the ban on transgender persons serving in the U.S. military; this now paves a path for existing military personnel to openly transition while enrolled, for already transitioning transgender persons to join the military, and for medical coverage important for such a transition identified by doctors (Rizzo & Cohen, 2016). In 2016, an Oregon court also ruled that a citizen could identify as third gender, a landmark ruling rendering Jamie Shupe the first legally nonbinary person in the United States (Foden-Vencil, 2016).

Current Oppression and Bias

Despite great strides in the social justice movement for affectional minority equality, there has been an equal and opposite reaction from the religious right. Following the string of positive LGBTQI+ civil rights legislation, there has been a backlash that can be seen in the rise of religious liberty bills or, as some refer to them, *anti-LGBT legislation* (Macgillivray, 2008). Although these laws are on a myriad of different topics, the basic tenet of all proposed legislation stipulates that the government does not have the right to force religious individuals to support or provide services to LGBTQI+ individuals. Proponents of the *liberty* laws do not see that the laws are allowing discrimination while taking liberty and freedom away from others; they only believe that these laws will allow them not to act in a way that goes against their religious beliefs. These same arguments were used to support discrimination against African Americans, from the abolition of slavery laws to the advent of civil rights legislation.

North Carolina passed a law in April 2016 that makes it illegal for people to use a public bathroom that does not match the sex designated on their birth certificate ("Session Law 2016-3, House Bill 2," 2016). It also prevents anyone from suing based on discrimination, in direct violation of an antidiscrimination law that has been in effect since 1985. This law is currently considered one of the most anti-LGBT laws in the country.

Likewise, on April 27, 2016, Tennessee's governor signed into law a bill that gives counselors the right to refuse service to anyone based on the counselors' sincerely held *principles* ("Tennessee Senate Bill 1556," 2016). This is a shift from legislation that previously used the term "sincerely held *religious beliefs.*" Many other states are also in the process of proposing similar bills. What these laws seek to do is to circumvent the *ACA Code of Ethics*, which explicitly states that no counseling professional may discriminate against a client based on the counselor's value conflicts with the client (ACA, 2014, Standard C.5.). On May 12, 2016, President Obama's administration issued a sweeping directive that interpreted Title IX requirements of public schools to grant transgender students access to bathrooms that match their gender identity, which reflects the specific update to Title IX by the U.S. Department of Education (U.S. Department of Justice, 2016). Although it may seem unnecessary for the federal government to become involved so that children can have access to bathroom facilities, this merely highlights the degree and level to which people will go to discriminate, oppress, and ostracize those in the LGBTQI+ community.

In November 2016, results of the U.S. presidential election revealed that the country elected a candidate who had espoused numerous prejudices, including those toward the LGBTQI+ population. Reactions following the election were quite profound, with a clear division on the importance of human rights for minority groups. At the time of this book's printing, the impact of this election is unclear. However, it seems unlikely that the pace of progress in LGBTQI+ rights will be maintained; many of the protections achieved thus far may indeed be at risk. Although only time will tell, it seems very unlikely that federal protections for LGBTQI+ persons will be reached in the next 4 years (Stack, 2016).

In the absence of a federal law or mandate, these battles for equal protection and rights under the law are occurring at the state level (Human Rights Campaign, 2016). Nondiscrimination issues include adoption laws, employment, housing, and public accommodations (e.g., restaurants, movie theaters, shops). For those who identify as transgender, current political movements include fighting the multiple statewide legislative proposals for bathroom laws, working toward gender marker change laws for identification documents, and working toward laws that allow for the inclusion of transgender issues in health care and insurance. Although the federal government now includes gender and affectional orientation as protected categories for hate crimes, many individual states do not. In terms of protection in schools, there is much work to be done on school nondiscrimination laws and policies. Although all states have antibullying laws, some states do not have protection for LGBTQI+ youth in them; some states go a step further to state that LGBTQI+ students are excluded from protection, and others restrict the inclusion of LGBTQI+ topics in schools.

These exclusionary and oppressive laws reflect the level of marginalization and bias toward LGBTQI+ persons. These attitudes and biases often result in verbal or physical harassment, bullying, and assault. LGBTQI+ youth report facing a hostile climate in schools as well as frequent harassment, bullying, and abuse (Kosciw, Greytak, Palmer, & Boesen, 2014). Twenty percent of all victims of hate crimes are affectional orientation and gender minorities (Federal Bureau of Investigation, 2014). Males, ethnic minorities, those who have a variant gender, and youth living in a rural areas are at the greatest risk for bullying, harassment, and hate crimes (Diaz & Kosciw, 2009; Roberts, Rosario, Slopen, Calzo, & Austin, 2013).

Much more subtle, yet still incredibly damaging, are microaggressions, which are daily indignities, slights, and insults reflecting discrimination and bias toward minorities that are, most often, unconscious (Sue et al., 2007). Microaggressions leave individuals questioning whether they are being too sensitive because microaggressions are not blatant discrimination but rather marginalization. Yet the outcomes of microaggressions are a heightened sense of awareness (hypervigilance) and low-level stress that research shows over time have the same impact as posttraumatic stress disorder (Robinson & Rubin, 2016).

Continuing Career and Health Care Disparities

Research shows that discrimination in the workplace based on affectional orientation is also a substantial problem. LGBTQI+ individuals who are out at work have a 40% chance of being discriminated against based solely on their affectional orientation, which is 4 times as much as LGBT individuals who are not out at work (Pizer, Sears, Mallory, & Hunter, 2012). Most commonly, LGBT individuals reported experiencing harassment, with many having lost their jobs following the harassment (Pizer et al., 2012). The situation is more severe for transgender employees: Their experience of discrimination increases dramatically (Sears & Mallory, 2011). Although research supports the fact that LGBT individuals experience discrimination at work, very little research has looked at intersectional identities, such as the greater bias that queer people of color might experience. One could argue, anecdotally speaking, that the intersectionality of these two identities creates discriminatory experiences at an exponential rate.

The Role of Media

In 1998, Ellen DeGeneres came out on national television, making history and paving the way for increased representation on television and in cinema of LGBTQI+ individuals and characters (Gomillion & Giuliano, 2011). Research suggests that the media may influence psychological domains, including individuals' self-perceptions (Hammack, 2005). Ochman (1996) found a link between self-esteem and storybook characters, as affectional minority children who were exposed to stories with strong, positive, same-sex characters exhibited increased self-concepts. Ochman was able to demonstrate that the positive examples, or portrayals, in the media of characters with whom the children shared qualities helped to increase the children's self-concepts. More contemporary research has found that people are more likely to have high self-esteem if they believe that they have more characteristics in common with their role models (Wohlford, Lochman, & Barry, 2004). This research supports the importance of how minority populations, both racial and sexual, are portrayed in the media, as the media is a powerful tool in crafting a dominant narrative. If research supports the idea that positive portrayals of characteristics in role models have the effect of increasing one's self-esteem, then it stands to reason that negative portrayals of characteristics in role models can have a deleterious effect on self-esteem. The portrayal of LGBTQI+ individuals in the news, on television, and in movies likewise paints a less than accurate picture of what it means to be an affectional minority (Houseman, 2010). The increase in television shows related to this population has been seen as a cause for celebration. Shows such as *Queer as Folk, The L Word, Queer Eye for the Straight Guy, RuPaul's Drag Race, Glee,* and *Orange Is the New Black* bring attention to LGBTQI+ persons in mainstream media. However, they may also sometimes give an unrealistic or skewed portrayal of LGBTQI+ life as hypersexual and feed into certain stereotypes of the LGBTQI+ communities. In reality, the truth of affectional orientation and gender minority life is substantially more mundane.

Skills

Culturally competent counselors also have skills in gaining self-awareness, communicating, and understanding how to assess their own biases and their impact. They also know how to adequately assess clients' cultures, privilege, and marginalization as well as use appropriate cross-cultural conceptualization and communication skills. These counselors know how to apply knowledge, theories, and research to connect with and enhance the counseling relationship with their clients. Counselors should be able to skillfully provide counseling interventions, which for LGBTQI+ clients are affirmative, strengths based, and designed to build empowerment and identity development. For example, the counselor working with Martin should provide a safe and warm environment; be prepared to discuss and feel comfortable discussing the differences in their experiences; and understand how to help him consider the influences in his life and develop strength, resilience, and coping skills in meeting his counseling goals.

Action

It is important that multiculturally competent counselors also take action to continually develop and maintain self-awareness; stay up to date on cultural variance and multicultural counseling skills; and actively explore issues of race, privilege, identity, and understanding. Counselors should also understand when and HOW to take advocacy action, as many states are in the process of proposing anti-LGBTQI+ bills. Advocacy and its role in counseling are discussed in Chapter 25. Counselors should additionally be aware of how to promote equity and remove barriers at institutional, community, and public policy levels.

Conclusion

When serving as a counselor for an LGBTQI+ client, a counselor must have multiple sets of skills. Although having competence in counseling is required, counselors also need the ability to understand which techniques work best for these populations, when they should be utilized, and how they should be modified for each client. As all clients have, in addition to their affectional orientation and gender identity, multiple intersectional identities of sex, ethnicity, socioeconomic status, religion/spirituality, age, and generation, to name a few, all must be considered when working with clients. Developing cultural competence for working with LGBTQI+ clients involves being aware of the overarching cultural bias against affectional orientation and gender variance as well as how these messages have impacted the counselor. Being LGBTQI+ culturally competent also involves gaining knowledge regarding how internal experiences of being LGBTQI+ and external treatment as an affectional orientation or gender minority have shaped the client's strengths and challenges. Counselors must be familiar with a wide variety of techniques that are empirically supported or, when there is a lack of empirical research, based on preliminary findings in the literature and sure not to cause harm. Internalizing all of these skills will lead the counselor to the important role of being an ally; advocating for social justice and equality for affectional orientation and gender minorities is also an important role for the counselor, client, and the counseling field.

Questions for Further Discussion

1. What precursory factors could be impacting Martin's reticence to come out as well as his depressive symptoms?
2. If you were Martin's counselor, what attitudes and beliefs would you need to be aware of that could impact Martin or the counseling relationship?
3. How would you gain knowledge about the Jamaican culture? About Church of God beliefs? About being a gay man in Jamaica?
4. What would be some appropriate counseling goals and strategies for Martin?
5. What type of advocacy might be helpful for Martin?

Resources

1. Develop your awareness of your biases by taking the Implicit Association Test with the sexuality and gender subtests at https://implicit.harvard.edu/implicit/takeatest.html.
2. Take the LGBTQI+ course created by ACA and the Human Rights Campaign at http://aca.digitellinc.com/aca/lessons/1.
3. Review the resources available through the ALGBTIC website at http://www.algbtic.org.
4. Be familiar with continuing education offered by ACA in order to stay up to date with your cultural knowledge. Visit https://www.counseling.org/continuing-education/overview for more information.

References

American Counseling Association. (2014). *ACA code of ethics*. Alexandria, VA: Author.

American Psychiatric Association. (2013). *Diagnostic and statistical manual of mental disorders* (5th ed.). Washington, DC: Author.

Association for Lesbian, Gay, Bisexual, and Transgender Issues in Counseling. (2010). *Competencies for counseling transgender clients*. Retrieved from http://www.algbtic.org/competencies.html

Association for Spiritual, Ethical, and Religious Values in Counseling. (2009). *Spiritual competencies endorsed by the American Counseling Association (ACA)*. Retrieved from http://www.aservic.org/resources/spiritual-competencies/

Bayer, R. (1987). *Homosexuality and American psychiatry: The politics of diagnosis*. Princeton, NJ: Princeton University Press.

Bogaert, A. F. (2004). Asexuality: Prevalence and associated factors in a national probability sample. *Journal of Sex Research, 41*, 279–287.

Campaign for Southern Equality et al. v. Mississippi Department of Human Services et al. (2016). Retrieved from http://www.southernequality.org/wp-content/uploads/2016/03/Judge-Jordan-III-opinion-in-Campaign-for-Southern-Equality-v.-Mississippi-Department-of-Human-Services-et-al.pdf

Carter, D. (2004). *Stonewall: The riots that sparked the gay revolution.* New York, NY: St. Martin's Press.

Cohen, J. (2012, July 13). And the band played on, Vol. 2. *Science, 337,* 174–175. doi:10.1126/science.337.6091.174

Conley, T. D., Moors, A. C., Matsick, J. L., & Ziegler, A. (2013). The fewer the merrier? Assessing stigma surrounding consensually non-monogamous romantic relationships. *Analyses of Social Issues and Public Policy, 13*(1), 1–30. doi:10.1111/j.1530-2415.2012.01286.x

Council for Accreditation of Counseling and Related Educational Programs. (2015). *2016 CACREP standards.* Alexandria, VA: Author.

Crethar, H. C., & Vargas, L. A. (2007). Multicultural intricacies in professional counseling. In J. Gregoire & C. Jungers (Eds.), *The counselor's companion: What every beginning counselor needs to know* (pp. 52–69). Mahwah, NJ: Erlbaum.

Defense of Marriage Act of 1996, 28 U.S.C. §§ 7–28 (1996).

Deitcher, D. (Ed.). (1995). *The question of equality: Lesbian and gay politics in America since Stonewall.* New York, NY: Scribner.

Diaz, E. M., & Kosciw, J. G. (2009). *Shared differences: The experiences of lesbian, gay, bisexual, and transgender students in our nation's schools.* New York, NY: GLSEN.

Don't Ask, Don't Tell Repeal Act of 2010, 10 U.S.C. §§ 654 (2010).

Drescher, J., & Merlino, J. P. (Eds.). (2007). *American psychiatry and homosexuality: An oral history.* New York, NY: Harrington Park Press.

Duberman, M. (1993). *Stonewall.* New York, NY: Penguin Books.

Edsall, N. (2003). *Toward Stonewall: Homosexuality and society in the modern Western world.* Charlottesville: University of Virginia Press.

Federal Bureau of Investigation. (2014). *FBI releases 2013 hate crime statistics.* Retrieved from https://www.fbi.gov/news/pressrel/press-releases/fbi-releases-2013-hate-crime-statistics

Foden-Vencil, K. (2016, June 17). *Neither male nor female: Oregon resident legally recognized as third gender.* Retrieved from the NPR Law website: http://www.npr.org/2016/06/17/482480188/neither-male-nor-female-oregon-resident-legally-recognized-as-third-gender

Fone, B. R. S. (2000). *Homophobia: A history.* New York, NY: Metropolitan Books.

Foster, T. (2007). *Long before Stonewall: Histories of same-sex sexuality in early America.* New York, NY: New York University Press.

Godbeer, R. (2002). *Sexual revolution in early America.* Baltimore, MD: Johns Hopkins University Press.

Gomillion, S. C., & Giuliano, T. A. (2011). The influence of media role models on gay, lesbian, and bisexual identity. *Journal of Homosexuality, 58*(3), 330–354. doi:10.1080/00918369.2011.546729

Green, P. (2007). *Alexander the Great and the Hellenistic Age.* London, UK: Phoenix.

Greenberg, D. F. (1988). *The construction of homosexuality.* Chicago, IL: University of Chicago Press.

Hammack, P. L. (2005). The life course development of human sexual orientation: An integrative paradigm. *Human Development, 48,* 267–290.

Harper, A., Finnerty, P., Martinez, M., Brace, A., Crethar, H., Loos, B., . . . Lambert, S. (2013). Association for Lesbian, Gay, Bisexual, and Transgender Issues in Counseling (ALGBTIC) competencies for counseling with lesbian, gay, bisexual, queer, questioning, intersex and ally individuals. *Journal of LGBT Issues in Counseling, 7*(1), 2–43. doi:10.1080/15538605.2013.755444

Hooker, E. (1956). A preliminary analysis of group behavior of homosexuals. *Journal of Psychology, 42,* 217–225.

Houseman, J. C. (2010). *The psychosocial impact of television on queer women.* Available from ProQuest Dissertations and Theses Global. (Order No. 3417162)

Hubbard, T. K. (2003). *Homosexuality in Greece and Rome: A sourcebook of basic documents.* Los Angeles, CA: University of California Press.

Human Rights Campaign. (2016). *Maps of state laws and policies.* Retrieved from http://www.hrc.org/state_maps

Jacobs, S., Thomas, W. (Navajo), & Lang, S. (1997). Introduction. In S. Jacobs, W. Thomas (Navajo), & S. Lang (Eds.), *Two-spirit people: Native American gender identity, sexuality, and spirituality* (pp. 1–20). Chicago, IL: University of Illinois Press.

Kinsey, A. C., Pomeroy, W. B., & Martin, C. E. (1948). *Sexual behavior in the human male.* Philadelphia, PA: W. B. Saunders.

Kinsey, A. C., Pomeroy, W. B., Martin, C. E., & Gebhard, P. H. (1953). *Sexual behavior in the human female.* Philadelphia, PA: W. B. Saunders.

Klein, F. (1993). *The bisexual option.* New York, NY: Hawthorne Press.

Kocet, M. (2008). *Power/privilege checklist.* Retrieved from http://vc.bridgew.edu/cgi/viewcontent.cgi?filename=2&article=1003&context=change&type=additional

Kosciw, J. G., Greytak, E. A., Palmer, N. A., & Boesen, M. J. (2014). *The 2013 National School Climate Survey: The experiences of lesbian, gay, bisexual and transgender youth in our nation's schools.* New York, NY: GLSEN.

Krajeski, J. (1996). Homosexuality and the mental health professions. In R. Cabaj & T. Stein (Eds.), *Textbook of homosexuality and mental health* (pp. 17–31). Washington, DC: American Psychiatric Press.

LeBeauf, I., Smaby, M., & Maddux, C. (2009). Adapting counseling skills for multicultural and diverse clients. In G. R. Walz, J. C. Bleuer, & R. K. Yep (Eds.), *Compelling counseling interventions: VISTAS 2009* (pp. 33–42). Alexandria, VA: American Counseling Association.

Macgillivray, I. K. (2008). Religion, sexual orientation, and school policy: How the Christian right frames its arguments. *Educational Studies, 43*(1), 29–44. doi:10.1080/00131940701796210

Marcus, E. (2002). *Making gay history.* New York, NY: HarperCollins.

Mussi, M. (2002). *Earliest Italy: An overview of the Italian paleolithic and mesolithic.* New York, NY: Springer.

Obergefell et al. v. Hodges et al., 575 U.S. 14-556 (2015).

Ochman, J. M. (1996). The effects of nongender-role stereotyped, same-sex role models in storybooks on the self-esteem of children in grade three. *Sex Roles, 35,* 711–736.

Pedersen, P. B. (2001). Multiculturalism and the paradigm shift in counseling: Controversies and alternative futures. *Canadian Journal of Counselling, 35*(1), 15–25.

Pizer, J. C., Sears, B., Mallory, C., & Hunter, N. D. (2012). Evidence of persistent and pervasive workplace discrimination against LGBT people: The need for federal legislation prohibiting discrimination and providing for equal employment benefits. *Loyola of Los Angeles Law Review, 45,* 715–779.

Ratts, M. J., Singh, A. A., Nassar-McMillan, S., Butler, S. K., & McCullough, J. R. (2015). *Multicultural and social justice counseling competencies.* Retrieved from https://www.counseling.org/docs/default-source/competencies/multicultural-and-social-justice-counseling-competencies.pdf?sfvrsn=20

Rizzo, J., & Cohen, Z. (2016, June 30). *Pentagon ends transgender ban.* Retrieved from the CNN Politics website: http://www.cnn.com/2016/06/30/politics/transgender-ban-lifted-us-military/

Roberts, A. L., Rosario, M., Slopen, N., Calzo, J. P., & Austin, S. (2013). Childhood gender nonconformity, bullying victimization, and depressive symptoms across adolescence and early adulthood: An 11-year longitudinal study. *Journal of the American Academy of Child & Adolescent Psychiatry, 52*(2), 143–152. doi:10.1016/j.jaac.2012.11.006

Robinson, J. L., & Rubin, L. J. (2016). Homonegative microaggressions and posttraumatic stress symptoms. *Journal of Gay & Lesbian Mental Health, 20*(1), 57–69. doi:10.1080/1935 9705.2015.1066729

Sears, B., & Mallory, C. (2011, July). *Documented evidence of employment discrimination & its effects on LGBT people.* Retrieved from http://williamsinstitute.law.ucla.edu/wp-content/uploads/Sears-Mallory-Discrimination-July-2011.pdf

Session Law 2016-3, House Bill 2. (2016). Retrieved from http://www.ncleg.net/sessions/2015e2/bills/house/pdf/h2v4.pdf

Shilts, R. (1987). *And the band played on: Politics, people and the AIDS (Acquired Immune Deficiency Syndrome) epidemic.* New York, NY: St. Martin's Press.

Singh, A., Merchant, N., Skudrzyk, B., & Ingene, D. (2012). *Association for Specialists in Group Work: Multicultural and social justice competence principles for group workers.* Retrieved from http://www.asgw.org/s/ASGW_MC_SJ_Priniciples_Final_ASGW.pdf

Stack, L. (2016, November 10). *Trump victory alarms gay and transgender groups.* Retrieved from the *New York Times* website: http://www.nytimes.com/2016/11/11/us/politics/trump-victory-alarms-gay-and-transgender-groups.html?_r=0

Sue, D. W., Capodilupo, C. M., Torino, G. C., Bucceri, J. M., Holder, A. B., Nadal, K. L., & Esquilin, M. (2007). Racial microaggressions in everyday life: Implications for clinical practice. *American Psychologist, 62*(4), 271–286. doi:10.1037/0003-066X.62.4.271

Talalay, L. E. (2005). The gendered sea: Iconography, gender, and Mediterranean prehistory. In E. Blake & A. Bernard Knapp (Eds.), *The archaeology of Mediterranean prehistory* (pp. 130–148). Oxford, UK: Blackwell.

Tennessee Senate Bill 1556 (in recess). (2016). Retrieved from https://legiscan.com/TN/text/SB1556/2015

United States v. Windsor et al., 570 U.S. 12-307 (2013).

U.S. Department of Justice. (2016). *Dear colleague letter on transgender students.* Retrieved from http://www2.ed.gov/about/offices/list/ocr/letters/colleague-201605-title-ix-transgender.pdf

VandenBos, G. R. (2015). *APA dictionary of psychology* (2nd ed.). Washington, DC: American Psychological Association.

Wilhelm, A. D. (2008). *Tritiya-Prakriti: People of the third sex. Understanding homosexuality, transgender identity, and intersex conditions through Hinduism.* Philadelphia, PA: Xlibris.

Wohlford, K. E., Lochman, J. E., & Barry, T. D. (2004). The relation between chosen role models and the self-esteem of men and women. *Sex Roles, 50,* 575–582.

Chapter 2

The Science of Gender and Affectional Orientation

Misty M. Ginicola

If you hear someone say that homosexuality is unnatural,
you can be pretty sure you are not listening
to a scientist.

—Dr. Marc Breedlove

• • •

Awareness of Attitudes and Beliefs Self-Check

1. Have you ever heard the argument that gay or transgender individuals choose to be gay or transgender? In what context were those arguments made? By whom in your life?
2. Do you think that gender and affectional orientation are caused by nature or nurture?
3. Why do you think same-sex affectional orientation is present across cultures and species?

Case Study

Marley is a 5-year-old biracial Japanese American and Caucasian preschooler. Her mother, Marin, has come to counseling to discuss concerns she has with Marley. Since Marley was incredibly young (approximately 18 months), she acted very differently than Marin's other daughter. She did not want to wear dresses; rejected all of her sister's toys; and gravitated to her older brothers' toys, cars, and trucks. At 3, she wanted her mother to cut her hair short and asked to wear "boy clothes." Marin's husband was opposed to "giving in" to Marley, so they kept her hair long and kept Marley in girls' clothes. Marin was concerned because when Marley turned 4, she refused to attend her birthday party and became withdrawn and sad. Marin asks the counselor what she should do to help Marley.

• • •

What Is Gender and Affectional Orientation?

Although the science on gender and affectional orientation is still developing, much is known about the development of gender and affectional orientation variance as it is experienced in heterosexual and lesbian, gay, bisexual, transgender, queer, questioning, intersex, asexual, ally, pansexual/polysexual, and two-spirited (LGBTQI+) populations. It should be noted that as with all successful variation in nature, differences are important, remarkable, and to be celebrated. The key to human survival is attributable to diversity. Diversity of biology is equally important to human survival. However, differences are not always interpreted in an advantageous way by the larger society. This chapter seeks to explore biology as a determination of this variation while at the same time underscoring that affectional orientation and gender variance are part of a spectrum that should be celebrated.

As previously defined, gender orientation involves the *experience* of being feminine or masculine in the mind (Harper et al., 2013; VandenBos, 2015). Sexual or affectional orientation involves the biological and physiological impulse of attraction or arousal and the psychological impulse for romantic and emotional attraction, both of which provide a foundation for sexual behavior and bonding (Harper et al., 2013; VandenBos, 2015). Whereas these social definitions are based on self-identity and bonding behavior, the biology of variant gender and affectional orientation is based on sex-linked behavior, acting in stereotypically male or female patterns, which includes sexual activity (LeVay, 2011). These gendered behavior patterns are then evaluated as they are linked to genetics, physiological expressions of hormones and behavior, and other physiological markers (LeVay, 2011).

The biological nature of gender and affectional orientation is complex (LeVay, 2011). Although these four areas—gender identity, physical attraction, romantic attraction, and sexual behavior/bonding—are correlated, they are distinct biological systems and vary between and within individuals. These systems can also be completely disconnected in individuals with "same-sex" and opposite-sex attractions. For example, heterosexual individuals could feel romantic attachment to their spouse, be sexually attracted to someone they work with, but choose to stay monogamous to their partner. An individual could have just a gender variance, which would result in being transgender. Another person could have no changes to gender identity but have a strong attraction to members of the same sex, resulting in a gay, lesbian, or queer identity.

What Is the Biological Basis for Sexual Attraction?

The biological nature of sexual arousal and romantic attachment also indicates that they have distinct physiological processes (Buss & Schmitt, 1993; Fisher, Aron, Mashek, Li, & Brown, 2002; Sanders et al., 2015). Whereas estrogens and androgens are primarily associated with sexual development and attraction, initial affectional attraction is strengthened by pheromones and neurochemicals in the bonding process (Buss & Schmitt, 1993; Fisher et al., 2002; Sanders et al., 2015). This involves increases in both dopamine and norepinephrine in the central nervous system and lowered serotonin (Kohl, 2006). Initial romantic attraction can be measured in neural activity in the caudate nucleus, an area of the brain associated with pleasure and excitement (Buss & Schmitt, 1993; Fisher et al., 2002; Sanders et al., 2015). Sustained bonding and attachment are associated with the expression of neuropeptides, vasopressin, and oxytocin (Buss & Schmitt, 1993; Fisher et al., 2002; Sanders et al., 2015). Attachment is also associated with the ventral tegmental area, the same area of the brain associated with addiction; this area of the brain activates when individuals think of their romantic partners (Buss & Schmitt, 1993; Fisher et al., 2002; Sanders et al., 2015). Therefore, affectional attachment is associated with a neurochemistry of both pleasure and reward; in many ways, our brain shows an *addiction* to our chosen partners (Buss & Schmitt, 1993; Fisher et al., 2002; Sanders et al., 2015). The insula and striatum have also been associated with sexual attraction; even though romantic love has a similar process, these areas of the brain are separate (Buss & Schmitt, 1993; Fisher et al., 2002; Sanders et al., 2015). In the majority of individuals, these systems are correlated and aligned, with the individual being attracted to and romantically bonded with the same person. However, it is also possible that these systems do not develop differentially and are not correlated; this could explain why some individuals (e.g., asexual persons) may feel romantic attraction but not sexual attraction.

What Is the Evidence for a Biological Cause for Gender and Affectional Orientation?

It is clear that biology provides a foundation for behavior; in regard to same-sex bonding, there is no shortage of evidence pointing to a biological cause (Bem, 2000; Goy, Bercovitch, & McBrair, 1988; LeVay, 2011). Other species of animals, such as sheep, rams, dolphins, penguins, swans, dragonflies, fruit flies, apes, lions, and giraffes, to name a few, have been found to exhibit same-sex partnerships (Adkins-Regan, 2002, 2005; Bagemihl, 1999; De Waal, 2006; Ferveur & Savarit, 1997; Roselli & Stormshak, 2009; Sommer & Vasey, 2006). Some of these bonds, such as in penguins, persist for the entire life span (Pincemy, Dobson, & Jouventin, 2010). Another tenet of support for a biological influence is the expression of psychological and physiological gender characteristics: These gender characteristics are variant in the population and do not follow a strict male–female continuum (LeVay, 2011).

Sex hormones play a role in the development of sexual attraction and orientation (Ellis & Ames, 1987). In particular, disruptions in androgens in the fetal period have been linked to gender-differentiated behavior in children (Auyeng et al., 2009; Berenbaum, 1999) as well as sexual attraction and same-sex sexual behavior in human and animal studies (Bakker, Brand, Van Ophemert, & Slob, 1993; Chapman & Stern, 1978; Ellis & Ames, 1987; Lephart et al., 2001). These hormones are responsible for creating structural and functional differences in the brain that are indeed measurable in youth and adults.

Heterosexual, cisgender males and females typically differ in brain anatomy and circuitry (Byne et al., 2001; Fine, 2014; Garcia-Falgueras & Swaab, 2008; Gorski, Gordon, Shryne, & Southam, 1978; Morris, Jordan, & Breedlove, 2008). For example, a region of the hypothalamus, the medial preoptic area, an area of the brain that is involved in sexual behavior, is larger in males than in females (Byne et al., 2001; Garcia-Falgueras & Swaab, 2008; Gorski et al., 1978; Morris et al., 2008). There are also differences between the sexes in other areas of the hypothalamus, amygdala, and stria terminalis; neurochemical patterns, hormone expression, and activity patterns in the brain are also measurably different between males and females (Byne et al., 2001; Garcia-Falgueras & Swaab, 2008; Gorski et al., 1978; Morris et al., 2008). Researchers call this phenomenon the *gendered brain* (LeVay, 2011). The research on affectional orientation indicates that the gendered brain is measurably different among the LGBTQI+ population and the heterosexual population, with some exhibiting cross-gender characteristics and others statistically increased variance (Allen & Gorski, 2007; LeVay, 1991, 2011; Savic, Berglund, Lindström, & Gustafsson, 2005).

These differences should not be thought of as disorders; rather, they are natural variations (LeVay, 2011). Current theory indicates that genes, random variability, and in utero environmental influences at specific periods of time influence the differentiation of the brain in a gendered manner (Bocklandt & Vilain, 2007). Gender nonconformity and affectional orientation have been found to have a genetic basis and can be passed on in family generations; this could indicate a genetic predisposition to cellular androgen (e.g., testosterone) receptiveness as well as baseline levels of sex hormone expression (Alanko et al., 2010; Bailey & Pillard, 1991; Bailey, Pillard, Neale, & Agyei, 1993; Bocklandt & Vilain, 2007; Zuloaga, Puts, Jordan, & Breedlove, 2008). The intrauterine environment, including exposure to androgens in fetal development and how many males a mother has carried previously, also has a relationship to the gendered brain: The theory that after carrying a male son mothers create antibodies when they detect testosterone in subsequent male pregnancies is currently favored (Blanchard, 2004; Blanchard & Lippa, 2007; Bocklandt & Vilain, 2007; Meyer-Bahlburg, Dolezal, Baker, Ehrhardt, & New, 2006). The current working hypothesis is that there is a complex biological system in place to ensure variability in terms of gender and personality in offspring (LeVay, 2011). In terms of behavior, these brain differences result in verbal and visuospatial skills, vocal pattern and postural differences, personality differences, aesthetic and occupational interests, socialization patterns, perception of masculinity and femininity, body shape, sexual interests, and sexual attraction to males and/ or females (Buss, 1989; Smyth, Jacobs, & Rogers, 2003).

The outcome of this biological variability could be gender nonconformity and/or same-sex relationships, behavior, and identity (Bailey & Bell, 1993; Goy et al., 1988; Hines, Golombok, Rust, Johnston, & Golding, 2002; LeVay, 2011). Regardless, the result of these hormonal and neuroanatomical differences is not full *gender inversion,* in which a gay male, for example, presents entirely with a feminized brain. Rather, there appears to be a shift in some but not all areas. Transgender individuals may experience a larger shift or more of an inversion than others. There are also substantial individual biological differences and cultural and social influences on the expression of behavior and presentation of gender. In other words, in one community in the LGBTQI+ population, such as lesbians, the full spectrum of gender expression could be represented, from overtly masculine to overtly feminine.

What is clear from the significant amount of research that exists is that (a) there is a biological foundation for the gender appearance of the brain; (b) the genetic and intrauterine environment impacts hormones, which in turn impact gender and stereotypical gendered behavior, including sexual attraction and bonding; (c) the brains of LGBTQI+ individuals have been found to indicate significant differences from their heterosexual and cisgender counterparts in terms of cross-gender similarities and increased variance; and (d) mountains of evidence point to a physiological cause for these affectional orientation and gender orientation differences (LeVay, 2011). This body of research strongly discredits choice, trauma, or rearing practices as viable influences for same-sex relationships and bonding (LeVay, 2011). Because gender and orientation differences have persisted and are found in every culture, it has been theorized that there must be some adaptive qualities for this variance (Mbugua, 2015; Zietsch et al., 2008).

Evolutionary biologists and psychologists have theorized that this variation in gender identity and affectional orientation actually serves adaptive purposes, such as increasing the mating success of heterosexuals, providing population control, and a kin selection benefit of increased survival rates for family members (Mbugua, 2015; Zietsch et al., 2008). Specifically, the kin selection hypothesis stipulates that because gay or lesbian individuals may have very few offspring, they would be more available to assist siblings with their children, with whom they share a blood bond and genetic characteristics (Mbugua, 2015). Another more recent hypothesis, based on historical information and animal studies, is that same-sex sexual encounters as a normative phenomenon bonded males to each other in building a lasting alliance, which could be linked to their survival in maintaining protection and providing food (Mbugua, 2015). For females, the same-sex alliance could benefit their reproductive survival and shared rearing of children (Mbugua, 2015).

Despite this scientific evidence and the fact that such biological diversity increases the adaptive nature of the species, diversity in a society is not always met with acceptance.

This leads to some severe environmental consequences for children who exhibit these gender-nonconforming characteristics, which can result in immense distress and impairments in psychological functioning. However, when children grow up feeling normative and valued for these differences, they are protected from distress and negative outcomes (van Beusekom, Bos, Overbeek, & Sandfort, 2015).

Conclusion

Sex, gender, and affectional orientation are complex in both development processes and expression. Research indicates that there is a biological and physiological cause for both gender and affectional orientation. The evidence is vast: This variance is found in other species, can be detected in early childhood, can be empirically observed, and has associations with genetic and hormonal variance. Although many in society currently view affectional orientation and gender variance as abnormal, the evidence does not support abnormal development in any way. The evidence supports a natural, perhaps advantageous variation that has persisted throughout time and across cultures. Although individuals have control over their behavior and what they choose to do with the attractions they have, research indicates that attractions, both romantic and sexual, may already be established at birth. Counselors should be comfortable discussing this scientific evidence in providing psychoeducation to LGBTQI+ clients and their families.

Questions for Further Discussion

1. What is Marley experiencing?
2. What are the possible biological explanations for Marley's experience?
3. How should the counselor describe this physiological evidence to Marin?
4. How might understanding the biology of gender and affectional orientation help Marin and her family?
5. What could protect Marley from her distress, evidenced through her withdrawal and sadness?

Resources

1. Learn about the most up-to-date scientific studies through LGBT Science at http://www.lgbtscience.org/.

References

Adkins-Regan, E. (2002). Development of sexual partner preference in the zebra finch: A socially monogamous, pair-bonding animal. *Archives of Sexual Behavior, 31*(1), 27–33. doi:10.1023/A:1014023000117

Adkins-Regan, E. (2005). *Hormones and animal social behavior.* Princeton, NJ: Princeton University Press.

Alanko, K., Santtila, P., Harlaar, N., Witting, K., Varjonen, M., Jern, P., . . . Sandnabba, N. K. (2010). Common genetic effects of gender atypical behavior in childhood and sexual orientation in adulthood: A study of Finnish twins. *Archives of Sexual Behavior, 39*(1), 81–92. doi:10.1007/s10508-008-9457-3

Allen, L. S., & Gorski, R. A. (2007). Sexual orientation and the size of the anterior commissure in the human brain. In G. Einstein (Ed.), *Sex and the brain* (pp. 725–729). Cambridge, MA: MIT Press.

Auyeng, B., Baron-Cohen, S., Ashwin, E., Knickmeyer, R., Taylor, K., Hackett, G., & Hines, M. (2009). Fetal testosterone predicts sexually differentiated childhood behavior in girls and in boys. *Psychological Science, 20*(2), 144–148. doi:10.1111/j.1467-9280.2009.02279.x

Bagemihl, B. (1999). *Biological exuberance: Animal homosexuality and natural diversity.* New York, NY: St. Martin's Press.

Bailey, J. M., & Bell, A. P. (1993). Familiality of female and male homosexuality. *Behavior Genetics, 23*(4), 313–322. doi:10.1007/BF01067431

Bailey, J. M., & Pillard, R. C. (1991). A genetic study of male sexual orientation. *Archives of General Psychiatry, 48,* 1089–1096. doi:10.1001/archpsyc.1991.01810360053008

Bailey, J. M., Pillard, R. C., Neale, M. C., & Agyei, Y. (1993). Heritable factors influence sexual orientation in women. *Archives of General Psychiatry, 50*(3), 217–223. doi:10.1001/archpsyc.1993.01820150067007

Bakker, J., Brand, T., Van Ophemert, J., & Slob, A. K. (1993). Hormonal regulation of adult partner preference behavior in neonatally ATD-treated male rats. *Behavioral Neuroscience, 107,* 480–487. doi:10.1037/0735-7044.107.3.480

Bem, D. J. (2000). Exotic becomes erotic: Interpreting the biological correlates of sexual orientation. *Archives of Sexual Behavior, 29,* 531–548. doi:10.1023/A:1002050303320

Berenbaum, S. A. (1999). Effects of early androgens on sex-typed activities and interests in adolescents with congenital adrenal hyperplasia. *Hormones and Behavior, 35*(1), 102–110. doi:10.1006/hbeh.1998.1503

Blanchard, R. (2004). Quantitative and theoretical analyses of the relation between older brothers and homosexuality in men. *Journal of Theoretical Biology, 230,* 173–187.

Blanchard, R., & Lippa, R. A. (2007). Birth order, sibling sex ratio, handedness, and sexual orientation of male and female participants in a BBC Internet Research Project. *Archives of Sexual Behavior, 36*(2), 163–176. doi:10.1007/s10508-006-9159-7

Bocklandt, S., & Vilain, E. (2007). Sex differences in brain and behavior: Hormones versus genes. *Advanced Genetics, 59,* 245–266.

Buss, D. M. (1989). Sex differences in human mate preference: Evolutionary hypothesis tested in 37 cultures. *Behavioral & Brain Sciences, 12,* 1–49.

Buss, D. M., & Schmitt, D. P. (1993). Sexual strategies theory: A contextual evolutionary analysis of human mating. *Psychological Review, 100,* 204–232.

Byne, W., Tobet, S., Mattiace, L. A., Lasco, M. S., Kemether, E., Edgar, M. A., . . . Jones, L. B. (2001). The interstitial nuclei of the human anterior hypothalamus: An investigation of variation with sex, sexual orientation and HIV status. *Hormones and Behavior, 40,* 86–92.

Chapman, R. H., & Stern, J. M. (1978). Maternal stress and pituitary–adrenal manipulations during pregnancy in rats: Effects on morphology and sexual behavior of male offspring. *Journal of Comparative and Physiological Psychology, 92,* 1074–1083. doi:10.1037/h0077509

De Waal, F. M. (2006). *Bonobo sex and society.* Retrieved from https://www.scientificamerican.com/article/bonobo-sex-and-society-2006-06/

Ellis, L., & Ames, M. A. (1987). Neurohormonal functioning and sexual orientation: A theory of homosexuality–heterosexuality. *Psychological Bulletin, 101*(2), 233–258. doi:10.1037/0033-2909.101.2.233

Ferveur, J., & Savarit, F. (1997, June 6). Genetic feminization of pheromones and its behavioral consequences in *Drosophila* males. *Science, 276,* 1555–1558.

Fine, C. (2014, November 21). His brain, her brain? *Science, 346,* 915–916. doi:10.1126/science.1262061

Fisher, H. E., Aron, A., Mashek, D., Li, H., & Brown, L. L. (2002). Defining the brain systems of lust, romantic attraction, and attachment. *Archives of Sexual Behavior, 31,* 413–419. doi:10.1023/A:1019888024255

Garcia-Falgueras, A., & Swaab, D. F. (2008). A sex difference in the hypothalamic uncinate nucleus: Relationship to gender identity. *Brain, 131,* 3132–3146. doi:10.1093/brain/awn276

Gorski, R. A., Gordon, J. H., Shryne, J. E., & Southam, A. M. (1978). Evidence for a morphological sex difference within the medial preoptic area of the rat brain. *Brain Research, 148*(2), 333–346. doi:10.1016/0006-8993(78)90723-0

Goy, R. W., Bercovitch, F. B., & McBrair, M. C. (1988). Behavioral masculinization is independent of genital masculinization in prenatally androgenized female rhesus macaques. *Hormones and Behavior, 22,* 552–571. doi:10.1016/0018-506X(88)90058-X

Harper, A., Finnerty, P., Martinez, M., Brace, A., Crethar, H., Loos, B., . . . Lambert, S. (2013). Association for Lesbian, Gay, Bisexual, and Transgender Issues in Counseling (ALGBTIC) competencies for counseling with lesbian, gay, bisexual, queer, questioning, intersex and ally individuals. *Journal of LGBT Issues in Counseling, 7,* 2–43. doi:10.1080/1 5538605.2013.755444

Hines, M., Golombok, S., Rust, J., Johnston, K. J., & Golding, J. (2002). Testosterone during pregnancy and gender role behavior of preschool children: A longitudinal, population study. *Child Development, 73,* 1678–1687.

Kohl, J. V. (2006). The mind's eyes: Human pheromones, neuroscience, and male sexual preferences. *Journal of Psychology & Human Sexuality, 18*(4), 313–369. doi:10.1300/ J056v18n04_03

Lephart, E. D., Call, S. B., Rhees, R. W., Jacobson, N. A., Weber, K. S., Bledsoe, J., & Teuscher, C. (2001). Neuroendocrine regulation of sexually dimorphic brain structure and associated sexual behavior in male rats is genetically controlled. *Biology of Reproduction, 64,* 571–578.

LeVay, S. (1991, August 30). A difference in hypothalamic structure between heterosexual and homosexual men. *Science, 253,* 1034–1037.

LeVay, S. (2011). *Gay, straight, and the reason why: The science of sexual orientation.* New York, NY: Oxford University Press.

Mbugua, K. (2015). Explaining same-sex sexual behavior: The stagnation of the genetic and evolutionary research programs. *Journal for General Philosophy of Science, 46*(1), 23–43. doi:10.1007/s10838-014-9273-5

Meyer-Bahlburg, H. L., Dolezal, C., Baker, S. W., Ehrhardt, A. A., & New, M. I. (2006). Gender development in women with congenital adrenal hyperplasia as a function of disorder severity. *Archives of Sexual Behavior, 35,* 667–684.

Morris, J. A., Jordan, C. L., & Breedlove, S. M. (2008). Sexual dimorphism in neuronal number of the posterodorsal medial amygdala is independent of circulating androgens and regional volume in adult rats. *Journal of Comparative Neurology, 506,* 851–859.

Pincemy, G., Dobson, F. S., & Jouventin, P. (2010). Homosexual mating displays in penguins. *Ethology, 116,* 1210–1216. doi:10.1111/j.1439-0310.2010.01835.x

Roselli, C. E., & Stormshak, F. (2009). The neurobiology of sexual partner preferences in rams. *Hormones and Behavior, 55,* 611–620. doi:10.1016/j.yhbeh.2009.03.013

Sanders, A. R., Martin, E. R., Beecham, G. W., Guo, S., Dawood, K., Rieger, G., . . . Bailey, J. M. (2015). Genome-wide scan demonstrates significant linkage for male sexual orientation. *Psychological Medicine, 45,* 1379–1388. doi:10.1017/S0033291714002451

Savic, I., Berglund, H., Lindström, P., & Gustafsson, J. (2005). Brain response to putative pheromones in homosexual men. *Proceedings of the National Academy of Sciences, USA, 102,* 7356–7361. doi:10.1073/pnas.0407998102

Smyth, R., Jacobs, G., & Rogers, H. (2003). *Male voices and perceived sexual orientation: An experimental and theoretical approach.* Cambridge, UK: Cambridge University Press.

Sommer, V., & Vasey, P. L. (2006). *Homosexual behaviour in animals: An evolutionary perspective.* New York, NY: Cambridge University Press.

27

van Beusekom, G., Bos, H. W., Overbeek, G., & Sandfort, T. M. (2015). Same-sex attraction, gender nonconformity, and mental health: The protective role of parental acceptance. *Psychology of Sexual Orientation and Gender Diversity, 2*(3), 307–312. doi:10.1037/sgd0000118

VandenBos, G. R. (2015). *APA dictionary of psychology* (2nd ed.). Washington, DC: American Psychological Association.

Zietsch, B. P., Morley, K. I., Shekar, S. N., Verweij, K. H., Keller, M. C., Macgregor, S., . . . Martin, N. G. (2008). Genetic factors predisposing to homosexuality may increase mating success in heterosexuals. *Evolution and Human Behavior, 29,* 424–433. doi:10.1016/j.evolhumbehav.2008.07.002

Zuloaga, D. G., Puts, D. A., Jordan, C. L., & Breedlove, S. M. (2008). The role of androgen receptors in the masculinization of brain and behavior: What we've learned from the testicular feminization mutation. *Hormones and Behavior, 53,* 613–626. doi:10.1016/j.yhbeh.2008.01.013

Section II

COUNSELING CONSIDERATIONS and COUNSELING STRATEGIES

Developmental Issues for LGBTQI+ People

Counseling Treatment Issues With LGBTQI+ Clients

Chapter 8
  Disaffirming Therapy: The Ascent and Descent of
  Sexual Orientation Change Efforts

Chapter 9
  Evidence-Based Practice for Counseling the LGBTQI+ Population

Chapter 10
  Affirmative, Strengths-Based Counseling With LGBTQI+ People

• • •

In order to serve lesbian, gay, bisexual, transgender, queer, questioning, intersex, asexual, ally, pansexual/polysexual, and two-spirited (LGBTQI+) clients in a competent manner, counselors need to understand the lives of LGBTQI+ persons as well as what types of counseling interventions are appropriate for this population. In this section, authors explore how LGBTQI+ youth grow up differently than their heterosexual and cisgender peers. The additional specialized needs surrounding being an LGBTQI+ youth and adult are discussed. In addition to the many cultural and environmental stressors related to growing up as an affectional orientation and gender minority, the role of coming out and understanding one's own affectional orientation and gender identity can also alter the way a person develops. These additional stressors can cause physical and mental health challenges of which counselors must be aware. This section also covers the types of therapeutic interventions for LGBTQI+ individuals that are ethical and empirically based as well as the history of sexual orientation change efforts, which are considered unethical and harmful, and are not to be used under any circumstances.

DEVELOPMENTAL ISSUES FOR LGBTQI+ PEOPLE

Chapter 3

Growing Up LGBTQI+:
The Importance of Developmental
Conceptualizations

Anneliese A. Singh, Kristopher M. Goodrich, Amney J. Harper, and Melissa Luke

*I wasn't always this confident. Growing up as the awkward gay kid
in a small town in Pennsylvania, you're constantly told,
"Don't be yourself, don't be proud of who you are."*
—Carson Kressley

• • •

Awareness of Attitudes and Beliefs Self-Check

1. What messages did you receive in regard to being a boy or a girl as you grew up?
2. Did you grow up with someone who did not conform to their gender? How did others react to them?
3. From early school age to adulthood, which was the most difficult age for you? Why?

Case Study

As a 9-year-old in fourth grade, Erik, a Caucasian male, was a student in the gifted and talented program at Smithville Elementary School. Records indicate that Erik had some difficulty with peers in physical education class, and teachers reporting incidences of Erik acting out when entering the locker room to change. When the school contacted Erik's mother to discuss their concerns, she informed them that Erik would be dressing up as a Disney princess for Halloween. She reported that Erik dressed in this manner consistently at home and that she and her partner were supportive of Erik's choice of costume for this school event. In seventh grade, Erik switched school districts and requested to be addressed as Erika, with increasingly changing gender expression. Although

Erika did not consistently express a male gender identity, all acting-out behaviors had ceased. That said, Erika was reported as being somewhat isolated from peers. She noted to a teacher that she was sometimes uncomfortable in school, especially when hearing comments like "That's so gay" and "No homo." Erika's parents called the school once, reporting that an unidentified group of students blocked her from entering the bathroom.

Once in high school, Erika developed a small group of friends who were supportive of her gender expression, was on the honor roll, and became active in student leadership in both the GSA and Peer Helpers. (Although GSA once stood for *gay–straight alliance,* many individual clubs are changing their names to *gender and sexualities alliance* or other similar names to remove the term *straight* and represent gender minorities in the organization.) That said, Erika's good friend Jaid reported concerns about Erika to the school counselor. Jaid noted that Erika had just broken up with Emory, a fellow female student, and that Erika was despondent about Emory's Facebook posts, as Emory was suggesting that Erika was "unattractive" and "mental." Furthermore, Jaid indicated that Erika had isolated herself, saying that she "hated life" because Emory had outed her as a lesbian to others.

• • •

Typical Development

Although educational settings organize students by chronological age and grade level, a student's development progresses unevenly across physical, cognitive, personal, social-emotional, moral, and cultural domains (Goodrich & Luke, 2015). Thus, what follows is a discussion of some key tenets of development that have the potential to influence the ways in which a lesbian, gay, bisexual, transgender, queer, questioning, intersex, asexual, ally, pansexual/polysexual, and two-spirited (LGBTQI+) student's basic needs of safety, belonging, love, and respect (Maslow, 1968) can be addressed. In order to illustrate the differences associated with growing up LGBTQI+, we review developmental theory and apply it to a developmental conceptualization of the case of Erika.

Physical

Although the most dramatic human growth takes place from birth to age 2 (Berger, 2003), changes in children's and adolescents' height, weight, and physical abilities continually progress throughout their development. Children in early childhood are in perpetual motion (Vernon, 2009), and they are continually practicing and refining their gross motor and fine motor skills (Owens, 2002). Although growth spurts in middle childhood and adolescence are common, there is wide variation in when such development, including the onset of puberty, takes place (Owens, 2002). Thereafter, the physiological similarities in children's body size, shape, and proportion shift and secondary sexual characteristics become more visible. These include increases in height, weight, and body hair as well as the broadening of hips and development of breasts in females and the widening of shoulders and deepening of the voice in males. During this period of physical development, changes in appetite and the need for sleep are evident, as are differing requirements for hygiene (Sussman & Rogel, 2004).

Cognitive

Piaget described preoperational thinking marking early childhood, with children engaging in fantasy play (Piaget & Cook, 1952; Wadsworth, 2004). Over time such magical thinking is punctuated by increasing incidents of logic (Rathus, 2004). That said, children at this point in development tend toward dichotomous and reductionist thinking (Trawick-Smith, 2000) as opposed to using a multiplistic and broad view. By middle childhood, children become more able to implement sequential thought, displaying concrete operational thinking (Piaget & Cook, 1952; Wadsworth, 2004). This development is marked by an understanding and awareness of concepts such as reversibility, reciprocity, identity, and classification. In early adolescence, thinking progresses toward more formal operations, wherein adolescents can increasingly take multiple perspectives, hypothesize, and use abstract reasoning (Wigfield, Lutz, & Wagner, 2005). Although more relativistic thinking is typical of later adolescence (Owens, 2002), the ability to philosophize in an abstract fashion continues to be used inconsistently (Sussman & Rogel, 2004).

Personal

Children display egocentrism in early childhood, unable to see the world outside of their own perspective (Vernon, 2009). Thus, it is not surprising that children's self-concept is typically quite positive in early childhood; as self-control and attention increase in early childhood, children's self-efficacy grows (Berger, 2003) and they evidence high levels of motivation. In middle childhood, children begin to recognize a multidimensional self composed of many traits and abilities and also begin to compare themselves to others (Owens, 2002). Dependent on a unique combination of internal and contextual strengths and challenges, children's self-concept can strengthen and moments of self-doubt arise (Bee, 2000). By early adolescence, self-definition and integration begin (Martin, 2003), with adolescents increasingly considering their identity and where they fit into the social world. Early adolescents have been described as having conflicting desires to be unique while also submitting to perceived pressures from imaginary audiences (Elkind, 2007). Egocentrism continues throughout adolescence, with a belief in one's specialness. At this point in development, a sense of invincibility (Elkind, 1984) comingles with a drive for increased autonomy (Owens, 2002), wherein later adolescents exhibit an increased ability to resist peer pressure and establish independent "vocational, political, social, sexual, moral, and religious identities" (Vernon, 2009, p. 28).

Social-Emotional

Children progress from engagement in primarily parallel play to increased abilities for associative and cooperative play in early childhood (Vernon, 2009). Children at this stage operate fluidly, without assigned roles or adhering to structure or rules (Owens, 2002). By school age, children increasingly select same-gender playmates (Owens, 2002; Rathus, 2004), with growing preferences for gender-typical play activities (Owens, 2002; Rathus, 2004). By middle childhood, children have often selected a preferred or best friend, and they begin to develop abilities to navigate difference across values, personality, behavior, and perspectives (Bee, 2000). At this point, children understand others' perspectives and exhibit more prosocial behaviors (Vernon, 2009). Aided by their burgeoning multiplistic thinking, children can recognize nuances in and discrepancies among what people think, feel, and do (Vernon, 2009). On a related note, in middle childhood children may experience a broader range of emotions that continues into early adolescence. Peers remain a significant force in adolescents' socialization, with particular sensitivity to group belonging and exclusion (Vernon, 2009). Gender differences in expectations for competence become increasingly relevant in establishing peer credibility, with athletic abilities stressed for males and prosocial leadership for females (Bee, 2000). Adolescents' volatile internal emotional experiences may be exacerbated by such expectations (Bee, 2000), and early adolescents frequently experience decreased self-concept and increased feelings of social vulnerability (Vernon, 2009). In middle and late adolescence, self-confidence increases as tolerance of individual difference expands. Intimate emotional connection also increases, and desires for romantic and sexual engagement often develop (Vernon, 2009).

Moral

Kohlberg (1958) described children moving through three multistage levels of moral development, with preconventional morality lasting until middle childhood. Preconventional morality is defined by reliance on an external authority (others) and direct consequences to establish right and wrong. In early adolescence, conventional morality develops in most people. The ability to think abstractly assists in the internalization of authority, with the adolescent increasingly able to understand the role of interpersonal relationships and social order. Kohlberg hypothesized that not all people develop postconventional morality. Often not manifested until full adulthood, postconventional morality is marked by the late adolescent's ability to apply moral reasoning based on individual rights and justice. As Kohlberg's theory was based on an all-male sample, Gilligan (1977) raised concerns that the theory purports a male definition of morality, not accounting for women approaching moral problems with an ethic of care, as opposed to justice, perspective.

Cultural

Children develop in a cultural context wherein there is a shared "way of life, including customs, traditions, laws, knowledge, shared meanings, norms, and values" (Henderson & Thompson, 2016, pp. 46–47). Generally transmitted by caretakers, children's cultural development includes a recognition of race, ethnicity, gender, religion, affectional orientation, gender identities, social class, and age cohort. Thus, in early childhood, children's ability to recognize cultural belonging and difference is simplistic and is based on visible, concrete, and sometimes stereotypic understanding. Although children may not be able to fully understand or articulate all of the elements of cultural identity, group membership can influence other aspects of development (Pedersen, Darguns, Lonner, & Trimble, 2008). In later childhood, children start to distinguish beliefs from behaviors, and they start to realize the complexities and intersectionality with respect to their own culture and that of others. With increased social interaction, later childhood and early adolescence bring increased exposure to people from other cultural groups. This process and the varied experiences can influence acculturation and the development of cultural bias or pluralism. Holcomb-McCoy (2005) noted that in early adolescence, ethnicity and race can play a critical role in identity development; it would follow that affectional orientation and gender identity are similarly relevant. In fact, Meece (2002) noted that adolescents whose identity is juxtaposed with those more privileged in the majority culture may experience increased anxiety and depression that contribute to additional struggles in establishing a cultural identity.

The Application of Developmental Theories
to LGBTQI+ Youth

In order to understand the key aspects of LGBTQI+ development as it differs across the varied domains, we discuss here the elements of Erika's identity, specifically in the preschool through 12th-grade school context. From an ecological perspective (Bronfenbrenner, 2005), multiple overlapping systems may have the potential to influence Erika's development. There are several ways in which school counselors or other counseling professionals might reflect on their work with Erika to best serve her needs. These techniques should consider her development to ensure that she is safe and supported as she progresses through her familial, social, emotional, and cognitive experiences in school.

The Elementary School Context

Using Erikson's (1959) stages of psychosocial development as a frame, we can say that Erika at age 9 is probably in the industry versus inferiority stage of development. This stage of development typically occurs for youth between the ages of 5 and 12 years. In this stage, peers, teachers, and parents take on importance in children's lives, and youth begin to recognize their special talents as well as have these recognized by others. Youth continue to explore and hone their skills and receive feedback from others about their performance. At this stage of development, crises can occur for youth, which can lead to low motivation, lower self-esteem, and lethargy.

At this stage of development, Erika is exploring her uniqueness in school and using her industriousness to state her need to come to a school event dressed as a Disney princess. Although a one-time occurrence in elementary school, there appears to be a pattern in which her peers may bully her, demonstrating a potential issue that may need to be dealt with in a systemic way. When children or adolescents are forming their identities, negative experiences can complicate that process for them, possibly halting or altering other aspects of their development until the issue is resolved. These developmental blocks can vary in how they present with each child in terms of duration, intensity, overall effect, and developmental focus. An example might be a child who begins to suppress their identity or withdraw from family and friends after being bullied about this identity. Specifically, Erika's mother shares that she is having difficulty with peers, and some of this has to stem from her peers' reaction when it comes time for Erika to change for physical education classes. Thus, one can see a potential developmental block for the client in this situation, as she is not receiving positive messages from her peers about who she is, and they appear not to understand her needs. She is aided, however, by support from her parents, who do express affirmation of her choice of Halloween costume.

In this case, the client is struggling with social-emotional relationships with peers and potentially facing some confusion from a moralistic standpoint, as she has received differing external messages about her identity from her parents, her school-based peers, and authority figures. She probably does not feel congruent with her physical body, as there may not be positive messages about her experience or opportunities for her to explore these feelings openly with others. If this does ring true for Erika, she might be a candidate for consideration of hormone blockers to prevent or delay the onset of puberty and the development of secondary sex characteristics of the sex with which she does not identify. Erika is evidencing high cognitive development; she still looks to deviate from dichotomous thinking and share her more concrete operationalist view of herself and her gender expression in a school environment that appears more rigid. Though it is not explicitly stated by cognitive theory, counselors might find persons exploring their identity to have given deep cognitive consideration to it prior to the onset of secondary sex characteristics that come with puberty, especially as they become aware of the impending nature of puberty. This can be explored in counseling to understand both who clients are internally and how they view themselves in the world; it would also be important to consider how this view might influence ongoing developmental processes at the individual, group, and societal levels.

For counselors and educators working with students in elementary school, the nonprofit educational organization the Human Rights Campaign (2015) offers the Welcoming Schools curriculum and campaign, which provides a group of resources for elementary educators to use to address issues of culture and difference in a developmentally appropriate way. The curriculum helps students to understand what it means to be an "other" and learn how to have a broader view of the experiences of others. The curriculum offers excellent resources made specifically for early childhood and elementary students, so it is developmentally appropriate both in language and in content. Thus, not much formatting is needed in terms of implementation in schools, and preliminary research has shown some effectiveness with diverse student groups, specifically around LGBTQI+ issues, a prime focus of the curriculum. It should be noted, however, that the Human Rights Campaign has had a challenging relationship with the transgender community because of some political decisions it made in the past, which have been seen by some as lacking advocacy. Although the Human Rights Campaign has made strides in recent years to address this concern, counselors should be aware of this history.

The Middle School Context

In the middle school context, Erika is beginning her transition by asserting her name and pronouns to others, a marker of increased identity development. We have learned a lot from persons in the transgender community about the need to help allies in having a *mental shift* when it comes to interacting with and advocating for transgender individuals. For example, instead of thinking of transgender people as who they used to be first and who they are now second (mental gymnastics that often result in mistakes), allies are asked to begin with who the transgender person is now, as the previous identity is no longer relevant. References to previous identities can cause distress for transgender people because previous identities are often used as ways to invalidate who they are (e.g., *dead naming* is a term used in transgender communities to refer to situations in which typically cisgender people refer to transgender people by their dead or previous name or misgender them). This often happens in journalism, in which a point is made ad nauseam about a transgender person, using incorrect pronouns and their dead name, when it is irrelevant to the story. However, this issue often happens interpersonally, too, when cisgender people continue to refer to these former identities or misgender an individual. Some transgender people do want to talk about their previous identities, but this should be driven by the transgender people themselves, not by the ally. Counselors who work with transgender clients should similarly allow the person to lead when it comes to how much of this previous history is relevant and important to the client. When there is a need for this type of historical information to be gathered, the purpose for doing so should be clearly communicated to clients with the understanding and validation of their current identity.

In terms of Erikson's (1959) psychosocial stages of development, Erika may be transitioning between the industry versus inferiority stage (5–12 years of age) and the identity versus role confusion stage (13–19 years of age). In this stage, identity crises occur as youth attempt to figure out who they are as whole people. They utilize feedback provided by others as well as learn to have a deeper understanding of whom they perceive themselves to be. In addition, developmental delays may be associated with one's sexual/affectional or gender identity not being accepted. If Erika suppressed aspects of her identity or had fewer opportunities to enact and practice social interaction than her peers, it would be possible to see discrepancies across areas of her development. This is, however, an area that deserves greater study for persons who identify as transgender. Often to claim their identities, transgender people have to ignore the opinions and beliefs of others because rejection rates by cisgender people can be so high. For some persons, it might present as an altered path of development, although this is certainly not true for everyone.

In Erika's case, she appears to have a growing comfort with her identity and an ability to speak this clearly to others despite the messages she has received from unsupportive people in her life. She has transitioned to better reflect how she sees herself, not necessarily the gender that was based on her assigned sex at birth. Hormone blockers could be utilized with Erika to allow her to delay the onset of puberty, to assist her in not developing physically in ways with which she does not identify. From a cognitive and moral standpoint, she will continue to grow into more abstract thinking and not necessarily rely on external authority or peers to guide her actions. A hallmark of her development is her speaking up to teachers in her classroom, expressing her discomfort with pejorative language, such as "That's so gay" and "No homo." These changes, however, have negatively impacted her social-emotional development, as they have isolated her from her peer group. This may prompt some egocentrism in her personal development, as she would be forced to feel unique while being isolated from her peers.

There are a number of resources available to middle school educators to address some of these concerns. GLSEN (http://www.glsen.org/) has a group of resources and a curriculum for both middle and high school students, including a guide for creating and facilitating GSAs or acceptance coalitions. These resources can be utilized to have challenging conversations with students across schools to better understand and relate to LGBTQI+ student issues. In addition, PFLAG (https://community.pflag.org) has resources, including an ally guide for transgender persons, to help to explain to laypeople who transgender people are and how best to support their needs publicly and privately. Both of these resources could provide support to Erika in her current school environment as well as some of her peers who are not out.

The High School Context

In high school, Erika would face similar developmental concerns in terms of Erikson's (1959) model as in middle school, although toward the end of the high school experience she would prepare to move to the next developmental phase, intimacy versus isolation (typically beginning around age 20). Erika is active in these developmental phases by exploring both her affectional orientation and gender identity as well as tentatively beginning to form intimate relationships with others. As is true for other high school students, her first relationship has challenges and probably will not be the last relationship that she seeks in her life span. What Erika has to attend to, however, are concerns related to the level of disclosure of her identity to others and issues related to trust of others to keep these specific confidences.

In high school, Erika is beginning to socialize with others, thereby increasing her social-emotional development. It appears that many of her trusted peers are also members of the GSA, which demonstrates that homophily, or friendships between youth with similar characteristics, is a critical feature of her school experience (Martin-Stoney, Cheadle, Skalamera, & Crosnoe, 2015). Erika also appears to be stretching herself socially and successfully seeking leadership positions through a Peer Helpers group, which assists her in growing in other areas she has not yet been able to explore. However, not all transgender youth will find homes in LGBTQI+ organizations, because many organizations do not fully address the needs of their transgender members. There may be some critical issues in terms of how Erika views herself and her world following her breakup, specifically that her trust was lost and that someone attempted to out her before she may have been ready to publicly disclose. This issue has the possibility of threatening not only Erika's development but also her physical and emotional safety.

Coming Out

Coming out, or disclosure, is a topic that is addressed in much more detail in Chapter 6 of this text. However, disclosure can be an important issue for youth in schools, as students during this time tend to spend more time with their peers in school than anyone else in their lives (Crosnoe, 2011). Numerous reports by GLSEN (Kosciw, Greytak, Palmer, & Boesen, 2014) have reported on the experiences of LGBTQ youth in schools, expressing the fear, harassment, lack of safety, and perceived lack of support that these students face. According to one report, LGBTQ students reported verbal (74.1%) and physical (36.2%) harassment as well as assault (16.5%) due to their affectional orientation; students also reported verbal (55.2%) and physical (22.7%) harassment and assault (11.4%) due to their gender expression. Most students (56.7%) claimed they did not report incidents to school staff because they doubted that school staff would respond, and of students who did report incidents, 61.6% stated that school staff did nothing in response. Thus, disclosure can be a difficult issue for youth to navigate in schools and can be a huge safety factor for one to consider when thinking about coming out. Counselors should discuss safety plans as well as other considerations when students discuss coming out in schools (Goodrich & Luke, 2015).

As expressed in the case study, there are many opportunities for Erika to come out as part of her schooling experience. This also demonstrates part of the process of her coming out, moving to more active voicing of her identity to others, and expressing different manifestations of her identity as she explores who she is in the world. Erika first publicly expressed her gender identity while in fourth grade, by deciding to dress up as a Disney princess for Halloween, although she had dressed consistently in this manner at home prior to this. Without an active and explicit announcement, she first displayed her gender identity to her classmates and school through a holiday that has historically allowed members of the LGBTQI+ communities to explore gender congruence in a socially acceptable way. Later, in the seventh grade, Erika began the process of living more congruently with her gender identity on a more ongoing basis through switching schools and being around new persons with whom she did not already have established identities and relationships.

Later, the difference between her affectional orientation and her gender identity is evident when Erika enters into and terminates a relationship with Emory, a fellow female classmate. This relationship appears to be private, only shared with those close to the couple. When the relationship ends, however, aspects of that relationship are made more public in ways that make Erika feel uncomfortable. Thus, it appears that Erika was ready to discuss and be out related to her gender identity but not necessarily her affectional orientation at that time. This then highlights the process of identity development for Erika, demonstrating that there is different salience and comfort with identity and how public that identity is with others. Counselors cannot assume that this will be a similarly timed process for youth or that once a student identifies in one way (e.g., gender identity as transgender, intersex, genderqueer, or questioning), this will trump other identities (e.g., affectional orientation as lesbian, gay, bisexual, or questioning). Counselors must find ways to express affirmation for youth in their identity process and work with students to ensure that all are provided with respect and privacy as part of their lived experience. The Internet, social media networking, and the availability of technology have served as a way to expand how and where students can identify with others, but has also complicated relationships and presented potential risks or barriers for students in schools.

Conclusion

Counselors must be able to conceptualize clients as well as to understand what normative responses to an oppressive environment are. When working with LGBTQI+ persons, it is important to have knowledge regarding how LGBTQI+ persons' childhood and adolescence impact their development. By using traditional developmental theories, a counselor can assess how internal experiences of being LGBTQI+ and external experiences of oppression can impact clients' physical and mental health, social-emotional lives, relationships, and sense of self. This developmental conceptualization is what all counselors will base their interventions on when planning treatment for an LGBTQI+ client. Therefore, it is crucial that counselors can perform a developmental conceptualization with ease.

Questions for Further Discussion

1. How did being transgender and gay impact Erika's physical development?
2. How would Erika's gender and affectional orientation impact her personal and social-emotional development?
3. If Erika is already out as transgender, why would coming out as gay still be difficult?
4. What would Erika's risk factors be?
5. As a school counselor, what would your immediate concerns for Erika be? How might this translate into counseling and advocacy work?

Resources

1. Find more information on the Welcoming Schools program at http://www.welcomingschools.org/.
2. Find resources for LGBTQI+ youth through GLSEN at http://www.glsen.org/.
3. Find resources for LGBTQI+ youth and their families at https://community.pflag.org.
4. Learn more about supporting transgender students in school settings through the *Schools in Transition* guide at http://hrc-assets.s3-website-us-east-1.amazonaws.com/files/assets/resources/Schools-In-Transition.pdf.

References

Bee, H. (2000). *The developing child* (9th ed.). Needham Heights, MA: Allyn & Bacon.

Berger, S. K. (2003). *The developing person through childhood* (3rd ed.). New York, NY: Worth.

Bronfenbrenner, U. (2005). *Making human beings human: Bioecological perspectives on human development.* Thousand Oaks, CA: Sage.

Crosnoe, R. (2011). *Fitting in, standing out: Navigating the social challenges of high school to get an education.* New York, NY: Cambridge University Press.

Elkind, D. (1984). *All grown up and no place to go: Teenagers in crisis.* Reading, MA: Addison-Wesley.

Elkind, D. (2007). *The hurried child: Growing up too fast too soon* (25th anniversary ed.). Reading, MA: Addison-Wesley.

Erikson, E. H. (1959). *Identity and the life cycle: Selected papers.* New York, NY: International Universities Press.

Gilligan, C. (1977). In a different voice: Women's conceptions of self and of morality. *Harvard Educational Review, 47,* 481–517.

Goodrich, K. M., & Luke, M. (2015). *Group counseling with LGBTQI persons.* Alexandria, VA: American Counseling Association.

Henderson, D. A., & Thompson, C. L. (2016). *Counseling children* (9th ed.). Belmont, CA: Brooks/Cole.

Holcomb-McCoy, C. (2005). Ethnic identity development in early adolescence: Implications and recommendations for middle school counselors. *Professional School Counseling, 9,* 120–127.

Human Rights Campaign. (2015). *Welcoming schools.* Retrieved from http://www.welcomingschools.org/

Kohlberg, L. (1958). *The development of modes of thinking and choices in years 10 to 16* (Unpublished doctoral dissertation). University of Chicago, IL.

Kosciw, J. G., Greytak, E. A., Palmer, N. A., & Boesen, M. J. (2014). *2013 National School Climate Survey: LGBT students experience pervasive harassment and discrimination, but school-based resources and supports are making a difference.* Retrieved from http://www.glsen.org/article/2013-national-school-climate-survey

Martin, D. G. (2003). *Clinical practice with adolescents.* Pacific Grove, CA: Brooks/Cole.

Martin-Stoney, A., Cheadle, J. E., Skalamera, J., & Crosnoe, R. (2015). Exploring the social integration of sexual minority youth across high school contexts. *Child Development, 86,* 965–975. doi:10.1111/cdev.12352

Maslow, A. H. (1968). *Toward a psychology of being* (2nd ed.). Princeton, NJ: Van Nostrand.

Meece, J. L. (2002). *Child and adolescent development for educators* (2nd ed.). New York, NY: McGraw-Hill.

Owens, K. B. (2002). *Child and adolescent development: An integrated approach.* Belmont, CA: Wadsworth.

Pedersen, P. B., Darguns, J. G., Lonner, W. J., & Trimble, J. E. (2008). *Counseling across cultures* (6th ed.). Thousand Oaks, CA: Sage.

Piaget, J., & Cook, M. T. (1952). *The origins of intelligence in children.* New York, NY: International Universities Press.

Rathus, S. A. (2004). *Voyages in childhood.* Belmont, CA: Wadsworth.

Sussman, E. J., & Rogel, A. (2004). Puberty and psychological development. In R. M. Lerner & L. D. Steinberg (Eds.). *Handbook of adolescent psychology* (2nd ed., pp. 15–44). New York, NY: Wiley.

Trawick-Smith, J. (2000). *Early childhood development* (2nd ed.). Upper Saddle River, NJ: Prentice Hall.

Vernon, A. (2009). *Counseling children and adolescents* (4th ed.). Denver, CO: Love.

Wadsworth, B. J. (2004). *Piaget's theory of cognitive and affective development: Foundations of constructivism.* New York, NY: Longman.

Wigfield, A., Lutz, S. L., & Wagner, A. L. (2005). Early adolescents' development across the middle school years: Implications for school counselors. *Professional School Counseling, 9,* 112–119.

Chapter 4

LGBTQI+ Youth Development

Melissa Luke, Amney J. Harper, Kristopher M. Goodrich, and Anneliese A. Singh

*Every gay and lesbian person who has been lucky enough to survive the
turmoil of growing up is a survivor.*

—Bob Paris

• • •

Awareness of Attitudes and Beliefs Self-Check

1. How important has your parent's/guardian's approval been for you in your life?
2. What strengths do you think lesbian, gay, bisexual, transgender, queer, questioning, intersex, asexual, ally, pansexual/polysexual, and two-spirited (LGBTQI+) youth are likely to have?
3. Why do you believe there are such high rates of suicide among LGBTQI+ youth?

Case Study

Sam (a nickname for Seung) is a 16-year-old Korean American teenager who immigrated with her family at the age of 2 years. She has a good academic history and has never had any issues at school. But in the past few months, she has appeared withdrawn from her friends, and her grades have been slipping. When she is called into the school counselor's office, she is reluctant at first but finally admits that about a year ago she fell in love with her best friend, Joon. When she told her friend, Joon became irate; she yelled at Sam and broke off their friendship. Unfortunately, Joon told another friend, and because the Korean community is so small and tight-knit where Sam lives, it made its way back to her mother and father. She was immediately sent to the pastor at her parents' Christian church, where she has been attending "ex-gay" classes designed to help her reorient her sexual attractions to men. Sam says that she has never been attracted to boys; she knew from a very young age that she was gay. Sam speaks of her love for her religion as well but says that she has "failed" at changing her attractions. She began acting as if her attractions had changed about 3 months ago; last week, her church held her up to the congregation as a success story. However, Sam says, "I'm a fraud. And worse than that, I'm going to hell. And I haven't even been able to change my attractions. I've prayed to God, but nothing has happened." She says that the news about her being gay has now made it to school because the pastor openly talked about her during a church service. Other kids at school have begun to make fun of her, both for being gay and for being ex-gay. She admits that she has considered suicide: She has thought about taking the pills in her mother's medicine cabinet and ending her struggle. She says, "I'm going to hell anyway, so it doesn't matter."

• • •

Risks for LGBTQI+ Youth

There are numerous studies indicating that the experiences of marginalization and bullying that youth commonly experience lead to negative outcomes for LGBTQI+ youth (Birkett, Espelage, & Koenig, 2009; Collier, Beusekom, Bos, & Sandfort, 2013; Eisenberg & Resnick, 2006; Kosciw, Greytak, Palmer, & Boesen, 2014; Kosciw, Palmer, Kull, & Greytak, 2013; Russell, Ryan, Toomey, Diaz, & Sanchez, 2011). In discussing these negative outcomes, it is also important to note that most LGBTQI+ youth "grow up to lead happy, healthy, and productive lives" (Eisenberg & Resnick, 2006, p. 663). Probably the most well-known studies on these outcomes were conducted by GLSEN, which found that LGBTQI+ youth who experience bullying, victimization, or harassment at school are at far greater risk than their heterosexual and cisgender peers for negative mental health and academic outcomes (Kosciw et al., 2014). LGBTQI+ youth are at a high risk for "depression, substance use, violence victimization . . . family conflict, ostracism at school, and broader stigmatizing socio-cultural factors, such as homophobia" (Eisenberg & Resnick, 2006, p. 663). Increased risk for sexually transmitted infections, including HIV, is also linked to LGBTQI+ youth's experiences of peer victimization at school, as are mental health risks, commonly anxiety, depression, and suicidality (Eisenberg & Resnick, 2006; Russell et al., 2011).

Most of these studies also note that there are factors that moderate the relationship between LGBTQI+ identity and negative outcomes, such as school climate and peer victimization or bullying (Birkett et al., 2009; Collier et al., 2013; Eisenberg & Resnick, 2006; Kosciw et al., 2013, 2014; Russell et al., 2011). In other words, the oppression that LGBTQI+ youth face in schools directly relates to their level of risk for negative outcomes. This, along with certain supportive or resiliency factors, can help explain how some individuals adjust and thrive, whereas others face struggles in maintaining adaptive functioning. Peer victimization is a broader umbrella phenomenon of which bullying is considered to be one subtype (Collier et al., 2013). Bullying is a type of peer victimization in which there are repeated negative aggressive behaviors with a varied power differential between the individuals involved (Collier et al., 2013). Youth who are bullied by their peers are at greater risk for negative mental health outcomes, but they are at even greater risk when the victimization or bullying is motivated by bias or hate, such as anti-LGBTQI+ bullying (Russell et al., 2011). Experiences of peer victimization leave male youth at an increased risk for delinquency, violence and aggression, and substance use compared to their female peers at school (Russell et al., 2011).

The GLSEN study clearly noted a link between school climate, including the availability of support services and supportive personnel, and negative outcomes for LGBTQI+ youth (Kosciw et al., 2014). Birkett et al. (2009) reported that school personnel, such as administrators and teachers, often are not supportive of LGBTQI+ youth despite the growing literature acknowledging the importance of that support. They noted that 70% of LGBTQI+ youth reported harassment due to affectional orientation or gender identity, and of that group, 59% stated that it happened in the presence of school personnel (Birkett et al., 2009). These hostile climates, particularly ones that are homophobic, significantly increase the risk for negative outcomes (Birkett et al., 2009), whereas supportive environments significantly minimize this risk (Kosciw et al., 2014).

With regard to these outcomes, some other factors appear to increase risk. One area of potential jeopardy is during the transition from middle to high school (Birkett et al., 2009). Middle school is a time when peer victimization (e.g., bullying) typically increases (Birkett et al., 2009). Early adolescence marks a time when many LGBTQI+ youth are first beginning to understand their affectional orientation or experiment with same-sex sexual behaviors (Birkett et al., 2009). These milestones do not differ significantly for transgender and gender-nonconforming youth; however, it is true that children become aware of gender much earlier than affectional orientation (Grossman & D'Augelli, 2007). Most agree that children understand themselves to be boys or girls by age 2 and begin using pronouns (*he* and *she*) by age 3 (Grossman & D'Augelli, 2007). However, most transgender youth assert that they came to better understand their identities around puberty (Grossman & D'Augelli, 2006). These developmental milestones may be complicated for nonbinary transgender youth who identify not as boys or girls but as no gender, more than one gender, or a mix of genders. Because there are currently very few role models and roadmaps for this developmental path, this can provide particular challenges for youth. Because of the changes happening in their bodies, puberty can be a particularly difficult time for transgender youth if they are not supported by adults who will help them to access puberty-delaying hormone suppressants. Therefore, it would stand to reason that the transition to middle school may also prove difficult for transgender youth.

Another important factor that can indicate higher risk relates to which identity one holds under the LGBTQI+ umbrella. Birkett et al. (2009) found that questioning youth experience higher rates of negative outcomes than their lesbian, gay, or bisexual peers. They report higher levels of bullying and homophobic victimization, drug use, depression and suicidality, and truancy (Birkett et al., 2009; Russell et al., 2011). Developmentally speaking, it is believed that being in a homophobic or hostile environment can interrupt people's identity development; as the negative environment adds additional stressors when people are questioning their identity, in the absence of positive support, the homophobia could become internalized (Birkett et al., 2009).

Lesbian, gay, and bisexual youth are more likely to report suicide attempts than their heterosexual peers (Friedman, Koeske, Silvestre, Korr, & Sites, 2006). Eisenberg and Resnick (2006) noted that in their study of 2,255 lesbian, gay, and bisexual participants, more than 50% reported suicidal ideation, and a little fewer than 40% reported at least one attempt. This makes lesbian, gay, and bisexual youth more than 4 times as likely than heterosexuals to attempt suicide (Eisenberg & Resnick, 2006). One study showed around a 50% prevalence rate for suicidal ideation among transgender youth, and approximately one third of transgender youth reported at least one suicide attempt (Grossman & D'Augelli, 2007; Olson, Schrager, Belzer, Simons, & Clark, 2015). Ybarra, Mitchell, and Kosciw (2015) found that bullying victimization also increases the risk of suicidality. However, there is a need for more research on transgender youth and suicidality (Grossman & D'Augelli, 2007), so it is possible that these rates may not be reflective of all transgender youth. In addition, there is no information available on how a nonbinary transgender or genderqueer identity may further increase risks.

Whenever anyone talks about LGBTQI+ individuals as a whole community, it is important to keep in mind that these individuals are not a homogenous group when it comes to risk factors such as suicidality (Eisenberg & Resnick, 2006). Bisexuals in particular have been noted to experience higher rates of suicidality than their lesbian and gay peers (Birkett et al., 2009). When people have gender or affectional variance, they are at greater risk as well (Friedman et al., 2006). Friedman and colleagues (2006) suggested that health professionals regularly screen for experiences of bullying and, when present, perform suicide assessments with LGBTQI+ youth. Also, they encouraged professionals to ask about suicidality and bullying when they note gender-nonconforming behavior (Friedman et al., 2006). Given the high rates of suicidality among LGBTQI+ youth, this should be a standard protocol for counselors and mental health professionals.

Resilience and Well-Being

As important as it is to understand the negative experiences and mental health stressors that LGBTQI+ students experience as children and adolescents, it is also vital to recognize the resilience and stress coping skills that LGBTQI+ students may have (Singh & Jackson, 2012). Masten (2001) defined *resilience* as "a class of phenomena characterized by good outcomes in spite of serious threats to adaptation or development" (p. 228). Resilience exists in both individuals and communities and may develop in response to experiences of oppression (Hartling, 2005). *Stress coping* is another term often used along with *resilience* to describe an individual's responses to managing various life stressors. Resilience and stress coping influence well-being, as the more resilience and coping methods youth have, the more enhanced their well-being is (Hartling, 2005).

For LGBTQI+ students, resilience and stress coping may be enhanced in many ways. Some research with affectional orientation and gender minority youth suggested that identity disclosure or *coming out* was correlated with greater experiences of heterosexism; however, it was also correlated with lower depression and increased self-esteem (Kosciw, Palmer, & Kull, 2015). Research with transgender youth has identified several resilience strategies that they may use in response to transgender oppression: (a) the ability to self-define and theorize one's gender, (b) proactive agency and access to supportive educational systems, (c) connection to a transgender-affirming community, (d) reframing of mental health challenges, and (e) navigation of relationships with family and friends (Singh, Meng, & Hansen, 2014). Resilience and stress coping with regard to LGBTQI+ students must also take into account the experiences of resilience that LGBTQI+ students of diverse backgrounds have. Research with transgender youth of color, for instance, has identified that resilience strategies may include the following: (a) an evolving, simultaneous self-definition of racial/ethnic and gender identities; (b) an awareness of adultism experiences; (c) self-advocacy in educational systems; (d) the finding of one's place in the LGBTQI+ youth community; and (e) the use of social media to affirm one's identity as a transgender youth of color (Singh et al., 2014).

School and Community Support

Schools may use resilience-based interventions to reduce heterosexism and develop affirmative learning environments for LGBTQI+ students. Craig (2013) described a group counseling modality developed specifically to support LGBQ students in school settings called Affirmative Supportive Safe and Empowering Talk (ASSET). ASSET addressed common LGBTQI+ themes of identity disclosure, family and peer interactions, and school experiences in the context of resilience. This particular group intervention also attended to intersectionality, as it was geared toward multiethnic LGBQ students.

Extracurricular activities may also have positive influences on the resilience of LGBTQI+ students. Research on GSAs has indicated that participation in a GSA promotes increased well-being for LGBTQI+ students of color, and LGBTQI+ students in GSAs that were in affirming schools with long-term advisors had more positive health outcomes (Poteat et al., 2015). (Although GSA once stood for *gay–straight alliance,* many individual clubs are changing their names to *gender and sexualities alliance* or other similar names to remove the term *straight* and represent gender minorities in the organization.) Although GSAs are commonly situated in schools, community contexts may also provide environments that enhance LGBTQI+ student resilience. For example, organizations that serve LGBTQI+ youth and community LGBTQI+ youth support groups can be places where LGBTQI+ students are able to feel safe, affirmed, and empowered. Students are simultaneously able to expand their social support by connecting to other LGBTQI+ students like themselves. In these environments, there are often LGBTQI+ student proms and other extracurricular activities that support positive LGBTQI+ student development and overall well-being. Also, it is important to keep in mind that GSA faculty advisors use education and advocacy in GSAs to ensure that these groups are inclusive and welcoming of all LGBTQI+ identities (e.g., transgender, bi, queer, nonbinary) as well as keep intersectional issues in LGBTQI+ communities (e.g., racism, sexism, classism, ableism) at the forefront.

Family Support

Research has begun to identify family support as a key indicator of LGBTQI+ resilience. A study examining the role of family acceptance as a protective factor found that this variable increased health outcomes in terms of higher self-esteem, social support, and general health, as well as reduced depression, suicidal ideation and suicide attempts, and substance abuse (Ryan, Russell, Huebner, Diaz, & Sanchez, 2010). Because family acceptance is such a protective factor for LGBTQI+ students, resilience-based scholarship on working with the families of LGBTQI+ students has emerged.

Working with LGBTQI+ students and their families requires that counselors have strong competencies not only with LGBTQI+ youth but also with family counseling. Research has suggested the negative health outcomes that occur when family support is low (Mustanski & Liu, 2013); however, it is important to share with families the fact that the more support LGBTQI+ students have, the better their long-term health outcomes will be. In addition, families come in many forms—blended, multiracial, and families of choice, among other family constellations. Therefore, it is also important for counselors to be able to use resilience-based family interventions with diverse families. Poirier and colleagues (2012), for example, articulated the need for cultural and linguistic competence when working with LGBTQI+ students and their families from diverse backgrounds so that family interventions are effective. Finally, supporting family acceptance and resilience also often entails being able to engage in grief work with families, helping families to let go of the image of what they intended for their LGBTQI+ child and process the fear and anxiety they may have for their child. It is also important to provide resources for families as well as connect them with other families undergoing similar experiences, as they may not have access to LGBTQI+-affirming networks and resources.

Conclusion

As noted in this chapter, there are gender and affectional orientation identity–based challenges and risks for LGBTQI+ youth; it is imperative that families, educators, and counselors who work with youth be informed about these issues and how to best serve these clients. In the face of all these challenges and risks, youth can be resilient and may have protective factors assisting their growth and development. It is important for families, educators, and counselors to explore clients' strengths and protective factors and serve as allies and advocates, thereby increasing the supportive environment for youth in a developmental framework. In conclusion, how counselors understand, approach, and intervene with respect to youth, including LGBTQI+ youth, always reflects their own as well as larger cultural biases and prejudices. Accordingly, counselors should seek continued consultation and supervision as part of best practices with youth. In addition, this chapter serves to reinforce a call to action for counselors to address systemic and institutional oppressions that impact LGBTQI+ youth, as the majority of negative outcomes experienced relate mostly to the absence of protective factors and the presence of oppression, discrimination, and marginalization.

Questions for Further Discussion

1. What are Sam's risk factors? What types of resilience factors might Sam have? How about coping factors?
2. What is Sam's current school and community support like? In what way might this be complicated for her as an immigrant, ethnic minority, lesbian female?
3. What are the complications that Sam might face in gaining family support?
4. As a school counselor, what would your immediate concerns for Sam be? How could a counselor handle her suicidality ethically and yet still maintain the confidentiality surrounding her affectional orientation?
5. What types of referrals and resources might Sam's school counselor provide for her?

Resources

1. Peruse the list of resources for LGBTQI+ youth available through the Centers for Disease Control and Prevention at http://www.cdc.gov/lgbthealth/youth-resources.htm.
2. Watch some of the videos through the It Gets Better Project at http://www.itgets-better.org.
3. Find networks and resources through the Trevor Project at http://www.thetrevor-project.org.
4. Read through the *Young Gay America* magazine at http://ygamag.com.

References

Birkett, M., Espelage, D. L., & Koenig, B. (2009). LGB and questioning students in schools: The moderating effect of homophobic bullying and school climate on negative outcomes. *Journal of Youth and Adolescence, 38,* 989–1000.

Collier, K. L., Beusekom, G. V., Bos, H. M. W., & Sandfort, T. G. M. (2013). Sexual orientation and gender identity/expression related peer victimization in adolescence: A systemic review of associated psychosocial and health outcomes. *Journal of Sex Research, 50*(3–4), 299–317.

Craig, S. L. (2013). Affirmative Supportive Safe and Empowering Talk (ASSET): Leveraging the strengths and resiliencies of sexual minority youth in school-based groups. *Journal of LGBT Issues in Counseling, 7*(4), 372–386.

Eisenberg, M. E., & Resnick, M. D. (2006). Suicidality among gay, lesbian, and bisexual youth: The role of protective factors. *Journal of Adolescent Health, 39,* 662–668.

Friedman, M. S., Koeske, G. F., Silvestre, A. J., Korr, W. S., & Sites, E. W. (2006). The impact of gender-role nonconforming behavior, bullying, and social support on suicidality among gay male youth. *Journal of Adolescent Health, 38,* 621–623. doi:10.1016/j.jadohealth.2005.04.014

Grossman, A. H., & D'Augelli, A. R. (2006). Transgender youth: Invisible and vulnerable. *Journal of Homosexuality, 51*(1), 111–128.

Grossman, A. H., & D'Augelli, A. R. (2007). Transgender youth and life threatening behaviors. *Suicide and Life Threatening Behaviors, 37,* 527–537.

Hartling, L. M. (2005). Fostering resilience throughout our lives: New relational possibilities. In D. Camstock (Ed.), *Diversity and development: Critical contexts that shape our lives and relationships* (pp. 337–354). Belmont, CA: Thomson Brooks/Cole.

Kosciw, J. G., Greytak, E. A., Palmer, N. A., & Boesen, M. J. (2014). *2013 National School Climate Survey: LGBT students experience pervasive harassment and discrimination, but school-based resources and supports are making a difference.* Retrieved from http://www.glsen.org/article/2013-national-school-climate-survey

Kosciw, J. G., Palmer, N. A., & Kull, R. M. (2015). Reflecting resiliency: Openness about sexual orientation and/or gender identity and its relationship to well-being and educational outcomes for LGBT students. *American Journal of Community Psychology, 55*(1–2), 167–178. doi:10.1007/s10464-014-9642-6

Kosciw, J. G., Palmer, N. A., Kull, R. M., & Greytak, E. A. (2013). The effect of negative school climate on academic outcomes for LGBT youth and the role of in-school supports. *Journal of School Violence, 12*(1), 45–63.

Masten, A. S. (2001). Ordinary magic: Resilience processes in development. *American Psychologist, 56*(3), 227–238. doi:10.1037/0003-066X.56.3.227

Mustanski, B., & Liu, R. T. (2013). A longitudinal study of predictors of suicide attempts among lesbian, gay, bisexual, and transgender youth. *Archives of Sexual Behavior, 42,* 437–448. doi:10.1007/s10508-012-0013-9

Olson, J., Schrager, S. M., Belzer, M., Simons, L. K., & Clark, L. F. (2015). Baseline physiologic and psychosocial characteristics of transgender youth seeking care for gender dysphoria. *Journal of Adolescent Health, 57*(4), 374–380. doi:10.1016/j.jadohealth.2015.04.027

Poirier, J. M., Martinez, K. J., Francis, K. B., Denney, T., Roepke, S., & Cayce-Gibson, N. A. (2012). Providing culturally and linguistically competent services and supports to address the needs of LGBT youth and their families. In S. K. Fisher, J. M. Poirier, & G. M. Blau (Eds.), *Improving emotional and behavioral outcomes for LGBT youth: A guide for professionals* (pp. 9–24). Baltimore, MD: Brookes.

Poteat, V. P., Yoshikawa, H., Calzo, J. P., Gray, M. L., DiGiovanni, C. D., Lipkin, A., . . . Shaw, M. P. (2015). Contextualizing gay-straight alliances: Student, advisor, and structural factors related to positive youth development among members. *Child Development, 86*(1), 176–193. doi:10.1111/cdev.12289

Russell, S. T., Ryan, C., Toomey, R. B., Diaz, R. M., & Sanchez, J. (2011). Lesbian, gay, bisexual, and transgender adolescent school victimization: Implications for young adult health and adjustment. *Journal of School Health, 81*(5), 223–230.

Ryan, C., Russell, S. T., Huebner, D., Diaz, R., & Sanchez, J. (2010). Family acceptance in adolescence and the health of LGBT young adults. *Journal of Child and Adolescent Psychiatric Nursing, 23*(4), 205–213. doi:10.1111/j.1744-6171.2010.00246.x

Singh, A. A., & Jackson, K. (2012). Queer and transgender youth: Education and liberation in our schools. In T. Quinn & E. R. Meiners (Eds.), *Sexualities in education: A reader* (pp. 175–186). New York, NY: Peter Lang.

Singh, A. A., Meng, S., & Hansen, A. (2014). "I am my own gender": Resilience strategies of trans youth. *Journal of Counseling & Development, 92,* 208–218.

Ybarra, M. L., Mitchell, K. J., & Kosciw, J. (2015). The relation between suicidal ideation and bullying victimization in a national sample of transgender and non-transgender adolescents. In P. Goldblum, D. L. Espelage, J. Chu, & B. Bongar (Eds.), *Youth suicide and bullying: Challenges and strategies for prevention and intervention* (pp. 134–145). New York, NY: Oxford University Press.

Chapter 5

LGBTQI+ Persons in Adulthood

Amy Moore-Ramirez, Melanie Kautzman-East, and Misty M. Ginicola

I transitioned 15 years ago; I've gotten a pretty thick skin,
but there's a part that just hurts.
If someone looks at me and doesn't see me, it's just hurtful.
—Laverne Cox

• • •

Awareness of Attitudes and Beliefs Self-Check

1. What concerns have you had for acceptance in your education and work experiences? Have you ever been fearful to share information about your partner/spouse?
2. If you are married, did everyone whom you love attend the ceremony? If you are not yet married, who would you wish to attend your wedding? How would it feel if someone important in your life refused?
3. If you have (or decide to have) children, what process did (would) you need to go through to make that happen? How might that be different for a same-sex couple?

Case Study

Chris is a 24-year-old Puerto Rican female enrolled in a secondary education major at her local college. Chris is in her junior year and came to the counseling center because she is contemplating coming out on her college campus. Chris states that she is in a committed relationship with her partner, who attends a different university. When Chris visits her girlfriend, she feels free to be herself in the relationship on that college campus. At her own college campus, however, she is hesitant to come out, as she is unsure of how her peers will respond. Chris reports feeling comfortable in her affectional orientation; however, based on her experiences of being harassed for being gay while at a previous job and her perception that the campus is not open to "sexual minorities," she is not sure how those who are close to her will respond. Chris reports that she is tired of "living a lie" and wants to be who she is without having to censor her actions when around others. Chris also shares her concerns about graduating next year and seeking employment in a school setting. She is afraid that she will not be able to find employment if she is open about her affectional orientation.

• • •

Early Adulthood

Identity and Intimacy

Identity and the development of platonic and romantic relationships become central to development in adolescence and early adulthood. For the lesbian, gay, bisexual, transgender, queer, questioning, intersex, asexual, ally, pansexual/polysexual, and two-spirited (LGBTQI+) community, experiences in their adolescence predict the difficulty of development in early adulthood (D'Augelli, 2006). As presented in the previous chapter, the effects of bullying and physical and emotional abuse can prevent identity formation and authentic bonding with peers. Coming out, if within an accepting environment, can help facilitate development in early adulthood. However, if individuals come out in a negative environment, they may face additional challenges that impair their mental health, physical health, and ability to approach early adulthood in the same manner as their heterosexual peers (Schiemann, 1995).

Not being able to explore your identity fully or what it means to be *authentically yourself* causes struggles at every level of development and interaction with others (Flanders, Dobinson, & Logie, 2015). Understanding your affectional orientation and coming out can also interfere with other important developmental tasks. For example, while heterosexual young adults may be bonding with new friends and openly experimenting with dating the opposite sex, LGBTQI+ individuals may be hiding their identity, thereby halting developmental progress in terms of pursuing intimacy with others (Flanders et al., 2015). Therefore, they are not bonding with peers authentically to strengthen their relationship skills; they also may be fearful of openly dating members of the same sex, which can impact not only their authenticity and identity but also their mental health (Flanders et al., 2015). Elevated rates of depression, anxiety, and posttraumatic stress disorder can cause further disruption in early adulthood developmental tasks such as finding a partner, learning relationship skills, participating in healthy sexual relationships, developing one's education and career, and strengthening one's identity (Roberts, Rosario, Corliss, Koenen, & Austin, 2012).

College and Occupation

Recent events have revealed that heterosexism continues to be a prevalent issue in society as well as on college campuses. A study by Rankin (2003) revealed that roughly 30% of LGBTQI+ college students reported experiencing harassment due to their affectional orientation or gender identity; 51% stated that they chose not to disclose their affectional orientation or gender identity for fear of harassment. This unreceptive environment can negatively affect an LGBTQI+ student's physical health, academic performance, and identity development (Woodford, Silverschanz, Swank, Scherrer, & Raiz, 2012). Many LGBTQI+ students struggle with making career development decisions as well as engaging in an initial exploration of their sexual identity (Mobley & Slaney, 1996). Research has further identified that the distinctive experiences of LGBTQI+ students affect their career development, as these individuals experience more career indecision and career confusion than their heterosexual counterparts (Schmidt, Miles, & Welsh, 2011).

It is imperative that culturally competent counselors be aware of the stigma and discrimination LGBTQI+ students face when preparing for and entering the labor force (Eddy, Schweitzer, & Lyons, 2012). LGBTQI+ students may benefit from discussing how they plan to manage their sexual identities and cope with potential discrimination in their place of employment (Russon & Schmidt, 2014). Furthermore, counselors need to consider the social supports of an LGBTQI+ student, which serve as a significant protective factor (Schmidt et al., 2011). In this vein, counselors can connect their students with career support for LGBTQI+ job seekers. Developing mentoring programs may be another way for counselors to provide students with the tools to connect to a supportive community (Russon & Schmidt, 2014).

Career Consideration and Workplace Rights

Although there needs to be more research in the area of career planning for LGBTQI+ individuals, the literature indicates that many factors unrelated to affectional orientation (i.e., abilities, interests) influence career choices. For the LGBTQI+ community, however, some career differences, particularly those related to heteronormative attitudes, can result in both individual and institutional prejudice and discrimination (Chung, 2001; Parnell, Lease, & Green, 2012). Examples of formal discrimination include LGBTQI+ individuals not being hired or promoted as a result of their affectional orientation and discriminatory institutional policies. Informal discrimination may consist of harassment from coworkers (Parnell et al., 2012). Although not every LGBTQI+ individual has directly experienced workplace discrimination, most LGBTQI+ persons anticipate or fear that discrimination would occur if their affectional orientation were discovered (Chung, 2001).

Currently, no federal laws protect LGBTQI+ employees from discrimination, and fewer than half of U.S. states have laws prohibiting employment discrimination based on an individual's affectional orientation or gender identity (Human Rights Campaign, 2016). Although increasingly accepting attitudes from coworkers are on the rise, LGBTQI+ individuals continue to report experiencing discrimination in the workplace; lesbian and bisexual women are significantly more likely to experience barriers related to sex discrimination, partially related to issues for women in the workplace (Parnell et al., 2012). An example of these barriers is the conflict between children and career demands (Parnell et al., 2012). However, this discrimination can also be related to certain types of careers (i.e., it is not safe to be out in some careers), which could affect LGBTQI+ individuals' career choice, coming out, and adjustment to their work environment (Parnell et al., 2012). Counselors must be familiar with the discrimination faced by this population and assist clients in carefully examining their coping strategies related to career choice and work adjustment (Parnell et al., 2012).

Military Experiences

Lesbian, gay, and bisexual individuals have a longstanding history of honorable service in the U.S. military. The affectional orientation of these individuals was forced to remain concealed, as LGBTQI+ service members were discriminated against whenever their affectional orientation became known because of exclusionary military policies (Estrada, Dirosa, & Decostanza, 2013). Recently these prohibitive policies were changed by the Don't Ask, Don't Tell Repeal Act of 2010, which eliminated all restrictions barring LGBQ individuals from openly serving in the military. This change, however, did not affect transgender people, who continued to be barred from military service until 2016 (Yerke & Mitchell, 2013).

The concerns of LGBQ individuals serving in the military historically included unit cohesion, military readiness, and unit effectiveness (Estrada et al., 2013). By and large, research on these concerns has revealed that issues other than affectional orientation influence these processes (Estrada et al., 2013). Ensuring the participation and inclusion of openly LGBTQI+ individuals in the military involves individual, organizational, and societal variables (Estrada et al., 2013). Examples of these variables include interpersonal contact with openly LGBTQI+ personnel, proper training and education, and leadership support in a supportive command climate (Estrada et al., 2013). Transgender individuals have been barred from military service reportedly because of concerns related to medical or physical problems, which may hinder their functioning in the armed forces (Yerke & Mitchell, 2013). However, models of inclusion and sensitivity toward these issues in other nations address the concerns of transgender individuals who are service members by treating the transgender individual's medical concerns just like the medical concerns of any other person serving in the armed forces (Yerke & Mitchell, 2013). Such an approach would certainly alleviate some of the mental health concerns resulting from the discrimination, harassment, and marginality faced by transgender individuals (Yerke & Mitchell, 2013).

Working with LGBTQI+ military families can be challenging for several reasons. As with heterosexual military members, there are fears about help-seeking behaviors being considered weak. However, unlike other populations, there is virtually no support or resources for the LGBTQI+ population, and they face the additional stigma of being out as an affectional minority. There are many things that counselors can do to support this population, such as gaining knowledge by attending workshops or reading articles, using gender-neutral language, creating support groups, or engaging in research related to LGBTQI+ military families (Sternberg, 2012).

Middle Adulthood

Relationships

This section highlights the research on this population, which has only included research on monogamous relationships. However, it is important to note that polyamory may be part of LGBTQI+ relationships as it is with heterosexual partnerships. Presenting problems in therapy for LGBTQI+ couples are categorized as either internal or external (contextual) concerns that are a direct reflection of the influences in an oppressive culture and a gender-biased society (Bepko & Johnson, 2000). Unfortunately, as a direct result of historical heterosexual bias and a lack of training directly linked to counseling LGBTQI+ couples, counselors often demonstrate heteronormativity bias and insufficiencies in preparation to serve LGBTQI+ couples. It is clear that there is a need for graduate-level training of clinical mental health counselors that explicitly identifies both counseling considerations and counseling strategies for working with LGBTQI+ couples.

LGBTQI+ couples who seek therapy primarily view their committed relationships as similar to those of heterosexual couples; most LGBTQI+ couples' issues include many of the same issues that are relevant for heterosexuals: intimacy, personal growth, individual responsibility, parenting, or financial stressors, to name a few (Bepko & Johnson, 2000; Macapagal, Greene, Rivera, & Mustanski, 2015). However, LGBTQI+ couples face additional stress that is often directly related to external, sociocultural, and familial sources (Bepko & Johnson, 2000). Introducing their partner to their families can be stressful in families that are not accepting (Macapagal et al., 2015). Other unique challenges that LGBTQI+ couples face include resolving relationship agreements in regard to commitment, boundaries, and gender-linked behaviors as well as family planning related to adoption and insemination

(Bepko & Johnson, 2000; Macapagal et al., 2015). In addition, they may face discrimination and prejudice at the occupational or community level (Macapagal et al., 2015). LGBTQI+ couples often navigate these external complexities associated with being an affectional minority without certain civil and legal rights, potentially without the support of family and the larger culture, that their heterosexual equivalents injoy (Bepko & Johnson, 2000; Macapagal et al., 2015). Family planning and raising children, in general, bring up an assortment of issues for the queer community that heterosexual couples do not share (Bepko & Johnson, 2000; Macapagal et al., 2015). Another relationship issue can involve coming out: There are intrinsic problems when one person is not out and the relationship is kept a secret (Bepko & Johnson, 2000). Finally, dealing with *small-town* issues in a small queer community or, conversely, with isolation from other gay couples if a couple lives outside a gay or lesbian community may interfere with the couple's relationship satisfaction (Bepko & Johnson, 2000; Macapagal et al., 2015).

LGBTQI+ couples should anticipate that their relationships will be affirmed by the counselor as being authentic and as meaningful as heterosexual ones (Bepko & Johnson, 2000). Because of the unique nature of the experiences LGBTQI+ couples encounter, it is important for counselors to remember that the most important traits in a couples counselor are the capacity to actively listen to, empathize with, and assist the members of the couple in regard to communicating their feelings and needs to each other (Bepko & Johnson, 2000; Macapagal et al., 2015). As in heterosexual couples counseling, the counselor will need to identify ground rules so that each person has the opportunity to be heard and the couple does not fall into negative communication habits in the session that might also be present in their home (Bepko & Johnson, 2000; Macapagal et al., 2015). All counselors who work with LGBTQI+ couples would also directly benefit from seeking consultation and supervision from a counselor who is culturally competent with this population (Bepko & Johnson, 2000; Macapagal et al., 2015). Being collaborative, being effective, and maintaining trusting therapeutic alliances are likely the most critical factors to ensuring positive and successful outcomes for LGBTQI+ couples in counseling (Bepko & Johnson, 2000; Macapagal et al., 2015).

Marriage

Although the United States now has marriage equality, negative attitudes and opinions related to the right of LGBTQI+ individuals to marry have long-term direct and negative consequences (Rostosky, Riggle, Horne, & Miller, 2009). For example, these individuals may still face negative attitudes regarding the validity of their marriage from unsupportive heterosexual friends and family. The American Psychological Association Council of Representatives in 2004 recognized that negative attitudes toward marriage equality and the passage of marriage amendments have a negative impact on the psychological health of LGBTQI+ individuals. According to Rostosky et al. (2009), "The denial of marriage rights to LGB individuals creates second-class citizens without access to the federal, state, and local rights, benefits, and privileges that are contingent on marital status" (p. 56). The years of discrimination have taken a toll on the queer community.

Heteronormativity, in reference to marriage and family, has a similar negative impact; it suggests that a sustainable family consists of a heterosexual mother and father rearing heterosexual children jointly (Hudak & Giammattei, 2010). Heteronormativity is supported by assertions about what is considered *normal* and *healthy* for individuals, couples, and families (Hudak & Giammattei, 2010). It is important for counselors to distinguish that valuable work with lesbian and gay couples will require them to be aware of these heterosexist attitudes; counselors must also be aware of the distinctive norms of the queer community to circumvent pathologizing what may be normative behavior for LGBTQI+ couples (Bepko & Johnson, 2000). A counselor should be able to consider all pertinent issues, including heteronormativity from the external environment and sexual behavior in the couple, with competence (Bepko & Johnson, 2000).

Family Planning and Raising Children

Some LGBTQI+ couples are not interested in having children. However, many couples are, and it appears that more LGBTQI+ couples are interested in starting families now that marriage equality is legal and the culture has become significantly more accepting (Riskind & Patterson, 2010). Research has indicated that in fact many LGBTQI+ couples currently have a strong desire to be parents (Burnett, 2006). For many LGBTQI+ couples who wish to have children, family planning is not as easy as it is for heterosexual couples (Eyler, Pang, & Clark, 2014; Holley & Pasch, 2015). Deciding to become parents can be both exciting and stressful for LGBTQI+ couples, as it can be for heterosexual couples (Eyler et al., 2014; Holley & Pasch, 2015). However, the financial commitment needed to begin the path to parenthood can be a major burden on affectional minority couples (Eyler et al., 2014; Holley & Pasch, 2015). There are ways to help a same-sex couple realize their parenting goals; however, many of these possibilities are costly and intensive. Given the nature of the costly process to become a family, socioeconomic limitations directly impact LGBTQI+ couples in regard to their ability to become parents (Eyler et al., 2014; Holley & Pasch, 2015).

Many lesbian women choose to explore options for conceiving through intrauterine insemination by using donor sperm and potentially in vitro fertilization if there are fertility issues (Eyler et al., 2014; Holley & Pasch, 2015). Sperm can be acquired from a known donor, who is frequently a friend or family member, or it can be procured from one of the many sperm banks throughout the United States; at-home insemination is also an option for lesbian couples and can be cost effective and private (Eyler et al., 2014; Holley & Pasch, 2015). All donor sperm is required to be screened for infectious diseases, including hepatitis B, hepatitis C, HIV, syphilis, gonorrhea, and chlamydia (Eyler et al., 2014; Holley & Pasch, 2015). In addition to choosing the method by which to start a family, many lesbian couples must also consider which partner will carry the child (Eyler et al., 2014; Holley & Pasch, 2015). This can be a very private and emotional experience for couples, and many couples will often seek help from a counselor during this time (Eyler et al., 2014; Holley & Pasch, 2015). Lesbian couples who choose not to become pregnant through the intrauterine insemination process will often explore options related to adoption (Eyler et al., 2014; Holley & Pasch, 2015). In addition to determining the process of adoption as a means of starting a family, lesbian couples must also consider whether they will adopt a child from another country and, if so, the cost associated with that adoption (Eyler et al., 2014; Holley & Pasch, 2015). Prior to a federal court decision in 2016, many states had laws barring same-sex couples from adopting; however, they still face barriers in these states, which are not yet honoring the court decision (Human Rights Campaign, 2016). In addition, bias is still very prevalent in the adoption process: Birth parents may refuse to adopt to an LGBTQI+ couple in open adoption contexts (Adoptions Together, 2016). Unfortunately, LGBTQI+ couples adopting children internationally may face legal exclusions or cultural biases against affectional orientation minorities, rendering international adoptions nearly impossible (Adoptions Together, 2016).

Unless adoption is the chosen method, gay males might experience a slightly more complicated process for family planning than lesbian couples (Eyler et al., 2014; Holley & Pasch, 2015). Often gay male couples will select an egg donor as well as a surrogate.

Similar to obtaining sperm, gay male couples can often choose someone they know or an anonymous egg donor who is screened by an infertility center. Selecting and supporting a surrogate can also be a stressful process. Considerations about family planning that are seemingly common for heterosexual individuals can be challenging, frightening, and financially draining for LGBTQI+ couples.

Beliefs about fertility and parenthood are often amplified in LGBTQI+ couples (Burnett, 2006). LGBTQI+ parents face heterosexist and homophobic attitudes that queer couples should not become parents because of the possible psychological risk to their children (Burnett, 2006). This stereotype persists despite the fact that researchers in multiple studies have proposed that children of gay and lesbian parents do not encounter significantly greater psychological or emotional adjustment difficulties, relationship problems, or social stigmatization than children of heterosexual parents (Burnett, 2006; Goldberg, 2010). However, these harmful attitudes can impact the LGBTQI+ parent in relation to microaggressions, prejudice, and overt discrimination, such as previous state laws not allowing same-sex couples to foster or adopt children.

The intersectionalities of couples' identities in terms of race, sex, and class differences are additional complexities that LGBTQI+ families face on their path to becoming parents (Ariel & McPherson, 2000). LGBTQI+ individuals who seek counseling for family planning issues would benefit greatly from working with a counselor who is both informed and able to competently understand intersectional issues; fertility; reproductive choices; and the ways in which sociocultural, gender, legal, and ethical issues can shape couples' choices in regard to family planning in order to support couples with their emotional experiences surrounding this process (Ariel & McPherson, 2000; Burnett, 2006). Counseling interventions must be adapted to accommodate LGBTQI+ couples' needs, open a dialogue regarding the differences they will experience with parenting, and develop coping skills and strong communication to counter the negative emotional and psychological impacts of being an LGBTQI+ family in a heterosexist culture (Burnett, 2006).

Some children being raised by LGBTQI+ parents were conceived during a previous heterosexual marriage or relationship (Alderson, 2013; Goldberg, 2010). Although this eases the issues surrounding planning a family, it complicates them as well because there is the issue of separation/divorce and coparenting. Having shared custody as well as one member of the LGBTQI+ couple being a stepparent mean that typical blended family issues will emerge.

For lesbian women and gay men, raising children tends to *out* them in public situations because of the nature of increased visibility in schools, communities, and public gathering spots (Alderson, 2013). Caring for the children and being responsible for daily caretaking tasks will make the couple's relationship status more transparent. A more public profile increases the risk of exposure to heteronormative attitudes and beliefs, homophobia, discrimination, and minority stress for LGBTQI+ parents. In living with these negative experiences, parents can also fear how these biases will impact their children.

Many LGBTQI+ clients seeking counseling will have questions related to parenting and raising children; lesbian women, for example, may wonder about the importance of a strong male role model for their son (Alderson, 2013). Often individuals will question the need for increased emotional support for children of LGBTQI+ parents due to the unique social stressors that each child might face. Clients may need psychoeducational support regarding the research that indicates that the quality of the relationship between both LGBTQI+ parents and heterosexual parents and their children, rather than a parent's affectional orientation or gender identity, is often the necessary element in positive development (Alderson, 2013; Goldberg, 2010). Unfortunately, some LGBTQI+ families will face discrimination in their communities and children may be bullied by peers (Goldberg,

2010). Like all children, those with LGBTQI+ parents will have both good and bad experiences and are no more likely than children of heterosexual parents to develop negative behaviors or coping skills (Alderson, 2013; Goldberg, 2010).

Intimate Partner Violence (IPV)

A preponderance of LGBTQI+ families are healthy, comparable to a healthy heterosexual partnership. However, IPV takes place at comparable rates in same-sex couples as in heterosexual couples (Baker, Buick, Kim, Moniz, & Nava, 2012; Murray, Mobley, Buford, Seaman-DeJohn, 2008). IPV for LGBTQI+ couples includes a pattern of abuse that is a cruel cycle of physical, emotional, and psychological exploitation, leaving the victim with feelings of isolation, fear, and guilt (Baker et al., 2012; Murray et al., 2008). Despite the similarities to heterosexual IPV, LGBTQI+ couples will experience unique stressors related to their affectional minority status (Carvalho, Lewis, Derlega, Winstead, & Viggiano, 2011). In LGBTQI+ relationships, a unique stressor associated with IPV is the threat of outing one's partner to coworkers, family, and friends (Carvalho et al., 2011). This risk is magnified by the sense of isolation among LGBTQI+ victims due to the fact that LGBTQI+ individuals have fewer civil rights protections and often lack access to legal systems (Messinger, 2014). Many LGBTQI+ individuals are hesitant to seek help because of the fear associated with being outed, not to mention the fear that others will view their same-sex relationship as innately dysfunctional (Baker et al., 2012; Messinger, 2014; Murray et al., 2008). Many LGBTQI+ persons also hesitate to report any incidence of IPV to local authorities out of fear that they will be required to disclose their affectional orientation or gender identity in an unsafe situation (Messinger, 2014). Additional considerations unique to LGBTQI+ individuals include the fear of losing contact with a child due to custodial parenting and adoption laws that vary from state to state (Messinger, 2014). Often LGBTQI+ abusers will threaten to no longer allow the victim to see the child if the abuser has custodial and legal parental custody (Messinger, 2014). The commonly recognized archetypal male aggressor and female survivor of IPV is not the case for LGBTQI+ couples; therefore, same-sex couples face barriers to having their IPV issues acknowledged and attended to that a heterosexual female victim may not (Messinger, 2014). It is also important to note that there are considerable challenges for LGBTQI+ individuals in regard to addressing IPV: Many law officials lack training related to handling LGBTQI+ IPV cases (Messinger, 2014). Many cases of IPV also go unfiled by police officers because the two partners are not ready to share the nature of their relationship (Messinger, 2014). In addition, many domestic violence shelters across the United States appear to be increasing their services to include lesbian or bisexual female victims, but it is still very difficult to locate services for gay men and transgender individuals (Messinger, 2014).

Late Adulthood

It is estimated that by 2030, as many as 6 million LGBTQI+ adults will be senior citizens (Dentato, Orwat, Spira, & Walker, 2014; Hash & Rogers, 2013). The majority of LGBTQI+ individuals' concerns appear to be related to aging and are similar to those of heterosexual seniors (Hughes, 2009; Kimmel, 2014). These concerns surround physiological and cognitive decline, loss of mobility and independence, financial strain, depression, lowered self-esteem, and issues with body image (Hughes, 2009; Kimmel, 2014). The main developmental tasks also appear to be similar, with LGBTQI+ individuals coming to terms with aging and the end of life as well as reviewing their life stories and choices, just as heterosexual seniors do.

However, aging in the LGBTQI+ communities can also bring about specific challenges that are different from those of their heterosexual peers (Dentato et al., 2014; Fenkl, 2012; Hash & Rogers, 2013; Hughes, 2009). Expression of sexual health and education may be hampered in LGBTQI+ seniors related to issues surrounding their orientation and generation, which may have been significantly less affirmative. These seniors are also still at risk for sexually transmitted infections, although this risk varies based on gender, education, and culture. They may face continued discrimination in housing, employment, and medical and mental health care, which further complicates issues surrounding aging and loss of independence. For example, individuals who identify as transgender need a competent and compassionate practitioner to understand the physiological and psychological components of their gender orientation in the aging process (e.g., a transgender female may need a prostate exam). However, just as in earlier stages of development, LGBTQI+ individuals face major barriers in accessing quality, compassionate, and educated practitioners.

In addition, a significant number of older adults remain in the closet and have not come out fully to their loved ones, nor do they identify with an LGBTQI+ community, which indicates that they may not have extensive support systems (Dentato et al., 2014; Fenkl, 2012; Hash & Rogers, 2013). Their developmentally appropriate life review may leave them with significant depression, especially if they were not able to live authentically (Kimmel, 2014). Even if they were able to come out, the lived experience of these seniors, which includes fighting for civil rights as well as legal, psychiatric, and moral oppression, makes them significantly different from not only heterosexual seniors but also younger LGBTQI+ generations. This can also be somewhat isolating and result in increased physical and mental health challenges (Hughes, 2009).

Although these factors give the impression that LGBTQI+ seniors might be holistically impaired by these life experiences, research also indicates that many have a higher level of resiliency in response to overcoming such adversity, especially those who were active in advocacy and social justice change (Dentato et al., 2014; Hash & Rogers, 2013). In addition, the changes associated with late life could result in a more open approach to their identity, with a greater acceptance of self and their sexual and/or gender orientation. In either instance, it is clear that earlier stages of development and the associated events have a large impact on late-life development, identity, and psychological needs.

Conclusion

Although the earlier developmental periods of childhood and adolescence are crucial for conceptualizing a client's developmental base, considering the developmental expectations and milestones in adulthood is also important. Being an affectional and gender minority can impact a person's development across the life span through profound experiences of marginalization and oppression. Adult issues with college education, career, relationships, starting a family, and aging with grace can all be made more difficult for the LGBTQI+ community. Counselors should be able to assess clients' developmental progress; understand the influence of negative societal beliefs, such as heteronormativity and homoprejudice; discuss the experiences and meanings that clients have attached to their difficulties; and plan interventions tailored to meet clients' specific goals at their developmental level.

Questions for Further Discussion

1. What concerns do you hear in Chris's narrative, as discussed in this chapter?
2. What types of discrimination and marginalization may Chris realistically face in her adult life?

3. How might you support Chris in moving forward in her coming out process based on strategies provided in this chapter?
4. What types of issues could you expect Chris to experience in middle adulthood?
5. What types of concerns could you expect Chris to have in late adulthood?

Resources

1. View career planning resources for LGBTQI+ persons at http://www.career.cornell.edu/resources/Diversity/lgbt.cfm.
2. Find resources and information for LGBTQI+ couples from the Partners Task Force at http://buddybuddy.com/partners.html.
3. Learn about LGBTQI+ family advocacy work at http://www.familyequality.org/.
4. Visit Children of Lesbians and Gays Everywhere to read more about support for LGBTQI+ families at http://www.colage.org/.
5. Find more information on aging in the LGBTQI+ communities at https://www.lgbtagingcenter.org/.

References

Adoptions Together. (2016). *Gay, lesbian, same sex adoption (LGBT adoption).* Retrieved from https://www.adoptionstogether.org/adopting/lgbt-adoption/

Alderson, K. (2013). *Counseling LGBTI clients.* Thousand Oaks, CA: Sage.

Ariel, J., & McPherson, D. (2000). Therapy with lesbian and gay parents and their children. *Journal of Marital and Family Therapy, 26,* 421–432.

Baker, N., Buick, J., Kim, S., Moniz, S., & Nava, K. (2012). Lessons from examining same-sex intimate partner violence. *Sex Roles, 69,* 182–192. doi:10.1007/s11199-012-0218-3

Bepko, C., & Johnson, T. (2000). Gay and lesbian couples in therapy: Perspectives for the contemporary family therapist. *Journal of Marital and Family Therapy, 24,* 409–419. doi:10.1111/j.1752-0606.2000.tb00312.x

Burnett, J. (2006). Use of assisted reproductive technology and gay and lesbian couples: What counselors need to know. *Journal of LGBT Issues in Counseling, 1,* 115–125. doi:10.1300/J462v01n01_08

Carvalho, A., Lewis, R., Derlega, V., Winstead, B., & Viggiano, C. (2011). Internalized sexual minority stressors and same-sex intimate partner violence. *Journal of Family Violence, 26,* 501–509. doi:10.1007/s10896-011-9384-2

Chung, Y. B. (2001). Work discrimination and coping strategies: Conceptual frameworks for counseling lesbian, gay, and bisexual clients. *The Career Development Quarterly, 50,* 33–44. doi:10.1002/j.2161-0045.2001.tb00887.x

D'Augelli, A. R. (2006). Developmental and contextual factors and mental health among lesbian, gay, and bisexual youths. In A. M. Omoto & H. S. Kurtzman (Eds.), *Sexual orientation and mental health: Examining identity and development in lesbian, gay, and bisexual people* (pp. 37–53). Washington, DC: American Psychological Association. doi:10.1037/11261-002

Dentato, M. P., Orwat, J., Spira, M., & Walker, B. (2014). Examining cohort differences and resilience among the aging LGBT community: Implications for education and practice among an expansively diverse population. *Journal of Human Behavior in the Social Environment, 24*(3), 316–328. doi:10.1080/10911359.2013.831009

Don't Ask, Don't Tell Repeal Act of 2010. (2010). Retrieved from http://www.gpo.gov/fdsys/pkg/BILLS-111hr2965enr/pdf/BILLS-111hr2965enr.pdf

Eddy, S. W., Schweitzer, L., & Lyons, S. T. (2012). Anticipated discrimination and a career choice in nonprofit: A study of early career lesbian, gay, bisexual, transgendered (LGBTQI+T) job seekers. *Review of Public Personnel Administration, 32*(4), 332–352. doi:10.1177/0734371×12453055

Estrada, A. X., Dirosa, G. A., & Decostanza, A. H. (2013). Gays in the U.S. military: Reviewing the research and conceptualizing a way forward. *Journal of Homosexuality, 60,* 327–355. doi:10.1080/00918369.2013.744676

Eyler, A. E., Pang, S. C., & Clark, A. (2014). LGBT assisted reproduction: Current practice and future possibilities. *LGBT Health, 1*(3), 151–156. doi:10.1089/lgbt.2014.0045

Fenkl, E. A. (2012). Aging gay men: A review of the literature. *Journal of LGBT Issues in Counseling, 6*(3), 162–182. doi:10.1080/15538605.2012.711514

Flanders, C. E., Dobinson, C., & Logie, C. (2015). "I'm never really my full self": Young bisexual women's perceptions of their mental health. *Journal of Bisexuality, 15,* 454–480. doi:10.1080/15299716.2015.1079288

Goldberg, A. (2010). *Lesbian and gay parents and their children: Research on the family life cycle.* Washington, DC: American Psychological Association.

Hash, K. M., & Rogers, A. (2013). Clinical practice with older LGBT clients: Overcoming lifelong stigma through strength and resilience. *Clinical Social Work Journal, 41*(3), 249–257. doi:10.1007/s10615-013-0437-2

Holley, S. R., & Pasch, L. A. (2015). Counseling lesbian, gay, bisexual and transgender patients. In S. N. Covington (Ed.), *Fertility counseling: Clinical guide and case studies* (pp. 180–196). New York, NY: Cambridge University Press. doi:10.1017/CBO9781107449398.014

Hudak, J., & Giammattei, S. V. (2010). Doing family: Decentering heteronormativity in "marriage" and "family" therapy. In T. Nelson & H. Winawer (Eds.), *Critical topics in family therapy: AFTA monograph series highlights* (pp. 105–115). New York, NY: Springer.

Hughes, M. (2009). Lesbian and gay people's concerns about ageing and accessing services. *Australian Social Work, 62*(2), 186–201. doi:10.1080/03124070902748878

Human Rights Campaign. (2016). *Support the Equality Act.* Retrieved from http://www.hrc.org/campaigns/support-the-equality-act

Kimmel, D. (2014). Lesbian, gay, bisexual, and transgender aging concerns. *Clinical Gerontologist, 37*(1), 49–63. doi:10.1080/07317115.2014.847310

Macapagal, K., Greene, G. J., Rivera, Z., & Mustanski, B. (2015). "The best is always yet to come": Relationship stages and processes among young LGBT couples. *Journal of Family Psychology, 29*(3), 309–320. doi:10.1037/fam0000094

Messinger, A. M. (2014). Marking 35 years of research on same-sex intimate partner violence: Lessons and new directions. In D. Peterson & V. Panfil (Eds.), *Handbook of LGBT communities, crime, and justice* (pp. 65–85). New York, NY: Springer Science + Business Media. doi:10.1007/978-1-4614-9188-0_4

Mobley, M., & Slaney, R. B. (1996). Holland's theory: Its relevance for lesbian women and gay men. *Journal of Vocational Behavior, 48*(2), 125–135. doi:10.1006/jvbe.1996.0013

Murray, C., Mobley, A., Buford, A., & Seaman-DeJohn, M. (2008). Same-sex intimate partner violence: Dynamics, social context, and counseling implications. *Journal of LGBT Issues in Counseling, 1*(4), 7–30.

Parnell, M. K., Lease, S. H., & Green, M. L. (2012). Perceived career barriers for gay, lesbian, and bisexual individuals. *Journal of Career Development, 39*(3), 248–268.

Rankin, S. R. (2003). *Campus climate for gay, lesbian, bisexual, and transgender people: A national perspective.* New York, NY: National Gay and Lesbian Task Force Policy Institute.

Riskind, R., & Patterson, C. (2010). Parenting intentions and desires among childless lesbian, gay, and heterosexual individuals. *Journal of Family Psychology, 24*(1), 78–81.

Roberts, A. L., Rosario, M., Corliss, H. L., Koenen, K. C., & Austin, S. B. (2012). Elevated risk of posttraumatic stress in sexual minority youths: Mediation by childhood abuse and gender nonconformity. *American Journal of Public Health, 102*, 1587–1593. doi:10.2105/AJPH.2011.300530

Rostosky, S., Riggle, E., Horne, S., & Miller, A. (2009). Marriage amendments and psychological distress in lesbian, gay, and bisexual (LGB) adults. *Journal of Counseling Psychology, 56*(1), 56–66.

Russon, J. M., & Schmidt, C. K. (2014). Authenticity and career decision-making self-efficacy in lesbian, gay, and bisexual college students. *Journal of Gay & Lesbian Social Services, 26*(2), 207–221. doi:10.1080/10538720.2014.891090

Schiemann, J. S. (1995). Staying in or coming out: A biographical study of early adulthood among gay men. *Dissertation Abstracts International: Section B. Sciences and Engineering, 55*(8), 3601.

Schmidt, C. K., Miles, J. R., & Welsh, A. C. (2011). Perceived discrimination and social support: The influences on career development and college adjustment of LGBT college students. *Journal of Career Development, 38*(4), 293–309.

Sternberg, M. M. (2012). Unique challenges of lesbian, gay, and bisexual military families. *ALGBTIC Newsletter, 36*(1), 22.

Woodford, M. R., Silverschanz, P., Swank, E., Scherrer, K. S., & Raiz, L. (2012). Predictors of heterosexual college students' attitudes toward LGBT people. *Journal of LGBT Youth, 9*(4), 297–320. doi:10.1080/19361653.2012.716697

Yerke, A. F., & Mitchell, V. (2013). Transgender people in the military: Don't ask? Don't tell? Don't enlist! *Journal of Homosexuality, 60*(2–3), 436–457.

Chapter 6

Identity Development, Coming Out, and Family Adjustment

Kristopher M. Goodrich and Misty M. Ginicola

I've endured years of misery and come to enormous lengths to live a lie.
I was certain that my world would fall apart if anyone knew,
and yet when I acknowledged my sexuality
I felt whole for the first time.

—Jason Collins

• • •

Awareness of Attitudes and Beliefs Self-Check

1. How much does your own affectional orientation and gender factor into your own identity?
2. What experiences have you had that are either confirming or disaffirming of your affectional orientation—of whom you love?
3. What messages have you sent others, either verbally or nonverbally, regarding how you feel about being lesbian, gay, bisexual, transgender, queer, questioning, intersex, asexual, ally, pansexual/polysexual, or two-spirited (LGBTQI+)?

Case Study

Carl, a 12-year-old Hispanic male, comes to a school counselor with complaints of anxiety and not feeling liked by his peers. After several visits, he tells the counselor that he knows he is gay but does not feel safe talking about his feelings openly. He tells the counselor that kids already make fun of him for being too "girly." Carl says that he has told no one about his feelings of being gay. He also feels that it is not an option to talk about this with his family, which is Catholic, as he fears being kicked out of his house. In the same school, the school counselor is working with a 17-year-old Caucasian female, Amanda, who identifies as a lesbian and is out to her friends. She came out at 13 years old; her family is Episcopalian and she has an uncle who is also gay. Her family and friends are supportive. She helps to organize the GSA in school and is well liked among the student population. (Although GSA once stood for *gay–straight alliance,* many individual clubs are changing their names to *gender and sexualities alliance* or other similar names to remove the term *straight* and represent gender minorities in the organization.) She works with the school counselor to create her schedule and prepare for college applications. She does not seem to experience much difficulty surrounding her orientation.

• • •

Identity Formation

These two clients represent a crucial difference in LGBTQI+ individuals to which counselors must attend: identity development. All LGBTQI+ persons must come to an understanding of the differences that their affectional orientation means for their lives in a context of heteronormativity. Understanding that one's experiences do not represent the *norm* can be confusing and isolating. As individuals seek to make sense of their attractions, experiences, and identity, they will have various struggles at different time periods in their development. In the case narrative, Carl is very much struggling with what his gay identity means and how it will impact others, whereas Amanda has a fully integrated identity. How clients currently identify in their sexual or gender orientation identity is important for a counselor to assess; it will guide the counselor's understanding of clients as well as what types of interventions are appropriate. For example, Amanda does not currently need any assistance with understanding herself as a lesbian; the interventions her school counselor uses will likely be targeted toward college readiness. However, Carl needs support related to his gay identity but is not yet in a place where coming out may be feasible. Therefore, the school counselor will want to find safe places, both inside and outside of the school, for Carl to progress in his identity. As described in previous chapters, disclosure, or *coming out*, is the process of revealing one's sexual/affectional orientation or gender identity to others in one's life.

Research shows that along with social support, a healthy affectional orientation identity can aid in the development of positive mental health (Feldman & Wright, 2013; Gallor & Fassinger, 2010; Zoeterman & Wright, 2014). The research on identity development is, therefore, crucial for counselors to understand (Pachankis & Goldfried, 2013). Affectional orientation identity integration is associated with lower rates of depression, anxiety, and conduct problems; it is also associated with higher levels of self-esteem (Rosario, Schrimshaw, & Hunter, 2011).

LGBTQI+ Identity Formation Models

Research on identity development in this population began in the late 1970s with the emergence of stage models, in which it was theorized that individuals progress to embrace a queer identity in sequential steps. All of the identity models to date share some significant factors (Gonsiorek & Weinrich, 1995). They describe defensive strategies that are used initially in response to experiencing attraction to a member of the same sex. In response to experiencing this attraction, individuals usually spend time minimizing, denying, and rejecting their orientation, which leads to compromised mental health. One undergoes a gradual realization and acceptance of one's affectional orientation identity, with the environment playing a large role in how quickly or slowly someone progresses toward an integrated identity. The models also acknowledge coming out as a milestone, but many models recognize that this is sometimes a fluid, partial, or back-and-forth process. Several of the most influential LGBTQI+ models are discussed next.

The first such model was presented by Cass (1979, 1984) to explain identity development in gay males and lesbian women. According to Cass, individuals first enter the stage of conscious awareness, in which they identify that their feelings may not be heterosexual. They then compare the various components of a gay or lesbian identity with their feelings and beliefs in the identity comparison stage. They may find themselves rejecting a gay or lesbian identity, staying in the closet while privately embracing their feelings, or embracing a queer identity on their own terms. In the identity/tolerance stage, individuals move to immerse themselves in the LGBTQI+ culture, connect with other similar individuals, and distance themselves from heterosexuals. In the next stage, identity acceptance, they move toward an active commitment to the queer community and a gay or lesbian identity. In the identity pride stage, they become committed to their identity and may exhibit some public activism. Finally, they will fully integrate their gay or lesbian identity with the remainder of their other cultural identities in the identity synthesis stage.

Troiden (1979, 1988) then proposed a four-stage model of affectional orientation development. The first stage is sensitization, in which individuals do not see themselves as LGBQ but rather are exposed to the negative stigma surrounding affectional orientation variance. In the second stage, identity confusion, individuals begin to recognize that their feelings do not represent a heterosexual identity but experience inner turmoil, uncertainty, and anxiety surrounding what these feelings do represent. In this stage they experience denial, repair (in which they attempt to change), avoidance, redefining, and acceptance. The third stage is identity assumption, in which individuals accept their gay identity for themselves and work toward coming out to others. Finally, individuals may reach the fourth stage of commitment, in which they have internalized and integrated being LGBQ into their social, professional, and private lives.

Falco (1991) also proposed a general model of sexual identity development. In the first stage, individuals become aware that their attractions are different from others'. The second stage marks when they begin to accept these feelings and tell others. The third stage represents the progression into finding an LGBTQI+ intimate partner and a supportive community. The final stage is when true private and social identity integration occurs.

D'Augelli (1994) changed the discussion of affectional orientation identity formation by presenting a life span framework for affectional orientation and gender identity development, with the recognition that this identity is not isolated from other areas of social, emotional, physical, and cognitive development. This theory includes *identity processes*, not stages, that are somewhat independent from one another. These are exiting heterosexuality, developing a personal LGB identity, developing an LGB social identity, becoming an LGB offspring (parental relations), developing an LGB intimacy status, and entering an LGB community. This theory recognizes the complexity of identity development and the fact that, although related, each process can progress at different rates with varied milestones.

McCarn and Fassinger (1996) also recognized the complexity of identity formation when they proposed a lesbian identity model in which individuals develop both an individual sexual identity and a group membership identity as a lesbian. In this model, individuals first become aware of an affectional orientation difference in the awareness stage. Then they explore these feelings, along with affiliation with LGBTQI+ communities, in the exploration stage. In the next stage of deepening/commitment, they develop self-fulfillment and commitment to both their individual affectional orientation and their identification with the label of *lesbian* as well as a lesbian community. Finally, individuals reach internalization/synthesis, in which they incorporate their identity as a lesbian and a member of a minority group into their other identities.

Weinberg, Williams, and Pryor (1994) hypothesized that the bisexual experience, even though it is included in many of the previous models, was not similar to the gay and lesbian experiences. They found that bisexuals initially feel anxiety about selecting a gay or heterosexual identity in the stage of initial confusion. These individuals then work toward being more comfortable with the broader identity of bisexual in the stage of finding and applying the label of bisexuality. The next stage, settling into the identity, represents individuals' acceptance of a bisexual identity, with an understanding of how it is significantly different from both a heterosexual and a gay or lesbian identity. It is interesting that this model represents a final stage that is not a fully integrated achievement of identity; rather, the authors hypothesized that individuals continue to feel intermittent uncertainty about their bisexual identity, as their gender, attraction, and identities are more fluid than others'.

Although most identity models center on affectional orientation, individuals who identify as transgender or gender dysphoric also go through developmental stages on the way to establishing their transgender identity (Morgan & Stevens, 2012). It is important to note, however, that because gender dysphoria has been seen through the lens of medical or psychopathological disorders, it has a lack of nonstigmatizing identity models. Although Mallon (1999) called for such models to be created in the late 1990s, only one such model exists to date: a transgender identity model developed by Morgan and Stevens (2012). Morgan and Stevens found that transgender individuals initially experience an early sense of mind–body dissonance, which typically occurs in early childhood with experiences of a disconnect between their gender and their physiological appearance. However, this disconnect can remain hidden from others well into adulthood in the absence of a supportive environment (Morgan & Stevens, 2012). In the next stage, transgender individuals negotiate and manage their identities, continuing to hide their secret and feeling shame surrounding their gender (Morgan & Stevens, 2012). The next stage is the process of transition, in which individuals reach a breaking point and decide to change their circumstances via either surgery, hormones, or dress (Morgan & Stevens, 2012).

New research indicates that although many of these models group people of varied affectional orientations together, such people actually may differ strongly in *how* they develop their identities. Martos, Nezhad, and Meyer (2015) found significant differences in the establishment of identity among lesbians, gay men, and bisexuals. For example, men tended to experience milestones earlier than women; in addition, younger generations tended to both experience milestones and disclose their orientation to others earlier than older generations (Martos et al., 2015). However, bisexual individuals tended to disclose their orientation significantly later than others (Martos et al., 2015). This research is a good example of the importance of considering the influence of other demographic variables on identity formation. In fact, Kenneady and Oswalt (2014) contended that although there is research support for Cass's original developmental model, individuals do not progress linearly through these stages. The stage models also exclude the experiences of individuals who identify as bisexual, pansexual, queer, or transgender and fail to adequately address intersectional identities, such as gender and ethnic differences (Kenneady & Oswalt, 2014).

The Influence of Other Demographic Factors

Although these models are helpful to counselors, new research has indicated that multiple cultural variables complicate identity development quite significantly; a linear model of stage progression, therefore, is simply not realistic. Although major affectional orientation and gender orientation identity milestones are consistent, the pace and plateauing of movement through the stages are different for individuals based on their demographic backgrounds and experiences (Calzo, Antonucci, Mays, & Cochran, 2011). Individuals from nonaffirmative religious and cultural backgrounds move more slowly to acceptance stages and often experience self-rejection multiple times throughout the entire course of development (Figueroa & Tasker, 2014).

In the context of heteronormativity, many will struggle to find their unique identity and feel isolated from others and fearful to discuss their variant experiences (Page & Peacock, 2013). In cultures in which being LGBTQI+ is taboo, individuals may face open hostility and rejection, which will impact their identity formation (Bates, 2010). However, in cultures in which a gay identity either carries significant stigma or is legally punishable, identity development can be completely halted, as coming out could be a potentially fatal decision (Ikizler & Szymanski, 2014). Counselors, therefore, must always consider the context from which clients have originated and how supportive their current environment is when counseling clients who are considering coming out or are fearful of doing so.

These religious and cultural backgrounds, the experience of oppression, and other significant life experiences lead individuals to attach meaning to their sexual identity, which can either complicate or accelerate their development depending on the positivity of their interpretation (Julian, Duys, & Wood, 2014; Lapinski & McKirnan, 2013). For example, the presence of appropriate sexual education, positive or negative media messages, an LGBTQI+ mentor, familial and peer rejection or acceptance, and the importance of a religion in an ethnic culture can alter the course of someone's development (Bates, 2010; Bregman, Malik, Page, Makynen, & Lindahl, 2013; Dentato, Craig, Messinger, Lloyd, & McInroy, 2014; Sheran & Arnold, 2012; Shilo & Savaya, 2011; Testa, Jimenez, & Rankin, 2014).

The Benefits and Challenges of Coming Out

Although often discussed as if it were a singular, one-time event, disclosure is actually a process that occurs over the course, and in different contexts, of a person's life (Goodrich & Luke, 2015). This process was illustrated by the Substance Abuse and Mental Health Services Administration (2013) as involving first the identification, recognition, and acknowledgment of the person as holding this identity, followed by self-acceptance, which then can move the person toward disclosing to others. Coming out is traditionally viewed as a normal developmental milestone for LGBTQI+ persons and has been defined as a stage in a number of the different LGB identity development models, as previously discussed. Although most theories have discussed disclosure from the standpoint of LGB individuals (Herek, 2003), there also are distinct stages or milestones for transgender and intersex persons who come out (Bilodeau, 2005; Poynter & Washington, 2005). Most scholars who have explored this, however, have only overlaid LGB identity development/disclosure processes on transgender persons without strong empirical research or the voice of transgender participants (Goodrich, 2012). It is therefore clear that this process has been underexplored and is in need of additional research to demonstrate the similarities and differences among those who identify as lesbian, gay, or bisexual; those who identify as transgender or intersex; and persons who identify with both groups of identities (Chaney, Filmore, & Goodrich, 2011; Goodrich, 2012; Goodrich & Luke, 2015).

Many benefits, as well as challenges, are faced by those who make the decision to share their identity with others. Potential benefits of disclosure include self-integration, self-growth, and empowerment for the LGBTQI+-identified person (Corrigan & Matthews, 2003). This empowerment results from being authentic (Corrigan & Matthews, 2003), honest, and open in communication with others; the impact of empowerment can be seen in psychological and social growth as well as physical health for the LGBTQI+-identified person (Goodrich, 2009; Goodrich & Luke, 2015; Phillips & Ancis, 2008; Trahan & Goodrich, 2015). The process of disclosure also opens up LGBTQI+ people to explore social and cultural experiences that they would not otherwise be allowed to explore openly and moves them beyond the isolation that can occur when people are keeping their identity secret.

With these potential benefits also come some potential challenges or costs. The literature has numerous examples of familial and social rejection that can follow LGBTQI+ persons' disclosure experience (Bowers, 2015; Goodrich, 2009; Goodrich & Gilbride, 2010; Phillips & Ancis, 2008). This rejection can lead to a number of emotional, physical, and financial consequences for LGBTQI+-identified youth, including elevated risks of verbal or physical abuse (Kosciw, Greytak, Bartkiewicz, Boesen, & Palmer, 2012), financial insecurity and homelessness (Bidell, 2014), and alienation or isolation from others (Goodrich & Luke, 2015). Extreme cases of rejection can lead to depression, anxiety, and suicidal ideation or suicide attempts for LGBTQI+ youth or adults. As discussed in Chapters 3 and 4, the school environment can be a challenging place to identify as LGBTQI+, as the social environment is often heterosexist and unwelcoming to persons outside the norm (Bidell, 2014; Kosciw et al., 2012; Payne & Smith, 2011). Bidell (2014) found greater social and emotional wellness for homeless youth who dropped out of school compared to those who persisted to graduation. In older populations, rejection by others can lead to the loss of a job, the loss of one's family or social circle, verbal or physical harassment, incidents of interpersonal violence, and so forth (Goodrich & Luke, 2015).

Most research in the area of disclosure has occurred among the White LGBTQI+ population, and few scholars have explored the experiences of persons of color (e.g., Hom, 1994; Merighi & Grimes, 2000; Trahan & Goodrich, 2015). Scholars have discussed this gap in the identity development literature, noting the centrality of intersectional identities (including race/ethnicity, sexual/affectional orientation, and gender identity) and the need for better research to understand the influence of each identity on the others for LGBTQI+ persons (e.g., see Budge, Tebbe, & Howard, 2010; Lindsey, 2005). Even though scholars have identified the importance of intersectionality (Sue & Sue, 2016) and the potential influence that one's race and gender identity development have on the coming out process (Rosario, Schrimshaw, & Hunter, 2004), few scholars have actually attended to this in the extant empirical literature.

Only a small number of empirical studies can inform counselors about what persons of color and their families might experience in the disclosure process. Merighi and Grimes (2000) explored the experiences of African, European, Mexican, and Vietnamese American gay males (from 18 to 24 years of age) as they disclosed their sexual/affectional orientation to their families. The researchers found similarities across participants, regardless of race, in both how the disclosure process occurred and the reactions they received from family members. This study provides limited evidence that perhaps the disclosure process is similar across families, and what researchers know about potential opportunities or benefits might be similar across different racial/ethnic groups.

Hom (1994) provided the results of a more targeted study exploring the experiences of Asian American families following the disclosure process. She found that parents expressed a wide range of emotions and reactions after the disclosure, although most parents were able to accept their lesbian daughter or gay son's identity with time. Cultural issues appeared to influence the parents' process of acceptance as well as whether and how they disclosed their children's identity to others. Specifically, cultural concerns raised by participants related to how affectional orientation is discussed (or not discussed), and messages related to "homosexuality" appeared to impact how parents shared this news with others. Thus, even though there is a wide array of languages and cultures across Asian families as a whole, there did appear to be a larger cultural component to the disclosure process when Asian American families were compared to other larger cultural groups.

Finally, Trahan and Goodrich (2015) found similar and different experiences for African American LGBTQI+ persons and their families compared to the previous literature.

Similarities between the families in this study and previous research included the fact that many families had a range of reactions during the disclosure experience and typically took time to adjust to the news. However, the unique findings from this study included the fact that half of the participants did not disclose their identities themselves but instead were *outed* by others. For some participants, the outing was due to a prior disclosure, with one family member taking on the responsibility of disclosing the identity to others without the explicit permission of the LGBTQI+-identified person. One participant had a different experience, with their outing occurring after they were found romancing a person they were in a relationship with by their partner's family member; the participant in the study was outed by their sexual partner so that they could protect themselves from being outed to their own family. This occurred because the sexual partner denied their place in the relationship and instead accused the study participant of taking advantage of them. The type of disclosure (whether active by the participant or outed by others) appeared to influence the study participants' immediate relationships with family and others. Additional findings included the influence of the African American church and the cultural phenomenon of being on the *down low,* which means secretly having sex with members of the same sex while identifying as heterosexual and maintaining heterosexual romantic relationships in public. Both specific African American phenomena appeared to impact how these LGBTQI+-identified persons and their families viewed disclosure, understood their identity, and shared it with others.

Although each of these studies paints a different picture of how different cultural communities responded to LGBTQI+ family members' identity disclosure, taken together, these findings appear to reflect the fact that racial/ethnic identity and culture have meaning in the disclosure process and that counselors need to speak with clients about how this can impact or influence their disclosure and family reactions. Thus, varying advantages and disadvantages may occur in different cultural groups. Careful decisions need to be made prior to the disclosure experience, as they could influence comfort and safety for clients and their families as they attempt to navigate their new lives following the disclosure of their identity as LGBTQI+.

Working With Families of Individuals Who Come Out

Research into the disclosure experience has suggested that often LGBTQI+ persons disclose their identities to one or more friends prior to family (D'Augelli & Hershberger, 1993; Savin-Williams, 2001); they often then disclose to siblings prior to disclosing to their parents (Goodrich, 2009; Goodrich & Gilbride, 2010; Savin-Williams, 2001). Although parents are often the last to know about their child's affectional orientation, this does not diminish its importance to the LGBTQI+ person or that person's family; instead, research has pointed to the importance of this milestone as described by both the LGBTQI+-identified person and that person's family members (Elizur & Ziv, 2001; Savin-Williams, 2001).

Even though it has long been recognized that disclosing to family, friends, and allies (FFA) is a step in the coming out process and a potential source of resiliency and coping for the LGBTQI+-identified person (Kosciw et al., 2012; Scourfield, Roen, & McDermott, 2008), few scholars have explored strategies that could be utilized with FFA to assist them in supporting the disclosure process (Luke & Goodrich, 2015). This is disturbing, as FFA have been shown to have their own experiences in attempting to adjust to and cope with the identity of their loved ones; in addition, FFA need to understand how to better work with, love, and address the LGBTQI+ persons in their lives (Goodrich, 2009; Goodrich & Gilbride, 2010; Hom, 1994; Merighi & Grimes, 2000; Trahan & Goodrich, 2015). Therefore, it is important for counselors to have interventions available so that they can work with

FFA to better integrate their new knowledge of their loved ones' identity as well as receive the knowledge, skills, and awareness necessary to act as supportive resources for the LGBTQI+ loved ones in their lives.

Luke and Goodrich (2015) utilized Bronfenbrenner's (1979, 2005) ecological model of counseling to illustrate the numerous ways in which counselors might be able to intervene with FFA to both recognize the vital role of social support in the health development of LGBTQI+ persons (Berk, 2000) and provide a structure for understanding the levels of intervention that might be useful based on the needs of FFA in the moment. They constructed interventions across the micro-, meso-, exo-, and macrolevels to educate and provide resources for FFA clients so that they could both understand and advocate for the persons they loved.

At the microlevel, Luke and Goodrich (2015) provided group work interventions so that FFA could come together with others to both receive psychoeducation and support to better understand their experiences on an intrapersonal level and be provided with experiences at the interpersonal level to learn how to discuss issues related to sexual/ affectional orientation and gender identity with others. These were provided so that FFA might be better prepared to engage in those discussions with their LGBTQI+-identified loved ones as well as other persons with positive or negative attitudes toward LGBTQI+ persons with whom they might interact in the future. Similarly, Bowers (2015) provided group interventions to allow a structure for families to discuss their personal experiences related to their disclosure experience and understand the similarities and differences they might have had compared to other families in a similar situation. Group interventions included discussions of personal beliefs and values and how these may need to shift or change, the nature of a *family of origin,* and how LGBTQI+ identity can both complicate and support future families. Families will need to individually and collectively construct a new narrative about their familial experience. Scholars such as Goodrich (2009) and Phillips and Ancis (2008) have discussed the importance of noncounseling groups, such as PFLAG, in supporting parents in different stages of identity adjustment following disclosure as well as the opportunity to be exposed to early-level advocacy on behalf of one's child or friend. Similarly, Goodrich and Luke (2010) found that it was helpful for both students and counselors-in-training to be exposed to GSAs and acceptance coalitions to understand the similarities and differences across LGBTQI+ persons and their friends and to be exposed to counseling interventions occurring in an important context of LGBTQI+ youth's lives and schools. Others have additionally discussed the utility of these groups (e.g., Kosciw et al., 2012; Lee, 2002).

Luke and Goodrich (2015) identified ways in which counselors and other stakeholders could utilize the different levels of Bronfenbrenner's (1995, 2005) model in understanding the needs of LGBTQI+ persons. At these levels, counselors and FFA would explore how they and their families intersect and interact with larger groups in the community, such as community and religious leaders as well as others. Interventions at this level explored how forming collaborations and coalitions with stakeholders in one's community can provide both education and support to FFA of LGBTQI+ persons. In addition, it may serve to help the family as a whole by bringing a positive outlook and messages about LGBTQI+ identity to a larger social circle. Larger scale advocacy and outreach occurred at the macrolevel, exploring (a) counselors working with clients around political advocacy and action as well as (b) education about how to navigate these different types of systems.

Although not an intervention for FFA, Goodrich and Luke (2015) presented a safety plan for LGBTQI+ persons as a means of providing structure to allow LGBTQI+ persons to consider the potential benefits and costs of disclosure, including specific issues around financial and personal safety. It is important to make note of this intervention, as not all LGBTQI+ persons may be fully prepared to deal with the outcomes of disclosure, especially if reactions are negative and they face physical abuse or rejection on emotional, financial, or relational levels. Thus, Goodrich and Luke (2015) provided a structured exercise for both the counselor and client to explore, either in a group or together as a dyad, to fully understand both the positive and negative implications that the client might anticipate as part of the coming out process. This intervention was constructed not to force clients to reconsider disclosing to others but instead to help them make an educated decision related to what they think they might anticipate as part of that process. Counselors can be instructed to inform clients that even if they decide not to disclose at the time of the intervention, this does not preclude them from disclosing later, such as when clients may have more financial security, physical safety, and independence from those who might reject them. Students in kindergarten through 12th grade might see benefits outweighing the risks and disclose while in school. However, certain students may wait until college, when different living arrangements are available and they may feel more independence. Adult clients may disclose to their family or at work, although some clients might decide to remain in the closet at work and disclose to close friends and/or family. All clients must see that everyone's life circumstances are different and that they each have the opportunity to change over time. Intentionality, as with other interventions in the counseling process, is most important in any type of decision making.

Conclusion

Although there are many different identity models for the LGBTQI+ population, the overarching message from this area of research indicates that developing a positive identity surrounding affectional orientation and gender variance is crucial for positive mental health and well-being. Counseling strategies will be highly dependent on how clients currently interpret their affectional orientation and/or gender differences. These models additionally help a counselor strategize how to move a client toward greater acceptance. Although counselors have a significant amount of influence in this process, they should never push clients to move too quickly or to disclose their feelings and identity before they are ready. Counseling a client in these areas involves conveying two specific messages to the client: (a) "There is nothing wrong with who you are or how you feel" and (b) "You live in a flawed culture that does not always accept culturally different persons, requiring you to plan for safety and support in being authentic to who you are." Working with families to internalize a positive identity surrounding their LGBTQI+ family member is also important in supporting the client.

Questions for Further Discussion

1. What are the potential benefits and risks of Carl disclosing his identity to others?
2. What forms of resiliency are present in Amanda and her system that might have supported her coming out?
3. What types of safety plans might be necessary to develop with Carl in the event that disclosure does not result in a positive outcome?
4. How might Carl's counselor support him through intentional work in his ecological system (FFA)?
5. How might Carl's counselor respond when Carl inquires about what he should do with his family?

Resources

1. Review the Human Rights Campaign's resource guides on coming out at http://www.hrc.org/resources/topic/coming-out.
2. Read the Trevor Project's "Coming Out as You" resource at http://www.thetrevor-project.org/section/YOU.
3. Review the coming out resources at http://www.huffingtonpost.com/2013/10/11/coming-out-resources_n_4085658.html.

References

Bates, D. D. (2010). Once-married African-American lesbians and bisexual women: Identity development and the coming-out process. *Journal of Homosexuality, 57*(2), 197–225. doi:10.1080/00918360903488848

Berk, L. E. (2000). *Child development* (5th ed.). Boston, MA: Allyn & Bacon.

Bidell, M. P. (2014). Is there an emotional cost to completing high school? Ecological factors and psychological distress among lesbian, gay, bisexual, and transgender homeless youth. *Journal of Homosexuality, 61*(3), 366–381.

Bilodeau, B. (2005). Beyond the gender binary: A case study of two transgender students at a midwestern research university. *Journal of Gay & Lesbian Issues in Education, 3,* 29–44.

Bowers, H. (2015). Groups for couples and families. In K. Goodrich & M. Luke, *Group counseling with LGBTQI persons* (pp. 113–134). Alexandria, VA: American Counseling Association.

Bregman, H. R., Malik, N. M., Page, M. L., Makynen, E., & Lindahl, K. M. (2013). Identity profiles in lesbian, gay, and bisexual youth: The role of family influences. *Journal of Youth and Adolescence, 42,* 417–430. doi:10.1007/s10964-012-9798-z

Bronfenbrenner, U. (1979). Contexts of child rearing: Problems and prospects. *American Psychologist, 34,* 844–850. doi:10.1037/0003-0066X.34.10.844

Bronfenbrenner, U. (1995). Developmental ecology through space and time: A future perspective. In P. Moen, G. H. Elder, Jr., & K. Lüscher (Eds.), *Examining lives in context: Perspectives on the ecology of human development* (pp. 619–647). Washington, DC: American Psychological Association.

Bronfenbrenner, U. (2005). *Making human beings human: Bioecological perspectives on human development.* Thousand Oaks, CA: Sage.

Budge, S. L., Tebbe, E. N., & Howard, K. A. S. (2010). The work experience of transgender individuals: Negotiating the transition and career decision-making process. *Journal of Counseling Psychology, 57,* 377–393.

Calzo, J. P., Antonucci, T. C., Mays, V. M., & Cochran, S. D. (2011). Retrospective recall of sexual orientation identity development among gay, lesbian, and bisexual adults. *Developmental Psychology, 47,* 1658–1673. doi:10.1037/a0025508

Cass, V. C. (1979). Homosexual identity formation: A theoretical model. *Journal of Homosexuality, 4*(3), 219–235. doi:10.1300/J082v04n03_01

Cass, V. C. (1984). Homosexual identity formation: Testing a theoretical model. *Journal of Sex Research, 20*(2), 143–167. doi:10.1080/00224498409551214

Chaney, M. P., Filmore, J. M., & Goodrich, K. M. (2011, May 1). No more sitting on the sidelines. *Counseling Today, 53*(11), 34–37.

Corrigan, P. W., & Matthews, A. K. (2003). Stigma and disclosure: Implications for coming out of the closet. *Journal of Mental Health, 12,* 235–248.

D'Augelli, A. R. (1994). Identity development and sexual orientation: Toward a model of lesbian, gay and bisexual development. In E. J. Trickett, R. J. Watts, & D. Birham (Eds.), *Human diversity: Perspectives on people in context* (pp. 312–333). San Francisco, CA: Jossey-Bass.

D'Augelli, A. R., & Hershberger, S. L. (1993). Lesbian, gay, and bisexual youth in community settings: Personal challenges and mental health problems. *American Journal of Community Psychology, 21,* 421–448.

Dentato, M. P., Craig, S. L., Messinger, L., Lloyd, M., & McInroy, L. B. (2014). Outness among LGBTQ social work students in North America: The contribution of environmental supports and perceptions of comfort. *Social Work Education, 33,* 485–501. doi:10.1080/02615479.2013.855193

Elizur, Y., & Ziv, M. (2001). Family support and acceptance, gay male identity formation, and psychological adjustment: A path model. *Family Process, 40,* 125–144.

Falco, K. L. (1991). *Psychotherapy with lesbian clients: Theory into practice.* Philadelphia, PA: Brunner/Mazel.

Feldman, S. E., & Wright, A. J. (2013). Dual impact: Outness and LGB identity formation on mental health. *Journal of Gay & Lesbian Social Services, 25,* 443–464. doi:10.1080/1053 8720.2013.833066

Figueroa, V., & Tasker, F. (2014). "I always have the idea of sin in my mind . . .": Family of origin, religion, and Chilean young gay men. *Journal of GLBT Family Studies, 10*(3), 269–297. doi:10.1080/1550428X.2013.834424

Gallor, S. M., & Fassinger, R. E. (2010). Social support, ethnic identity, and sexual identity of lesbians and gay men. *Journal of Gay & Lesbian Social Services, 22*(3), 287–315. doi:10.1080/10538720903426404

Gonsiorek, J. C., & Weinrich, J. D. (1995). Definition and measurement of sexual orientation. *Suicide and Life-Threatening Behavior, 25*(Suppl.), 40–51.

Goodrich, K. M. (2009). Mom and Dad "come out": The process of identifying as a heterosexual parent with a lesbian, gay or bisexual child. *Journal of LGBT Issues in Counseling, 3*(1), 37–61.

Goodrich, K. M. (2012). Lived experiences of college-age transsexual individuals. *Journal of College Counseling, 15,* 215–232. doi:10.1002/j.2161-1882.2012.00017.x

Goodrich, K. M., & Gilbride, D. D. (2010). The refinement and validation of a model of family functioning after child's disclosure as lesbian, gay or bisexual. *Journal of LGBT Issues in Counseling, 4*(2), 92–121.

Goodrich, K. M., & Luke, M. (2010). Experiences of school counselors-in-training in group work with LGBTQ adolescents. *Journal for Specialists in Group Work, 35,* 143–159.

Goodrich, K. M., & Luke, M. (2015). *Group counseling with LGBTQI persons.* Alexandria, VA: American Counseling Association.

Herek, G. M. (2003). Why tell if you're not asked? Self-disclosure, intergroup contact, and heterosexuals' attitudes toward lesbians and gay men. In L. D. Garnets & D. C. Kimmel (Eds.), *Psychological perspectives on lesbian, gay, and bisexual experiences* (2nd ed., pp. 270–298). New York, NY: Columbia University Press.

Hom, A. Y. (1994). Stories from the homefront: Perspectives of Asian American parents with lesbian daughters and gay sons. *Amerasia Journal, 20*(1), 19–32.

Ikizler, A. S., & Szymanski, D. M. (2014). A qualitative study of Middle Eastern/Arab American sexual minority identity development. *Journal of LGBT Issues in Counseling, 8*(2), 206–241. doi:10.1080/15538605.2014.897295

Julian, N., Duys, D. K., & Wood, S. M. (2014). Sexual identity formation of women who love women: A contextual view point. *Journal of LGBT Issues in Counseling, 8*(2), 189–205. doi: 10.1080/15538605.2014.895665

Kenneady, D. A., & Oswalt, S. B. (2014). Is Cass's model of homosexual identity formation relevant to today's society? *American Journal of Sexuality Education, 9*(2), 229–246. doi:10 .1080/15546128.2014.900465

Kosciw, J. G., Greytak, E. A., Bartkiewicz, M. J., Boesen, M. J., & Palmer, N. A. (2012). *The 2011 National School Climate Survey: Experiences of lesbian, gay, bisexual and transgender youth in our nation's schools.* New York, NY: GLSEN.

Lapinski, J., & McKirnan, D. (2013). Forgive me father for I have sinned: The role of a Christian upbringing on lesbian, gay, and bisexual identity development. *Journal of Homosexuality, 60,* 853–872. doi:10.1080/00918369.2013.774844

Lee, C. (2002). The impact of belonging to a high school gay/straight alliance. *The High School Journal, 85,* 13–26.

Lindsey, E. S. (2005). Reexamining gender and sexual orientation: Revisioning the representation of queer and trans people in the 2005 edition of *Our Bodies, Ourselves. NWSA Journal, 17,* 184–189.

Luke, M., & Goodrich, K. M. (2015). Working with family, friends, and allies of LGBT youth. *Journal for Social Action in Counseling and Psychology, 7*(1), 63–83.

Mallon, G. P. (1999). A call for organizational trans-formation. *Journal of Gay & Lesbian Social Services: Issues in Practice, Policy & Research, 10*(3–4), 131–142. doi:10.1300/ J041v10n03_09

Martos, A. J., Nezhad, S., & Meyer, I. H. (2015). Variations in sexual identity milestones among lesbians, gay men, and bisexuals. *Sexuality Research & Social Policy, 12*(1), 24–33. doi:10.1007/s13178-014-0167-4

McCarn, S. R., & Fassinger, R. E. (1996). Revisioning sexual minority identity formation: A new model of lesbian identity and its implications. *The Counseling Psychologist, 24,* 508–534. doi:10.1177/0011000096243011

Merighi, J. R., & Grimes, M. D. (2000). Coming out to families in a multicultural context. *Families in Society, 81*(1), 32–41.

Morgan, S. W., & Stevens, P. E. (2012). Transgender identity development as represented by a group of transgendered adults. *Issues in Mental Health Nursing, 33*(5), 301–308. doi: 10.3109/01612840.2011.653657

Pachankis, J. E., & Goldfried, M. R. (2013). Clinical issues in working with lesbian, gay, and bisexual clients. *Psychology of Sexual Orientation and Gender Diversity, 1*(S), 45–58. doi:10.1037/2329-0382.1.S.45

Page, A. D., & Peacock, J. R. (2013). Negotiating identities in a heteronormative context. *Journal of Homosexuality, 60,* 639–654. doi:10.1080/00918369.2012.724632

Payne, E. C., & Smith, M. (2011). The reduction of stigma in schools: A new professional development model for empowering educators to support LGBTQ students. *Journal of LGBT Youth, 8*(2), 174–200.

Phillips, M. J., & Ancis, J. R. (2008). The process of identity development as the parent of a lesbian or gay male. *Journal of LGBT Issues in Counseling, 2*(2), 126–158.

Poynter, K. J., & Washington, J. (2005). Multiple identities: Creating community on campus for LGBT students. *New Directions for Student Services, 2005,* 41–47.

Rosario, M., Schrimshaw, E. W., & Hunter, J. (2004). Ethnic/racial differences in the coming out process of lesbian, gay, and bisexual youths: A comparison of sexual identity development over time. *Cultural Diversity and Ethnic Minority Psychology, 10*(3), 215–228.

Rosario, M., Schrimshaw, E. W., & Hunter, J. (2011). Different patterns of sexual identity development over time: Implications for the psychological adjustment of lesbian, gay, and bisexual youths. *Journal of Sex Research, 48*(1), 3–15. doi:10.1080/00224490903331067

Savin-Williams, R. C. (2001). *Mom. Dad. I'm gay.* Washington, DC: American Psychological Association.

Scourfield, J., Roen, K., & McDermott, L. (2008). Lesbian, gay, bisexual and transgender young people's experiences of distress: Resilience, ambivalence and self-destructive behaviour. *Health and Social Care in the Community, 16*(3), 329–336.

Sheran, N., & Arnold, E. A. (2012). Fairy godmothers and guardian angels: A qualitative study of the gay mentorship relationship. *Journal of Gay & Lesbian Social Services, 24*(3), 201–220. doi:10.1080/10538720.2012.697050

Shilo, G., & Savaya, R. (2011). Effects of family and friend support on LGB youths' mental health and sexual orientation milestones. *Family Relations, 60*(3), 318–330. doi:10.1111/j.1741-3729.2011.00648.x

Substance Abuse and Mental Health Services Administration. (2013). *Building bridges: LGBT populations: A dialogue on advancing opportunities for recovery from addictions and mental health problems* (HHS Publication No. [SMA] 13-4774). Rockville, MD: Author.

Sue, D. W., & Sue, D. (2016). *Counseling the culturally diverse: Theory and practice* (7th ed.). New York, NY: Wiley.

Testa, R. J., Jimenez, C. L., & Rankin, S. (2014). Risk and resilience during transgender identity development: The effects of awareness and engagement with other transgender people on affect. *Journal of Gay & Lesbian Mental Health, 18*(1), 31–46. doi:10.1080/19359705.2013.805177

Trahan, D. P., Jr., & Goodrich, K. M. (2015). "You think you know me, but you have no idea": Dynamics in African American families following a son's or daughter's disclosure as LGBT. *The Family Journal, 23*, 147–157.

Troiden, R. R. (1979). Becoming homosexual: A model of gay identity acquisition. *Psychiatry: Journal for the Study of Interpersonal Processes, 42*(4), 362–373.

Troiden, R. R. (1988). Homosexual identity development. *Journal of Adolescent Health Care, 9*(2), 105–113. doi:10.1016/0197-0070(88)90056-3

Weinberg, M. S., Williams, C. J., & Pryor, D. W. (1994). *Dual attraction: Understanding bisexuality.* New York, NY: Oxford University Press.

Zoeterman, S. E., & Wright, A. J. (2014). The role of openness to experience and sexual identity formation in LGB individuals: Implications for mental health. *Journal of Homosexuality, 61*(2), 334–353. doi:10.1080/00918369.2013.839919

Chapter 7

Physical and Mental Health Challenges Found in the LGBTQI+ Population

Misty M. Ginicola, Joel M. Filmore, Cheri Smith, and Jahaan Abdullah

> *Where LGBT and mental health issues collide is over stigma.*
> *And stigma is society's problem, not the problem of the LGBT or*
> *mental health community. What we have to deal with is the ignorance,*
> *fear, and prejudice that blight the lives of those who have nothing*
> *wrong with them in any moral or transgressive sense.*
> *It is society that is ill.*
>
> —Stephen Fry

• • •

Awareness of Attitudes and Beliefs Self-Check

1. What parts of your identity carry a negative stigma from within your family or the overall culture?
2. What negative coping behaviors do you have when you experience stress?
3. When you go to seek health or mental health services, do you ever fear that they will discriminate against you?

Case Study

Liv, a 30-year-old female transgender and African American client, comes to your office with symptoms of depression and anxiety. She reports multiple digestive problems (ulcerative colitis and stomach ulcers) as well as previous addiction issues before her complete gender transition at age 25. In her intake, you learn that her family has very strained relations with Liv: Most will not talk to her, and those who do often call her by her previous male name or make comments about how they do not understand her "choices." She was also the victim of a hate-based attack at age 23 when she was beginning her transition: She was physically assaulted one night when she was walking alone. She was recently outed as transgender by someone at work and has been noticing people acting strangely toward her lately. She is worried that she could be fired because she lives in a state without employment protections for transgender individuals.

• • •

Causes of Physical and Mental Health Impairments

Those in the lesbian, gay, bisexual, transgender, queer, questioning, intersex, asexual, ally, pansexual/polysexual, and two-spirited (LGBTQI+) communities are at a substantially greater risk for a variety of physical, psychological, and emotional issues. In addition to the factors that put heterosexual individuals at risk for mental or physical illness (e.g., abuse, trauma, stress), LGBTQI+ individuals carry more risk related to their minority status. The minority stress model best explains this greater prevalence among the LGBTQI+ population (Meyer, 2003). *Minority stressors* are events and experiences associated with being a minority that cause disruption and maladjustment (Meyer, 2003). For the LGBTQI+ population, these experiences typically fall into three categories: the direct experience of prejudicial events and discrimination, internalizations of society's heterosexist and homophobic attitudes, and expectations of rejection (Kelleher, 2009; Sutter & Perrin, 2016).

For queer people of color, the minority stress experienced can be amplified as it is impacted by their intersectional cultural backgrounds (Sutter & Perrin, 2016). In addition, the additive nature of social stress related to affectional and gender orientation, ethnic minority status, gender issues, and socioeconomic prejudices can have a massive impact. These intersectional experiences can lead to increases in overall physiological issues, psychological distress, mental health disorders, and overall reduced quality of life (Díaz, Ayala, Bein, Henne, & Marin, 2001; Lewis, Derlega, Griffin, & Krowinski, 2003; Mays & Cochran, 2001; Schneeberger, Dietl, Muenzenmaier, Huber, & Lang, 2014).

The increased violence and abuse that impact LGBTQI+ youth is an additional complex factor impacting the prevalence of physical and psychological disorders (Saewyc et al., 2006; Schneeberger et al., 2014). This increase in violence and abuse is directly related to negative societal attitudes regarding affectional and gender orientation. If children exhibit gender nonconformity or openly acknowledge varied sexual attractions in childhood or adolescence, they may experience violence from family, peers, or other authority figures in attempts to force them to conform (Saewyc et al., 2006). Both LGBTQI+ males and females are more likely than their heterosexual counterparts to be physically abused. For example, up to 33% of bisexual and gay males report having been physically abused in their childhood, in contrast to 20% of heterosexual males (Saewyc et al., 2006). In addition, their isolation from others, as well as these societal attitudes, appears to increase their vulnerability to sexual abuse: Up to 50% of lesbian and bisexual women, 20% of bisexual men, and 25% of gay men report sexual abuse (Saewyc et al., 2006). Once they have experienced victimization in any form, they are also more vulnerable to being revictimized, which is similar for heterosexual populations (Schneeberger et al., 2014).

General Physical Health Challenges

The physical challenges for the LGBTQI+ community are as varied as the communities themselves. For some, unhealthy coping mechanisms can result in substance abuse and addiction; for others, overeating may occur. Demographic variables, the extent of stress and trauma, and the types of unhealthy coping mechanisms used will predict the type of physical health problems each group and individual will face. Research has primarily focused on the LGB community, with some initial research on the transgender population.

Lesbian and bisexual females face higher rates of heart disease and breast cancer than heterosexual women; lower physical fitness and higher obesity rates are linked to this increase in risk (Boehmer, Bowen, & Bauer, 2007; Brittain, Baillargeon, McElroy, Aaron, & Gyurcsik, 2006; Cochran et al., 2001; Dibble, Roberts, & Nussey, 2004; National Women's Health Information Center, 2016). For lesbians, lower physical fitness rates have been found to be influenced by high levels of fatigue, no partner with whom to work out, and a lack of lesbian-themed or lesbian-friendly workout groups and gyms (including facilities lacking same-sex partner memberships). Lesbians are also less likely than heterosexual women to visit a doctor for routine physical screenings. Among lesbians, African American women, those who live in either a rural or urban environment, and those with a lower income and education level are at the highest risk for physical health problems (Dobinson, 2007). Bisexual women are at a higher risk for participating in sexually risky behavior and contracting sexually transmitted infections (Dobinson, 2007). Lesbians are also at an increased risk for injury due to physical harassment, physical violence surrounding their sexual/affectional orientation, and intimate partner violence (Gross, Aurand, & Addessa, 2000). Bisexual women are also at a drastically increased greater risk (more than 30% increase) for intimate partner violence compared to heterosexual adults (VanKim & Padilla, 2010).

Gay and bisexual men are at a high risk for heart disease and increased risk for prostate, testicular, anal, and colon cancers, as well as sexually transmitted infections (including HIV, syphilis, human papillomavirus, and hepatitis); this increased risk is related to increased rates of tobacco and alcohol use as well as a higher risk of infection for anyone who has sex with a male or who has receptive anal sex (Asencio, Blank, & Descartes, 2009; Centers for Disease Control and Prevention, 2007, 2012; Chin-Hong et al., 2005; Hall et al., 2008; Ostrow & Stall, 2008; Urbanus, van Houdt, van de Laar, & Coutinho, 2009). Although gay males are at risk for sexually transmitted infections, practicing safe sex is an incredibly effective way to reduce this risk and has been successfully embraced in the gay male community (Hall et al., 2008). Although HIV was originally conceptualized as an LGBTQI+ disease, this myth has long been debunked, and it is understood that the high risk for the queer community resulted from having sex with men as well as anal intercourse (Hall et al., 2008). However, the impact of HIV/AIDS on the LGBTQI+ community is widespread—from the members who died of AIDS in the 1980s and 1990s, to those who are now living with HIV/AIDS, to all of the challenges (financial and physical) that accompany the virus (Hall et al., 2008). Gay and bisexual males are also at an increased risk for injury due to physical victimization based on their affectional orientation and intimate partner violence (Houston & McKirman, 2007; VanKim & Padilla, 2010; Willis, 2004).

Research on transgender persons is very limited. However, there is some evidence that both the feminizing and masculinizing therapies may increase the risk of certain types of cancers and other physical issues, such as venous thromboembolic disease (blood clots in the legs) from estrogen–progestin combinations; increased risks of liver cancer, ovarian cancer, and bone density loss are also linked to taking testosterone (Dizon, Tejada-Berges, Koelliker, Steinhoff, & Granai, 2006; Moore, Wisniewski, & Dobs, 2003). Transgender persons, particularly male-to-female transgender youth, are at an increased risk for HIV and other sexually transmitted infections (Kenagy & Hsieh, 2005; Reback, Simon, Bemis, & Gatson, 2001). The risk of violence against transgender persons is one of the largest issues that faces the community; as indicated earlier, research indicates that more than half of transgender persons are at risk for injury as a result of physical assault or abuse as well as sexual assault (Reback et al., 2001; Xavier et al., 2005). Transgender individuals are also at a higher risk for intimate partner violence (Reback et al., 2001; Xavier, Bobbin, Singer, & Budd, 2005).

Emotional and Mental Health Challenges

Significant disparities in mental health have been noted for this population compared to the heterosexual population. However, the full extent of disparities in the LGBTQI+ community is uncertain, as there remains a noticeable paucity of research on this group. Although some information is known, information regarding the transgender community and LGBTQI+ people of color overall is substantially lacking. Empirical studies note greater overall levels of anxiety, depression, distress, substance abuse, and unsafe sexual practices among this population. King et al. (2008) conducted a systematic review and meta-analysis of the prevalence of mental disorders, substance abuse, self-harm, suicide, and suicidal ideation in LGB people. It was found that on average the risks of depression and anxiety disorders were at least 1.5 times higher in LGB people; the incidence of alcohol and other substance abuse was also 1.5 times higher than in the heterosexual population (King et al., 2008). Body image issues are also associated with the LGBTQI+ population. Unlike lesbians, who are at risk for obesity, gay men are at a higher risk for negative body images, which results in bulimia or anorexia (Deputy & Boehmer, 2010; Siconolfi, Halkitis, & Allomong, 2009). Equally important is the transgender community; research and theoretical literature is limited but emerging for this population. Although a great deal of research has been conducted, further investigations to help better understand this population are warranted.

Depression and Suicide

There is well-established literature and research on increased levels of depression among LGBTQI+ persons (Case et al., 2004; Fergusson, Horwood, & Beautrais, 1999; McLaren, 2009; Westefeld, Maples, Buford, & Taylor, 2001) as well as an increased suicide risk (Fergusson et al., 1999; Garcia, Adams, Friedman, & East, 2002; Skegg, Nada-Raja, Dickson, Paul, & Williams, 2003). As described previously, being a sexual or gender minority can cause great distress; the virulent and hostile environments that an LGBTQI+ person encounters could certainly lead to distress and depression. Various factors contribute to depression and suicidality for LGBTQI+ people, among them poor self-esteem, internalized homophobia, the experiencing of microaggressions, alienation from family and friends, homelessness, fear of violence, and a lack of overall societal and cultural acceptance (Case et al., 2004; Fergusson et al., 1999; McLaren, 2009; Westefeld et al., 2001). Rejecting environments that hold rigid views of gender and affectional orientation have been linked to increases in depression and suicidal ideation in this population (Ryan, Huebner, Diaz, & Sanchez, 2009). Many LGBTQI+ individuals also experience isolation or bullying from their families, their peers, and the communities in which they live, which thus creates feelings of abandonment and loneliness; this in turn often leads to feelings of depression and suicidality. For example, out lesbian and bisexual women were more than twice as likely as heterosexual women to have suicidal ideation (Koh & Ross, 2006). Unfortunately, being closeted also comes with an extra cost: LGB persons who are not out are more likely to attempt suicide than their heterosexual counterparts (Gilman et al., 2001; Koh & Ross, 2006). Transgender individuals appear to be at the highest risk, with suicidal ideation ranging from 38% to 65% in research findings; approximately 32% of transgender persons attempt suicide (Clements-Nolle, Marx, & Katz, 2006; Mathy, 2002).

Anxiety Disorders

In the LGBTQI+ community, anxiety disorders are also common (Meyer, 2003). The experience of anxiety disorders, including posttraumatic stress disorder, is significantly higher among members of the LGBTQI+ communities as yet another symptom of self-hatred, internalized homophobia and shame, institutionalized prejudice, oppression (Mays & Cochran, 2001), a lack of social support (Safren & Pantalone, 2006), and violence toward this population due to affectional minority status (King et al., 2008). Increased levels of anxiety have also been associated with low self-esteem: Internalized homophobia and negative self-evaluations have been noted in the LGBTQI+ community (Gilman et al., 2001; Pachankis & Bernstein, 2012; Pachankis & Goldfried, 2006; Potoczniak, Aldea, & DeBlaere, 2007; Safren & Pantalone, 2006). Studies have shown that LGB individuals have increased levels of psychiatric burden in terms of stress and distress; this can result in heightened depression and anxiety, where individuals attempt to self-medicate with substances in order to relieve their symptoms (Cochran, 2001; Cochran & Mays, 2009; Cochran, Sullivan, & Mays, 2003; King et al., 2008).

Substance Abuse

Because of this high level of distress and drive to self-medicate, there is a high overlap in symptomatology of depression, anxiety, and substance abuse (Case et al., 2004; Fergusson et al., 1999; Ngamake, Walch, & Raveepatarakul, 2016; Orenstein, 2001). "Sexual minorities" who use substances to cope report higher levels of psychological distress, lending support to the minority stress model (Ngamake et al., 2016). Experiences of discrimination and internalized homophobia have been linked to substance abuse in lesbians (Nyitray, Corran, Altman, Chikani, & Negrón, 2006). Research indicates that abuse of tobacco, marijuana, and alcohol is higher among lesbians than heterosexuals (Diamant, Wold, Spritzer, & Gelberg, 2000; Nyitray et al., 2006). Use of tobacco, alcohol, and illicit substances also occurs at a higher rate among gay men; however, this use is significantly predicted by age, level of stress, and whether the person is closeted (Centers for Disease Control and Prevention, 2010; Ostrow & Stall, 2008). Bisexuals have been found to have the highest smoking rates of any other population; they also have significantly higher rates of binge drinking (VanKim & Padilla, 2010). Homelessness has also been associated with subsequent symptoms of anxiety, depression, conduct problems, and substance abuse (Rosario, Schrimshaw, & Hunter, 2012). Stressful life events, negative social relationships, and lack of social support from friends strengthen the association between homelessness and depression symptomatology (Rosario et al., 2012).

Barriers to Health Care

Compounding the increased physical and mental health risks for the LGBTQI+ population is the experience of significant barriers to accessing high-quality health care (Brotman, Ferrer, Sussman, Ryan, & Richard, 2015; Daulaire, 2014; Whitehead, Shaver, & Stephenson, 2016). Access to health insurance and financial costs are a large barrier for LGBTQI+ populations. In addition, finding quality, culturally competent care can be a challenge. Not all doctors and clinicians will understand what types of medical care a transgender individual will need— for example, a transwoman will need prostate exams as she ages. A doctor needs to both understand the physical needs a transgender individual will have and remain sensitive to the emotional impact that these procedures might have on the patient. In terms of mental health, counselors and other helping professionals need to know how to culturally accommodate the queer community into existing intervention programs. For example, bisexual individuals who are attending a substance abuse counseling program will have different needs and different stressors than their heterosexual and gay counterparts; they also may have gender variance, which may not translate well to an all-female or all-male counseling group.

Unfortunately, experiences of homophobia and transphobia in the health care and mental health fields are still common. The combination of little training and experience with LGBTQI+ persons as well as personal biases can create disaffirming and uncomfortable contexts. Therefore, many in the LGBTQI+ community may fear seeking help or may fear coming out to health care professionals. Members of the LGBTQI+ communities have reported experiencing microaggressions. For example, a lesbian mother reported the following after the birth of her first child: "An employee stopped me and asked me who I was. When I said 'the other mom,' she rolled her eyes and walked away saying, 'I don't believe this'" (Human Rights Campaign, 2016, p. 5). This discrimination can also include inappropriate health care, as one transgender woman reported: "I went to the [emergency room] because I broke a rib. Once the doctor found out I was transgender he wanted to do a genital exam on me. When I refused, they refused to treat me" (p. 5). It can also include humiliating experiences, as this transgender woman waiting for a physical reported: "When I walked towards the women's bathroom in the waiting area, the receptionist jumped up and told me to use a McDonald's restroom down the street. I felt like leaving and never going back" (p. 5). Often the discrimination may be subtle but still apparent, as a gay man who was hospitalized experienced: "After I mentioned that my husband would be visiting me, the staff, who had been very friendly, turned very cool—and I saw a lot less of them, even when I really needed help" (p. 6). Fear of being outed, being treated with little dignity, or experiencing discrimination or marginalization can prevent members of the LGBTQI+ communities from getting regular and preventive health care (Human Rights Campaign, 2016).

Protective Factors

More recent research has identified mediating and protective factors for both physical and mental health outcomes for LGBTQI+ individuals. Internal factors, such as feeling self-confident, accepting one's own identity, experiencing feelings of authenticity, and feeling hope, are related to positive health and mental health outcomes. In terms of external protective factors, being connected to the LGBTQI+ communities, being part of a collective that is affirmative and has high self-esteem in relation to LGBTQI+ identities, having support from meaningful relationships, and having positive role models in life are protective factors against physical and psychological distress as well as the associated negative outcomes (Mason, Lewis, Winstead, & Derlega, 2015; Meyer, 2015; Moody, Fuks, Peláez, & Smith, 2015; Puckett, Levitt, Horne, & Hayes-Skelton, 2015). Counselors working with LGBTQI+ clients will want to not only increase these resilient characteristics but teach self-advocacy skills for use in the medical system. Advocacy groups like the Center of Excellence for Transgender Health (http://transhealth.ucsf.edu/) and the Human Rights Campaign (http://www.hrc.org/campaigns/healthcare-equality-index) have materials for clients to educate themselves on proper standards of care.

Conclusion

On receiving LGBTQI+ or other minority clients, counselors may only see evidence of the client's maladaptive behavior in causing physical and mental health problems. Although clients should take responsibility for their own choices, this view does not consider the actual source of their negative behaviors: minority stress. In order to cope with internalized negative feelings surrounding their affectional orientation and gender variance and external experiences of oppression and marginalization, LGBTQI+ persons, like other minorities, often develop negative coping behaviors in order to survive. Understanding this process can improve the treatment of both physical and mental health problems in clients. By targeting the real culprit, clients can feel understood, accepted, and empowered to change their behaviors once they learn positive coping skills and improve their resiliency.

Questions for Further Discussion

1. What risk factors or minority stressors should a counselor identify in Liv's story?
2. What additional stressors may Liv face being both African American and transgender?
3. What types of physical issues are individuals from the LGBTQI+ community more at risk for developing? What about transgender individuals specifically?
4. What types of mental health issues are individuals from the LGBTQI+ community more at risk for developing? What about transgender individuals specifically?
5. Knowing the research on protective factors, what should Liv's counselor focus on to help develop her resiliency?

Resources

1. Read about LGBT health and mental health at https://www.healthypeople. gov/2020/topics-objectives/topic/lesbian-gay-bisexual-and-transgender-health.
2. Become familiar with how to use the Gay and Lesbian Medical Association provider directory at http://www.glma.org/index.cfm?fuseaction=Page.viewPage&pageId =939&grandparentID=534&parentID=938&nodeID=1.
3. Review the *Top Health Issues for LGBT Populations Information and Resource Kit* at http://store.samhsa.gov/product/Top-Health-Issues-for-LGBT-Populations/ SMA12-4684.
4. Read through the Healthcare Equality Index at http://www.hrc.org/apps/hei/.
5. Visit LGBT-friendly standards of practice at http://www.glbthealth.org/CommunityStandardsofPractice.htm.

References

Asencio, M., Blank, T., & Descartes, L. (2009). The prospect of prostate cancer: A challenge for gay men's sexualities as they age. *Sexuality Research & Social Policy, 6*(4), 38–51.

Boehmer, U., Bowen, D. J., & Bauer, G. R. (2007). Overweight and obesity in sexual-minority women: Evidence from population-based data. *American Journal of Public Health, 97,* 1134–1140.

Brittain, D. R., Baillargeon, T., McElroy, M., Aaron, D. J., & Gyurcsik, N. C. (2006). Barriers to moderate physical activity in adult lesbians. *Women & Health, 43*(1), 75–92.

Brotman, S., Ferrer, I., Sussman, T., Ryan, B., & Richard, B. (2015). Access and equity in the design and delivery of health and social care to LGBTQ older adults: A Canadian perspective. In N. A. Orel & C. A. Fruehauf (Eds.), *The lives of LGBT older adults: Understanding challenges and resilience* (pp. 111–140). Washington, DC: American Psychological Association.

Case, P., Austin, S. B., Hunter, D. J., Manson, J. E., Malspeis, S., Willett, W. C., & Spiegelman, D. (2004). Sexual orientation, health risk factors, and physical functioning in the Nurses' Health Study II. *Journal of Women's Health, 13,* 1033–1047. doi:10.1089/ jwh.2004.13.1033

Centers for Disease Control and Prevention. (2007). *CDC fact sheet, syphilis and MSM (men who have sex with men).* Atlanta, GA: Author.

Centers for Disease Control and Prevention. (2010). *CDC fact sheet, substance abuse among gay and bisexual men.* Atlanta, GA: Author.

Centers for Disease Control and Prevention. (2012). *Viral hepatitis.* Retrieved from http://www.cdc.gov/hepatitis/

Chin-Hong, P. V., Vittinghoff, E., Cranston, R. S., Browne, L., Buchbinder, S., Colfax, G., . . . Palefsky, J. M. (2005). Age-related prevalence of anal cancer precursors in homosexual men: The EXPLORE study. *Journal of the National Cancer Institute, 97,* 896–905.

Clements-Nolle, K., Marx, R., & Katz, M. (2006). Attempted suicide among transgender persons: The influence of gender-based discrimination and victimization. *Journal of Homosexuality, 51*(3), 53–69. doi:10.1300/J082v51n03_04

Cochran, S. D. (2001). Emerging issues in research on lesbians' and gay men's mental health: Does sexual orientation really matter? *American Psychologist, 56,* 931–947. doi:10.1037/0003-066X.56.11.931

Cochran, S. D., & Mays, V. M. (2009). Burden of psychiatric morbidity among lesbian, gay, and bisexual individuals in the California Quality of Life Survey. *Journal of Abnormal Psychology, 118,* 647–658. doi:10.1037/a0016501

Cochran, S. D., Mays, V. M., Bowen, D., Gage, S., Bybee, D., Roberts, S. J., . . . White, J. (2001). Cancer-related risk indicators and preventative screening behaviors between lesbian and bisexual women. *American Journal of Public Health, 91,* 591–597.

Cochran, S. D., Sullivan, J. G., & Mays, V. M. (2003). Prevalence of mental disorders, psychological distress, and mental health services use among lesbian, gay, and bisexual adults in the United States. *Journal of Consulting and Clinical Psychology, 71*(1), 53–61. doi:10.1037/0022-006X.71.1.53

Daulaire, N. (2014). The importance of LGBT health on a global scale. *LGBT Health, 1*(1), 8–9. doi:10.1089/lgbt.2013.0008

Deputy, N. P., & Boehmer, U. (2010). Determinants of body weight among men of different sexual orientation. *Preventive Medicine, 51*(2), 129–131.

Diamant, A. L., Wold, C., Spritzer, K., & Gelberg, L. (2000). Health behaviors, health status, and access to and use of health care: A population-based study of lesbian, bisexual, and heterosexual women. *Archives of Family Medicine, 9,* 1043–1051.

Díaz, R. M., Ayala, G., Bein, E., Henne, J., & Marin, B. V. (2001). The impact of homophobia, poverty, and racism on the mental health of gay and bisexual Latino men: Findings from 3 US cities. *American Journal of Public Health, 91,* 927–932.

Dibble, S. L., Roberts, S. A., & Nussey, B. (2004). Comparing breast cancer risk between lesbians and their heterosexual sisters. *Women's Health Issues, 14*(2), 60–68.

Dizon, D. S., Tejada-Berges, T., Koelliker, S., Steinhoff, M., & Granai, C. O. (2006). Ovarian cancer associated with testosterone supplementation in a female-to-male transsexual patient. *Gynecologic & Obstetric Investigation, 62*(4), 226–228.

Dobinson, C. (2007). Top ten bisexual health issues. In M. Miller, A. André, J. Ebin, & L. Bessonova, *Bisexual health: An introduction and model practices for HIV/STI prevention programming* (pp. 106–109). New York, NY: National Gay and Lesbian Task Force Policy Institute, the Fenway Institute at Fenway Community Health, and BiNet USA.

Fergusson, D., Horwood, J., & Beautrais, A. (1999). Is sexual orientation related to mental health problems and suicidality in young people? *Archives of General Psychiatry, 56,* 876–880.

Garcia, J., Adams, J., Friedman, L., & East, P. (2002). Links between past abuse, suicide ideation, and sexual orientation among San Diego college students. *Journal of American College Health, 51*(1), 9–14. doi:10.1080/07448480209596322

Gilman, S. E., Cochran, S. D., Mays, V. M., Hughes, M., Ostrow, D., & Kessler, R. C. (2001). Risk of psychiatric disorders among individuals reporting same-sexual partners in the National Comorbidity Survey. *American Journal of Public Health, 91,* 933–939.

Gross, L., Aurand, S., & Addessa, R. (2000). *The 1999–2000 study of discrimination and violence against lesbian and gay men in Philadelphia and the Commonwealth of Pennsylvania.* Philadelphia, PA: Philadelphia Lesbian and Gay Task Force.

Hall, H. I., Song, R., Rhodes, P., Prejean, J., An, Q., Lee, L. M., . . . Janssen, R. S., for the HIV Incidence Surveillance Group. (2008). Estimation of HIV incidence in the United States. *Journal of the American Medical Association, 300,* 520–529.

Houston, E., & McKirman, D. J. (2007). Intimate partner abuse among gay and bisexual men: Risk correlates and health outcomes. *Journal of Urban Health, 84,* 681–690.

Human Rights Campaign. (2016). *Healthcare equality index 2016: Promoting equitable and inclusive care for lesbian, gay, bisexual and transgender patients and their families.* Washington, DC: Author.

Kelleher, C. (2009). Minority stress and health: Implications for lesbian, gay, bisexual, transgender, and questioning (LGBTQ) young people. *Counselling Psychology Quarterly,* 22(4), 373–379. doi:10.1080/09515070903334995

Kenagy, G., & Hsieh, C. M. (2005). The risk less known: Female-to-male transgender persons' vulnerability to HIV infection. *AIDS Care, 17*(2), 195–207.

King, M., Semlyen, J., Tai, S. S., Killaspy, H., Osborn, D., Popelyuk, D., & Nazareth, I. (2008). A systematic review of mental disorder, suicide, and deliberate self-harm in lesbian, gay and bisexual people. *BMC Psychiatry, 8*(70). doi:10.1186/1471-244X-8-70

Koh, A. S., & Ross, L. K. (2006). Mental health issues: A comparison of lesbian, bisexual and heterosexual women. *Journal of Homosexuality, 51,* 33–57.

Lewis, R. J., Derlega, V. J., Griffin, J. L., & Krowinski, A. C. (2003). Stressors for gay men and lesbians: Life stress, gay-related stress, stigma consciousness, and depressive symptoms. *Journal of Social and Clinical Psychology, 22,* 716–729.

Mason, T. B., Lewis, R. J., Winstead, B. A., & Derlega, V. J. (2015). External and internalized heterosexism among sexual minority women: The moderating roles of social constraints and collective self-esteem. *Psychology of Sexual Orientation and Gender Diversity,* 2(3), 313–320. doi:10.1037/sgd0000115

Mathy, R. M. (2002). Transgender identity and suicidality in a nonclinical sample—Sexual orientation, psychiatric history, and compulsive behaviors. *Journal of Psychology & Human Sexuality, 14*(4), 47–65.

Mays, V. M., & Cochran, S. D. (2001). Mental health correlates of perceived discrimination among lesbian, gay, and bisexual adults in the United States. *American Journal of Public Health, 91,* 1869–1876.

McLaren, S. (2009). Sense of belonging to the general and lesbian communities as predictors of depression among lesbians. *Journal of Homosexuality, 56*(1), 1–13. doi:10.1080/00918360802551365

Meyer, I. H. (2003). Prejudice, social stress, and mental health in lesbian, gay, and bisexual populations: Conceptual issues and research evidence. *Psychological Bulletin, 129,* 674–697.

Meyer, I. H. (2015). Resilience in the study of minority stress and health of sexual and gender minorities. *Psychology of Sexual Orientation and Gender Diversity, 2*(3), 209–213. doi:10.1037/sgd0000132

Moody, C., Fuks, N., Peláez, S., & Smith, N. G. (2015). "Without this, I would for sure already be dead": A qualitative inquiry regarding suicide protective factors among trans adults. *Psychology of Sexual Orientation and Gender Diversity, 2*(3), 266–280. doi:10.1037/sgd0000130

Moore, E., Wisniewski, A., & Dobs, A. (2003). Endocrine treatment of transsexual people: A review of treatment regimens, outcomes, and adverse effects. *Journal of Clinical Endocrinology & Metabolism, 88*, 3467–3473.

National Women's Health Information Center. (2016). *Lesbian and bisexual health fact sheet.* Retrieved from https://www.womenshealth.gov/publications/our-publications/fact-sheet/lesbian-bisexual-health.html

Ngamake, S. T., Walch, S. E., & Raveepatarakul, J. (2016). Discrimination and sexual minority mental health: Mediation and moderation effects of coping. *Psychology of Sexual Orientation and Gender Diversity, 3*(2), 213–226. doi:10.1037/sgd0000163

Nyitray, A., Corran, R., Altman, K., Chikani, V., & Negrón, E. V. (2006). *Tobacco use and interventions among Arizona lesbian, gay, bisexual and transgender people.* Phoenix: Arizona Department of Health Services.

Orenstein, A. (2001). Substance use among gay and lesbian adolescents. *Journal of Homosexuality, 41*(2), 1–15. doi:10.1300/J082v41n03_01

Ostrow, D. G., & Stall, R. (2008). Alcohol, tobacco, and drug use among gay and bisexual men. In R. J. Wolitski, R. Stall, & R. O. Valdiserri (Eds.), *Unequal opportunity: Health disparities affecting gay and bisexual men in the United States* (pp. 121–158). New York, NY: Oxford University Press.

Pachankis, J. E., & Bernstein, L. B. (2012). An etiological model of anxiety in young gay men: From early stress to public self-consciousness. *Psychology of Men & Masculinity, 13*(2), 107–122. doi:10.1037/a0024594

Pachankis, J. E., & Goldfried, M. R. (2006). Social anxiety in young gay men. *Journal of Anxiety Disorders, 20*, 996–1015. doi:10.1016/j.janxdis.2006.01.001

Potoczniak, D. J., Aldea, M. A., & DeBlaere, C. (2007). Ego identity, social anxiety, social support, and self-concealment in lesbian, gay, and bisexual individuals. *Journal of Counseling Psychology, 54*, 447–457. doi:10.1037/0022-0167.54.4.447

Puckett, J. A., Levitt, H. M., Horne, S. G., & Hayes-Skelton, S. A. (2015). Internalized heterosexism and psychological distress: The mediating roles of self-criticism and community connectedness. *Psychology of Sexual Orientation and Gender Diversity, 2*, 426–435. doi:10.1037/sgd0000123

Reback, C., Simon, P., Bemis, C., & Gatson, B. (2001). *The Los Angeles transgender health study: Community report.* Los Angeles, CA: University of California at Los Angeles.

Rosario, M., Schrimshaw, E. W., & Hunter, J. (2012). Homelessness among lesbian, gay, and bisexual youth: Implications for subsequent internalizing and externalizing symptoms. *Journal of Youth and Adolescence, 41*, 544–560. doi:10.1007/s10964-011-9681-3

Ryan, C., Huebner, D., Diaz, R. M., & Sanchez, J. (2009). Family rejection as a predictor of negative health outcomes in White and Latino lesbian, gay, and bisexual young adults. *Pediatrics, 23*(1), 346–352.

Saewyc, E. M., Skay, C. L., Pettingell, S. L., Reis, E. A., Bearinger, L., Resnick, M., . . . Combs, L. (2006). Hazards of stigma: The sexual and physical abuse of gay, lesbian, and bisexual adolescents in the United States and Canada. *Child Welfare, 85*(2), 195–214.

Safren, S. A., & Pantalone, D. W. (2006). Social anxiety and barriers to resilience among lesbian, gay, and bisexual adolescents. In A. M. Omoto & H. S. Kurtzman (Eds.), *Sexual orientation and mental health: Examining identity and development in lesbian, gay, and bisexual people* (pp. 55–71). Washington, DC: American Psychological Association. doi:10.1037/11261-003

Schneeberger, A. R., Dietl, M. F., Muenzenmaier, K. H., Huber, C. G., & Lang, U. E. (2014). Stressful childhood experiences and health outcomes in sexual minority populations: A systematic review. *Social Psychiatry and Psychiatric Epidemiology, 49*, 1427–1445. doi:10.1007/s00127-014-0854-8

Siconolfi, D., Halkitis, P. N., & Allomong, T. W. (2009). Body dissatisfaction and eating disorders in a sample gay and bisexual men. *International Journal of Men's Health, 8*(3), 254–264.

Skegg, K., Nada-Raja, S., Dickson, N., Paul, C., & Williams, S. (2003). Sexual orientation and self-harm in men and women. *American Journal of Psychiatry, 160,* 541–546. doi:10.1176/appi.ajp.160.3.541

Sutter, M., & Perrin, P. B. (2016). Discrimination, mental health, and suicidal ideation among LGBTQ people of color. *Journal of Counseling Psychology, 63*(1), 98–105. doi:10.1037/cou0000126

Urbanus, A. T., van Houdt, R., van de Laar, T. J., & Coutinho, R. A. (2009). Viral hepatitis among men who have sex with men, epidemiology and public health consequences. *Euro Surveillance, 14*(47), 11–16.

VanKim, N. A., & Padilla, J. L. (2010). *New Mexico's progress in collecting lesbian, gay, bisexual, and transgender health data and its implications for addressing health disparities.* Albuquerque: New Mexico Department of Health, Chronic Disease Prevention and Control Bureau.

Westefeld, J. S., Maples, M. R., Buford, B., & Taylor, S. (2001). Gay, lesbian, and bisexual college students: The relationship between sexual orientation and depression, loneliness, and suicide. *Journal of College Student Psychotherapy, 15*(3), 71–82. doi:10.1300/J035v15n03_06

Whitehead, J., Shaver, J., & Stephenson, R. (2016). Outness, stigma, and primary health care utilization among rural LGBT populations. *PLoS ONE, 11*(1). doi:10.1371/journal.pone.0146139

Willis, D. G. (2004). Hate crimes against gay males: An overview. *Issues in Mental Health Nursing, 25*(2), 115–132.

Xavier, J., Bobbin, M., Singer, B., & Budd, E. (2005). A needs assessment of transgendered people of color living in Washington, DC. *International Journal of Transgenderism, 8*(2/3), 31–47.

COUNSELING TREATMENT ISSUES WITH LGBTQI+ CLIENTS

Chapter 8

Disaffirming Therapy: The Ascent and Descent of Sexual Orientation Change Efforts

Peter Finnerty, Michael M. Kocet, Jeff Lutes, and Chad Yates

I am sorry for the pain and hurt that many of you have experienced. I am sorry some of you spent years working through the shame and guilt when your attractions didn't change. I am sorry we promoted sexual orientation change efforts and reparative theories about sexual orientation that stigmatized parents . . . I am sorry that when I celebrated a person coming to Christ and surrendering their sexuality to Him, I callously celebrated the end of relationships that broke your heart. I am sorry I have communicated that you and your families are less than me and mine. . . . More than anything, I am sorry that so many have interpreted this religious rejection by Christians as God's rejection. I am profoundly sorry that many have walked away from their faith and that some have chosen to end their lives.

—Alan Chambers, apologizing for
the damage caused by Exodus International,
a faith-based ex-gay organization

• • •

Awareness of Attitudes and Beliefs Self-Check

1. What have been your experiences of acceptance when seeking counseling services? What do you expect mental health professionals to be like in terms of their acceptance of you and your life?
2. What are your feelings and experiences of acceptance within a religious/spiritual orientation?
3. Have you ever tried to change your affectional orientation or sexual attractions? If not, what impact do you think that would have?

Case Study

Angie is a 29-year-old Chinese American who emigrated from Hong Kong to the United States with her parents at the age of 6. Her parents were incredibly hard working and identified strongly with their Chinese culture. They immigrated into a Chinese Christian community, which represented a change in religious beliefs for the family. Growing up in this cultural and religious context, when Angie began to understand that she was attracted to other girls, she kept it a secret from everyone. She dated men, but the relationships went nowhere without any real emotional attachments. She began to read about ex-gay theology: She read that if she acted in more feminine ways and trusted her faith, she could be cured. Angie became involved in an online support group for ex-gays and also prayed to God every day that He would help her change. Once in college, she became more depressed; one summer, she secretly went to an ex-gay camp. She also began seeing a reparative therapist. When nothing was working, she began to drink excessively and her depression deepened; she began cutting as well. On one weekend home from college, Angie came out to her parents and told them the secrets, including the years of ex-gay therapy that she had attempted. They embraced her, accepted her affectional orientation, and asked her to go to professional counseling for the depression. Although she is now coming to counseling, she reports being uncomfortable in sessions sometimes, as some elements remind her of the reparative therapy sessions. She also reports that any reminder of church also sends her into a deep depression—even hearing worship music can make her cry.

● ● ●

Disaffirming Therapies

The antithesis of person-centered, affirmative counseling is reparative therapy, conversion therapy, and ex-gay ministries—a variety of methodologies under the umbrella term of *sexual orientation change efforts* (SOCE) that aim to change non-heterosexual persons into heterosexuals. SOCE in mainstream psychology emerged during the 19th century when "homosexuality" was classified as both a medical disease and a criminal activity (Katz, 1976). Affectional orientation variance continued to be pathologized in the mental health professions until halfway through the 20th century, when a growing body of research found heterosexual and "homosexual" individuals to be identical on measures of emotional and psychological health (American Psychological Association Task Force on Appropriate Therapeutic Responses to Sexual Orientation [APA Task Force], 2009; Freedman, 1971; Gonsiorek, 1991; Hart et al., 1978; Hooker, 1957; Reiss, 1980).

SOCE and Their Effects

Empirical data and the declassification of "homosexuality" as a disorder led to resolutions by the major health and mental health organizations opposing representations of affectional orientation variance as a mental illness (APA Task Force, 2009). In 1999, a primer on the emotional and psychological injuries resulting from SOCE was endorsed by the American Counseling Association (ACA), the American Psychological Association, the National Association of Social Workers, the American Academy of Pediatrics, the American Association of School Administrators, the American Federation of Teachers, the American School Counselor Association, the American School Health Association, the National Association of School Psychologists, the National Association of Secondary School Professionals, the School Social Work Association of America, the National Association of Education, and the Interfaith Alliance Foundation (Just the Facts Coalition, 2008).

The popularity of SOCE continued to grow in the 1980s and 1990s, developed and supported largely by religious groups (APA Task Force, 2009) who viewed heterosexuality as normative and "same-sex attraction" as psychopathology, a developmental disorder, and an indication of poor moral character (Drescher, 1998). Faith-based *ex-gay ministries* include an array of modalities ranging from Bible study to prayer, worship services, group educational activities, and self-help exercises to help individuals overcome "same-sex attraction" (Erzen, 2006). Ex-gay ministries can be as simple as weekly meetings with a pastor or church counselor or as intensive as residential programs in which individuals live together for several months while engaging in activities aimed at changing them from gay to heterosexual. Examples of such programs include Love in Action (now known as Restoration Path), Desert Stream, and New Hope.

From 1998 to 2009, the conservative Christian organization Focus on the Family brought its large Love Won Out conferences to American cities and by 2005 had reached an estimated audience of 25,000 with the message that for individuals with affectional orientation variance, change is possible (Gilgoff, 2007). Focus on the Family eventually turned the conference over to Exodus International, an organization promoting "Change is possible" on billboards across the United States and claiming to support more than 230 ex-gay ministries in the United States and Canada. Other groups, such as Jews Offering New Alternatives for Healing (JONAH) for the Jewish community, Courage for Catholics, and Evergreen International for followers of The Church of Jesus Christ of Latter-Day Saints, emerged during this period alongside Witness Freedom Ministries for African Americans; Exodus Latinoamerica, Courage Latino, and Camino de Salida for Latin Americans; Exodus Youth; Homosexuals Anonymous; and Parents and Friends of Ex-Gays and Gays (Lutes & McDonough, 2012).

In addition to religious ministries, there is a small but active group of licensed mental health professionals who ignore the social science research, view "homosexuality" as a mental illness or addiction, and offer psychotherapy to change affectional orientation based on debunked theories that affectional orientation variance is caused by family dysfunction, trauma, or developmental delays (Drescher, 1998). This form of affectional orientation change effort is often referred to as *reparative therapy, conversion therapy,* or *reorientation therapy.* The largest organization promoting such therapies is the National Association for Research and Therapy of Homosexuality. Although most reparative therapists claim to be secular, they are in fact often connected to conservative religious organizations (Besen, 2003).

In 2003, Robert Spitzer, MD, a professor of psychiatry at Columbia University, published a study claiming that 200 highly motivated individuals had changed their orientation from "homosexual" to heterosexual. Supporters of SOCE highlighted this study largely because Spitzer was a leader in the declassification of "homosexuality" from the *Diagnostic and Statistical Manual of Mental Disorders* (Drescher, 2006). The methodologies of Spitzer's 2003 study were widely criticized by social scientists (Besen, 2006). In 2009, the *Report of the Task Force on Appropriate Therapeutic Responses to Sexual Orientation* published by the American Psychological Association, determined that affectional orientation change is rare and warned of potential harm caused by programs and providers promoting change efforts (APA Task Force, 2009, p. 30). Programs promoting SOCE have since appeared, facing increased public scrutiny. In 2012, Robert Spitzer retracted his 2003 study and made a media statement in which he publicly apologized to the lesbian, gay, bisexual, transgender, queer, questioning, intersex, asexual, ally, pansexual/polysexual, and two-spirited (LGBTQI+) communities for making unproven claims regarding reparative therapy (Becker, 2012). In

2013, the leaders of Exodus International shut down operations after 37 years in business and issued a public apology for the years of judgment and damage caused by the organization and by the Christian church (Payne, 2013).

The practice of conversion therapy with minors is now banned in California, New Jersey, Oregon, Illinois, New York, and Washington, DC (Movement Advancement Project, 2016). In 2015, a jury found JONAH guilty of violating New Jersey's Consumer Fraud Act by claiming to provide services that change a client from gay to heterosexual, and JONAH agreed to permanently cease operations (Southern Poverty Law Center, 2015). In May 2015, the Therapeutic Fraud Prevention Act was introduced in the House of Representatives, which is a bill that seeks to ban conversion therapy throughout the United States (Lieu, 2015). Despite the recent decline in SOCE practices, programs and providers promoting SOCE persist. Counselors and other affirming mental health professionals will inevitably encounter clients traumatized by this form of institutional heterosexism (McGeorge & Carlson, 2009). Thus, the reasons for practitioners not to utilize these methodologies must be explored through a critique of empirical research supporting SOCE and a discussion of how evidence-based practice can instead be utilized (Yates, 2013) to serve LGBTQI+ clients affirmatively and competently (Malyon, 1982; McGeorge & Carlson, 2009).

As Angie faced nonaffirming therapeutic modalities as a young person, it is likely that the trauma and distrust of counseling fester in her today (Lutes & McDonough, 2012). Negotiating building a positive, non-shame-based therapeutic relationship will be essential in attaining positive treatment outcomes (Harper et al., 2013; McGeorge & Carlson, 2009). In order to do this, counselor allies and the client must treat and explore previous trauma at the pace set by Angie. Coming out may be impacted negatively by these traumas, so understanding and deep empathy are ideal for moving the relationship forward while also attaining treatment goals set collaboratively by Angie and her counselor (Haldeman, 2002; Legate, Ryan, & Weinstein, 2012). Counselors who understand how trauma impacts the counseling relationship and timeline for growth recognize the slower speed clients such as Angie may take (Lutes & McDonough, 2012).

Empirical Research Concerning SOCE and Evidence-Based Practice

The questionable efficacy of SOCE is well documented (Serovich et al., 2008; Shidlo & Schroeder, 2002). However, the debate still rages today about the use of these treatments for clients. These debates often revolve around religious freedoms and client preferences versus LGBTQI+ rights and protection from unsafe treatments (Rosik, 2003; Throckmorton, 2002; Yarhouse & Throckmorton, 2002). Despite the debate, the overall efficacy of these treatments and their well-documented iatrogenic effects (Haldeman, 2002; Shidlo & Schroeder, 2002) make them unfit and unethical to carry out with clients. Mental health professionals have an ethical obligation to practice from an evidence-based approach that minimizes the potential for client harm (ACA, 2014).

The evidence-based practice model ensures that interventions available to clinicians are both efficacious and safe. This model calls for application of the best available researched interventions, clinician expertise, and client preferences and culture to be taken into account when choosing and applying interventions with clients. In the framework of the evidence-based practice model, the APA Task Force (2009) reviewed an extensive range ($N = 88$) of past and current (1960–2007) peer-reviewed literature on reparative therapies and aversion therapies. This review critiqued the methodologies of these studies and the generalizability of the reported effectiveness of these treatments. This investigation is the most comprehensive to date in terms of exploring the numerous concerns found in studies supportive of reparative or aversion therapies. These concerns undermine SOCE being seen as an evidence-based practice.

The APA Task Force (2009) reported that investigations supporting SOCE contained methodological concerns such as attrition, retrospective pretests, poor or inconsistent outcome measures, and construct validity concerns related to the assessment and definitions of affectional orientation. In addition, the report concluded that few studies conducted could be classified as experimental because of the lack of a control group design. This limits the generalizability of any such study because of the inability to isolate treatment effects.

Studies utilizing experimental designs often faced substantial attrition rates. Reviewing 31 studies on reparative and aversion therapies, Adams and Sturgis (1977) reported participant dropout typically ranged from 36% to 58% of the sample. Furthermore, most studies examining reparative or aversion therapies utilized penile circumference as a predictor of treatment efficacy. Penile circumference as an outcome measure has come under great scrutiny in recent years because of its inaccuracy, its tendency to produce false positives, and the difficulty participants face registering readings of any type in a research laboratory setting (Castonguay, Proulx, Aubut, McKibben, & Campbell, 1993; Kuban, Barbaree, & Blanchard, 1999; Lalumiere & Earls, 1992).

In addition, the APA Task Force (2009) reported that recent studies on SOCE (conducted from 1999 to 2007) primarily utilized qualitative research methodologies or retrospective pretests. Studies utilizing retrospective pretests often survey self-selected participants about changes in their affectional orientation (typically gay, lesbian, and bisexual to heterosexual) in a specified time frame. These studies do not utilize experimental methods and cannot be used to indicate causality. Generalizability of these experimental studies is also severely reduced by the limited sample variety of the investigations. Most studies also included White men who were highly religious.

Furthermore, studies often utilized participants attending mandated treatment against their will and those who did not identify as LGBTQI+, instead receiving treatment for pedophilia, exhibitionism, and fetishism. Investigation of the results provided by these inquiries demonstrates that enduring change to participant affectional orientation was not likely. The evidence failed to demonstrate that SOCE can increase attraction to the opposite sex. Some findings indicated that participants experienced significant decreases in sexual desire altogether, especially during studies utilizing aversion treatments (APA Task Force, 2009). These methodological concerns and the scarcity of results demonstrating efficacy further advance the arguments against reparative, aversion, and other SOCE treatments.

Ethical Implications of SOCE

Lee (2008) and Sheperis, Henning, and Kocet (2016) connected the importance of cultural competence to sound ethical practice. The *ACA Code of Ethics* (ACA, 2014) designates knowledge of culturally competent, strengths-based approaches developed from both quantitative and qualitative research as critical to developing evidence-based, ethical practice. Lee advanced the *Code*'s language by stating that research must frame culture as multifaceted while investigating inter- and intragroup differences. This framework solidifies the importance of cross-cultural research to progress in ethical practice (Lee, 2008; Sheperis et al., 2016). In this section we explore the ethics of affirmative treatment versus SOCE through the contextual lens of cultural competence.

The *ACA Code of Ethics* (ACA, 2014) provides clear guidelines that govern practicing with diverse populations, which includes LGBTQI+ individuals. The *Code* addresses the core values of the counseling profession:

1. Enhancing human development throughout the life span
2. Honoring diversity and embracing a multicultural approach in support of the worth, dignity, potential, and uniqueness of people within their social and cultural contexts
3. Promoting social justice
4. Safeguarding the integrity of the counselor–client relationship
5. Practicing in a competent and ethical manner (p. 3)

Several standards in the *ACA Code of Ethics* (ACA, 2014) provide guidance in understanding the prohibition of SOCE. The *Code* states that counselors must avoid harming clients (Standard A.4.a.). As noted previously, research in the field indicates the emotional, psychological, and in some cases physical harm that SOCE can have on sexual or gender minorities. Although counselors with a religious or spiritually conservative worldview are entitled to maintain their personal belief systems, the *Code* mandates that counselors not impose their personal values on clients in the counseling relationship (Standard A.4.b.). Counselors are also required to seek additional training when personally held beliefs prevent them from providing comprehensive, quality care to all clients, including LGBTQI+ persons (Standard A.11.b.). Furthermore, the *Code* includes a new standard intended to address unproven or harmful interventions that lack a scientific basis, such as SOCE. Standard C.7.c., Harmful Practices, states, "Counselors do not use techniques/procedures/ modalities when substantial evidence suggests harm, even if such services are requested" (p. 10). The last phrase of this ethical standard is critical. Even if clients (or their legal guardians) request reparative or conversion therapy, counselors are obligated to explain that SOCE are unethical and that counselors are not qualified to offer such interventions because these interventions go against the core ethical foundation of the profession. Angie chose to attend an ex-gay camp and reparative therapy to alter or change her affectional orientation. Thus, for counselors, the ethical principle of maleficence (do no harm) trumps autonomy (the client's or guardian's right to self-determination), as this approach was detrimental to Angie's mental health (ACA, 2014).

When counselors lack the training or skills to intervene with a client, they have the ethical responsibility to refer the client to another provider. However, in the case of SOCE, because the major mental health organizations have banned such practices, there is literally no person to refer the client to. It is recommended that the counselor, instead of focusing on changing the client's affectional orientation as the client has requested, take a strengths-based perspective focusing on deeper exploration of the reasons why the client (or guardian) wishes to attempt to alter affectional orientation (Kocet, 2014). Significant negative self-esteem or internalized homoprejudice may exist, likely causing internal dissonance. When LGBTQI+-affirming counselors find themselves in a values conflict with a client or legal guardian around affectional orientation or gender identity, they are encouraged to consult the counseling values-based conflict model (Kocet & Herlihy, 2014). This model is useful in providing sequential steps that foster deeper reflection when sorting out a dilemma involving a counselor and client whose personal values may be opposite of one another, which can create an ethical impasse in the therapeutic relationship.

Conclusion

As a result of growing up in a heteronormative and transphobic society, some LGBTQI+ individuals may want to change their affectional orientation or gender identity. Learning that SOCE are not available and learning about the evidence that reparative therapies are not efficacious can be a disappointing experience; clients may be suicidal and feel that they have no other options than to become heterosexual and cisgender. No matter the request, counselors cannot provide a service that has no empirical basis, is unethical, and has a high potential of harming the client. However, counselors' responsiveness to the underlying and presenting emotions that clients have in regard to this desire to change themselves can help save clients' lives and set them on a path to self-acceptance.

Questions for Further Discussion

1. Why might Angie have difficulty coming to counseling given her history?
2. In what ways did the SOCE that Angie experienced harm her?
3. What are the ethical violations associated with the SOCE that Angie experienced?
4. In what way can the counselor help to educate Angie about why these therapies failed?
5. How can Angie's counselor build rapport with Angie?

Resources

1. Read about SOCE on the Human Rights Campaign website at http://www.hrc.org/resources/the-lies-and-dangers-of-reparative-therapy.
2. Look through the Truth Wins Out website, which has stories of ex-gay survivors, advocacy efforts, and many resources, at https://www.truthwinsout.org/category/videos/survivors/.
3. Read ex-gay survivor experiences at http://beyondexgay.com/.

References

Adams, H. E., & Sturgis, E. T. (1977). Status of behavioral reorientation techniques in the modification of homosexuality: A review. *Psychological Bulletin, 84,* 1171–1188.

American Counseling Association. (2014). *ACA code of ethics.* Alexandria, VA: Author.

American Psychological Association Task Force on Appropriate Therapeutic Responses to Sexual Orientation. (2009). *Report of the Task Force on Appropriate Therapeutic Responses to Sexual Orientation.* Washington, DC: American Psychological Association.

Becker, J. (2012, April 25). *Exclusive: Dr. Robert Spitzer apologizes to gay community for infamous "ex-gay" study.* Retrieved from the Truth Wins Out website: https://www.truthwinsout.org/news/2012/04/24542/

Besen, W. (2003). *Anything but straight: Unmasking the scandals and lies behind the ex-gay myth.* Binghamton, NY: Harrington Park Press.

Besen, W. (2006). Political science. In J. Drescher & K. J. Zucker (Eds.), *Ex-gay research: Analyzing the Spitzer study and its relation to science, religion, politics, and culture* (pp. 291–308). Binghamton, NY: Haworth Press.

Castonguay, L. G., Proulx, J., Aubut, J., McKibben, A., & Campbell, M. (1993). Sexual preference assessment of sexual aggressors: Predictors of penile response magnitude. *Archives of Sexual Behavior, 22,* 325–334.

Drescher, J. (1998). *Psychoanalytic therapy and the gay man.* Hillsdale, NJ: Analytic Press.

Drescher, J. (2006). The Spitzer study and the culture wars. In J. Drescher & K. J. Zucker (Eds.), *Ex-gay research: Analyzing the Spitzer study and its relation to science, religion, politics, and culture* (pp. 107–112). Binghamton, NY: Harrington Park Press.

Erzen, T. (2006). *Straight to Jesus: Sexual and Christian conversions in the ex-gay movement.* Berkeley, CA: University of California Press.

Freedman, M. (1971). *Homosexuality and psychological functioning.* Belmont, CA: Brooks/Cole.

Gilgoff, D. (2007). *The Jesus machine: How James Dobson, Focus on the Family, and evangelical Americans are winning the culture war.* New York, NY: St. Martin's Press.

Gonsiorek, J. C. (1991). The empirical basis for the demise of the illness model of homosexuality. In J. C. Gonsiorek & J. D. Weinrich (Eds.), *Homosexuality: Research implications for public policy* (pp. 115–136). Newbury Park, CA: Sage.

Haldeman, D. C. (2002). Gay rights, patient rights: The implications of sexual orientation conversion therapy. *Professional Psychology, 33,* 200–204.

Harper, A., Finnerty, P., Martinez, M., Brace, A., Crethar, H., Loos, B., . . . Lambert, S. (2013). Association for Lesbian, Gay, Bisexual, and Transgender Issues in Counseling (ALGBTIC) competencies for counseling with lesbian, gay, bisexual, queer, questioning, intersex and ally individuals. *Journal of LGBT Issues in Counseling, 7*(1), 2–43. doi:10.1080/15538605.2013.755444

Hart, M., Roback, H., Tittler, B., Weitz, L., Walston, B., & McKee, E. (1978). Psychological adjustment of nonpatient homosexuals: Critical review of the research literature. *Journal of Clinical Psychiatry, 39,* 604–608.

Hooker, E. A. (1957). The adjustment of the male overt homosexual. *Journal of Projective Techniques, 21,* 18–31.

Just the Facts Coalition. (2008). *Just the facts about sexual orientation and youth: A primer for principals, educators and school personnel.* Retrieved from the American Psychological Association website: http://www.apa.org/pi/lgbt/resources/just-the-facts.aspx

Katz, J. (1976). *Gay American history: Lesbians and gay men in the U.S.A.* New York, NY: Thomas Crowell.

Kocet, M. (Ed.). (2014). *Counseling gay men, adolescents, and boys: A guide for helping professionals and educators.* New York, NY: Routledge.

Kocet, M., & Herlihy, B. (2014). Addressing value-based conflicts within the counseling relationship: A decision-making model. *Journal of Counseling & Development, 92,* 180–186. doi:10.1002/j.1556-6676.2014.00146.x

Kuban, M., Barbaree, H. E., & Blanchard, R. (1999). A comparison of volume and circumference phallometry: Response magnitude and method agreement. *Archives of Sexual Behavior, 28,* 345–359.

Lalumiere, M. L., & Earls, C. M. (1992). Voluntary control of penile responses as a function of stimulus duration and instructions. *Behavioral Assessment, 14,* 121–132.

Lee, C. C. (2008). *Elements of culturally competent counseling* (ACAPCD-24). Alexandria, VA: American Counseling Association.

Legate, N., Ryan, R. M., & Weinstein, N. (2012). Is coming out always a "good thing"? Exploring the relations of autonomy support, outness, and wellness for lesbian, gay, and bisexual individuals. *Social Psychological and Personality Science, 3*(2), 145–152. doi:10.1177/1948550611411929

Lieu, T. (2015, May 19). *Congressman Lieu announces Therapeutic Fraud Prevention Act.* Retrieved from https://lieu.house.gov/media-center/press-releases/congressman-lieu-announces-therapeutic-fraud-prevention-act

Lutes, J., & McDonough, M. (2012). Helping individuals and families recover from sexual orientation change efforts and heterosexism. In J. Bigner & J. Wetchler (Eds.), *Handbook of LGBT-affirmative couple and family therapy* (pp. 443–458). New York, NY: Routledge.

Malyon, A. K. (1982). Psychotherapeutic implications of internalized homophobia in gay men. *Journal of Homosexuality, 7*(2/3), 56–69. doi:10.1300/J082v07n02_08

McGeorge, C., & Carlson, T. (2009). Deconstructing heterosexism: Becoming an LGB affirmative heterosexual couple and family therapist. *Journal of Marital and Family Therapy, 37*(1), 14–26.

Movement Advancement Project. (2016). *Conversion therapy laws.* Retrieved from http://www.lgbtmap.org/equality-maps/conversion_therapy

Payne, E. (2013, July 8). *Group apologizes to gay community, shuts down "cure" ministry.* Retrieved from the CNN website: http://www.cnn.com/2013/06/20/us/exodus-international-shutdown/

Reiss, B. F. (1980). Psychological tests in homosexuality. In J. Marmor (Ed.), *Homosexual behavior: A modern reappraisal* (pp. 296–311). New York, NY: Basic Books.

Rosik, C. H. (2003). Motivational, ethical, and epistemological foundations in the treatment of unwanted homoerotic attractions. *Journal of Marital and Family Therapy, 29,* 13–28.

Serovich, J. M., Craft, S. M., Toviessi, P., Gangamma, R., McDowell, T., & Grafsky, E. L. (2008). A systematic review of the research base on sexual reorientation therapies. *Journal of Marital and Family Therapy, 34*(2), 227–238. doi:10.1111/j.1752-0606.2008.00065.x

Sheperis, D. S., Henning, S. L., & Kocet, M. M. (2016). *Ethical decision making for the 21st century counselor.* Thousand Oaks, CA: Sage.

Shidlo, A., & Schroeder, M. (2002). Changing sexual orientation: A consumer's report. *Professional Psychology: Research and Practice, 33,* 249–259.

Southern Poverty Law Center. (2015). *Michael Ferguson, et al., v. JONAH, et al.* Retrieved from https://www.splcenter.org/seeking-justice/case-docket/michael-ferguson-et-al-v-jonah-et-al

Spitzer, R. L. (2003). Can some gay men and lesbians change their sexual orientation? 200 participants reporting a change from homosexual to heterosexual orientation. *Archives of Sexual Behavior, 32,* 403–417. doi:0004-0002/03/1000-0403/0

Throckmorton, W. (2002). Initial empirical and clinical findings concerning the change process for ex-gays. *Professional Psychology: Research and Practice, 33,* 242–248.

Yarhouse, M. A., & Throckmorton, W. (2002). Ethical issues in attempts to ban reorientation therapies. *Psychotherapy: Theory, Research, Practice, Training, 39,* 66–75.

Yates, C. (2013). Evidence-based practice: The components, history and process. *Counseling Outcome Research and Evaluation, 4*(1), 41–54. doi:10.1177/2150137812472193

Chapter 9

Evidence-Based Practice for Counseling the LGBTQI+ Population

Kristopher M. Goodrich and Misty M. Ginicola

In my early professional years I was asking the question: How can I treat, or cure, or change this person? Now I would phrase the question in this way: How can I provide a relationship which this person may use for his own personal growth?

—Carl Rogers

• • •

Awareness of Attitudes and Beliefs Self-Check

1. What types of evidence-based practice (EBP) do you know of that work for a client with depression or suicidality? As a counselor, how well do you expect these techniques to work?
2. How applicable are those techniques to minorities who may experience oppression, discrimination, and marginalization?
3. When a client does not respond to treatment, what are your thoughts about the treatment? About the client? About your skills?

Case Study

Mara, a clinical mental health counselor, has a new client, Kishana, who is African American. Kishana tells Mara that she is asexual. She is exhibiting comorbid symptoms of depression and anxiety. Mara knows that the EBP for depression and anxiety is the use of cognitive–behavioral techniques. She also is aware that she should consider her client's characteristics and values when choosing the most promising intervention. As she reviews EBP manuals and surfs through the topics on PsycINFO and Google, she makes a startling discovery. There are *no* EBP studies for the treatment of depression or anxiety in asexual clients, much less African American asexual clients. She is disheartened and not sure where to go from here: Clearly, using cognitive behavior therapy (CBT) techniques may not be entirely appropriate or effective when this client's symptoms are from real experiences of oppression, discrimination, and marginalization. Mara is left wondering which of Kishana's symptoms are related to differences in gender and affectional orientation as well as what is the best way to help her client.

• • •

The Current State of EBP in the LGBTQI+ Population

As highlighted by the case study presented above, there is currently a dearth of empirical research on which counseling interventions or therapies are most effective for lesbian, gay, bisexual, transgender, queer, questioning, intersex, asexual, ally, pansexual/polysexual, and two-spirited (LGBTQI+) persons. A host of studies have discussed the concept of LG-BTQI+ affirmative (or, as more typically identified in the literature, gay affirmative) practice, although the research has been fragmented (Harrison, 2000) and predominantly qualitative. Little research has tangibly explored what LGBTQI+ affirmative practice is or which interventions rise to the level of therapeutic outcome effectiveness for this population. A coherent definition of practice and true process and outcome studies of counselors practicing this type of work are missing, which thus calls into question the utility of these models beyond the face validity of their work. National organizations and research-sponsoring organizations have noted this gap and have begun to call for further research into this practice. A combined report by the Institute of Medicine (2011) and the Substance Abuse and Mental Health Services Administration discussed the need for further exploration and evaluation of LGBTQI+-responsive services and called on federal organizations to fund studies to better focus funded research in this area. In response to this call, the National Institutes of Health (2013) has funded randomized clinical trials and other empirical studies to better understand how effective clinical work can occur with this historically and culturally marginalized group of persons.

EBPs for Building Rapport

Although currently few large-scale studies have explored clinical work with this population, some qualitative research has examined what LGBTQI+ clients have considered to be helpful when seeking different forms of counseling. Lebolt (1999) utilized phenomenological methods to explore nine gay male clients' experiences of gay affirmative psychotherapy. Findings centered on clients' experiences of the counselor (i.e., the "therapist," as described in the study), the type of counseling pursued (i.e., substance abuse or addiction), and the effects of treatment. Specifically, clients discussed the fact that warm and intimate environments were important therapeutic qualities that enhanced their sense of trust. In terms of counselors, the experience was best with sensitive, kind, warm, and caring counselors who expressed openness; expressed a nonjudgmental and accepting attitude; and could demonstrate an active, attentive, and fully present stance with their client. Clients also discussed counselors' ability to give them space to think, reflect, talk, and feel, as well as provide support and reassurance, through either their verbal or nonverbal cues.

Furthermore, Lebolt (1999) explored how counselors dealt with clients' issues specific to affectional orientation. All participants felt that their counselors accepted their identity from the start of the counseling relationship. The way in which issues were addressed, however, varied across counselors. It appeared that gay-identified counselors increased clients' awareness of homophobia and heterosexism and assisted clients in understanding the diversity of the LGBTQI+ experience. Conversely, heterosexual-identified counselors appeared to normalize and equalize gay and heterosexual relationships and legitimize the experiences of pain and loss experienced in LGBTQI+ relationships. Clients in recovery reported that counselors' self-disclosure of experiences in recovery, confrontation of self-destructive behaviors, and exploration of clients' relationship with their Higher Power were perceived as beneficial. Across all types of treatment, gay male clients reported feeling increased comfort in their bodies and in their sexual selves and improvement in their sexual, romantic, and social relationships with other gay-identified persons while engaged in treatment. This study was limited in its qualitative design (and thus nongeneralizable results) as well as its lack of adherence to a rigorous qualitative approach in the way it was conducted. However, this study does provide a preliminary introduction to what LGBTQI+ clients may find effective in building a therapeutic relationship.

Pixton (2003) explored the experiences of lesbian and gay clients who claimed to have experienced gay affirmative counseling. Using grounded theory, Pixton found similar results to Lebolt (1999) across participants. Specifically, Pixton found that a counselor's demonstration of a nonpathologizing view of LGBTQI+ identity, a sense of closeness or relationship between the counselor and the client, and a therapeutic space in which to do the work were all contributing elements to a strong therapeutic relationship. In addition, counselors brought knowledge and skills as well as a sense of humanity to the sessions. For example, counselors who self-disclosed their own experiences in counseling to facilitate client growth allowed clients to experience their own humanity and uniqueness as well. In addition, counselors' use of a holistic approach to counseling through conceptualizing and treating clients as whole people with other concerns not related to their affectional orientation also appeared to add to the therapeutic experience across all clients. Counselor affectional orientation did not appear to influence or impact the results across client respondents, which suggested to the study's author that counselors' knowledge and awareness of LGBTQI+ issues were more important than their own affectional orientation and underscores the importance of counselors increasing their knowledge and awareness of LGBTQI+ persons to effectively do this work.

Both the Lebolt (1999) and Pixton (2003) studies provide a wonderful introduction on how to form effective therapeutic relationships with LGBTQI+ clients and provide preliminary evidence of important therapeutic ingredients that might be necessary to do gay affirmative work. Neither study, however, provides strong empirical support on specific methodology, as both studies lack rigor in terms of their implementation of their stated qualitative approaches and generalizability to other samples. They both, however, reaffirm the importance of a strong working alliance with clients, LGBTQI+ or heterosexual, and introduce the importance of counselors having knowledge and awareness of specific cultural factors that influence LGBTQI+ persons' lives.

EBPs for Assessment, Diagnosis, and Goals

Beyond the issues discussed by previous scholars, other authors have conceptually laid out specific issues that clinicians may need to be aware of when working with LGBTQI+ persons. There is the connection of the LGBTQI+ person's experience to the minority stress model, or microaggressions that LGBTQI+ persons may feel in their daily lives. As discussed in Chapter 7, the minority stress model states that persons from nondominant backgrounds encounter chronic stress due to the experiences of prejudice and discrimination they face from others, which in turn can create greater psychological disturbances (Meyer, 2003). This is described as a stress unique to marginalized populations. *Microaggressions* were described by Sue and colleagues (2007) as "brief and commonplace daily verbal, behavioral, or environmental indignities, whether intentional or unintentional, that communicate hostile, derogatory, or negative" slights or insults toward persons of a certain cultural background (p. 273). Although originally described in terms of race, other scholars have applied the term *microaggressions* to the LGBTQI+ community (Nadal, 2013; Nadal et al., 2011).

The minority stress model and the microaggressions model are similar in that both express the fact that LGBTQI+ persons are more likely to encounter daily experiences of stress or anxiety due in part to being a member of a nondominant cultural group. Through their lived experiences of being LGBTQI+, they may feel, either internally or externally, as if they have not lived up to set cultural expectations and that others may think or behave differently toward them. They may also have the view that institutions or systems might be set up in a way that minimizes or silences them or their relationships compared to their cisgender and heterosexual peers. Being aware of this, counselors should be cautious in how they assess and view their LGBTQI+ clients and not necessarily pathologize them based solely on their presentations. Experiences of posttraumatic stress, anxiety, depression, or paranoia may be best explained not as organic issues but as due to environmental stress caused by living in an unjust and oppressive environment (Goodrich & Luke, 2015). Clinicians may work to normalize and legitimize the experiences of being a member of the LGBTQI+ community and work with clients to teach them how to advocate for and nurture themselves while living in environments that may be systemically unjust or oppressive. Clinicians also should become sensitive to issues such as internalized heterosexism (or internalized homophobia), which is the shame that some LGBTQI+ persons may experience as part of being *other than* in a heterosexual and cisgender culture. Instead of diagnosing clients as needing to change their affectional orientation or pathologizing those clients for their experiences of self-hatred, clinicians should attend to how these concerns might manifest either emotionally or through behavior; this can include suicidal ideation or suicide attempts (Rutter, 2008; Silverman, Smith, & Burns, 2013), substance abuse (Hughes & Eliason, 2002), relationship difficulties (Green & Mitchell, 2002), or other self-destructive behaviors. Counselors should also understand ways to legitimize, normalize, and bring value to the LGBTQI+ experience. Although the mental health culture and professions have a long history of focusing on negativity and labeling, clinicians could instead utilize elements of positive psychology to raise awareness of the strengths and other beneficial elements of being LGBTQI+ (Craig, Austin, & Alessi, 2013).

Identity Development

As explored in Chapter 6, identity development is something that all LGBTQI+ persons undergo as part of their experiences. Clinicians should familiarize themselves with traditional models of LGBTQI+ identity development, such as those by Cass (1979), Troiden (1979), and D'Augelli (1994), to understand how clients may be understanding themselves internally and in relation to their larger world. Cass's model is the most commonly cited and is based on Cross's (1991) model of Black identity development. As in other models, most persons begin in a state that reflects a lack of awareness of difference, which is followed by events or milestones that promote some level of awareness of difference. Persons then typically move through stages of identity confusion, tolerance, acceptance, and then pride. Some persons are able to move beyond pride toward a greater synthesis of their identity with the larger world, seeing both the similarities and differences across different identities and learning to accept persons from different cultural or identity-based groups.

As discussed in Chapter 6, across different identity development models there is traditionally a process of disclosure, or *coming out* to oneself and others, as part of the process (e.g., Cass, 1979; D'Augelli, 1994; Goodrich & Luke, 2015; Troiden, 1979). In the literature related to this topic, disclosure is often a treatment goal for closeted (or undisclosed) clients. Although most see this as a necessary part of the process, as previously discussed, it is not always wise for all persons to disclose their identity to others because of safety or other concerns.

Clients may suffer from familial, occupational, social, religious, or other rejections as part of this experience, and some might also face safety risks as well. Thus, clinicians need to be knowledgeable about how to negotiate these concerns with clients, including having intentional discussions about with whom, when, and how clients may wish to disclose their identity and when it might be better to wait or not disclose their status. Exercises that clinicians can utilize with clients regarding these topics can be found in Goodrich and Luke (2015). Prior to setting disclosure as a treatment goal, however, clinicians and clients need to carefully review these topics and understand in what circumstances it might be best for a client to come out.

Other topics clinicians should have a good working knowledge of include couples' relationships and parenting, the experiences of LGBTQI+ persons as members of the family, and legal and workplace issues related to these experiences (Pachankis & Goldfried, 2013). Each of these issues was discussed in Chapter 5. In addition to these experiences, and in need of additional study, is the intersectionality of identities, such as for ethnic minority persons, persons with disabilities, religious/spiritual persons, older individuals, and other multiply marginalized persons who also identify as LGBTQI+ (Pachankis & Goldfried, 2013). Little has been written about members of these other populations and the effective ways in which clinicians might work with them, which is disappointing, as members from these multiply marginalized groups might benefit most from counseling and may have additional needs beyond their other counterparts. With these persons, clinicians may need to not only be LGBTQI+ or affirming but also demonstrate affirming qualities and cultural competence related to other groups as well. As no client or clinician exists in a vacuum, one might assume that all LGBTQI+ affirmative counseling might also be intersectional in nature. The lack of research, however, tells us little about the experiences of racial/ethnic minority LGBTQI+ persons and others, so we know even less about the application of these forms of counseling with these persons compared to their Caucasian peers.

Empirically Based Interventions

Affirmative Therapy

As mentioned previously, affirmative therapy is the typical intervention referred to when working with LGBTQI+ clients. It is not a specific treatment protocol but rather a collection of components important for a minority population. The components of affirmative therapy include therapists striving for certain qualities: They should espouse a supportive, nonpathological framework for viewing the client; have knowledge and skills relevant to working with this population; and have increased self-awareness of how their experience of privilege and oppression may impact the client (Harrison, 2000). The affirmative therapist should seek to take a feminist or social justice approach by focusing on empowerment, openly challenging oppression, and actively building resilience and coping skills (Harrison, 2000; Rutter, 2012). In terms of interventions, affirmative therapists work carefully to match client issues with existing counseling interventions and make necessary cultural adaptations to meet the needs of the client (Harrison, 2000).

Craig et al. (2013) delineated specific directives for counselors who are involved in affirmative therapy. Therapists should affirm the client's identity, providing a warm, accepting space for healing. Similarly, they should empower the client by taking a collaborative approach in treatment. When counselors are transparent with assessment, diagnosis, and treatment selection, clients are helped to feel part of the process. Allowing clients to help choose their treatment or to comment on what they are feeling in terms of the process or specific interventions the counselor has chosen serves to help disempowered clients to feel the onus for their healing as well as to build empowerment.

Taking a strengths-based approach allows the counselor to help build the client's confidence and esteem (Craig et al., 2013). When it comes to using specific interventions, the counselor should take care to distinguish between dysfunctional thoughts, which may be treated with CBT, and real experiences of oppression and discrimination in clients' environment due to their affectional or gender orientation. For example, an individual may describe that he is being talked about and others are treating him harshly in the work environment; this could be a reality, not a cognitive distortion. In either case, it is important to build up the client's coping skills and resilience.

In providing interventions and seeking change, the counselor should generally seek to collaborate more than confront as well as to work toward creating helpful thoughts and strategies (Craig et al., 2013). All interventions need to be matched not only to developmental level and culture but also to identity development and clients' level of self-acceptance. For example, a counselor might suggest that a client watch an *It Gets Better* video on her own when she is struggling with self-acceptance rather than having her attend a queer community event with others, an experience that she may interpret negatively given her sense of internalized homophobia. Assigning homework that is culturally congruent with clients' intersectional identities can also be very helpful. Finally, all interventions should have cultural accommodations or adaptations to make them stronger in their approach. Much more information on the nature and importance of affirmative therapy is provided in Chapter 10.

Cultural Accommodations and Adaptions

Although there are varying definitions of cultural accommodation, the basic definition involves adapting intervention content and strategies to be congruent with the cultural norms and experiences of a particular minority group (Duarté-Vélez, Bernal, & Bonilla, 2010). Blending EBPs with multicultural competence means that the counselor must also take a multifaceted and thoughtful approach to understanding clients within their intersectional identities (Hays, 2009). Applying cultural considerations begins with assessing the client's needs while maintaining cultural respect (Hays, 2009). As applied to LGBTQI+ issues, it could mean being careful to ask what identity and terms the client wishes to use. It would also mean building rapport before asking questions that may be very personal or allowing clients to tell their stories at their own pace (e.g., asking transgender people if they have had sexual reassignment surgery). The counselor should also identify any culturally relevant support networks (Hays, 2009). In the case of the LGBTQI+ community, it would be important to consider how accepting the community surrounding the client's ethnic identity or the client's spiritual community is of the client's affectional orientation. In many cases, LGBTQI+ individuals with intersectional identities (i.e., ethnic minority status, low socioeconomic status, elderly, or religious, etc.) can feel isolated, as they do not *belong* in any specific community. It is equally important to consider the strengths associated with their identity and who in their lives are supportive and affirmative.

The counselor should also seek to clarify external influences versus cognitive influences on clients' issues (Hays, 2009). Even when using CBT, the focus should be on questioning the helpfulness of a thought to clients' goals rather than questioning the validity of the thought or belief (Hays, 2009). Counselors should always validate reports of discrimination and help clients to understand that they are not to blame for this negative treatment

(Craig et al., 2013). Exploring the effects of discrimination and oppression and developing resilience, coping skills, and empowerment to survive and thrive in an unfair world are of key importance (Hays, 2009). However, changing one's thought structure to more helpful beliefs when using CBT can also be very important (Craig et al., 2013; Hays, 2009). Applying these types of cultural accommodations to CBT in the treatment of LGBTQI+ clients' substance abuse symptoms has been investigated and found to be helpful (Jerome & Halkitis, 2014; Reback & Shoptaw, 2014).

Integrating With Traditional Approaches

Most affirmative and culturally adaptive therapies for the LGBTQI+ community have been integrated with CBT, as discussed previously (Craig et al., 2013; Hart, Tulloch, & O'Cleirigh, 2014; Jerome & Halkitis, 2014; Reback & Shoptaw, 2014). However, two studies have discussed the integration of affirmative therapy with family-based therapy. Diamond and Sphigel (2014) modified attachment-based family therapy. They described the importance of building an alliance with the youth client as well as preparing adults to reach out and communicate clearly with their child. The counselor works to build an alliance with parents, simultaneously preparing all members for discourse; this will lead to ultimately conducting *attachment episodes* in which everyone speaks openly and honestly, allows themselves to be vulnerable and scared, and communicates in a compassionate and nonblaming manner (Diamond & Sphigel, 2014). The counselor is also required to help parents navigate the child's and, ultimately, the family's coming out process and find resources and support networks such as PFLAG (Diamond & Sphigel, 2014). LaSala (2013) took a similar approach but focused on the needs of the family, including fears surrounding the child being gay as well as nonacceptance. Counselors should seek to accept families in their current state, support them to grow and develop, and build families as a resource for the LGBTQI+ individual (Diamond & Sphigel, 2014; LaSala, 2013).

Creative Therapies

Although the research is predominantly qualitative, one area of intervention that has some empirical support for use with the LGBTQI+ population is that of creative therapies (Loue, 2009; Pelton-Sweet & Sherry, 2008; Silverman et al., 2013). Creative approaches encourage clients to explore painful experiences and tell their stories as well as heal from psychological trauma and stressors (Pelton-Sweet & Sherry, 2008). Art therapy in particular has been successful in treating anxiety, panic, hopelessness, and low self-esteem in LGBTQI+ clients (Pelton-Sweet & Sherry, 2008). These clients' stories can be explored through artwork; the experience of internalized and generalized homophobia, trauma, and abuse they have suffered because of their sexual or gender orientation and the coming out process could all be themes to be explored in therapy (Pelton-Sweet & Sherry, 2008). The use of art-based projects has also been identified as a way to explore complex issues such as intersectionality, invisibility, and suicide (Silverman et al., 2013). Sandplay has been studied in relation to posttraumatic stress disorder in gay males (Loue, 2009). Psychodrama has also been utilized to address silencing and oppression, giving a voice to the emotions that LGBTQI+ individuals have experienced (Shpungin, Allen, Loomis, & DelloStritto, 2012).

Practice Issues

In preparing to perform EBPs for the LGBTQI+ community, counselors must develop self-awareness of not only their own feelings and beliefs but also how clients are likely to perceive them (Holahan & Gibson, 1994). If a counselor is a heterosexual ally, clients may initially be very cautious because of potentially having had negative previous experiences. For example, if a counselor wears a cross as a religious symbol, some clients may be reluctant to share their affectional orientation until they are sure that the counselor is affirmative of their identity. If counselors are LGBTQI+ themselves, there may be opportunities for self-disclosure that can be very helpful for clients in terms of building rapport as well as their own recovery.

Counselors should also fully understand what a helping relationship looks like for an LGBTQI+ client. The Association for Lesbian, Gay, Bisexual, and Transgender Issues in Counseling LGBQQIA Competencies Taskforce (Harper et al., 2013) delineated these elements (see http://www.algbtic.org/competencies.html). In addition to understanding how their own gender/affectional orientation may impact clients, competent counselors are open about and accepting of the evolution of a client's affectional orientation; in addition, they do not make assumptions, they acknowledge and accept identities espoused by the client, and they use appropriate language and terms. Counselors must be knowledgeable about affectional orientation and gender identity as well as resources for this community; they need to be aware of myths surrounding these populations as well as unique issues experienced within the identities for each letter of the LGBTQI+ acronym. They must incorporate a social justice approach in terms of attending to prejudice and discrimination and see the client as a whole person (physically, socially, emotionally, spiritually, etc.). Counselors should never use reparative therapies, as mentioned in Chapter 8. Counselors should always seek consultation and supervision while they are working to increase their competence and ensure ethical responses. They should also continue to seek training in this area and better their skills with the LGBTQI+ population. Much more information on this topic is presented in Chapter 10.

In school systems, some communities may be openly hostile toward the LGBTQI+ community; some school counselors additionally face ethical and legal conflicts, as some states have discriminatory laws that may impact what type of resources a counselor can use in the school setting (Meyer & Bayer, 2013). For example, in some places, bullying of LGBTQI+ students is allowed if it is based on religious beliefs, and in 2016, North Carolina passed legislation regarding transgender individuals' use of bathrooms. Ginicola, Smith, and Rhoades (2016) discussed a step-by-step strategy for schools to use to overcome such negative environments and continue to support their LGBTQI+ students in an affirming manner.

Conclusion

The lack of EBPs for the LGBTQI+ populations requires counselors to think critically about what types of counseling strategies they will use with a client. Although the methodology of an affirmative approach is not always well delineated, it serves as a framework for building rapport, performing assessment, and selecting interventions. Providing a space for clients that is safe, nonjudgmental, and affirming helps all clients develop their authenticity and acceptance of self; for LGBTQI+ clients this space may be a rare oasis in a desert of rejection and marginalization. Having a culturally competent awareness and knowledge of the LGBTQI+ populations will help the counselor create developmentally appropriate conceptualizations. Focusing on the empowerment and acceptance of the LGBTQI+ client, counselors can make an informed choice about which strategies will be best for each client.

Questions for Further Discussion

1. What resources might a counselor seek out in order to plan treatment for Kishana?
2. What would affirmative therapy look like for Kishana?

3. How might counselors practice CBT differently if they use it with Kishana?
4. How might counselors track whether they are practicing in an LGBTQI+ affirmative way?
5. What types of research studies would need to be conducted to help a client like Kishana?

Resources

1. Read the American Psychological Association report on appropriate therapeutic responses to affectional orientation at http://www.apa.org/pi/lgbt/resources/sexual-orientation.aspx.
2. Recognize anti-LGBTQI+ fringe organizations that support sexual orientation change efforts at https://www.pflag.org/antilgbtq.

References

Cass, V. C. (1979). Homosexual identity formation: A theoretical model. *Journal of Homosexuality, 4*(3), 219–235. doi:10.1300/J082v04n03_01

Craig, S. L., Austin, A., & Alessi, E. (2013). Gay affirmative cognitive behavioral therapy for sexual minority youth: A clinical adaptation. *Clinical Social Work Journal, 41*(3), 258–266. doi:10.1007/s10615-012-0427-9

Cross, W. J. (1991). *Shades of black: Diversity in African-American identity.* Philadelphia, PA: Temple University Press.

D'Augelli, A. R. (1994). Identity development and sexual orientation: Toward a model of lesbian, gay and bisexual development. In E. J. Trickett, R. J. Watts, & D. Birham (Eds.), *Human diversity: Perspectives on people in context* (pp. 312–333). San Francisco, CA: Jossey-Bass.

Diamond, G. M., & Sphigel, M. S. (2014). Attachment-based family therapy for lesbian and gay young adults and their persistently nonaccepting parents. *Professional Psychology: Research and Practice, 45*(4), 258–268. doi:10.1037/a0035394

Duarté-Vélez, Y., Bernal, G., & Bonilla, K. (2010). Culturally adapted cognitive-behavioral therapy: Integrating sexual, spiritual, and family identities in an evidence-based treatment of a depressed Latino. *Adolescent Journal of Clinical Psychology, 66*, 895–906.

Ginicola, M. M., Smith, C., & Rhoades, E. (2016). Love thy neighbor: A guide for implementing safe school initiatives for LGBTQ students in nonaffirming religious communities. *Journal of LGBT Issues in Counseling, 10*, 159–173. doi:10.1080/15538605.2016.1199992

Goodrich, K. M., & Luke, M. (2015). *Group counseling with LGBTQI persons.* Alexandria, VA: American Counseling Association.

Green, R., & Mitchell, V. (2002). Gay and lesbian couples in therapy: Homophobia, relational ambiguity, and social support. In A. S. Gurman & N. S. Jacobson (Eds.), *Clinical handbook of couple therapy* (3rd ed., pp. 546–568). New York, NY: Guilford Press.

Harper, A., Finnerty, P., Martinez, M., Brace, A., Crethar, H., Loos, B., . . . Lambert, S. (2013). Association for Lesbian, Gay, Bisexual, and Transgender Issues in Counseling (ALGBTIC) competencies for counseling with lesbian, gay, bisexual, queer, questioning, intersex and ally individuals. *Journal of LGBT Issues in Counseling, 7*(1), 2–43. doi:10.1080/15538605.2013.755444

Harrison, N. (2000). Gay affirmative therapy: A critical analysis of the literature. *British Journal of Guidance & Counselling, 28*(1), 24–53. doi:10.1080/030698800109600

Hart, T. A., Tulloch, T. G., & O'Cleirigh, C. (2014). Integrated cognitive behavioral therapy for social anxiety and HIV prevention for gay and bisexual men. *Cognitive and Behavioral Practice, 21*(2), 149–160. doi:10.1016/j.cbpra.2013.07.001

Hays, P. (2009). Integrating evidence-based practice, cognitive–behavior therapy, and multicultural therapy: Ten steps for culturally competent practice. *Professional Psychology: Research and Practice, 40,* 354–360.

Holahan, W., & Gibson, S. A. (1994). Heterosexual therapists leading lesbian and gay therapy groups: Therapeutic and political realities. *Journal of Counseling & Development, 72,* 591–594. doi:10.1002/j.1556-6676.1994.tb01687.x

Hughes, T. L., & Eliason, M. (2002). Substance use and abuse in lesbian, gay, bisexual and transgender populations. *Journal of Primary Prevention, 22*(3), 263–298. doi:10.1023/A:1013669705086

Institute of Medicine. (2011). *The health of lesbian, gay, bisexual, and transgender people: Building a foundation for better understanding.* Retrieved from http://www.nationalacademies.org/HMD/Reports/2011/The-Health-of-Lesbian-Gay-Bisexual-and-Transgender-People.aspx

Jerome, R. C., & Halkitis, P. N. (2014). An exploratory investigation of treatment strategies for Black, gay, bisexual, and heterosexual men-who-have-sex-with-men who use methamphetamine. *Journal of LGBT Issues in Counseling, 8*(1), 2–24. doi:10.1080/15538605.2014.853636

LaSala, M. C. (2013). Out of the darkness: Three waves of family research and the emergence of family therapy for lesbian and gay people. *Clinical Social Work Journal, 41*(3), 267–276. doi:10.1007/s10615-012-0434-x

Lebolt, J. (1999). Gay affirmative psychotherapy: A phenomenological study. *Clinical Social Work Journal, 27*(4), 355–370. doi:10.1023/A:1022870129582

Loue, S. (2009). A prologue to sandplay: With an inner-city self-identified gay man. *Journal of Sandplay Therapy, 18*(1), 107–115.

Meyer, I. H. (2003). Prejudice, social stress, and mental health in lesbian, gay, and bisexual populations: Conceptual issues and research evidence. *Psychological Bulletin, 129,* 674–697.

Meyer, I. H., & Bayer, R. (2013). School-based gay-affirmative interventions: First amendment and ethical concerns. *American Journal of Public Health, 103,* 1764–1771. doi:10.2105/AJPH.2013.301385

Nadal, K. L. (2013). *That's so gay! Microaggressions and the lesbian, gay, bisexual, and transgender community.* Washington, DC: American Psychological Association.

Nadal, K. L., Wong, Y., Issa, M., Meterko, V., Leon, J., & Wideman, M. (2011). Sexual orientation microaggressions: Processes and coping mechanisms for lesbian, gay, and bisexual individuals. *Journal of LGBT Issues in Counseling, 5*(1), 21–46.

National Institutes of Health. (2013). *Plans for advancing LGBT health research.* Retrieved from https://www.nih.gov/about-nih/who-we-are/nih-director/statements/plans-advancing-lgbt-health-research

Pachankis, J. E., & Goldfried, M. R. (2013). Clinical issues in working with lesbian, gay, and bisexual clients. *Psychology of Sexual Orientation and Gender Diversity, 1,* 45–58. doi:10.1037/2329-0382.1.S.45

Pelton-Sweet, L. M., & Sherry, A. (2008). Coming out through art: A review of art therapy with LGBT clients. *Art Therapy, 25*(4), 170–176. doi:10.1080/07421656.2008.10129546

Pixton, S. (2003). Experiencing gay affirmative therapy: An exploration of clients' views of what is helpful. *Counselling & Psychotherapy Research, 3*(3), 211–215. doi:10.1080/14733140312331384372

Reback, C. J., & Shoptaw, S. (2014). Development of an evidence-based, gay-specific cognitive behavioral therapy intervention for methamphetamine-abusing gay and bisexual men. *Addictive Behaviors, 39,* 1286–1291. doi:10.1016/j.addbeh.2011.11.029

Rutter, P. (2008). Suicide protective and risk factors for sexual minority youth: Applying the cumulative factor model *Journal of LGBT Issues in Counseling, 2*(1), 81–92. doi:10.1080/15538600802077681

Rutter, P. A. (2012). Sex therapy with gay male couples using affirmative therapy. *Sexual and Relationship Therapy, 27*(1), 35–45. doi:10.1080/14681994.2011.633078

Shpungin, E., Allen, N., Loomis, C., & DelloStritto, M. (2012). Keeping the spirit alive: Using feminist methodology to address silencing as a structural issue. *Journal of Community Psychology, 40*(1), 44–61. doi:10.1002/jcop.20481

Silverman, Y., Smith, F., & Burns, M. (2013). Coming together in pain and joy: A multicultural and arts-based suicide awareness project. *The Arts in Psychotherapy, 40*(2), 216–223. doi:10.1016/j.aip.2013.02.003

Sue, D. W., Capodilupo, C. M., Torino, G. C., Bucceri, J. M., Holder, A. B., Nadal, K. L., & Esquilin, M. (2007). Racial microaggressions in everyday life: Implications for clinical practice. *American Psychologist, 62*(4), 271–286. doi:10.1037/0003-066X.62.4.271

Troiden, R. R. (1979). Becoming homosexual: A model of gay identity acquisition. *Psychiatry, 42*(4), 362–373.

Chapter 10

Affirmative, Strengths-Based Counseling With LGBTQI+ People

Peter Finnerty, Michael M. Kocet, Jeff Lutes, and Chad Yates

Counselors work with and within the sentience of human beings,
not against or in spite of it. Counseling is not about telling
people what to do, even when you think you know,
even when you think God told you so.
—Ryan Thomas Neece

• • •

Awareness of Attitudes and Beliefs Self-Check

1. How many experiences have you had in your life that have been affirming—in which others have communicated their approval of who you are and what you do?
2. What does it feel like to be affirmed?
3. In what ways do you use affirming techniques in your counseling practice?

Case Study

Tony, a 24-year-old Mexican American cisgender man, attends counseling after being referred by his college advisor. Tony notes, "I think I need to figure some stuff out about my sexuality." He begins by saying, "My girlfriend dumped me because she found out I like guys and women . . . guess she couldn't handle that." Tony reports having had several relationships with women and men before dating this girlfriend and the desire to date either gender "if they are the right person for me . . . but to be honest, I don't know who the right person is because I thought my friend Jose was, but he freaked out when I said I was into him." He reports difficulty identifying as any orientation in the lesbian, gay, bisexual, transgender, queer, questioning, intersex, asexual, ally, pansexual/

polysexual, and two-spirited (LGBTQI+) community, noting, "Bisexual doesn't feel right, gay isn't right, so I don't know." Tony reports a traumatic history regarding his orientation, as his parents sent him to what he calls "Be straight or else camp." During this time, Tony became depressed, even suicidal at times, but he made it through by "doing what they said, at least they thought." After he turned 18, Tony left his parents' home and has not "looked back since." He worked several jobs before landing his current position, tending bar at a busy downtown restaurant where management works with his school schedule. Tony demonstrates high motivation for completing his bachelor's degree so he can go to graduate school to become a counselor himself. Tony notes, "I want to work with other people like me. I don't want any young person to deal with what I went through." Tony's motivation is high, yet he knows "I need to work stuff out. I never got help after that camp, and I want a relationship with my parents someday."

• • •

The Need for Affirmative Counseling

Many LGBTQI+ persons do not develop a positive identity without accomplishing several developmental milestones, including coming out internally and later externally to friends, family, and coworkers (Cass, 1996; Eliason, 1996; Meyer & Wilson, 2009). Tony demonstrates some evidence of these types of concerns with identification, but he may also represent a significant portion of the populace that does not wish to identify at all (Harper et al., 2013). Cultural values may also impact Tony, who identifies as Mexican American and whose identity may be altered because of ethnic, racial, gender, and other perceptions of LGBTQI+ identity (Balsam, Molina, Beadnell, Simoni, & Walters, 2011; Jamil, Harper, & Fernandez, 2009; Jones & McEwen, 2000). Gonzalez (2007) spoke to the ethnic factor of culture, noting how many Latino men do not identify as LGBTQI+ for fear of violating gender roles important to Latin American families and the Latin American ethnic community.

These groupings of factors are relevant and crucial, as the LGBTQI+ communities embody a wide spectrum of identifications (Firestein, 1996). Fassinger and Arseneau (2007) described concern over the umbrella identity, noting how acronyms like LGBTQI+ designating diverse affectional orientation and gender do not necessarily account for distinctions among members (Moe, Perera-Diltz, Sepulveda, & Finnerty, 2014). Foucault (1978) applied a critical lens in studying the notion of the classification of affectional orientation and how this classification became a commanding part of personal identity in the 19th and 20th centuries, later becoming a progressive political identity (Finnerty, 2016). Labeling a specific identity can be problematic for all those represented in the LGBTQI+ community, as members can exist both inside and in between groups (Israel & Mohr, 2004). This constitutes an important reminder for counselors working with clients who do not identify, such as Tony, to be careful about labeling and rather allow clients to narrate their own experience (Moe, Finnerty, Sparkman, & Yates, 2015).

Foucault (1978) expressed how power and oppression inform the classification of sexuality through the lens of the European feudal age. It was not uncommon for those identified as *sinners* by religious and/or governmental authorities to be rejected, abused, and murdered (Foucault, 1978). This concept of law intruding on one's sexuality continues today, even as LGBTQI+ rights advance in terms of both the legal system and community attitudes (Chaney, Filmore, & Goodrich, 2011). Alongside the reversal of government-sanctioned bans on marriage equality and adoption and the movement to end the practice of sexual orientation change efforts (SOCE) in the counseling sphere, ridicule and violence linger both in the United States and globally, as evidenced by terrorist groups such as Daesh tormenting and murdering suspected LGBTQI+ persons (Associated Press, 2015). In the United States, the passage of the North Carolina law preventing transgender individuals from using the restrooms associated with their gender identity, as well as similar legislation considered in multiple other states, represents only a single law among hundreds created and/or passed to hinder the rights of LGBTQI+ persons (Bendery & Signorile, 2016; Harper et al., 2013; Nord & Burbach, 2016). Tony has experienced at least the threat of ridicule if not outright oppression from significant others, family members, and certain members of the helping profession. Thus, to counsel Tony means to create affirming dialogue that resists the creation of further oppression, to heal previous trauma, and to foster a safe space for the exploration of presenting and identity concerns (Lutes & McDonough, 2012; McGeorge & Carlson, 2009).

As discussed previously, the LGBTQI+ population experiences compromised mental health and overall wellness due to oppression, discrimination, and systemic heterosexism and transphobia, even when being cared for by helping professionals (Carter, Mollen, & Smith, 2013; Dermer, Smith, & Barto, 2010; Harper et al., 2013; Kocet, 2014). Particular populations, such as transgender, asexual, intersex (American Counseling Association [ACA], 2010), and even affectionally fluid (Finnerty, 2016) persons, exhibit heightened risk due to rejection from both heterosexual and exclusively gay or lesbian communities (Ochs, 1996), which contributes to increased mental health (D'Augelli, 1998; Kocet, 2014; National Alliance for Mental Health, 2007) and physical (Amola & Grimmett, 2015; Herek, 2002) problems.

Culturally Competent and LGBTQI+ Affirmative Counseling

As discussed earlier in the book, counseling with the LGBTQI+ community is conducted through an affirming approach (Kocet, 2014; Kort, 2008; McGeorge & Carlson, 2009). An affirmative counselor recognizes affectional and gender development as vibrant, organic, and ceaseless during the lifetime (Moe, Finnerty, et al., 2015). Professional ethics codes (ACA, 2014; Hermann & Herlihy, 2006; Kaplan, 2014) and the practice of culturally competent counseling (Lee, 2008) show how affirmation strengthens the holistic framework, designating counselors as allies of LGBTQI+ persons (Finnerty, Goodrich, Brace, & Pope, 2014; Poynter, 1999). Efficacious and ethical counseling (ACA, 2014; Harper et al., 2013) includes culturally competent wellness approaches that inspire clients to live mentally and physically beneficial lives (Lee, 2008; Myers & Sweeney, 2005).

Courtland Lee, a pioneer in culturally competent counseling, summarized these elements by noting several concepts inherent to suitable practice (Lee, 2008). Perhaps the most pertinent is to place the counseling relationship within the constraints of a "social and historical context" that speaks to each person's lived experience (p. 1). For example, a recent significant historical event for many LGBTQI+ persons, the U.S. Supreme Court decision in *Obergefell et al. v. Hodges et al.* (2015) granting marriage equality to all U.S. citizens, demonstrates a culturally noteworthy occurrence such as Lee described. Jack Evans and George Harris, partners for 54 years, present the human face of this social change as the first couple to wed in Dallas County, Texas, on June 26, 2015 (Mosbergen, 2015). Lee (2008) noted that many ostracized groups began to demand inclusion over the past 300 years through social or political struggles, effectively fostering change in society; marriage equality, then, is a symbol of the greater LGBTQI+ struggle for acceptance and equality.

Another milestone moment was the attaining of high state office by the first *out* bisexual governor, Kate Brown, in Oregon in early 2015 (State of Oregon, 2015). This model of a person who identifies along the affectional orientation continuum can be helpful for Tony, as he does not currently identify but reports attraction to and a desire for relationships with people of multiple genders. A counselor unfamiliar with these significant events neglects countless attitudes, values, and behaviors of clients. This is true in the LGBTQI+ community, as historical connotations include "homosexuality" as a mental disorder in the *Diagnostic and Statistical Manual of Mental Disorders*, which pathologized affectional orientation variance (American Psychiatric Association, 1973; Harper et al., 2013; Hooker, 1957). Attending to Tony's experiences in his family, in previous therapeutic modalities such as the SOCE groups, and with his dismissal by his girlfriend and best friend are relevant to providing competent treatment.

Lee and Diaz (2009) outlined another key realm of cultural competence in the "cross-cultural zone" (p. 95). In this zone the counselor studies variances in culture between client and counselor. Counselors, supervisors, educators, and consultants must appreciate that distinctions involve intersecting factors (Robinson & Howard-Hamilton, 2000) and thus design efficacious (Yates, 2013) and culturally comprehensive (Lee, 2008) interventions. Factors can include but are not limited to ability, affectional orientation, social class, education, ethnicity, gender expression, race, religion and/or spirituality, and socioeconomic status (Harper et al., 2013; Lee, 2008). Assessing the converging cultural factors affecting Tony's clinical concerns is critical, as he has a wide breadth of experiences informed by the systems and environments he inhabits (Moe, Finnerty, et al., 2015). Without proper assessment, treatments cannot be described as affirmative, as each does not attend to the individual system Tony occupies.

Intersectionality and the assimilation of multiple identities have led to higher levels of wellness and mental health for both heterosexual and LGBTQI+ clients (Ketz & Israel, 2002; Myers & Sweeney, 2005) and have engaged counselors in a critical internal dialogue regarding subjective assumptions about those who are culturally different (Griffith, 2004; Wilcox, 2003). Tony's experience includes integrating the ethnic, orientation, and religious components of identity, any of which may be more salient day to day, even hour to hour (Moe et al., 2014). Assisting Tony in moving toward a healthy, balanced integration of cultural identity in which shame is cast aside, pride is prevalent, and his orientation is noted as a celebrated piece of the overall puzzle is ideal (Abes, Jones, & McEwen, 2007; American Association for Marriage and Family Therapy [AAMFT], 2014).

Empowerment with and for Tony is a model outcome of culturally competent counseling. Empowerment captures both optimized wellness and positive mental health outcomes along individual, collective, and systemic levels (Harley, Stebnicki, & Rollins, 2000; Prilleltensky, 2003). Empowerment fosters client counteracting of internalized inferiority "in societal relationships with powerful others" (Lee, 2008, p. 1; see also Harley et al., 2000). Empowerment is also an essential tool for developing positive coping skills while battling the discrimination, oppression, and violence experienced by LGBTQI+ persons (Savage, Harley, & Nowak, 2005). The use of empowerment strategies with Tony is therefore an ideal intervention in the spectrum of culturally competent and LGBTQI+ affirmative counseling (Association for Multicultural Counseling and Development, 2015; Ratts & Hutchins, 2009). This process can include specific advocacy interventions, such as providing psychoeducation for Tony (and family members, if desired) along with addressing gaps in community support, wellness, and/or academic or career support and guidance (Ratts & Hutchins, 2009). Incorporating empowerment into counseling is just one step counselors can take toward providing affirming modalities in counseling services, education, and supervision, discussed at length below.

The Methodology of LGBTQI+ Affirmative Counseling

Alan Malyon (1982) created affirmative methodologies for counseling with gay men (later utilized across the LGBTQI+ community) during a research project in 1982 when he noted a necessary therapeutic sphere affirming his gay participants' personhood while validating cultural elements. Affirmative therapy, more of a lens for viewing practice than a specific modality, grew mostly from marriage and family therapy literature and practice, including inquiries piloted by members of AAMFT (Kort, 2008). Affirmative therapy was noted by AAMFT (2014) as "an approach to therapy that embraces a positive view of lesbian, gay, bisexual, transgender, and queer identities and relationships and addresses the negative influences that homophobia, transphobia, and heterosexism have on the lives of LGBTQ clients" (p. 1). Tony can benefit from this approach, as although he does not identify his orientation specifically, he reports previous discrimination from significant others and trauma from both family and therapeutic modalities.

Kort (2008) and later AAMFT (2014) expressed essential qualities in applying affirmative therapy. Both understanding and resisting heterosexism and heterosexual privilege are the base from which counselors must operate throughout counseling (Kort, 2008), but this is not sufficient for dynamic affirmative counseling (McGeorge & Carlson, 2009). Singh and Gonzalez (2014) placed particular importance on defying heterosexism, an advocacy act conducted by the counselor in each meeting with an LGBTQI+ client. This microlevel process combats microaggressions found in everyday life, creating an environment free of negativity and resonant with comfort (Lewis, Arnold, House, & Toporek, 2003). This requires counselors to identify their heteronormative privilege and biases as well as to evaluate how these attitudes may emerge in their behavior in a counseling session.

Another essential element of these processes is counselor growth beyond mere tolerance of all orientations and gender expressions (AAMFT, 2014). Tolerance actually represents a low-level and negative view of LGBTQI+ clients (Riddle, 1994). Riddle (1994) created the Riddle Scale, which evaluates the attitudes that an individual or institution might possess toward LGBTQI+ persons. Although tolerance is above the initial levels of repulsion and pity, it is lower than the levels of acceptance, support, admiration, appreciation, and nurturance (Riddle, 1994). The higher levels clearly represent an affirmation that is important for counseling. The need for this level of affirmation of clients has been addressed through simple statements and advanced competencies by ACA (2004, 2005, 2010, 2014; see also Harper et al., 2013), the American Psychological Association (American Psychological Association, Division 44/Committee on Lesbian, Gay, and Bisexual Concerns Joint Task Force on Guidelines for Psychotherapy With Lesbian, Gay and Bisexual Clients, 2000; American Psychological Association Task Force on Appropriate Therapeutic Responses to Sexual Orientation, 2009), and many others. In these statements, all affirming organizations not only denounce SOCE but also define affirmation as extending beyond tolerance to a celebration of the experiences of LGBTQI+ persons (Harper et al., 2013). All of these organizations utilize empirical, qualitative, and theoretical literature to promote affirmative modalities in combating the onslaught of negative experiences among LGBTQI+ persons across all of their intersectional cultural identities (Harper et al., 2013; Selvidge, Matthews, & Bridges, 2008).

In counseling LGBTQI+ persons, clinicians (especially those who identify as heterosexual) must explore and initiate removal of entrenched heterosexist social customs, such as asking a female whether she has a boyfriend rather than a partner (Israel, 2015; Israel, Gorcheva, Walther, Sulzner, & Cohen, 2008). Counselors can then take collaborative measures with clients in fostering wellness and optimal mental health through advocacy and clinical interventions (Kocet, 2014; Lewis et al., 2003). It is important to note that counselors must also combat internalized homophobia in their clients as well as a myriad of other symptoms influenced by heterosexism (McGeorge & Carlson, 2009; Sophie, 1987).

Tackling homophobia, biphobia, transphobia, heterosexism, and other prejudices is imperative when clients internalize these injustices and/or counselors have not utilized self-reflection to analyze their own personal background (Kort, 2008). Without the first step of the counselor examining personal biases from "living in a heteronormative and gender-binaristic society" (AAMFT, 2014, p. 1), recognizing personal privilege, and reflecting on belief systems regarding gender, family, relationships, sexuality, and affectionality, affirmative counseling cannot occur (Bradford, 2012; Rock, Carlson, & McGeorge, 2010).

Bradford (2012) extended the use of counselor self-reflection regarding belief systems and relationships to the experience of bisexuals and other nonidentifying affectionally fluid persons (Finnerty, 2016), who are even more likely than gay and lesbian persons to experience discrimination and oppression in counseling (Israel et al., 2008; Pachankis & Goldfried, 2004). Bradford described clinical situations similar to concerns raised by Tony, including relational issues with his presumed heterosexual girlfriend and best friend. Bradford noted that resolution can be achieved through individual, couples, and/or family therapy affirmative interventions only after the destruction of a counselor's heterosexist or biphobic thoughts and beliefs.

AAMFT (2014) noted how becoming personally "involved" through living "an affirmative life" (p. 2) is part of developing supportive stances through familiarity with LGBTQI+ issues and struggling for societal transformation and justice. Many counseling authors (Lewis et al., 2003; Ratts & Hutchins, 2009) describe advocacy through the lens of "with and for" the "client/student, community and public level" (Lewis et al., 2003, pp. 1–3) as pertinent to creating a just world for LGBTQI+ clients (Harley et al., 2000). The individual level may entail the counselor simply engaging in small individualized efforts (Ratts & Hutchins, 2009), such as direct counseling (Savage et al., 2005). This would include assisting Tony with succeeding in academics and discovering an occupation in which his orientation is celebrated or at least not vilified. In this stage, the counselor would take part in assisting Tony to build his self-advocacy to empower himself toward his goals. Referrals to resources may be made during this level or in the community level (Ratts & Hutchins, 2009).

The community-level concerns Tony faces include a lack of acceptance from his parents and quite conceivably the particular church he may or may not attend. Empowering *with* can include Tony and the counselor constructing a supportive group of friends with similar interests while suggesting, when he is prepared, that Tony possibly include his parents in sessions to implement changes (Ratts & Hutchins, 2009). Empowering *for* can include reaching out to bisexual, queer, and college-level groups in the area to assess safety and interest for Tony to join (Savage et al., 2005). In the public arena, the counselor can advocate for Tony by becoming part of movements showing support within social and other support groups for bisexual or nonidentifying affectionally fluid persons. Counselors can invest professional time advocating for affirming clinical practice through taking leadership positions in counseling organizations such as the Association for Lesbian, Gay, Bisexual, and Transgender Issues in Counseling (ALGBTIC; www.algbtic.org).

Fostering a welcoming therapeutic setting for the client is essential to affirmative practice (AAMFT, 2014). Often a counselor who is also an ally of LGBTQI+ persons creates such an atmosphere by implementing localized interventions (Harper et al., 2013). Interventions for Tony in particular can include placing relevant LGBTQI+ periodicals and resources in the office waiting room; creating affirming paperwork absent of checkbox identifications for gender, sex, or orientation; and using culturally competent and affirming terminology, such as *partner* and the client's name, that reflects the client's identity (AAMFT, 2014; Harper et al., 2013; Poynter, 1999). Tony can benefit from bisexual and nonidentifying titles being displayed in the counselor's office; referrals to bisexual and nonidentifying community resources; and current local, regional, national, and global events (Rock et al., 2010). Other LGBTQI+-friendly signage and, if possible, "Safe Zone" or "Safe Place" stickers on office doors and in windows also present a sense of safety and openness (Harper et al., 2013).

Openness on the part of the counselor in pledging to utilize affirmative therapy with affectionally and gender-diverse persons (Moe et al., 2014) is also very important to identifying as an affirming clinician (AAMFT, 2014). Openness is represented by the discussion of such modalities with clients and colleagues and/or the conducting of research related to the efficacy of affirming interventions and techniques (AAMFT, 2014; Finnerty et al., 2014; Harper et al., 2013). Remaining cognizant of, and gaining continuing education in, LGBTQI+-affirming practices and research through workshops and conventions (such as ALGBTIC's biennial conference and ACA's annual conference) is essential; counselors should also stay up to date with current LGBTQI+ popular literature and events (ALGBTIC, 2016; Harper et al., 2013). Informed consent regarding the affirmative therapeutic stance held by the counselor, alongside consultation with other affirming professionals, can help set the stage for a productive therapeutic relationship. In addition, connecting Tony with other allies at his school and in the workplace can create the systemic safety and support that Tony needs to flourish (Poynter, 1999; Ratts & Hutchins, 2009).

Pachankis, Hatzenbuehler, Rendina, Safren, and Parsons (2015) recently studied the effect of a cognitive–behavioral affirmative strategy in creating a marked decrease in minority stress symptoms such as substance abuse, depression, anxiety, and compulsive sexual behaviors alongside improvements in condom use for gay and bisexual men. These treatment effects translate to some of the first evidence-based affirmative practice modalities (Lambert & Barley, 2001; Pachankis et al., 2015). The common factors referred to by Lambert and associates over the years include "empathy, warmth, congruence and the therapeutic alliance" (Lambert & Barley, 2001, p. 357). To create an affirmative stance is to develop a positive therapeutic alliance, as one cannot provide affirmative therapy from any other place. Unfortunately, no specific studies have measured characteristics of LGBTQI+ affirmative therapy as actual predictors of outcome, although many studies and task forces have denounced and repudiated SOCE, the exact opposite of affirming practice (Haldeman, 2002; Lutes & McDonough, 2012).

Perhaps one of the most relevant characteristics of an affirmative counselor is present when the client is not present: being an ally and an advocate. The "challenging [of] heterosexism and the gender binary" (AAMFT, 2014, p. 1) with persons who identify outside the LGBTQI+ community is pertinent, as it demonstrates consistency, authenticity, and continual advocacy (Harper et al., 2013; Ratts & Hutchins, 2009). This demonstration of the counselor/advocate role shows that advocacy does not end with clinical work with LGBTQI+ persons but pervades all counseling interventions, professionalism, and ways of being for the affirmative counselor (Harper et al., 2013). Before affirmative counseling and advocacy takes place, the seed must be planted through effective education, training, and supervision.

Education and Training for Affirmative Counseling

Several authors have designated adequate training of counselors as essential to providing effectual and affirmative therapy (Frank & Cannon, 2010; Matthews, 2005; Wells, 1989). Counselor education programs display a disturbing deficiency of training in affirmative therapies, as LGBTQI+ issues are often only covered in cultural diversity courses through a single lesson, even as accreditation standards (Council for Accreditation of Counseling and Related Educational Programs, 2015) demonstrate stringent requirements for counselor education students. Marriage and family therapy programs demonstrate further training and research in such endeavors (McGeorge & Carlson, 2009; Rock et al., 2010).

Contextual reasoning regarding why counselor education programs often lack an emphasis on affirmative training may be found in research conducted by McGeorge, Carlson, and Toomey (2015) in marriage and family therapy programs. These authors found that faculty members who exhibited more "positive beliefs about LGB clients appear to be more likely to include LGB affirmative therapy content" in course curriculum (p. 57). Issues of anti-LGBTQI+ beliefs and lack of appropriate education with faculty members inherently trickle down to counseling students and, ultimately, clients; thus, critical analysis of affirmative practice training in counselor education is pertinent (Matthews, 2005). If a lack of pro-LGBTQI+ beliefs is also present in counselor education faculty, diversity training for instructors can be conducted to increase knowledge, leading to affirmation and inclusion of LGBTQI+ material in counselor education programs (Mathews, 2005; McGeorge et al., 2015).

The critical thinking desired to combat heterosexism, transphobia, and other systemic and internalized negative beliefs present in beginning counselors must be developed in counselor education students (Frank & Cannon, 2010). The literature presented here, although limited in scope, provides a starting point for engagement for educators. Wells (1989) was one of the first theorists to suggest specific pedagogical methods, as he implemented the use of "explicit films," films depicting sexuality and affection between LGBTQI+ couples, to decrease bias and homophobia (p. 19). Matthews (2005) later noted specific suggestions for developing competence through the infusion of affectional orientation information in counselor education in a multitude of courses from the likely confines of a cultural course to psychopathology and even research courses. Later, Frank and Cannon (2010) theorized how queer theory can be formatted both as a critique of current curriculum and as a pedagogical tool for teaching LGBTQI+ issues going forward. As a critical lens for viewing counseling processes, assessment protocols, and theoretical assumptions, queer theory is also ideal for instructing about affirmative therapies, as it forces students to critique the social construction of beliefs, gender, and orientation (Frank & Cannon, 2010).

Several years later, LaMantia, Wagner, and Bohecker (2015) posited the use of another critical tool, feminist pedagogy, for ally development through an intersectional lens (of converging cultural factors). These authors challenged educators to incorporate the use of competencies in the classroom, utilizing students to create attentiveness to oppressions and foster ally behaviors, abilities, and activism (LaMantia et al., 2015). There is a gap in the literature in pedagogical methods for instructing students about affirmative modalities for LGBTQI+ persons, especially minorities in the community, such as nonidentifying persons, affectionally fluid persons, persons who are transgender, and those who are intersex (Finnerty, 2016; Harper et al., 2013; Matthews, 2005). Research in LGBTQI+-affirming pedagogies is needed to focus more on developing effective affirmative counselors.

Affirmative Supervision

Phillips and Fischer (1998) noted that many affirmative and feminist counseling leaders believe that concentrated training and supervision are essential for counselors to provide adequate services. As supervision is assumed to be fundamental to the professional progress of counselors, affirmative supervision is also necessary; through challenging counseling and theoretical heterosexist traditions and biases, counselors can seek assistance in their own development (Halpert & Pfaller, 2001; Phillips & Fischer, 1998). Depending on the experience and knowledge base of Tony's counselor, there is a need for supervision (of counseling students and new professionals) and/or consultation (between affirmative practitioners) to negotiate ideal treatment (Halpert & Pfaller, 2001).

The clinical supervision literature demonstrates "heterosexual bias and discrimination" in supervisors as well (Burkard, Knox, Hess, & Schultz, 2009, p. 177), which fosters unfavorable effects for supervisees and clients (Rose, Moore, Kautzman-East, & Burton, 2015). Well-trained and well-practiced supervisors who evaluate their own subjective attitudes and utilize efficacious clinical and counseling approaches can reconcile such biases and discriminatory practices (Halpert, Reinhardt, & Toohey, 2007; Rock et al., 2010). Affirmative supervisors critically engage the prejudices, assumptions, and harmful attitudes of students and supervisees noted in the literature (Dillon et al., 2004; Rainey & Trusty, 2007). Overall, research in the helping professions notes affirmative supervision as imperative to adequately serving the LGBTQI+ community (Aducci & Baptist, 2011; Halpert & Pfaller, 2001; Halpert et al., 2007; Moe, Perera-Diltz, & Sepulveda, 2015; Rock et al., 2010). Before clinical experience begins, counseling students must be educated to provide culturally competent and affirming counseling; this amounts to a reconstructive reeducation of societal and systemic influences for counselors-in-training.

Counselor as Ally

Poynter (1999) first developed a strengthened sense of what an ally is in describing student affairs with college students with a set of behaviors and characteristics. Later Poynter's ally behaviors, along with guidelines originated by the LGBT Center Resource Library at the Minnesota State University at Mankato (n.d.), were translated for the counseling sphere in the ALGBTIC competencies (Harper et al., 2013; see http://www.algbtic.org/competencies.html) for both "counselors as allies" (Harper et al., 2013, p. 22) and "competencies for counseling allies" (Harper et al., 2013, p. 24). The section for counselors as allies applies to this review, including sections on awareness, knowledge, supporting coming out decisions, and supportive environments. A description of counselor allies is presented next.

The ALGBTIC Competencies Taskforce (Harper et al., 2013) responded to a multitude of clinical issues surrounding LGBTQI+ work, including the referral of LGBTQI+ persons to self-identified LGBTQI+ counselors. The automatic assumption that LGBTQI+ counselors exhibit the training to work with LGBTQI+ clients is not realistic, nor should administrators or supervisors decide that it is only self-identified LGBTQI+ counselors who must provide this therapy. Instead, creating an atmosphere in which all counselors are versed in LGBTQI+ issues, exhibit ally behaviors, and self-identify as allies must be promoted (Harper et al., 2013). Ally identification also extends to the therapeutic environment's functionality for LGBTQI+ persons through inclusive paperwork, policies, and nondiscrimination attitudes for all aspects of culture (Finnerty et al., 2014; Harper et al., 2013, p. 24).

A focus on the intersectionality of cultural diversity is noted throughout the ALGBTIC competencies, with an emphasis on demonstrating competent ally behavior, as gender and affectional orientation does not describe the sum of a person's culture or identity (Harper et al., 2013). Intersectionality was later affirmed as pertinent in other theoretical literature on allies (LaMantia et al., 2015). Tony's orientation cannot be separated from his ethnic, religious, or familial background for conceptualizing clinical interventions; all identities are salient at specific times, even as each affects the others as a composite figure (Moe et al., 2014). Ally behavior often goes a step beyond affirmative behaviors, as counselor allies do more than object to stereotypical depictions of LGBTQI+ identities (Harper et al., 2013). There is little doubt that Tony will react to negative statements regarding his fluid identity. Counselor allies combat these statements not only in session but also across their lives and work with all clients, colleagues, and policymakers. An intersectional focus forges past barriers in counseling to celebrate the unique experiences of LGBTQI+ persons (Harper et al., 2013).

Besides gaining more experience in affirmative interventions, competent allies not only participate in self-reflection but also engage directly with and learn about LGBTQI+ community members to discover their stories (Harper et al., 2013, p. 22). To supplement affirming practitioners' focus on cultural systems, we mirror Lee (2008) in calling for deeper understanding of "political and economic climates and the resulting institutional practices, laws, and policies" along with the effects on LGBTQI+ persons (Harper et al., 2013, p. 23). Decisions about coming out are relevant for affirmative counselors, as displaying one's true self is up to the individual client and must be done safely and thoughtfully (Legate, Ryan, & Weinstein, 2012). Tony must decide when and to whom coming out will be functional, as this process may represent deep anxiety regarding acceptance and safety; thus, core counseling skills such as "empathic listening and reflective feedback" are functional not only in developing a therapeutic relationship but also in achieving positive outcomes (Harper et al., 2013, p. 23). Counselor allies who demonstrate competence and knowledge of the systemic injustices facing clients such as Tony not only develop more succinct interventions but also can create positive therapeutic outcomes.

Providing Tony's affirmative therapeutic treatment is not as simple as providing a nonjudgmental stance or as difficult as knowing all there is to know, because being an ally means listening to his unique individual story (Harper et al., 2013). Allies/affirmative counselors do not succumb to stereotypes about those like Tony who are questioning or do not identify as a particular LGBTQI+ identity. Allies create a space for continual, affirming personal growth through evidence-based treatment modalities from a myriad of therapeutic approaches (Finnerty et al., 2014). To be an ally is not only to be competent in specific mental health treatments but also to extend one's professional and experiential education to include cultural competence and affirmation of all those who are LGBTQI+ (Harper et al., 2013; LaMantia et al., 2015; Lee, 2008).

Ethical Issues in LGBTQI+ Counseling

Connected to ethical practice, counselors working with LGBTQI+ clients must demonstrate the requisite training and competency to work affirmatively, effectively, and ethically with LGBTQI+ individuals (Rutter, Estrada, Ferguson, & Diggs, 2008). In the case of Tony, because he has disclosed the fact that his sexual/affectional orientation is more fluid and does not adhere to traditional labels, such as *gay* or *bisexual,* the counselor working with Tony needs to possess the expertise, knowledge, and skills necessary to work with clients who do not conform to traditional binary labels. In addition, it is important for counselors to assess the role religion or spirituality plays in the lives of LGBTQI+ individuals. In the scenario involving Tony, it is important for the counselor to assess whether the camp experience was affiliated with a religious or spiritual tradition. Because Tony has expressed being harmed by the camp experience, it is critical to explore Tony's own religious or spiritual beliefs and whether religion or spirituality warrants a deeper exploration in counseling. Some LGBTQI+ clients may need to integrate their spiritual or religious identities with their sexual, affectional, or gender identities in an affirming manner (Kocet, Sanabria, & Smith, 2011).

In addition to the ethical issues surrounding SOCE covered in Chapter 8, there are other pertinent ethical concerns that counselors should be mindful of when treating LGBTQI+ individuals. Whether in a large metropolitan area or a rural community, the LGBTQI+ community is often considered small. Therefore, it is likely that LGBTQI+-identified counselors may unknowingly share friends or acquaintances with their LGBTQI+ clients (Goodrich & Luke, 2015). For example, a current client's Facebook profile may appear to the counselor through "People You May Know," or when the counselor clicks on a friend's profile, they may discover that a client is a mutual friend. Some counselors and clients may even serve in the same LGBTQI+ organization in their community.

Social gatherings, establishments, or other LGBTQI+ organizations may be common places for LGBTQI+ counselors and clients to inadvertently encounter one another. Prior to such possible sightings, counselors should discuss these potential scenarios during the informed consent process in the counseling relationship (Goodrich & Luke, 2015; Sheperis, Henning, & Kocet, 2016; Welfel, 2013) and discuss the limitations regarding professional and nonprofessional interactions (Jungers & Gregoire, 2013). LGBTQI+ counselors must take careful steps to manage professional boundaries and take proactive steps in working through ethical dilemmas involving interpersonal relationships with clients outside of the therapeutic setting. Although the *ACA Code of Ethics* does not prohibit LGBTQI+ affirmative counselors from engaging in interactions with LGBTQI+ clients outside of counseling, counselors must explore the risks and benefits of extending professional counseling boundaries (Standard A.6.b.) and ensure that such boundary crossings are not exploitive or harmful to the client (ACA, 2014).

Counselors must also be mindful of possibly harmful issues related to client confidentiality and record keeping. When counseling LGBTQI+ minors, professionals must respect minors' ability to explore their affectional orientation or gender identity in a private, confidential manner while keeping in mind that parents or legal guardians have legal access to client records (Kocet, 2014). Children or adolescents who are questioning or exploring their affectional orientation or gender identity and have not disclosed this to their parents or legal guardians may be in harm's way if clinical documentation refers to such issues and the parents are not informed prior to their discovery of it in the clients' records. A delicate balance is struck in creating a therapeutic environment in which children and adolescents can feel safe to explore such identity issues, but this can pose challenges when parents or guardians demand detailed information about a minor client's disclosures in treatment (Kocet, 2014; Legate et al., 2012).

When faced with an ethical concern involving an LGBTQI+ client, counselors are encouraged to seek ethical tools for guidance. Practitioners are encouraged to utilize an ethical decision-making model, such as the intercultural model of ethical decision making (Goodrich & Luke, 2015), Kocet's relational ethical decision-making model (Sheperis et al., 2016), or other similar models, when facing an ethical conundrum with LGBTQI+ clients. Counselors working with the LGBTQI+ population need to demonstrate ethical sensitivity when faced with these critical ethical dilemmas (Houser & Thomas, 2013; Welfel, 2013).

Conclusion

Overall, utilization of affirming counseling practice is demonstrated as effective, ethical, and appropriate to support growth for Tony. As a previous experience with shame-based therapy meant to reorient his attractions created negative effects and adversity for Tony, affirming practice from a counselor ally is optimal for personal and professional growth. Practitioners must demonstrate competence in responding to requests for SOCE therapeutic practices by citing a lack of evidence and demonstrating ethical and safety issues (Kocet, 2014) in noting the ability to provide an effective, affirming practice. Counselors must also demonstrate active engagement with ally behaviors, both in and outside the counseling office, as these characteristics demonstrate both affirmative counseling and acting as a continual advocate and ally for persons like Tony (Finnerty et al., 2014).

Questions for Further Discussion

1. How could affirmative counseling meet Tony's current needs?
2. What type of preparatory work would Tony's counselor need to do to be able to affirm Tony in a counseling context?
3. What would affirmative counseling look like for Tony?

4. What type of education, training, or supervision should Tony's counselor seek out to improve their competence?
5. What are potential ethical issues for Tony's counselor?

Resources

1. Read the *Counseling Today* article "No More Sitting on the Sidelines" at http://ct.counseling.org/2011/05/no-more-sitting-on-the-sidelines/.
2. Read the *Counseling Today* article "Connecting With Clients of Faith" at http://ct.counseling.org/2009/08/connecting-with-clients-of-faith/.
3. Read the journal article "Adapting Counseling Skills for Multicultural and Diverse Clients" at http://www.counseling.org/Resources/Library/VISTAS/2009-V-Print/Article%204%20LeBeaufSmabyMaddux.pdf.
4. Read PFLAG Metro DC's page on mental health for clients at http://pflagdc.org/learn/mental-health/.

References

Abes, E. S., Jones, S. R., & McEwen, M. K. (2007). Reconceptualizing the model of multiple dimensions of identity: The role of meaning-making capacity in the construction of multiple identities. *Journal of College Student Development, 48,* 1–22. doi:1353/csd.2007.0000

Aducci, C. J., & Baptist, J. A. (2011). A collaborative-affirmative approach to supervisory practice. *Journal of Feminist Family Therapy, 23*(2), 88–102. doi:10.1080/08952833.2011.574536

American Association for Marriage and Family Therapy, California Division. (2014). *LGBT affirmative therapy: Tips for creating a more lesbian, gay, bisexual, transgender, and gender inclusive practice from the AAMFT Queer Affirmative Caucus.* Retrieved from https://education.uoregon.edu/sites/default/files/affirmative_therapy_handout_0.pdf

American Counseling Association. (2004). *Compilation of resolutions adopted by the association: 2001–present.* Retrieved from http://www.counseling.org/Sub//Minutes/Resolutions/Resolutions-2001-Present.pdf

American Counseling Association. (2005). *Code of ethics.* Alexandria, VA: Author.

American Counseling Association. (2010). American Counseling Association competencies for counseling with transgender clients. *Journal of LGBT Issues in Counseling, 4*(3), 135–159. doi:10.1080/15538605.2010.524839

American Counseling Association. (2014). *ACA code of ethics.* Alexandria, VA: Author.

American Psychiatric Association. (1973). *Homosexuality and sexuality orientation disturbance: Proposed change in* DSM-II (APA Document Reference No. 730008). Washington, DC: Author.

American Psychological Association, Division 44/Committee on Lesbian, Gay, and Bisexual Concerns Joint Task Force on Guidelines for Psychotherapy With Lesbian, Gay and Bisexual Clients. (2000). Guidelines for psychotherapy with lesbian, gay and bisexual clients. *American Psychologist, 55,* 1440–1451.

American Psychological Association Task Force on Appropriate Therapeutic Responses to Sexual Orientation. (2009). *Report of the Task Force on Appropriate Therapeutic Responses to Sexual Orientation.* Washington, DC: American Psychological Association.

Amola, O., & Grimmett, M. A. (2015). Sexual identity, mental health, HIV risk behaviors, and internalized homophobia among Black men who have sex with men. *Journal of Counseling & Development, 93,* 236–246. doi:10.1002/j.1556-6676.2015.00199.x

Associated Press. (2015, December 2). *Inside look at ISIS' brutal persecution of gays.* Retrieved from the CBS News website: http://www.cbsnews.com/news/isis-persecution-gay-men-murder-lgbt-muslim-society/

Association for Lesbian, Gay, Bisexual, and Transgender Issues in Counseling. (2016, February 25). *ALGBTIC webpage.* Retrieved from www.algbtic.org

Association for Multicultural Counseling and Development. (2015). *Multicultural and social justice counseling competencies.* Retrieved from https://www.counseling.org/knowledge-center/competencies

Balsam, K. F., Molina, Y., Beadnell, B., Simoni, J., & Walters, K. (2011). Measuring multiple minority stress: The LGBT People of Color Microaggressions Scale. *Cultural Diversity and Ethnic Minority Psychology, 17*(2), 163–174. doi:10.1037/a0023244

Bendery, J., & Signorile, M. (2016, April 16). *Everything you need to know about the wave of 100+ anti-LGBT bills pending in states.* Retrieved from the Huffington Post website: http://www.huffingtonpost.com/entry/lgbt-state-bills-discrimination_us_570ff4f2e4b0060ccda2a7a9

Bradford, M. (2012). Affirmative bisexual couple therapy. In J. J. Bigner & J. L. Wetchler (Eds.), *Handbook of LGBT-affirmative couple and family therapy* (pp. 57–68). New York, NY: Routledge.

Burkard, A. W., Knox, S., Hess, S. A., & Schultz, J. (2009). Lesbian, gay, and bisexual supervisees' experiences of LGB-affirmative and nonaffirmative supervision. *Journal of Counseling Psychology, 56*(1), 176–188. doi:10.1037/0022-0167.56.1.176

Carter, L. W., II, Mollen, D., & Smith, N. G. (2013). Locus of control, minority stress, and psychological distress among lesbian, gay, and bisexual individuals. *Journal of Counseling Psychology.* Advance online publication. doi:10.1037/a0034593

Cass, V. C. (1996). Sexual orientation identity formation: A Western phenomenon. In R. Cabaj & T. Stein (Eds.), *Textbook of homosexuality and mental health* (pp. 227–251). Washington, DC: American Psychiatric Press.

Chaney, M. P., Filmore, J. M., & Goodrich, K. M. (2011). No more sitting on the sidelines. *Counseling Today, 53*(11), 34–37.

Council for Accreditation of Counseling and Related Educational Programs. (2015). *2016 CACREP standards.* Alexandria, VA: Author.

D'Augelli, A. R. (1998). Developmental implications of victimization of lesbian, gay and bisexual youths. In G. Herek (Ed.), *Psychological perspective on lesbian and gay issues: Vol. 4. Stigma and sexual orientation: Understanding prejudice against lesbians, gay men, and bisexuals* (pp. 187–201). Thousand Oaks, CA: Sage.

Dermer, S. B., Smith, S. D., & Barto, K. K. (2010). Identifying and correctly labeling sexual prejudice, discrimination and oppression. *Journal of Counseling & Development, 88,* 325–331.

Dillon, F. R., Worthington, R. L., Savoy, H., Rooney, S., Becker-Schutte, A., & Guerra, R. M. (2004). On becoming allies: A qualitative study of lesbian-, gay-, and bisexual affirmative counselor training. *Counselor Education and Supervision, 43,* 162–178.

Eliason, M. J. (1996). Identity formation for lesbian, bisexual, and gay persons: Beyond a "minoritizing" view. *Journal of Homosexuality, 30*(3), 31–58.

Fassinger, R. E., & Arseneau, J. R. (2007). "I'd rather get wet than be under the umbrella": Differentiating the experiences and identities of lesbian, gay, bisexual, and transgender people. In K. J. Bieschke, R. M. Perez, & K. A. DeBord (Eds.), *Handbook of counseling and psychotherapy with lesbian, gay, bisexual, and transgender clients* (2nd ed., pp. 19–49). Washington, DC: American Psychological Association.

Finnerty, P. S. (2016). *Affectionally fluid persons' subjective attitudes of wellness* (Unpublished doctoral dissertation). Kent State University, Kent, OH.

Finnerty, P., Goodrich, K., Brace, A., & Pope, A. (2014). Charting the course of ally development. *Journal of LGBT Issues in Counseling, 8*(4), 326–330. doi:10.1080/15538605.2014.974385

Firestein, B. (Ed.). (1996). *Bisexuality: The psychology and politics of an invisible minority.* Thousand Oaks, CA: Sage.

Foucault, M. (1978). *The history of sexuality: Vol. 1. An introduction.* London, UK: Allen Lane.

Frank, D. A., & Cannon, E. P. (2010). Queer theory as pedagogy in counselor education: A framework for diversity training. *Journal of LGBT Issues in Counseling, 4*(1), 18–31. doi:10.1080/15538600903552731

Gonzalez, M. A. (2007). Latinos on da down low: The limitations of sexual identity in public health. *Latino Studies, 5*(1), 25–52.

Goodrich, K., & Luke, M. (2015). *Group counseling with LGBTQI persons.* Alexandria, VA: American Counseling Association.

Griffith, B. A. (2004). The structure and development of internal working models: An integrated framework for understanding clients and promoting wellness. *Journal of Humanistic Counseling, Education and Development, 43,* 163–177. doi:10.1002/j.2164-490X.2004.tb00016.x

Haldeman, D. C. (2002). Gay rights, patient rights: The implications of sexual orientation conversion therapy. *Professional Psychology, 33,* 200–204.

Halpert, S. C., & Pfaller, J. (2001). Sexual orientation and supervision: Theory and practice. *Journal of Gay & Lesbian Social Services, 13*(3), 23–40. doi:10.1300/J041v13n03_02

Halpert, S. C., Reinhardt, B., & Toohey, M. J. (2007). Affirmative clinical supervision. In K. J. Bieschke, R. M. Perez, & K. A. DeBord (Eds.), *Handbook of counseling and psychotherapy with lesbian, gay, bisexual, and transgender clients* (2nd ed., pp. 341–358). Washington, DC: American Psychological Association.

Harley, D. A., Stebnicki, M., & Rollins, C. W. (2000). Applying empowerment evaluation as a tool for self-improvement and community development with culturally diverse populations. *Journal of the Community Development Society, 31,* 348–364.

Harper, A., Finnerty, P., Martinez, M., Brace, A., Crethar, H., Loos, B., . . . Lambert, S. (2013). Association for Lesbian, Gay, Bisexual, and Transgender Issues in Counseling (ALGBTIC) competencies for counseling with lesbian, gay, bisexual, queer, questioning, intersex and ally individuals. *Journal of LGBT Issues in Counseling, 7*(1), 2–43. doi:10.1080/15538605.2013.755444

Herek, G. M. (2002). Heterosexuals' attitudes toward bisexual men and women in the United States. *Journal of Sex Research, 39,* 264–274. doi:10.1080/00224490209552150

Hermann, M. A., & Herlihy, B. J. (2006). Legal and ethical implications of refusing to counsel homosexual clients. *Journal of Counseling & Development, 84,* 414–418. doi:10.1002/j.1556-6678.2006.tb00425.x

Hooker, E. A. (1957). The adjustment of the male overt homosexual. *Journal of Projective Techniques, 21,* 18–31.

Houser, R., & Thomas, S. (2013). *Ethics in counseling and therapy: Developing an ethical identity.* Los Angeles, CA: Sage.

Israel, T. (2015, July 7). *Bisexuality and beyond: Tania Israel* [Video file]. Retrieved from http://tedxucla.org/project/bisexuality-and-beyond-tania-israel/

Israel, T., Gorcheva, R., Walther, W., Sulzner, J., & Cohen, J. (2008). Therapists' helpful and unhelpful situations with LGBT clients: An exploratory study. *Professional Psychology: Research & Practice, 39,* 361–368. doi:10.1037/0735-7028.39.3.361

Israel, T., & Mohr, J. (2004). Attitudes towards bisexual women and men: Current research, future directions. In R. Fox (Ed.), *Current research on bisexuality* (pp. 73–92). New York, NY: Harrington Park Press.

Jamil, O. B., Harper, G. W., & Fernandez, M. I. (2009). Sexual and ethnic identity development among gay-bisexual-questioning (GBQ) male ethnic minority adolescents. *Cultural Diversity and Ethnic Minority Psychology, 15,* 203–214.

Jones, S. R., & McEwen, M. K. (2000). A conceptual model of multiple dimensions of identity. *Journal of College Student Development, 41,* 405–414.

Jungers, C., & Gregoire, J. (Eds.). (2013). *Counseling ethics: Philosophical and professional foundations.* New York, NY: Springer.

Kaplan, D. M. (2014). Ethical implications of a critical legal case for the counseling profession: *Ward v. Wilbanks. Journal of Counseling & Development, 92,* 142–146. doi:10.1002/j.1556-6676.2014.00140.x

Ketz, K., & Israel, T. (2002). The relationship between women's sexual identity and perceived wellness. *Journal of Bisexuality, 2*(2), 227–242.

Kocet, M. (Ed.). (2014). *Counseling gay men, adolescents, and boys: A guide for helping professionals and educators.* New York, NY: Routledge.

Kocet, M., Sanabria, S., & Smith, M. (2011). Finding the spirit within: Religion, spirituality, and faith development in gay, lesbian, and bisexual individuals. *Journal of LGBT Issues in Counseling, 5,* 163–179.

Kort, J. (2008). *Gay affirmative therapy for the straight clinician: The essential guide.* New York, NY: Norton.

LaMantia, K., Wagner, H., & Bohecker, L. (2015). Ally development through feminist pedagogy: A systemic focus on intersectionality. *Journal of LGBT Issues in Counseling, 9*(2), 136–153. doi:10.1080/15538605.2015.1029205

Lambert, M. J., & Barley, D. E. (2001). Research summary on the therapeutic relationship and psychotherapy outcome. *Psychotherapy, 38*(4), 357–361.

Lee, C. C. (2008). *Elements of culturally competent counseling* (ACAPCD-24). Alexandria, VA: American Counseling Association.

Lee, C. C., & Diaz, J. M. (2009). The cross-cultural zone in counseling. In C. C. Lee, D. A. Burnhill, A. L. Butler, C. P. Hipolito-Delgado, M. Humphrey, O. Muñoz, & H. Shin (Eds.), *The elements of culture in counseling* (pp. 95–104). Columbus, OH: Pearson.

Legate, N., Ryan, R. M., & Weinstein, N. (2012). Is coming out always a "good thing"? Exploring the relations of autonomy support, outness, and wellness for lesbian, gay, and bisexual individuals. *Social Psychological and Personality Science, 3*(2), 145–152. doi:10.1177/1948550611411929

Lewis, J. A., Arnold, M. S., House, R., & Toporek, R. L. (2003). *ACA advocacy competencies.* Retrieved from http://www.counseling.org/resources/competencies/advocacy_competencies.pdf

Lutes, J., & McDonough, M. (2012). Helping individuals and families recover from sexual orientation change efforts and heterosexism. In J. Bigner & J. Wetchler (Eds.), *Handbook of LGBT-affirmative couple and family therapy* (pp. 443–458). New York, NY: Routledge.

Malyon, A. K. (1982). Psychotherapeutic implications of internalized homophobia in gay men. *Journal of Homosexuality, 7*(2/3), 56–69. doi:10.1300/J082v07n02_08

Matthews, C. R. (2005). Infusing lesbian, gay, and bisexual issues into counselor education. *Journal of Humanistic Counseling, Education and Development, 44,* 168–184.

McGeorge, C., & Carlson, T. (2009). Deconstructing heterosexism: Becoming an LGB affirmative heterosexual couple and family therapist. *Journal of Marital and Family Therapy, 37*(1), 14–26.

McGeorge, C. R., Carlson, T. S., & Toomey, R. B. (2015). Assessing lesbian, gay, and bisexual affirmative training in couple and family therapy: Establishing the validity of the faculty version of the Affirmative Training Inventory. *Journal of Marital and Family Therapy, 41*(1), 57–71. doi:10.1111/jmft.12054

Meyer, I. H., & Wilson, P. A. (2009). Sampling lesbian, gay, and bisexual populations. *Journal of Counseling Psychology, 56*(1), 23–31.

Minnesota State University at Mankato, LGBT Center Resource Library. (n.d.). *How to be an ally.* Retrieved from http://www.mnsu.edu/lgbtc/resource.html

Moe, J., Finnerty, P., Sparkman, N., & Yates, C. (2015). Initial assessment and screening with LGBTQ clients: A critical perspective. *Journal of LGBT Issues in Counseling, 9*(1), 1–34. doi: 10.1080/15538605.2014.997332

Moe, J., Perera-Diltz, D., Sepulveda, V., & Finnerty, P. (2014). Salience, valence, context and integration: Conceptualizing the needs of sexually and gender diverse youth in P-12 schools. *Journal of Homosexuality, 61,* 435–451. doi:10.1080/00918369.2013.842437

Moe, J. L., Perera-Diltz, D., & Sepulveda, V. (2015). Beyond competence: Fostering LGBTQQI ally development through supervision. *Journal of LGBT Issues in Counseling, 8,* 389–401. doi:10.1080/15538605.2014.960129

Mosbergen, D. (2015, June 29). *After 54 years together, Jack Evans and George Harris become first same-sex couple to marry in Dallas.* Retrieved from the Huffington Post website: http://www.huffingtonpost.com/2015/06/29/first-same-sex-couple-dallas-jack-evans-george-harris_n_7684464.html

Myers, J. E., & Sweeney, T. J. (Eds.). (2005). *Counseling for wellness: Theory, research, and practice.* Alexandria, VA: American Counseling Association.

National Alliance for Mental Health. (2007). *LGBTQ.* Retrieved from http://www.nami.org/Find-Support/LGBTQ

Nord, J., & Burbach, K. (2016, February 16). *Transgender bathroom bill sent to South Dakota governor.* Retrieved from http://www.record-bee.com/article/ZZ/20160216/NEWS/160216840

Obergefell et al. v. Hodges et al., 575 U.S. 14-556 (2015).

Ochs, R. (1996). Biphobia: It goes more than two ways. In B. A. Firestein (Ed.), *Bisexuality: The psychology and politics of an invisible minority* (pp. 217–239). Thousand Oaks, CA: Sage.

Pachankis, J. E., & Goldfried, M. R. (2004). Clinical issues in working with lesbian, gay, and bisexual clients. *Psychotherapy: Theory, Research, Practice, Training, 41*(3), 227–246.

Pachankis, J. E., Hatzenbuehler, M. L., Rendina, H. J., Safren, S., & Parsons, J. T. (2015). LGB-affirmative cognitive-behavioral therapy for young adult gay and bisexual men: A randomized controlled trial of a transdiagnostic minority stress approach. *Journal of Consulting and Clinical Psychology, 83,* 875–889. doi:10.1037/ccp0000037

Phillips, J. C., & Fischer, A. R. (1998). Graduate students' training experiences with lesbian, gay and bisexual issues. *The Counseling Psychologist, 26,* 712–734. doi:10.1177/0011000098265002

Poynter, K. (1999, March). *Development of heterosexual allies: Their role in the learning community.* Paper presented at the American College Personnel Association annual conference, Atlanta, GA.

Prilleltensky, I. (2003). Understanding, resisting, and overcoming oppression: Towards psychopolitical validity. *American Journal of Community Psychology, 31,* 195–202.

Rainey, S. J., & Trusty, J. (2007). Attitudes of master's level counseling students toward gay men and lesbians. *Counseling and Values, 52,* 12–24.

Ratts, M. J., & Hutchins, A. M. (2009). ACA advocacy competencies: Social justice advocacy at the client/student level. *Journal of Counseling & Development, 87,* 269–275.

Riddle, D. (1994). Attitudes towards differences: The Riddle Scale. In *Alone no more: Developing a school support system for gay, lesbian and bisexual youth* (pp. 34–35). St. Paul: Minnesota State Department of Education.

Robinson, T. L., & Howard-Hamilton, M. F. (2000). *The convergence of race, ethnicity, and gender: Multiple identities in counseling.* Upper Saddle River, NJ: Merrill.

Rock, M., Carlson, T. S., & McGeorge, C. R. (2010). Does affirmative training matter? Assessing CFT students' beliefs about sexual orientation and their level of affirmative training. *Journal of Marital and Family Therapy, 36*(2), 171–184.

Rose, J. S., Moore, A. M., Kautzman-East, M., & Burton, S. (2015, October). *Affirmative approach to supervision: Working with LGBQ+ supervisees and clients.* Presentation at biennial conference of the Association for Counselor Education and Supervision, Philadelphia, PA.

Rutter, P., Estrada, D., Ferguson, L., & Diggs, G. (2008). Sexual orientation and counselor competency: The impact of training on enhancing awareness, knowledge, and skills. *Journal of LGBT Issues in Counseling, 2,* 109–125. doi:10.1080/15538600802125472

Savage, T. A., Harley, D. A., & Nowak, T. M. (2005). Applying social empowerment strategies as tools for self-advocacy in counseling lesbian and gay male clients. *Journal of Counseling & Development, 83,* 131–137.

Selvidge, M. M. D., Matthews, C. R., & Bridges, S. K. (2008). The relationship of minority stress and flexible coping to psychological well being in lesbian and bisexual women. *Journal of Homosexuality, 55,* 450–470.

Sheperis, D. S., Henning, S. L., & Kocet, M. M. (2016). *Ethical decision making for the 21st century counselor.* Thousand Oaks, CA: Sage.

Singh, A. A., & Gonzalez, M. (2014). *LGBTQQ-affirmative counseling practice brief.* Alexandria, VA: American Counseling Association.

Sophie, J. (1987). Internalized homophobia and lesbian identity. *Journal of Homosexuality, 14*(1–2), 53–65.

State of Oregon. (2015). *Governor Kate Brown.* Retrieved from http://www.oregon.gov/gov/Pages/index.aspx

Welfel, E. R. (2013). *Ethics in counseling and psychotherapy: Standards, research, and emerging issues* (6th ed.). Boston, MA: Cengage.

Wells, J. W. (1989). Teaching about gay and lesbian sexual and affectional orientation using explicit films to reduce homophobia. *Journal of Humanistic Education and Development, 28,* 18–34.

Wilcox, M. M. (2003). Innovation in exile: Religion and spirituality in lesbian, gay, bisexual and transgender communities. In D. W. Machacek & M. M. Wilcox (Eds.), *Sexuality and the world's religions* (pp. 323–357). Santa Barbara, CA: ABC-CLIO.

Yates, C. (2013). Evidence-based practice: The components, history and process. *Counseling Outcome Research and Evaluation, 4,* 41–54. doi:10.1177/2150137812472193

Section III

SPECIALIZED POPULATIONS

• • •

Although the queer community is often aggregated into one population, it actually consists of multiple identities that are incredibly varied in their counseling needs. Understanding these different identities, as well as how intersectionality impacts each population, is incredibly important for counselors. This section includes chapters addressing lesbian, gay male, bisexual, pansexual, polysexual, transgender, queer and genderqueer, questioning, intersex, asexual, and two-spirited persons. The unique differences for each specific population, including prevalence and identity development, relationships, experiences of bias, physical and mental health challenges, and appropriate counseling skills and techniques, are presented.

Chapter 11

Counseling Lesbian Clients

Cindy Anderton and Lindsay Woodbridge

*Growing up, I felt there was something about me that truly
set me apart from other kids. But I didn't have a grasp of what it was. I
had a few fleeting crushes on girls, then, a full-blown crush.
Inside, they felt right and normal. But at the same time,
I didn't have any way to process those feelings because
I didn't know any gay people or know that I knew them.
I felt that I would risk something if I expressed my feelings.
Then I started playing on my college rugby team—which had
some lesbian players—and for the first time I saw women being
openly affectionate to each other. It was like being dropped into
what was originally a foreign country but, once there,
I realized it was my country of origin. I thought,
Wow, the feelings I've been having are normal.
It is okay to be who I am.*

—Candace Gingrich

• • •

Awareness of Attitudes and Beliefs Self-Check

1. Close your eyes and picture someone who is a lesbian. What do you see? How are your biases and stereotypes present in your image?
2. What people do you know who are out as lesbian, including celebrities? What lesbian characters have you seen in movies or on television? How are they usually represented?
3. What messages have you received regarding femininity in your family of origin? What are the typical expectations of a feminine gender role in your family? How are these different from mainstream American culture?

Case Study[1]

Maggie is a 49-year-old single mother and White female who self-identifies as lesbian. Maggie grew up as a "tomboy" in a family with four sisters who were very feminine and "matched what the cultural expectations were of a female" in The Church of Jesus Christ of Latter-Day Saints. She recalls a specific time talking to a friend on the phone late at night that resulted in her mother angrily confronting her and asking her if she were gay. At the time, Maggie denied it. She further states, "I knew that it would create real problems in my family. I knew that my parents would be angry. That at school and in my life I would be cut-off actually . . . from friends, and peers, and my family." It was not until Maggie was approximately 14 and she began playing organized sports that she first heard "rumors of things related to being gay going around on the team" and at the same time heard negative comments that being gay was "terrible and wrong." In high school, Maggie did not date very much because she felt awkward and uncomfortable and did not know "how to relate to" or "connect with the guys" she was dating. She states, "Mentally I had learned the process of dating, but emotionally there was no connection." She eventually became engaged (to a man) and got married, as there were religious expectations "of getting married and having kids and living happily ever after." At the time, she was very tied to her religion, and she says, "Doing what was right was paramount." Maggie states that while she was married she was occasionally attracted to women and that she was "actually more aware of it . . . but [her] fidelity to her husband was absolute," and it was during this time that she "actually became quite anti-gay." She made anti-gay statements about people and believes it was completely out of fear of her own feelings. Maggie divorced and continued to date men. One night when she was on a date with a male, she said to herself, "I cannot do this again. I can't pretend to be able to be here in this relationship with men. I can't do it." She had decided that she was going to be alone and celibate for the rest of her life because the "physical, sexuality stuff was way too complicated and confusing" for her. After her divorce, Maggie came into contact with and began experiencing strong feelings for a friend who had come back into her life. It was during this time that Maggie was finally able to say to her therapist, "I'm gay." However, when her therapist mentioned her being a lesbian, Maggie says, "My whole body just shut down." She could talk "about loving this person and that was the most [she] could acknowledge because even then identifying [herself] with the term *lesbian* was still not possible." Maggie states that the most difficult thing for her has been coming out to her family. She states that dealing with her family's reaction "was and still is my greatest concern in relation to being gay." Two of her siblings continue to be open and understanding toward her, but the rest "mostly pretend that [she] doesn't exist right now." One brother has cut all ties with her; they do not talk at all. Another sister refuses to allow her daughter to go to Maggie's house. Maggie's relationship with her parents continues to be "friendly" but stays "guarded on their side as well" as hers.

• • •

[1]The following narrative, a specific case study, was chosen from previous research (Anderton, 2010) with specific demographic information updated and/or changed (to preserve anonymity), with actual quotes interspersed throughout the narrative.

Awareness of Differences

To date, the U.S. Census has never included a question regarding affectional orientation. Estimating the actual percentage of lesbians living in the United States is difficult for many of the following reasons: (a) Lesbians, like other "sexual minorities," may be reluctant to self-identify because of fears of discrimination and stigmatization (Waterman & Voss, 2015), (b) most studies trying to determine the population of lesbians living in the United States have not utilized large population-based samples (Black, Gates, Sanders, & Taylor, 2000; Savin-Williams, 2006), (c) researchers have varied methods for defining and measuring affectional orientation (e.g., sexual behaviors, emotional/sexual attractions, or self-identification; Black et al., 2000; Savin-Williams, 2006; Worthington, 2004), and (d) researchers who want to do research with "sexual minorities" struggle to find funding sources (Coulter, Kenst, Bowen, & Scout, 2014). The way in which researchers choose to define and measure affectional orientation has been shown to impact estimations of the rates or percentages of "sexual minorities" in the general population (Black et al., 2000; Savin-Williams, 2006). Research that uses behavioral estimates to identify affectional minority populations tends to produce higher population rates of "sexual minorities." Self-identification estimates tend to produce lower percentages, and research using emotional/sexual attraction tends to produce percentages somewhere in between (Savin-Williams, 2006).

Black et al. (2000) completed a large population-based study using samples drawn from the General Social Survey, the National Health and Social Life Survey, and the 1990 U.S. Census. Findings indicated that 3.5% of women indicated that they had sex with at least one woman since the age of 18, whereas 1.4% had engaged exclusively in same-sex sexual intimacy the preceding year, with only 0.6% of women self-identifying as lesbian. Taking into consideration the fact that some participants might not have indicated sexual behaviors or self-identified as lesbian, the findings from this study appear to indicate a U.S. lesbian population of approximately 1% to 3%.

Lesbian Identity Development

As discussed in Chapter 6, McCarn and Fassinger (1996) integrated previous models on racial/ethnic identity, gender identity, and gay and lesbian identity in the development of a model of lesbian identity formation. It has been argued that McCarn and Fassinger's model is "the most advanced developmental model of lesbian identity development" (Worthington, Navaro, Savoy, & Hampton, 2008, p. 23). The model has been validated empirically (Fassinger & McCarn, 1997; McCarn, 1991; Mohr & Fassinger, 2000), with results indicating "its usefulness in describing the experiences of diverse lesbians, as expected" (McCarn & Fassinger, 1996, pp. 530–531). It is for these reasons that we believe that McCarn and Fassinger's model of lesbian identity development is the best model for understanding specific lesbian identity. However, it is important to emphasize that this model of lesbian identity development might only be applicable to women whose process of forming a non-heterosexual identity has been problematic for one reason or another. This specific model of identity development might not be representative of the identity development process of women who do not struggle in forming a non-heterosexual identity.

As discussed in Chapter 6, McCarn and Fassinger's (1996) model sees identity development as a progression through phases that are continuous and circular, with each new relationship raising issues regarding sexuality and each new situation requiring renewed awareness of minority group status and oppression. McCarn and Fassinger's model theorizes a dual process (although not necessarily a simultaneous process) that involves a woman's personal sexual identity developing and the experiences in this process possibly causing a shift in her self-defined group membership. As a woman comes to identify more and more as a lesbian, her self-identified reference group might shift from a heterosexual reference group (family, friends, church, ethnic culture) to a reference group that consists of the queer community. However, some women coming into contact with the lesbian, gay, bisexual, transgender, queer, questioning, intersex, asexual, ally, pansexual/polysexual, and two-spirited (LGBTQI+) communities might also have negative experiences and, as a result, these women might distance themselves from and even express hostility toward LGBTQI+ persons. These women might argue that they should be seen as unique individuals rather than individuals of a group defined on the basis of affectional orientation and frame their sexual identity on a personal basis. Thus, according to McCarn and Fassinger, lesbian identity formation follows two parallel processes or branches. This model could explain why women who experience romantic attraction for women and engage in sexual behaviors with other women might dis-identify with a specific term or label and/or dis-identify with the lesbian community.

Individual Sexual Identity Development
In McCarn and Fassinger's (1996) model, the process of individual sexual identity development involves four phases: awareness, exploration, deepening and commitment, and internalization/synthesis. The *awareness* phase involves a general feeling of being different or a developing awareness that one's feelings or desires are different from both the heterosexual norm and one's assumed heterosexual self. In the *exploration* phase, a person will examine the questions that surfaced in the first phase and will experience strong relationships with women or feelings for them, but these experiences do not necessarily involve an exploration of sexual behaviors. In the *deepening and commitment* phase, previous explorations provide the basis for a deeper understanding of self, and the emerging lesbian will begin to identify her desires for other women as residing within her. Some women in this phase might see relationships with women as only one option (bisexual), and others could opt in favor of men as sexual partners. However, it is in the deepening and commitment phase that a woman will become more committed to her self-fulfillment as a sexual being, and she will recognize that her forms of intimacy imply certain things about her identity. This commitment to self-fulfillment will intersect with previously held assumptions regarding her heterosexuality and will most likely have an effect on her group identity processes.

In the final phase, *internalization/synthesis*, a woman becomes more accepting of herself and her desires for other women. She is likely to have resolved most if not all of the difficult decisions regarding her affectional orientation, and she might show an unwillingness to change her lesbian identity. Once she has formed a commitment to her lesbian identity, she must begin facing decisions about what to do regarding her public identity. At the very least, she will have to wrestle with what it means to be a lesbian in current society and must make choices regarding when, where, and how to be open about her affectional orientation (McCarn & Fassinger, 1996).

McCarn and Fassinger (1996) argued that it is possible for a woman, closeted in various environments (work, family, other reference groups of importance), to be just as integrated in terms of her sexual identity as a woman who is out of the closet as long as this choice has been acknowledged and addressed. However, a woman cannot be fully integrated without answering some of the questions related to the group membership branch of the model.

Group Membership Identity Development
The separate but parallel branch of group membership identity development also has four phases: awareness, exploration, deepening and commitment, and internalization/synthesis, as described previously. Group membership tasks involve addressing society's atti-

tudes toward one's own same-sex desires, the labeling of self, and one's identification as a member of a minority reference group. What becomes important to consider when using this model are the experiences of women of color who identify as non-heterosexual. In fact, it has been noted that lesbians of color can experience conflict between their racial/ethnic identity and affectional orientation identity (Morales, 1989; Sarno, Mohr, Jackson, & Fassinger, 2015). Resolving conflict between one's racial/ethnic identity and affectional orientation identity was seen by Morales (1989) as an important step in the greater identity integration process (Sarno et al., 2015). Morales introduced the construct of *conflict of allegiances* to define a state in which an ethnic identity and LGB identity cause anxiety and present an obstacle to identity integration. The lesbian client may develop anxiety surrounding the conflicts these two identities may cause in each community (Morales, 1989).

Thus, women of color who are in the process of identifying as non-heterosexual are working through feelings and attitudes toward themselves, other gays and lesbians, heterosexuals, and their own racial/ethnic minority culture. Consider a woman experiencing conflict of allegiances with her religious culture and it quickly becomes evident that this intersectionality of aspects of identity could cause a person to experience multiple layers of conflict and cause reassessment of her feelings and attitudes toward multiple groups.

It is also important to note that women who come into contact with the queer community might not have positive experiences and might not experience a sense of belonging because of other salient aspects of their identity (e.g., ethnic/racial identity, disability, and/or religious/spiritual identity). During the coming out process, a woman is making decisions about what her affectional orientation identity means for her both in heterosexual society and in other minority groups of which she is a member (e.g., racial/ethnic culture, religious/spiritual culture). Women from other minority identity statuses could essentially both reject heterosexual culture and reject the LGBTQI+ community, which has been viewed as predominantly representative of White, middle-class persons (Chan, 1989; Han, 2007; Harper, Jernewall, & Zea, 2004; Loiacano, 1989; Logie & Rwigema, 2014).

It has been identified in the literature that Black lesbians feel pressure to conform to heterosexual norms in which one woman plays the more masculine role and her partner frequently plays the more feminine role (Wilson, 2009). In this case, one could argue that these women are not totally rejecting heterosexual culture. They are, however, committing to a lesbian identity (or at the very least a non-heterosexual identity) and operating in a lesbian culture (situated in an ethnic culture) with more rigid norms surrounding gender roles. In addition, a woman whose racial/ethnic identity is the most salient aspect of her identity might dis-identify with certain terms (accepted in a dominant White gay community) and identify with other labels being used by lesbians who identify as such in her own racial/ethnic culture. She might also, if the option is available, prefer to interact with LGBTQI+ persons in her ethnic/racial culture (this also could be seen as part of the deepening and commitment phase). If this option is not available, she might only be out to herself (and partner) and might try to "pass" for heterosexual in her ethnic/racial culture. Similarly, a woman whose religious/spiritual identity is the most salient aspect of self might also dis-identify with certain labels (only out to herself or a select few) and feel a sense of belonging and/or acceptance in her religious/spiritual community rather than in the LGBTQI+ communities.

Lesbian Relationships

Research has shown that romantic relationships between same-sex partners are similar in many ways to heterosexual relationships. Same-sex couples and heterosexual couples report similar levels of affective expression, intimacy, conflict, relationship commitment, and overall satisfaction (Kurdek, 1998, 2001, 2004). In addition, various predictors of relationship satisfaction (e.g., agreeableness) are also similar between same-sex couples and heterosexual couples in regard to relationship quality and arguments (Malouff, Thorsteinsson, Schutte, Bhullar, & Rooke, 2010).

More specifically, recent research has revealed that lesbians are similar to their heterosexual counterparts in terms of relationship satisfaction, commitment, passion (Cusack, Hughes, & Cook, 2012), and work–family conflict (Brashier, Hughes, & Cook, 2013). Furthermore, for lesbians, length of relationship is a positive predictor of relationship satisfaction (Cusack et al., 2012). Lesbians also report less gender-role-differentiated behavior than heterosexual couples (Cardell, Finn, & Marecek, 1981) and more equity in their relationships in terms of sharing household responsibilities (Littlefield, Lim, Canada, & Jennings, 2000); balances in power have been positively correlated with relationship satisfaction (Peplau, Padesky, & Hamilton, 1982).

From the research literature and personal narratives in lesbian studies, it is clear that there are various forms of lesbian communities both within and outside the United States that differ according to race, ethnicity, and geographic region, among other variables (Clarke & Spence, 2013; Enteen, 2007; Hammidi & Kaiser, 1999; Kowalska, 2011; Lapovsky-Kennedy & Davis, 1993; Maree, 2007; Moore, 2006; B. Morris, 2005; Rabin & Slater, 2005; Vanita, 2007; Wilson, 2009). Regardless of the specific lesbian community, it has been shown that a core feature of these groups is expression of gender through one's appearance and dress (Clarke & Spence, 2013; Moore, 2006; Welker, 2010; Wilson, 2009). Appearance and the way a lesbian may serve a function can indicate expectations regarding personal identity, social interactions, and romantic exchanges (Levitt, Puckett, Ippolito, & Horne, 2012; Moore, 2006; Wilson, 2009). In fact, lesbian women have reported feeling pressured to change their dress and appearance in order to conform to expectations in lesbian communities (Clarke & Spence, 2013; Huxley, Clarke, & Halliwell, 2013; Moore, 2006; Welker, 2010; Wilson, 2009). In the past decade much has been written on changes related to lesbian gender appearance, labels and terms that accompany lesbian gender appearance, and the historical and political transformations that correspond to these changes (Levitt et al., 2012).

In the 1940s and 1950s, lesbian gender appearance was seen as binary and synonymous with traditional masculine and feminine gender appearance (i.e., butch or femme). *Butch* is a term used to describe a lesbian who takes on stereotypical masculine roles, is masculine in appearance (e.g., in clothing and hair) and mannerisms, and rejects cultural norms surrounding femininity (Rothblum, 2010; Walker, Golub, Bimbi, & Parsons, 2012). The identity of butch has several iterations, including *stone butch* and *soft butch* (Walker et al., 2012), as well as cultural interpretations. In African American culture this identity is usually referred to as *stud, hard stud, soft stud, dom,* and *aggressive* (Moore, 2006; Wilson, 2009). Among Chinese lesbians this identity is known as *T* (Zheng & Zheng, 2011). In Thai culture, this presentation is known as *tom;* it has also been used as a synonym for *lesbian* (Enteen, 2007).

A *femme* is a lesbian who stereotypically acts and dresses more feminine (Levitt, Gerrish, & Hiestand, 2003). This term is also used in African American lesbian communities to represent women who identify as feminine in appearance, behavior, erotic expression, and relationship roles (Moore, 2006; Wilson, 2009). Other iterations of this identity include *lipstick* (Wilson, 2009). In African American cultures, the terms for a feminine identity include *ultra-femme* (Wilson, 2009). Chinese lesbians may refer to this identity as *P* (Zheng & Zheng, 2011). In Thailand, the term used to describe women who would be interested in the tom presentation is *dees* (Enteen, 2007).

However, at that time, it was argued that lesbian gender identities transcended traditional gender roles through butch women (through masculine dress and appearance) stretching the image of what it meant to be a female. Similarly, femme women were thought to be strong female activists rather than viewed as passive or weak because they oriented their affectional orientation toward butch women instead of men. This led to femme invisibility as well as femme-based discrimination among lesbian women; women presenting as femme may be seen, even today, as compromising feminist ideals or giving in to masculine desires of female presentation (Speciale, Gess, & Speedlin, 2015).

In the 1960s and 1970s, the feminist movement was hitting full stride, and not only were butch–femme lesbians accused of perpetuating gender stereotypes, but more specifically butch women were accused of benefitting from male privilege (Levitt et al., 2012). At this time, butch and femme lesbians either withdrew from the lesbian community or adopted a more androgynous look in order to conform to new expectations regarding lesbian gender appearance. In the 1980s, lesbians in the United States reclaimed butch–femme gender identities, and this remained consistent into the 1990s. Over time, lesbian gender appearance (as well as terminology) in some lesbian communities has moved away from the binary of masculine and feminine to being viewed on a continuum or within a sphere (Spade, 2008), and this has allowed for various lesbian gender identities to emerge (e.g., butch, soft butch, stud, femme, high femme, boi, sporty femme, stem).

It is important to note that the term *lesbian* and butch–femme gender identities are viewed as Western concepts (Enteen, 2007; Kowalska, 2011; Welker, 2010). In the United States, the butch–femme identity as well as identities that exist in between are viewed as constructs belonging to White (European) lesbian communities (Adams & Phillips, 2009; Moore, 2006; Walters, Campbell, Simoni, Ronquillo, & Byuhan, 2006; Wilson, 2009), and though it might seem that non-White lesbians might be using different terms to describe butch–femme lesbian identities, the meanings they place on these terms differ.

Many peoples indigenous to the Americas use the term *two-spirit* to capture gender and affectional orientation differences in LGBTQI+ persons (Adams & Phillips, 2009; Garrett & Barret, 2003; Walters et al., 2006). More specifically, this term has been used to refer to Native people who identify as lesbian, gay, or transgender and adhere to "some or all of the parameters of alternate gender roles (may include specific social roles, spiritual roles, and same-sex relationships) specific to their tribe or panethnicity" (Adams & Phillips, 2009, p. 960). This identity is discussed in much more detail in Chapter 19. *Queer* is a term that younger generations of women both in the United States (Russell, Clarke, & Clary, 2009) and outside (Kowalska, 2011; Welker, 2010) are reclaiming; many might prefer to use this term rather than the term *lesbian*, as is fully explored in Chapter 15. African American and Latino communities use the term *gender blender* to refer to a person who has an androgynous look with aspects of both masculine and feminine clothing (Moore, 2006); this person is known as an *aggressive femme* in Caucasian communities (Wilson, 2009). In Thai culture, *anjaree* is used to describe women who are nonconformist (Enteen, 2007).

When working with lesbians, counselors need to be knowledgeable about the various terms or labels that lesbians might use to self-identify. Knowing the language that lesbians use to identify their sexual identity will facilitate a safe and comfortable environment and facilitate the building of the therapeutic alliance (Garofalo & Bush, 2008). Labels or terms used to refer to lesbians have traditionally and historically been linked to certain mannerisms, behaviors (including sexual behaviors and preferences), and clothing styles and/or appearance (e.g., masculine and/or feminine). Specific terms used by lesbians can vary widely based on age (Russell et al., 2009), sexual behavior, gender appearance, ethnicity, socioeconomic class, geographic location, and religious background and can result from relationships between these same factors. Some women might choose to dis-identify with any label and have been referred to in the literature as "unlabeled women" (Brooks & Quina, 2009; Diamond, 2005) or "post-gay" (Coleman-Fountain, 2014). Counselors working with lesbians (or women who are romantically and sexually attracted to women) need to take the time to understand how each client prefers to self-identify or dis-identify with a certain label or term.

Terms that were once used by lesbians in past generations (e.g., *kiki,* a now derogatory term that several decades ago meant a lesbian who was not butch or femme) have fallen out of favor and new terms are being created by younger generations. Thus, it is important to understand that any classification of terms or labels related to affectional orientation identity exists in a social, historical, political, and cultural context (Hammack, Thompson, & Pilecki, 2009; Weston, 2009).

Knowledge of Issues and Problems

Experiences of Bias

Intersectionality

When considering the various identities of lesbians, it is important to understand the framework of intersectionality. Bowleg (2012) defined *intersectionality* as a way of understanding how an individual's multiple identities (sexual identity, age, race, gender, disability status, and others) "intersect at the micro level of individual experience to reflect interlocking systems of privilege and oppression . . . at the macro social-structural level" (p. 1267). Although it is not feasible to address all permutations of intersecting identities in this text, this section explores some ways in which lesbians' sexual identities intersect with other identities in ways that have real impacts on the women's lives.

Age

Age is an underrepresented area of research in lesbian studies (Westwood, 2013). Westwood (2013) hypothesized that one reason for the dearth of research is that older lesbians are "not only a hidden population but also a population in hiding" (p. 383). Accordingly, disclosure and invisibility are two issues that arise at the intersection of age and sexual identity. Other issues include loneliness, discomfort using social services, and bereavement. The research indicates that older lesbian women face the same issues as all elders, with additional complications related to being "sexual minorities" in a heteronormative culture. For example, one study revealed substantial concerns about a perceived lack of senior housing that is both affordable and affirmative of all facets of lesbian elders' identities (Gardner, de Vries, & Mockus, 2014).

In their survey of 101 lesbian women living in Riverside County, California, 80% of whom were older than age 50, Gardner et al. (2014) found that 29% of respondents expressed fear of openly disclosing their sexual identity in the larger community compared to only 18.5% of gay men. The researchers concluded that heterosexism in communities, including in social service agencies, discourages some older lesbians from disclosing their sexual identity and thus can lead to invisibility for LGBTQI+ seniors (Gardner et al., 2014). Wilkens (2015), who conducted qualitative research with 10 older lesbian women in the United Kingdom, reached a similar conclusion, finding that although "many participants initially asserted that they were 'out' . . ., reflection on this topic often revealed nuances and degrees of concealment" (p. 92).

Issues with disclosure can result in an increased sense of isolation and loneliness. Wilkens (2015) described her participants' reality of feeling "silent and unseen" in their communities (p. 92). This isolation extends to the media, in which there is a critical lack of portrayals of older LGBTQI+ individuals (Gardner et al., 2014). Thus, older lesbians are doubly invisible, rendered unseen as a result of both their age and their sexual identity. As a result of this invisibility, it becomes more difficult for older lesbians to find one another and establish crucial structures for social support (Jenkins, Edmundson, Averett, & Yoon, 2014).

136

The loss of a partner is an important contributor to older lesbians' sense of isolation. In addition to losing a partner, older lesbians may also face a loss of support from their partners' families as well as other social groups (Wilkens, 2015). Although partner loss is an issue for many older adults, lesbians' bereavement experiences can be complicated when those around them do not recognize their grief as legitimate. This phenomenon, known as *disenfranchised grief*, can deeply complicate the grieving process (Jenkins et al., 2014). A lack of recognition for the legitimacy of the partnership, and thus the legitimacy of the loss, can have significant financial and legal impacts. Lesbians living in jurisdictions that do not recognize same-sex partnerships can lose access to their deceased partners' financial assets, be denied their partners' Social Security benefits and/or pension, and be forced to pay inheritance tax on any assets owned jointly (Jenkins et al., 2014).

Race

Like older lesbians, there is also a paucity of research on the lives and experiences of lesbian women of color (Hill, Woodson, Ferguson, & Parks, 2012). Again, this underrepresentation in the literature reflects invisibility in society at large. Qualitative research with 16 lesbian or bisexual women of color in Toronto revealed experiences of exclusion both in the queer community (for being a person of color) and in racially bound communities (for being an affectional minority; Logie & Rwigema, 2014). Woody (2015) described one example of the stigma that lesbian women face in African American communities: She wrote that in these communities, the term *lesbian* is "perceived as a *bad* word—a label that disenfranchises Black women" (p. 53, emphasis in the original). Research participants identified numerous negative impacts of their intersecting minority identities, ranging from internalized stigma, to less access to services, to daily experiences of stigma and fear (Logie & Rwigema, 2014).

Discomfort in seeking out social services can be a significant issue for these women. For example, in a 2014 qualitative study of 16 lesbian or bisexual Black women who had been the victims of intimate partner violence, participants identified a number of societal and institutional barriers that prevented them from seeking help (Simpson & Helfrich, 2014). They reported that "homophobia was the most pervasive and powerful obstacle to their safety" (p. 452). This homophobia was present in the very institutions that victims of intimate partner violence are most likely to seek out, including hospitals and mental health centers (Simpson & Helfrich, 2014). It is interesting that these reports of homophobia as the biggest barrier contradict the findings of other studies that indicate that the challenges of racism are more constant and detrimental than the challenges of homophobia (Logie & Rwigema, 2014; Woody, 2015).

Intersections Among Three or More Identities

The limited studies that have addressed intersections of three or more identities reveal some findings aligned with those presented previously. For example, participants in Woody's (2015) study of 15 Black lesbian elders described experiences of social isolation. This finding is also apparent in Witten's (2015) study of older transgender lesbians, who are transwomen who bond romantically with women. The studies also illustrate how intersections of three or more minority identities may result in compounded isolation and fear. For instance, the study of older transgender lesbians revealed deep concerns about lack of access to high-quality, affirmative health care; these concerns reflect "fear around the normative consequences of aging" that is compounded by "the endemic negativity against and fear of healthcare providers" in the transgender community (Witten, 2015, p. 85). Thus, in evaluating the social and emotional concerns of lesbians, it is imperative for mental health professionals to recognize the multiple dimensions of clients' identities and to consider how these identities may intersect in clients' lives.

Social Aggression

Lesbians are at risk for social aggression as a function of their sexual identity; as seen in the previous section, intersecting identities serve to increase this risk. This section explores two dimensions of social aggression that may impact lesbian clients: bullying and intimate partner violence.

Bullying

A California study of 245 LGBT individuals ages 21 to 25 years revealed that, for adolescents, "the simple, daily routine of going to school is fraught with harassment and victimization" (Russell, Ryan, Toomey, Diaz, & Sanchez, 2011, p. 228). Although the study indicated that lesbians and bisexual women faced less victimization than males or transgender individuals, experiences of bullying were still pervasive. The study noted that bullying resulted in negative impacts across various measures of mental and physical well-being. The distressing thing is that it appears that these negative impacts of bullying in school persist beyond adolescence (Greene, Britton, & Fitts, 2014; Russell et al., 2011). A 2014 study of more than 100 adult lesbian women revealed that victimization through bullying as an adolescent was predictive of future victimization as an adult. Findings further indicated that adult lesbians who had been bullied as adolescents were more likely to experience social anxiety and to engage in maladaptive coping strategies such as withdrawal and avoidance (Greene et al., 2014).

Intimate Partner Violence

Lesbian women and gay men are at equal or greater risk than heterosexuals for experiencing intimate partner violence and sexual violence (Breiding et al., 2014). The researchers estimated that 43.8% of lesbian women have experienced rape, physical violence, and/or stalking at some point in their lifetime compared to 35% of heterosexual women; the rate for bisexual women was even greater—a staggering 61.1%. A statistic that is particularly relevant to counselors is that one third of lesbian women who were raped, physically abused, or stalked by a partner reported negative impacts, such as missing work or school because of symptoms of posttraumatic stress disorder.

Physical Issues and Health Care

Barriers to Equitable Health Care

Lesbians encounter substantial barriers to finding quality health care free from discrimination (M. J. Johnson & Nemeth, 2014). More specifically, these barriers include lack of health insurance (Cochran, Ackerman, Mays, & Ross, 2004; Herrick, Matthews, & Garofalo, 2010; Tracy, Schluterman, & Greenberg, 2013), lack of a physician or physician referral (Tracy et al., 2013), discrimination or stigma due to their affectional minority status, and lack of access to culturally sensitive health care and health-related education materials (M. J. Johnson & Nemeth, 2014). When lesbians seek out health care, they often encounter health care professionals who are insensitive, are discriminatory, and lack education regarding the health care needs of lesbians (Clift & Kirby, 2012). Lesbians also report commonly receiving treatment in health care systems that is discriminatory and culturally insensitive (M. J. Johnson & Nemeth, 2014).

It is no wonder that many lesbians report underutilization of health care services. More specifically, it has been found that lesbians are less likely than heterosexual women to seek out gynecological care (Agenor, Krieger, Austin, Haneuse, & Gottlieb, 2014; Waterman & Voss, 2015). Some of the cited reasons for lack of gynecological care are a focus on contraception and pregnancy, negative health care experiences, and misinformation regarding preventive health care needs (Waterman & Voss, 2015). A specific barrier to the utilization of routine gynecological care is the fact that health care professionals have been misinformed about the likelihood of lesbians contracting human papillomavirus (Waterman & Voss, 2015). Unfortunately, health care professionals have passed on this misinformation, and lesbians have reported believing that they are at less risk than heterosexual women for contracting human papillomavirus (Curmi, Peters, & Salamonson, 2014).

Self-disclosure of affectional orientation and provider attributes have been identified as positive factors in lesbian health care experiences (M. J. Johnson & Nemeth, 2014). Lesbians have reported that it is important to be able to disclose their affectional orientation status and that a pivotal point in the health care experience is what occurs after this disclosure (M. J. Johnson & Nemeth, 2014). Factors associated with a positive health care experience following disclosure of affectional orientation were (a) the degree to which health care professionals had specific knowledge regarding same-sex relationships, sexuality, and health care concerns specific to lesbians; (b) health care professionals' ability to communicate using culturally sensitive terms; and (c) providers' conveyance of a caring and accepting attitude. Furthermore, it was noted that when negative experiences with health care professionals occurred, it delayed health care visits and caused lesbians to disguise their affectional orientation during subsequent health care visits.

The Health Needs of Lesbians

Population-based studies have documented important health differences between LGB adults and heterosexuals that include higher risks of mental health issues, higher rates of smoking and excessive drinking, and less physical activity (Conron, Mimiaga, & Landers, 2010; Dilley, Simmons, Boysun, Pizacani, & Stark, 2010; Fredriksen-Goldsen, Kim, Barkan, Muraco, & Hoy-Ellis, 2013). More specifically, it has been shown that lesbians have higher rates of smoking and excessive drinking (Dilley et al., 2010; Farmer, Jabson, Bucholz, & Bowen, 2013; Fredriksen-Goldsen et al., 2013; Marshal et al., 2012), obesity (Boehmer, Bowen, & Bauer, 2007; Boehmer et al., 2011; Dilley et al., 2010; Fredriksen-Goldsen et al., 2013; Jun et al., 2012), drug use (K. Kerr, Ding, Burke, & Ott-Walter, 2015), and cardiovascular disease (Farmer et al., 2013; Fredriksen-Goldsen et al., 2013) and are at increased risk for cervical cancer (Waterman & Voss, 2015). This increased risk of cervical cancer is due to a combination of risk factors (smoking, drinking, obesity) and underutilization of routine gynecological care (Agenor et al., 2014; Waterman & Voss, 2015).

There is some evidence that lesbians could be more at risk for developing breast cancer than their heterosexual counterparts (Meads & Moore, 2013). In their comprehensive review of the literature, Meads and Moore (2013) examined three different types of studies on breast cancer comparisons between lesbians and heterosexual women: prevalence and risk rate studies, risk factor model studies, and studies examining risk factors associated with the development of breast cancer. Despite mixed results and problems with research design and sampling, Meads and Moore concluded that there is uncertainty regarding whether there is a higher incidence of breast cancer in lesbians; however, "the balance of the evidence is starting to suggest a higher incidence" (para. 1). However, these conclusions are tentative given the lack of large population-based studies that include affectional orientation in routine statistics (Meads & Moore, 2013).

In the scarce body of research on lesbian breast cancer survivors are a handful of studies that have examined differences or similarities in quality of life, coping and resilience, sexual functioning, and sexual frequency between affectional minority women and heterosexual women (Arena et al., 2006; Fobair et al., 2001; Jabson, Donatelle, & Bowen, 2011; Meyer, 2003). Three studies (Boehmer & White, 2012; Jabson et al., 2011; Meyer, 2003) reported findings suggesting that as a result of dealing with ongoing minority stress, lesbians may develop resilience associated with positive effects on health and quality of life. In fact, a growing body of research (Arena et al., 2006; Boehmer, Glickman, Winter, & Clark, 2015; Fobair et al., 2001) indicates that affectional minority women who have had breast cancer use more adaptive coping skills (e.g., less denial, less cognitive avoidance, more expressions of anger, more positive reframing) and report similar levels of sexual frequency and sexual satisfaction as heterosexual women with less disruption in their sexual relationships.

Finally, one study discovered that lesbians report higher rates of childhood and adulthood victimization (Andersen, Hughes, Zou, & Wilsnack, 2014). This finding is consistent with previous research that found that lesbians have a higher likelihood of victimization because of their affectional minority status in a heterosexist society (Andersen & Blosnich, 2013; Wilsnack, Kristjanson, Hughes, & Bensen, 2012). These lifetime victimization rates are also associated with physical health problems.

Potential Mental Health Challenges

A review of the literature reveals that lesbian, gay, and bisexual individuals are at greater risk for mental disorders, suicidal ideation, and deliberate self-harm compared to their heterosexual counterparts (King et al., 2008; Silenzio, Pena, Duberstein, Cerel, & Knox, 2007). More specifically, lesbians are more likely to report depression and/or anxiety (Burgess, Lee, Tran, & Van Ryn, 2008; D. L. Kerr, Santurri, & Peters, 2013; King et al., 2008), self-harm (D. L. Kerr et al., 2013), suicidal ideation, and suicide attempts (Conron et al., 2010; D. L. Kerr et al., 2013).

Research has shown a connection between mental health issues (e.g., depression, anxiety, and substance abuse) and stigma, discrimination, internalized homophobia (Newcomb & Mustanski, 2010), and oppression dynamics related to a person's affectional minority orientation (Lewis, Milletich, Mason, & Verlega, 2014). A recent study found that lesbians' expectations of rejection and discrimination influenced the concealment of their affectional orientation identity (Lewis et al., 2014). This in turn impacted their ability to talk with friends and family about their affectional orientation, leading to increased brooding and rumination and ultimately increased psychological distress (Lewis et al., 2014).

Counseling Skills and Techniques

At this time, there is a marked lack of empirically based interventions for counselors working with lesbian clients. This lack of knowledge is well documented in the literature. For example, Borden, Lopresto, Sherman, and Lyons (2010) wrote that "although counselors are certainly beginning to incorporate relevant practical and ethical guidelines into their counseling experiences with LGB clients, research on evidence-based practices . . . with this population [is] lacking" (p. 67). This lack of empirical knowledge is particularly striking when one considers that lesbian and other affectional minority individuals make use of counseling at higher rates than those who identify as heterosexual (Borden et al., 2010; S. D. Johnson, 2012).

A study of the use of counselor self-disclosure in working with LGB college students indicates the potential usefulness of this intervention. Working from the previously documented finding that counselor self-disclosure can positively impact the therapeutic relationship, Borden and colleagues (2010) designed a study measuring 275 lesbian, gay, and bisexual college students' ratings of a counselor's expertness, attractiveness, and trustworthiness after subjects read written vignettes portraying a client–counselor interaction with differing levels of therapist self-disclosure. Their findings indicated that participants were more likely to rate highly those counselors who engaged in disclosure of both personal and professional information. The researchers concluded that "since helpful therapeutic interactions can produce reported improvement in psychosocial functioning, these findings may have beneficial implications for using careful, relevant self-disclosure with LGB clients" (p. 64). There are a number of possible limitations to these findings. Because the participant sample was relatively homogeneous (university students) the generalizability of the findings to other populations is unclear. The sample was also nonclinical: Researchers recruited participants through LGBTQI+ campus organizations, and current participation in counseling was not an inclusion criterion. In addition, although it is known that lesbian women made up 30% of the sample, it is unclear whether and how their responses may have varied from those of the sample population as a whole.

Despite the lack of empirically validated interventions, the recent literature includes a number of articles presenting treatment approaches that, their authors argue, offer useful interventions for counseling lesbians. Examples include feminist multicultural counseling (Hagen, Arczynski, Morrow, & Hawxhurst, 2011), acceptance and commitment therapy (Stitt, 2014), and narrative therapy (Galarza, 2013).

Some authors have put forth comprehensive, though so far not empirically validated, therapeutic models for addressing specific issues LGBTQI+ clients face. For example, Bozard and Sanders (2011) authored the GRACE (goals, renewal, action, connection, and empowerment) model for integrating sexual and religious identities, presented in Chapter 23. M. Pope's (2011) career counseling with underserved populations model offers information on the specialized career needs of lesbians and other affectional minority clients and puts forth 13 keys to effective practice with these individuals. Matthews and Salazar (2012) published a suggested framework for counselors working with adolescents during their coming out process. The framework emphasizes a holistic approach and includes specific interventions such as facilitating the exploration of fears associated with coming out, dispelling myths, and being an advocate for clients in schools and other settings.

Others have offered suggestions for how to modify existing treatment approaches to better meet the needs of lesbian and other affectional minority clients. In addressing the treatment of substance use disorders in affectional minority women, Drabble and Eliason (2012) emphasized the usefulness of trauma-informed treatment, interventions focused on developing coping skills, and the provision of referrals for community organizations that provide support for affectional minority women. McNutt and Yakushko (2013) presented suggestions for counselors working with grieving lesbian and gay clients. They advised counselors to be aware of possible additional stressors for lesbian and gay individuals who have lost their partner (such as legal concerns); counselors should also be aware that such clients may have sources of support that differ from those of grieving heterosexual clients. In addition, several writers have advocated for the use of various developmental approaches in work with lesbian and other affectional minority clients, stating that such approaches offer a framework for conceptualizing clients' issues as well as a source for potential interventions. A. L. Pope, Mobley, and Myers (2010) wrote about the use of developmental constructivist theory, whereas Zubernis, Snyder, and McCoy (2011) addressed the use of Cass's and Chickering's models of development in counseling work with lesbian and gay college students.

As discussed in Section I, the term *affirmative therapy* appears frequently in the literature. However, at this point, this approach to therapy has not been fully operationalized (S. D. Johnson, 2012). There are even questions as to how to categorize affirmative therapy: S. D. Johnson (2012) identified it as a therapeutic approach, whereas Pachankis and Goldfried (2013) defined it as a stance that is compatible with many different theoretical approaches. Thus, there are varying descriptions of the approach. It is not surprising that basic counseling values such as empathy, positive regard, and emphasis on the therapeutic alliance are components of affirmative counseling (S. D. Johnson, 2012; Pachankis & Goldfried, 2013). In addition, counselors who practice from an LGBTQI+ affirmative stance pay particular attention to understanding their own feelings, biases, and attitudes toward LGBTQI+ individuals in order to achieve maximum competency (Pachankis & Goldfried, 2013).

Others have illustrated the ways in which affirmative therapy may vary from other approaches to therapy. S. D. Johnson (2012) suggested that clinicians incorporate questions about the client's coming out experience into their initial assessment. Walker and Prince (2010) emphasized the importance of counselor advocacy both on a personal level, such as by connecting lesbian and other affectional minority clients to community groups and resources, and at the institutional level. They also suggested making use of cognitive–behavioral techniques to confront internalized messages of homophobia and affirm the use of positive self-talk (Walker & Prince, 2010). Finally, Pachankis and Goldfried (2013) provided a list of issues to explore that may be particularly useful in work with LGBTQI+ clients. This list includes sexual identity development, issues related to family of origin, exploration of the client's chosen family, legal issues, and intersections among the client's multiple dimensions of identity (e.g., sexual, racial, socioeconomic, and ability status).

Non-heterosexuals who actively participate in an affectional minority community report less psychological distress than those who do not (J. Morris, Waldo, & Rothblum, 2001). This may be because a collective identity affords an individual additional resources beyond those available through a purely personal identity. Thus, in comparison with other non-heterosexuals, individuals who adopt an affectional minority identity may be better equipped to cope with minority stress. By identifying and affiliating with similarly stigmatized others, they are able to experience social environments in which they are not stigmatized. In such environments, they can more readily develop a worldview that invalidates negative stereotypes and biases while affirming positive evaluations of the group and its members. This worldview can reduce an individual's level of internalized stigma while fostering a positive collective identity. Minority communities can also provide emotional and instrumental support for dealing with stigma and teach survival skills for meeting the challenges created by sexual stigma (Ueno, 2005). Adopting a collective identity also increases the likelihood that affectional minority individuals will come out to their heterosexual family members, friends, and acquaintances. To the extent that significant others respond favorably, coming out can make additional social support available in the face of societal stigma (Hershberger & D'Augelli, 1995; Luhtanen, 2003). This discussion highlights an important limitation of research that combines all affectional minority respondents into a single non-heterosexual group. That undifferentiated category inevitably includes not only individuals with a collective LGBTQI+ identity but also those who regard their affectional orientation in purely personal terms. Indeed, two leading researchers in this area estimated that only half of the individuals who report sexual contact with a same-sex adult actually identify as lesbian, gay, or bisexual (Cochran & Mays, 2006).

Conclusion

As affectional orientation minorities, lesbians experience multiple layers of prejudice. Sexism can have a large impact on the physical and mental health of all women; however, lesbians additionally face heterosexism, heteronormativity, homophobia, and homoprejudice. If they are people of color, they additionally face racism and lack of acceptance, even in the LGBTQI+ communities. Developing a positive identity surrounding their affectional orientation, both as an individual and in a collective, will help them find increased life and relationship satisfaction. Lesbian identity and relationships have been influenced throughout time by political movements, a sense of gender differences, cultural markers, and minority stress. As a result of minority stress, lesbians can have physical and mental health problems. By using affirmative, feminist, and multicultural approaches, counselors can best help these clients work toward their counseling goals and find acceptance.

Questions for Further Discussion

1. Based on the case narrative, how would you work with Maggie if she presented to you as an adolescent during her teenage years?
2. What types of mental health challenges did Maggie experience likely as a result of being an affectional minority?
3. What are the possible reasons why Maggie at one point expressed homophobic attitudes?
4. How would you work with Maggie if she had come to you after her divorce?
5. What types of strategies might you use with Maggie if she were struggling over whether to disclose her identity to her child?

Resources

1. Visit the international website by, for, and about lesbians at http://www.lesbian.com/.
2. Read more about the *herstory* of lesbians at http://www.lesbianherstoryarchives.org/.
3. Surf the website of the National Center for Lesbian Rights at http://www.nclrights.org/.
4. Read more about advocacy and resources for lesbians of color at http://womeninthelife.com/.

References

Adams, H. L., & Phillips, L. (2009). Ethnic related variations from the Cass model of homosexual identity formation: The experiences of two-spirit, lesbian and gay Native Americans. *Journal of Homosexuality, 56*, 959–976. doi:10.1080/00918360903187895

Agenor, M., Krieger, N., Austin, S. B., Haneuse, S., & Gottlieb, B. R. (2014). Sexual orientation disparities in Papanicolaou test use among US women: The role of sexual and reproductive health services. *American Journal of Public Health, 104*(2), 68–73.

Andersen, J. P., & Blosnich, J. (2013). Disparities in adverse childhood events among sexual minority and heterosexual adults: Results from a multi-state probability based sample. *PLoS ONE, 8.* doi:10.1371/journal.pone.0054691

Andersen, J. P., Hughes, T. L., Zou, C., & Wilsnack, S. C. (2014). Lifetime victimization and physical health outcomes among lesbian and heterosexual women. *PLoS ONE, 9*(7). doi:10.1371/journal.pone.0101939

Anderton, C. (2010). *Reconciling disparate identities: A qualitative study with women in the LDS church experiencing same-sex attractions* (Doctoral dissertation). Retrieved from https://www.researchgate.net/publication/45542802_Reconciling_Disparate_Identities_A_Qualitative_Study_with_women_in_the_LDS_Church_Experiencing_Same-sex_Attractions?ev=prf_pub

Arena, P. L., Carver, C. S., Antoni, M. H., Weiss, S., Ironson, G., & Duran, R. E. (2006). Psychosocial responses to treatment for breast cancer among lesbian and heterosexual women. *Women's Health, 44*, 81–102.

Black, D., Gates, G., Sanders, S., & Taylor, L. (2000). Demographics of the gay and lesbian population in the United States: Evidence from available systematic sources. *Demography, 37*(2), 139–154.

Boehmer, U., Bowen, D. J., & Bauer, G. R. (2007). Overweight and obesity in sexual-minority women: Evidence from population-based data. *American Journal of Public Health, 97*, 1134–1140.

Boehmer, U., Glickman, M., Winter, M., & Clark, M. A. (2015). Coping and benefit finding among long-term breast cancer survivors of different sexual orientations. *Women & Therapy, 37*(3/4), 222–241. doi:10.1080/02703149.2014.897548

Boehmer, U., Mertz, M., Timm, A., Glickman, M., Sullivan, M., & Potter, J. (2011). Overweight and obesity in long term breast cancer survivors: How does sexual orientation impact BMI? *Cancer Investigation, 29*(3), 220–228.

Boehmer, U., & White, J. L. (2012). Sexual minority status and long-term breast cancer survivorship. *Women & Health, 52*(1), 71–87. doi:10.1080=03630242.2011.643349

Borden, L. A., Lopresto, C. T., Sherman, M. F., & Lyons, H. Z. (2010). Perceptions of self-disclosing counselors among lesbian, gay, and bisexual individuals. *Journal of LGBT Issues in Counseling, 42*(2), 54–69. doi:10.1080/15538605.2010.481958

Bowleg, L. (2012). The problem with the phrase women and minorities: Intersectionality—an important theoretical framework for public health. *American Journal of Public Health, 102*, 1267–1273.

Bozard, R. L., & Sanders, C. J. (2011). Helping Christian lesbian, gay, and bisexual clients recover religion as a source of strength: Developing a model for assessment and integration of religious identity in counseling. *Journal of LGBT Issues in Counseling, 5*(1), 47–74. doi:10.1080/15538605.2011.554791

Brashier, E., Hughes, J. L., & Cook, R. E. (2013). A comparison of women in lesbian and heterosexual dual-income couples: Communication and conflict. *Psi Chi Journal of Psychological Research, 18*(4), 170–175.

Breiding, M. J., Smith, S. G., Basile, K. C., Walters, M. L., Jieru, C., & Merrick, M. T. (2014). Prevalence and characteristics of sexual violence, stalking, and intimate partner violence victimization—National Intimate Partner and Sexual Violence Survey, United States, 2011. *MMWR Surveillance Summaries, 63*(8), 1–18.

Brooks, K. D., & Quina, K. (2009). Women's sexual identity patterns: Differences among lesbians, bisexuals, and unlabeled women. *Journal of Homosexuality, 56,* 1030–1045. doi:10.1080/00918360903275443

Burgess, D., Lee, R., Tran, A., & Van Ryn, M. (2008). Effects of perceived discrimination on mental health and mental health services utilization among gay, lesbian, bisexual and transgender persons. *Journal of LGBT Health Research, 3*(4), 1–14.

Cardell, M., Finn, S., & Marecek, J. (1981). Sex-role identity, sex-role behavior, and satisfaction in heterosexual, lesbian, and gay male couples. *Psychology of Women Quarterly, 5,* 488–494. doi:10.1111/j.1471-6402.1981.tb00588.x

Chan, C. S. (1989). Issues of identity development among Asian-American lesbians and gay men. *Journal of Counseling & Development, 68,* 16–20.

Clarke, V., & Spence, K. (2013). "I am who I am"? Navigating norms and the importance of authenticity in lesbian and bisexual women's accounts of their appearance practices. *Psychology & Sexuality, 4*(1), 25–33. doi:10.1080/19419899.2013.748240

Clift, J. B., & Kirby, J. (2012). Healthcare access and perceptions of provider care among individuals in same-sex couples: Findings from the Medical Expenditure Panel Survey (MEPS). *Journal of Homosexuality, 59,* 839–850. doi:10.1080/0091836 9.2012.694766

Cochran, S. D., Ackerman, D., Mays, V. M., & Ross, M. W. (2004). Prevalence of non-medical drug use and dependence among homosexually active men and women in the US population. *Addiction, 99,* 989–998.

Cochran, S. D., & Mays, V. M. (2006). Estimating prevalence of mental and substance-using disorders among lesbians and gay men from existing national health data. In A. M. Omoto & H. S. Kurtzman (Eds.), *Sexual orientation and mental health: Examining identity and development in lesbian, gay, and bisexual people* (pp. 143–165). Washington, DC: American Psychological Association. doi:10.1037/11261-007

Coleman-Fountain, E. (2014). Lesbian and gay youth and the question of labels. *Sexualities, 17,* 802–817.

Conron, K. J., Mimiaga, M. J., & Landers, S. J. (2010). A population based study of sexual orientation identity and gender differences in adult health. *American Journal of Public Health, 100,* 1953–1960.

Coulter, R. W., Kenst, K. S., Bowen, D. J., & Scout, N. (2014). Research funded by the National Institutes of Health on the health of lesbian, gay, bisexual, and transgender populations. *American Journal of Public Health, 104*(2), 105–112.

Curmi, C., Peters, K., & Salamonson, Y. (2014). Lesbians' attitudes and practices of cervical cancer screening: A qualitative study. *BMC Women's Health, 14,* 153. doi:10.1186/s12905-014-0153-2

Cusack, C. E., Hughes, J. L., & Cook, R. E. (2012). Components of love and relationship satisfaction: Lesbians and heterosexual women. *Psi Chi Journal of Psychological Research, 17*(4), 171–179.

Diamond, L. M. (2005). A new view of lesbian subtypes: Stable versus fluid identity trajectories over an 8-year period. *Psychology of Women Quarterly, 29,* 119–128. doi:10.1111/j.1471-6402.2005.00174.x

Dilley, J. A., Simmons, K. W., Boysun, M. J., Pizacani, B. A., & Stark, M. J. (2010). Demonstrating the importance and feasibility of including sexual orientation in public health surveys: Health disparities in the Pacific Northwest. *American Journal of Public Health, 100,* 460–467.

Drabble, L., & Eliason, M. J. (2012). Substance use disorders treatment for sexual minority women. *Journal of LGBT Issues in Counseling, 6*(4), 274–292. doi:10.1080/15538605.2012.726150

Enteen, J. (2007). Lesbian studies in Thailand. *Journal of Lesbian Studies, 11*(3/4), 255–263.

Farmer, G. W., Jabson, J. M., Bucholz, K. K., & Bowen, D. J. (2013). A population based study of cardiovascular disease risk in sexual-minority women. *American Journal of Public Health, 103,* 1845–1850.

Fassinger, R. E., & McCarn, S. (1997). *Lesbian Identity Questionnaire* [Unpublished measurement instrument]. College Park, MD: University of Maryland.

Fobair, P., O'Hanlan, K., Koopman, C., Classen, C., Dimiceli, S., & Drooker, N. (2001). Comparison of lesbian and heterosexual women's response to newly diagnosed breast cancer. *Psycho-Oncology, 10*(1), 40–51.

Fredriksen-Goldsen, K. I., Kim, H. J., Barkan, S. E., Muraco, A., & Hoy-Ellis, C. P. (2013). Health disparities among lesbian, gay, and bisexual older adults: Results from a population-based study. *American Journal of Public Health, 103,* 1802–1809.

Galarza, J. (2013). Borderland queer: Narrative approaches in clinical work with Latina women who have sex with women (WSW). *Journal of LGBT Issues in Counseling, 7*(3), 274–291. doi:10.1080/15538605.2013.812931

Gardner, A. T., de Vries, B., & Mockus, D. S. (2014). Aging out in the desert: Disclosure, acceptance, and service use among midlife and older lesbians and gay men. *Journal of Homosexuality, 61*(1), 129–144. doi:10.1080/00918369.2013.835240

Garofalo, R., & Bush, S. (2008). Addressing LGBTQ youth in the clinical setting. In H. J. Makadon, K. H. Mayer, J. Potter, & H. Goldhammer (Eds.), *The Fenway guide to lesbian, gay, bisexual, and transgender health* (pp. 75–99). Philadelphia, PA: American College of Physicians.

Garrett, M. T., & Barret, B. (2003). Two-spirit: Counseling Native American gay, lesbian, and bisexual people. *Journal of Multicultural Counseling and Development, 31,* 131–142.

Greene, D. C., Britton, P. J., & Fitts, B. (2014). Long-term outcomes of lesbian, gay, bisexual, and transgender recalled school victimization. *Journal of Counseling & Development, 92,* 406–417. doi:10.1002/j.1556-6676.2014.00167.x

Hagen, W. B., Arczynski, A. V., Morrow, S. L., & Hawxhurst, D. M. (2011). Lesbian, bisexual, and queer women's spirituality in feminist multicultural counseling. *Journal of LGBT Issues in Counseling, 5*(3–4), 220–236. doi:10.1080/15538605.2011.633070

Hammack, P., Thompson, E., & Pilecki, A. (2009). Configurations of identity among sexual minority youth: Content, desire and narrative. *Journal of Youth and Adolescence, 38,* 867–883.

Hammidi, T. N., & Kaiser, S. B. (1999). Doing beauty: Negotiating lesbian looks in everyday life. *Journal of Lesbian Studies, 3*(3), 55–63. doi:10.1300/J155v03n04_07

Han, C. (2007). They don't want to cruise your type: Gay men of color and the racial politics of exclusion. *Social Identities, 13*(1), 51–67.

Harper, G. W., Jernewall, N., & Zea, M. C. (2004). Giving voice to emerging science and theory for lesbian, gay, and bisexual people of color. *Cultural Diversity and Ethnic Minority Psychology, 10,* 187–199. doi:10.1037/1099-9809.10.3.187

Herrick, A. L., Matthews, A. K., & Garofalo, R. (2010). Health risk behaviors in an urban sample of young women who have sex with women. *Journal of Lesbian Studies, 14,* 80–92. doi:10.1080/10894160903060440

Hershberger, S. L., & D'Augelli, A. R. (1995). The impact of victimization on the mental health and suicidality of lesbian, gay, and bisexual youths. *Developmental Psychology, 31*(1), 65–74. doi:10.1037/0012-1649.31.1.65

Hill, N., Woodson, K., Ferguson, A., & Parks, C. (2012). Intimate partner abuse among African American lesbians: Prevalence, risk factors, theory, and resilience. *Journal of Family Violence, 27,* 401–413. doi:10.1007/s10896-012-9439-z

Huxley, C., Clarke, V., & Halliwell, E. (2013). Resisting and conforming to the "lesbian look": The importance of appearance norms for lesbian and bisexual women. *Journal of Community & Applied Social Psychology, 24*(3), 205–219. doi:10.1002/casp.2161

Jabson, J. M., Donatelle, R. J., & Bowen, D. J. (2011). Relationship between sexual orientation and quality of life in female breast cancer survivors. *Journal of Women's Health, 20,* 1819–1824. doi:10.1089/jwh.2011.2921

Jenkins, C. L., Edmundson, A., Averett, P., & Yoon, I. (2014). Older lesbians and bereavement: Experiencing the loss of a partner. *Journal of Gerontological Social Work, 57*(2–4), 273–287. doi:10.1080/01634372.2013.850583

Johnson, M. J., & Nemeth, L. S. (2014). Addressing health disparities of lesbian and bisexual women: A grounded theory study. *Women's Health Issues, 24,* 635–640.

Johnson, S. D. (2012). Gay affirmative psychotherapy with lesbian, gay, and bisexual individuals: Implications for contemporary psychotherapy research. *American Journal of Orthopsychiatry, 82,* 516–522. doi:10.1111/j.1939-0025.2012.01180.x

Jun, H., Corliss, H. L., Nichols, L. P., Pazaris, M. J., Spiegelman, D., & Austin, S. B. (2012). Adult body mass index trajectories and sexual orientation. *Journal of Preventive Medicine, 42*(2), 348–354. doi:10.1016/j.amepre.2011.11.011

Kerr, D. L., Santurri, L., & Peters, P. (2013). A comparison of lesbian, bisexual, and heterosexual college undergraduate women on selected mental health issues. *Journal of American College Health, 61*(4), 185–194.

Kerr, K., Ding, K., Burke, A., & Ott-Walter, K. (2015). An alcohol, tobacco, and other drug use comparison of lesbian, bisexual, and heterosexual undergraduate women. *Substance Use & Misuse, 50,* 340–349. doi:10.3109/10826084.2014.980954

King, M., Semlyen, J., Tai, S., Killaspy, H., Osborn, D., & Popelyuk, D. (2008). A systematic review of mental disorder, suicide, and deliberate self-harm in lesbian, gay and bisexual people. *BMC Psychiatry, 8*(1), 70.

Kowalska, A. (2011). Polish queer lesbianism: Sexual identity without a lesbian community. *Journal of Lesbian Studies, 15,* 324–336. doi:10.1080/10894160.2010.530152

Kurdek, L. A. (1998). Relationship outcomes and their predictors: Longitudinal evidence from heterosexual married, gay cohabiting, and lesbian cohabiting couples. *Journal of Marriage and Family, 60,* 553–568.

Kurdek, L. A. (2001). Differences between heterosexual-nonparent couples, and gay, lesbian, and heterosexual-parent couples. *Journal of Family Issues, 22,* 727–754.

Kurdek, L. A. (2004). Gay men and lesbians: The family context. In M. Coleman & L. H. Ganong (Eds.), *Handbook of contemporary families: Considering the past, contemplating the future* (pp. 96–115). Thousand Oaks, CA: Sage.

Lapovsky-Kennedy, E., & Davis, M. (1993). *Boots of leather, slippers of gold: The history of a lesbian community.* New York, NY: Routledge.

Levitt, H. M., Gerrish, E. A., & Hiestand, K. R. (2003). The misunderstood gender: A model of modern femme identity. *Sex Roles, 4*(3/4), 99–113.

Levitt, H. M., Puckett, J. A., Ippolito, M. R., & Horne, S. G. (2012). Sexual minority women's gender identity and expression: Challenges and supports. *Journal of Lesbian Studies, 16*(2), 153–176. doi:10.1080/10894160.2011.605009

Lewis, R. J., Milletich, R. J., Mason, T. B., & Verlega, V. J. (2014). Pathways connecting sexual minority stressors and psychological distress among lesbian women. *Journal of Gay & Lesbian Social Services, 26*(2), 147–167.

Littlefield, G. D., Lim, M., Canada, R. M., & Jennings, G. (2000). Common themes in long-term lesbian relationships. *Family Therapy, 27*(2), 71–79.

Logie, C. H., & Rwigema, M. J. (2014). The normative idea of "queer is a White person": Understanding perceptions of White privilege among lesbian, bisexual, and queer women of color in Toronto, Canada. *Journal of Lesbian Studies, 18*(2), 174–191. doi:10.10 80/10894160.2014.849165

Loiacano, D. K. (1989). Gay identity issues among Black Americans: Racism, homophobia, and the need for validation. *Journal of Counseling & Development, 68,* 21–25.

Luhtanen, R. K. (2003). Identity, stigma management, and well-being: A comparison of lesbians/bisexual women and gay/bisexual men. *Journal of Lesbian Studies, 7*(1), 85–100. doi:10.1300/J155v07n01_06

Malouff, J. M., Thorsteinsson, E. B., Schutte, N. S., Bhullar, N., & Rooke, S. E. (2010). The five factor model of personality and relationship satisfaction of intimate partners: A meta-analysis. *Journal of Research in Personality, 44,* 124–127.

Maree, C. (2007). The un/state of lesbian studies: An introduction to lesbian communities and contemporary legislation in Japan. *Journal of Lesbian Studies, 11*(3/4), 291–301.

Marshal, M. P., Sucato, G., Stepp, S. D., Hipwell, A., Smith, H. A., & Friedman, M. S. (2012). Substance use and mental health disparities among sexual minority girls: Results from the Pittsburgh Girls Study. *Journal of Pediatric and Adolescent Gynecology, 25,* 15–18. doi:10.1016/j.jpag.2011.06.011

Matthews, C. H., & Salazar, C. F. (2012). An integrative, empowerment model for helping lesbian, gay, and bisexual youth negotiate the coming-out process. *Journal of LGBT Issues in Counseling, 6*(2), 96–117. doi:10.1080/15538605.2012.678176

McCarn, S. R. (1991). *Validation of a model of sexual minority (lesbian) identity development* (Unpublished doctoral dissertation). University of Maryland, College Park.

McCarn, S. R., & Fassinger, R. E. (1996). Revisiting sexual minority identity formation: A new model of lesbian identity and its implications for counseling and research. *The Counseling Psychologist, 24,* 508–534.

McNutt, B., & Yakushko, O. (2013). Disenfranchised grief among lesbian and gay bereaved individuals. *Journal of LGBT Issues in Counseling, 7*(1), 87–116. doi:10.1080/15538605.2013758345

Meads, C., & Moore, D. (2013). Breast cancer in lesbians and bisexual women: Systematic review of incidence, prevalence and risk studies. *BMC Public Health, 13.* doi:10.1186/1471-2458-13-1127

Meyer, I. H. (2003). Prejudice, social stress, and mental health in lesbian, gay, and bisexual populations: Conceptual issues and research evidence. *Psychological Bulletin, 129,* 674–697.

Mohr, J., & Fassinger, R. E. (2000). Measuring dimensions of lesbian and gay male experience. *Measurement and Evaluation in Counseling and Development, 33,* 66–91.

Moore, M. R. (2006). Lipstick or Timberlands? Meanings of gender presentation in Black lesbian communities. *Signs, 32*(1), 83–111.

Morales, E. S. (1989). Ethnic minority families and minority gays and lesbians. *Marriage & Family Review, 14*(3–4), 217–239. doi:10.1300/J002v14n03_11

Morris, B. (2005). Negotiating lesbian worlds: The festival communities. In E. Rothblum & P. Sablove (Eds.), *Lesbian communities: Festivals, RVs, and the Internet* (pp. 55–62). Binghamton, NY: Routledge.

Morris, J., Waldo, C., & Rothblum, E. (2001). A model of predictors and outcomes of outness among lesbian a bisexual women. *American Journal of Orthopsychiatry, 71*(1), 61–71.

Newcomb, M. E., & Mustanski, B. (2010). Internalized homophobia and internalizing mental health problems: A meta-analytic review. *Clinical Psychology Review, 30,* 1019–1029. doi:10.1016/j.cpr.2010.07.003

Pachankis, J. E., & Goldfried, M. R. (2013). Clinical issues in working with lesbian, gay, and bisexual clients. *Psychology of Sexual Orientation and Gender Diversity, 1*(S), 45–58. doi:10.1037/2329-0382.1.S.45

Peplau, L. A., Padesky, C., & Hamilton, M. (1982). Satisfaction in lesbian relationships. *Journal of Homosexuality, 8*(2), 23–35. doi:10.1300/J082v08n02_04

Pope, A. L., Mobley, A. K., & Myers, J. E. (2010). Integrating identities for same-sex clients: Using developmental counseling and therapy to address sexual orientation conflicts. *Journal of LGBT Issues in Counseling, 4*(1), 32–47.

Pope, M. (2011). The career counseling with underserved populations model. *Journal of Employment Counseling, 48*(4), 153–155.

Rabin, J., & Slater, B. (2005). Lesbian communities across the United States: Pockets of resistance and resilience. In E. Rothblum & P. Sablove (Eds.), *Lesbian communities: Festivals, RVs, and the Internet* (pp. 169–182). Binghamton, NY: Harrington Park Press.

Rothblum, E. (2010). The complexity of butch and femme among sexual minority women in the 21st century. *Psychology of Sexualities Review, 1*(1), 29–42.

Russell, S. T., Clarke, T. J., & Clary, J. (2009). Are teens "post-gay"? Contemporary adolescents' sexual identity labels. *Journal of Youth & Adolescence, 38,* 884–890. doi:10.1007/s10964-008-9388-2

Russell, S. T., Ryan, C., Toomey, R. B., Diaz, R. M., & Sanchez, J. (2011). Lesbian, gay, bisexual, and transgender adolescent school victimization: Implications for young adult health and adjustment. *Journal of School Health, 81*(5), 223–230.

Sarno, E. L., Mohr, J. J., Jackson, S. D., & Fassinger, R. E. (2015). When identities collide: Conflicts in allegiances among LGB people of color. *Cultural Diversity and Ethnic Minority Psychology, 21,* 550–559. doi:10.1037/cdp0000026

Savin-Williams, R. C. (2006). Who's gay? Does it matter? *Current Directions in Psychological Science, 51*(1), 40–44.

Silenzio, V. M., Pena, J. B., Duberstein, P. R., Cerel, J., & Knox, K. L. (2007). Sexual orientation and risk factors for suicidal ideation and suicide attempts among adolescents and young adults. *American Journal of Public Health, 97,* 2017–2019.

Simpson, E. K., & Helfrich, C. A. (2014). Oppression and barriers to service for Black, lesbian survivors of intimate partner violence. *Journal of Gay & Lesbian Social Services, 26*, 441–465. doi:10.1080/10538720.2014.951816

Spade, J. V. (2008). *The kaleidoscope of gender: Prisms, patterns, and possibilities.* Thousand Oaks, CA: Sage.

Speciale, M., Gess, J., & Speedlin, S. (2015). You don't look like a lesbian: A coautoethnography of intersectional identities in counselor education. *Journal of LGBT Issues in Counseling, 9*(4), 256–272. doi:10.1080/15538605.2015.1103678

Stitt, A. L. (2014). The cat and the cloud: ACT for LGBT locus of control, responsibility, and acceptance. *Journal of LGBT Issues in Counseling, 8*(3), 282–297. doi:10.1080/15538605.2014.933469

Tracy, J. K., Schluterman, N. H., & Greenberg, D. R. (2013). Understanding cervical cancer screening among lesbians: A national survey. *BMC Public Health, 13*, 442. doi:10.1186/1471-2458-13-442

Ueno, K. (2005). Sexual orientation and psychological distress in adolescence: Examining interpersonal stressors and social support processes. *Social Psychology Quarterly, 68*(3), 258–277.

Vanita, R. (2007). Lesbian studies and activism in India. *Journal of Lesbian Studies, 11*(3/4), 245–253.

Walker, J. A., Golub, S. A., Bimbi, D. S., & Parsons, J. T. (2012). Butch bottom-femme top? An exploration of lesbian stereotypes. *Journal of Lesbian Studies, 16*, 90–107. doi:10.1080/10894160.2011.557646

Walker, J. A., & Prince, T. (2010). Training considerations and suggested counseling interventions for LGBT individuals. *Journal of LGBT Issues in Counseling, 4*(1), 2–17. doi:10.1080/15538600903552756

Walters, K. L., Campbell, T. E., Simoni, J. M., Ronquillo, T., & Byuhan, R. (2006). My spirit in my heart: Identity experiences and challenges among American Indian two-spirit women. *Journal of Lesbian Studies, 10*(1/2), 125–149. doi:10.1300/J155v10n01_07

Waterman, L., & Voss, W. (2015). HPV, cervical cancer risks, and barriers to care for lesbian women. *The Nurse Practitioner, 40*(1), 46–53. doi:10.1097/01.NPR.0000457431.20036.5c

Welker, J. (2010). Telling her story: Narrating a Japanese lesbian community. *Journal of Lesbian Studies, 14*, 359–380. doi:10.1080/10894161003677265

Weston, K. (2009). The lady vanishes: On never knowing, quite, who is a lesbian. *Journal of Lesbian Studies, 13*(2), 136–148.

Westwood, S. (2013). Researching older lesbians: Problems and partial solutions. *Journal of Lesbian Studies, 17*(3–4), 380–392. doi:10.1080/10894160.2013.773840

Wilkens, J. (2015). Loneliness and belongingness in older lesbians: The role of social groups as "community." *Journal of Lesbian Studies, 19*(1), 90–101. doi:10.1080/10894160.2015.960295

Wilsnack, S. C., Kristjanson, A. F., Hughes, T. I., & Bensen, P. W. (2012). Characteristics of childhood sexual abuse in lesbians and heterosexual women. *Child Abuse & Neglect, 36*, 260–265.

Wilson, B. D. M. (2009). Black lesbian gender and sexual culture: Celebration and resistance. *Culture, Health & Sexuality, 11*(3), 297–313. doi:10.1080/13691050802676876

Witten, T. M. (2015). Elder transgender lesbians: Exploring the intersection of age, lesbian sexual identity, and transgender identity. *Journal of Lesbian Studies, 19*(1), 73–89. doi:10.1080/10894160.2015.959876

Woody, I. (2015). Lift every voice: Voices of African-American lesbian elders. *Journal of Lesbian Studies, 19*(1), 50–58. doi:10.1080/10894160.2015.972755

Worthington, R. L. (2004). Sexual identity, sexual orientation, religious identity and change: Is it possible to de-polarize the debate? *The Counseling Psychologist, 32*, 741–749.

Worthington, R. L., Navaro, R. L., Savoy, H. B., & Hampton, D. (2008). Development, reliability, and validity of the Measure of Sexual Identity Exploration and Commitment (MoSIEC). *Developmental Psychology, 44*(1), 22–33. doi:10.1037/0012-1649.44.1.22

Zheng, Y., & Zheng, L. (2011). Sexual self-labels and personality differences among Chinese lesbians. *Social Behavior and Personality, 39,* 955–962. doi:10.2224/sbp.2011.39.7.955

Zubernis, L., Snyder, M., & McCoy, V. A. (2011). Counseling lesbian and gay college students through the lens of Cass' and Chickering's developmental models. *Journal of LGBT Issues in Counseling, 5*(2), 122–150.

Chapter 12

Counseling Gay Male Clients

Misty M. Ginicola, Samuel Sanabria, Joel M. Filmore, and Michael DeVoll

Gay is not about fashion, being rich, drag queens, or queer,
or the color pink. What gay is about is love, self-happiness,
unity, contentment, emotions. Gay is a lot of things.
I'm gay, but gay is not what I'm about.
Gay is just a part of me.

—Brad Matthew Fuglei

• • •

Awareness of Attitudes and Beliefs Self-Check

1. Close your eyes and picture a gay man. What do you see? How are your biases and stereotypes present in your image?
2. What people do you know who are out as gay men, including celebrities? What gay male characters have you seen in movies or on television? How are they usually represented?
3. What messages have you received regarding masculinity in your family of origin? What are the typical expectations of a masculine gender role in your family? Are they different from mainstream American culture?

Case Study

Matias, a 35-year-old Ecuadorian male, and Thomas, a 32-year-old African American male, are a same-sex couple looking to start a family either through adoption or through surrogacy. They have been together for 8 years and have been talking about starting a family for the past 2 years. They are both excited about being fathers but have a few reservations about their ability to raise children in an environment that has historically been unsupportive of gay individuals. Matias and Thomas live in a politically and religiously conservative community. Recently there was a petition going around in their neighborhood from "concerned parents" about a high school teacher in their school district who was recently outed as gay. Last year there was a tragic incident involving a gay couple that was assaulted coming out of a local gay bar. Matias and Thomas grew up in this community and are very aware of the anti-gay beliefs of its citizens. Both Matias and Thomas work for the same company and have a long history with and love for their community.

In addition to living in an anti-gay community, both Matias and Thomas have family members who are unsupportive of their relationship and have expressed outright disapproval of their "lifestyle." One is Matias's mother, with whom he is very close: She has been openly hostile toward Thomas and did not attend their wedding 2 years ago. Matias is not allowed to bring Thomas with him during family visits. Thomas has a sister and brother who have kept their distance from him since he came out as gay 15 years ago. These experiences have caused stress in their personal lives as well as in their relationship; however, they do find strength with each other. They have a group of friends they consider their chosen family. Despite finding their strength and support with each other and their friends, they are very concerned about how their children will be treated by the community and their family members. Matias and Thomas decided to see a counselor to talk through their concerns and work toward better comfort surrounding their decision to start a family.

• • •

Awareness of Differences

Prevalence

It is estimated that gay men represent 1% to 2% of the U.S. population (Chandra, Mosher, & Copen, 2011; Gates, 2011; Jones & Cox, 2015). A major limitation to collecting information on affectional orientation is that the measurement of prevalence is based on identity, and some males may not want to disclose their affectional orientation, whereas others may identify as heterosexual despite having sexual contact with males. In his famous sexuality studies, Kinsey (1948) found that approximately 37% of men had had sexual contact with another male. Although modern surveys identify the percentage of men who have sex with men as much higher than the percentage of men who identify as gay, it is not nearly as high as Kinsey's estimates (Chandra et al., 2011; Gates, 2011; Jones & Cox, 2015). Approximately 6% of men report that they have had sexual contact with another male (Chandra et al., 2011). There is also some evidence that younger generations, specifically millennials, may be more apt to identify as bisexual or some associated identity rather than as gay (Jones & Cox, 2015).

Identity Development

As discussed in Chapter 6, Troiden's (1989) model of affectional orientation development is an excellent framework because it acknowledges early childhood experiences with gay identity development. The following is a brief description of each stage in Troiden's model. In Stage 1, *sensitization,* which usually occurs before puberty, the boy has a sense of being different. This is usually experienced by having interests that are more gender neutral or gender variant. However, he is unable to identify the source of the differences that he feels. In Stage 2, *confusion,* the young male begins to have an increasing awareness of his thoughts and feelings and begins to experience attraction to and arousal by other males. However, he is not ready to accept these thoughts and feelings. Therefore, the young male may actively engage in strategies to cope, like denial, avoidance, and rationalization. This stage usually occurs during adolescence. In Stage 3, *identity assumption,* the gay male may experience a reduction in social isolation in pursuit of other gay individuals. The man is still keenly aware of social stigma and may choose to accept his gay identity but hold on to negative views, accept his gay identity and reject heterosexual society, or live a double life in which he comes out to certain individuals or groups but not the rest of society. This usually occurs during late adolescence. The final stage, Stage 4, *commitment,* involves the male becoming increasingly more comfortable with his gay identity and integrating being gay into his internal and external lives. The individual also begins to seek out same-sex relationships.

It is important to know that not every gay male experiences all of these stages in this exact formation or at the same rate. However, McDonald (1982) found that gay youth on average were aware of their attractions at the age of 13 years, had their first sexual experience at the age of 15 years, and had a gay relationship at the age of 23; the average age at which gay men reported obtaining a positive gay identity was 24. McDonald found that the social context of the youth, whether affirming or rejecting, could influence the trajectory of development.

Coleman (1987) also theorized specifically about gay males and how the disclosure of one's sexual identity is experienced in stages. In the first stage, *pre–coming out,* the youth as well as his parents know that the child has a variant gender presentation. When the young gay male realizes that he is different, he will reference his parents' values as well as their messages surrounding his potential gender nonconformity. If the family has been punitive surrounding potential evidence of an affectional orientation variance, the son is likely to feel isolated and hopeless. Depression and suicide can appear in this stage, along with a profoundly lowered self-esteem, internalized homophobia, or conflicted feelings. In the second stage, *coming out,* the gay male discloses his identity to someone with a feeling of self-acceptance but also fear. How the gay male proceeds from this stage is greatly influenced by the reactions that others have to his disclosure. Coleman felt that counselors should help their clients come out to likely supportive persons first before family. The more support clients have, the better they will be able to process and cope with potential negative familial responses. The third stage is called *exploration:* In this stage the gay male may have his first experiences with other males. In this realm, he should develop social and dating skills, a sense of sexual attractiveness, and a sense of self-esteem or self-worth. Coleman noted that gay men, regardless of their age, can become enraptured by the adolescent adventure of sexual intimacy, particularly if they have not fully developed a sense of self-esteem and self-worth. *First relationships,* the next stage, is when the gay male has his first relationship, which, as with heterosexual ones, is unlikely to succeed. The final stage, *integration,* is when the gay male's personal identity and public persona merge and he feels more comfortable in his own skin.

When it comes to understanding gay male youth, the differential developmental trajectories framework (Savin-Williams, 2005) can be helpful for counselors in their conceptualizations of gay males' issues. This model operates on multiple assumptions. First, it is believed that gay adolescents are in all ways adolescents first and therefore will share the same developmental issues as heterosexual males. Second, what is different for gay male youth development compared with heterosexual development is the trajectory of their experiences, which is likely because of rejecting reactions in the culture. Expectations of heteronormativity have a profound impact on the psyche of the gay youth. Third, the developmental trajectory varies among gay youth as a result of intersectionality: The child's ethnicity, socioeconomic status, generation, religion/spirituality, and regional location will impact his progression to acceptance of his identity. Finally, the gay youth's path to acceptance will not look like any other person's path. Because of the significant diversity and varied socioemotional experiences in youth's lives, each person's development will be unique in significant ways.

Relationships

The limiting nature of the definition of masculinity in U.S. culture and many minority cultures may impact gay males whether or not they are gender nonconforming; the nature and acceptability of relationships, even friendships between males, have rigid behavioral expectations (Duck, 1983; Fassinger, 1991; Price, 1999). This rigid sense of masculinity can be harmful to both gay and heterosexual men (Sullivan, 2003). It impacts how close males, regardless of their orientation, feel that they can be with each other, and how they approach expressions of affection and friendship will also be judged against their masculinity (Sullivan, 2003). Growing up, gay men may intuitively know that their peers will not accept their affectional orientation, as it violates standard assumptions surrounding the culture's attitudes toward masculinity (Duck, 1983; Fassinger, 1991; Price, 1999). This can create a sense of isolation and secrecy that can harm their developmental growth and lead to psychological distress (Duck, 1983; Fassinger, 1991; Price, 1999). Gay male youth may also fear serious emotional or physical abuse as a result of disclosing, which research indicates may be a founded fear (Price, 1999). Conversely, having gay friendships can serve as social support and a protective factor toward gay males' resiliency (Kocet, 2001; Nardi, 1992). They can improve their feelings of safety and belonging (Kocet, 2001; Nardi, 1992).

Another area of awareness development is understanding how cultural norms regarding relationships influence commitment and intimacy among gay men. Because of long-held religious and cultural beliefs that long-term, monogamous, and opposite-sex relationships are superior to other forms of relationships, gay men sometimes internalize the idea that an intimate, romantic desire is unattainable and unacceptable (Weiten & Lloyd, 2000). As heteronormativity and homoprejudice impact their development of core attitudes and beliefs, gay males may internalize a sense that their relationships are not as important or valued as heterosexual ones (Frost & Meyer, 2009). There is still social stigma attached to being gay, which includes historically and widely held stereotypes that gay men are incapable of maintaining long-term intimate relationships (Frost & Meyer, 2009; Meyer & Dean, 1998).

This stereotype is untrue: Gay males desire and are very often in monogamous relationships (LaSala, 2004). However, it is important to note that some gay couples do decide to have open relationships that incorporate polyamory. However, this practice is not isolated to gay males: It is common in heterosexuals as well as persons with other affectional orientations. As described in Chapter 1, polyamory is a relationship status unlinked to affectional orientation.

However, gay males' sense of intimacy in a relationship can be an issue for couples (Coleman, Rosser, & Strapko, 1992). As a result of experiences of homophobia, often anxiety, shame, and feelings of inferiority are associated with same-sex romantic feelings, which inevitably affects how gay men enter into and experience intimacy (Frost & Meyer, 2009). As these feelings and beliefs are further internalized, the capability of having a meaningful intimate relationship and the quality of such a relationship are compromised (Coleman et al., 1992). The influence of internalized messages of homophobia is not the only risk to gay men's relationships. The threat of violence also plays a role in the intimacy expressed by a couple. Depending on their environment, showing affection with each other may be unsafe: Two males who are publicly affectionate are at the highest risk for harassment compared to other lesbian, gay, bisexual, transgender, queer, questioning, intersex, asexual, ally, pansexual/polysexual, and two-spirited (LGBTQI+) populations (Garnets & Kimmel, 1993). This self-monitoring of affection to ensure a safe context also takes a toll on a relationship (Garnets & Kimmel, 1993). The struggle to obtain and maintain a meaningful intimate relationship is stressful under these conditions; in addition to the stressors that occur among heterosexual couples, gay male couples may have to cope with a significantly higher level of stress and psychological distress due to their minority status (Meyer, 2003).

Knowledge of Issues and Problems

Experiences of Bias

It is important that counselors have knowledge of the various experiences found in gay individuals and groups, including the effects that homoprejudice, homonegativity, heterosexism, and homophobia have on gay men. All gay men face societal sexual stigma that pathologizes, implies inferiority, and applies negative regard to non-heterosexual relationships (Parrott & Peterson, 2008). This stigma is prevalent in all aspects of society, from a gay man's family to his religion; to the language used in the culture; and to media, community organizations, and institutions (Parrott & Peterson, 2008).

This marginalization can vary; when it is based on heterosexism, gay males are not considered. Sears and Williams (1997) described the impact of heterosexism as exclusion and omission. When heterosexuals evaluate laws, policies, procedures, and activities, the needs of the LGBTQI+ communities are not always considered, which can further lead to oppression (Sears & Williams, 1997). This can range from a lack of benefits for same-sex partners at a place of employment, to a church that has a standard wedding service that only includes language for opposite-sex couples, to school forms that only have space for mother and/or father. None of these allow for the opportunity for same-sex couples to access the same benefits or be included in an official capacity (Sears & Williams, 1997). In many cases, these policies are in place because of tradition and simply have not been updated to consider minorities. This creates a subversive environment in which LGBTQI+ members of the community feel excluded, underrepresented, or simply ignored.

The issues for a gay man go beyond heterosexism: Gay men are often the target of discrimination. In a career context, Chojnacki and Gelberg (1994) identified four issues in the workplace that LGBTQI+ individuals frequently experience. Gay males may encounter overt discrimination, often legal or policy based, which may include the unjust termination of gay male employees or the creation of such a hostile environment that they decide to leave the workplace (Chojnacki & Gelberg, 1994). They also may experience covert discrimination, in which no written policies exist that openly discriminate against LGBTQI+ persons but informal procedures may be greatly impacted by homoprejudice (Chojnacki & Gelberg, 1994). At this level, a climate can still be hostile, and a gay man may still end his career in that workplace. Some gay employees may encounter a tolerant work environment in which their needs are minimally met; however, they do feel safe from discrimination (Chojnacki & Gelberg, 1994). Finally, an affirmative work environment has both support and formal antidiscrimination protections. This is an ideal workplace, in which the gay man feels comfortable and safe. However, even if career settings are supportive, the workplace may exhibit a *lavender ceiling*, which means that LGBTQI+ people may be overlooked for career advancement because of their affectional orientation (Conklin, 2000).

Beyond discrimination, gay males may also experience others' externalized behaviors impacted by homophobia. Homophobia can lead to aggressive and dangerous behavior. A homophobic individual may target a victim specifically; because of experiences of masculinity, this can very often be a gay male or a transwoman (Sears & Williams, 1997). As defined earlier, homophobia includes prejudice, discrimination, and possible verbal or physical harassment toward non-heterosexual persons; homophobia can be seen in visceral, hateful reactions others have to gender and affectional minority issues, sometimes involving threats or real violence (Sears & Williams, 1997). Homophobia can be seen in hate crimes, also referred to as *gay bashings*.

Having an affectional minority status puts one at an increased risk for experiencing a hate crime as well: Lesbian, gay, bisexual, and queer persons experience roughly 20% of all hate crimes reported to the Federal Bureau of Investigation (Federal Bureau of Investigation, 2014). Of the entire LGBTQI+ community, gay males experience the largest number of hate crimes of all types; the risk is even higher if the males are ethnic minorities, are gender nonconforming, and/or reside in rural areas (Diaz & Kosciw, 2009; Federal Bureau of Investigation, 2014; Roberts, Rosario, Slopen, Calzo, & Austin, 2013). Approximately a quarter of all gay men report having been physically assaulted because of their orientation (Carragher & Rivers, 2002; Wells & Tsutsumi, 2005). Half of cases of physical assault actually involve family members of the gay male, which can serve as an additional layer of betrayal on top of the trauma (Bohan, 1996). In addition, gay males are also at risk for sexual abuse in childhood (Neisen & Sandall, 1990).

Violence can also come from within a gay man's relationship, and this is known as intimate partner violence (IPV). In a sample of young gay men, 39% reported having been the victim of IPV (Stults et al., 2015). IPV among gay men has similar causes and consequences as heterosexual IPV; however, when it is experienced between two men, themes of masculinity and internalized homophobia can lead the gay men to normalize or conceal the violence at greater rates (Bartholomew, Regan, Oram, & White, 2008; Finneran & Stephenson, 2014; Oliffe et al., 2014). In addition to overt violence, coercive control can be used in a relationship: If a gay man is not out, his partner's threat of disclosing his affectional orientation can be a significant method of controlling and keeping him in the relationship despite the violence (Frankland & Brown, 2014). The impact of oppression seems to have a link to IPV in gay men: Experiencing gay-related stigma, a closeted status, childhood abuse, level of minority stress, internalized homophobia, and a posttraumatic stress disorder diagnosis are all associated with IPV in gay males (Bartholomew et al., 2008; Stults et al., 2015; West, 2012). There is also some evidence that in ethnic minority cultures in which the masculine gender role is more rigid, the incidence of IPV is increased (Nowinski & Bowen, 2012; Santaya & Walters, 2011).

Bartlett (2007) found that the riskiest time in a gay male's life is his youth; adolescent gay males were at the highest risk of being severely beaten or killed. Research indicates that most LGBTQI+ students attend schools in an unsafe climate; more than 50% feel unsafe in school, with students reporting regular physical (36%), verbal (74%), and electronic (49%) harassment (Kosciw, Greytak, Palmer, & Boesen, 2014). Often students do not report the abuse (57%), but among students who did make a report, almost two thirds did not experience staff support or intervention (Kosciw et al., 2014).

When it comes to intersectionality, there does exist prejudice in the gay male community (Green, 2008). Caucasian, middle-class, and younger males (ages 20 to 30 years) are valued, whereas males who are Black, Asian, of low socioeconomic status, and older than 40 years of age are devalued (Green, 2008). Some gay men face additional challenges due to their intersectionality and context. Aging gay men have been reported to face special challenges in retirement facilities, as they encounter prejudice and discrimination (Kean, 2006). Although homophobia can be seen in every region of the United States, gay males living in southeastern and mid-South states have been found to be the least tolerant of LGBTQI+ persons (Sullivan, 2003).

Some who are supportive of the LGBTQI+ community may feel that with the rapid changes in acceptance of the gay community and the political advancements that have been made in recent years, the environment for LGBTQI+ individuals has improved significantly. Although it is true that the sociopolitical climate is significantly better than it was during the times of Stonewall, there are still significant problems. The fact that LGBTQI+ persons are reluctant to disclose their identity, a high percentage of hate crimes against gay men still occur, heteronormative attitudes abound, and political battles for equality are still occurring indicate that there is a long road to true inclusion and acceptance. This homophobia is also seen very clearly in the backlash following proposed legislation on marriage equality. Under the guise of religious freedom laws, this proposed legislation is incredibly anti-LGBT. These laws allow overt discrimination against LGBTQI+ persons due to religious convictions or sincerely held beliefs (Bendery & Signorile, 2016).

Although individual attitudes have changed drastically over the past 10 years, it takes much longer for culture to change. Urie Bronfenbrenner (1979) addressed this in his eco-logical systems developmental model. In the outer constellation of influences around an individual, he posited the exosystem, or the social settings and institutions that influence the individual, and, beyond that, the macrosystem, or the culture in which the individual lives. These two outer layers of the ecological system influence the thoughts and beliefs of the individual above and beyond the people who have direct interaction with the in-dividual. In other words, although the people in a gay man's life may be accepting and affirming, if the culture in which he exists is not accepting and affirming, there will be increased experiences of homoprejudice and discrimination as well as high levels of inter-nalized homophobia.

Physical Issues and Health Care

Gay men have the worst general health of all demographic populations, including ethnic minorities (Boehmer, Miao, Linkletter, & Clark, 2012; Boehmer, Miao, & Ozonoff, 2011; Porche, 2010; Ward, Dahlhamer, Galinsky, & Joestl, 2014). Lack of access to quality health care and fear surrounding encountering discrimination in the health care system, as well as real experiences of discrimination, lead gay men to avoid physical preventive care and early treatment (Brooks, Etzel, Hinojos, Henry, & Perez, 2005). Gay men are more likely to have general health problems, including lung and heart issues; high blood pressure; can-cer; and sexually transmitted infections (STIs), including HIV and human papillomavirus (Durso & Meyer, 2013; Institute of Medicine, 2011; Mayer, 2011).

In terms of STIs, gay men are at an increased risk because of two factors: having sex with a male (which also puts heterosexual women at risk) and increased rates of engaging in anal sex. Because anal sex is the riskiest type of sex for transmitting STIs, it is crucial that gay males have protected sex (Centers for Disease Control and Prevention [CDC], 2016). Although the message of safe sex is prominent in the gay male community, issues related to oppression still put these men at higher risk (CDC, 2016). Some gay and bisexual men may have unprotected sex under the influence when they are using substances to cope and/or have been diagnosed with addiction (CDC, 2016). In addition, some men are not comfortable coming out, so rather than date openly, they may have sex on the *down low* or meet men in risky situations to have anonymous and unprotected sex (CDC, 2016). In terms of HIV, gay men are one of the most affected populations in the United States: White men who have sex with men account for the highest number of persons affected in the United States, followed by Black men who have sex with men and then Hispanic/ Latino men who have sex with men (CDC, 2016). In 2010, gay and bisexual men accounted for more than 60% of all new HIV cases (CDC, 2016). African American gay and bisexual men are at the highest risk, with a 20% increase in new HIV cases in 2 years, from 2008 to 2010 (CDC, 2016). It should be noted that having HIV can cause gay men to experience higher rates of depression and suicidality (Theodore & Koegel, 2002). In addition to HIV, gay males have high rates of hepatitis A, B, and C; tuberculosis; gonorrhea; chlamydia; syphilis; and human papillomavirus (Mayer, 2011).

Because of increased rates of smoking and drinking alcohol, gay males have a higher in-cidence of respiratory disorders and lung cancer (Storholm, Halkitis, Siconolfi, & Moeller, 2011) as well as liver diseases and liver failure (Barrett et al., 1995). Significantly increased

157

rates of blood pressure are also prevalent in gay men whether or not they have a history of substance use (Everett & Mollborn, 2013). This can often lead to the onset of heart disease, for which gay men are also at an increased risk (Ungvarski & Grossman, 1999). Gay males are also at an increased risk for cancer of the lung, rectum, and liver and some lymphomas (Boehmer et al., 2011). These increased cancer rates can be linked to poor overall health, increased use of substances, and untreated STIs (Boehmer et al., 2011).

For many, these health issues are the result of undue stressors related to isolation, stereotyping, poor social support, and oppression at the individual and the institutional levels. In fact, Burchell et al. (2010) found that gay and bisexual men were more likely to be infected with HIV when they were experiencing high levels of stress. The result of these unique experiences is often called *minority stress* (Meyer, 2003), and proponents of this model posit that minorities, especially LGBTQI+ individuals, who experience a high degree of stress over a period of time are more likely to develop psychological and physical health problems.

Potential Mental Health Challenges

Gay men have a greater risk of mental health issues than the general population (Durso & Meyer, 2013). The most common mental health symptoms that gay men may experience are depression and suicidality, anxiety, eating disorders, and substance abuse (S. D. Cochran, 2001; Herek & Garnets, 2007; King et al., 2008). The experience of being a minority can lead to increased minority stress, as previously discussed (Meyer, 2003). Experiences of homophobia, harassment, and violence not only lead to increased psychological distress for gay men but lead to an increase in negative coping behaviors, such as substance use and risky sexual behavior; this in turn leads to significant increases in health and mental health problems (Lock & Steiner, 1999; Wong, Weiss, Ayala, & Kipke, 2010). For a gay man of color, this stress is increased exponentially, as racism and homophobia make the gay man a target of multiple prejudices (Brooks et al., 2005). Other increased risks for gay men include concealing their affectional orientation or going through the coming out process, particularly when they are rejected by family or close friends (Bybee, Sullivan, Zielonka, & Moes, 2009). Both being closeted and coming out increase the risks of depression, low self-esteem, and substance abuse (Bybee et al., 2009).

Gay male adolescents are approximately 3 times as likely as heterosexual males to have suicidal ideation or attempt suicide (Morrison & L'Heureux, 2001). The most common mental health disorder among gay males, suicide can become a risk at multiple stages of identity development (Bybee et al., 2009). Depression and suicidality can occur when individuals first realize that they are gay or if they conceal their attractions, come out partially, disclose to rejecting family members and peers, experience harassment for being fully out, or experience abuse and violence (Bybee et al., 2009). It is important to remember that depression and suicidality will also occur in response to stressors and relationship difficulties, just as they do in heterosexual relationships (Iwasaki & Ristock, 2007). High levels of depression are also linked to chronically low levels of self-esteem in gay males as well as isolation and loneliness due to rejection (D'Augelli, Grossman, Hershberger, & O'Connell, 2001; Kuyper & Fokkema, 2010).

As a result of high rates of bullying, abuse, and trauma, gay males may commonly present with anxiety and trauma symptoms (Dworkin, 2000). Gay men are commonly diagnosed with conditions along the spectrum of anxiety disorders (Pachankis & Goldfried, 2006). This anxiety is present across the life span and influenced by ageism, homophobia, classism, discrimination, and exclusion (D'Augelli et al., 2001; Hatzenbuehler, McLaughlin, Keyes, & Hasin, 2010). The trauma experienced as a result of being a victim of a hate crime can be even more extensive, with anger, anxiety, and depression persisting years after the attack (Bridgewater, 1992). Diagnosing and treating posttraumatic stress disorder are common in counseling gay males; the external homophobia and traumatic experiences can be compounded by the person's own internal homophobia (Dworkin, 2000).

Beginning in adolescence, gay males are at a higher risk for substance use and abuse, with poorer outcomes even after treatment (B. N. Cochran & Cauce, 2006). With excessive alcohol use, the gay male is also likely to increase his depressive symptoms and increase his risk of STIs (Halkitis & Parsons, 2002). The use of illicit recreational drugs, including marijuana, cocaine, methamphetamine, amyl nitrate, and heroin, is also increased in this population (Barrett et al., 1995; Boehmer, Ozonoff, & Miao, 2012). Off-label use of erectile dysfunction drugs can also occur in this population and can lead to serious physical issues (Prestage et al., 2009). Another issue surrounding substance abuse is that the gay bar represents a community of support where the individual can be free to be authentic and express himself openly; his uniqueness is celebrated, feelings of isolation are lowered, and feelings of joy are increased (Cheng, 2003). Unfortunately, in this same setting, alcohol and illicit drugs flow freely, making the gay bar scene also one of increased risk for those susceptible to addiction (Cheng, 2003).

The prevalence of eating disorders is also high in gay male populations: Gay men are much more likely than heterosexual men to be diagnosed with and receive treatment for eating disorders (Feldman & Meyer, 2010). The current theory behind the etiology of this increased risk is that, similar to heterosexual females, gay males experience being sexually objectified by males (Fredrickson & Roberts, 2006). Wiseman and Moradi (2010) presented data to support this theory. They found that gay males who experience higher rates of reported body objectification also evidence high rates of body surveillance, body-related shame, and eating disorder symptomatology. Marino Carper, Negy, and Tantleff-Dunn (2010) reported that gay culture exhibits norms related to appearance more so than heterosexual male culture. Gay men diagnosed with anorexia nervosa may restrict eating as well as exercise excessively (Marino Carper et al., 2010). Other theories are that gay males are more sensitive to media and social expectations of attractiveness in the gay male community (Siconolfi, Halkitis, Allomong, & Burton, 2009). Gay males also commonly experience bulimia nervosa (Feldman & Meyer, 2007) and muscle dysmorphia in body dysmorphic disorder, which is an obsessive and compulsive preoccupation with having a muscular body (Chaney, 2008).

However, if a male exhibits a positive gay identity and is out, his incidence of physical diseases and mental health conditions is lower than among gay males who are not out to others (Cole, Kemeny, Taylor, & Visscher, 1996). The empowerment that results from fully accepting and integrating one's affectional orientation appears to serve as a protective factor (Garnets & Kimmel, 1993). Alderson (2000) described a positive gay identity as involving high regard for oneself and for the fact that one is gay. Men with a positive gay identity believe that they are equal to heterosexuals and should be treated as such; their internal sense of homophobia and homonegativity has been resolved (Alderson, 2000). When asked, these persons would state that they prefer their affectional orientation to being heterosexual and value their unique selves (Alderson, 2000). Although they may not disclose their orientation in all contexts, they are out with most people who play major roles in their lives (Alderson, 2000).

Counseling Skills and Techniques

Counselor Self-Awareness

Given that gay men experience stressors in addition to the common occurrence of stress, gay men are more likely than heterosexual males to seek counseling and for a longer period of time

(Graham, Carney, & Kluck, 2012). As a result, counselors, whether in community counseling agencies or in private practice, are likely to work with gay clients. In fact, in a study conducted by Murphy, Rawlings, and Howe (2002), 56% of mental health professionals reported working with a gay client in the past week. This statistic does not take into account the percentage of mental health professionals who reported ever having worked with gay clients during their professional career. Thus, it is important that counselors develop an acceptable level of competency when they are likely to have gay male clients. This requires a strong basis in awareness, knowledge, and skills as they relate to providing services to the LGBTQI+ communities, with special attention to the unique needs of gay men (Harper et al., 2013). The *ACA Code of Ethics* (American Counseling Association, 2014) states, "Whereas multicultural counseling competency is required across all counseling specialties, counselors gain knowledge, personal awareness, sensitivity, dispositions, and skills pertinent to being a culturally competent counselor in working with a diverse client population" (Standard C.2.a.).

Although the American Counseling Association is clear in its mandate for counselors, it is uncertain whether training programs are adequately preparing counselors to provide effective and affirming services to gay men. Many counselors have reported a lack of sufficient training in working with LGBTQI+ populations during their education (Graham et al., 2012). In fact, many counselors and other helping professionals have received little to no training on LGBTQI+ issues (Alderson, 2004; Dillon et al., 2004; Eubanks-Carter, Burckell, & Goldfried, 2005; Pearson, 2003). Other studies suggest that progress is being made in counselors' awareness of attitudes and beliefs, but more is needed to develop their knowledge and skills competencies (Farmer, Welfare, & Burge, 2013). Despite the progress counselor education programs are making in integrating opportunities to develop LGBTQI+ competencies, many counseling professionals in the field work with gay men but have not acquired the necessary knowledge, awareness, and skills to effectively provide them with services. In addition, counselor education programs need to identify whether counseling students have existing prejudices against vulnerable groups, including ethnic minorities and LGBTQI+ clients; students with prejudicial attitudes are more likely to have had previous negative experiences with a member of the LGBTQI+ community and score high on religiosity and conservatism measures (Rainey & Trusty, 2007). Helping students overcome prejudices and learn how not to impose their own values is of great import for maintaining ethical behavior (Rainey & Trusty, 2007). Counselors with low competence and/or existing prejudices against the LGBTQI+ communities are at risk for not only violating ethical standards but also exacting harm on this population.

Gay males, like other members of the LGBTQI+ populations, may be reticent to come to counseling and to disclose their orientation to their counselors. Because of previous experiences of oppression and discrimination, as well as internalized homophobia, LGBTQI+ clients may look for indicators of disapproval in a counselor's reactions. In order to stay multiculturally competent, counselors must first address their own attitudes and beliefs and understand the client's worldview (Ratts, Singh, Nassar-McMillan, Butler, & McCullough, 2015). In reviewing their own attitudes toward masculinity, counselors should ensure that they are treating their gay male clients the same as their heterosexual ones (Pixton, 2003).

Gay men, especially those who have not come to terms with their affectional orientation, may be wary of coming out to their counselor if they are not certain that the counselor will be affirming or able to appropriately empathize with their experience. Many clients directly or indirectly screen counselors to ascertain whether it is safe to come out. This is done either through direct interviewing or through observation of counselors' language and behavior (Liddle, 1997). Thus, it is possible that counselors have worked with gay clients without realizing it; if this is the case, then it is uncertain how the services provided without this knowledge could have negatively impacted the client. The use of affirmative counseling strategies with a developmental counseling framework will be the most effective approach for gay males.

Developmental Counseling

Burlew, Pulliam, and Grant (2014) stipulated that one of the more important strategies for counseling gay male youth and adults is to match techniques to their identity development. Counselors should assess development according to identity level and work toward successful resolution of each developmental identity milestone (Burlew et al., 2014). Many negative outcomes can be prevented if the counselor guides the individual through each stage, providing psychoeducation, assisting in the building of a social support network, and strengthening resiliency and coping factors (Burlew et al., 2014). If a crisis does occur, the counselor should approach the client with age-appropriate interventions, which should include advocacy and social justice work (Burlew et al., 2014). Special attention should also be given to the client's cognitive development as well as the level of insight he has developed into his mental health and psychological distress (Marszalek, Cashwell, Dunn, & Jones, 2004).

In this effort, counselors can utilize the integrative empowerment model (Matthews & Salazar, 2012) to help LGBTQI+ youth with the coming out process. The counselor should first explore the *internal and external factors* that bring the client in to the counselor's office. As these issues are explored and processed, the counselor should move to explore all variables that can impact disclosure and psychological distress. These can include the client's current stage of identity development, internalized homoprejudice, self-esteem, and mental health. The counselor should also explore family acceptance or rejection, school experiences, access to an LGBTQI+ support network, intersectional identities and related pressures (including ethnicity/culture, spirituality, and religion), and previous counseling experiences. The counselor then should move to match the factors with *strategies and interventions* that will best meet the client's goals. Using an affirmative therapy approach, the counselor should choose empowering and strengths-based therapeutic interventions.

Affirmative Therapy

It is also important to understand affirmative therapy, as described in Chapter 10, when working with gay men and boys. It is important for counselors to maintain self-awareness and question how their standard practice (e.g., intake questions, common assessment protocols) might be different if they knew the client was gay (Morrow, 1997). Ensuring the use of non-heteronormative language (such as *partner* and *spouse*) is a good way to begin (Morrow, 1997). Also, creating a waiting room that represents LGBTQI+ persons and resources can indicate acceptance, safety, and representativeness of LGBTQI+ persons in a counseling practice (Morrow, 1997). LGBTQI+ counselor self-disclosures can also be valuable in facilitating a connection with a client as well as increasing feelings of hope (Kronner, 2005).

The main counseling goals that should occur in an affirmative counseling practice are combatting isolation and stigma as well as exploring cognitions, emotions, and fears surrounding affectional orientation (Matthews & Salazar, 2012). Assisting clients to progress in their understanding and development of their affectional orientation identity is a main counseling goal for gay men (Pope & Barret, 2002; Sanabria, 2014). If they have not yet disclosed, clients may need support surrounding issues of coming out, including the advantages and disadvantages of disclosure and a safety plan (Matthews & Salazar, 2012). One of the more important goals for gay males across the life span is to increase their resiliency and coping skills (Matthews & Salazar, 2012).

A key aspect of affirmative therapy with gay men is highlighting the experience of external and internal messages surrounding homophobia, heterosexism, and, when the client is an ethnic minority, racism (Rutter & Camarena, 2015). Exploring the broad concepts involved in marginalized clients' experiences can help them to view their mental health symptoms in a nonshameful way; it is important for gay males to externalize their struggle as the impact of being different in the context of a culture with rigid gender and sexual roles and norms (Rutter & Camarena, 2015). A trauma-informed approach that involves processing the damage caused by homophobia and related experiences will be important for work with gay men, particularly ones who have been victimized by homophobic harassment and violence (Cheng, 2004). Because these experiences are quite common for gay men, experiences of trauma and symptoms of posttraumatic stress disorder should also be assessed (Cheng, 2004). It is important to note that if a gay male experienced sexual abuse as a child, his presentation of posttraumatic stress disorder will be much more complex, as he experiences the stigma of being a sexual abuse survivor along with the many other stigmas a gay male encounters in his developmental experiences (Cheng, 2003).

Exploring spirituality with gay male clients can be beneficial (Sanabria & Suprina, 2014). As spirituality is a key aspect of wellness, having an existential purpose can be a protective factor for gay youth (Sanabria & Suprina, 2014). In addition, many clients may have directly experienced religious rejection or, at the very least, heard associated religious messages of intolerance of same-sex relationships (Sanabria & Suprina, 2014). If a client has religious objections to his affectional orientation, introducing the client to alternative spiritual interpretations to understanding LGBTQI+ issues as well as connecting him to a positive, affirming religious community can help the client resolve this conflict (Marshall, 2010). The issue of religion, the GRACE (goals, renewal, action, connection, and empowerment) counseling model, and discussions pertinent to religion-based trauma are presented later in this book.

A potentially helpful strategy for empowering gay male clients is queer affirmative narrative therapy (Hart, 2012). Narrative strategies provide a framework for exploring values, culture, privilege, and marginalization and how they shape each person's story (McLean & Marini, 2008). By helping gay clients to explore their stories, the counselor can help them understand how the internalization and experiences surrounding homophobia and heteronormativity have influenced their personal narrative (Hart, 2012; McLean & Marini, 2008). By retelling their story from a positive empowerment viewpoint, individuals can increase their self-esteem and reduce other mental health symptoms (Hart, 2012; McLean & Marini, 2008).

Additional counseling techniques may be of use when working with gay male clients. Using grief counseling strategies, a counselor may need to help gay men explore grief and loss in their lives (Knapp & Myer, 2000). The loss of significant relationships, loss of acceptance and affirmation in social contexts, experiences of rejection, and acceptance of health problems (such as HIV) are moments when grief-based counseling strategies may be applicable for some clients (Knapp & Myer, 2000; Kocet, 2014). Because LGBTQI+ persons also commonly experience crises related to their affectional orientation, utilizing crisis counseling techniques may be helpful as well (Thomas, 2013).

As gay males often experience isolation, it is crucial that when they are ready (e.g., are not actively homophobic), the counselor refer them to an affirming LGBTQI+ organization (Burlew et al., 2014). This may also include resources for their families, who may also be struggling with acceptance and affirmation of their gay family member. Counselors should work to connect their clients to a positive gay male community, as research has shown that affiliation with other gay males increases positive gay identity development (Frable, Wortman, & Joseph, 1997). Prescreening community organizations is important for gay clients, particularly when they have other intersectional identities, such as being a person of color, being an immigrant, having a disability, or having spiritual or religious needs.

Normalizing and valuing clients' affectional orientation through psychoeducation is also important (Burlew et al., 2014). Gay youth may often need additional psychoeducation on the importance of safe sex as well as support surrounding the common mental and physical health risks associated with being an affectional minority (Burlew et al., 2014). In a school and family context, counselors may also provide education on issues central to the LGBTQI+ populations as well as the importance of affirmation and support (Burlew et al., 2014). Working toward a more affirming social context through social justice and advocacy efforts can also improve the mental health of LGBTQI+ persons (Burlew et al., 2014; Luke & Goodrich, 2014).

Exploring the strength associated with being a gay male can also help clients build esteem from a strengths-based approach (Riggle, Whitman, Olson, Rostosky, & Strong, 2008). Lesbians and gay males have reported that belonging to a community, creating a family of choice, and forging strong and immeasurable bonds with other marginalized persons are among the reasons for feeling positive about being an affectional minority. Gay men have also cited being able to be a positive role model and mentor for younger LGBTQI+ individuals as a chance to serve as the mentor they never had or pay forward a relationship they did experience. Being able to live authentically, with freedom from gender roles, and openly explore sexuality and relationships are also among the favored benefits of being gay or lesbian. Many gay males also find esteem and fulfillment in fighting for civil rights and being activists for social justice efforts.

Conclusion

Working with gay male youth and adults can reveal the multiple negative impacts of heterosexism, rigid expectations of masculinity, homoprejudice, and homophobia. As a response to high levels of stigma, harassment, and violence, gay men experience relationship difficulties, physical health issues, and mental health problems, which can very often include suicidality. When counselors work with gay male clients, they must be aware of all of the societal, familial, and media-based influences on the gay male's schema. He may have created a narrative of his experiences from a framework of abnormality, immorality, and pain. Working to expose these negative beliefs in a safe, affirmative, and nonjudgmental context can provide gay clients with the space to process the impact of these negative messages and experiences. Helping a client to become empowered and valued can help improve his mental health symptoms as well as his overall quality of life.

Questions for Further Discussion

1. What messages may Matias and Thomas have internalized regarding their affectional orientation and relationship together?
2. What types of bias are Matias and Thomas likely to have experienced? What biases might they experience in the future when they become parents?
3. How does disclosing their orientation in their lives impact them? How would their relationship be difficult if one of them were closeted?
4. What negative coping mechanisms are Matias and Thomas at risk for to deal with the stress they are experiencing in terms of relational, physical, and mental health issues?
5. What can a counselor provide Matias and Thomas during this time? What should their counseling goals be? What strategies may be the most effective?

Resources

1. Read the positive messages surrounding Gay Men of Wisdom at http://www.gay-menofwisdom.com/.

2. Find a community center through CenterLink at http://www.lgbtcenters.org/.
3. Review photos from the Gay Men Project, which visually represents positive images of gay men from around the world, at http://thegaymenproject.com/.
4. Visit the Gay Men of African Descent website at www.gmad.org.
5. Review resources from the CDC for health professionals working with gay and bisexual men at http://www.cdc.gov/msmhealth/professional-resources.htm.

References

Alderson, K. (2000). *Beyond coming out: Experiences of positive gay identity.* Toronto, Ontario, Canada: Insomniac Press.

Alderson, K. (2004). A different kind of outing: Training counsellors to work with sexual minority clients. *Canadian Journal of Counselling, 38,* 193–210.

American Counseling Association. (2014). *ACA code of ethics.* Alexandra, VA: Author.

Barrett, D. C., Bolan, G., Joy, D., Counts, K., Doll, L., & Harrison, J. (1995). Coping strategies, substance use, sexual activity, and HIV sexual risks in a sample of gay male STD patients. *Journal of Applied Social Psychology, 25,* 1058–1072.

Bartholomew, K., Regan, K. V., Oram, D., & White, M. A. (2008). Correlates of partner abuse in male same-sex relationships. *Violence and Victims, 23*(3), 344–360.

Bartlett, P. (2007). Killing gay men, 1976–2001. *British Journal of Criminology, 47,* 573–595.

Bendery, J., & Signorile, M. (2016, April 16). *Everything you need to know about the wave of 100+ anti-LGBT bills pending in states.* Retrieved from the Huffington Post website: http://www.huffingtonpost.com/entry/lgbt-state-bills-discrimination_us_570ff4f2e4b0060ccda2a7a9

Boehmer, U., Miao, X., Linkletter, C., & Clark, M. A. (2012). Adult health behaviors over the life course by sexual orientation. *American Journal of Public Health, 102*(2), 292–300.

Boehmer, U., Miao, X., & Ozonoff, A. (2011). Cancer survivorship and sexual orientation. *Cancer, 117,* 3796–3804.

Boehmer, U., Ozonoff, A., & Miao, X. (2012). An ecological approach to examine lung cancer disparities due to sexual orientation. *Public Health, 126,* 605–612. doi:10.1016/j.puhe.2012.04.004

Bohan, J. S. (1996). *Psychology and sexual orientation: Coming to terms.* New York, NY: Routledge.

Bridgewater, D. (1992). A gay male survivor of anti-gay violence. In S. H. Dworkin & F. J. Gutierrez (Eds.), *Counseling gay men and lesbians: Journey to the end of the rainbow* (pp. 219–230). Alexandria, VA: American Association of Counseling and Development.

Bronfenbrenner, U. (1979). *The ecology of human development: Experiments by nature and design.* Cambridge, MA: Harvard University Press.

Brooks, R. A., Etzel, M. A., Hinojos, E., Henry, C. L., & Perez, M. (2005). Preventing HIV among Latino and African American gay and bisexual men in a context of HIV-related stigma, discrimination, and homophobia: Perspectives of providers. *AIDS Patient Care and STDs, 19,* 737–744.

Burchell, A. N., Calzavara, L. M., Myers, T., Remis, R. S., Raboud, J., Corey, P., & Swantee, C. (2010). Stress and increased HIV infection risk among gay and bisexual men. *AIDS, 24,* 1757–1764. doi:10.1097/QAD.0b013e32833af7c9

Burlew, L. D., Pulliam, N. P., & Grant, K. L. (2014). The mental health and counseling needs of gay men, adolescents, and boys. In M. M. Kocet (Ed.), *Counseling gay men, adolescents, and boys: A strengths-based guide for helping professionals and educators* (pp. 90–108). New York, NY: Routledge.

Bybee, J., Sullivan, E., Zielonka, E., & Moes, E. (2009). Are gay men in worse mental health than heterosexual men? The role of age, shame and guilt, and coming-out. *Journal of Adult Development, 16*(3), 144–154. doi:10.1007/s10804-009-9059-x

Carragher, D. J., & Rivers, I. (2002). Trying to hide: A cross-national study of growing up non-identified gay and bisexual male youth. *Clinical Child Psychology and Psychiatry, 7,* 457–474.

Centers for Disease Control and Prevention. (2016). *HIV among gay and bisexual men.* Retrieved from http://www.cdc.gov/hiv/group/msm/index.html

Chandra, A., Mosher, W. D., & Copen, C. (2011). *Sexual behavior, sexual attraction, and sexual identity in the United States: Data from the 2006–2008 National Survey of Family Growth* (National Health Statistics Report No. 36). Retrieved from http://www.cdc.gov/nchs/data/nhsr/nhsr036.pdf

Chaney, M. P. (2008). Muscle dysmorphia, self-esteem, and loneliness among gay and bisexual men. *International Journal of Men's Health, 7*(2), 157–170.

Cheng, Z. (2003). Issues and standards in counseling lesbians and gay men with substance abuse concerns. *Journal of Mental Health Counseling, 25,* 323–336.

Cheng, Z. (2004). Hate crimes, posttraumatic stress disorder and implications for counseling lesbians and gay men. *Journal of Applied Rehabilitation Counseling, 35*(4), 8–16.

Chojnacki, J. T., & Gelberg, S. (1994). Toward a conceptualization of career counseling with gay/lesbian/bisexual persons. *Journal of Career Development, 21*(1), 3–10. doi:10.1007/BF02107099

Cochran, B. N., & Cauce, A. M. (2006). Characteristics of lesbian, gay, bisexual, and transgender individuals entering substance abuse treatment. *Journal of Substance Abuse Treatment, 30*(2), 135–146.

Cochran, S. D. (2001). Emerging issues in research on lesbians' and gay men's mental health: Does sexual orientation really matter? *American Psychologist, 56,* 931–947.

Cole, S. W., Kemeny, M. E., Taylor, S. E., & Visscher, B. R. (1996). Elevated physical health risk among gay men who conceal their homosexual identity. *Health Psychology, 15,* 243–251.

Coleman, E. (1987). Assessment of sexual orientation. *Journal of Homosexuality, 14*(1/2), 9–24.

Coleman, E., Rosser, B. R. S., & Strapko, N. (1992). Sexual and intimacy dysfunction among homosexual men and women. *Psychiatric Medicine,10,* 257–271.

Conklin, W. (2000). Employee resources groups: A foundation for support and change. *Diversity Factor, 9*(1), 12–25.

D'Augelli, A., Grossman, A., Hershberger, S., & O'Connell, T. (2001). Aspects of mental health among older lesbian, gay, and bisexual adults. *Aging & Mental Health, 5*(2), 149–158.

Diaz, E. M., & Kosciw, J. G. (2009). *Shared differences: The experiences of lesbian, gay, bisexual, and transgender students in our nation's schools.* New York, NY: GLSEN.

Dillon, F. R., Worthington, R. L., Savoy, H. B., Rooney, S. C., Becker-Schutte, A., & Guerra, R. M. (2004). On becoming allies: A qualitative study of lesbian-, gay-, and bisexual affirmative counselor training. *Counselor Education and Supervision, 43,* 162–178.

Duck, S. (1983). *Friends for life: The psychology of close relationships.* New York, NY: St. Martin's Press.

Durso, L. E., & Meyer, I. H. (2013). Patterns and predictors of disclosure of sexual orientation to healthcare providers among, lesbian, gay men, and bisexuals. *Sexuality Research and Social Policy, 10*(1), 35–42. doi:10.1007/s13178-012-0105-2

Dworkin, S. H. (2000). Individual therapy with lesbian, gay and bisexual clients. In R. M. Perez, K. A. Debord, & K. J. Bieschke (Eds.), *Handbook of counseling and psychotherapy with lesbian, gay, and bisexual clients* (pp. 157–182). Washington, DC: American Psychological Association.

Eubanks-Carter, C., Burckell, L. A., & Goldfried, M. R. (2005). Enhancing therapeutic effectiveness with lesbian, gay, and bisexual clients. *Clinical Psychology: Science and Practice, 12*(1), 1–18.

Everett, B. E., & Mollborn, S. (2013). Differences in hypertension by sexual orientation among U.S. young adults. *Journal of Community Health, 38,* 588–596.

Farmer, L. B., Welfare, L. E., & Burge, P. L. (2013). Counselor competence with lesbian, gay, and bisexual clients: Differences among practice settings. *Journal of Multicultural Counseling and Development, 41,* 194–209. doi:10.1002/j.2161-1912.2013.00036.x

Fassinger, R. E. (1991). The hidden minority: Issues and challenges in working with lesbians and gay men. *Counseling Psychologist, 19,* 157–176.

Federal Bureau of Investigation. (2014). *FBI releases 2013 hate crime statistics.* Retrieved from https://www.fbi.gov/news/pressrel/press-releases/fbi-releases-2013-hate-crime-statistics

Feldman, M. B., & Meyer, I. H. (2007). Eating disorders in diverse lesbian, gay, and bisexual populations. *International Journal of Eating Disorders, 40*(3), 218–226. doi:10.10002/eat.20360

Feldman, M. B., & Meyer, I. H. (2010). Comorbidity and age of onset of eating disorders in gay men, lesbians, and bisexuals. *Psychiatry Research, 180*(2), 126–131.

Finneran, C., & Stephenson, R. (2014). Antecedents of intimate partner violence among gay and bisexual men. *Violence and Victims, 29,* 422–435. doi:10.1891/0886-6708.VV-D-12-00140

Frable, D. E. S., Wortman, C., & Joseph, J. (1997). Predicting self-esteem, well-being, and distress in a cohort of gay men: The importance of cultural stigma, personal visibility, community networks, and positive identity. *Journal of Personality, 65,* 599–624.

Frankland, A., & Brown, J. (2014). Coercive control in same-sex intimate partner violence. *Journal of Family Violence, 29*(1), 15–22. doi:10.1007/s10896-013-9558-1

Fredrickson, B. L., & Roberts, T. A. (2006). Objectification theory: Toward understanding women's lived experiences and mental health risks. *Psychology of Women Quarterly, 21*(2), 173–206. doi:10.1111/j.1471-6402.1997.tb00108.x

Frost, D. M., & Meyer, I. H. (2009). Internalized homophobia and relationship quality among lesbians, gay men, and bisexuals. *Journal of Counseling Psychology, 56*(1), 97–109.

Garnets, L. D., & Kimmel, D. C. (1993). Introduction: Lesbian and gay male dimensions in the psychological study of human diversity. In L. D. Garnets & D. C. Kimmel (Eds.), *Psychological perspectives on lesbian and gay male experiences* (pp. 1–51). New York, NY: Columbia University Press.

Gates, G. J. (2011). *How many people are lesbian, gay, bisexual, and transgender?* Retrieved from the Williams Institute website: http://williamsinstitute.law.ucla.edu/wp-content/uploads/Gates-How-Many-People-LGBT-Apr-2011.pdf

Graham, S. R., Carney, J. S., & Kluck, A. S. (2012). Perceived competency in working with LGB clients: Where are we now? *Counselor Education and Supervision, 51,* 2–16. doi:10.1002%2Fj.l556-6978.2012.00001.x

Green, A. I. (2008). Health and sexual status in an urban gay enclave: An application of the stress process model. *Journal of Health & Human Behavior, 49,* 436–451.

Halkitis, P. N., & Parsons, J. T. (2002). Recreational drug use and HIV-risk sexual behavior among men frequenting gay social venues. *Journal of Gay & Lesbian Social Services, 14*(4), 19–38.

Harper, A., Finnerty, P., Martinez, M., Brace, A., Crethar, H. C., Loos, B., . . . Lambert, S. (2013). Association for Lesbian, Gay, Bisexual, and Transgender Issues in Counseling (ALGBTIC) competencies for counseling with lesbian, gay, bisexual, queer, questioning, intersex, and ally individuals. *Journal of LGBT Issues in Counseling, 7*(1), 2–43. doi:10.1080/15538605.2013.755444

Hart, D. W. (2012). Counseling HIV-positive gay men. In S. H. Dworkin & M. Pope (Eds.), *Casebook for counseling lesbian, gay, bisexual, and transgender persons and their families* (pp. 269–279). Alexandria, VA: American Counseling Association.

Hatzenbuehler, M., McLaughlin, K., Keyes, K., & Hasin, D. (2010). The impact of institutional discrimination on psychiatric disorders in lesbian, gay, and bisexual populations: A prospective study. *American Journal of Public Health, 100,* 452–459. doi:10.2105/AJPH.2009.168815

Herek, G. M., & Garnets, L. D. (2007). Sexual orientation and mental health. *Annual Review of Clinical Psychology, 3,* 353–375.

Institute of Medicine. (2011). *The health of lesbian, gay, bisexual, and transgender people: Building a foundation for better understanding.* Washington, DC: National Academies Press.

Iwasaki, Y., & Ristock, J. L. (2007). The nature of stress experienced by lesbians and gay men. *Anxiety, Stress & Coping, 20*(3), 299–319.

Jones, R. P., & Cox, D. (2015). *How race and religion shape millennial attitudes on sexuality and reproductive health.* Washington, DC: Public Religion Institute.

Kean, R. (2006). Understanding the lives of older gay people. *Gerontological Care and Practice, 18*(8), 31–36.

King, M., Semlyen, J., See Tai, S., Killaspy, H., Osborn, D., Popelyuk, D., & Nazareth, I. (2008). A systematic review of mental disorder, suicide, and deliberate self harm in lesbian, gay and bisexual people. *BMC Psychiatry, 18,* 70–87.

Kinsey, A. (1948). *Sexual behavior in the human male.* New York, NY: W. B. Saunders.

Knapp, A. W., & Myer, R. A. (2000). Layers of grief: Counseling the seropositive gay male. *Crisis Intervention & Time-Limited Treatment, 6*(2), 141–150. doi:10.1080/10645130008951138

Kocet, M. M. (2001). *An examination of friendship between gay men and its impact on psychological well-being and identity disclosure: A case study* (Unpublished doctoral dissertation). University of Arkansas, Fayetteville.

Kocet, M. M. (Ed.). (2014). *Counseling gay men, adolescents, and boys: A strengths-based guide for helping professionals and educators.* New York, NY: Routledge.

Kosciw, J. G., Greytak, E. A., Palmer, N. A., & Boesen, M. J. (2014). *The 2013 National School Climate Survey: The experiences of lesbian, gay, bisexual and transgender youth in our nation's schools.* New York, NY: GLSEN.

Kronner, H. W. (2005). The importance of therapist self-disclosure in the therapeutic relationship as perceived by gay male patients in treatment with gay male therapists: A mixed methods approach. *Dissertation Abstracts International: Section A. Humanities and Social Sciences, 66*(3), 1959.

Kuyper, L., & Fokkema, T. (2010). Loneliness among older lesbian, gay, and bisexual adults: The role of minority stress. *Archives of Sexual Behavior, 39,* 1171–1180. doi:10.1007/s10508-009-9513-7

LaSala, M. C. (2004). Extradyadic sex and gay male couples: Comparing monogamous and nonmonogamous relationships. *Families in Society, 85,* 405–412.

Liddle, B. J. (1997). Gay and lesbian clients' selection of therapists and utilization of therapy. *Psychotherapy, 34,* 11–18. doi:10.1037%2Fh0087742

Lock, J., & Steiner, H. (1999). Gay, lesbian, and bisexual youth risks for emotional, physical, and social problems: Results from a community-based survey. *Journal of the American and Child and Adolescent Psychiatry, 38,* 297–304.

Luke, M. M., & Goodrich, K. M. (2014). Recognizing the needs of sexual minority boys and adolescents in schools. In M. M. Kocet (Ed.), *Counseling gay men, adolescents, and boys: A strengths-based guide for helping professionals and educators* (pp. 129–142). New York, NY: Routledge.

Marino Carper, T. L., Negy, C., & Tantleff-Dunn, S. (2010). Relations among media influence, body image, eating concerns, and sexual orientation in men: A preliminary investigation. *Body Image, 7*(4), 301–309.

Marshall, J. L. (2010). Pro-active intercultural pastoral care and counseling with lesbian women and gay men. *Pastoral Psychology, 59,* 423–432. doi:10.1007/s11089-009-0203-0

Marszalek, J. I., Cashwell, C. S., Dunn, M. S., & Jones, K. H. (2004). Comparing gay identity development theory to cognitive development: An empirical study. *Journal of Homosexuality, 48*(1), 103–123. doi:10.1300/J082v48n01_05

Matthews, C. H., & Salazar, C. F. (2012). An integrative, empowerment model for helping lesbian, gay, and bisexual youth negotiate the coming-out process. *Journal of LGBT Issues in Counseling, 6*(2), 96–117. doi:10.1080/15538605.2012.678176

Mayer, K. H. (2011). Sexually transmitted diseases in men who have sex with men. *Clinical Infectious Diseases, 53*(3), S79–S83.

McDonald, G. J. (1982). Individual differences in the coming out process for gay men: Implications for theoretical models. *Journal of Homosexuality, 8*(1), 47–60.

McLean, R., & Marini, I. (2008). Working with gay men from a narrative counseling perspective: A case study. *Journal of LGBT Issues in Counseling, 2*(3), 243–257. doi:10.1080/15538600802120085

Meyer, I. H. (2003). Prejudice, social stress, and mental health in lesbian, gay, and bisexual populations: Conceptual issues in research evidence. *Psychological Bulletin, 129,* 674–697.

Meyer, I. H., & Dean, L. (1998). Internalized homophobia, intimacy, and behavior among gay and bisexual men. In G. M. Hereck (Ed.), *Stigma and sexual orientation: Understanding prejudice against lesbians, gay men, and bisexuals* (pp. 160–186). Thousand Oaks, CA: Sage.

Morrison, L. L., & L'Heureux, J. (2001). Suicide and gay/lesbian/bisexual youth: Implications for clinicians. *Journal of Adolescence, 24,* 39–49.

Morrow, S. L. (1997). Career development of lesbian and gay youth: Effects of sexual orientation, coming out, and homophobia. *Journal of Gay and Lesbian Social Services, 7*(4), 1–15.

Murphy, J. A., Rawlings, E. I., & Howe, S. R. (2002). A survey of clinical psychologists on treating lesbian, gay, and bisexual clients. *Professional Psychology: Research and Practice, 33,* 183–189.

Nardi, P. (1992). *Men's friendships: Research on men and masculinities.* Newbury Park, CA: Sage.

Neisen, J. H., & Sandall, H. (1990). Alcohol and other drug abuse in a gay/lesbian population: Related to victimization? *Journal of Psychology & Human Sexuality, 3*(1), 151–168.

Nowinski, S. N., & Bowen, E. (2012). Partner violence against heterosexual and gay men: Prevalence and correlates. *Aggression and Violent Behavior, 17*(1), 36–52. doi:10.1016/j.avb.2011.09.005

Oliffe, J. L., Han, C., Maria, E. S., Lohan, M., Howard, T., Stewart, D. E., & MacMillan, H. (2014). Gay men and intimate partner violence: A gender analysis. *Sociology of Health & Illness, 36,* 564–579. doi:10.1111/1467-9566.12099

Pachankis, J. E., & Goldfried, M. R. (2006). Social anxiety in young gay men. *Journal of Anxiety Disorders, 20,* 996–1015. doi:10.1016/j.janxdis.2006.01.001

Parrott, D. J., & Peterson, J. L. (2008). What motivates hate crimes based on sexual orientation? Mediating effects of anger on antigay aggression. *Aggressive Behavior, 34*(3), 306–318. doi:10.1002/ab.20239

Pearson, Q. M. (2003). Breaking the silence in the counselor education classroom: A training seminar on counseling sexual minority clients. *Journal of Counseling & Development, 81,* 292–300.

Pixton, S. (2003). Experiencing gay affirmative therapy: An exploration of clients' views of what is helpful. *Counselling & Psychotherapy Research, 3*(3), 211–215.

Pope, M., & Barret, B. (2002). Counseling gay men toward an integrated sexuality. In L. D. Burlew & D. Capuzzi (Eds.), *Sexuality counseling* (pp. 149–175). Hauppauge, NY: Nova Science.

Porche, D. J. (2010). Healthy men 2020. *American Journal of Men's Health, 4*(1), 5–6. doi:10.1177/1557988309361158

Prestage, G., Jin, F., Kipax, S., Zablotska, I., Imrie, J., & Grulich, A. (2009). Use of illicit drugs and erectile dysfunction medications and subsequent HIV infection among gay men in Sydney, Australia. *Journal of Sexual Medicine, 6,* 2311–2320. doi:10.1111.j.1743-6109.2009.01323.x

Price, J. (1999). *Navigating differences: Friendships between gay and straight men.* New York, NY: Hayworth Press.

Rainey, S., & Trusty, J. (2007). Attitudes of master's-level counseling students toward gay men and lesbians. *Counseling and Values, 52,* 12–24. doi:10.1002/j.2161-007X.2007.tb00084.x

Ratts, M. J., Singh, A. A., Nassar-McMillan, S., Butler, S. K., & McCullough, J. R. (2015). *Multicultural and social justice counseling competencies.* Retrieved from http://www.multiculturalcounseling.org/index.php?option=com_content&view=article&id=205:amcd-endorses-multicultural-and-social-justice-counseling-

Riggle, E. B., Whitman, J. S., Olson, A., Rostosky, S. S., & Strong, S. (2008). The positive aspects of being a lesbian or gay man. *Professional Psychology: Research and Practice, 39*(2), 210–217. doi:10.1037/0735-7028.39.2.210

Roberts, A. L., Rosario, M., Slopen, N., Calzo, J. P., & Austin, S. (2013). Childhood gender nonconformity, bullying victimization, and depressive symptoms across adolescence and early adulthood: An 11-year longitudinal study. *Journal of the American Academy of Child & Adolescent Psychiatry, 52*(2), 143–152. doi:10.1016/j.jaac.2012.11.006

Rutter, P. A., & Camarena, J. (2015). Decolonizing sex: A multicultural and gay affirmative approach to counseling with African American and Latino men who have sex with men. *Journal of LGBT Issues in Counseling, 9*(1), 57–68. doi:10.1080/15538605.2014.997330

Sanabria, S. (2014). Affirmative therapy with sexual minority men. In M. Englar-Carlson, M. P. Evans, & T. Duffey (Eds.), *A counselor's guide to working with men* (pp. 113–133). Alexandria, VA: American Counseling Association.

Sanabria, S., & Suprina, J. S. (2014). Addressing spirituality when counseling gay boys, adolescents, and men. In M. M. Kocet (Ed.), *Counseling gay men, adolescents, and boys: A strengths-based guide for helping professionals and educators* (pp. 52–65). New York, NY: Routledge.

Santaya, P. T., & Walters, A. S. (2011). Intimate partner violence within gay male couples: Dimensionalizing partner violence among Cuban gay men. *Sexuality & Culture, 15*(2), 153–178. doi:10.1007/s12119-011-9087-0

Savin-Williams, R. C. (2005). *The new gay teenager.* Cambridge, MA: Harvard University Press.

Sears, J. T., & Williams, W. L. (1997). *Overcoming heterosexism and homophobia: Strategies that work.* New York, NY: Columbia University Press.

Siconolfi, D., Halkitis, P. N., Allomong, T. W., & Burton, C. L. (2009). Body dissatisfaction and eating disorders in a sample of gay and bisexual men. *International Journal of Men's Health, 8*(3), 254–264. doi:10.3149/jmh.0803.254

Storholm, E. D., Halkitis, P. P., Siconolfi, D. E., & Moeller, R. W. (2011). Cigarette smoking as part of a syndemic among young men who have sex with men ages 13–29 in New York City. *Journal of Urban Health, 88,* 663–676.

Stults, C. B., Javdani, S., Greenbaum, C. A., Barton, S. C., Kapadia, F., & Halkitis, P. N. (2015). Intimate partner violence perpetration and victimization among YMSM: The P18 cohort study. *Psychology of Sexual Orientation and Gender Diversity, 2*(2), 152–158. doi:10.1037/sgd0000104

Sullivan, M. K. (2003). Homophobia, history, and homosexuality: Trends for sexual minorities. *Journal of Human Behavior in the Social Environment, 8*(2–3), 1–13.

Theodore, J. L., & Koegel, H. M. (2002). The impact of depression on sexual risk-taking behavior of HIV-negative gay men. *NYS Psychologist, 14*(1), 22–27.

Thomas, S. R. (2013). Lesbian, gay, bisexual, transgender, and questioning (LGBTQ) youth. In J. Sandoval (Ed.), *Crisis counseling, intervention, and prevention in the schools* (3rd ed., pp. 264–290). New York, NY: Routledge.

Troiden, R. R. (1989). The formation of homosexual identities. *Journal of Homosexuality, 17*(1/2), 43–73.

Ungvarski, P., & Grossman, A. (1999). Health problems of gay and bisexual men. *Nursing Clinics of North America, 34*(2), 313–331.

Ward, B. W., Dahlhamer, J. M., Galinsky, A. M., & Joestl, S. S. (2014). Sexual orientation and health among U.S. adults: National Health Interview Survey, 2013. *National Health Statistical Report, 77,* 1–10.

Weiten, W., & Lloyd, M. (2000). *Psychology applied to modern life: Adjustment at the turn of the century.* Stamford, CT: Wadsworth.

Wells, K., & Tsutsumi, L. M. (2005). *Creating safe and caring schools for lesbian, gay, bisexual, and trans-identified students: A guide for counselors.* Edmonton, Alberta, Canada: Society for Safe and Caring Schools and Communities.

West, C. M. (2012). Partner abuse in ethnic minority and gay, lesbian, bisexual, and transgender populations. *Partner Abuse, 3*(3), 336–357. doi:10.1891/1946-6560.3.3.336

Wiseman, M. C., & Moradi, B. (2010). Body image and eating disorder symptoms in sexual minority men: A test and extension of objectification theory. *Journal of Counseling Psychology, 57*(2), 154–166. doi:10.1037/a0018937

Wong, C., Weiss, G., Ayala, G., & Kipke, M. (2010). Harassment, discrimination, violence, and illicit drug use among young men who have sex with men. *AIDS Education & Prevention, 22*(4), 286–298. doi:10.1521/aeap.2010.22.4.286

Chapter 13
Counseling Bisexual/Pansexual/Polysexual Clients

Amney J. Harper and Misty M. Ginicola

The world is so obsessed with defining sexuality for everyone and at-taching labels to it. Any time any person openly leaves the sexual norm, their sexuality becomes, more often than not, the absolute defining char-acteristic of that person. It becomes the first thing people think about and often the first thing they mention. Every other part of that person all but disappears.

—Dan Pearce

• • •

Awareness of Attitudes and Beliefs Self-Check

1. Close your eyes and picture someone who is bisexual. What do you see? How are your biases present in your image? Does the image change if you picture a male versus a female?
2. What people do you know who are out as bisexual/pansexual/polysexual, includ-ing celebrities? What bisexual characters have you seen in movies or on television? How are they usually represented?
3. If your spouse or partner were to tell you that they were bisexual/pansexual/poly-sexual, what would be your reaction? Your fears?

Case Study

Miranda is a 26-year-old cisgender, Italian, bisexual female. She has been out as bisexual since she was 17 years old. Growing up, she knew that she was at-tracted to others based on their personality and similar characteristics, not their sex or gender presentation. She is currently in a relationship with a male and comes to counseling regarding relationship issues. She reports that although she has dated women in the past and is fully out as a bisexual, her orientation is still misunderstood by her friends and family. Her heterosexual friends and her family have told her that she was just going through a phase now that she

171

is with a man. Her gay and lesbian friends also continue to question her affectional orientation and are somewhat less interested in spending time with her and her boyfriend than they were in spending time with her when she was with a woman. Miranda says she gets frustrated with the constant questioning and challenging of her identity; she reports feeling isolated and alone.

• • •

Awareness of Differences

In the past, bisexuals (biindividuals) were defined as those who were attracted to either males or females. Some individuals feel that because this term was used to describe someone's sexual attraction, this definition does not completely capture their complete affectional orientation (Callis, 2014; Elizabeth, 2013; GLAAD, 2014; Rice, 2009; Soble, 2006). *Bisexuals* are currently defined as people who are "emotionally, physically, mentally, and/or spiritually oriented to bond and share affection with" people of their own gender and those of other genders (Harper et al., 2013, p. 39). However, despite this new definition, some found the term *bi* and how it was used in the past to still be too limiting. As a result, some groups developed identities that moved beyond this scope. Pansexuals (panindividuals) so identify because they are attracted to individuals regardless of sex or gender identity and expression; they report being attracted to *all* genders and sexes. Polysexuals (polyindividuals) identify with affection and bonding with *multiple* gender orientations. There is much overlap among these three identities, but the common thread among them is that sex and gender presentation may not or does not serve as a discriminating factor in the experience of attraction and bonding with others. This attraction is not seen as equivalent for many individuals, however. Some bisexuals report a stronger attraction to one gender or sex, whereas pansexuals and polysexuals typically report being inclusive of all or most gender presentations. It is important to note that members of all three groups experience diversity, and many experience fluidity in the extent to which they are attracted to one gender or another. The defining quality of all three identities is that these attractions are not exclusive and their existence directly challenges the gender binary.

In this landscape of nonbinary gender and affectional orientation reside incredibly diverse identities. In addition to identifying as bisexual, an individual may recognize other intersecting identities, including nonbinary/genderqueer or transgender (Kuper, Nussbaum, & Mustanski, 2012). Gender presentation in bisexuals and pansexuals can also be fluid, meaning that it may shift from masculine to feminine to genderqueer/nonbinary and back (Gonel, 2013). Individuals who are bisexual, and pansexual cannot be easily placed into distinct gender and affectional categories; they exhibit a personhood that identifies with a contextual and shifting sense of gender and affectional orientation (Fallas, 2011). Bisexual and pansexual orientations can also become more challenging in ethnic minority cultures and in those who are biracial because of rigid gender expectations surrounding a male and female binary (King, 2010).

Prevalence

Identifying the prevalence of bisexuals is difficult, because reports vary widely. In his groundbreaking work on sexuality, Kinsey (1948) found that 46% of the male population had engaged in sexual behavior with both males and females. This fits in the theoretical perspective that affectional orientation is a continuum, and therefore the majority of individuals in a population would likely be in the middle of the continuum, which represents bisexuality or attraction to both sexes. However, a recent Centers for Disease Control and

Prevention (2014) study using data from the National Health Interview Survey indicated that only 0.7% of the population *identifies* as bisexual. A recent study by YouGov in the United Kingdom noted that many people identified as not 100% heterosexual (YouGov, 2015). The number of those identifying on a bisexual continuum increased as age decreased (YouGov, 2015). For example, 43% of 18- to 24-year-olds identify as a 1 to 5 on the Kinsey scale, whereas 29% of 25- to 39-year-olds do, 16% of 40- to 59-year-olds do, and only 7% of those older than 60 do (YouGov, 2015). This study found that 19% of the total population placed themselves as bisexual on the Kinsey scale (YouGov, 2015).

Identity Development

Becoming aware of the unique culture, issues, and challenges of bi/pan/poly individuals is imperative to providing competent services. A part of that is understanding the unique and specific developmental paths that bisexuals may follow to understanding and asserting their identities. Many individuals suggest that models of affectional orientation development geared toward understanding lesbian and gay development, such as the Cass (1979) model, are sufficient and can be applied to bisexual individuals. Although certain aspects of these models may indeed ring true for bisexuals, often these models fail to recognize the ways in which the lesbian, gay, bisexual, transgender, queer, questioning, intersex, asexual, ally, pansexual/polysexual, and two-spirited (LGBTQI+) communities as a whole can promote biphobia, which can make it more difficult for individuals to secure acceptance in the queer community. In addition, lesbian and gay identity models often do not address the unique challenges associated with the need to integrate the different aspects of a bisexual identity and instead focus solely on accepting the "homosexual" aspect of one's identity. There is a bias present in the assumption that one only needs to accept one's same-gender attractions, because this assumes that these are the only parts of their identity that bi/pan/poly people may struggle to accept. However, as seen in a study by Ross, Dobinson, and Eady (2010), sometimes bisexuals struggle to come out in the LGBTQI+ community because they feel, or are afraid of being deemed, not legitimate in the LGBTQI+ communities.

Some alternative models have been utilized to understand some of the unique challenges of bisexual identity. It is important to recognize that despite the existence of these models, individual pathways to understanding, developing, and accepting one's identity vary from person to person (Pachankis & Goldfried, 2013). As discussed in Chapter 6, Weinberg, Williams, and Pryor (1994) presented a model of bisexual identity in which individuals begin their development in Stage 1, *initial confusion,* as they experience anxiety, fear, and uncertainty surrounding their attraction to both sexes. When they discover the word *bisexual,* this moves them into Stage 2, *finding and applying the label.* As they learn more about others who are bisexual, they feel comforted that they are not alone in their feelings and identity (Weinberg et al., 1994). During this stage, they will likely seek additional support and information from other bisexuals as well as the larger queer community (Weinberg et al., 1994). In Stage 3, *settling into the identity,* bi/pan/poly people become generally more accepting of their affectional orientation and surround themselves with more supportive friends (Weinberg et al., 1994). In Stage 4, *continued uncertainty,* bi/pan/poly people continue to feel confusion surrounding their identity, particularly because there is a lack of validation from both their heterosexual family and peers and their gay and lesbian friends and family (Weinberg et al., 1994).

Bleiberg, Fertmann, Friedman, and Godino (2005) proposed the layer cake model of bisexual identity development. This model differs in that it discusses the first stage, or layer, as socialization into a heterosexual world with a heterosexual identity (Bleiberg et al., 2005). In the second layer, bi/pan/poly individuals experience attractions to members of the same sex accompanied by feelings and thoughts regarding a non-heterosexual identity; in this stage, they may identify completely with these attractions and identify as gay (Bleiberg et al., 2005). Because of misunderstandings associated with the fluid and nonbinary nature of bisexuality, their exposure to gay and lesbian individuals, and the relative invisibility of bisexuality, these individuals may feel pressure to identify as gay or lesbian (Deschamps, 2008). In the third layer, they accept that they have both types of sexual attractions; however, not until the fourth layer do they integrate and assimilate these identities (Bleiberg et al., 2005). Finally, in the fifth layer, they embrace the bisexual label (Bleiberg et al., 2005).

One of the important developmental differences that may be found in the bi/pan/poly community is that because of stigmatization and bi-invisibility, many individuals may come out later in life than their lesbian or gay peers. Ross et al. (2010) noted that many of the participants in their study stated that they were unaware of bisexual identity as a possible identity during adolescence and early adulthood. It is also noteworthy that ages for coming out likely vary based on generation, because visibility is increasing. This means that younger generations are more likely to become aware of role models and possible identity development pathways at a younger age than their older counterparts were. The impact of coming out later in life on one's affectional orientation development has not been sufficiently studied, but it is fair to assume that models designed for lesbians or gay men may not fit for bi/pan/poly people who come out later in life.

Relationships

Like many marginalized communities, the bisexual/pansexual/polysexual community has been underrepresented in research. One way in which this is most evident is that when research does exist, it focuses almost entirely on those who identify as bisexual, not pansexual or polysexual or other labels under the same umbrella. This focus is often the result of bisexual being the only option for participants to use to describe their identities. This forces many who might identify with a term outside of *bisexual* to either mislabel themselves or be excluded from a study. Many times research studies aggregate bi/poly/pan persons into studies on LGB participants, but often the research is not truly representative, as too few participants identify as bisexual to generalize the results (Pachankis & Goldfried, 2013). Therefore, this research can fail to uncover the unique relationship experiences of bisexuals, pansexuals, or polysexuals (Pachankis & Goldfried, 2013). The San Francisco Human Rights Campaign (2011) noted that the presence of bisexuals in studies of lesbians and gay people will conflate the data and skew the results. Therefore, the research on bisexuals is limited in most areas.

Although most estimates show that bisexuals make up a large percentage of the LGBTQI+ community, in the context of heteronormativity, many bisexuals never come out or identify as bisexual in their lifetime (San Francisco Human Rights Campaign, 2011). The bisexual community has some additional terms for those who do not identify as bi/pan/poly but do engage in both same-sex and opposite-sex relationships. Some individuals may identify as *bi-curious*, which indicates that they wish to experiment sexually as bi but may not wish to settle into an identity as bisexual. Some individuals only engage in same-sex activity as a result of being in restrictive conditions (e.g., gender-segregated schools, prisons; the slang term is *prison gay*) or are paid for engaging in same-sex activity (e.g., a male who identifies as heterosexual but will have sex with other men in pornography; the slang term is *gay for pay*). These individuals do not typically identify as bisexual (or pansexual or polysexual) despite having same-sex sexual activity, known as *conditional bisexuality.* In addition, because of heteronormative and monosexual cultural pressures, many individuals may present as monosexual but have *latent bisexuality,* a part of their attractions that they have never acted on.

Research from the Pew Research Center (2013) showed that in comparison to lesbians and gay men, bisexuals were more likely to be married. The Pew Research Center also reported that bisexuals are more likely to be with partners of the opposite sex versus partners of the same sex. This could lead to many experiencing an invalidation of their affectional orientation as either heterosexual (which suggests that they are not bisexual) or promiscuous (which suggests that they cannot be truly happy with one gender).

Bisexuals, pansexuals, and polysexuals frequently have to field numerous questions surrounding the legitimacy of their orientation as well as judgmental questions surrounding polyamory and promiscuity. Although affectional orientation has little to do with having more than one partner in a single relationship, many question bisexuals regarding how they can stay monogamous, confusing affectional orientation with an unrelated relationship status. Therefore, it is crucial for counselors working with these individuals to have an awareness of the bi/poly/pan experience, knowledge of key definitions and issues, and the skills needed to serve this population (Dworkin, 2001).

Knowledge of Issues and Problems

Experiences of Bias

Being bisexual has many challenges, some of which can be noted in Miranda's case narrative. Having a foot in both the heterosexual and gay or lesbian worlds, bisexuals do not have a limited or dichotomous sexual identity, which can be confusing for them as well as their queer and heterosexual friends and families (Dworkin, 2001). Because bisexuality is a complex identity, it can be difficult for others to comprehend if they do not experience it directly (Deschamps, 2008). Both bisexuals and pansexuals/polysexuals may face negative attitudes and beliefs from those who identify with a monosexual orientation, who might apply pressure to bisexuals, pansexuals, and polysexuals to identify as either gay/lesbian or heterosexual, a phenomenon known as *monosexism* (Dworkin, 2001). This pressure is further complicated by the fact that some individuals who are gay or lesbian identify as bisexual prior to fully accepting their gay or lesbian identity; therefore, these individuals may look at bi/pan/poly persons as not fully achieving their gay or lesbian identity, or it can reinforce the myth that these bisexual identities are just a phase (Dworkin, 2001).

Another factor that leads to stigma for bisexuals in the queer community is that they can benefit from heterosexual privilege, which means that if their partner appears to be heterosexual, they will not face as much discrimination in the heterosexual community (Ochs, 2007). They can also, if they are in a heterosexual relationship, hide their affectional orientation, which again leads to less overt discrimination in the heterosexual community (Ochs, 2007). Bisexuals themselves may feel guilt over this privilege, and it can lead to additional discrimination and invalidation of bisexuals by others in the LGBTQI+ communities (Ochs, 2007). Although outsiders may grant heterosexual privilege when one is read as heterosexual, this type of privilege for bisexuals also promotes oppression because it increases bisexual invisibility. Even though bisexuality has existed throughout history, in various societies, and in other animal species, bisexuals continually face others' contentions that bisexuality does not exist, a phenomenon known as *bisexual erasure* (Crompton, 2003; Roughgarden, 2004).

Bi/pan/poly individuals specifically face challenges under biphobia as well as monosexism (Ross et al., 2010). Biphobia (alternatively known as *biprejudice*) is understood as a system of oppression that consists of "negativity, prejudice, or discrimination against bisexual people" (Ross et al., 2010, p. 496). Biphobia can come in many forms and is often experienced from both the heterosexual and LGBTQI+ communities (Ross et al., 2010). Biphobia, particularly from heterosexual communities in the form of homophobia, means the bias targets the same-gender aspect of a couple without perhaps full knowledge of their identity as bi/pan/poly (Ross et al., 2010).

As mentioned previously, another aspect of biphobia is bisexual invisibility. The San Francisco Human Rights Campaign (2011) noted, "Bisexuals experience high rates of being ignored, discriminated against, demonized, or rendered invisible by both the heterosexual world and lesbian and gay communities. Often the entire affectional orientation is branded as invalid, immoral, or irrelevant" (p. 1). This goes hand in hand with bisexual erasure, in which bisexual histories and identities are erased by being labeled as something else (e.g., historical figures or famous people are labeled as lesbian or gay when they were bisexual). This invisibility and erasure have a significant impact on the mental health of bisexual individuals.

Both bisexual invisibility and bisexual erasure are influenced by not only biphobia but also monosexism, which is a bias against anything outside of the monosexual orientations (gay, lesbian, and heterosexual) and gender (male or female) binary (Ochs, 2007). Monosexism only acknowledges a binary of affectional orientation, with lesbian/gay on one side and heterosexual on the other (Ross et al., 2010). The term *monosexism* reflects the idea that lesbian, gay, and heterosexual sexualities are directed at a single (or mono) gender, whereas bi/pan/poly people are attracted to more than one, all, or multiple genders. The system of monosexism privileges those who fall into the binary and makes invisible those who do not fit neatly into either of those boxes (Ochs, 2007).

Ross and colleagues (2010) described some specific examples of these oppressive experiences in their qualitative study. Participants reported constantly coming out or reminding people of their bisexuality, as well as being frustrated with others labeling them as monosexual (Ross et al., 2010). They also reported that they commonly experienced questioning surrounding their affectional orientation when they were not in relationships and faced assumptions about their sexual behavior (e.g., promiscuity, interest in threesomes; Ross et al., 2010). Participants noted that they faced other negative stereotypes: bisexual men as carriers of HIV into heterosexual communities and bisexual women as sexual objects for heterosexual men (Ross et al., 2010). These bisexual participants also reported experiencing biphobic and monosexist reactions from their romantic partners and those in the LGBTQI+ community (Ross et al., 2010). They expressed that they struggled to understand and accept their bisexual identity in the context of these reactions (Ross et al., 2010).

The San Francisco Human Rights Campaign (2011) noted additional forms of biphobia as well. Many lesbians and gay men may have briefly identified as bisexual before settling into their current identities; bisexuals report that lesbian and gay persons have stated that they have been told that they just have not settled into their true identity yet (San Francisco Human Rights Campaign, 2011). In addition, bi/pan/poly persons' affectional orientation identity is labeled by others depending on the sex of the person with whom they are partnered (San Francisco Human Rights Campaign, 2011). Other negative attitudes include believing that bisexual women infect lesbians with HIV/AIDS and assuming that bisexuals need to make up their minds. Bisexuals report prejudice surrounding not acknowledging the bisexual identity of celebrities or bisexual issues in the media and not accepting people's self-identification if they have not been with multiple genders (San Francisco Human Rights Campaign, 2011). In addition to these negative experiences, participants also noted positive or protective factors that they experienced that positively impacted their mental health, including having a supportive partner; being out at work; having supportive people in their lives, such as counselors or friends/family; having access to a bisexual community; and engaging in self-care activities (Ross et al., 2010).

The reality is that in addition to being oppressed by monosexual, heterosexual, and cisgender communities, most bi/pan/poly people also internalize biphobia, homophobia, and monosexism (Ross et al., 2010). Internalized oppression occurs when individuals take in the negative messages in society about themselves and believe them to be true. This can be seen in direct ways (e.g., a desire to be monosexual or heterosexual) or indirect ways (e.g., relationship problems that come from shame about certain types of relationships).

It is also important to keep in mind the ways in which other marginalized identities can intersect with biphobia and/or monosexism. For example, transgender individuals who are also bi/pan/poly may experience others' ideas that transgender people cannot be both bisexual and transgender (Ross et al., 2010). Polyamorous individuals, or people who wish to or do have consensual relationships with more than one individual at a time, who are also bi/pan/poly can experience another layer of invisibility as well. Because bi/pan/poly people may defend their identities by asserting their monogamy, this can marginalize those who are not monogamous. There is very little research into the number of bi/pan/poly people who are polyamorous, but one study found that 7% of participants were currently in polyamorous relationships, though others indicated that they were open to it (Ross et al., 2010). People of color and ethnic minorities may also have unique experiences of oppression related to how racism or ethnocentrism interacts with a bi/pan/poly identity (Pachankis & Goldfried, 2013). Although there is limited research on this particular intersection, the ways in which cultural and family values may intersect with biphobia and monosexism are particularly important considerations (Pachankis & Goldfried, 2013). Another consideration is how spiritual or religious identities or age intersect with bisexual identities and what that might mean for the intersection of oppressive experiences (Pachankis & Goldfried, 2013). Another example is found in communities with disabilities, in which invisibility can be twofold for people who are also bi/pan/poly (Caldwell, 2010). An example of this offered by Caldwell (2010) is that although the disability rights movement has centered around the fight to be visible and to be heard, in the movement, equal voice is not given to people of all sexualities and affectional orientations.

Bisexuals are unique in the fact that a single identity can result in multiple oppressions through biphobia and monosexism (Ross et al., 2010). In addition, because they are often treated as though their concerns are the same as those of lesbians and gay men, they can be further negatively impacted when those concerns are not understood or considered (Ross et al., 2010). This is even truer when it comes to the dearth of research on those who use different labels, like pansexual or polysexual. Additional layers are added when individuals hold another marginalized identity. This can create intersecting oppressions that converge in particular ways that are not necessarily easily understood through a single lens of oppression (e.g., biphobia or racism) and for which little research exists as a guide. Bisexual oppression impacts bisexuals in unique ways from lesbian or gay people. For example, one study in the United Kingdom found that bisexuals were less likely than lesbian or gay persons to be discriminated against in housing and employment (most likely because of bisexual invisibility) but were more likely to experience discrimination from their friends (Colledge, Hickson, Reid, & Weatherburn, 2015).

Other life experiences can further isolate bisexuals. Ross and colleagues (2010) found that bisexuals who are pregnant or become parents feel further isolated, as most people assume that a pregnant woman or a mother or father is heterosexual. Bisexual and pansexual mothers in particular reported feeling further invalidated in the queer community, having little to no support and role models for non-gender-binary parenting. The identities of queer-identified individuals (see Chapter 15) and two-spirited individuals (see Chapter 19), who are part of a Native/indigenous cultural community, also sometimes overlap with bisexual and pansexual definitions.

Potential Physical and Mental Health Challenges

Research indicates that bi/pan/poly people often experience greater negative physical and mental health outcomes in comparison to their heterosexual counterparts; some newer research has also supported the notion of greater negative mental health consequences compared to lesbian and gay peers as well (Ross et al., 2010). Biphobia, monosexism, and other forms of oppression that bisexuals face have negative repercussions for physical and mental health. One particular area of concern is the high rates of depression and anxiety faced by bisexuals (San Francisco Human Rights Campaign, 2011). In addition, bisexuals have been found to experience higher rates of hypertension, general poor or fair physical health, and more high-risk behaviors like smoking and drinking than gay men, lesbians, or heterosexuals (San Francisco Human Rights Campaign, 2011). In addition, rates of domestic violence are substantially higher among bisexual women than heterosexual women when their partner is monosexual (San Francisco Human Rights Campaign, 2011).

It is hypothesized that the different layers of bisexual oppression contribute to greater negative outcomes for bisexuals (Ross et al., 2010). A study of almost 1,500 women who identified as "sexual minorities" found that compared with lesbians, bisexuals had higher rates of poverty, had more children, had less education, were less likely to be covered by insurance, and had higher rates of mental distress and poor health (San Francisco Human Rights Campaign, 2011). For both bisexual women and men, the San Francisco Human Rights Campaign (2011) reported higher rates of suicidality than in lesbian, gay, or heterosexual populations.

Some important qualitative research has come out of Canada showing a connection between experiences of biphobia and monosexism and negative mental health outcomes (Ross et al., 2010):

> Experiences of discrimination were perceived to affect mental health both directly (e.g. anxiety associated with fear of affectional orientation-based violence) and indirectly, through their effects on interpersonal relationships (e.g. distress associated with relationship problems) and on individuals' senses of self-worth and self-esteem. (p. 501)

These same researchers found that 69% of their participants experienced mental health problems (Eady, Dobinson, & Ross, 2011). In the United Kingdom, studies have shown mixed results in terms of greater negative outcomes for bisexuals than lesbian or gay people, with some finding no differences and some finding statistically higher rates of negative outcomes or health disparities for bisexuals (Colledge et al., 2015). In one study, however, Colledge et al. (2015) found significant differences, with bisexuals having poorer outcomes for the following: suicidality and suicide attempts, self-harm, eating concerns, mood concerns, poor physical health, some drug use (marijuana and tranquilizers), lack of LGBTQI+ community connections, lower rates of being out to family and friends, and being less likely to have a partner.

Counseling Skills and Techniques

LGB individuals, and bisexuals in particular, have also been found in the literature to have higher rates of utilization of mental health services (Pachankis & Goldfried, 2013), which means that they often encounter services that are not able to meet their unique needs (Ross et al., 2010). In addition to the shortage of research, the literature consistently points to the fact that mental health professionals are inadequately trained to address the unique needs of bisexual clients or, for that matter, lesbian or gay clients (Pachankis & Goldfried, 2013).

This need is heightened when one considers that almost all therapists report having at least one LGB client (Pachankis & Goldfried, 2013). Mental health professionals often can inadvertently promote homophobia (or biphobia more specifically) and heterocentrism because they themselves are unaware of their own biases and may use models and interventions that emerge from these worldviews (Pachankis & Goldfried, 2013). Some common negative experiences with counseling reported by bi/pan/poly individuals have been that counselors expressed judgment, invalidated their bisexual identity as a real identity, pathologized their bisexual identity, or posed excessively personal and unnecessary questions (Eady et al., 2011). It is also important to note that, to add to the difficulty bi/pan/poly people may experience when seeking mental health services, mental health professionals may need to overcome negative attitudes that come from historical (and current) oppression of LGBTQI+ people by mental health professionals. Historically, and in many cases currently as well, LGBTQI+ persons have had negative relationships with mental health professionals because of the ways in which their identities have been pathologized (Ross et al., 2010). This can be seen in more overt forms through practices such as conversion therapy and diagnosis (in the case of gender dysphoria for transgender people) and in more covert forms, as when therapists may inadvertently use microaggressions in their interactions with bi/pan/poly clients (e.g., when clients' identity becomes the focus of therapy even though it is unrelated to their presenting concern).

Pachankis and Goldfried (2013) laid out some important considerations for affirming practice as a way to combat the heterocentrism and homophobia that are present in the mental health field. They suggested that therapists increase their contact with LGBTQI+ individuals in their own lives and communities to gain more familiarity with their lived experiences (Pachankis & Goldfried, 2013). They noted that counselors should reflect on their own values, biases, and assumptions about LGBTQI+ identities as well as explore the meaning that their own affectional orientation provides in their life; counselors should similarly become aware of how their own identity may impact their client conceptualizations (Pachankis & Goldfried, 2013). *Counseling Competencies for Counseling LGBQQIA Individuals* (Harper et al., 2013) promotes reflecting around one's own personal identity, gaining knowledge of the rich history and culture of LGBTQI+ individuals, understanding systemic oppressions these individuals may face, engaging in regular supervision, and using a strengths-based approach instead of a deficit model. An additional consideration found in the work by Pachankis and Goldfried is that therapists who also identify as LGB are not immune from bias. Specifically, lesbian and gay therapists may find particular challenges with bisexual clients; all LGBTQI+ helping professionals may also promote acceptance of identities to the point that there is little space to explore shame that clients may experience or that clients are encouraged to come out before they are ready (Pachankis & Goldfried, 2013). In addition, there can be boundary crossings in small LGBTQI+ communities, and confidentiality and appropriate professional boundaries can be difficult to maintain (Pachankis & Goldfried, 2013).

No studies to date have examined specific theoretical approaches in therapy and their effectiveness with bi/pan/poly populations (Pachankis & Goldfried, 2013). Some suggest that a variety of theoretical interventions may be effective, particularly if mental health professionals use an affirmative approach (Pachankis & Goldfried, 2013). As stated previously, Harper and colleagues (2013) encouraged the use of a strengths-based approach. They also noted the particular benefit of a feminist and social justice lens because of the ability to understand and conceptualize concerns in a framework that considers the effects of oppression on individuals and their mental health.

Some guidelines for the tasks of therapy are present in the literature. One suggests the following as important tasks: promoting the establishment of a support network of other

LGBTQI+ individuals; assisting clients in examining and becoming aware of the ways in which they experience oppression/marginalization; addressing and reducing shame and guilt associated with sexual behaviors, thoughts, and feelings; and demonstrating explicit respect and value for clients' identity and experiences (Pachankis & Goldfried, 2013). Others have also noted the importance of advocacy in working with LGBTQI+ clients as a means of addressing institutional barriers and systemic injustices that LGBTQI+ clients may face (Pachankis & Goldfried, 2013). Of equal importance is for mental health professionals to be aware of resources for bi/pan/poly clients that are available in the community, with special prescreening to ensure that the queer community is affirmative of bisexual identities (Harper et al., 2013; Pachankis & Goldfried, 2013).

Conclusion

Bisexuals, pansexuals, and polysexuals can face the same issues that lesbians and gay men encounter; however, in a binary-coded world, the fluidity of their affectional orientation and gender identities can cause confusion for them as well as those around them. Bisexuals face marginalization and prejudice from both heterosexual and LGBTQI+ communities. In addition to overt discrimination, bi/pan/poly persons encounter monosexism, biphobia, bisexual invisibility, and bisexual erasure. As a result of these additional minority stressors, bi/pan/poly people have been found to have worse physical and mental health than their heterosexual and lesbian/gay peers. Affirmative therapy strategies are thought to work well with bi/pan/poly persons. Using a feminist and social justice view, counselors can help bi/pan/poly clients develop a positive identity, coping skills, an affirmative social network, and the resources needed to promote wellness.

Questions for Further Discussion

1. What types of bias is Miranda experiencing? How might this be different if Miranda were an ethnic minority as well?
2. How is bisexual erasure impacting Miranda in her current relationship?
3. How might Miranda's experience be different if she identified as pansexual or polysexual?
4. What common errors do you think counselors might make when working with bi/pan/poly clients? Which would be the most damaging to a client like Miranda? What can be done after such mistakes are made?
5. What are the most important things you think a counselor can do in working with Miranda to provide bisexual affirmative counseling?

Resources

1. Visit the American Institute of Bisexuality information and advocacy site at https://bisexual.org/.
2. Surf the Bisexual Resource Center to learn more at http://www.biresource.net/.
3. Read the article "Pansexuality 101: It's More Than 'Just Another Letter'" at http://everydayfeminism.com/2014/11/pansexuality-101/.
4. Review a glossary of polysexual terms at https://www.morethantwo.com/poly-glossary.html.
5. Surf the website of Robyn Ochs, educator, writer, and activist for bisexual issues, at https://robynochs.com/.

References

Bleiberg, S., Fertmann, A., Friedman, A. T., & Godino, C. (2005). The layer cake model of bisexual identity development: Clarifying preconceived notions. *Campus Activities Programming, 37*(8), 53–58.

Caldwell, K. (2010). We exist: Intersectional in/visibility in bisexuality and disability. *Disability Studies Quarterly, 30*(3/4). Retrieved from http://dsq-sds.org/article/view/1273/1303

Callis, A. S. (2014). Bisexual, pansexual, queer: Non binary identities and the sexual borderlands. *Sexualities, 17*, 63–80. doi:10.1177/1363460713511094

Cass, V. C. (1979). Homosexual identity formation: A theoretical model. *Journal of Homosexuality, 4*(3), 219–235.

Centers for Disease Control and Prevention. (2014). *National Health Interview Survey.* Retrieved from http://www.cdc.gov/nchs/nhis/

Colledge, L., Hickson, F., Reid, D., & Weatherburn, P. (2015). Poorer mental health in UK bisexual women than lesbians: Evidence from the UK 2007 Stonewall Women's Health Survey. *Journal of Public Health.* Advance online publication. doi:10.1093/pubmed/fdu105

Crompton, L. (2003). *Homosexuality and civilization.* Cambridge, MA: Belknap Press.

Deschamps, C. (2008). Visual scripts and power struggles: Bisexuality and visibility. *Journal of Bisexuality, 8*, 131–139.

Dworkin, S. H. (2001). Treating the bisexual client. *Journal of Clinical Psychology, 57*, 671–680.

Eady, A., Dobinson, C., & Ross, L. E. (2011). Bisexual people's experiences with mental health services: A qualitative investigation. *Community Mental Health Journal, 47*, 378–389. doi:10.1007/s10597-010-9329-x

Elizabeth, A. (2013). Challenging the binary: Sexual identity that is not duality. *Journal of Bisexuality, 13*, 329–337. doi:10.1080/15299716.2013.813421

Fallas, J. A. (2011). *Disrupting patriarchal norms and languages: Narrative and rhetorical analyses of bi and pansexual feminist blogs* (Doctoral dissertation). Available from ProQuest dissertations and theses database. (ProQuest Document ID No. 1221035559)

GLAAD. (2014). *GLAAD media reference guide* (9th ed.). Retrieved from http://www.glaad.org/reference

Gonel, A. H. (2013). Pansexual identification in online communities: Employing a collaborative queer method to study pansexuality. *Graduate Journal of Social Science, 10*(1), 36–59.

Harper, A., Finnerty, P., Martinez, M., Brace, A., Crethar, H. C., Loos, B., . . . Lambert, S. (2013). Association for Lesbian, Gay, Bisexual, and Transgender Issues in Counseling (ALGBTIC) competencies for counseling with lesbian, gay, bisexual, queer, questioning, intersex, and ally individuals. *Journal of LGBT Issues in Counseling, 7*, 2–43.

King, A. R. (2010). Are we coming of age? A critique of Collins's proposed model of biracial-bisexual identity development. *Journal of Bisexuality, 11*, 98–120. doi:10.1080/15299716.2011.545314

Kinsey, A. (1948). *Sexual behavior in the human male.* Bloomington: Indiana University Press.

Kuper, L. E., Nussbaum, R., & Mustanski, B. (2012). Exploring the diversity of gender and sexual orientation identities in an online sample of transgender individuals. *Sex Research, 49*, 244–254. doi:10.1080/00224499.2011.596954

Ochs, R. (2007). What's in a name? Why women embrace or resist bisexual identity. In B. A. Firestein (Ed.), *Becoming visible: Counseling bisexuals across the lifespan* (pp. 72–87). New York, NY: Columbia University Press.

Pachankis, J. E., & Goldfried, M. R. (2013). Clinical issues in working with lesbian, gay, and bisexual clients. *Psychology of Sexual Orientation and Gender Diversity, 1*(S), 45–58. doi:10.1037/2329-0382.1.S.45

Pew Research Center. (2013). *A survey of LGBT Americans: Attitudes, experiences and values in changing times.* Retrieved from http://www.pewsocialtrends.org/2013/06/13/a-survey-of-lgbt-americans/

Rice, K. (2009). Pansexuality. In M. Cavendish (Ed.), *Sex and society* (p. 593). Stockbridge, MA: Hard Press.

Ross, L. E., Dobinson, C., & Eady, A. (2010). Perceived determinants of mental health for bisexual people: A qualitative examination. *American Journal of Public Health, 111,* 496–502.

Roughgarden, J. (2004). *Evolution's rainbow: Diversity, gender and sexuality in nature and people.* Berkeley, CA: University of California Press.

San Francisco Human Rights Campaign, LGBT Advisory Committee. (2011). *Bisexual invisibility: Impacts and recommendations.* Retrieved from http://sf-hrc.org/sites/default/files/Documents/HRC_Publications/Articles/Bisexual_Invisiblity_Impacts_and_Recommendations_March_2011.pdf

Soble, A. (2006). Bisexuality. In *Sex from Plato to Paglia: A philosophical encyclopedia* (p. 115). Westport, CT: Greenwood.

Weinberg, M. S., Williams, C. J., & Pryor, D. W. (1994). *Dual attraction: Understanding bisexuality.* New York, NY: Oxford University Press.

YouGov. (2015). *1 in 2 young people say they are not 100% heterosexual.* Retrieved from https://yougov.co.uk/news/2015/08/16/half-young-not-heterosexual

Chapter 14

Counseling Transgender Clients

Robyn Brammer and Misty M. Ginicola

But you can only lie about who you are for so long without going crazy.
—Ellen Wittlinger

• • •

Awareness of Attitudes and Beliefs Self-Check

1. Close your eyes and picture someone who is transgender. What do you see? How are your biases present in your image? Does the image change if you picture a male versus a female?
2. What people do you know who are out as transgender, including celebrities? What transgender characters have you seen in movies or on television? How are they usually represented?
3. If one of your parents were to tell you that they were transgender, what would be your reaction? Your fears?

Case Study

Michelle is a 49-year-old African American transwoman. She tells her story in her own words: "I wish I could describe where things slipped out of control. I spent the first 40 years of my life trying to convince myself of the lie: that I was supposed to be a boy. Despite the veracity of the inner voice shouting my true gender, I wanted to live for others. I tried my best. I played football, married a woman, adopted children, started a masculine career, and tried settling into the role. The part I can't describe is why it didn't work. Although I earned material possessions, love, status, and a respected identity, none of it felt real. How can you feel content when everything you do and think feels like a lie?

"I tried breaking out of the narrative. In my early teens, I told various members of my family about my need to transition. In my later teens, I told my girlfriend. In my 20s, I told my counselor and subsequently a psychologist and psychiatrist. The latter two told me I had 'fantasy delusions.' But I felt content and substantive when I engaged in the world as a woman. I would sneak out to shop, study, or just have coffee somewhere. I needed to know that people could see me—that I was real. These feelings mounted and mounted until I sought out doctors, who always told me that transitioning would ruin my life. I then pushed the feelings deeper, creating a black hole in my soul. It was soul shattering.

"One night I walked through the door of my home, and it hit me: I didn't exist. I wept for an hour until my wife came home. I confessed that I could not continue as a male. She was kind and understanding, knowing of my struggle, but she also divorced me. I felt lost, confused, happy, strong, broken, content, and frightened. When the hormones kicked in, the second puberty made me more reactive. I lost even more friends, people questioned my leadership at work, and I started to wonder whether I could survive. Without conscious thought, I grabbed a knife, clutched it in my hand, and walked toward the bathroom. I had no conscious thought of suicide. I had been mildly suicidal for nearly a decade, but on this occasion I only knew that life was too hard. I felt unloved, insignificant, valueless, and hopeless. After two steps, I collapsed on the floor and wept. I threw the knife, called a friend, and continued on my journey.

"Things slowly improved. The darkness, once all encompassing, showed glimpses of light. I moved to a new state, started a new job, gained new friends, and everything started fitting together. Today, most days are finally bright. I shudder when I think of how close I came to death. What would have happened if my friend had not been available? What would have happened if I had lost my job? We don't realize how tenuous life can be until we find ourselves dangling from the edge of our rope."

• • •

Awareness of Differences

As evidenced in Michelle's case, people who are transgender experience a disconnect between their sense of gender and the one seemingly represented in their body (Chang, Singh, & Rossman, 2017; Harper et al., 2013; Killermann, 2013; Singh, Hwahng, Chang, & White, 2017). The term *transgender* is used to describe a broad array of people who share this discordance between their designated sex at birth and their gender identity. In order to have a true understanding of gender, it is important to be clear on terminology. A person's *sex* is the classification of being male or female, as designated by the medical or birthing professional based on a cursory examination of the external genitalia. The result of this process is referred to as *designated sex at birth*. This examination is made with the assumption that people's external genitalia will match their internal genitalia, gendered brain, sex hormones, and sex chromosomes. However, this cursory inspection has no way of revealing people's *gender,* which is their feelings, attitudes, and behavior associated with their sex, or their *gender identity,* which involves people's sense of themselves related to the cultural concepts of male, female, or neither. These cultural concepts are conventionally defined as *masculinity* and *femininity* and are evidenced through *gender expression* and *presentation,* which can include behavior, demeanor, body language, hairstyle, clothing, and accessories. The majority of people are *gender normative,* which means that their gender identity is not largely disconnected from their designated sex. When people do not experience a discordance between their designated sex at birth and their gender identity, they are known as *cisgender.* However, transgender persons are a *gender minority,* as their gender identity differs from that of the majority of the population. As minorities, their experiences and needs are likely to be misunderstood and marginalized.

As children, transgender persons are typically *gender nonconforming* because they exhib-it a gender identity and gender presentation that is not aligned with cultural expectations surrounding masculinity or femininity (Chang et al., 2017; Harper et al., 2013; Killermann, 2013; Singh et al., 2017). However, under the transgender and gender-nonconforming um-brella, there are distinctly different experiences. In some cases, gender nonconforming has to do with typical gender variation in heterosexual and cisgender populations. For ex-ample, a male child may wish to paint his fingernails and play with dolls. This may just be *gender variant* or *gender expansive,* as it expands past the conventional, culturally assigned notions of masculine and feminine. Toys and dress do not truly carry a gender; it is quite normative for a child to explore and wish to participate in a variety of activities and play. However, in a *binary* culture, in which sex and gender are seen as distinct and opposite ways of being, gender variation may be seen as problematic or pathological.

In other cases, gender nonconforming can be related to variant affectional orientation (Chang et al., 2017; Harper et al., 2013; Killermann, 2013; Singh et al., 2017). For example, a female child who will later identify as a lesbian may not want to play with dolls or wear dresses and may prefer playing with stereotypically and culturally assigned male toys, such as cars and trucks. Her gender identity is also gender expansive, but she may later connect her sense of gender to an *affectional orientation,* or indication of the type of person with whom she is predisposed to bond emotionally, physically, sexually, psychologically, and spiritually. Gender and affectional orientation are distinctly different concepts: Who one *is* and whom one *loves* are separate constructs. However, they can be connected in one's identity. For ex-ample, this female child may grow up and identify as a butch lesbian, which indicates an identification with masculine cultural traits. This identification could also include *drag queens* and *drag kings,* who are predominantly of a variant affectional orientation but cross-dress for entertainment purposes and identify with drag culture, in which gender expression, gender play, and exploration of femininity or masculinity are common.

A child with gender nonconformity may also identify as *genderqueer,* which indicates a person whose gender identity is not adequately captured by a binary male or female designation (Chang et al., 2017; Harper et al., 2013; Killermann, 2013; Singh et al., 2017). As adolescents or adults, genderqueer individuals may view their gender as outside the conventional expectations of male or female. They could think of themselves as being both male and female, known as *bigender,* or as having no gender, known as *agender.* They may also identify as *third gender,* which is another gender altogether; many cultures and societ-ies formally and historically recognize a third gender category option. They may also see themselves as having multiple genders, known as *pangender* or *omnigender.* They may see themselves as *genderfluid,* which indicates that one's gender shifts and changes over time. Genderqueer individuals may reject *gender binary* (i.e., only male and female) identities and may wish to use nonbinary pronouns such as *ze, per, sie, hir, v, they, them, one, e,* and *eir.* It is important to note that some may also consider the word *queer* offensive and prefer al-ternatives, such as *gender variant, gender questioning,* or *gender neutral.* Genderqueer persons are discussed further in Chapter 15.

Finally, gender nonconforming can be present in childhood for someone who identi-fies as transgender with a strong wish to transition. To *transition* means to move from a designated sex at birth to a gender expression and presentation congruent, authentic, and in harmony with one's gender identity (Chang et al., 2017; Harper et al., 2013; Killermann, 2013; Singh et al., 2017). People can make a *social transition,* which involves moving toward their gender identity through expression and presentation, evidenced in their behavior and clothing. It can also mean changing their name and legal docu-ments. A person could also wish to transition physically through the use of *hormone replacement therapy,* a medical process of administering hormone blockers (for the sex that does not match the person's gender identity) and sex hormones (for the sex that does match the person's gender identity). *Second puberty* can be the result of hormone replacement therapy. Second puberty is often just as confusing, emotional, and challenging as the first puberty—only the individual may lack peer support or a sense of normality in the process. A person may wish to transition through *gender confirmation surgery*, which can involve *top surgery* (modification to the chest or breasts), *bottom surgery* (modification to genitalia), and plastic surgery (in order to create secondary sex characteristics, such as feminine facial features, etc.). It is important to note that not all transgender persons who wish to transition will wish to have surgical intervention. Transgender people may or may not transition socially; they also may or may not transition physically and surgically. If they do choose to have surgery, they may or may not have all forms of surgery. This often depends on the severity of the discordance between their designated sex and gender identity, their ability to pay for the high costs of surgery, the acceptance in their environment for gender nonconforming, the risks associated with surgical intervention, and their satisfaction with making a social transition and/or receiving hormone replacement therapy. It may also be related to their ability to *pass,* which is a term used by the transgender community to indicate the ability to be accepted by others as a person's gender identity. Being able to "pass" can result in fewer experiences of harassment, abuse, and/or discrimination, known as *bias incidents.* Those who are not readily identified by others as transgender may harbor guilt for "passing," as it is considered a privilege in the transgender community; some may even consider those who "pass" to be cisgender.

When people desire to transition in any manner, it indicates that their gender identity is strongly different from their designated sex at birth (Chang et al., 2017; Harper et al., 2013; Killermann, 2013; Singh et al., 2017). For example, a female child who states, "I am not a girl. I am a boy," in the context of gender nonconformity may wish to transition. Transgender people may also often experience distress and impairment from not being able to express themselves as their authentic gender. Like Michelle from the case study, the discordance can be so pervasive and distressful that it can only be described as "soul shattering." This chapter focuses on these persons, who are most commonly associated with the term *transgender.* Transgender persons who desired to transition were once called *transsexuals.* However, this is an outdated term that many find derogatory; it should be avoided unless someone specifically identifies as a transsexual man or transsexual woman.

A transgender person may identify in many different ways (Chang et al., 2017; Harper et al., 2013; Killermann, 2013; Singh et al., 2017). A person may identify as a transgender man, transman, or FtM/F2M, meaning the person is transitioning from being a female designated at birth to a male gender identity. A person may identify as a transgender woman, transwoman, or MtF/M2F, meaning the person is transitioning from being designated male at birth to a female gender identity. These persons wish to recognize and/or honor both their gender identity and their transgender identity, meaning that they had a different designated sex at birth. It is very important to note that many transgender persons will not wish to do this and may simply identify as male or female. This is partly because of the antipathy toward their history and their designated sex at birth, which may be very painful and a narrative that they do not wish to own. When individuals grow up with a sense of dysphoria, they may attempt to resist any identity with the journey that caused them harm. Some clients avoid any identity associated with being transgender; however, others may identify strongly with the transgender label. However, it is important to ask how clients identify and what terms, including pronouns, they use in reference to their gender.

Changing Terminology

Terminology in the transgender culture is always shifting and changing (Chang et al., 2017; Harper et al., 2013; Killermann, 2013; Singh et al., 2017). The sheer number of terms and conflicting information about which terms are acceptable can be overwhelming to a professional new to transgender clinical work and research. The reasons for these shifting terms are complex. First, as American culture is predominantly heteronormative, cisnormative (the assumption that all persons are cisgender), and binary, the initial terms used to describe gender issues often indicated a lack of understanding and bias. Gender identity issues are relatively new to research. Even though affectional orientation has been recognized and studied for a long period of time, transgender identity was not always recognized as having unique needs. Karl Heinrich Ulrichs (1864/1994), arguably the first author to publish a scientific justification for affectional orientation variance in the mid-1800s, unfortunately blended together affectional orientation and gender identity. As a gay man who believed that his feminine instincts were associated with his love of men, he published a series of 12 tracts on "homosexuality" in which he argued that some men have feminine temperaments. Unfortunately, this has led others to conflate gender identity with affectional orientation. As more research is conducted, the faulty assumptions in the terminology are exposed.

For example, it was once common to refer to a transgender person's "biological" or "genetic" sex, as in "a biological female" (Brammer, 2012; Chang et al., 2017; Harper et al., 2013; Killermann, 2013; Singh et al., 2017). This term is created on the assumption that someone is either "biologically female" or "biologically male." However, intersex persons experience a discordance among their chromosomes, hormones, internal and external genitalia, and secondary sex characteristics. It is also a problematic term because it assumes that all of biology is visible or measurable and that transgender people wish to live contrary to their biology. Neither of these assumptions is accurate: The gendered brain, which is very likely also a biological and physiological phenomenon, can differ from a person's designated sex at birth. Similarly, the terms *born a man* or *born a woman* are problematic for the same reasons. In addition, they are very technically inaccurate, as people are born babies, not men and women. The term *sex change* is similarly inaccurate, as it suggests that people are changing their sex rather than aligning their designated sex with their gender identity. Similarly, some people may think of a transman as "a man trapped in a woman's body." Even though there is a recognition of this individual as a *woman,* there is a tacit conceptualization of her as a *him. He* is a man even if he still has a vagina. His journey should be recognized through terminology, pronouns, and titles. It is also incredibly important that counselors investigate their own subconscious thoughts and assumptions surrounding gender and transgender issues, as counselors are also impacted by heteronormative and cisnormative cultural attitudes and messages.

Second, because American culture is heteronormative, cisnormative, and binary, any variation from the culturally sanctioned gender roles can result in marginalization and stigma (Chang et al., 2017; Harper et al., 2013; Killermann, 2013; Singh et al., 2017). A term used historically in a medical or a clinical context over time can begin to carry stigma (Chang et al., 2017; Killermann, 2013). Similar to what has happened with the term *homosexuality,* terms for marginalized groups of people can become slang or carry so much stigma that they must be changed (Chang et al., 2017; Killermann, 2013). This was similarly experienced with terms describing intellectual disability, which changed from *simpleton, moron, feeble-minded,* and *retarded* to *intellectual disability* (Reynolds, Zupanick, & Dombeck, 2013). The term *cross-dresser* has replaced the term *transvestite,* as the latter term has become pathologized by its use as the mental disorder and paraphilia transvestic disorder

(Killermann, 2013). The term *transsexual* has also shifted out of common use, as it carried stigma, and is no longer used by most in the transgender community (Killermann, 2013). It is also associated with the term *tranny*, which is derogatory. The word *transgender* is also sometimes used incorrectly, reflecting the stigma associated with gender variance (Killermann, 2013). For example, some people will say "transgenders" or "a transgender"; however, *transgender* is an adjective, not a noun. Therefore, saying "Mark is a transgender" is as incorrect as saying "Mark is a gay." Similarly, "transgendered" is a misuse of the term as well: "Sue is transgendered" is as incorrect as "Sue is gayed."

Finally, the reason there have been so many additional terms, often confused with another, is simply that gender is based on one's subjective sense of self (Chang et al., 2017; Harper et al., 2013; Killermann, 2013; Singh et al., 2017). Gender identity is on a spectrum (see Chapter 15 for a full discussion), which means that there are many points on that spectrum with which a person can identify. In addition, if people consider their gender identity in the context of their intersectional identities, such as their affectional orientation and/or ethnicity, they have even more ways to identify. For example, an African American person who identifies as queer may self-identify as BlaQ, a Latin American genderqueer person may describe themselves as Latinx, or a lesbian who identifies very strongly with femininity may describe herself as femme. Because of this, there could be millions of different gender identities and labels to match different intersectional identities.

Regardless of the reasons for the shifting terminology, it is very important that counselor educators provide training on affirming language and practices for work with lesbian, gay, bisexual, transgender, queer, questioning, intersex, asexual, ally, pansexual/polysexual, and two-spirited (LGBTQI+) clients (Gess, 2016). Counselors must continue to seek out additional professional development and networking with transgender communities in order to continue to learn and stay up to date on terminology. In order to provide competent services to transgender and gender-nonconforming clients, counselors must recognize that some language can serve as microaggressions; counselors must learn which terms can be offensive and which terms should be avoided (see the Glossary of Terms at the end of the book).

Third Gender as a Cultural Phenomenon

An Oregon court recently ruled that a citizen, Jamie Shupe, could legally identify as a third-gender person (Foden-Vencil, 2016). However, the United States is behind several other countries in recognizing gender identity as a social construct (Andrist, 2014; Park & Dhitavat, 2015; Quinto, 2003; Totman, 2003). Argentina and Denmark were the first countries to let citizens self-label. In these countries, if people view themselves as members of a gender, they may change their legally recognized gender. There is also a similar movement emerging to include a third gender option on legal documentation. Nepal was the first country to implement a third gender option, in 2007, with Pakistan, Bangladesh, Germany, New Zealand, and Australia following suit. In these countries, individuals may identify as neither gender. In Australia, for example, an X rather than an M or F indicates the third gender. Although these legal designations are relatively new, the third-gender or transgender identity has a long history in several different cultures.

Thailand has recognized a transgender identity called the *Kathoey*, which are typically transwomen (Totman, 2003). Although the Kathoey are a recognized group, they are still highly marginalized (Byung'chu-Käng, 2014). Many Kathoey are exposed to transphobia and violence (often from brothers or fathers) from an early age (Nemoto et al., 2012). They are often prohibited from upper-class professions and may also struggle financially; thus, they may engage in the sex trade, which can make them vulnerable to sexually transmitted infections such as HIV (Nemoto et al., 2012; Totman, 2003). In 2015, the Thai government moved to change the constitution to protect those who do not identify as male or female but as a third gender termed *phet thi sam* (Park & Dhitavat, 2015). The presence of the Kathoey helped move this legislation forward.

Similar debates are occurring in Indonesia for its identified group, the Waria, which represent people designated male at birth with a female soul; Waria can include gay males, transwomen, cross-dressers, and drag queens (Andrist, 2014). Like the Kathoey and Waria cultures, Hijra culture in India has gained international prominence (Kalra & Shah, 2013). Hijra culture has existed in India for thousands of years, and it includes individuals who may be eunuchs, intersex, or transgender (Kalra & Shah, 2013). Although not by name, Hijra culture is even celebrated in the *Mahabharata* and the *Kama Sutra* (sacred religious texts; Kalra & Shah, 2013). Despite this history, many people who identify as Hijra are unable to find employment (Kalra & Shah, 2013). They were regarded as one of the lowest castes and often turned to the sex trade for survival (Kalra & Shah, 2013). However, in 2014, the Indian supreme court required legal protections for these third-gender persons (Kalra & Shah, 2013). This followed similar legislation from Nepal, Pakistan, and Bangladesh (Kaldera, 2007).

These other countries often have a history of acceptance for these groups; however, following modernization and/or colonization, the third gender identification became marginalized and stigmatized. The United States has a similar history of marginalizing gender minorities following colonization. In numerous Native cultures, people have identified as two-spirited, indicating that they have both feminine and masculine spirits in them (Lehavot, Walters, & Simoni, 2009). Although two-spirit persons can be transgender, *two-spirit* is an umbrella term used to describe a person who has gender and/or affectional orientation variance (Lehavot et al., 2009). Two-spirit persons were historically a blessing to the tribe, as they were associated with tribal social and spiritual significance. Although traditionally accepted and valued, following colonization, two-spirit persons have faced increased rates of violence in their homes, community, and society, leading to increases in posttraumatic stress disorder and other psychological symptoms (Balsam, Huang, Fieland, Simoni, & Walters, 2004). As Raven Heavy Runner said, "The two-spirit movement if anything is a decolonization process, to support the Native community and to reclaim those roles we used to have" (Quinto, 2003, p. 15).

Where ancient cultures remain intact, there appears to be significantly more acceptance. For example, in the Isthmus of Tehuantepec in Mexico, the Juchitán have a gendered group called *muxe* that is highly respected and valued (Brunjes, 2011). The Siberian shamans valued a group of individuals called the Ergi, who could transform to become the gender needed (to complete love, a specific task, etc.; Kaldera, 2007). *Fa'afafine* is a recognized third gender designation in Samoa and the Samoan diaspora (Bartlett & Vasey, 2006). Such individuals are usually birth-assigned males whose behaviors range from very feminine to moderately masculine (Bartlett & Vasey, 2006). The sworn virgins of Albania and Montenegro are usually birth-assigned females who take on masculine roles but remain celibate (Young, 2000).

Prevalence

Transgender and gender-nonconforming people are more visible in American society today than in recent history (Hendricks & Testa, 2012). When Caitlyn Jenner came out, a national conversation emerged about what it means to be transgender. Gates (2011) reported that based on population studies in California and Massachusetts, approximately 0.3% of the adult population identifies as transgender. However, newer data from the Centers for Disease Control and Prevention's Behavioral Risk Factor Surveillance System indicate that the prevalence is closer to 0.6% of the adult population (Flores, Herman, Gates, & Brown, 2016). Flores and colleagues (2016) also found that younger adults (0.66%) had a higher prevalence of transgender identity than elderly adults (0.50%), which may reflect improving knowledge and acceptance of gender variance and transgender issues. However, because the definition of transgender may be different across research (as an umbrella term or only including those who wish to transition), estimates may vary widely. Although population studies to date have not included youth, Steensma, McGuire, Kreukels, Beekman, and Cohen-Kettenis (2013) did investigate the persistence of gender dysphoria from childhood to adolescence. Their findings suggest that the intensity of discordance significantly predicts whether transgender identity will persist into adulthood.

Knowledge of Issues and Problems

Identity Development

Although various accepting cultural groups throughout history openly allowed people to identify as third gender, transitioning in modern-day society is challenging and involves several stages. Pinto and Moleiro (2015) identified five developmental stages for transgender persons seeking to transition. First, people feel confusion and an increasing sense of gender difference. The intensity of this discordance leads them to seek a label, identity, or cause for their experience. Second, they explore a new identity and find an explanation and a label; they understand themselves as transgender or see that their designated sex at birth does not match their gender identity. Third, they begin actively exploring transition options and deciding what to do and when to do it. They will be thinking critically about all different types of transitions, what fits them best, and what the consequences and benefits of each type of transition are. Fourth, they embrace their gender identity with their chosen transition. Fifth, they may experience their transgender identity as part of their experience rather than as an all-encompassing identity. They may also seek to make their transgender status invisible, seeking to be recognized by others as their true gender identity and not recognized as transgender in any way.

Experiences of Bias

When transgender people come out, they may experience numerous microaggressions from their friends, family, and community (Galupo, Henise, & Davis, 2014). Microaggressions are understated, subtle forms of discrimination (Galupo et al., 2014). Whether intentional or unintentional, microaggressions shape the daily experience of transgender individuals; they play a central role in social and personal relationships (Galupo et al., 2014). Galupo and colleagues (2014) reported the greatest incidence of microaggressions from cisgender, heterosexual friends, but the most painful aggressions came from those in the LGBTQI+ communities. Individuals from the queer community do not always understand or acknowledge identities different from their own, particularly if they are nonbinary; thus, transgender persons may face significant negative attitudes from both their heterosexual and queer peers (Farmer & Byrd, 2015). LGBTQI+ persons may internalize these heterosexist and transphobic attitudes, which can cause pain to themselves as well as others in the LGBTQI+ communities (Puckett & Levitt, 2015). In the context of queer friendships, words of criticism may be felt more painfully from persons the transgender individual expects will have greater understanding (Galupo et al., 2014).

Microaggressions, regardless of the speaker, can be incredibly hurtful and isolating. Microaggressive statements regarding a person's transgender status might include (Heffernan, 2015) "Why can't you just be okay being butch?" "You will never be a real woman," and "Did you transition because you thought you were an ugly girl?" Microaggressions can also include questions about "real" body parts, questions about whether or not someone has had surgery, and intimate sexual questions (Galupo et al., 2014). Counselors may also inadvertently commit microaggressions by misunderstanding some of the key components of gender (e.g., referring to "biological" sex), confusing affectional and gender orientation (e.g., assuming that transfemales are gay because they bond with men—if they identify as female, they more likely identify as heterosexual), using a term incorrectly (e.g., saying "transgendered"), and/or making assumptions regarding transitioning (e.g., assuming that all transgender persons wish to transition surgically).

Many of these microaggressions, as well as the experience of discrimination and violence, can be linked to how congruent transgender persons' gender expression is with their gender identity; in other words, can the individuals "pass" as the other gender without others knowing that they are transgender (Velez, Breslow, Brewster, Cox, & Foster, 2016)? Other people in a transgender person's life may openly comment on or question the transgender person's body, dress, and genitalia. These microaggressions and discrimination related to "passing" can cause body surveillance and image issues, preoccupation with societal cultural standards of attractiveness, eating disorders, and/or a desire for surgery. In essence, transgender persons commonly experience objectification of their bodies.

Similar to other members of the LGBTQI+ communities, transgender persons are at risk for increased bullying and violence, including physical assault and sexual assault violence (Dank, Lachman, Zweig, & Yahner, 2014; Langenderfer-Magruder, Walls, Whitfield, Brown, & Barrett, 2016; Wilson, 2013). Many transgender persons live in poverty partially because of employment and social discrimination (Grant et al., 2011). If they have performed some kind of sex work to survive, they are also at a significantly higher risk for violence and suicide attempts (Nemoto et al., 2012). Transgender-based harassment and discrimination in school systems are incredibly common, as almost 80% of transgender youth report being harassed, 35% being physically assaulted, and 12% being sexually assaulted while at school (Grant et al., 2011). Transgender individuals have reported high rates of experiences of stigma, bullying, verbal and emotional harassment and abuse, physical abuse, and sexual abuse related not only to homophobia but also to transphobia in particular (Dank et al., 2014; Langenderfer-Magruder et al., 2016; Wilson, 2013). Homophobia and transphobia can put many transgender persons at risk for anti-LGBT hate crimes, which can include homicide (Kelley & Gruenewald, 2015; Woods & Herman, 2015). Those who commit these crimes reportedly do so with a goal of protecting or accomplishing their masculinity (Kelley & Gruenewald, 2015). It is important to understand that the experience of bias, assault, and discrimination can significantly increase the risk of suicide in transgender persons (Grant et al., 2011).

Transgender individuals are considered double minorities when their gender minority status intersects with their ethnic minority status; in these cases, they may experience an increased risk for violence, discrimination, and harassment (Graham, 2014). Not only is discrimination greater for transgender people of color, but the physical and mental health impacts are increasingly devastating (Grant et al., 2011). Much of this increased harassment and violence occurs in structural and social institutions (Wilton & Short, 2016). For example, Black transwomen report high rates of violence in their schools and churches, as well as in the criminal justice system (Graham, 2014). The ethnic minority transgender person in these contexts encounters racism, genderism, and the combination of intersectional prejudice; this can lead to an internalization of negative attitudes and increased shame surrounding being a person of color and a transgender person (Meyer, 2012).

Employment issues and discrimination are significant problems for transgender persons (Grant et al., 2011). Transgender persons have twice the rate of unemployment as the general population; transgender persons of color have up to 4 times the unemployment rate as the general population (Grant et al., 2011). To date in the United States, gender identity remains unprotected at the federal level. In the majority of states, individuals may be dismissed from employment because of their gender identity. More than 25% of transgender persons have lost a job because of being transgender, with 47% experiencing an adverse job outcome, which includes being denied a promotion because of being gender nonconforming or transgender. Issues surrounding employment can lead to work in an underground economy (such as the drug or sex trade). Persons who experience employment discrimination are 4 times more likely to experience homelessness; they are also more likely to be incarcerated and use drugs.

Budge, Tebbe, and Howard (2010) identified the fact that the process of transitioning at work requires multiple phases. There is a preparation phase, in which the individual must decide how and when to come out. After coming out, there are then considerations regarding how to dress, act, and interact. Regardless of how well the transgender person handles this phase, there are probable complications from some at work, including microaggressions and discrimination. In addition, if the person is transitioning to female, she may experience female-based sexism and gender discrimination.

Transgender persons frequently experience bias, verbal harassment, and discrimination in housing, with more than 19% reporting having been refused an apartment or house (Grant et al., 2011). Even when they find shelter in a homeless shelter, more than half of transgender persons (55%) report being harassed by shelter staff or residents. These experiences of bias are common in public accommodations (such as retail stores, airports, hotels, doctor's offices, legal services, treatment programs, and counseling centers) as well. Transgender persons also report experiences of harassment, physical assault, and sexual assault at the hands of the police and in the correctional system: The highest rates of harassment and assault occur among Black transgender persons. Experiences of discrimination in health care are also common, with 19% reporting being refused medical care because of their gender identity. These refusals, along with a lack of money and fear surrounding discrimination in the health care system, can clearly lead to postponed medical care and additional poor health outcomes.

In addition to significant experiences of bias, discrimination, and harassment, a transgender person must also cope with the potential loss of relationships (e.g., possible rejection from parents, partners, children, friends, employers, and more; Dank et al., 2014; Langenderfer-Magruder et al., 2016; Wilson, 2013). Another significant loss may be the person's history. Although many transgender persons are eager to let go of a history as the sex designated at birth, they may also feel conflicted about abandoning some elements of that history. For example, it is difficult for a transgender person to discuss playing traditional football or wrestling in high school if everyone knows that person as a female; she may be required to disclose her transgender identity or status. It is similarly difficult to discuss one's experience with painful menstruation or pregnancy if everyone knows that person as a male. Although there are contexts in which such conversations may be appropriate, transgender clients quickly learn to hide these past identities from others and then from themselves. Grieving these losses may take time, and it may be painful for clients to reclaim even a portion of what was lost.

Potential Physical and Mental Health Challenges

As previously discussed, when people have a diverse gender identity, presentation, or expression, they are very likely to face discrimination and bias in their context—this can include family, peers, school, work, and partners (Tebbe & Moradi, 2016). With this increased minority stress comes increasing physical and mental health concerns (Tebbe & Moradi, 2016). Physical health concerns for transgender persons include high rates of HIV (Grant et al., 2011). Transgender persons are also at a high risk for injury due to physical assault and abuse, sexual assault and abuse, and intimate partner violence (Reback, Simon, Bemis, & Gatson, 2001; Xavier, Bobbin, Singer, & Budd, 2005).

Rates of anxiety, depression, substance use, and suicidality are particularly high in the transgender population (Borden, 2015; Grant et al., 2011). Most striking is the risk for suicide among transgender people. Haas, Rodgers, and Herman (2014) reported suicide attempts of 46% among transmen and 42% among transwomen. These are 10 times as great as the national average (4.6%). Suicide rates are high prior to transition, with one study finding 81% of respondents considering suicide before transition (Transgender Equality Network Ireland, 2012). Rates for suicide may increase during the transition phase (DeCuypere et al., 2006). Although after transition, suicide rates decrease dramatically, they are still higher than for cisgender individuals. However, this could be because of the ongoing bias a transgender person may experience. For example, Haas and colleagues found that 69% of transgender people who experienced homelessness because of gender identity had attempted suicide. Similar effects (above 60%) were found for those who had been turned away from a doctor or had been physically assaulted by family members (Haas et al., 2014). Nonsuicidal self-injury, which usually involves cutting, is also very high among transgender clients. In one study, 41.9% of transgender participants had a lifetime history of nonsuicidal self-injury (dickey, Reisner, & Juntunen, 2015). Similar to the role of bias in suicidality, Liu and Mustanski (2012) found a relationship among suicidal ideation, self-harm, and victimization.

Borden (2015) noted that when transgender persons seek mental health services, their common issues (like depression, anxiety, or relationship concerns) are incredibly complicated further by the bias and prejudice they face. Because of these multiple experiences of bias and their internalization of American culture's genderism and cisnormativity, their struggles are often compounded by feelings of shame (Borden, 2015). They feel different and often feel like freaks (Borden, 2015). They may also face bias related to affectional orientation and being part of the LGBTQI+ community, whether they are heterosexual or not (Sutter & Perrin, 2016). Because of the high probability of increased bias incidents and experiences, they may additionally experience isolation and limited support systems in their environment (Borden, 2015; Tebbe & Moradi, 2016). Therefore, these internal and external sources of bias cause mental health issues, complicated presentations, and issues with recovery (Tebbe & Moradi, 2016).

Suicide attempts are significantly less common among transgender individuals when families are accepting of their gender identity (Grant et al., 2011; Haas et al., 2014). For many, the process of coming out or medical transition also brings significant relief (Transgender Equality Network Ireland, 2012). However, coming out may contribute to a risk of suicide if it leads to homelessness, the loss of significant relationships, unemployment, or physical abuse (Haas et al., 2014). Developing strong support mechanisms helps mitigate these effects, as does learning how to cope with and respond to microaggressions (Haas et al., 2014). Budge, Adelson, and Howard (2013) found that social support directly explained experience of distress variables. They advocated for the simultaneous use of counseling strategies of increasing coping skills and developing social support as a way to reduce mental health risks (Budge et al., 2013). They also noted that coping strategies changed between early stages of transition and later stages (Budge et al., 2013).

Transitioning

If transgender individuals decide to transition, they will experience substantial physical and emotional changes, some related to being transgender, some related to their marginalized minority status, and some due to the medical process of transitioning (Deutsch, 2016a, 2016b, 2016c; Dhejne, Öberg, Arver, & Landén, 2014). Once people have been diagnosed with gender dysphoria, they are able to seek gender-affirming hormone therapy from a medical provider. The individual must be assessed and be able to provide informed consent; assessment and consent do not necessarily have to come from a mental health provider. A range of medical physicians can prescribe and oversee hormone therapy, including primary care physicians, endocrinologists, physician assistants/advanced practice nurses, gynecologists, and in some states naturopathic providers and nurse midwives. If transitioning people seek hormone replacement therapy, they will first experience a blocking of the hormones that do not match their gender identity. After a period of time, or at around age 16 for youth, they will be introduced to the hormones (i.e., estrogen or testosterone) that match their gender identity. This could happen before they ever reach puberty from their assigned sex at birth or after they have experienced puberty of an assigned sex at birth. Either way, the experience of hormones and blockers will be cause for comfort as their physical body begins becoming more congruent with their gender identity. However, it can also cause heightened emotions and stress, as is experienced with a typical puberty. If a transgender person has experienced puberty before, the second puberty can be just as difficult. During this second puberty, the individual may lack solidarity from peers, support from parents, or a social context (like school) in which the system understands and supports the process.

Hormone therapy is significantly different for male-to-female (called MtF or M2F) transition and female-to-male (called FtM or F2M) transition (Deutsch, 2016a; Dhejne et al., 2014). For the MtF transition, the process involves blocking androgens and introducing estrogens (Deutsch, 2016a; Dhejne et al., 2014). However, some estrogens, such as ethinyl estradiol, have been found to carry specific health risks: Ethinyl estradiol is associated with venous thrombosis and cardiovascular disease and should no longer be used for hormone replacement therapy (Gooren & Asscheman, 2014). If a male puberty has not occurred, then the introduction of estrogen can slow bone growth and slow or halt the development of height (Deutsch, 2016a; Dhejne et al., 2014). If a male puberty has occurred, this process will not undo bone development from the first puberty (Deutsch, 2016a; Dhejne et al., 2014). However, there are considerable changes to the body irrespective of a previous puberty. Other changes include breast growth (which may be painful during the first few months), fat redistribution (especially around the hips, thighs, waist, and face), softer and thinner skin, fluctuations in the experience of pain and temperature, loss of muscle mass, decreased body hair growth, change in orgasm sensation (less frequent, longer lasting, and more related to a whole-body experience), reduced testicle size, and fluctuations in emotions (Gooren & Asscheman, 2014).

If androgens are blocked prior to a male puberty, then feminization of facial features will also occur (Gooren & Asscheman, 2014; Meltzer, 2016). However, if a transgender person is transitioning MtF after a male puberty, she may desire facial feminization, which will not occur through hormone replacement following a male puberty. This can be a painful and expensive process that may include years of electrolysis, jaw contouring, chin contouring/reduction, face/neck lift, reduction rhinoplasty, forehead/brow ridge contouring, upper eyelid surgery (upper blepharoplasty), lower eyelid surgery (lower blepharoplasty), and/or trachea shave surgery. When gender confirmation surgery is performed, insurance companies may cover some or all of the costs. Top surgery for the MtF transition refers to breast augmentation, which will involve breast implants. Some surgeons recommend that breast augmentation be performed a year after bottom surgery to ensure that hormones will not result in even larger breasts. Bottom surgery for the MtF transition refers to penectomy (removal of the penis), orchiectomy (removal of the testicles), vaginoplasty (creation of a vaginal cavity), and labiaplasty (formation of the external female genitalia). Sexual functioning and ability to orgasm can be maintained, although that is not a guarantee from the surgery. The genital surgery has some risks, including infection and bleeding, as well as necrosis, urinary retention, or vaginal prolapse (falling out of position). Postoperative care, including vaginal dilation, is an important piece of gender affirmation surgical recovery.

For a FtM transition, the desired outcome may be accomplished through hormone affirmation therapy alone (Crane, 2016; Gooren & Asscheman, 2014). Testosterone deepens the voice, increases facial and body hair, enlarges the clitoris, creates fairly rapid male pattern baldness (if one is genetically so inclined), improves muscle development, increases libido, and redistributes body fat (though hip development will likely not reduce); moreover, ovulation and menstruation cease, sweat increases, veins become more prominent, skin coarsens, acne may increase, and some individuals may experience outbursts or irritability. If a person seeks a FtM surgical transition, the surgery is often broken into stages. Top surgery will involve a subcutaneous mastectomy, which is a removal of the breasts. Bottom surgery will include a hysterectomy. After this, a genital transformation can begin, which includes a vaginectomy, reconstruction of the urethra, a scrotoplasty, and a penile reconstruction (phalloplasty or metaoidioplasty). A penile prosthesis (for erections) and testicular prostheses can also be implanted, typically in stages. The penis may not have any erotic sensation if a phalloplasty is completed. The successful completion of a penile transplant in South Africa has many hopeful that alternative options will be available to transmen soon. As with any type of surgery, there are significant risks involved; for FtM genital surgeries, these can include infections, wound breakdown, urinary difficulties, bleeding, rectal injury, and scarring.

Given the difficult nature of transitioning surgically, it is essential for the client to self-examine and fully understand the process. If a person is unhappy with the surgical transition, retransitioning is extremely difficult. Fortunately, most people who transition surgically are satisfied with their decision. Suicide rates fall to one tenth of pretransition levels; this may also be influenced by hormone replacement therapy, which for the MtF transition has been found to increase serotonin in the brain, similar to antidepressants (Kranz et al., 2014). Both MtF and FtM hormonal transitions are associated with lower depression, anxiety, and somatization problems (Dhejne et al., 2014; Kranz et al., 2014). Other studies have found evidence that hormonal and surgical intervention can significantly reduce symptoms of gender dysphoria and improve overall psychological outcomes, overall quality of life, and sexual function (Delemarre-van de Waal & Cohen-Kettenis, 2006; Murad et al., 2010). A Swedish study spanning 50 years found that only 2.2% of those who had undergone gender affirmation surgery regretted their decision (Dhejne et al., 2014). The regret rates for FtM and MtF patients were not significantly different, and the regret rates for both groups decreased over the years (Dhejne et al., 2014). When individuals are unhappy with their transition, it is most often because of the continued experience of discrimination and bias by others, which may not improve for them after surgery.

Although hormone replacement surgery and/or surgery are perceived as vastly positive for transgender persons wishing to transition, there can be some negative physical experiences (Khatchadourian, Amed, & Metzger, 2014). Wierckx and colleagues' (2012) study of long-term hormone use found no significant cardiovascular events, hormone-related cancers, or osteoporosis among transmen. However, a quarter of transwomen had osteoporosis at the lumbar spine and radius. Even more disturbing is that 6% of transwomen experienced at least one thromboembolic event (blood clot), and another 6% experienced other cardiovascular problems after on average 11.3 years of hormone treatment. Despite these physical challenges and potential risks, transgender persons seeking to transition may find hormonal and surgical intervention necessary. As one individual said to me (Robyn Brammer), "To transition is pricey, painful, yet essential. My life sucks, yet I've never been happier. Life as a transperson is WAY better than suicide." It is important to remember, however, that a transgender person may validly desire no, some, or all gender-affirming hormone treatments and/or surgeries. The choices need to be carefully considered by the individual in terms of the benefits versus risks of the interventions. Even if people choose not to transition, they are still transgender.

Counseling Skills and Techniques

Understanding the Role of the
Diagnostic and Statistical Manual of Mental Disorders (DSM)

Transsexualism was not included in the *DSM* until the third edition (American Psychiatric Association, 1980). This marked the beginning of the recognition of gender identity issues in psychiatry but was based on limited field tests (Zucker, 2010). The *DSM–III–R* strengthened the phrasing by adding gender identity disorder of adolescence and adulthood, non-transsexual type (American Psychiatric Association, 1987), and added intense distress regarding assigned gender, but there were still several limitations of the diagnostic criteria. Specifically, there were no formal guidelines for assessment or studies of reliability, and there were also differences in the wording for diagnosing males and females. Rather than forcing a single perspective in diagnoses, the authors of the *DSM–IV* took a different tactic. They explored and refined requisite conditions—in particular, the stated desire to be of the opposite sex was demoted from a requisite condition to an optional criterion. However, evidence published since the *DSM–IV* has indicated that cross-gender identification may be the single greatest factor in the diagnosis (Elliott-Pascal, 2006; Steensma et al., 2013). Indeed, Cohen-Kettenis and Pfäfflin (2010) noted that in the *DSM–IV–TR*, gender identity disorder was a single diagnosis, but there was recognition that it could develop along divergent routes and that it differed in children and adults. These changes in the *DSM* reflect the complex and varied nature of gender identity issues, but difficulties remained with respect to defining transgender as a mental health disorder versus a medical or physiological condition (Cohen-Kettenis & Pfäfflin, 2010). There was also extensive discussion about whether to rule out intersex conditions and whether distress is necessary for a diagnosis (Cohen-Kettenis & Pfäfflin, 2010). Another controversial issue was that the *DSM* diagnosis applied before and after individuals had transitioned to their gender identity; Cohen-Kettenis and Pfäfflin (2010) disagreed with this idea and concluded that "as having a mental disorder diagnosis may have adverse implications for employment, insurance, etc., the diagnosis should exclude treated individuals who are no longer gender dysphoric" (p. 505).

The *DSM–5* (American Psychiatric Association, 2013) moved gender identity issues out of the sexual and gender identity disorders category, changed the diagnosis from *gender identity disorder* to *gender dysphoria*, and clarified key constructs. *Gender identity* is defined as a social identity and indicates an individual's identification as male, female, or another gender category, whereas "*gender dysphoria* . . . refers to an individual's affective/cognitive disconnect with the assigned gender but is more specifically defined when used as a diagnostic category" (p. 451, emphasis added). This reflects an attempt to recognize the full spectrum of gender variance phenomena but focus on better meeting the mental health needs of individuals who specifically seek to transition.

Rather than focus on the gender incongruence, the *DSM–5* definition focuses on the "dysphoria as the clinical problem, not the identity per se" (American Psychiatric Association, 2013, p. 451). In clarifying the potential permanence of the gender dysphoria diagnosis, the *DSM–5* now includes a posttransition specifier. This specifier applies to individuals who have transitioned socially and either are preparing to or have completed at least hormone or surgical intervention. The wording, however, is ambiguous, and it is unclear whether the authors expect the specifier to be used in all cases or whether the diagnosis need not apply to individuals who are no longer distressed. Given the emphasis on the incongruence between birth assignment and gender identity, it is likely to imply a permanent condition. In addition, although the *DSM* has removed gender dysphoria as having any connection to transvestic disorder, it has kept both disorders. Although the *DSM–5* has progressed to a better understanding and presentation of transgender and gender issues, it still clearly pathologizes transgender issues, treating them as psychopathology and hence as a disease or illness. The possibility that the diagnosis may create more hardship or lead to increased discrimination and mistreatment instead of provide any psychiatric benefit has led many advocates to question the diagnosis even being included in the *DSM* and International Classification of Diseases, in which it is still identified as gender identity disorder (World Health Organization, 2016). Yet because gender dysphoria is a requisite condition for transitioning in terms of medical care and/or reimbursement, it is currently necessary (Lev, 2013; Whalen, 2013; Winters, 2013). However, the continued conceptualization of transgender persons as having psychopathology is problematic and needs to be recognized as such by counselors and other health professionals working with transgender clients.

Preparing to Work With Transgender Clients

Developing Competencies for Counseling Transgender People

The Association for Lesbian, Gay, Bisexual, and Transgender Issues in Counseling (ALGBTIC) published counseling competencies for working with transgender clients in 2010 (Burnes et al., 2010; see http://www.algbtic.org/competencies.html). The ALGBTIC competencies emphasize an understanding of human growth and development in transgender persons, allowing a counselor to conceptualize the client's case with attention to biological, familial, social, cultural, socioeconomic, and psychological factors. Counselors should have knowledge surrounding social and cultural foundations impacting transgender clients, which include intersectional identities and the complex experiences of oppression, transphobia, classism, and discrimination. Counselors are also expected to have competencies related to creating helping relationships, which include avoiding the use of reparative therapies or attempts to change one's gender identity to match one's designated sex at birth. ALGBTIC also warns against counselors using their own gender identity as a guide for understanding the client. Counselors should also recognize the whole person, seeing the client as more than someone with gender identity issues. As they do with other clients, counselors need to take special care in creating a nurturing environment for healing work. Another competency area is that of group work, which involves expressing nonjudgmental attitudes, using facilitative skills, focusing on the client's goals, and providing psychoeducation while emphasizing diversity and creating a safe environment. Professional orientation competencies include understanding the history of institutional and professional discrimination against transgender clients, learning the American Counseling Association ethical guidelines for treatment, knowing referral resources, and serving as an advocate. Understanding transgender needs as they relate to career issues, assessment, and research is also covered in this document (see http://www.algbtic.org/competencies.html).

The World Professional Association for Transgender Health (WPATH) has published standards of care since 1979 (WPATH, 2011). The current seventh iteration of the standards recognizes that not all transgender persons will seek to transition; having a flexible client-centered approach is now underscored. WPATH's (2011) standards include a description of mental health professionals' competencies for working with transgender clients, which include continual education on gender dysphoria and transgender issues. WPATH also recognizes the role of mental health professionals in assessment, referral, psychoeducation (including knowledge regarding hormonal and surgical interventions), assisting with informed consent for treatment options, treating comorbid mental health concerns, and working with an interdisciplinary team for treatment. Mental health professionals take on the role of assessing, preparing, and referring to medical professionals in the cases in which the client is seeking to transition with hormones and/or surgery. WPATH is also clear that therapy is not required for medical interventions, as it previously was required; it is recommended for transgender clients only to improve their well-being and quality of life.

The Center of Excellence for Transgender Health (dickey, Karasic, & Sharon, 2016) has also presented a statement on mental health care for transgender clients. They recognize the importance of mental health care for treatment in terms of the trauma and depression for which transgender clients are at risk due to increased bias incidents and discrimination. They are careful to consider that the mental health system has historically pathologized and mistreated transgender clients, leading to many transgender people being reluctant to seek mental health care. Competent counselors need to understand the role of the *DSM;* affirmative therapy techniques; and how to assess and prepare clients for transition, if needed.

Understanding Ethical and Legal Issues

In addition to developing competence related to working with transgender people, understanding the unique ethical and legal issues involved with working with this population is also important (Campbell & Arkles, 2017). Avoiding harm is more complex than when one is working with cisgender clients, as harm may occur through unintended microaggressions involving the use of problematic terms. For example, asking people for their "preferred pronoun" suggests that they are not truly their gender identity but rather are "choosing" a gender identity. With a simple phrase or word, a mental health professional could minimize or pathologize a client's experience, damaging the therapeutic relationship and causing harm (Campbell & Arkles, 2017; Chang et al., 2017). When working with transgender clients, counselors should prioritize client self-determination and emotional well-being over their own opinion of and frustration with the complex terminology (Chang et al., 2017). For example, staying up to date with appropriate terminology can feel cumbersome and frustrating; a counselor may also feel that transgender persons are being too sensitive or demanding surrounding their word or pronoun use. However, it is crucial to remember that it is not the client's obligation to manage counselor frustration and opinion—it is the counselor's ethical responsibility (Chang et al., 2017). It is also an ethical requirement to explore one's own values: Being aware of one's own beliefs and attitudes surrounding femininity, masculinity, gender, and binary conceptualizations is crucial when one is working with transgender and genderqueer populations (Chang et al., 2017). Counselors also need to understand the difference between affectional orientation and gender identity (Chang et al., 2017). For example, if a person is transitioning MtF and is bonded romantically to women, she may identify as a lesbian. Likewise, if a MtF transitioning client is attracted to males, he may identify as heterosexual. Counselors must educate themselves, challenge traditional gender assumptions, and work toward gaining a better understanding of gender variation to be able to provide more affirmative counseling to their transgender clients. It is also important that counselors keep an open mind and not assume when people identify as transgender what their experience, identity, or destination will be (Chang et al., 2017).

Counselors working with transgender clients should be prepared to advocate for their clients in traditional (i.e., working toward social justice) and transgender-specific ways (Campbell & Arkles, 2017). For example, counselors may need to provide documentation indicating that clients are transgender and should be allowed to use the public accommodation of their gender identity. They may also need to provide letters indicating diagnosis and consent to medical health professionals. In addition, counselors may assist in name and gender marker changes on legal documents. Counselors working with this population need to be aware of the state laws regarding changing gender markers on identification documents. In addition, counselors must be conscious of finding gender-affirming care when making referrals of any type but in particular referrals to health care practitioners. Knowing that the client will receive respectful, quality care in any referral that a counselor provides is very important. All care, including counseling, should be affirmative in nature; no conversion or change efforts should ever be used.

Affirmative and Interdisciplinary Care Guidelines

Understanding the medical and mental health guidelines for working with a transgender client is important to providing quality interdisciplinary care (dickey & Singh, 2016). Utilizing their training and understanding of biological, neuroanatomical, social, emotional, cognitive, and psychological case conceptualization skills, counselors can help facilitate communication across the varied medical and other professionals who may be involved in a transgender client's case (Ducheny, Hendricks, & Keo-Meier, 2017). This could include physicians, endocrinologists, surgeons, employers, school officials, and attorneys (Ducheny et al., 2017). Services for transgender clients may be coordinated through one organization (such as the LA LGBT Center in Los Angeles) or through separate locations and organizations (Ducheny et al., 2017). All interdisciplinary care providers need to establish communication with appropriate and full informed consent releases to share information (Ducheny et al., 2017).

As mental health professionals, counselors may be required to work with all providers in using the most up-to-date best practices of care for working with transgender clients (Ducheny et al., 2017). For example, best practices for hormone therapy no longer require a confirmed diagnosis of gender dysphoria from a mental health professional (WPATH, 2011). Currently, best practices for puberty suppression and/or hormone replacement therapy do involve obtaining informed consent: Medical professionals need to provide comprehensive information on the benefits versus risks of the medical procedures and assist patients in the decision-making process (Ducheny et al., 2017). However, most youth providers and many adult health providers still require a letter confirming a diagnosis of gender dysphoria—sometimes two from separate mental health providers—depending on the type of medical intervention (Ducheny et al., 2017). The process can also vary significantly based on how familiar a health professional is with working with transgender patients (Ducheny et al., 2017).

Counselors may also need to provide psychoeducation in their interdisciplinary work (Ducheny et al., 2017). For example, medical professionals new to working with transgender patients may be unaware of best practices. School professionals may be unaware of the difference between genderqueer or nonconforming students and transgender students who wish to transition. Employers or schools may be unaware of the Title IX laws that require them to accommodate requests for access to public accommodations, such as restrooms that match one's gender identity. Therefore, in the realm of the collaborative care guidelines, counselors may find themselves making specific advocacy efforts for their clients.

Counseling Practices With Transgender Clients

Rapport Building

In addition to traditional rapport-building practices, counselors must be aware of specific challenges to building rapport with transgender clients. Clients may feel that therapy is necessary to gain access to their desired transition with hormones and/or surgery, which may lead them to be guarded in therapy (Borden, 2015). Some counselors may also focus on this gatekeeping role, which is very problematic and can damage rapport (Mizock &

Lundquist, 2016). In addition, counselors may inadvertently commit microaggressions as a result of a lack of knowledge surrounding transgender issues. Mizock and Lundquist (2016) found that therapists made several missteps in their work with transgender clients that could have severely impacted rapport building and the efficacy of treatment. Some mental health professionals relied on clients to provide them with education, asking for multiple clarifications and/or using inappropriate language, which required clients to educate them on appropriate terminology (Mizock & Lundquist, 2016). Some mental health professionals also applied binary or restrictive gender conceptualizations to all clients when they did not fit all transgender clients (Mizock & Lundquist, 2016). Therapists also showed gender inflation, in which they overlooked other important life issues beyond gender identity, and gender avoidance, in which they sidestepped discussion of gender identity (Mizock & Lundquist, 2016). Through their interactions, counselors may have inadvertently communicated that "the client is a problem to be fixed" or stigmatized and pathologized clients as mentally ill (Mizock & Lundquist, 2016, p. 151). These missteps underscore the importance of counselors receiving continual education on transgender issues and being connected to the transgender community.

Affirmative Therapy

As with all LGBTQI+ clients, affirmative therapy is the best practice for working with transgender clients. Positive psychology practices can be utilized in this effort; however, it should be noted that much of the literature on positive psychology has emphasized cisgender and heterosexual reference groups (Lytle, Vaughan, Rodriguez, & Shmerler, 2014). There are, however, two primary goals of positive psychology that are important for transgender affirmative counseling: (a) developing self-affirmation and (b) building resilience and coping skills.

Developing Self-Affirmation. In building self-affirmation, counselors may wish to focus on developing client self-awareness and authenticity, based on the research on positive identity development in transgender people (Riggle & Mohr, 2015). Part of this self-affirmation will include a depathologizing of clients' gender identity: The counselor should recognize them and affirm them as gender variant rather than abnormal or clinically disturbed (Singh et al., 2017).

Some transgender clients may wish to further explore their internal gender identity or their affectional orientation in a questioning process (see Chapter 16), whereas many will be secure in their gender and affectional identity and will not wish to further explore these issues. However, exploring clients' identity and need to potentially transition socially, hormonally, or surgically will be important. This process involves not only exploration and affirmation of client identity and values but also potentially psychoeducation and informed consent. If the client decides to pursue transition, other decisions must be considered, including whether hormonal and/or surgical interventions may be part of the process. Informed consent includes psychoeducation surrounding the fact that although hormones will likely impact cognitive, affective, and physical processes (e.g., Keo-Meier et al., 2015), they will not resolve all of clients' negative symptoms and do carry some risks.

Balancing psychoeducation and encouragement can be very helpful. If clients do transition with hormone replacement therapy, they may look to the counselor to reflect on how they are changing. Budge (2014) encouraged counselors to model support and self-disclose when appropriate. For example, one client described her therapist's self-disclosure to me (Robyn Brammer) in this way:

> Five months after starting estrogen, I noticed something happen to my thought process. I was in the shower, and I developed a stream of consciousness about what I planned to do for the day. Typically, this list would comprise 10 to 15 items. Mentally, I would logically rank them, then start with the first few items after grooming. On this day, however, one of the items on my list "felt" more important. For no apparent reason, I felt

compelled to start with this item, even though I could not justify why. I even felt energy through my body, emphasizing the significance of this item. It was as if my body was telling me something different from my mind. I found this so disturbing that I called my counselor and asked for an appointment. I feared I might be developing some neurological problem. When I told my counselor that I had a "body voice" commanding me to do things, she laughed. "You have never had a body voice before?" my counselor asked. "All women have body voices." I stayed with this counselor for 3 years. Looking back, this moment was the most important event. With one laugh and one normalization, she helped me accept myself as a woman and embrace the transition process.

In order to better understand the experiences throughout transition, clients often need reassurance and psychoeducation surrounding cisgender experiences. Even though clients have likely been aware of their gender identity most of their lives, they have also been acting out the role of their assigned gender at birth. They may lack awareness of what is typically experienced by cisgender persons or of what typically happens in the puberty for the sex associated with their gender identity. For example, FtM clients may not understand how the process of voice changes occurs. Counselors who self-reveal part of their own puberty experiences may greatly benefit clients who lack an understanding of the physical transitions.

In addition, transgender persons may wish to discuss issues of gender after a transition. Transgender clients have often lived their lives according to the rules and guidelines American culture has dictated to them. When liberated into the gender of their identity, they sometimes switch one stereotypical gender role for another, which may or may not improve their quality of life. For some persons, having a stereotypical gender presentation and "passing" may be affirming. In learning to present themselves more authentically, some clients may need to explore beliefs regarding the variance in their gender identity. One of my (Robyn Brammer) clients summarized the process this way: "I lived my whole life trying to be the 'boy' they wanted me to be; even though I now feel like me, I fear I am subconsciously trying to be the type of girl they want me to be." When they are helped to redefine gender for themselves, clients may be able to feel more fully authentic.

The use of a transgender-affirming adaptation of cognitive behavior therapy may be helpful (Austin & Craig, 2015). In Austin and Craig's (2015) model, transgender-affirming practice applications focus on providing psychoeducation (regarding transition, relationships, and gender), modifying problematic thinking styles (including instilling hope and addressing catastrophizing), enhancing social support, and preventing suicidality. Overcoming shame and instilling hope have been viewed as essential components for creating positive outcomes (Budge, 2014).

It is also important to assist transgender clients in building effective relationships to support positive affirmation of their identity as well as to offset the rejection, discrimination, and harassment often shown to gender minorities (Domínguez, Bobele, Coppock, & Peña, 2015). Successful outcomes of any intervention are intertwined with social support, which is essential in reducing depression, suicidality, and hopelessness (Budge, 2013). Although not all transgender persons will wish to identify as transgender (i.e., they may just identify as male or female), for many, identifying as transgender and feeling part of the transgender community can serve to improve positive conceptions of self (Barr, Budge, & Adelson, 2016). Counselors working with this community should be aware of local, national, and online advocacy and resource organizations for transgender persons in order to improve their knowledge of and connection with the transgender community. As mentioned previously, it is important to ensure that LGBTQI+ organizations will be understanding, nonbinary, and validating of transgender or gender-nonconforming persons. Counselors need to fully prescreen any referrals or resources that they give to clients.

It is important to note that there can be animosity between transgender persons who become *stealth* because they are able to "pass" as cisgender and those who identify strongly with the transgender identity. Those who specifically identify as transgender may do so out of advocacy and empowerment of others to create social change; an identity with the community for these reasons does have positive impacts (Riggle & Mohr, 2015). However, clients who wish to go stealth and identify and live as cisgender males or females should also be supported.

Counselors working with this population will frequently provide psychoeducation and resources to family members (dickey & Bower, 2017). Whether clients are young and the counselor is working with their family, or they are older and their transition impacts their spouse and/or children, clients may need special care in coming out to their families. The families may need psychoeducation and support around what transitioning *with* their family member will be like. Many parents or guardians will be completely unfamiliar with gender variance and transgender issues. They may struggle with terminology and pronoun use as well as experience their own struggle with their loved one's transgender status and transition. For example, parents may experience grief over the loss of the child they thought they had as well as heightened fear and anxiety surrounding the discrimination their child will potentially endure as a transgender person. They may also require support surrounding *coming out* or revealing their child's transgender identity to other family members and friends. Likewise, a spouse may be confused, uncertain, and/or angry at a transgender partner. If a spouse identifies as gay or lesbian, the transgender partner transitioning may challenge not only their identity but also their sexuality and attractions. If a spouse identifies as heterosexual, the transgender spouse will challenge their sexuality and affectional orientation identity in a similar way. Children of a transgender person may find it difficult to reconceptualize their father or mother as something different; they may also grieve the loss of the parent they envisioned or be angry that their parent kept this secret from them. Connecting families to resources is crucial for helping them cope with their transgender loved one's transition; it is also of benefit to the transgender client to have family who can serve as social support and a positive resource in their life.

Building Resilience and Coping Skills. Given the immense influence of minority stress associated with being transgender or gender nonconforming, counselors must first recognize the adverse bias incidents and trauma that a client may have experienced (Hendricks & Testa, 2012; Liao, Kashubeck-West, Weng, & Deitz, 2015). In addition, counselors must be aware of how mental health symptoms, particularly depression, suicidality, and anxiety, are associated with victimization, rejection, or internalized transphobia (Liao et al., 2015). In addition to experiencing previous trauma, after transition, transgender clients may continue to be at a heightened risk for mental health issues, with continual experiences of microaggressions and transgender bias. However, now they may additionally experience gender-related victimization (e.g., a MtF person may also experience sexism and the disempowerment of females) and encounter persons who refuse to affirm their gender identity, misgendering them and using the incorrect pronoun (Testa, Habarth, Peta, Balsam, & Bockting, 2015).

Using a trauma-informed approach is important when working with transgender clients who have experienced past trauma (Burnes, Dexter, Richmond, Singh, & Cherrington, 2016; Richmond, Burnes, Singh, & Ferrara, 2017). For many transgender persons, experiences of trauma may have begun with their family, persisting throughout their transition (Burnes et al., 2016; Richmond et al., 2017). They may have additionally experienced self-hatred surrounding their bodies, including self-mutilation, self-injury, and/or purposeful self-care neglect (Burnes et al., 2016). Many transgender persons also report feeling fearful of using public restrooms and experiencing potential violence (Burnes et al., 2016). It is important for counselors to appropriately assess experiences of trauma as well as to include the treatment of trauma symptoms in their intervention plans (Richmond et al., 2017). Counselors should consider trauma developmentally, in terms of what impact the trauma may have had on the client at the specific ages when it occurred (Richmond et al., 2017).

Developing a positive self-identity, a sense of empowerment, and self-advocacy skills are essential components of treating trauma in transgender clients (Richmond et al., 2017).

In addition to affirming and validating transgender clients' gender identities and exploring past trauma, counselors should help prepare clients for potential negative consequences of coming out or transitioning openly, especially if clients are living with their parents or working in an unstable position. The key to balancing both affirmation and risk management is to underscore that these bias incidents and negative reactions have to do with pathology and problems in others, not the client (Budge, 2013). Preparing clients to cope with these unfortunately real biases is important. In addition to there being a general lack of understanding about transgender issues and the increased threat of violence, some groups of people view this population as a public threat. In 2015, the Texas House of Representatives proposed a bill that would define sex (and gender) only by chromosomes (Texas House Bill 1748, 2015). North Carolina was recently successful in passing a similar law requiring persons to use the bathrooms associated with the sex listed on their birth certificate (Session Law 2016-3, 2016). There are also a number of other proposed anti-transgender bills currently under review in many other states. This underscores the importance of fighting against discriminatory laws, policies, and statutes in being an ally and an advocate for transgender clients.

Helping clients to manage internalized transphobia and negativity is also important to reducing psychological symptoms from potential bias incidents. For example, people who have high internalized transnegativity and experiences of rejection will evidence greater psychological distress and mental health symptomology, including shame for their identity, limited peer relationships, loneliness, depression, suicidality, anxiety, and distressing physical symptoms (Breslow et al., 2015; Mereish & Poteat, 2015). It is also important to help the client process the idea that negative coping behaviors may be a result of attempting to cope with the increased minority stress of being transgender (Dank et al., 2014; Langenderfer-Magruder et al., 2016; Wilson, 2013).

In addition to fostering resilience and self-acceptance, experts recommend using interpersonal therapy with transgender clients (Budge, 2013). The first stage of interpersonal therapy for transgender clients is to identify the target diagnosis and the interpersonal context. Rather than focusing on someone being transgender, the emphasis is on identifying the dysphoria, related affective conditions, and risk for suicidality. The therapist also reviews the client's relationships. The client will have to work through bereavement with those who have been or will be rejecting. The client will also have to identify how to come to terms with struggles involving individual relationships (referred to as *role dispute*) and the factors associated with important life changes (referred to as *role transition*). Next, interpersonal therapy emphasizes developing clients' ability to assert needs and explore interpersonal encounters. During these discussions, clients' frustration or anger is viewed as a normal part of their interpersonal struggles, but taking risks is the only way to move forward. Finally, specific self-advocacy and behavioral techniques are put into place to identify and manage future internal and interpersonal conflicts.

Developmental Issues

Specific developmental issues need to be addressed when working with transgender youth (Edwards-Leeper, 2017; Edwards-Leeper, Leibowitz, & Sangganjanavanich, 2016). New guidelines and scientific evidence suggest that transgender youth who wish to transition experience better outcomes if they are allowed to begin a transition to their gender identity. However, the research is scarce and relatively new. Therefore, there is no truly empirically validated treatment plan for transgender youth clients. At this point, although it can still be controversial, the best course of action appears to support a social transition and, before

puberty, receipt of pubertal hormone suppression. This completely reversible medical intervention can allow some time for child clients to decide another course of action if they
wish. Even though many adolescents do continue their transition, not all gender dysphoric
youth seek a transition once they are older. Because adolescents' sense of consequences
and long-term decision making are still developing with the frontal lobe of their brain, it is
currently believed that other medical interventions need to wait.

Like adults, children and adolescents who experience a strong mismatch between their
assigned gender at birth and their gender identity have increased mental health symptoms
associated with an internal struggle; perception of stigma; and experience of abuse, harassment, rejection, and other bias incidents (Edwards-Leeper, 2017; Edwards-Leeper et al.,
2016). However, youth who wish to transition also have to contend with caregivers who
may or may not be supportive. Even supportive parents may go through a grieving process, be confused, and be fearful of what a transition will mean for their child. Even if the
youth are lucky enough to have supportive and educated guardians, pubertal suppression
is expensive and not often covered by insurance.

Counselors will use similar affirmative counseling practices with child and adolescent clients in terms of strengths-based and resiliency practices (Edwards-Leeper, 2017;
Edwards-Leeper et al., 2016). Although counselors should affirm the youth's gender identity, current ethical guidelines indicate that counselors should have conversations with the
child and caregiver on how gender may be fluid and change, and may later be recognized
as affectional orientation variance, based on the research. However, some see this as unethical and disaffirming. This process may also reflect the prejudice of adultism, in which
youth have very little autonomy and ability to make decisions about their own lives and
bodies. Therefore, counselors need to be careful to still affirm, empower, and explore the
medical guidelines without disempowering the child. This will also require work with
clients' parents, providing support, referrals, and psychoeducation. In conversations with
clients and their guardians, informed consent should be reviewed and the benefits and
risks of all potential medical interventions should be discussed. In addition, counselors
working with youth may find themselves playing a more pivotal role in an interdisciplinary team, particularly with school professionals.

For elderly transgender clients, later life transitions, as well as health issues and finding
affirmative medical care, can emerge as complex issues (dickey & Bower, 2017; Elder, 2016).
Although older individuals often feel more resilient as they get older, they may face fami-
ly-of-origin issues that have resulted in negative experiences for decades (dickey & Bower,
2017; Elder, 2016). It is common that they will still find it difficult to come out to their family of origin as well as potential partners and children (dickey & Bower, 2017; Elder, 2016).
In addition, elderly clients may have more difficulty rejecting traditional and rigid gender
stereotypes, as the beliefs surrounding gender during their childhood formative years may
have been exceptionally rigid (dickey & Bower, 2017). Navigating a relationship with a
spouse and children while transitioning can also be difficult, as stated earlier. Counselors
need to also consider and support intersectional issues with their clients, such as age and
development as well as ethnicity and religion/spirituality (dickey & Bower, 2017).

Transgender Persons of Color

For transgender persons of color, their contexts and experiences can provide increased challenges for physical and mental health as well as obstacles to transition (Chang & Singh, 2016;
Singh et al., 2017). Despite precolonization acceptance of third-gender and transgender persons in many areas of the globe, minorities may now face additional stigma and discrimination
in their ethnic communities (this is discussed further in Chapter 20). Research on transgender
persons in the public health literature does not tend to include ethnically diverse participants,

with the exception of HIV research, which may limit the knowledge on counseling transgender persons of color (Chang & Singh, 2016; Singh et al., 2017). When working with transgender clients of color, counselors should be aware of the power differential between themselves and their clients and increased experiences of trauma and discrimination (Chang & Singh, 2016; Singh et al., 2017). The experience of multiple oppressions not only clearly adds to minority stress experienced but underscores the importance of developing coping skills and resiliency through counseling (Chang & Singh, 2016; Singh et al., 2017). In addition, intersectional socio-economic issues must be considered, as they can create a barrier to accessing expensive medical interventions for transition (Chang & Singh, 2016; Singh et al., 2017). Finally, intersectional issues surrounding spirituality and religion can be important for all transgender clients but can carry a different community significance for people of color (Hopwood & Witten, 2017; Rosenkrantz, Rostosky, Riggle, & Cook, 2016). Section IV of this book further explores the emerging issues of intersectional ethnic and racial issues as well as religion and spirituality.

Conclusion

After reading this chapter, some readers may feel overwhelmed by the complexity of issues in work with transgender clients; they may also worry that their lack of knowledge may harm clients. However, becoming culturally competent and knowledgeable, being open, building resilience, and improving self-concept are techniques most counselors use regularly. With some additional work, counselors can have a significant influence on transgender persons' lives. These clients, who are the highest risk for suicide in the LGBTQI+ community, can greatly benefit from a professional who actively listens, validates and affirms their experiences, advocates for them, and helps them find their authenticity when their world is often so rejecting.

Questions for Further Discussion

1. What themes do you hear in Michelle's narrative, as discussed in the chapter?
2. What counseling strategies would have been most helpful to use with Michelle when she was "in the blackness"?
3. What resources would be important to connect her with outside of her counseling sessions?
4. What are some ethical and multicultural considerations in work with a client like Michelle?
5. What challenges do you think may arise next for Michelle?

Resources

1. View the transgender resources listed through GLAAD at http://www.glaad.org/transgender/resources.
2. Understand medical best practices by reading through information from the Center of Excellence for Transgender Health (http://transhealth.ucsf.edu)_and Informed Consent for Transgender Health (https://icath.info/).
3. Read through resources for transgender individuals at the Human Rights Campaign (http://www.hrc.org/resources/topic/transgender) and Susan's Place (https://www.susans.org/).
4. Be aware of the *Schools in Transition* guide for supporting transgender youth in schools at http://hrc-assets.s3-website-us-east-1.amazonaws.com//files/assets/resources/Schools-In-Transition.pdf.

5. Surf through resources for family members of transgender individuals at http://www.hrc.org/resources/resources-for-people-with-transgender-family-members.

References

American Psychiatric Association. (1980). *Diagnostic and statistical manual of mental disorders* (3rd ed.). Washington, DC: Author.

American Psychiatric Association. (1987). *Diagnostic and statistical manual of mental disorders* (3rd ed., rev.). Washington, DC: Author.

American Psychiatric Association. (2013). *Diagnostic and statistical manual of mental disorders* (5th ed.). Arlington, VA: Author.

Andrist, L. (2014). Review of tales of the Waria. *Men and Masculinities, 17*(3), 349–350. doi:10.1177/1097184X14533704

Austin, A., & Craig, S. L. (2015). Transgender affirmative cognitive behavioral therapy: Clinical considerations and applications. *Professional Psychology: Research and Practice, 46*(1), 21–29.

Balsam, K. F., Huang, B., Fieland, K. C., Simoni, J. M., & Walters, K. L. (2004). Culture, trauma, and wellness: A comparison of heterosexual and lesbian, gay, bisexual, and two-spirit Native Americans. *Cultural Diversity and Ethnic Minority Psychology, 10*(3), 287–301.

Barr, S. M., Budge, S. L., & Adelson, J. L. (2016). Transgender community belongingness as a mediator between strength of transgender identity and well-being. *Journal of Counseling Psychology, 63*(1), 87–97. doi:10.1037/cou0000127

Bartlett, N. H., & Vasey, P. L. (2006). A retrospective study of childhood gender-atypical behavior in Samoan Fa'afafine. *Archives of Sexual Behavior, 35,* 659–666. doi:10.1007/s10508-006-9055-1

Borden, K. A. (2015). Introduction to the special section transgender and gender nonconforming individuals: Issues for professional psychologists. *Professional Psychology: Research and Practice, 46*(1), 1–2.

Brammer, R. (2012). *Diversity in counseling* (2nd ed.). Pacific Grove, CA: Brooks/Cole.

Breslow, A. S., Brewster, M. E., Velez, B. L., Wong, S., Geiger, E., & Soderstrom, B. (2015). Resilience and collective action: Exploring buffers against minority stress for transgender individuals. *Psychology of Sexual Orientation and Gender Diversity, 2*(3), 253–265. doi:10.1037/sgd0000117

Brunjes, A. (2011, November 29). *Juchitán: A place like no other.* Retrieved from the *Oaxaca Times* website: http://www.oaxacatimes.com/inprint/currentissuemenu/34-culture

Budge, S. L. (2013). Interpersonal psychotherapy with transgender clients. *Psychotherapy, 50*(3), 356–359. doi:10.1037/a0032194

Budge, S. L. (2014). Navigating the balance between positivity and minority stress for LGBTQ clients who are coming out. *Psychology of Sexual Orientation and Gender Diversity, 1*(4), 350–352. doi:10.1037/sgd0000077

Budge, S. L., Adelson, J. L., & Howard, K. A. S. (2013). Anxiety and depression in transgender individuals: The roles of transition status, loss, social support, and coping. *Journal of Consulting and Clinical Psychology, 81,* 545–557.

Budge, S. L., Tebbe, E. N., & Howard, K. A. S. (2010). The work experiences of transgender individuals: Negotiating the transition and career decision-making processes. *Journal of Counseling Psychology, 57*(4), 377–393.

Burnes, T. R., Dexter, M. M., Richmond, K., Singh, A. A., & Cherrington, A. (2016). The experiences of transgender survivors of trauma who undergo social and medical transition. *Traumatology, 22*(1), 75–84. doi:10.1037/trm0000064

Burnes, T., Singh, A., Harper, A., Harper, B., Maxon-Kann, W., Pickering, P., . . . Hosea, J. (2010). American Counseling Association competencies for counseling with transgender clients. *Journal of LGBT Issues in Counseling, 4,* 135–159. doi:10.1080/15538605.2010.524839

Byung'chu-Käng, D. (2014). Conceptualizing Thai genderscapes: Transformation and continuity in the Thai sex/gender system. In P. Liamputtong (Ed.), *Contemporary socio-cultural and political perspectives in Thailand* (pp. 409–429). New York, NY: Springer Science.

Campbell, L. F., & Arkles, G. (2017). Ethical and legal concerns for mental health professionals. In A. Singh & l. m. dickey (Eds.), *Affirmative counseling and psychological practice with transgender and gender nonconforming clients* (pp. 95–118). Washington, DC: American Psychological Association.

Chang, S. C., & Singh, A. A. (2016). Affirming psychological practice with transgender and gender nonconforming people of color. *Psychology of Sexual Orientation and Gender Diversity, 3*(2), 140–147. doi:10.1037/sgd0000153

Chang, S. C., Singh, A. A., & Rossman, K. (2017). Gender and sexual orientation diversity within the TGNC community. In A. Singh & l. m. dickey (Eds.), *Affirmative counseling and psychological practice with transgender and gender nonconforming clients* (pp. 19–40). Washington, DC: American Psychological Association.

Cohen-Kettenis, P. T., & Pfäfflin, F. (2010). The *DSM* diagnostic criteria for gender identity disorder in adolescents and adults. *Archives of Sexual Behavior, 39,* 499–513. doi:10.1007/s10508-009-9562-y

Crane, C. (2016). *Phalloplasty and metaoidioplasty—overview and postoperative considerations.* Retrieved from the Center of Excellence for Transgender Health website: http://transhealth.ucsf.edu/trans?page=guidelines-phalloplasty

Dank, M., Lachman, P., Zweig, J. M., & Yahner, J. (2014). Dating violence experiences of lesbian, gay, bisexual, and transgender youth. *Journal of Youth and Adolescence, 43,* 846–857. doi:10.1007/s10964-013-9975-8

DeCuypere, G., Elaut, E., Heylens, G., Van Maele, G., Selvaggi, G., T'Sjoen, G., . . . Monstrey, S. (2006). Long-term follow-up: Psychosocial outcome of Belgian transsexuals after sex reassignment surgery. *Sexologies, 15,* 126–133.

Delemarre-van de Waal, H., & Cohen-Kettenis, P. T. (2006). Clinical management of gender identity disorder in adolescents: A protocol on psychological and paediatric endocrinology aspects. *European Journal of Endocrinology, 155,* S131–S137. doi:10.1530/eje.1.02231

Deutsch, M. B. (2016a). *Initiating hormone therapy.* Retrieved from the Center of Excellence for Transgender Health website: http://transhealth.ucsf.edu/trans?page=guidelines-initiating-hormone-therapy

Deutsch, M. B. (2016b). *Overview of feminizing hormone therapy.* Retrieved from the Center of Excellence for Transgender Health website: http://transhealth.ucsf.edu/trans?page=guidelines-feminizing-therapy

Deutsch, M. B. (2016c). *Overview of masculinizing hormone therapy.* Retrieved from the Center of Excellence for Transgender Health website: http://transhealth.ucsf.edu/trans?page=guidelines-masculinizing-therapy

Dhejne, C., Öberg, K., Arver, S., & Landén, M. (2014). An analysis of all applications for sex reassignment surgery in Sweden, 1960–2010: Prevalence, incidence, and regrets. *Archives of Sexual Behavior, 43,* 1535–1545. doi:10.1007/s10508-014-0300-8

dickey, l. m., & Bower, K. L. (2017). Aging and TGNC identities: Working with older adults. In A. Singh & l. m. dickey (Eds.), *Affirmative counseling and psychological practice with transgender and gender nonconforming clients* (pp. 161–174). Washington, DC: American Psychological Association.

dickey, l. m., Karasic, D. H., & Sharon, N. (2016). *Mental health considerations with transgender and gender nonconforming clients.* Retrieved from the Center of Excellence for Transgender Health website: http://transhealth.ucsf.edu/trans?page=guidelines-mental-health

dickey, l. m., Reisner, S. L., & Juntunen, C. L. (2015). Non-suicidal self-injury in a large online sample of transgender adults. *Professional Psychology: Research and Practice, 46*(1), 3–11. doi:10.1037/a0038803

dickey, l. m., & Singh, A. A. (2016). Training tomorrow's affirmative psychologists: Serving transgender and gender nonconforming people. *Psychology of Sexual Orientation and Gender Diversity, 3*(2), 137–139. doi:10.1037/sgd0000175

Domínguez, D. G., Bobele, M., Coppock, J., & Peña, E. (2015). LGBTQ relationally based positive psychology: An inclusive and systemic framework. *Psychological Services, 12*(2), 177–185. doi:10.1037/a0038824

Ducheny, K., Hendricks, M. L., & Keo-Meier, C. L. (2017). TGNC-affirmative interdisciplinary collaborative care. In A. Singh & l. m. dickey (Eds.), *Affirmative counseling and psychological practice with transgender and gender nonconforming clients* (pp. 69–93). Washington, DC: American Psychological Association.

Edwards-Leeper, L. (2017). Affirmative care of TGNC children and adolescents. In A. Singh & l. m. dickey (Eds.), *Affirmative counseling and psychological practice with transgender and gender nonconforming clients* (pp. 119–141). Washington, DC: American Psychological Association.

Edwards-Leeper, L., Leibowitz, S., & Sangganjanavanich, V. F. (2016). Affirmative practice with transgender and gender nonconforming youth: Expanding the model. *Psychology of Sexual Orientation and Gender Diversity, 3*(2), 165–172. doi:10.1037/sgd0000167

Elder, A. B. (2016). Experiences of older transgender and gender nonconforming adults in psychotherapy: A qualitative study. *Psychology of Sexual Orientation and Gender Diversity, 3*(2), 180–186. doi:10.1037/sgd0000154

Elliott-Pascal, A. (2006). About Indians and Eskimos . . . *Journal of Psychosomatic Obstetrics & Gynecology, 27*(1), 1–3. doi:10.1080/01674820500509686

Farmer, L. B., & Byrd, R. (2015). Genderism in the LGBTQQIA community: An interpretative phenomenological analysis. *Journal of LGBT Issues in Counseling, 9*(4), 288–310. doi: 10.1080/15538605.2015.1103679

Flores, A. R., Herman, J. L., Gates, G. J., & Brown, T. N. T. (2016). *How many adults identify as transgender in the United States.* Retrieved from the Williams Institute website: http://williamsinstitute.law.ucla.edu/research/how-many-adults-identify-as-transgender-in-the-united-states/

Foden-Vencil, K. (2016, June 17). *Neither male nor female: Oregon resident legally recognized as third gender.* Retrieved from the NPR Law website: http://www.npr.org/2016/06/17/482480188/neither-male-nor-female-oregon-resident-legally-recognized-as-third-gender

Galupo, M. P., Henise, S. B., & Davis, K. S. (2014). Transgender microaggressions in the context of friendship: Patterns of experience across friends' sexual orientation and gender identity. *Psychology of Sexual Orientation and Gender Diversity, 1,* 461–470.

Gates, G. J. (2011). *How many people are lesbian, gay, bisexual, and transgender?* Retrieved from the Williams Institute website: http://williamsinstitute.law.ucla.edu/wp-content/uploads/Gates-How-Many-People-LGBT-Apr-2011.pdf

Gess, J. M. (2016). *Queering counselor education: Situational analysis of LGBTQ+ competent faculty* (Unpublished doctoral dissertation). Idaho State University, Pocatello.

Gooren, L., & Asscheman, H. (2014). Sex reassignment: Endocrinological interventions in adults with gender dysphoria. In B. P. C. Kreukels, T. D. Steensma, & A. L. C. de Vries (Eds.), *Gender dysphoria and disorders of sex development: Progress in care and knowledge* (pp. 277–297). New York, NY: Springer Science + Business Media.

Graham, L. F. (2014). Navigating community institutions: Black transgender women's experiences in schools, the criminal justice system, and churches. *Sexuality Research & Social Policy, 11*(4), 274–287. doi:10.1007/s13178-014-0144-y

Grant, J. M., Mottet, L. A., Tanis, J., Harrison, J., Herman, J. L., & Keisling, M. (2011). *Injustice at ever turn: A report of the National Transgender Discrimination Survey.* Retrieved from http://endtransdiscrimination.org/report.html

Haas, A. P., Rodgers, P. L., & Herman, J. L. (2014). *Suicide attempts among transgender and gender non-conforming adults: Findings of the National Transgender Discrimination Survey.* Retrieved from the Williams Institute website: http://williamsinstitute.law.ucla.edu/wp-content/uploads/AFSP-Williams-Suicide-Report-Final.pdf

Harper, A., Finnerty, P., Martinez, M., Brace, A., Crethar, H., Loos, B., . . . Lambert, S. (2013). Association for Lesbian, Gay, Bisexual, and Transgender Issues in Counseling (ALGBTIC) competencies for counseling with lesbian, gay, bisexual, queer, questioning, intersex and ally individuals. *Journal of LGBT Issues in Counseling, 7*(1), 2–43. doi:10.1080/15538605.2013.755444

Heffernan, D. (2015). *GLAAD launches trans microaggressions photo project #transwk.* Retrieved from https://www.glaad.org/blog/glaad-launches-trans-microaggressions-photo-project-transwk

Hendricks, M. L., & Testa, R. J. (2012). A conceptual framework for clinical work with transgender and gender nonconforming clients: An adaptation of the minority stress model. *Professional Psychology: Research and Practice, 43,* 460–467.

Hopwood, R. A., & Witten, T. M. (2017). Spirituality, faith, and religion: The TGNC experience. In A. Singh & l. m. dickey (Eds.), *Affirmative counseling and psychological practice with transgender and gender nonconforming clients* (pp. 213–230). Washington, DC: American Psychological Association.

Kaldera, R. (2007). *Wightriden: Paths of northern-tradition Shamanism.* Hubbardston, MA: Asphodel Press.

Kalra, G., & Shah, N. (2013). The cultural, psychiatric, and sexuality aspects of Hijras in India. *International Journal of Transgenderism, 14*(4), 171–181. doi:10.1080/15532739.2013.876378

Kelley, K., & Gruenewald, J. (2015). Accomplishing masculinity through anti-lesbian, gay, bisexual, and transgender homicide: A comparative case study approach. *Men and Masculinities, 18*(1), 3–29. doi:10.1177/1097184X14551204

Keo-Meier, C. L., Herman, L. I., Reisner, S. L., Pardo, S. T., Sharp, C., & Babcock, J. C. (2015). Testosterone treatment and MMPI-2 improvement in transgender men: A prospective controlled study. *Journal of Consulting and Clinical Psychology, 83*(1), 143–156.

Khatchadourian, K., Amed, S., & Metzger, D. L. (2014). Clinical management of youth with gender dysphoria in Vancouver. *Journal of Pediatrics, 164,* 906–911. doi:10.1016/j.jpeds.2013.10.068

Killermann, S. (2013). *The social justice advocate's handbook: A guide to gender.* Austin, TX: Impetus Books.

Kranz, G. S., Wadsak, W., Kaufmann, U., Savli, M., Baldinger, P., Gryglewski, G., . . . Lanzenberger, R. (2014). High-dose testosterone treatment increases serotonin transporter binding in transgender people. *Biological Psychiatry, 78,* 525–533. doi:10.1016/j.biopsych.2014.09.010

Langenderfer-Magruder, L., Walls, N. E., Whitfield, D. L., Brown, S. M., & Barrett, C. M. (2016). Partner violence victimization among lesbian, gay, bisexual, transgender, and queer youth: Associations among risk factors. *Child & Adolescent Social Work Journal, 33*(1), 55–68. doi:10.1007/s10560-015-0402-8

Lehavot, K., Walters, K. L., & Simoni, J. M. (2009). Abuse, mastery, and health among lesbian, bisexual, and two-spirit American Indian and Alaska Native women. *Cultural Diversity and Ethnic Minority Psychology, 15*(3), 275–284.

Lev, A. I. (2013). Gender dysphoria: Two steps forward, one step back. *Clinical Social Work Journal, 41,* 288–296. doi:10.1007/s10615-013-0447-0

Liao, K. Y., Kashubeck-West, S., Weng, C., & Deitz, C. (2015). Testing a mediation framework for the link between perceived discrimination and psychological distress among sexual minority individuals. *Journal of Counseling Psychology, 62*(2), 226–241.

Liu, R. T., & Mustanski, B. (2012). Suicidal ideation and self-harm in lesbian, gay, bisexual, and transgender youth. *American Journal of Preventive Medicine, 42*(3), 221–228.

Lytle, M. C., Vaughan, M. D., Rodriguez, E. M., & Shmerler, D. L. (2014). Working with LGBT individuals: Incorporating positive psychology into training and practice. *Psychology of Sexual Orientation and Gender Diversity, 1*(4), 335–347.

Meltzer, T. (2016). *Vaginoplasty procedures, complications and aftercare.* Retrieved from the Center of Excellence for Transgender Health website: http://transhealth.ucsf.edu/trans?page=guidelines-vaginoplasty

Mereish, E. H., & Poteat, V. P. (2015). A relational model of sexual minority mental and physical health: The negative effects of shame on relationships, loneliness, and health. *Journal of Counseling Psychology, 62,* 425–437. doi:10.1037/cou0000088

Meyer, D. (2012). An intersectional analysis of lesbian, gay, bisexual, and transgender (LGBT) people's evaluations of anti-queer violence. *Gender & Society, 26,* 849–873. doi:10.1177/0891243212461299

Mizock, L., & Lundquist, C. (2016). Missteps in psychotherapy with transgender clients: Promoting gender sensitivity in counseling and psychological practice. *Psychology of Sexual Orientation and Gender Diversity, 3*(2), 148–155. doi:10.1037/sgd0000177

Murad, M. H., Elamin, M. B., Garcia, M. Z., Mullan, R. J., Murad, A., Erwin, P. J., & Montori, V. M. (2010). Hormonal therapy and sex reassignment: A systematic review and meta-analysis of quality of life and psychosocial outcomes. *Clinical Endocrinology, 72,* 214–231.

Nemoto, T., Iwamoto, M., Perngparn, U., Areesantichai, C., Kamitani, E., & Sakata, M. (2012). HIV-related risk behaviors among Kathoey (male-to-female transgender) sex workers in Bangkok, Thailand. *AIDS Care, 24*(2), 210–219.

Park, M., & Dhitavat, K. (2015, January 16). *Thailand's new constitution could soon recognize third gender.* Retrieved from the CNN website: http://www.cnn.com/2015/01/16/world/third-gender-thailand/

Pinto, N., & Moleiro, C. (2015). Gender trajectories: Transsexual people coming to terms with their gender identities. *Professional Psychology: Research and Practice, 46*(1), 12–20.

Puckett, J. A., & Levitt, H. M. (2015). Internalized stigma within sexual and gender minorities: Change strategies and clinical implications. *Journal of LGBT Issues in Counseling, 9*(4), 329–349. doi:10.1080/15538605.2015.1112336

Quinto, J. (2003). Northwest two-spirit society. *Colors NW, 3*(3), 12–15.

Reback, C., Simon, P. A., Bemis, C. C., & Gatson, B. (2001). *The Los Angeles transgender health study: Community report.* Los Angeles, CA: University of California at Los Angeles.

Reynolds, T., Zupanick, C. E., & Dombeck, M. (2013). *History of stigmatizing names for intellectual disabilities continued.* Retrieved from the MentalHelp.net website: https://www.mentalhelp.net/articles/history-of-stigmatizing-names-for-intellectual-disabilities-continued/

Richmond, K., Burnes, T. R., Singh, A. A., & Ferrara, M. (2017). Assessment and treatment of trauma with TGNC clients: A feminist approach. In A. Singh & l. m. dickey (Eds.), *Affirmative counseling and psychological practice with transgender and gender nonconforming clients* (pp. 191–212). Washington, DC: American Psychological Association.

Riggle, E. D. B., & Mohr, J. J. (2015). A proposed multi-factor measure of positive identity for transgender identified individuals. *Psychology of Sexual Orientation and Gender Diversity, 2*(1), 78–85.

Rosenkrantz, D. E., Rostosky, S. S., Riggle, E. B., & Cook, J. R. (2016). The positive aspects of intersecting religious/spiritual and LGBTQ identities. *Spirituality in Clinical Practice, 3*(2), 127–138. doi:10.1037/scp0000095

Session Law 2016-3, House Bill 2, General Assembly of North Carolina (2016) (enacted).

Singh, A. A., Hwahng, S. J., Chang, S. C., & White, B. (2017). Affirmative counseling with trans/gender-variant people of color. In A. Singh & l. m. dickey (Eds.), *Affirmative counseling and psychological practice with transgender and gender nonconforming clients* (pp. 41–68). Washington, DC: American Psychological Association.

Steensma, T. D., McGuire, J. K., Kreukels, B. C., Beekman, A. J., & Cohen-Kettenis, P. T. (2013). Factors associated with desistence and persistence of childhood gender dysphoria: A quantitative follow-up study. *Journal of the American Academy of Child & Adolescent Psychiatry, 52*, 582–590. doi:10.1016/j.jaac.2013.03.016

Sutter, M., & Perrin, P. B. (2016). Discrimination, mental health, and suicidal ideation among LGBTQ people of color. *Journal of Counseling Psychology, 63*(1), 98–105. doi:10.1037/cou0000126

Tebbe, E. A., & Moradi, B. (2016). Suicide risk in trans populations: An application of minority stress theory. *Journal of Counseling Psychology.* Advance online publication. doi:10.1037/cou0000152

Testa, R. J., Habarth, J., Peta, J., Balsam, K., & Bockting, W. (2015). Development of the Gender Minority Stress and Resilience Measure. *Psychology of Sexual Orientation and Gender Diversity, 2*(1), 65–77. doi:10.1037/sgd0000081

Texas House Bill 1748. (2015, February 20). Retrieved from https://legiscan.com/TX/bill/HB1748/2015

Totman, R. (2003). *The third sex-Kathoey: Thailand's ladyboys.* London, UK: Souvenir Press.

Transgender Equality Network Ireland. (2012). *Ireland's trans mental health and well-being survey.* Retrieved from http://www.teni.ie/attachments/1ceee942-ac62-4dac-8741-5f9e752f3e86.PDF

Ulrichs, K. H. (1994). *Forschungen über das Räthsel der mannmännlichen Liebe* [The riddle of "man-manly" love: The pioneering work on male homosexuality] (M. A. Lombardi-Nash, Trans.). Buffalo, NY: Prometheus. (Original work published 1864)

Velez, B. L., Breslow, A. S., Brewster, M. E., Cox, R. J., & Foster, A. B. (2016). Building a pan-theoretical model of dehumanization with transgender men: Integrating objectification and minority stress theories. *Journal of Counseling Psychology.* Advance online publication. doi:10.1037/cou0000136

Whalen, K. (2013). *(In)validating transgender identities: Progress and trouble in the* DSM-5. Retrieved from the National LGBTQ Task Force website: http://www.thetaskforce.org/invalidating-transgender-identities-progress-and-trouble-in-the-dsm-5/

Wierckx, K., Mueller, S., Weyers, S., Van Caenegem, E., Roef, G., Heylens, G., & T'Sjoen, G. (2012). Long-term evaluation of cross-sex hormone treatment in transsexual persons. *Journal of Sexual Medicine, 9*, 2641–2651.

Wilson, M. (2013). *Violence and mental health in the transgender community* (Unpublished doctoral dissertation). Ohio University, Athens.

Wilton, L., & Short, E. L. (2016). "Black lives matter": Structural violence, agency, and resiliency in Black transgender women's communities. In E. L. Short & L. Wilton (Eds.), *Talking about structural inequalities in everyday life: New politics of race in groups, organizations, and social systems* (pp. 139–164). Charlotte, NC: Information Age.

Winters, K. (2013). *GID reform in the* DSM-5 *and ICD-11: A status update.* Retrieved from http://gidreform.wordpress.com/2013/06/13/gid-reform-in-the-dsm-5-and-icd-11-a-status-update/

Woods, J. B., & Herman, J. L. (2015). Anti-transgender hate crime. In N. Hall, A. Corb, P. Giannasi, & J. D. Grieve (Eds.), *The Routledge international handbook on hate crime* (pp. 278–288). New York, NY: Routledge.

World Health Organization. (2016). *ICD-10 version: 2016: F64 gender identity disorders.* Retrieved from http://apps.who.int/classifications/icd10/browse/2016/en#/F64

World Professional Association for Transgender Health. (2011). *Standards of care for the health of transsexual, transgender, and gender nonconforming people* (7th version). Retrieved from https://s3.amazonaws.com/amo_hub_content/Association140/files/Standards%20 of%20Care%20V7%20-%202011%20WPATH%20(2)(1).pdf

Xavier, J., Bobbin, M., Singer, B., & Budd, E. (2005). A needs assessment of transgendered people of color living in Washington, DC. *International Journal of Transgenderism, 8*(2/3), 31–47.

Young, A. (2000). *Women who become men: Albanian sworn virgins.* New York, NY: Berg. doi:10.2752/9781847888990

Zucker, K. J. (2010). The *DSM* diagnostic criteria for gender identity disorder in children. *Archives of Sexual Behavior, 39,* 477–498. doi:10.1007/s10508-009-9540-4

Chapter 15

Counseling Queer and Genderqueer Clients

Jeffry Moe, Jamie Bower, and Madeline Clark

> *I like the word gay, though I think of myself more as queer.*
> *I believe the strength in my work comes from that perspective—*
> *my being an outsider.*
>
> —Holly Hughes

• • •

Awareness of Attitudes and Beliefs Self-Check

1. Close your eyes and picture someone who identifies as queer. What do you see? How are your biases present in your image? Does the image change if you picture a male versus a female?
2. What people do you know who are out as queer, including celebrities or television/movie characters? How might this lack of representation impact queer or genderqueer persons?
3. How do you feel about the cultural reclamation of a previously negative or pejorative term? As this has been done similarly in African American communities (e.g., the *n*-word) and by females (e.g., *bitch*), can you understand the desire or process of doing this?

Case Study

Bianca is a 29-year-old first-generation Chicana cisgender woman. Bianca has a bachelor's degree and works at a medium-size business as a graphic designer. Bianca is proud of her educational and professional achievements but reports that her interpersonal relationships are strained. She currently lives with her partner, Thomas, in a midwestern city. Bianca's family, especially her parents and grandparents, are not supportive of Bianca's identity as a queer woman, her relationship with a Euro-American man, and her preference to focus on her career rather than start a family. Bianca presents with symptoms of depression (lethargy, negative self-talk, change in sleep/eating/activity, and increased substance use). Bianca reports that she has been feeling depressed since college. For about 2 years she has been experiencing profound sadness, suicidal thoughts, loss of interest in life, and social embarrassment (especially when she is with her family). Bianca has also been struggling to manage her identity as a Chicana woman who identifies as queer. Bianca has attempted to connect with other lesbian, gay, bisexual, transgender, queer, questioning, intersex, asexual, ally, pansexual/polysexual, and two-spirited (LGBTQI+) persons but has felt excluded because she is currently in a relationship with a heterosexual cisgender man, even though she has had multiple long-term sexual and romantic relationships with women. Bianca has decided to ask for professional help because her depression and lack of interest in life activities are affecting her relationship with Thomas, her relationship with her family, and her productivity at work.

Jesse is 45 years old and identifies as both African American and gender-queer. Jesse was married and has two teenage children from his previous marriage. His marriage ended after he came out as gay 5 years ago. He was working as a medical assistant at a local hospital but was fired after being convicted of and serving jail time for driving under the influence. Jesse's former partner is uncomfortable with his gender expression and will not allow Jesse to see their teenage children. Jesse is working with an attorney to gain custody of their children. He has no extended family, as his mother passed away about 6 years ago and he is an only child. Jesse presents with polysubstance use, including use of alcohol, marijuana, and prescription medication. He reports feeling disconnected from friends and family and feeling that no one will accept him for who he is as a genderqueer person. Jesse is experiencing suicidal ideation and reports various suicide attempts across his life span. He is connected with the local LGBT center and other LGBTQI+-specific resources. Jesse periodically attends Alcoholics Anonymous with friends he has made from the LGBT center but does not attend on a regular basis.

• • •

Awareness of Differences

The term *queer* can be used to describe identity as a subjective mode of self-concept, which has its roots in theory and philosophy. Feminist scholar Judith Butler asserted queer theory as a logical development from poststructural feminism and other critical perspectives, including significant contributions from the philosophical work of Michel Foucault (Balick, 2011; Moore, 2013). Initially characterizing a paradigm for academic criticism based on deconstruction of heteronormative and patriarchal gender binary ideologies, queer theory and other aspects of queer subjectivity can be applied to diverse social phenomena (Carroll & Gilroy, 2001; Frank & Cannon, 2010). Tropes from feminist and critical philosophy, such as the personal being political and the role power serves in the construction of knowledge, are turned toward a consideration of how sociocultural norms saturate local and individual experiences of sex, gender, sexuality, and relationships (Moore, 2013). Commonalities across queer methodologies and practices include a critical analysis of power in the operation and performance of both dominant and marginalized affectional orientation and gender subjectivities (Zeeman, Aranda, & Grant, 2014). Practice grounded in a queer perspective also involves the deconstruction of gender and affectional orientation binaries and the perceived normativity of heterosexuality; these constructs are seen as artifacts of social power dynamics manifesting in the social construction of truth, mores, values, and knowledge. Along with the critical, deconstructive philosophies in queer theory are creative and productive modes based on valuing exploration; gender and affectional orientation fluidity; and the reclamation and expression of a diverse array of gender, sexual, relational, and intersecting subjectivities (Moore, 2013).

As a term, *queer* has historically been used as a pejorative to insult, marginalize, and discriminate against individuals who identify under the LGBTQI+ umbrella (Brontsema, 2004; Burn, 2000; University of California, Berkeley [UCB], 2015). To some, the term *queer* can be experienced as offensive and marginalizing; these feelings may be especially common in older LGBTQI+ persons who have experienced the word *queer* as an insult (Brontsema, 2004; UCB, 2015). The work of queer activists and queer theorists has aided in the deconstruction of a heteronormative paradigm that attempts to fit people into neat and exclusive boxes of heterosexual or gay. As a result, in recent years, some individuals have adopted the term *queer* to reclaim their own queer identity (Smith, Shin, & Office, 2012). *Queer* was not initially intended to be a term interchangeable with *gay* and *lesbian:* "Queer was associated with a radical, confrontational challenge to the status quo, and a constructionist understanding of sexuality and gender" (Brontsema, 2004, p. 5). The term *queer* is now understood as an affectional orientation as well as a political statement: Labeling oneself as queer can be viewed as taking a stand against hegemonic (dominant) social norms related to gender, sex, affectional orientation, and especially binary and gender conformity (UCB, 2015).

The 1980s and 1990s were groundbreaking decades for the United States with regard to both queer activism and queer theory. Queer activists in the 1980s and 1990s changed the way the LGBTQI+ community engaged with the term *queer,* which has led to the rise of queer identity in many LGBTQI+ communities. Activism surrounding several needs has increased the infusion of queer theory into LGBTQI+ issues. These events were (a) the AIDS crisis and the reactions and feelings of victimization, (b) the limitations associated with a categorization of identity beyond "homosexuality," and (c) Queer Nation's push for a reconceptualization of sexual identity (Brontsema, 2004). The term *queer* became somewhat of a newly reclaimed signifier of proud, provocative sexual identity and self-empowerment during the 20th century (Rand, 2014). Reclaiming the term *queer* can be seen as a way of promoting tolerance, regaining the right of self-definition, forging and naming one's own existence and identity, and gaining strength from past victimization in addition to challenging affectional orientation and gender dichotomies (Brontsema, 2004; Rand, 2014).

Terms used to identify gender (e.g., *male* and *female*) and affectional orientation (e.g., *heterosexual* and *gay*) are social constructs signifying a complex set of identity positions, experiences, and behavior (Moe, Reicherzer, & Dupuy, 2011). For example, society may label someone who is attracted to the opposite sex as heterosexual. Socially constructed identity categories (e.g., gender, affectional orientation) carry multiple meanings, including a context of power and privilege; they also perpetuate the notion that labeling one's gender and affectional orientation is a simple process. These labels also structure how individuals understand themselves and their position in relation to dominant and marginalized subjectivities in a social hierarchy. The dominant discourse in society reinforces a system of power and privilege through the use of identity labels; it also results in discrimination against groups espousing marginalized identities and further reifies the associated inequities (Smith et al., 2012). In addition, these simple labels are simply incorrect: Gender and affectional orientation variance exists in a continuum-based model of gender identity, gender expression, designated sex at birth, and sexual and romantic attraction. However, each of these variables is still subversive to dominant discourses (Moe et al., 2011). The gender Gumby (UCB, 2015) and genderbread person (Killermann, 2013) models serve as a depiction of the utility of continuum-based models wherein individuals may locate their gender and affectional orientation subjectivities.

The Gender Gumby and Genderbread Person Identity Models

Traditional roles related to gender identity, gender expression, sexual identity, and romantic attractions are prescribed, reinforced, and constructed by society. Traditional society

215

recognizes two binary genders: male and female (Killermann, 2013; UCB, 2015). The social construction of identity and language limits and categorizes individual identities and experiences into opposing binaries (i.e., gay or heterosexual, male or female). This binary does not allow for the possibility that identities outside of the gender and affectional orientation binaries exist (e.g., bisexual, pansexual, asexual, genderqueer, nonbinary, gender fluid), which therefore limits their social recognition through language.

The gender Gumby and genderbread person models (Killermann, 2013; UCB, 2015) deconstruct the majority social narrative of the gender and affectional orientation binary, thereby allowing individuals to identify in ways that are most authentic to their lived experiences. The gender Gumby model enables individuals to identify intersecting aspects of their identities (UCB, 2015). The domains in this model influence how individuals perceive their world in terms of sex, gender identity, gender presentation, and affectional orientation, each on a separate continuum (UCB, 2015). For example, the sex continuum ranges from male on one end to female on the other. These constructs are discussed and fully defined in Chapter 14. The genderbread person model Version 3.3 (see http://itspronouncedmetrosexual.com/2015/03/the-genderbread-person-v3/) contains the same constructs: gender identity, gender expression, designated sex at birth, and sexual attraction. It additionally contains romantic orientation, which is important to separate out, particularly for asexual individuals (Killermann, 2013). The genderbread person Version 3.3 model additionally breaks down the continuum to allow for a blend and combination in each category. For example, people can rate their gender identity on two continuums: woman-ness (from 0 to complete) and man-ness (from 0 to complete; Killermann, 2013). In both models, these identity domains exist independently and are expressed independently; that is, people's gender identity and/or expression are not the same as or in conjunction with their sexual or romantic attractions (Killermann, 2013; UCB, 2015).

Just as sex and gender identity/expression are not linked, gender and its domains are not linked to an individual's romantic or sexual attractions. The gender Gumby and genderbread person models outline how individuals have domains of sexual attraction and romantic attraction, which can be the same or different. These domains are related to varying levels of femaleness/femininity and maleness/masculinity to which a person is sexually or romantically attracted. This continuum of sexual and romantic attraction is related to principles outlined by Kinsey, Pomeroy, and Martin (1948) in the Heterosexual-Homosexual Rating Scale, sometimes referred to as the Kinsey Scale. This research found that people do not fit into neat and exclusive heterosexual or "homosexual" categories (Kinsey et al., 1948) and that sexual identity is more aptly described as being on a continuum. Though the majority of men and women reported being exclusively heterosexual, and a percentage reported exclusively gay behavior and attractions, many individuals disclosed behaviors or thoughts somewhere in between (Kinsey et al., 1948). This challenges typical ideas proposed by the gender binary and provides evidence for nonbinary identities such as bisexual, pansexual, polysexual, and queer.

Kinsey et al. (1948) found that sexual behavior, thoughts, and feelings toward the same or opposite sex were not always consistent across time and could evolve across the life span. In addition to feeling various levels of sexual and romantic attraction to femaleness/femininity and maleness/masculinity, individuals may identify as having no (e.g., asexual) or little (e.g., demisexual) sexual and/or romantic attraction toward others. The gender Gumby and genderbread person models outline the fluidity of human affectional orientation and gender expression. These models challenge gender binary ideals of how society groups and defines individual sexual identity, gender identity, and gender expression; they also assist individuals in learning the complex nature of gender and affectional orientation.

Genderqueer

An individual who identifies as genderqueer is "a person whose gender identity is neither man nor woman, is between or beyond genders, or is a combination of typical prescribed gender roles and/or expressions" (UCB, 2015, "genderqueer"). This identity is related to or in reaction to the social construction of gender, prescribed gender stereotypes, and the gender binary system. The gender binary system reinforces principles of genderism, or the belief that there are only two genders (Killermann, 2013). Genderism also insists that individuals' birth-assigned sex is related to their gender identity and expression (Killermann, 2013). Genderism and genderist attitudes discriminate against transgender, genderqueer, and gender-nonconforming individuals, reinforcing the belief that cisgender individuals and those who identify as either male or female are superior and deserving of privilege. Genderqueer individuals may choose to label themselves as a direct response to genderism and the gender binary.

Genderqueer individuals do not conform to society's prescribed gender roles and ideas of gender conformity (Killermann, 2013; UCB, 2015). Therefore, genderqueer is a gender identity and gender expression rather than a sexual identity. In addition, some genderqueer persons identify under the transgender umbrella, whereas others do not. Someone who identifies as genderqueer may identify with characteristics traditionally labeled as masculine and other characteristics typically labeled as feminine in various combinations. Genderqueer persons can express gender nonconformity through gender expression, behavior, social roles, and gender identity. However, it is not necessary to express one's gender identity to identify as genderqueer. Genderqueer persons may also identify with terms such as *bigender, androgynous, gender fluid, gender nonconforming, gender diverse, pangender,* and/or *nonbinary.* They may also use terms such as *androsexual* (attracted to males) or *gynesexual* (attracted to females) to indicate affectional orientation, as *heterosexual* and *gay* assume a gender in their definitions.

Knowledge of Issues and Problems

Information about different groups of individuals who may identify as queer, in relation to either their gender, sexual/relational/affectional orientation(s), behaviors, or other modes of expression, can be difficult to generalize; one hallmark of living a queer perspective is the valuing of complexity, fluidity, change, and the performance of idiosyncratic or innovative subjectivities (Downing & Gillett, 2011). Research on the psychosocial and physical health of people who express same-sex sexual and relational orientations and/or who subvert gender binaries in dress, behavior, identity, or any other means exists but may be limited in its generalizability and transferability across the queer and genderqueer identities. Here we discuss overarching themes related to the physical, social, emotional, and mental health needs of queer and genderqueer individuals synthesized from the literature. Collaborative biopsychosocial assessment with queer clients can be enriched through attention to these issues (Moe, Finnerty, Sparkman, & Yates, 2015). Assuming that these issues are universal, however, should be avoided in favor of honoring the lived experiences and capabilities of queer clients.

The Institute of Medicine (IOM; 2011) sponsored a nationwide task force addressing the need for best practice standards in health care for LGBTQ individuals that developed an integrated theoretical framework for conceptualizing health issues faced by these historically marginalized populations. Members of the task force, based on a critical review and analysis of the literature, identified the following four perspectives as vital to understanding the physical and mental health care needs of LGBTQ people: minority stress, social ecology, life span development, and intersectionality. The minority stress perspective attributes the physical and mental health disparities disproportionally impacting LGBTQI+ people to their experience of discrimination, both overt and subtle, including internalized oppression (IOM, 2011). Social ecology refers to situating queer subjectivities in interrelated contexts and discourses, in which the experience and expression of gender and affectional orientation diversity needs are textured by the interactions, mores, and expectations emergent in social relationships. The life span development viewpoint encompasses the ongoing growth and changes experienced by queer individuals as a result of aging, experiencing new roles (or the loss of old ones), and the impact of social change over the life span. The experience of identifying as queer, for example, is contextualized by social expectations for youth, young adults, middle-aged persons, and older persons in any historical moment. Finally, intersectionality involves intentional consideration of the dynamic interplay between multiple identities and subjectivities, including the operation of privilege and oppression. Expecting queer clients to prioritize their gender and affectional orientation identities over others, such as cultural or ethnicity-based identities, is tacitly heteronormative and cisgender biased, as it is based on viewing these aspects of identity as primary regardless of context or individual experiences (Moe et al., 2011).

Experiences of Bias

Self-awareness related to same-sex sexual and relational experiences or binary gender nonconformity may develop in early childhood (Cox, Dewaele, Van Houtte, & Vincke, 2010). How family and primary caregivers respond to this awareness has a lifelong impact on the sense of connection and personal well-being of people who identify as queer, with negative reactions being associated with undesirable psychosocial outcomes (Poteat, Mereish, DiGiovanni, & Koenig, 2011). It is very likely that queer persons are subject to the same degree of bullying, harassment, and abuse as other LGBTQI+ persons discussed in this book (Hines, Malley-Morrison, & Dutton, 2013; Kosciw, Greytak, Palmer, & Boesen, 2014). However, often the queer and genderqueer identities are not researched uniquely; rather, they are aggregated with LGBT data. Regardless, a nonaffirming social environment may foster a sense of isolation in children, adolescents, and adults. Isolation is a powerful contributing factor to a person's sense of self-worth, ability to cope with life challenges, and development of resiliency and overall wellness (Cox et al., 2010; Poteat et al., 2011). The effect of social context on the well-being and positive development of gender and affectional minorities (including queer people) is well documented (American Psychological Association Task Force on Appropriate Therapeutic Responses to Sexual Orientation, 2009; Cox et al., 2010). However, people who identify as queer may face unique challenges related to within-group social dynamics that manifest in spaces otherwise affirming of LGBTQI+ people (Moore, 2013).

For example, gender and affectionally divergent youth of color reported feeling misunderstood by older LGBTQI+ people (Giwa & Greensmith, 2012). This sense of feeling invalidated or misunderstood arose partially as a result of the adults expecting the youth to identify with and express their gender and affectional orientations through identity markers such as lesbian or gay (Giwa & Greensmith, 2012). It should be noted that the participants, despite describing this sense of disconnection, still felt that LGBTQI+ service providers were more competent and affirming in general compared to non-LGBTQI+-identifying providers (Giwa & Greensmith, 2012). Thus, people expressing queer and genderqueer subjectivities may feel isolated, judged negatively, or otherwise invalidated in groups and communities that embrace ethnic majority, binary, and/or heteronormative identities (Stone, 2013). This informs the therapeutic alliance, as queer clients may struggle to trust that their counselors, even those identifying as allies and/or LGBTQI+, will be authentically affirming and valuing of their lived experiences.

Life span considerations for queer individuals include being able to share their gender, sexual, and relational fluidity with family members (whether of origin or intent) and potential life partners (Moe et al., 2011). Adopting and expressing a queer identity after identifying as heterosexual, lesbian, bisexual, and so on may cause awkwardness and confusion among close friends and loved ones as the new identity is negotiated socially. Intimate partner violence has also been studied in queer-identified individuals. Queer individuals appear to experience rates of intimate partner violence comparable to cisgender and heterosexually identified couples (Ard & Makadon, 2011). The experience of intimate partner violence for queer and other LGBTQI+ people is nuanced by a lack of affirmation from intimate partner violence response providers, a lack of relationship recognition in many communities and states, and fear of having their sexualities or gender identities involuntarily disclosed to others as result of seeking help (Ard & Makadon, 2011; Carvalho, Lewis, Derlega, Winstead, & Viggiano, 2011). Older adults who identify as queer may face significant challenges to maintaining their standard of living, as services (such as group homes) for elders may expect or enforce strict codes of behavior based on heterosexism and patriarchal gender-role conformity; individuals presenting as ambiguous in any way in terms of affectional orientation or gender identity may be turned away from such facilities (Erdley, Anklam, & Reardon, 2014). Seeking out and connecting with other people who affirm queer values is an important wellness practice across the life span for people who identify as queer (Moe et al., 2011).

Queer-identified persons are infrequently included under the LGBT umbrella. The term *queer* sometimes serves as an umbrella term for LGBT-identified persons but is also a unique political and social identity that is not included in the LGBT spectrum. One person may identify as LGBT and queer, and another person could identify as queer and not under the LGBT identities, depending on personal identification preferences. Traditional paradigms regarding affectional orientation and gender insist that an individual must identify with a group (e.g., heterosexual or gay, male or female) without allowing for fluidity. This is sometimes reinforced in lesbian and gay communities through the nomenclature and language used to define an individual's affectional orientation or gender. For the counseling field to improve services for LGBTQI+ persons and advocate for social justice issues related to this group, counselors themselves must develop an awareness of the power of language and grouping on individual identities (Smith et al., 2012). In the case of queer-identified persons, cultural norms, traditions, grouping, and naming have reproduced a gender binary, which creates socially constructed either/or identity categories. These categories cannot accurately describe the fluidity of human sexuality or gender identity. This inaccuracy leads to the exclusion and marginalization of sexually diverse and gender-nonconforming individuals.

Queer-identified persons are also often misunderstood and marginalized, culturally and in mental health services. The deconstruction of heteronormative values, the gender binary, and genderist attitudes enable counselors to dismantle heteronormative mental health practices and research (Smith et al., 2012). Greater awareness of the affectional orientation and gender binary can enable well-intended counselors to construct their own understanding of affectional orientation, gender, and client status(es) (Burnes et al., 2010; Harper et al., 2013). Interrogating the construction of gender binary principles is essential for counselors and the field of counseling to gain an understanding of affectional orientation and gender minority concerns (Smith et al., 2012). This deconstruction will ensure that counselors develop a greater awareness of their own assumptions, values, and biases related to the affectional orientation and gender binary. This will assist in developing practice-appropriate interventions for affectional minority and gender-nonconforming clients (Smith et al., 2012). Increased understanding of the queer community requires that counselors and mental health professionals educate themselves about and advocate for efficacious services for queer-identified persons.

Physical Issues and Health Care

LGBTQI+ populations, including queer and genderqueer individuals, present with significant health disparities in the United States and globally (Haas et al., 2010). Negative physical health outcomes manifesting with greater prevalence across gender and affectional orientation variant groups include higher rates of HIV/AIDS and other sexually transmitted infections as well as greater risk of injury due to physical assault (IOM, 2011). Individuals with genderqueer and/or transgender identities and modes of expression, especially those with intersecting ethnic minority heritages, appear to be at the highest risk for interpersonal violence; deprivation due to poverty; financial insecurity; and the development of chronic health care conditions, including HIV seroconversion (Balsam, Molina, Beadnell, Simoni, & Walters, 2011). Access to competent and affirming providers of physical health care is also an important social justice issue for queer populations, with the real or perceived threat of prejudicial behavior on the part of providers being a factor in the decision of LGBTQI+ people to seek care (Carvalho et al., 2011).

The evolution of marriage equality laws to recognize non-heterosexual couples is a welcome structural development in terms of ensuring that queer clients are able to share insurance, to share information, and to act as decision makers in critical health care situations on behalf of their partners and spouses (Erdley et al., 2014). However, insurance coverage for gender transition and health care providers who are open, affirming, and competent relative to gender and affectional orientation variance are still relevant issues for LGBTQI+ persons.

Potential Mental Health Challenges

As previously delineated, individuals who identify as LGBTQI+, or whose behavior and experience does not conform to strict heterosexuality and/or binary gender-role conformity, appear to experience higher rates of mental disorder and stress than their heterosexual and cisgender counterparts (Haas et al., 2010; IOM, 2011). This includes higher rates of suicidality, depression, and anxiety (Haas et al., 2010), all conditions seen as related to minority stress and internalized prejudice (Balsam et al., 2011; Cox et al., 2010). These manifestations of mental distress appear to be common across LGBTQI+ groups and to be exacerbated further by social alienation and isolation (Mink, Lindley, & Weinstein, 2014). Trauma appears to be experienced at higher rates by LGBTQI+ groups, with the highest rates experienced by people who identify as transgender or genderqueer as well as LGBTQI+ people of color (Balsam et al., 2011). Accurate assessment of minority stress, internalized prejudice, and trauma that accounts for societal heterosexism and cisgender prejudice is an important standard of care for counselors seeking to provide services to queer individuals (IOM, 2011; Moe et al., 2015; Patton & Reicherzer, 2010).

In terms of unique aspects of queer individuals' mental health and ongoing development, Stone (2013) reported queer individuals place high value on being able to remain in a state of experiential fluidity regarding their gender and/or sexual-relational orientation(s) and identities in order to avoid a sense of feeling stuck or trapped. That is, challenging and questioning personal identities, relationships, and experiences (even positive or affirming ones) was seen as a motivating force by participants and as a healthy indicator of the queer individual's ability to avoid stagnation (Stone, 2013). Cherishing fluidity in identity and experience, as well as innovation in gender, sexual, and relational expression, may be both a strength and a potential source of stress for clients who identify as queer in terms of striving to enact an idealized queer subjectivity. It is also important to note the strengths and capabilities of queer individuals in any discussion of mental health and well-being: It is important to honor the achievements of members of this population and to counter the overpathologizing of nonbinary persons. Self-identifying queer, genderqueer, and other nonbinary-conforming individuals have been an integral and visible part of sociopolitical movements to address heterosexism, patriarchy, and cisgender prejudice, especially in previous generations when other identity markers (e.g., gay) were used less or not at all (Lee, 2013).

Counseling Skills and Techniques

To those familiar with the critical epistemologies (e.g., feminism) from which queer theory was developed, it should come as no surprise that the discourse of evidence-based practice (EBP) is also an object for deconstructive engagement along with heteronormativity and gender binary thinking. The framework of postpositivism, rooted in modernism and so-called scientific objectivity, promotes the seeking of unitary and universalist truths and related value-free causal explanations for phenomena (Balick, 2011). Information that is quantifiable, created using postpositivist methodologies such as the randomized controlled clinical trial, is privileged in the EBP perspective because of the apparent removal of both the observer and the observed from consideration of the knowledge claims supported by such research endeavors (Balick, 2011; Zeeman et al., 2014). Therefore, queering the discourse of EBP and reclaiming potentially useful knowledge and awareness are the goals in reviewing the existing research; expressly critiquing the operations of heteronormative and gender binary assumptions in the creation, implementation, analysis, and interpretations of research will help reveal the validity of the research. Just as a queer view of identity does not deny the valuing of nonqueer identities (Moore, 2013), a queer response to EBP does not reject the scientific method; rather, claims based solely on a postpositivist frame are considered incomplete without consideration of power, history, relationships, and other sources of context (Burnes et al., 2010; Harper et al., 2013). Thus, the paradigm of EBP, applied uncritically and differentially, itself can be used to support tacit and explicit heteronormativity and transgender prejudice (Smith, 2013; Zeeman et al., 2014), as has been done in the past (Daley & Mulé, 2014).

Another important consideration involving uncritical adherence to the EBP viewpoint is related to which populations and presenting concerns have any empirically supported counseling and psychotherapy approaches validated for work with queer and other LGBTQI+ individuals. According to the *ACA Code of Ethics* (American Counseling Association, 2014), counseling interventions that do not rest on a scientific and theoretical foundation for work with populations to which clients belong, and/or the presenting concerns of clients (e.g., social phobia), should be represented as developing or innovative. Assessment instrument reliability and validity, intervention efficacy studies with LGBTQI+ populations, and the development of therapeutic responses for specific presenting concerns are all underdeveloped domains in the existing knowledge base largely as a function of historical heteronormativity and transprejudice in the academy (Singh & Shelton, 2010). This is especially problematic given the apparent differential expectations for what kind of evidence is considered sufficient to justify continued use of diagnoses in the *Diagnostic and Statistical Manual of Mental Disorders, Fifth Edition,* whose criteria for gender dysphoria and some paraphilias appear to be informed more by social norms than by scientific evidence (Daley & Mulé, 2014).

To counter the potential for misappropriation of the EBP worldview, counselors working with queer individuals (and other gender and affectional minorities) can seek to enrich their awareness of valid approaches. Along with standards for evaluating quantitative research, such as reliability, validity, and generalizability, counselors can apply standards related to qualitative methodologies (e.g., trustworthiness, credibility, transferability) to an evaluation of counseling approaches. Counselors can use this combined approach when working with queer clients and developing a case conceptualization and related evaluation of EBP: (a) Is gender and/or sexual diversity related to the reason queer individuals are seeking counseling? (b) What are the presenting concerns, and how are these concerns informed by heterosexism and cisgender privilege? (c) What evidence (both quantitative and qualitative) exists to support counseling for the presenting concerns with any populations? (d) What evidence exists to support counseling with the specific populations with which queer individuals identify? and (e) How does a particular counseling approach resonate with the lived experiences of queer individuals, including tapping into their competence, strengths, and coping abilities (Moe et al., 2015; Zeeman et al., 2014)?

Scholars have sought to strengthen the empirical and theoretical synthesis of counseling models with affirmation of LGBTQI+ communities, including those identifying as queer. The framework of cognitive–behavioral counseling, an approach with breadth and depth of empirical support for a diverse array of presenting concerns, can be tailored to address issues specific to the lives of queer clients (Martell, 2014). Techniques such as challenging rigid or dichotomous thinking, engaging in and altering self-talk to be more self- and other affirming, thought stopping, behavioral rehearsal and experimentation, and reframing can be utilized to counter the influence of internalized prejudice and related minority stress concerns (Martell, 2014). Third-wave cognitive therapies based on mindfulness, such as acceptance and commitment therapy, can help deepen the ability of queer-identified clients to be more present oriented and confident in negotiating their values across the full spectrum of social contexts (Stitt, 2014). Paradigms based on cultivating a rich therapeutic rapport, such as relational-cultural theory (Patton & Reicherzer, 2010), are theoretically consonant with the queer values of engaging with the worldview, self-expression, and self-concept of individuals negotiating their life experience in an oppressive sociocultural milieu (Moe et al., 2011). Self-disclosure, immediacy, authenticity, radical valuing, and accurate empathic awareness are all appropriate counseling techniques for both fostering a sense of therapeutic alliance and subverting the potential objectification of the client (Patton & Reicherzer, 2010).

The framework of narrative therapy (Saltzburg, 2007) is based on deconstruction of counseling and psychotherapy as a social practice, which makes this approach theoretically and stylistically consistent with the poststructural philosophy on which queer theory is based (Saltzburg, 2007). Elements of narrative therapy, such as restorying, situating thoughts and beliefs in social discourse, and externalizing discourse(s) limiting the well-being of clients, are well matched to the lives and experiences of queer individuals. Externalizing heteronormativity, patriarchy, and cisgender prejudice as sociocultural discourses may in fact be second nature to clients already identifying as queer, and counselors should privilege the competence and strengths of queer clients related to coping with and resisting oppressive discourses. Strengths-based counseling and psychotherapy models, such as solution-focused brief therapy, are also helpful for reclaiming the successes, capabilities, and innovations that queer-identified individuals engage to not only cope with oppression but thrive as fully realized social agents (Mink et al., 2014). Identifying strengths and successes with queer clients can be helpful given the history (and current use) of stigma, overpathologizing, and medical discourse to objectify queer people as deviant or abnormal (Daley & Mulé, 2014; Moe et al., 2015).

The Competencies for Counseling LGBQQIA Individuals (Harper et al., 2013) and Competencies for Counseling Transgender Clients (Burnes et al., 2010) are frameworks that contain process guidelines for affirmative practice that should be synthesized with other counseling models. Standards such as cultivating self-awareness around heterosexist and cisgender biases, incorporating inclusive and client-affirming language in documentation as well as spoken dialogue, and seeking complementarity in the evidence used are all informed explicitly by queer theory and should be applied to any counseling situation with people who identify as queer (Burnes et al., 2010; Harper et al., 2013). Each framework is based on critical review and integration of available theoretical and empirical evidence on affirming counseling with LGBTQI+ populations.

Conclusion

Ongoing research and theory construction is still needed to validate counseling and psychotherapy approaches with queer individuals and groups, especially in terms of theory built on the foundation of queer peoples' values, strengths, and lived experiences. This chapter has predominantly considered queer subjectivity as one of many viewpoints relating to gender and affectional orientation, but a queer perspective can also be infused into consideration of the needs, experiences, and identities of heterosexual or cisgender individuals as well. Illustrating the operation of power in how individuals manifests their affectional orientation or gender identity, for example, may be liberating for any human; it can be quite oppressive for any person to negotiate a unique or minority identity in a patriarchal, heteronormative, and binary gender deterministic social ecology. Embracing the diversity within and between identity categories (including heterosexual or cisgender identities) creates space for continued innovation in the collective understanding of sexuality, relationships, affectional orientation, gender, and their myriad intersections and forms of expression in human development.

Questions for Further Discussion

1. What might it mean to Bianca to identify as queer? How about Jesse as genderqueer?
2. What types of bias and discrimination are Bianca and Jesse facing?
3. What are the possible reasons why Bianca and Jesse are experiencing physical/mental health symptoms?
4. What competencies does a counselor need to be able to work effectively with Bianca and Jesse?
5. What potential counseling interventions may be effective for these cases?

Resources

1. Review the following gender training tools online:
   a. Gender Gumby: http://www.pdxqcenter.org/wp-content/uploads/2013/02/gumby%20pp.pdf
   b. Gender Pokey: https://catchingwine.files.wordpress.com/2013/11/gender-pokey1.pdf
   c. Genderbread person version 3: http://itspronouncedmetrosexual.com/2015/03/the-genderbread-person-v3/
   d. Gender unicorn: http://www.transstudent.org/gender
2. Learn more about the genderqueer identity at http://genderqueerid.com/.
3. Read about the overlap of affectional orientation and genderqueer identity at http://itspronouncedmetrosexual.com/2012/02/sexual-orientation-for-the-genderqueer/.

References

American Counseling Association. (2014). *ACA code of ethics.* Alexandria, VA: Author.

American Psychological Association Task Force on Appropriate Therapeutic Responses to Sexual Orientation. (2009). *Report of the Task Force on Appropriate Therapeutic Responses to Sexual Orientation.* Washington, DC: American Psychological Association.

Ard, K., & Makadon, H. (2011). Addressing intimate partner violence in lesbian, gay, bisexual, and transgender patients. *Journal of General Internal Medicine, 26,* 930–933. doi:10.1007/s11606-011-1697-6

Balick, A. (2011). Speculating on sexual subjectivity: On the application and misapplication of postmodern discourse on the psychology of sexuality. *Psychology & Sexuality, 2*(1), 16–28. doi:10.1080/19419899.2011.536312

Balsam, K. F., Molina, Y., Beadnell, B., Simoni, J., & Walters, K. (2011). Measuring multiple minority stress: The LGBT People of Color Micro-aggressions Scale. *Cultural Diversity and Ethnic Minority Psychology, 17*(2), 163–174. doi:10.1037/a0023244

Brontsema, R. (2004). A queer revolution: Reconceptualizing the debate over linguistic reclamation. *Colorado Research in Linguistics, 7*(1), 1–17.

Burn, S. B. (2000). Heterosexuals' use of "fag" and "queer" to deride one another: A contributor to heterosexism and stigma. *Journal of Homosexuality, 40*(2), 1–11.

Burnes, T., Singh, A., Harper, A., Harper, B., Maxon-Kann, W., Pickering, P., . . . Hosea, J. (2010). American Counseling Association competencies for counseling with transgender clients. *Journal of LGBT Issues in Counseling, 4,* 135–159. doi:10.1080/15538605.2010.524839

Carroll, L., & Gilroy, P. (2001). Teaching "outside the box": Incorporating queer theory in counselor education. *Journal of Humanistic Counseling, Education and Development, 40,* 49–57.

Carvalho, A., Lewis, R., Derlega, V., Winstead, B., & Viggiano, C. (2011). Internalized sexual minority stressors and same-sex intimate partner violence. *Journal of Family Violence, 26,* 501–509. doi:10.1007/s10896-011-9384-2

Cox, N., Dewaele, A., Van Houtte, M., & Vincke, J. (2010). Stress-related growth, coming out, and internalized homo-negativity in lesbian, gay, and bisexual youth. An examination of stress-related growth within the minority stress model. *Journal of Homosexuality, 58,* 117–137.

Daley, A., & Mulé, N. J. (2014). LGBTQs and the *DSM-5:* A critical queer response. *Journal of Homosexuality, 61,* 1288–1312. doi:10.1080/00918369.2014.926766

Downing, L., & Gillett, R. (2011). Viewing critical psychology through the lens of queer. *Psychology & Sexuality, 2*(1), 4–15. doi:10.1080/19419899.2011.536310

Erdley, S. D., Anklam, D. D., & Reardon, C. C. (2014). Breaking barriers and building bridges: Understanding the pervasive needs of older LGBT adults and the value of social work in health care. *Journal of Gerontological Social Work, 57*(2–4), 362–385. doi:10.1080/01634372.2013.871381

Frank, D. A., & Cannon, E. P. (2010). Queer theory as pedagogy in counselor education: A framework for diversity training. *Journal of LGBT Issues in Counseling, 4*(1), 18–31. doi:10.1080/15538600903552731

Giwa, S., & Greensmith, C. (2012). Race relations and racism in the LGBTQ community of Toronto: Perceptions of gay and queer social service providers of color. *Journal of Homosexuality, 59*(2), 149–185. doi:10.1080/00918369.2012.648877

Haas, A., Eliason, M., Mays, V. M., Mathy, R. M., Cochran, S. D., D'Augelli, A., & Clayton, P. (2010). Suicide and suicide risk in lesbian, gay, bisexual, and transgender populations: Review and recommendations. *Journal of Homosexuality, 58,* 10–51.

Harper, A., Finnerty, P., Martinez, M., Brace, A., Crethar, H. C., Loos, B., . . . Lambert, S. (2013). Association for Lesbian, Gay, Bisexual, and Transgender issues in counseling (ALGBTIC) competencies for counseling with lesbian, gay, bisexual, queer, questioning, intersex, and ally individuals. *Journal of LGBT Issues in Counseling, 7*(1), 2–43. doi:10.1080/15538605.2013.755444

Hines, D. A., Malley-Morrison, K., & Dutton, L. B. (2013). *Family violence in the United States: Defining, understanding, and combating abuse* (2nd ed.). Thousand Oaks, CA: Sage.

Institute of Medicine. (2011). *The health of lesbian, gay, bisexual, and transgender people: Building a foundation for better understanding.* Washington, DC: National Academies Press.

Killermann, S. (2013). *The social justice advocate's handbook: A guide to gender.* Austin, TX: Impetus Books.

Kinsey, A., Pomeroy, W., & Martin, C. (1948). *Sexual behavior in the human male.* New York, NY: W. B. Saunders.

Kosciw, J. G., Greytak, E. A., Palmer, N. A., & Boesen, M. J. (2014). *The 2013 National School Climate Survey: The experiences of lesbian, gay, bisexual and transgender youth in our nation's schools.* New York, NY: GLSEN.

Lee, M. (2013). Between Stonewall and AIDS: Initial efforts to establish gay and lesbian social services. *Journal of Sociology & Social Welfare, 40,* 163–186.

Martell, C. (2014). The hybrid case study of "Adam": Perspectives from behavioral activation and the influence of heteronormativity on LGB-affirmative therapy. *Pragmatic Case Studies in Psychotherapy, 10*(2), 106–116.

Mink, M., Lindley, L., & Weinstein, A. (2014). Stress, stigma, and sexual minority status: The intersectional ecology model of LGBTQ health. *Journal of Gay & Lesbian Social Services, 26,* 502–521. doi:10.1080/10538720.2014.953660

Moe, J. L., Finnerty, P., Sparkman, N., & Yates, C. (2015). Initial assessment and screening with LGBTQ clients: A critical perspective. *Journal of LGBT Issues in Counseling, 9*(1), 36–56. doi:10.1080/15538605.2014.997332

Moe, J. L., Reicherzer, S., & Dupuy, P. (2011). Models of sexual and relational orientation: A critical review and synthesis. *Journal of Counseling & Development, 89,* 227–233.

Moore, D. L. (2013). Structurelessness, structure, and queer movements. *Women's Studies Quarterly, 41*(3&4), 257–260.

Patton, J., & Reicherzer, S. (2010). Inviting "Kate's" authenticity: Relational-cultural theory applied in work with a transsexual sex worker of color using the competencies for counseling with transgender clients. *Journal of LGBT Issues in Counseling, 4*(3–4), 214–227. doi:10.1080/15538605.2010.524846

Poteat, V., Mereish, E., DiGiovanni, C., & Koenig, B. (2011). The effects of general and homophobic victimization on adolescent psychosocial and educational concerns: The importance of intersecting identities and parent support. *Journal of Counseling Psychology, 58,* 567–609. doi:10.1037/a0025095

Rand, E. (2014). *Reclaiming queer: Activist and academic rhetorics of resistance.* Tuscaloosa: University of Alabama Press.

Saltzburg, S. (2007). Narrative therapy pathways for re-authoring with parents of adolescents coming-out as lesbian, gay, and bisexual. *Contemporary Family Therapy, 29,* 57–69. doi:10.1007/s10591-007-9035-1

Singh, A., & Shelton, K. (2010). A content analysis of LGBTQ qualitative research in counseling: A ten-year review. *Journal of Counseling & Development, 89,* 217–226.

Smith, L. (2013). How the ASCA national model promotes or inhibits safe schools for queer youth: An inquiry using critical theory. *Journal of LGBT Issues in Counseling, 7,* 339–354.

Smith, L., Shin, R., & Office, L. (2012). Moving counseling forward on LGB and transgender issues: Speaking queerly on discourses and micro-aggressions. *The Counseling Psychologist, 40,* 385–408.

Stitt, A. (2014). The cat and the cloud: ACT for LGBT locus of control, responsibility, and acceptance. *Journal of LGBT Issues in Counseling, 8*(3), 282–297. doi:10.1080/15538605.2014.933469

Stone, A. L. (2013). Flexible queers, serious bodies: Transgender inclusion in queer spaces. *Journal of Homosexuality, 60,* 1647–1665. doi:10.1080/00918369.2013.834209

University of California, Berkeley. (2015). *Definition of terms.* Retrieved from http://ejce.
    berkeley.edu/geneq/resources/lgbtq-resources/definition-terms
Zeeman, L., Aranda, K., & Grant, A. (2014). Queer challenges to evidence-based practice.
    Nursing Inquiry, 21(2), 101–111. doi:10.1111/nin.12039

Chapter 16

Counseling Clients Questioning Their Affectional Orientation

Jared S. Rose and Eric R. Baltrinic

*It's interesting that when young people state that they are
attracted to someone of the same gender, they're often told,
"You're too young to know," or, "This is probably just a phase."
Yet if that same young person were to say that he or she is attracted to
someone of the opposite gender, no one seems to question this.*
—Dr. Fishberger

• • •

Awareness of Attitudes and Beliefs Self-Check

1. How old were you when you had your first crush on or attraction to someone? Was it met with approval or disapproval by others?
2. What people do you know who openly admit that they are questioning their affectional orientation, including celebrities and television/movie characters? How might this lack of representation impact children or adolescents who are questioning their affectional orientation?
3. If a 10-year-old child told you that they had a crush on someone of the same sex, what would be your reaction? Your fears?

Case Study

Nina is a 15-year-old female who emigrated from Russia at age 10. She has come to the school counselor with feelings of depression and anxiety that are beginning to impact her school work. As the school counselor begins to build rapport with Nina, she learns that Nina feels that she may be in love with her best friend, Jackie. Nina is very fearful about these feelings and does not want to have them exposed. She is concerned about losing her friendship with Jackie if she discloses how she feels. She is also afraid of her parents finding out: In the Russian culture, being gay is not openly accepted. She is not sure whether she is gay but feels lonely, isolated, and confused.

• • •

Awareness of Differences

For many, the phrase "questioning one's affectional orientation" leaves the impression that the person questioning is pondering the very nature of their affectional orientation. Although this may be the case for some, it is not always a matter of questioning one's orientation. Often the act of questioning speaks to how affectional orientation fits in the social construct of sexuality. Are individuals who are questioning their affectional orientation asking "What (who) am I?" or are they asking "What does this mean for me?" In order to better understand clients who are questioning their affectional orientation, the term *social construction* and the process of how individuals identify their affectional orientation must first be addressed.

A plethora of definitions of *affectional orientation* can be found, but a succinct one comes from Reams (2016), who stated that it is "the preponderance of one's emotional and physical attractions—whether stable or fluid—to males, females, both, or neither" (p. 2). This definition illustrates key elements of affectional orientation, including one that is often overlooked: that one's orientation is complex and involves not merely physical or sexual attraction but also emotionality. In other words, individuals considering any orientation other than heterosexuality focus almost exclusively on sexual attraction, negating emotional attraction. This inherent element of orientation is important when working with any client, regardless of affectional identification, but is crucial with individuals questioning their orientation. In addition, what of the term *affectional orientation* itself? The use of the word *orientation* intends to describe a position of one's affectional orientation, but frequently individuals view orientation as one extreme or the other (i.e., heterosexual or gay), sometimes including a middle ground (i.e., bisexual). There is evidence to support the need to conceptually disaggregate the term *affectional orientation* from *gender identity* (see Galupo, Davis, Grynkiewicz, & Mitchell, 2014); the same holds true when considering affectional orientation. In fact, affectional orientation is better viewed as developing on a continuum (Kinsey, Pomeroy, & Martin, 1948; Laumann, Gagnon, Michael, & Michaels, 1994) and not as a static construct lacking fluidity. Perhaps the time has come to stop considering the term *orientation* and recognize that humans are sexual beings and have sexuality, regardless of their orientation. Perhaps the best starting place to reduce any confusion related to the classification of affectional orientation is to just talk about sexuality and affection instead of orientation.

Culture and the language in it changes over time (Carroll & Gilroy, 2001; Kramsch, 1998). With that in mind, we are led to another element of contemplation: the use of language. Care must be taken to understand what exactly a client is questioning. Often when people experience feeling attracted to a person or gender different from what they have been attracted to in the past, the initial consideration is how and why it is occurring, or what it means for them and their life. They are not necessarily questioning affectional orientation as a whole, although it is certainly possible that clients may say something relative to questioning their affectional orientation. Far too often, however, the *questioning* term is one the counselor considers when hearing clients conceptualizing their experiences. Sometimes individuals question not their affectional orientation per se but rather what it means for them. Clients will also use terms to describe themselves in ways that are unfamiliar to some counselors (e.g., *pansexual, polysexual, demisexual, allosexual, omnisexual,* and the list goes on and on). The point is that individuals today, especially youth, are more likely to use terms other than to describe themselves as they navigate their affectional orientation than *questioning* (Harvey & Stone, 2015; Savin-Williams, 2006, 2008). As in any work with clients, counselors must bracket their own assumptions about affectional orientation and see through their clients' lens instead. This can sometimes be a challenge because language surrounding affectional orientation changes frequently, sometimes leaving a counselor confused as to a client's intended meaning. This occurs because culture changes, and such changes influence and construct human interaction with varied affectional orientations.

Eagly's (1987) social theory emphasized how individuals develop traits that serve not just themselves as individuals but societal needs and expectations. Society sees this commonly through gender roles and gender expression. Twenge (1997) noted significant changes in masculine and feminine traits over time and within cultures. Consider the common, easily identifiable example of the working family. Fifty or 60 years ago gender roles were characterized by a heterosexual male in the household working and a heterosexual female caring for the home and raising the children. In today's modern United States, the nuclear family and expected gender roles have changed so much that no such common view of family even exists anymore (Cohen, 2014). From single-parent homes to same-sex married couples, more women in the workforce, blended families, and two-income households, the variability is to the point where the *typical* family no longer exists (Luscombe, 2014). These are but a few examples of variant gender roles, but what must be acknowledged is that the same types of changes in a culture happen with how individuals view and express their affectional orientation. This can be seen most prominently with today's youth.

Savin-Williams (2006) noted how youth engage in same- and opposite-sex encounters without necessarily prescribing themselves to any particular affectional orientation identification. In fact, youth may not consider categorized labels important at all. Harvey and Stone (2015) later explained how youth explore their gender and their affectional orientation, viewing affection as fluid and less dichotomous. For today's youth, expression and exploration are more important than labels or rigid classification. Yet society and culture play a significant role in the desire to neatly categorize people into groups so as to feel more secure with human interaction. It is not just youth, of course, who experience this or feel this way. Anyone, at any point in their life, may give consideration to their affectional orientation based on emerging or changing attractions and personal needs. An individual's sense of emotional and physical attraction may change over time based on both romantic relationships and social group inclusions (Diamond, 2009; Reams, 2016; Savin-Williams, 2006). This does not mean to suggest that affectional orientation identity is a choice but rather that it is a continuum, fluid over the life span, and at least in part socially constructed.

Identity Development

Case conceptualizations are a common and extremely helpful tool for practitioners. Although a case narrative is presented for this chapter, it should be noted that there is no prototype for clients questioning (CQ) their gender identity or affectional orientation. It could be the 17-year-old high school football quarterback dating the head female cheerleader who recently started finding himself physically attracted to some of his male teammates. Perhaps it is the 30-something woman who has begun to be emotionally attracted to her best female friend. Or maybe it is the 65-year-old retiree who spent his life identifying as gay but yesterday discovered that he rather enjoyed the opposite-sex advances of a fellow retirement home resident. The fact of the matter is that it could be any client, at any time during their life. As noted, affectional orientation is fluid, and it courses along a continuum. What is important for counselors working to conceptualize CQ is that they draw on their core client-centered principles of being genuine, providing unconditional positive regard, and being empathetic to the client's particular presentation (Rogers, 1951, 2003). The therapeutic setting must be one in which clients are comfortable expressing and discussing their affectional orientation. It may not always be a topic related to the client's issue(s), but counselors need to be professionals in which the client can confide, and this means being approachable on topics relating to sex. This is true for all clients, not just CQ, but those questioning may be particularly vulnerable should the questioning be relative to a shift in their very identity.

The question may arise for some as to why this firm stance is so important when trying to conceptualize CQ. The answer, simply, is because affectional orientation and sexuality are incredibly important to individuals' identity and the very nature of their needs as humans. Most mental health professionals subscribe to the ideas established by Maslow's hierarchy of needs (Maslow, 1943, 1954), at least insofar as individuals need to have certain foundational needs (e.g., biological needs, safety) met before higher order needs (e.g., love, self-actualization) can be realized. It is unrealistic, for example, to assume that a client can feel truly safe if he is living on the streets or for a client to decrease her anxiety if she has problems breathing and cannot afford the medical treatment needed to improve air flow. Likewise, it would be impossible for clients to reduce their depression if they are malnourished, with no power to acquire food. Examples abound, but the point is that counselors are frequently able to identify how a lack of even one physiological need can interfere with a client's overall well-being. What is frequently overlooked is how Maslow included sexual behavior as part of the foundational physiological needs of humans. In fact, Maslow argued that sexual needs are just as important to physiological homeostasis as food, water, warmth, and air. Maslow further contended that care should be taken not to confuse the needs sex and love because, although the two often go together, the needs are not mutually exclusive.

The levels and intensity of one's sexual needs may vary from person to person and from time to time, but they are inherently biologically present for all people, including asexual groups, although they experience their sexuality very differently (Reams, 2016). As a consequence, a client cannot reach the upper echelons of the needs hierarchy if one of the foundational elements is unstable, as can be expected for any CQ. When appropriate to the therapeutic needs of a client, to ignore or otherwise avoid conversations regarding the client's affectional orientation is to do a disservice to the client. Doing so could even pose harm to clients, especially for CQ who have hopes that their counselors will assist them with their concerns. Counselors need to address their own worldview, biases, stereotypes, and attitudes when it comes to affectional orientation and sexuality. Although the conversation about a client's affectional orientation must be navigated carefully, just like any interaction with a client, such topics should not, and cannot, be taboo.

Knowledge of Issues and Problems

Experiences of Bias

Members of the lesbian, gay, bisexual, transgender, queer, questioning, intersex, asexual, ally, pansexual/polysexual, and two-spirited (LGBTQI+) community face numerous challenges often leading to increased stress levels (Shipherd, 2015) and negative coping responses, including cognitive questioning and rumination (Borders, Guillen, & Meyer, 2014). These collective challenges contribute to increased physical, mental, and emotional challenges (Institute of Medicine, 2011), which may adversely affect affectional and gender minorities' access to, and quality of, health care and mental health treatment. As has been discussed previously, the literature is replete with evidence suggesting the risk factors for LGBTQI+ individuals, including bullying and victimization by peers and other adults (Hollander, 2000; Society for Adolescent Health and Medicine, 2013), increased risk of depression and suicide (Savin-Williams & Ream, 2003), and self-harm (Liu & Mustanski, 2012). Unfortunately, the preponderance of research aggregates questioning individuals in in the rest of the LGBTQI+ population; therefore, little is known about the unique physical and mental health of questioning persons.

To further complicate matters, LGBTQI+ clients are often served by counselors who are themselves working through their own identities and understandings of others' affectional identities. Although many counselors can effectively serve LGBTQI+ clients, counselors who are unaware of their biases, who are not conversant with the literature, or who are undertrained run the risk of applying approaches or models that are inappropriate or even marginalizing for the LGBTQI+ population (Ratts, Singh, Nassar-McMillan, Butler, & McCullough, 2015). This is particularly true for CQ who may not identify and therefore align with the queer or heterosexual communities. If a counselor is going to meet the needs of LGBTQI+ clients, and in particular CQ, an increased understanding of the therapy components and training elements for working with this population is needed (Shipherd, 2015).

Counseling Skills and Techniques

Up to this point, it has been argued that counselors adopt a broad and phenomenologically grounded stance regarding clients' concepts of affectional identity, which was described earlier as existing on a continuum, especially when working with CQ. This is a key component of self-awareness important for cultural competence with CQ. The recommendations put forth by the Society for Adolescent Health and Medicine (2013) are that counselors (and all health care providers for that matter) be trained to provide "competent and nonjudgmental care" for lesbian, gay, or transgender clients (p. 506). This recommendation should be extended to the provision of competent and nonjudgmental care to CQ. And although it is clear that counselors should observe established dimensions of sexuality (e.g., attraction, behavior, and identity; Savin-Williams, 2008), providers should also recognize that clients' affectional identities develop not just throughout adolescence but long into adulthood (Horner, 2007; Reams, 2016; Society for Adolescent Health and Medicine, 2013). Furthermore, counselors should use caution when assigning labels (i.e., LGBTQI+) to CQ. Instead, counselors would benefit from asking clients how they self-identify, accepting clients' uncertainties about their affectional identity (i.e., questioning) as an *expectation and not an exception.*

Counselor Self-Awareness

The *Multicultural and Social Justice Counseling Competencies* established by Ratts and colleagues (2015) include (a) counselor self-awareness, (b) client worldview, (c) the counseling relationship, and (d) counseling and advocacy interventions; these can all be addressed as they pertain to working with CQ. Clients may experience uncertainties of meaning and associated feelings when exploring their affectional identities. In some cases, CQ may simply refuse an affectional orientation identity label (Savin-Williams, 2006, 2008). For Horner (2007), the term *questioning* reflected a nontraditional perspective on affectional identity development; the term also suggests that counselors view affectional identity development as a fluid process (Diamond, 2009; Savin-Williams, 2006). Similarly, Russell, Clarke, and Clary (2009) found that it is wrong to conclude that labels (e.g., LGBTQI+) are unimportant for some individuals; rather, labels of affectional identity need to be understood by counselors in the context of a more fluid (vs. staged or static) view of affectional identity development. Russell et al. described the development of sexuality in terms of "developmental milestones rather than stages" (p. 885). In other words, when it comes to CQ, there is no single label-driven, stage-related line in the sand demarcating the moment CQ move from one stage of affectional identity development to another.

Most important, counselors need to (a) acknowledge their own biases (i.e., their own affectional identity and associated feelings about their own affectional identity and those of others) and (b) recognize that professional competencies serve as a foundation—but not a replacement—for conscientious interactions and careful listening as clients tell their stories in counseling sessions (Harper et al., 2013; Ratts et al., 2015). In addition, counselors need to be aware that the application of terms (e.g., *LGBTQI+*) on their part and recommendations for CQ to engage in activities or organizations may prematurely assume an LGBTQI+ identity (Hollander, 2000), thus failing to address other factors that influence affectional identity formulation (e.g., development, preferences, biases, violence; Institute of Medicine, 2011).

The Counseling Relationship

It is evident that CQ face stressors related to identity development, victimization, discrimination, marginalization, and multiple barriers to accessing treatment and other supports. To counter these stressors for CQ, counselors working with this population are charged with building welcoming, affirming counseling relationships. There is a clear link between a quality counseling relationship and positive client outcomes (for a good summary of the research and trends on the therapeutic relationship and client outcomes, see Duncan, Miller, Wampold, & Hubble, 2009). Ratts et al. (2015) identified that competent counselors engage in counseling relationships informed by a self-awareness of their biases. Furthermore, competent counselors possess the skills to initiate safe and appropriate conversations with clients, can comfortably broach the topic of affectional identity, and are capable of taking action to support clients' treatment needs (Day-Vines et al., 2007).

CQ struggle with identity issues while simultaneously navigating predominantly heteronormative environments. Given this reality, one negative counseling experience can be a significant setback for CQ who want assistance. Counseling relationships tailored to the needs of CQ are characterized by the counselor's use of affirming language and active listening skills. Competent counselors tune their ears to listen for conversational evidence of clients' concerns about affectional identity and all associated factors. Competent counselors take time to understand clients' struggles and themes for explorations, reflecting these issues back to clients while avoiding the temptation to pounce on a particular label or stage of development.

Counseling and Advocacy Interventions

Counselors need to proceed with cautious concern when working with CQ on both the individual and collective levels. On the individual level, counseling and advocacy interventions begin in counselors' offices. This means that counselors must (a) know themselves (in terms of their biases and stereotypes; heterosexual counselors must also know their position of privilege related to living in a heterosexist society), (b) be willing and able to broach issues of affectional identity with clients (Day-Vines et al., 2007), (c) make their unconditional positive regard status apparent (which is necessary if they are heterosexual), and (d) directly model the qualities of a safe person/space for people of *all* affectional identities.

For CQ, interventions need to be gradual and grounded in the client's comfort level with discussing sexuality. Grounded in affirmative therapy, part of working with CQ is creating a welcoming physical space in the counseling office or setting. Other professionals in the broader work setting and community are made aware of this safe space for counseling.

Empirically Based Interventions

Malyon originally coined the term *gay affirmative psychotherapy* in 1982 during his work with gay males. Malyon (1982) sought to alleviate a condition he was seeing in gay male clients that he referred to as "internalized homophobia." The term, which suggests a fear-related component to one's own sexuality, is a misnomer. More accurately, it refers to the internalized struggle gay individuals often experience when their true self conflicts with dominant societal values, beliefs, and attitudes. Specifically, in a society in which sex and gender are socially construed as binary (male/female), so too affectional orientation becomes constructed as one extreme or the other (heterosexual/gay). Therefore, individuals who do not identify with these fabricated silos find conflict during the normal developmental process. Malyon suggested that this internal conflict poses significant impairment to the individual's identity, self-esteem, defenses, cognitions, and psychological development. He further indicated that these complications have a tendency to cause feelings of guilt and self-inflicted psychological punishment. His answer was to call for a gay-affirming approach to psychotherapy.

LGBTQI+ Affirmative Therapy

Since its inception, gay affirmative psychotherapy has been reconceptualized to recognize that *gay* is not properly inclusive of all affectional and gender minorities. In attempts to account for lesbian, gay, bisexual, transgender, and questioning individuals, the most prominent current term is *LGBTQI+ affirmative therapy*. Yet there remains a gap for those who identify in other fashions, such as queer, intersex, transgender, asexual, or even allies of LGBTQI+ people. Carroll and Gilroy (2001), recognizing that language changes over time and is "used to assert power and control in our culture," argued that all such labels should be tossed aside (p. 49). They put forward that, given that such language was created by the heteronormative society in which we live, a more profound change should occur and the term *queer* should be used to describe all aspects of sex, affectional orientation, and gender minorities. As discussed in Chapter 15, by taking the term *queer* generated by the dominant culture and used negatively toward the LGBTQI+ communities, these theorists advocate the reclaiming of the term as a sense of power and as it is used with queer theory (the position that binary thinking about sex, affectional orientation, gender, and their consequent roles should be questioned and that these phenomena should be recognized for the continuums they are). To date, few have adopted viewing affirmative therapy from this position. In an attempt to recognize that neither *queer* nor *LGBTQ* may be the most encompassing, the more colloquially accepted *LGBTQI+*, signifies the extensive continuum.

Tenets of LGBTQI+ Affirmative Therapy and CQ

As discussed in Chapter 10, although there is a fair amount of literature on LGBTQI+ affirmative therapy, there is surprisingly no definitive agreement on exactly what constitutes this approach. Johnson (2012), in reviewing three decades of mental health literature, summarized by stating that "even though studies discuss gay affirmative therapy, no study has operationalized this construct" and that the field "lacks a unique theoretical framework one might expect given its application to a unique population" (p. 517). This leaves clinicians assuming that they are incorporating counseling techniques properly with clients, educators and clinical supervisors bewildered on how to teach it, and researchers confused on what the next steps should be for providing answers.

When considering how to incorporate the professional literature for working with CQ, two sources are helpful. The first is a guide provided by the American Association for Marriage and Family Therapy (AAMFT; 2014) that encapsulates a variety of work done by their various members. The second is the book *Gay Affirmative Therapy for the Straight Clinician: The Essential Guide* (Kort, 2008). Building on these two foundational sources, we reviewed the literature on affirmative therapy (e.g., American Psychological Association Task Force on Appropriate

Therapeutic Responses to Sexual Orientation, 2009; Chernin & Johnson, 2003; Harrison, 2000; Pixton, 2003; Ritter & Terndrup, 2002) and summarized it into eight themes, which are presented as the basis for implementing LGBTQI+ affirmative therapy when working with CQ.

1. *Understand and combat heterosexism.* The first theme for affirmative therapy is understanding and combating heterosexism (Kort, 2008). AAMFT (2014) describes this as recognizing the heteronormative and gender-normative assumptions throughout U.S. culture. Affirming counselors recognize and address how the dominant culture oppresses affectional orientation and gender minorities and that such oppression has an impact on their mental health. When a counselor is working with CQ, it is imperative to be ever mindful that the struggle clients are wrestling with is not just internal; rather, external pressures (e.g., family, society) contribute greatly as well.

2. *Understand and address heterosexual privilege.* The second theme of affirmative therapy deals with heterosexual privilege (Kort, 2008). Just as it should be clear to all counselors that dominant racial and ethnic populations automatically have privilege over minority groups (e.g., in the United States, Whites have privilege over Blacks/African Americans), so too heterosexuals have privilege over affectional orientation and gender minorities. This imbalance of power, like the heterosexism that influences it, has consequences for the LGBTQI+ communities that must be recognized and empathized with in order for treatment to be effective. CQ may be dealing with, for example, a heterosexist work environment and interposing other important concerns.

3. *Affirm, don't tolerate.* Another primary element of affirmative therapy is the affirming nature itself (AAMFT, 2014; Kort, 2008). Affirming psychotherapists recognize that regardless of whether they are privileged or marginalized, people's sex, affectional orientation, and gender identity and expression should be not merely tolerated or accepted but affirmed. Tolerance and acceptance are at their core based on the assumption that individuals are making a choice and therefore should have such a choice tolerated. Although it may be the case that individuals make choices in their gender expression, they do not have choices in their sex, affectional orientation, or gender identity beyond what they do with it. As a consequence, saying "I tolerate your affectional orientation" is akin to saying "I tolerate your skin color." Affirming denotes recognizing not that a choice is made but rather that the person is who they are, and therefore acceptance is just not good enough. An affirmative counselor does not view clients questioning their same- and/or opposite-sex attractions as people who should be tolerated or accepted. Nor does the counselor consider such clients to be people who are making a choice so much as people discovering who they are and how they wish to express and experience their identity.

4. *Understand and address homophobia.* The fourth affirmative therapy theme is that homophobia must be addressed. Kort (2008) identified two primary components when addressing homophobia, the first being what he termed "homo-avoidance" (p. 28). By this he was referring to uncomfortable feelings among both professionals and the general public as a result of interacting with the LGBTQI+ communities, which often lead to avoidance behavior. An example would be a clinician inquiring about a client's romantic partner, learning that the client is somewhere along the continuum of affectional orientation such that the client is questioning, and then never returning to the subject. If counselors avoid the topic because of their own issues, clients are likely to receive the same messages they receive in other parts of their lives, namely, that their questioning causes others to be uncomfortable and therefore must be wrong in some way. Clearly this does not help CQ. The second component of addressing homophobia deals with the original concept of internalized homophobia.

Because the internal conflict LGBTQI+ persons experience is really about the pressure to conform to societal constructions of sex, affectional orientation, and gender, the argument is made that the true issue is heterosexism, and therefore the real struggle is *internalized heterosexism* (Burkard, Knox, Hess, & Schultz, 2009). The American Counseling Association's Association for Lesbian, Gay, Bisexual, and Transgender Issues in Counseling division has thus far been reluctant to use this term. Harper and colleagues (2013) suggested that it may discount the nuances of homo-, trans-, and biphobia. What is important about this term, however, is that it speaks to the multilevel aspects of heterosexism and the various phobias surrounding affectional orientation and gender minorities. LGBTQI+ persons can expect to experience aggression and oppression in a variety of ways: individual (either overtly or covertly), institutionalized (e.g., most states do not protect affectional orientation and gender minorities from discrimination or ensure job security), and societal (e.g., legal battles over same-sex marriage occur throughout the country, even though it is now legal in the entire United States). When met with such issues on a daily basis, affectional orientation and gender minorities, including those questioning their identity, would naturally be struggling internally with a society that oppresses them externally.

5. *Construct appropriate pathology identification.* The fifth common element of LGBTQI+ affirmative therapy is the focus on appropriate identification of pathology both relative to and separate from a client's sex, affectional orientation, and/or gender. As Kort (2008) explained, "Because of the historical pattern of pathologizing homosexuality, [affirmative therapy] has tended to deemphasize emotional disorders and not examine any pathology" (p. 31). This therapeutic lens is intended to assist in recognizing and addressing the unique issues facing the LGBTQI+ client; it is not meant to remove consideration, diagnosis, and treatment of emotional and mental problems. Nor, for that matter, should LGBTQI+ persons be viewed as seeking services merely because of their sex, affectional orientation, or gender. In other words, affirmative counselors who learn that clients are questioning their affectional orientation should not assume that this is their primary reason for seeking treatment, nor should they discount the impact questioning one's affectional orientation may have on pathology. Clients' reasons for seeking treatment and how their affectional orientation does or does not contribute to these concerns would be explored with them by an affirmative counselor.

6. *Recognize and address countertransference.* The next premise of affirmative therapy is what Kort (2008) referred to as an element of countertransference in that psychotherapists must recognize and address their issues of heterosexism and homophobia. Professionals need to give serious consideration to their comfort level with variant continuums of sex, affectional orientation, and gender. This self-reflection can be a key element both in being more genuine with clients and in recognizing when clients themselves are struggling with such issues. Perhaps one of the best places for counselors to start, as previously mentioned, is to recognize and accept the fact that affectional orientation is on a continuum and that most people do not fit into one dichotomy (heterosexual) or the other (gay). Thus, it would be logical that many individuals at some point in their lives would be questioning where they feel most comfortable on such a continuum.

7. *Reflect on self and social justice.* The final two significant components of affirmative therapy are other self-reflection elements that were acutely identified by AAMFT (2014). LGBTQI+ affirmative counselors should consistently reflect on their own attitudes, values, and beliefs surrounding the impact of society's heteronormative and binary-assumed stance on sex, affectional orientation, and gender. Moreover, being a true affirmative therapist calls for active social justice and advocacy efforts. AAMFT

recommends that such clinicians be clear about their affirmative approach in both their professional and personal lives. This includes having an office setting that exudes affirmation in terms of surroundings, literature, speech, and behavior. The AAMFT further called on affirmative psychotherapists to advocate for and engage in social justice at all levels for affectional orientation and gender minorities. As noted earlier, this parlays well with the *Multicultural and Social Justice Counseling Competencies* (Ratts et al., 2015) advocated for by the American Counseling Association.

8. *Expand counselor training in affirmative therapy.* LGBTQI+ individuals may be considered minorities, but they are frequent consumers of mental health services. Research shows that psychotherapists can expect 40% to 90% of their clients to be affectional or gender minorities (Burkard et al., 2009; Johnson, 2012). Although LGBTQI+ clients are likely to be seen by non-LGBTQI+ practitioners (Johnson, 2012), affirmative therapy is needed because no clinician, regardless of that clinician's own affectional orientation, is able to be an expert on all levels of sex, affectional orientation, and gender when the continuums are so expansive (AAMFT, 2014; Kort, 2008). Furthermore, mental health providers trained

> in a generalist model are more likely to be harmful to [LGBTQI+] clients because of their own unchallenged . . . heterosexist biases, the biases of the traditional psychological therapist in which they have been trained, and/or their lack of familiarity with [LGBTQI+] issues. (Kort, 2008, p. 713)

These premises underscore the necessity for more practitioners to be trained in implementing affirmative therapy. The implications of this seem clear: better therapeutic relationships and more positive outcomes for LGBTQI+ clients.

Affirmative therapy goes beyond standard considerations of multiculturalism. Although the field of psychology in recent years has begun to enhance its position on multiculturalism in working with clients, professional counseling is arguably the mental health field that leads in this approach. For professional counselors, multiculturalism is not merely a focus; it is a necessary foundation from which everything else is built. Carroll and Gilroy (2001) argued that a true affirmative approach goes beyond what professional counseling currently considers multiculturalism and entails a consistent, ever-infused perspective of how society uses power, control, and language to oppress affectional orientation and gender minorities. These constructs cut across all races, ethnic heritages, and cultures while being situated in an overarching society that oppresses and marginalizes them. Individuals questioning themselves and their place in the dominant culture need more than multicultural counseling: They need an affirmative approach.

Conclusion

It is hoped that a better understanding of working with CQ is gained by considering the material provided here. We would argue, however, that the conversation has only just begun and that it is natural, even hoped, that additional questions arise when considering this client population. In closing, consider the outlined affirmative therapeutic foundations as a map for navigating the vast, endless sea of LGBTQI+ experiences. Shift the focus from seeking or wondering what an ideal exemplar of CQ might be to how it can be expected that many individuals at some point in their lives will question something about their sexuality. It may be who they are; it may be feelings, attractions, or thoughts that are new or different; it may be how they fit into the overall societal view and/or construction of affectional orientation—but at some point and on some level, there will be questioning. Affirming, ethical, competent counselors will be ready to give their best to their LGBTQI+

clients, all the while being comfortable acknowledging that they can always learn more from working with such clients.

Questions for Further Discussion

1. What types of biases will counselors need to check themselves for when working with Nina?
2. What types of fears might Nina be experiencing that are impacting her depression?
3. What types of bias and discrimination might Nina face if she reveals her feelings for her friend?
4. What types of symptoms might Nina present with during her discovery phase?
5. What types of counseling strategies should the school counselor use with Nina?

Resources

1. Learn more about the process of discovering one's identity through the Trevor Project at http://www.thetrevorproject.org/pages/spectrum.
2. Read through Dr. Reams's "Am I Gay?" website at http://www.yoursexualorientation.info/.
3. Review GLBT National Help Center resources at http://www.glbthotline.org/.
4. Surf the It Gets Better Project website at http://www.itgetsbetter.org/.

References

American Association for Marriage and Family Therapy, California Division. (2014). *LGBT affirmative therapy: Tips for creating a more lesbian, gay, bisexual, transgender, and gender inclusive practice from the AAMFT Queer Affirmative Caucus.* Retrieved from https://education.uoregon.edu/sites/default/files/affirmative_therapy_handout_0.pdf

American Psychological Association Task Force on Appropriate Therapeutic Responses to Sexual Orientation. (2009). *Report of the Task Force on Appropriate Therapeutic Responses to Sexual Orientation.* Washington, DC: American Psychological Association.

Borders, A., Guillen, L. A., & Meyer, I. H. (2014). Rumination, sexual orientation uncertainty and psychological distress in sexual minority university students. *The Counseling Psychologist, 42,* 497–523. doi:10.1177/0011000014527002

Burkard, A. W., Knox, S., Hess, S. A., & Schultz, J. (2009). Lesbian, gay, and bisexual supervisees' experiences of LGB-affirmative and nonaffirmative supervision. *Journal of Counseling Psychology, 56*(1), 176–188. doi:10.1037/0022-0167.56.1.176

Carroll, L., & Gilroy, P. J. (2001). Teaching "outside the box": Incorporating queer theory in counseling education. *Journal of Humanistic Counseling, Education and Development, 40,* 49–58. doi:10.1002/j.2164-490X.2001.tb00101.x

Chernin, J. N., & Johnson, M. R. (2003). *Affirmative psychotherapy and counseling for lesbians and gay men.* Thousand Oaks, CA: Sage.

Cohen, P. N. (2014). *The family: Diversity, inequality, and social change.* New York, NY: Norton.

Day-Vines, N. L., Wood, S. M., Grothaus, T., Craigen, L., Holman, A., Dotson-Blake, K., & Douglass, M. J. (2007). Broaching the subjects of race, ethnicity, and culture during the counseling process. *Journal of Counseling & Development, 85,* 401–409. doi:10.1002/j.1556-6678.2007.tb00608.x

Diamond, L. M. (2009). *Sexual fluidity: Understanding women's love and desire.* Cambridge, MA: Harvard University Press.

Duncan, B. L., Miller, S. D., Wampold, B. E., & Hubble, M. A. (Eds.). (2009). *The heart and soul of change: Delivering what works in therapy* (2nd ed.). Washington, DC: American Psychological Association.

Eagly, A. H. (1987). *Sex differences in social behavior: A social-role interpretation.* Hillsdale, NJ: Erlbaum.

Galupo, M. P., Davis, K. S., Grynkiewicz, A. L., & Mitchell, R. C. (2014). Conceptualization of sexual orientation identity among sexual minorities: Patterns across sexual and gender identity. *Journal of Bisexuality, 14,* 433–456. doi:10.1080/15299716.2014.933466

Harper, A., Finnerty, P., Martinez, M., Brace, A., Crethar, H. C., Loos, B., . . . Lambert, S. (2013). Association for Lesbian, Gay, Bisexual, and Transgender Issues in Counseling (ALGBTIC) competencies for counseling with lesbian, gay, bisexual, queer, questioning, intersex, and ally individuals. *Journal of LGBT Issues in Counseling, 7*(1), 2–43. doi:1 0.1080/15538605.2013.755444

Harrison, N. (2000). Gay affirmative therapy: A critical analysis of the literature. *British Journal of Guidance & Counseling, 28*(1), 37–53. doi:10.1080/030698800109600

Harvey, R. G., & Stone, L. F. (2015). Queer youth in family therapy. *Family Process, 54,* 396–417. doi:10.1111/famp.12170

Hollander, G. (2000). Questioning youths: Challenges to working with youths forming identities. *School Psychology Review, 29*(2), 173–179.

Horner, E. (2007). Queer identities and bisexual identities: What's the difference? In B. A. Firestein (Ed.), *Becoming visible: Counseling bisexuals across the lifespan* (pp. 287–296). New York, NY: Columbia University Press.

Institute of Medicine, Committee on Lesbian, Gay, Bisexual, and Transgender Health Issues and Research Gaps and Opportunities. (2011). *The health of lesbian, gay, bisexual, and transgender people: Building a foundation for better understanding.* Washington, DC: National Academies Press.

Johnson, S. D. (2012). Gay affirmative psychotherapy with lesbian, gay, and bisexual individuals: Implications for contemporary psychotherapy research. *American Journal of Orthopsychiatry, 82,* 516–522. doi:10.1111/j.1939-0025.2012.01180.x

Kinsey, A. C., Pomeroy, W. B., & Martin, C. E. (1948). *Sexual behavior in the human male.* Bloomington: Indiana University Press.

Kort, J. (2008). *Gay affirmative therapy for the straight clinician: The essential guide.* New York, NY: Norton.

Kramsch, C. (1998). *Language and culture.* Oxford, UK: Oxford University Press.

Laumann, E. O., Gagnon, J. H., Michael, R. T., & Michaels, S. (1994). *The social organization of sexuality: Sexual practices in the United States.* Chicago, IL: University of Chicago Press.

Liu, R. T., & Mustanski, B. (2012). Suicidal ideation and self-harm in lesbian, gay, bisexual, and transgender youth. *American Journal of Preventive Medicine, 42*(2), 221–228. doi:10.1016/j.amepre.2011.10.023

Luscombe, B. (2014, September 4). *There is no longer any such thing as a typical family.* Retrieved from the *Time Magazine* website: http://time.com/3265733/nuclear-family-typical-society-parents-children-households-philip-cohen/

Malyon, A. K. (1982). Psychotherapeutic implications of internalized homophobia in gay men. *Journal of Homosexuality, 7*(2/3), 56–69. doi:10.1300/J082v07n02_08

Maslow, A. H. (1943). A theory or human motivation. *Psychological Review, 50*(4), 370–396. doi:10.1037/h0054346

Maslow, A. H. (1954). *Motivation and personality.* New York, NY: Harper & Row.

Pixton, S. (2003). Experiencing gay affirmative therapy: An exploration of clients' views of what is helpful. *Counseling and Psychotherapy Research, 3*(3), 211–215. doi:10.1080/1473 3140312331384372

Ratts, M. J., Singh, A. A., Nassar-McMillan, S., Butler, S. K., & McCullough, J. R. (2015). *Multicultural and social justice counseling competencies.* Retrieved from https://www.counseling.org/knowledge-center/competencies

Reams, R. H. (2016). *"Am I gay?" A guide for people who question their sexual orientation.* Retrieved from http://www.yoursexualorientation.info/

Ritter, K. Y., & Terndrup, A. I. (2002). *Handbook of affirmative psychotherapy with lesbians and gay men.* New York, NY: Guilford Press.

Rogers, C. (1951). *Client-centered therapy: Its current practice, implications and theory.* London, UK: Constable.

Rogers, C. (2003). *Client-centered therapy: Its current practice, implications and theory.* London, UK: Constable.

Russell, S. T., Clarke, T. J., & Clary, J. (2009). Are teens "post-gay"? Contemporary adolescents' sexual identity labels. *Journal of Youth and Adolescence, 38,* 884–890. doi:10.1007/s10964-008-9388-2

Savin-Williams, R. C. (2006). *Adolescent lives: Vol. 3. The new gay teenager.* Cambridge, MA: Harvard University Press.

Savin-Williams, R. C. (2008). Refusing and resisting sexual identity labels. In D. L. Browning (Ed.), *Adolescent identities: A collection of readings* (pp. 67–91). New York, NY: Analytic Press.

Savin-Williams, R. C., & Ream, G. L. (2003). Suicide attempts among sexual minority male youth. *Journal of Clinical Child and Adolescent Psychology, 32,* 509–522. doi:10.1207/S15374424JCCP3204_3

Shipherd, J. C. (2015). Defining competence when working with sexual and gender minority populations: Training models for professional development. *Clinical Psychology: Science and Practice, 22*(2), 101–104. doi:10.1111/cpsp.12100

Society for Adolescent Health and Medicine. (2013). Recommendations for promoting the health and well-being of lesbian, gay, bisexual, and transgender adolescents: A position paper of the Society for Adolescent Health and Medicine. *Journal of Adolescent Health, 52,* 506–510.

Twenge, J. M. (1997). Changes in masculine and feminine traits over time: A meta-analysis. *Sex Roles, 36*(5/6), 305–325. doi:10.1007/BF02766650

Chapter 17

Counseling Intersex Clients

Misty M. Ginicola

Sometimes I still feel that there are two of me: one clean,
flawless picture, the other imperfect and cracked; one boy, one girl; one
voice that speaks aloud and one that whispers in my ear; . . .
I feel sometimes there are things that tear me in two directions,
that there are two sets of thoughts that grow side by side.
But then I realize that I am whole, whatever that means
and does not mean; I am complete without the need
for additions or alteration.

—Abigail Tarttelin

• • •

Awareness of Attitudes and Beliefs Self-Check

1. Close your eyes and picture an intersex person. What do you see? Now picture a "hermaphrodite." How are your biases and stereotypes present in both images? Were there connotations involved in your image of "hermaphrodite" that explain why this term is no longer used?
2. When you learn that someone is pregnant or recently had a baby, how often do you ask about the sex of the child?
3. If one of your children were born intersex, what would be your reaction? Your fears?

Case Study

Maria is a 14-year-old Hispanic female who was recently referred for counseling because of excessive school absences. At her intake, Maria tells you, "I am not a girl; I am a boy." When you probe further, Maria asks you to use the pronoun *he* and refer to him as *Mateo*. Mateo reports that he just recently discovered that he was born with a micropenis and female genitalia. He remembers having to go through multiple surgeries and having lots of genital pain from the multiple surgeries and healing. He states that his parents never explained to him the reasons for the surgeries and never discussed his birth. Mateo reports that he never felt like a girl, but when Mateo reached puberty, a stronger feeling that he was male, as well as his attraction to females, disturbed him. He confessed these feelings to his parents and also asked about the multiple surgeries. Although reticent to tell him at first, his parents revealed that he was intersex at birth; they had made the choice to surgically render him female based on the doctor's opinion. Mateo was livid and began acting out by being truant from school, withdrawing from his parents, dressing as a male, and staying out late at night. He reports feelings of depression as well as a general distrust of and anger toward his parents. He says he wishes to have sexual reassignment surgery to fix their mistake, but his parents have said that they will not support his decision or pay for the surgery.

• • •

Awareness of Differences

Intersex is a general term that refers to multiple types of conditions in which a person is born with ambiguous or both male and female genitalia. Often the variance in anatomy is outwardly visible, but sometimes the individual may have internal anatomy that matches one sex and external genitalia that matches the other sex. This means that sometimes the condition is not identified until puberty. There are many variations in the intersex category; there is not a uniform presentation among people who are born with this condition. Therefore, rather than representing a true *condition* or *disorder,* it is a socially constructed category that encompasses any variation in genitalia from the binary male or female presentation (Crocetti, 2013; Feder, 2009; Topp, 2013).

Understanding the biological nature of intersex requires knowledge regarding sex development and differentiation that happens in utero (Bakker, 2014; Crocetti, 2013; Ristvedt, 2014; Wilhelm, Palmer, & Koopman, 2007). As discussed in Chapter 2, the gender of the mind develops in response to genes and the expression of hormones. Sex, which is the physical manifestation of the sex chromosomes (male or female), develops in a similarly complex manner. Females carry XX chromosomes, whereas males carry XY chromosomes. These sex-determining chromosomes hinge on the Y chromosome. All fetuses begin with the potential for both sexes in an undifferentiated state externally. Internally, they carry duct systems for both male and female. By default, all fetuses are female; with no intervention of hormones, they will fully develop as female. Therefore, in the absence of the Y chromosome, the fetus continues to fully develop as female. When a fetus has a typically functioning Y chromosome, it develops as male.

The Y chromosome carries the sex-determining region of the Y chromosome (SRY) gene, which is linked to *maleness* as manifested physically in the fetus's genitalia (Bakker, 2014; Crocetti, 2013; Ristvedt, 2014; Wilhelm et al., 2007). The function of this gene is twofold: to start the expression of testosterone and to allow the expression of the anti-Müllerian hormone. Testosterone is expressed and created into an enzyme that is responsible for shaping the external genitalia: for enlarging the clitoris into a penis and for shaping the labiascrotal tissue to fuse and form a scrotum. The anti-Müllerian hormone is responsible for preventing the internal sexual anatomy from developing as female; it causes the destruction of all internal female ducts (the fallopian tubes and uterus). Ultimately, the testes then descend into the scrotal sac, and they develop the fully formed male Wolffian ducts, which include the epididymis, vas deferens, and seminal vesicle. Without this delicate process, the Wolffian ducts die off automatically, as they do normally in the typical development of females.

There are numerous ways in which this process can be altered (Bakker, 2014; Crocetti, 2013; Ristvedt, 2014). If a male has a genetic issue with the SRY gene, he will develop as a female. If testosterone is expressed but there is a problem with expression of the anti-Müllerian hormone, the fetus will develop internal female anatomy and external male anatomy. If a female fetus's mother's body floods with testosterone at the sensitive period of sex development, the fetus will appear male externally but will have female internal anatomy. If a male's cells carry a genetic condition in which they are insensitive to testosterone during the fetal period, they will develop externally as female. The infinite number of combinations and issues for this development could result in a range from both sexes present in the child's anatomy (e.g., a penis and a labia with a vaginal opening) to some variance (e.g., a micropenis).

As puberty involves another burst of hormones, either estrogen or testosterone, in some cases this will impact the individual's gender, physical primary sex characteristics, and/or secondary sex characteristics (Bakker, 2014; Crocetti, 2013; Ristvedt, 2014). An extreme example is the Guevedoces, who carry a gene common in a region of the Dominican Republic but also found in other cultures. This gene inhibits the formation of testosterone into the enzyme that impacts sex development. At birth, these children appear completely female. At puberty, they receive a surge of testosterone, which forms the secondary sex characteristics. This causes the clitoris to enlarge into a penis; the testes to descend; and a male body type to develop, complete with body hair and muscle tone.

There have been many different opinions on how to describe intersex. Formerly termed *hermaphrodite,* the change to call this set of anatomical variations intersex was due to associations with so-called freak shows; it was seen as a bizarre condition open to others' entertainment and scrutiny (Reis, 2007). Feder (2009) called for intersex to be renamed *disorders of sex development* (DSD) to capture the etiology and to normalize the condition. Many parents responded negatively to the term *intersex* because they associated it with transgender identity, believing, mistakenly for both intersex and transgender individuals, that the child was choosing a gender (Feder, 2009). Intersex is commonly referred to as DSD in the medical community across the globe (Reis, 2007). Topp (2013) has further called for the term to be changed to *differences of sex development* to reflect that it is a variation, not a disorder.

Although intersex is different than transgender, there are similarities in the mismatch between gender and sex, especially if there was surgical intervention for intersex individuals in their infancy and childhood (Reiner & Reiner, 2012). Intersex individuals may also identify strongly with a mixed gender presentation, identifying as a third gender altogether. The blend of male and female anatomy and hormones may present as a unique combination in both mind and body with which the individual is completely comfortable. However, when there is a mismatch between the gender of the mind and the sex expressed in one's anatomy, there is immense psychological distress equivalent to the transgender experience along with a desire to alter one's body and/or gender presentation.

Knowledge of Issues and Problems

Experiences of Bias

Children who are intersex face multiple social and emotional complications that cause psychological distress (Brinkmann, Schuetzmann, & Richter-Appelt, 2007; Canguçú-Campinho, de Sousa Bastos, & Oliveira Lima, 2014; Lev, 2006; Meoded-Danon & Yanay, 2016). These children may feel that they are *abnormal* or are seen as being *broken* with a problem that needs to be fixed. They often internalize messages surrounding shame and guilt about their intersex variance, which is further reinforced by family and medical messages that they should keep their condition secret. Their family may also have kept the condition secret from them, which can lead to feelings of betrayal, mistrust, and anger. When these secrets are kept from them, such children are not able to incorporate being intersex into their sense of meaning or identity; when it is revealed that they are intersex, this may lead to an identity crisis or feelings of hopelessness and depression. In fact, intersex individuals usually report the silence and secrecy surrounding being intersex to be the most damaging to their emotional and mental health. Having had surgical interventions, learning that their parents have kept this a secret, and being intersex can be traumatizing to some individuals.

Current views on gender in U.S. culture represent a predominantly binary presentation (male/female) rather than the continuum that has been argued by many theorists throughout the field as well as authors in this book. From the moment a woman is pregnant, friends and family (and sometimes strangers) ask her the sex of the baby. When a parent or parents greet a newborn baby, again people wish to know the sex of the baby, often before inquiring about the health of the baby or mother. Therefore, these gender expectations are present prior to birth. Imagine the difficulty parents of intersex individuals—and later the intersex persons themselves—face if they are unable to answer that question. The existence of intersex persons violates the gender binary; therefore, they can face immense scrutiny, marginalization, and prejudice (Fausto-Sterling, 2000).

Physical Issues and Health Care

When an infant is born with an intersex presentation, doctors are responsible for diagnosing the infant with either a DSD or normative variation (Byne & Reiner, 2015). Previous medical pediatric policy was to surgically correct any life-threatening conditions (such as a blocked urethra); educate the parents on the condition; assist the parents in choosing the most likely and/or surgically feasible sex that they wished for their infant; conceal the sex assignment surgeries from friends, family, and the child (reportedly to promote less bullying and misunderstandings); and then perform multiple surgeries in order to seek that typical sex presentation (Byne & Reiner, 2015). It is important to note that many pediatricians and medical organizations continue to support this model.

However, there are multiple ethical concerns with this process (Lathrop, Cheney, & Hayman, 2014). The sex assignment surgeries are completely cosmetic; therefore, the parents are unequivocally deciding the sex of the child without knowing the child's ultimate gender identity or receiving the child's consent (Thorn, 2014). In many cases people's gender as assigned by the doctor at birth does not match their later identity, which requires them to have expensive and painful gender reassignment surgery as adults (Kolesinska et al., 2014). These childhood surgeries carry the risk of causing irreparable damage to genitalia through the loss of sexual function or feeling (Thorn, 2014). In addition, it has been found that parents' decisions are highly based on information presented to them by medical staff (Streuli, Vayena, Cavicchia-Balmer, & Huber, 2013), which means that if they do not have complete information about all of these risks and ethical issues, parents may be vulnerable to choosing whatever the doctor suggests.

Potential Mental Health Challenges

Research has indicated that parents experience immense psychological distress on learning that their child is intersex; some even experience traumatic symptoms in response to having a child with DSD (Lev, 2006; Sanders, Carter, & Goodacre, 2011). As previously referenced, one of the most common questions for pregnant women is "Are you having a boy or a girl?" Among parents who do not find out the sex prior to birth, the first utterance after birth is "It's a boy!" or "It's a girl!" The highly gendered societal norms do not allow for ambiguity, and parents internalize these cultural messages that a gender that is not clear or binary (male vs. female) is wrong, shameful, and repulsive. In the moment they should be

244

celebrating the birth of their child, these parents experience feelings of fear, anxiety, grief, and horror. In this distressed state, they also have to make significant life-altering decisions for their child and family. Parents require significant emotional support as well as medical knowledge and psychoeducation (Sanders, Carter, & Goodacre, 2012).

Intersex individuals may grow up with body image issues due to having genital variance and/or due to cosmetic issues and scarring from the multiple surgeries (Alderson, Madill, & Balen, 2004; Brinkmann et al., 2007; Köhler, Jürgensen, Kleinemeier, & Thyen, 2014). Getting dressed or using a bathroom in front of others may become embarrassing or humiliating. A large percentage of intersex adults report feeling very negative about their surgeries, including the consent process, surgical procedures, and the outcomes.

In addition, they may experience variant gender identities and presentations that do not match their assigned gender (Köhler et al., 2014). This may range from small disparities to a complete blending of gender (third gender or genderqueer) to transgender identity (Köhler et al., 2014). Intersex individuals may feel that they have been rendered transgender as a result of the choices that their parents and doctors made in their infancy (Köhler et al., 2014). They additionally may have experienced stigmatizing experiences and bullying surrounding being intersex or their outward gender appearance and expression, which can cause increased depression, anxiety, and posttraumatic symptoms (Köhler et al., 2014). Hosey (2014) also reported that intersex individuals have reported engaging in nonsuicidal self-harm and injury. The reasons for this self-injury may be similar to what cisgender persons experience (depression, anxiety) but may additionally include their unhappiness with their bodies.

As they age into adulthood, intersex individuals may continue to have issues in romantic and sexual relationships (Alderson et al., 2004; Jürgensen et al., 2013; Köhler et al., 2014; Warne et al., 2005). Continued body image problems and genital variance may require them to *come out* as intersex to potential love interests early in the relationship. As a result of surgical intervention, hormone replacement therapy, or a genetic condition, they may also have sexual dysfunction and/or impaired fertility. If they do experience internalized shame and guilt, as well as low body esteem, it is likely to impact their partnerships in significant ways.

Although these physical and sexual issues are typical for those who are intersex, many such individuals are able to have positive mental health experiences (Warne et al., 2005). Those who successfully navigate this disorder and maintain a positive identity as intersex make meaning of their intersexuality in two specific ways: They accept that they are a variation of normal, and/or they come to the conclusion that there is no normal (Guntram, 2013).

Counseling Skills and Techniques

Because of these ethical issues, some countries have enacted laws banning cosmetic surgeries on intersex infants and children; these laws allow the children to be identified as intersex on their birth certificates and be protected from surgical intervention until they are able to choose and consent (Harper et al., 2013; Intersex Society of North America, 2006; Thorn, 2014; Warne & Mann, 2011). The Association for Lesbian, Gay, Bisexual, and Transgender Issues in Counseling's (ALGBTIC) standards regarding intersex clients can be found on their website (http://www.algbtic.org/competencies.html). The current recommendation for medical intervention from ALGBTIC, intersex organizations, and multiple researchers and advocates is to approach parents and the child in an open, honest, and shame-free manner. Doctors should continue to perform minimal corrective surgery for life-threatening conditions. Parents should be fully informed about the medical and ethical issues involved and should be provided with access to competent counselors for psychotherapy. Families should be connected with other families who are intersex as resources and social support. Doctors should complete a full diagnostic workup, including genetic and hormonal assessments, which result in them making a suggestion for gender *assignment.* This process should not include surgery but rather a data-based conclusion on what gender the child will likely feel as an adult. Surgery should not be completed until the child is capable of making an informed choice and providing consent.

When working with intersex individuals and families, it is important to coordinate service across both medical and mental health support (Harper et al., 2013; Sandberg & Mazur, 2014). It is also important to assess for posttraumatic stress disorder, as both parents and the intersex individual may experience the condition or the medical interventions and subsequent treatment from others as traumatic (Pasterski, Mastroyannopoulou, Wright, Zucker, & Hughes, 2014). A counselor must serve as an educator, an advocate, a family therapist, and a clinical mental health counselor when working with intersex individuals and families (Lev, 2006).

In the *Diagnostic and Statistical Manual of Mental Disorders, Fifth Edition,* intersex conditions in which individuals' assigned sex does not match their gender are now diagnosable with gender dysphoria through the specifier associated with DSD (American Psychiatric Association, 2013). This move was particularly controversial: The biological evidence does not support identifying intersex as a psychiatric disorder (Kraus, 2015). In addition, identifying intersex as transgender is problematic: Intersex individuals' physical sex at birth; may be the one with which they identify, potentially as a third gender (Kraus, 2015). Even if it is not, what they are experiencing may not be *reassignment* but rather assignment to a gender via surgery (Kraus, 2015). Finally, if they do choose reassignment, they are not reassigning the assigned sex from birth; they are reassigning the gender assigned to them by their parents and doctor without their consent (Kraus, 2015).

Counseling strategies for intersex individuals have not been well studied. The only research that exists on the topic is typically qualitative (case studies) and theoretical. However, this literature and intersex advocacy groups provide several strategies that are important for counselors to consider when working with intersex individuals and their families. Counselors need to provide empathic, sensitive support and psychoeducation to help intersex individuals understand their bodies as well as to help families understand what being intersex means (Sanders, Carter, & Lwin, 2015). Counselors should also work toward educating and empowering families to make informed decisions for their child, even when that means resisting biased medical advice (Harper et al., 2013). Reviewing the impact of intersectionality of background (e.g., ethnicity, affectional orientation, family education, and socioeconomic level), family dynamics, and messages surrounding gender is crucial (Lev, 2006). Counselors also need to be aware that intersex individuals commonly experience isolation in the lesbian, gay, bisexual, transgender, queer, questioning, intersex, asexual, ally, pansexual/polysexual, and two-spirited (LGBTQI+) community and may not feel welcome there; therefore, referring intersex individuals to a general LGBT community center may not always be helpful (Harper et al., 2013).

If the family was silent or secretive surrounding the child's intersex condition, the client will need to work through those internalized feelings of shame as well as externalized feelings of anger and betrayal (Lev, 2006). Counselors should explore what meaning clients have made regarding their intersex condition. Have they come to a healthy conclusion regarding normal sexual development, or do they see themselves as abnormal or broken (Murphy, 2015)? When a client is pursuing surgery, it is important to explore their expectations for surgery as well as their evaluation of the benefits and risks (Murphy, 2015). Assisting clients in learning how to communicate with others regarding their intersexuality is a very helpful part of counseling; in addition, counselors can help families learn how to communicate (Sanders et al., 2015).

Burnes and Richmond (2012) recommended approaching clients from an affirmative, relational-cultural, and feminist integrated approach. These approaches are appropriate for assisting with a minority's identity development in the presence of oppression. It can be important to reflect on a client's symptoms less as psychopathology and more as efforts to cope with environmental stressors and unfair treatment. It is also important to acknowledge clients' feelings about seeing the counselor, as they may view the medical community as wholly untrustworthy and as victimizers. Building rapport, promoting transparency in assessment and diagnosis, and developing trust in the professional counseling relationship will be fundamental to any strategy. Allowing individuals to voice their feelings, concerns, and reactions to others is useful in exploring the impact of the negative treatment they have experienced. Bibliotherapy and cinematherapy can help clients and families learn more about the intersex condition and common experiences and reactions. Visiting websites of intersex advocacy groups and connecting to other intersex individuals can also reduce a client's feelings of isolation. Learning communication and self-advocacy skills can lead the client to feelings of empowerment. Using a trauma-informed approach, in which trauma and its impact is discussed and reprocessed, is likely to lead to a reduction in mental health symptoms. It can be equally important to counter cognitive distortions and messages of shame and guilt with cognitive–behavioral strategies. The main goal of any counseling intervention for intersex clients should be for them to develop a positive identity, build on their strengths, and develop their resiliency and coping skills.

Conclusion

Intersex persons often present to counseling with a complex history: They face stigma, prejudice, and oppression for violating a gender binary both in the body and in their mind. The shame surrounding their body can be intense, the hegemonic messages profoundly binary and monosexist. Unlike other members of the LGBTQI+ communities, parents of intersex persons are almost always aware of their condition from their birth. This has benefits, in that the parent can gather information and research that can be incorporated into a child's developmental experiences in order to promote self-acceptance and self-esteem. However, most often that is not the case. In response to pressure from medical professionals, these parents, who are incredibly vulnerable after their child's birth, often make the decision to forever alter their child's body and life, without consent of the child. Intersex clients and their families often need psychoeducational support and trauma- and grief-based counseling interventions in addition to an affirming approach.

Questions for Further Discussion

1. How does knowledge regarding gender differentiation explain Mateo's physical intersex presentation?
2. What are ways to identify and acknowledge the terms that Mateo identifies with (e.g., *intersex, DSD*)?
3. In what ways did Mateo's early medical care contribute to his presenting symptoms?
4. What are other potential causes of Mateo's presenting symptoms?
5. What counseling strategies might be most successful in facilitating Mateo's acceptance of his identity and resiliency?

Resources

1. Learn more about intersex issues at http://www.isna.org/.
2. Surf an advocacy site for intersex individuals at http://oii-usa.org/.
3. Read more about what intersex youth wish doctors, parents, and friends knew about them at http://interactyouth.org/resources.
4. Review issues relevant to intersex persons through the interACT advocacy group at http://interactadvocates.org/.

References

Alderson, J., Madill, A., & Balen, A. (2004). Fear of devaluation: Understanding the experience of intersexed women with androgen insensitivity syndrome. *British Journal of Health Psychology, 9*, 81–100.

American Psychiatric Association. (2013). *Diagnostic and statistical manual of mental disorders* (5th ed.). Washington, DC: Author.

Bakker, J. (2014). Sex differentiation: Organizing effects of sex hormones. In B. C. Kreukels, T. D. Steensma, & A. C. de Vries (Eds.), *Gender dysphoria and disorders of sex development: Progress in care and knowledge* (pp. 3–23). New York, NY: Springer Science + Business Media. doi:10.1007/978-1-4614-7441-8_1

Brinkmann, L., Schuetzmann, K., & Richter-Appelt, H. (2007). Gender assignment and medical history of individuals with different forms of intersexuality: Evaluation of medical records and the patients' perspective. *Journal of Sexual Medicine, 4*, 964–980. doi:10.1111/j.1743-6109.2007.00524.x

Burnes, T. R., & Richmond, K. (2012). Counseling strategies with intersex clients: A process-based approach. In S. H. Dworkin & M. Pope (Eds.), *Casebook for counseling lesbian, gay, bisexual, and transgendered persons and their families* (pp. 35–44). Alexandria, VA: American Counseling Association.

Byne, W., & Reiner, W. (2015). Interview with William Reiner, MD, urologist and child psychiatrist, on approaches to care for individuals with disorders of sex development and somatic intersex conditions. *LGBT Health, 2*(1), 3–10. doi:10.1089/lgbt.2015.0008

Canguçú-Campinho, A. K., de Sousa Bastos, A. C., & Oliveira Lima, I. S. (2014). Gender identity in intersex adults: The interplay of voices and silences. In S. Salvatore, A. Gennaro, & J. Valsiner (Eds.), *Multicentric identities in a globalizing world* (pp. 3–20). Charlotte, NC: Information Age.

Crocetti, D. (2013). Genes and hormones: What makes up an individual's sex. In M. Ah-King (Ed.), *Challenging popular myths of sex, gender and biology* (pp. 23–32). New York, NY: Springer Science + Business Media.

Fausto-Sterling, A. (2000). *Sexing the body: Gender politics and the construction of sexuality*. New York, NY: Basic Books.

Feder, E. K. (2009). Normalizing medicine: Between "intersexuals" and individuals with "disorders of sex development." *Health Care Analysis, 17*(2), 134–143. doi:10.1007/s10728-009-0111-6

Guntram, L. (2013). "Differently normal" and "normally different": Negotiations of female embodiment in women's accounts of "atypical" sex development. *Social Science & Medicine, 98*, 232–238. doi:10.1016/j.socscimed.2013.09.018

Harper, A., Finnerty, P., Martinez, M., Brace, A., Crethar, H. C., Loos, B., . . . Lambert, S. (2013). Association for Lesbian, Gay, Bisexual, and Transgender Issues in Counseling (ALGBTIC) competencies with counseling lesbian, gay, bisexual, queer, questioning, intersex, and ally individuals. *Journal of LGBT Issues in Counseling, 7*(1), 2–43. doi:10.1080/15538605.2013.755444

Hosey, J. (2014). *Self-harming behavior in individuals with disorders of sex development*. Available from Sociological Abstracts. (Order No. AAI3611813)

Intersex Society of North America. (2006). *Clinical guidelines for the management of disorders of sex development in childhood*. Rohnert Park, CA: Author.

Jürgensen, M., Kleinemeier, E., Lux, A., Steensma, T. D., Cohen-Kettenis, P. T., Hiort, O., . . . Köhler, B. (2013). Psychosexual development in adolescents and adults with disorders of sex development—Results from the German Clinical Evaluation Study. *Journal of Sexual Medicine, 10*, 2703–2714. doi:10.1111/j.1743-6109.2012.02751.x

Köhler, B., Jürgensen, M., Kleinemeier, E., & Thyen, U. (2014). Psychosexual development in individuals with disorders of sex development. In B. C. Kreukels, T. D. Steensma, & A. C. de Vries (Eds.), *Gender dysphoria and disorders of sex development: Progress in care and knowledge* (pp. 115–134). New York, NY: Springer Science + Business Media. doi:10.1007/978-1-4614-7441-8_6

Kolesinska, Z., Ahmed, S. F., Niedziela, M., Bryce, J., Molinska-Glura, M., Rodie, M., . . . Weintrob, N. (2014). Changes over time in sex assignment for disorders of sex development. *Pediatrics, 134,* e710–e715. doi:10.1542/peds.2014-1088

Kraus, C. (2015). Classifying intersex in *DSM-5:* Critical reflections on gender dysphoria. *Archives of Sexual Behavior, 44,* 1147–1163. doi:10.1007/s10508-015-0550-0

Lathrop, B. L., Cheney, T. B., & Hayman, A. B. (2014). Ethical decision-making in the dilemma of the intersex infant. *Issues in Comprehensive Pediatric Nursing, 37*(1), 25–38. doi:10.3109/01460862.2013.855842

Lev, A. I. (2006). Intersexuality in the family: An unacknowledged trauma. *Journal of Gay & Lesbian Psychotherapy, 10*(2), 27–56. doi:10.1300/J236v10n02_03

Meoded-Danon, L., & Yanay, N. (2016). Intersexuality: On secret bodies and secrecy. *Studies in Gender and Sexuality, 17*(1), 57–72. doi:10.1080/15240657.2016.1135684

Murphy, T. F. (2015). Ethical aspects in the care of intersex patients. In J. Z. Sadler, W. W. van Staden, & K. M. Fulford (Eds.), *The Oxford handbook of psychiatric ethics* (Vol. 1, pp. 193–199). New York, NY: Oxford University Press.

Pasterski, V., Mastroyannopoulou, K., Wright, D., Zucker, K. J., & Hughes, I. A. (2014). Predictors of posttraumatic stress in parents of children diagnosed with a disorder of sex development. *Archives of Sexual Behavior, 43*(2), 369–375. doi:10.1007/s10508-013-0196-8

Reiner, W. G., & Reiner, D. (2012). Thoughts on the nature of identity: How disorders of sex development inform clinical research about gender identity disorders. *Journal of Homosexuality, 59,* 434–449. doi:10.1080/00918369.2012.653312

Reis, E. (2007). Divergence or disorder? The politics of naming intersex. *Perspectives in Biology and Medicine, 50,* 535–543. doi:10.1353/pbm.2007.0054

Ristvedt, S. L. (2014). The evolution of gender. *JAMA Psychiatry, 71*(1), 13–14. doi:10.1001/jamapsychiatry.2013.3199

Sandberg, D. E., & Mazur, T. (2014). A noncategorical approach to the psychosocial care of persons with DSD and their families. In B. C. Kreukels, T. D. Steensma, & A. C. de Vries (Eds.), *Gender dysphoria and disorders of sex development: Progress in care and knowledge* (pp. 93–114). New York, NY: Springer Science + Business Media. doi:10.1007/978-1-4614-7441-8_5

Sanders, C., Carter, B., & Goodacre, L. (2011). Searching for harmony: Parents' narratives about their child's genital ambiguity and reconstructive genital surgeries in childhood. *Journal of Advanced Nursing, 67,* 2220–2230. doi:10.1111/j.1365-2648.2011.05617.x

Sanders, C., Carter, B., & Goodacre, L. (2012). Parents need to protect: Influences, risks and tensions for parents of prepubertal children born with ambiguous genitalia. *Journal of Clinical Nursing, 21,* 3315–3323. doi:10.1111/j.1365-2702.2012.04109.x

Sanders, C., Carter, B., & Lwin, R. (2015). Young women with a disorder of sex development: Learning to share information with health professionals, friends and intimate partners about bodily differences and infertility. *Journal of Advanced Nursing, 71,* 1904–1913. doi:10.1111/jan.12661

Streuli, J. C., Vayena, E., Cavicchia-Balmer, Y., & Huber, J. (2013). Shaping parents: Impact of contrasting professional counseling on parents' decision making for children with disorders of sex development. *Journal of Sexual Medicine, 10,* 1953–1960. doi:10.1111/jsm.12214

Thorn, E. D. (2014). Drop the knife! Instituting policies of nonsurgical intervention for intersex infants. *Family Court Review, 52*, 610–621. doi:10.1111/fcre.12110

Topp, S. S. (2013). Against the quiet revolution: The rhetorical construction of intersex individuals as disordered. *Sexualities, 16*(1–2), 180–194. doi:10.1177/1363460712471113

Warne, G., Grover, S., Hutson, J., Sinclair, A., Metcalfe, S., Northam, E., & Freeman, J. (2005). A long-term outcome study of intersex conditions. *Journal of Pediatric Endocrinology & Metabolism, 18*, 555–567.

Warne, G. L., & Mann, A. (2011). Ethical and legal aspects of management for disorders of sex development. *Journal of Paediatrics and Child Health, 47*, 661–663. doi:10.1111/j.1440-1754.2011.02164.x

Wilhelm, D., Palmer, S., & Koopman, P. (2007). Sex determination and gonadal development in mammals. *Physiological Reviews, 87*(1), 1–28.

Chapter 18

Counseling Asexual Clients

Misty M. Ginicola and Angela Ruggiero

> *I realized that I was asexual because when I was young,*
> *all of my friends started being attracted to people,*
> *and I had no idea what they were talking about.*
>
> —David Jay

• • •

Awareness of Attitudes and Beliefs Self-Check

1. Imagine a client tells you that they hate any type of sexual activity. What are your immediate thoughts about the potential causes? How might these assumptions represent your biases about human sexuality?
2. What are your beliefs surrounding the role of sex in a relationship? Do you think people who never want to touch their partners sexually can have fulfilling relationships?
3. Have you ever experienced a period in your life when you did not wish to be sexual with others? What did you experience as the cause? How can your own experiences serve as a bias when thinking about other potential causes?

Case Study

As a child, Marlene, a Caucasian female, was attractive and well liked and was never without a boyfriend. However, during her high school years, while her friends shared their first sexual encounters, Marlene could not identify. She would always make excuses with her boyfriends such as "I like somebody else" whenever a relationship was about to become physical. While playing a college drinking game, Never Have I Ever, a player said, "Never have I ever had sex," and for the first time Marlene felt humiliated that she had never had sexual relations. She ran from the room and cried.

From that point, she began looking for the *right* one. Marlene spent many years dating, but to no avail. She became depressed, as she would become attached to her girlfriends but would continue to get hurt as they attached to significant others. Marlene came across information online about asexuality. Marlene was ecstatic, as she related to everything that was described, but at the same time she felt saddened by the thought of being officially different. She felt like she had a lifelong disease and questioned whether God would still love and accept her.

After 10 years of therapy (with some psychotherapists who told her she just needed to find the right man) and dating all types of men, Marlene asked the gynecologist if perhaps she had a hormone problem. The gynecologist quickly turned down that idea and told her that many women did not have an active sex drive. It was at that time Marlene found the Asexual Visibility and Education Network (AVEN) online and learned that 1% of the population identified as asexual. She immediately approached another counselor to ask about this identity. Her counselor told her that there was no such thing as asexuality; she must have a hormonal issue or a sexual dysfunction. Her counselor then immediately asked whether she had ever been raped. Marlene never returned.

Identifying as an asexual biromantic, Marlene attempted to have her first asexual relationship with an allosexual (a person who experiences sexual attraction) female. Marlene remained clear that she was not attracted to her female friend and did not care to touch her. She did allow the woman to touch her, and although she enjoyed the attention, she never felt any excitement or desire to be touched. Marlene soon felt uncomfortable, but no matter how many times she explicitly stated her feelings, her partner would push sexual relations to the point that Marlene felt assaulted.

• • •

Awareness of Differences

Asexuality as an identity generally refers to a lack of sexual desire toward others since birth (Bogaert, 2004; Pinto, 2014; Scherrer, 2008). Asexual individuals make up approximately 1% of the world's population. There are three components to an asexual identity: the absence of sexual behavior, the absence of sexual attraction or desire, and self-identification as an asexual (Bogaert, 2004; Chasin, 2011; Van Houdenhove, Gijs, T'Sjoen, & Enzlin, 2014). Although some asexual persons do report sexual attraction, they have no desire to engage in sexual activity. Most asexual individuals set a strong boundary between physical affection (cuddling, kissing, and hugging), which some enjoy, and sexual activity, which most do not (Bogaert, 2006; Van Houdenhove et al., 2014).

Although asexuality was mentioned by Kinsey in his sexuality studies, Storms (1980) was one of the first researchers to recognize it as a distinct affectional orientation: Asexual individuals were found to score low on attraction to both opposite-sex and same-sex members. However, there was relative silence on asexuality in the research literature for decades. In the absence of popular or scientific discourse, AVEN was founded in 2001 with goals of advocating for and creating public acceptance and discourse around the asexual community (AVEN, 2008; Chasin, 2011). As a result of extensive advocacy on the part of AVEN and renewed interest by researchers, asexuality has been identified as one of the affectional orientation continuums; heterosexual to gay is one continuum of affectional and sexual attraction, and many place bisexual attraction in the middle (Chasin, 2011; Yule, Brotto, & Gorzalka, 2013b). Thinking dimensionally, asexuality would be the flip side of the sexual continuum, on the reverse side of bisexuality. People could have romantic attraction anywhere on that continuum but do not experience sexual attraction (Chasin, 2011). The genderbread person model presented in Chapter 15 (Killermann, 2013) incorporates asexuality easily into its new version: The asexual person may select close to 0 for sexual attraction for males and females but may identify with a romantic attraction, which is a separate item of assessment.

Although the cause of asexuality is unknown, preliminary research has indicated a neurodevelopmental cause (Yule, Brotto, & Gorzalka, 2013a). Asexual men and women are more than 2 times as likely to be ambidextrous or left handed. Birth order is also associated with asexuality: Asexual men are likely to be born later, whereas asexual women are likely to be born earlier. As discussed in Chapter 2, it is likely that, as with other gender and affectional presentations, genetics and hormones play a role in the asexual person's sexuality. Variance in the genetic, hormonal, and fetal environment could also explain why the asexual population is not a singular homogenous group (Brotto, Knudson, Inskip, Rhodes, & Erskine, 2010; Chasin, 2011).

Although there is little consistency among all those who self-identify as asexual, it is clear that these individuals are not emotionless and that most seek relationships with others for companionship, affection, and intimacy. There is a noticeable distinction between romantic attraction and sexual attraction in asexual individuals. Although asexual individuals have diminished sexual attraction to others, they may place a strong emphasis on how they identify themselves based on romantic attraction (Bogaert, 2006; Chasin, 2011; Diamond, 2003; Hinderliter, 2009). Many asexual individuals do identify as romantic, fall in love, and seek partnerships (Pinto, 2014; Scherrer, 2008). Asexual persons self-identify in two categories: sexual and romantic orientation (Carrigan, 2011). For example, some identify as *demisexual*, which means that they have some sexual interest only on feeling intense romantic feelings (Carrigan, 2011). Some identify with the terms *aromantic* (no romantic feelings), *heteroromantic* (romantic feelings toward someone of the opposite sex), *homoromantic* (romance with someone of the same sex) or *biromantic* (both sexes), or *gray-A/hyposexual* (somewhere between sexual and asexual in terms of attraction), to name a few (Carrigan, 2011).

Some asexual individuals do engage in sexual activity to please a partner and/or to have children (Carrigan, 2011). Although asexual persons are able to achieve sexual arousal, they are likely to have little interest in engaging with their partners sexually (Bogaert, 2006). Some asexual members may fantasize and masturbate; however, their fantasies do not typically include another person (Yule et al., 2013a). Others may choose to avoid partnerships and be celibate (Pinto, 2014). The aromantic asexual will likely have little or no desire to be in a romantic relationship (Carrigan, 2011). Aromantic asexual individuals may still desire affection and close emotional connections, but they can achieve this level of satisfaction through platonic friendships.

Knowledge of Issues and Problems

Experiences of Bias

Asexual clients live in a world that does not fit their identity in one of the most basic ways: as regards sexuality and sexual attraction (Chasin, 2015; Przybylo, 2011). Sexual attraction and behavior are not only expressed as the norm in society but highlighted everywhere, from media to peers to basic cultural celebrations, such as weddings (Chasin, 2011). To not feel attraction in a highly sexualized culture is very difficult (Foster & Scherrer, 2014). Asexual individuals very often experience disbelief from others about the existence of their sexuality, challenging invalidations, and other marginalizing behavior, such as the belief that their lack of attraction must be due to sexual trauma (Cerankowski, 2012; Yule et al., 2013b).

In addition, asexual individuals often have a variant gender presentation: Their gender identity tends to be nonconforming (Przybylo, 2011). They could also identify as transgender or genderqueer. Asexual persons also report often identifying with "same-sex" romantic attractions (Yule et al., 2013b). They are thus also privy to all of the hostility and prejudice focused against the lesbian, gay, bisexual, transgender, queer, questioning, intersex, asexual, ally, pansexual/polysexual, and two-spirited (LGBTQI+) community (Przybylo, 2011).

People who identify as asexual are minorities, even in the LGBTQI+ community (Chasin, 2015; Przybylo, 2011). As allosexual individuals, neither heterosexual nor LGBTQI+ persons can identify with a lack of sexual attraction (Chasin, 2015). Reactions from others can range from mild confusion to open hostility: Both heterosexual and queer communities have sexual norms that are violated by asexual persons (Przybylo, 2011). Therefore, asexual persons are stigmatized and feel discrimination and prejudice from both communities (MacInnis & Hodson, 2012). Part of this devaluing behavior translates into being generally treated as having less value and being evaluated negatively by both heterosexual and queer friends and family (MacInnis & Hodson, 2012).

Even some in the helping professions do not believe that asexuality truly exists and can invalidate an asexual person's identity (Yule et al., 2013b; Zucker, 2013). When many counselors and psychotherapists met asexual clients in the past, they immediately pathologized their sexual behavior; they searched for a potential cause of their lack of sexual attraction. Hypotheses include having been sexually assaulted as a child, not having come to terms with being gay, or being abnormal in some deep neurological manner (Foster & Scherrer, 2014). Another common diagnosis that clients who present with asexuality are mistakenly given is either female sexual interest/arousal disorder or male hypoactive sexual desire disorder, which are sexual dysfunctions characterized by pathologically low sexual desire (American Psychiatric Association, 2013; Yule et al., 2013b; Zucker, 2013). With a clinical diagnosis, patients may feel that they are being told that they are broken when they actually feel whole and healthy (Foster & Scherrer, 2014). They may get referred to sex therapists or prescribed a drug to increase sexual drive. Some may spend years in therapy, confused and instructed to partake in sexual exploration that feels unnatural to an asexual person.

Many asexual persons will meet many of the *Diagnostic and Statistical Manual of Mental Disorders* criteria for arousal disorders; however, there are key differences between asexuality and a sexual dysfunction. One difference is that asexual persons experience the same amount of genital arousal as allosexuals; however, they report that this arousal does not correspond to sexual attraction to anyone when they are aroused (Brotto & Yule, 2011; Yule, Brotto, & Gorzalka, 2013b, 2014a, 2014b, 2014c). Individuals who identify as asexual are also less likely than those with sexual dysfunctions to masturbate (Yule et al., 2014b). Although about half of asexual persons masturbate, many do not report sexual attraction or fantasies about specific people; rather, they seek a release (Pinto, 2014; Yule et al., 2014b). Another main difference between those with asexuality and those with a sexual dysfunction is that most asexual individuals do not report any type of distress over not being sexually attracted to others (Brotto et al., 2010; Cerankowski & Milks, 2010; Yule et al., 2013b). Among those asexual persons who do report distress, it is due to their lack of acceptance in the culture and by their partners, which should not indicate a true mental health disorder with distress related to internal psychological functioning (Brotto et al., 2010; Cerankowski & Milks, 2010; Pinto, 2014; Yule et al., 2013b).

The minority stress model (Meyer, 2003) can also be used to help understand the social, emotional, and mental health experience of asexual clients. The lack of normative information about asexuality; growing up in a highly sexualized culture; and the negative reactions that peers, family, and partners have to learning that an individual is asexual can create immense psychological distress. Asexual individuals may feel not only different but broken and dysfunctional, as the culture and even medical diagnoses may inform them of their pathological state.

Asexual persons are also more likely to have greater interpersonal problems than others in the LGBTQI+ community (Yule et al., 2013a). If they can find another asexual near them with whom they are romantically attracted, they may be able to have a relationship free of much sexual pressure. However, if the stars do not align in that manner, they must negotiate sexual activity with their partners. To asexual persons, this is akin to allosexual persons having a close friend to whom they are not sexually attracted but for whom they feel great love and find to be beautiful. Most sexual people could picture being happy residing with and sharing their lives with this close friend. However, if they were asked to have sex on a regular basis with the friend to whom they were not attracted, their relationship would be difficult, to say the least. Asexual partners often need to negotiate this type of sexual activity as a condition of their romantic relationship with an allosexual partner (Scherrer, 2008).

Potential Physical and Mental Health Challenges

Similar to other subpopulations in the LGBTQI+ acronym, there is a complete dearth of research on the asexual population to clearly understand their experiences and issues of physical and mental health. Because their experiences of bias are quite frequent, it would be reasonable to assume that, like the rest of the LGBTQI+ population, asexual individuals experience increased minority-related stress that leads to greater health problems (Meyer, 2003). As a result of this increased stress, asexual persons have been found to have a greater incidence of a variety of mental health issues than other members of the LGBTQI+ community (Yule et al., 2013a). Preliminary research from Yule et al. (2014a) found that Caucasian asexual individuals face more psychiatric issues than their heterosexual peers, including depression, suicidality, anxiety, and psychosis.

Counseling Skills and Techniques

There is a shortage of literature on counseling asexual individuals. However, some research studies can be used to inform some elements of counseling practice. Taking an affirmative approach with asexual clients is important (Chasin, 2015; Crisp, 2006; Hill, 2009). Validating clients' feelings; providing psychoeducation; and drawing attention to the inequality, discrimination, and prejudice they have experienced can help to validate and empower them and teach self-advocacy skills (Chasin, 2015; Foster & Scherrer, 2014; Meyer, 2003). It is also important to discuss the isolation they may feel in the queer community as well (Hill, 2009).

It is important for counselors to be aware of their own beliefs and values surrounding sexuality; as allosexual persons, it may be inconceivable to imagine having no sexual attraction (Crisp, 2006; Hill, 2009). Counselors and other helping professionals immediately look to identify pathology; counselors are naturally curious about the underlying causes into which clients have little insight. Exploring one's own attitudes toward sexuality and pathology as well as one's own power and privilege is important in working with asexual clients (Meyer, 2003). It is also important for counselors to have an awareness of what seeking therapy with a mental health professional is like for asexual persons: They may expect that the therapist will dismiss them, pathologize them, or be rejecting, making disclosing very stressful (Foster & Scherrer, 2014).

On hearing clients report that they have no sexual attraction, it is important to formally assess their symptoms rather than immediately judge that they must have an arousal or desire disorder (Zucker, 2013). The overt and subtle reactions and messages that a counselor sends to the client should not be that these symptoms are pathological in nature (Zucker, 2013). Evaluating how long the client has had the symptoms is crucial, as asexual individuals, like other affectional orientations, most often report experiencing their affectional orientation for as long as they can remember (Zucker, 2013). For asexual individuals, it would be very noticeable around puberty, when other peers are beginning to act on sexual attraction and partake in sexual behavior (Zucker, 2013). In addition, assessing for the presence of psychological distress as well as understanding the source of this psychological distress also help to identify an affectional orientation versus a sexual dysfunction (Chasin, 2015; Zucker, 2013). Asexual persons are likely either to not have distress over their sexual attraction or to express distress over not fitting in with the sexualized society, having difficulty with their partnerships, or accepting their identity as asexuals (Chasin, 2015; Zucker, 2013). All things being equal, if individuals have never experienced sexual attraction, would be happy never partaking in sexual behavior, and wish for their current or prospective partners to accept these feelings, they are likely asexual (Chasin, 2011). In addition, if clients self-identify as asexual, they should absolutely be accepted as such and not be challenged or doubted (Chasin, 2015).

Exploring and fostering asexual identity development is an important task of counseling as well (Hill, 2009). Providing acceptance, as well as the time and space to discuss their thoughts and identity, can help asexual clients feel included and lead to better identity development and functioning (Foster & Scherrer, 2014). Clients may also have internalized sexual norm attitudes as well as heterosexism blocking identity development (Hill, 2009). Connecting asexual persons to a community in which they can feel normalized and validated is also very important for identity development (Carrigan, 2011; Foster & Scherrer, 2014). Sending a client to the AVEN website would be a good way to provide psychoeducation and help the client find a supportive community (Foster & Scherrer, 2014).

If asexual persons come to counseling for issues surrounding their affectional orientation, it is likely related to relevant identity issues or relationship issues (Van Houdenhove, Gijs, T'Sjoen, & Enzlin, 2015). They may be having issues with negotiating physical intimacy and sexuality with an allosexual partner or seeking to experience love and romantic relationships. Clients may also seek assistance with developing strength, a voice, and strategies to come out to others in their lives. The advantages and disadvantages of negotiating their sexual behavior with their partner may be a topic for counseling. It is also important that the counselor remember that being asexual may *not* be the presenting issue (Foster & Scherrer, 2014).

Conclusion

As affectional minorities, asexual persons face a unique set of challenges and minority stressors, as do other members of the LGBTQI+ communities. However, asexual clients face additional stigma, disbelief, relationship difficulties, and prejudice from allosexuals in both the LGBTQI+ and heterosexual populations. Asexual persons feel isolated from both their queer and heterosexual peers beginning in adolescence. Puberty typically brings with it a new sexual exploration and obsession for others, but an asexual person cannot identify and feels frightened to share these feelings. Further amplified by peers', parents', and professionals' commentary surrounding their perceived dysfunction, an asexual often is misdiagnosed and harmed, even in a counseling environment. It is important for counselors to provide a culturally competent assessment, affirm asexual persons' identity, and help them navigate the issues they face in relationships with others.

Questions for Further Discussion

1. In what ways is Marlene's case typical of asexual individuals' internal experiences?
2. What does Marlene's identity of asexual biromantic mean?

3. What damaging cultural messages, medical services, and mental health services did Marlene receive?
4. What types of social and emotional issues is Marlene experiencing? What might a counselor expect Marlene to have in terms of mental health symptoms?
5. As Marlene's new counselor, and in the absence of empirically based research, what approaches and strategies should you take in working with Marlene?

Resources

1. Read more about asexuality at http://www.asexuality.org/home/.
2. Read more about demisexuality at http://demisexuality.org/.
3. Learn more about asexual people's stories at https://asexualstories.wordpress.com/.
4. Watch the documentary *(A)sexual* (2011) as described at http://www.counseling.org/news/blog/aca-blog/2014/08/26/asexuality.

References

American Psychiatric Association. (2013). *Diagnostic and statistical manual of mental disorders* (5th ed.). Washington, DC: Author.

Asexuality Visibility Education Network. (2008). *AVEN survey 2008–Results.* Retrieved from http://www.asexuality.org/home/?q=2008_stats.html

Bogaert, A. F. (2004). Asexuality: Prevalence and associated factors in a national probability sample. *Journal of Sex Research, 41,* 279–287.

Bogaert, A. F. (2006). Toward a conceptual understanding of asexuality. *Review of General Psychology, 10,* 241–250.

Brotto, L. A., Knudson, G., Inskip, J., Rhodes, K., & Erskine, Y. (2010). Asexuality: A mixed methods approach. *Archives of Sexual Behavior, 39,* 599–618.

Brotto, L. A., & Yule, M. A. (2011). Physiological and subjective sexual arousal in self-identified asexual women. *Archives of Sexual Behavior, 40,* 699–712. doi:10.1007/s10508-010-9671-7

Carrigan, M. (2011). There's more to life than sex? Difference and commonality within the asexual community. *Sexualities, 14,* 462–478. doi:10.1177/1363460711406462

Cerankowski, K. (2012, November). *Trauma and asexuality: Uncovering a "digital archive of 'feelings.'"* Paper presented at the annual conference of the National Women's Studies Association, Berkeley, CA.

Cerankowski, K. J., & Milks, M. (2010). New orientations: Asexuality and its implications for theory and practice. *Feminist Studies, 36,* 650–664.

Chasin, C. D. (2011). Theoretical issues in the study of asexuality. *Archives of Sexual Behavior, 40,* 713–723.

Chasin, C. D. (2015). Making sense in and of the asexual community: Navigating relationships and identities in a context of resistance. *Journal of Community & Applied Social Psychology, 25*(2), 167–180. doi:10.1002/casp.2203

Crisp, C. (2006). The Gay Affirmative Practice scale (GAP): A new measure for assessing cultural competence with gay and lesbian clients. *Social Work, 51,* 115–126. doi:10.1093/sw/51.2.115

Diamond, L. M. (2003). What does sexual orientation orient? A biobehavioral model distinguishing romantic love and sexual desire. *Psychological Review, 110,* 173–192.

Foster, A. B., & Scherrer, K. S. (2014). Asexual-identified clients in clinical settings: Implications for culturally competent practice. *Psychology of Sexual Orientation and Gender Diversity, 1,* 422–430. doi:10.1037/sgd0000058

Hill, N. L. (2009). Affirmative practice and alternative sexual orientations: Helping clients navigate the coming out process. *Clinical Social Work Journal, 37,* 346–356. doi:10.1007/s10615-009-0240-2

Hinderliter, A. C. (2009). Methodological issues for studying asexuality. *Archives of Sexual Behavior, 38,* 619–621.

Killermann, S. (2013). *The social justice advocate's handbook: A guide to gender.* Austin, TX: Impetus Books.

MacInnis, C. C., & Hodson, G. (2012). Intergroup bias toward "group x": Evidence of prejudice, dehumanization, avoidance, and discrimination against asexuals. *Group Processes & Intergroup Relations, 15,* 725–743. doi:10.1177/1368430212442419

Meyer, I. H. (2003). Prejudice, social stress, and mental health in lesbian, gay, and bisexual populations: Conceptual issues and research evidence. *Psychological Bulletin, 129,* 674–697. doi:10.1037/0033-2909.129.5.674

Pinto, S. A. (2014). ASEXUally: On being an ally to the asexual community. *Journal of LGBT Issues in Counseling, 8*(4), 331–343. doi:10.1080/15538605.2014.960130

Przybylo, E. (2011). Crisis and safety: The asexual in sexusociety. *Sexualities, 14,* 444–461. doi:10.1177/1363460711406461

Scherrer, K. S. (2008). Coming to an asexual identity: Negotiating identity, negotiating desire. *Sexualities, 11,* 621–641. doi:10.1177/1363460708094269

Storms, M. D. (1980). Theories of sexual orientation. *Journal of Personality and Social Psychology, 38,* 783–792.

Van Houdenhove, E., Gijs, L., T'Sjoen, G., & Enzlin, P. (2014). Asexuality: Few facts, many questions. *Journal of Sex & Marital Therapy, 40*(3), 175–192. doi:10.1080/0092623X.2012.751073

Van Houdenhove, E., Gijs, L., T'Sjoen, G., & Enzlin, P. (2015). Stories about asexuality: A qualitative study on asexual women. *Journal of Sex & Marital Therapy, 41*(3), 262–281. doi:10.1080/0092623X.2014.889053

Yule, M. A., Brotto, L. A., & Gorzalka, B. B. (2013a). Biological markers of asexuality: Handedness, birth order, and finger length ratios in self-identified asexual men and women. *Archives of Sexual Behavior, 43,* 299–310.

Yule, M. A., Brotto, L. A., & Gorzalka, B. B. (2013b). Mental health and interpersonal functioning in self-identified asexual men and women. *Psychology & Sexuality, 4,* 136–151. doi:10.1080/19419899.2013.774162

Yule, M. A., Brotto, L. A., & Gorzalka, B. B. (2014a). Mental health and interpersonal functioning in self-identified asexual men and women. In M. Carrigan, K. Gupta, & T. G. Morrison (Eds.), *Asexuality and sexual normativity: An anthology* (pp. 25–40). New York, NY: Routledge.

Yule, M. A., Brotto, L. A., & Gorzalka, B. B. (2014b). Sexual fantasy and masturbation among asexual individuals. *Canadian Journal of Human Sexuality, 23*(2), 89–95. doi:10.3138/cjhs.2409

Yule, M. A., Brotto, L. A., & Gorzalka, B. B. (2014c). A validated measure of no sexual attraction: The asexuality identification scale. *Psychological Assessment.* Advance online publication. doi:10.1037/a0038196

Zucker, K. J. (2013). *DSM-5:* Call for commentaries on gender dysphoria, sexual dysfunctions, and paraphilic disorders. *Archives of Sexual Behavior, 39,* 477–498. doi:10.1007/s10508-013-0148-3

Chapter 19

Counseling Two-Spirit Clients

Misty M. Ginicola

We're reclaiming our place in the circle.
Until the two-spirit people are brought back into that circle,
that circle is never going to be completely mended.
—Steven Barrios (Blackfeet)

• • •

Awareness of Attitudes and Beliefs Self-Check

1. Close your eyes and picture a gay Native. What do you see? How are your biases and stereotypes of both being gay and being Native present in your image?
2. What changes are you aware of that occurred among the indigenous population as a result of European colonization?
3. Do you consider having an affectional orientation or gender variance to be spiritual? Why or why not?

Case Study

Wilma Black Fox is a 22-year-old biracial female who grew up in a rural area outside of tribal lands. Her father is from the Cherokee Nation and her mother is White (English and Irish). Wilma's mother was extremely religious, and she grew up with the influence of a Protestant religion. Wilma reports that she always felt different than the other children: She was darker skinned, and she always enjoyed both traditional girl and boy toys and games. As an early adolescent, she knew that she was attracted to both males and females but had learned from her mother at an early age that "homosexuality" was sinful and wrong. She never told anyone of her feelings until she left the area to go to college. At college, she briefly identified as lesbian because, in retrospect, she was trying very hard to fit into the gay community that she found there. She found that being attracted to men was not understood or accepted by her friends, nor were some of the traditional Native beliefs that she had grown up with through the influence of her father. Even with his influence, Wilma felt very disconnected from her Native heritage; she also felt that being half White made her not fit in with the few other Natives she had met. She began identifying as bisexual and reports that although she does not feel transgender, her gender is very different than other people's gender identities. She is currently dating a female and reports that she just came out, unplanned, to her mother. It resulted in a huge argument in which her mother said very hurtful things, including telling her she was going to hell. When her brother found out, he told her he wasn't sure he wanted her around his children. She slipped into a deep depression and has come to counseling to find a way to be happy on her own.

• • •

Awareness of Differences

Natives are composed of the groups referred to as American Indians and Alaska Natives (Fieland, Walters, & Simoni, 2007). Natives represent 5.2 million or 2% of the U.S. population, a number that has grown since their near extinction by the Europeans throughout the 1800s (Fieland et al., 2007). The term *two-spirit* refers to a person with indigenous American heritage who has gender and affectional orientation variance, which means it is inclusive of lesbian, gay, bisexual, transgender, intersex, and queer identities (Jacobs, Thomas, & Lang, 1997). The modern term of *two-spirit* reflects identities and terms used in many different tribes: *adanvdo tali* (Cherokee), *heemaneh'* (Cheyenne), *bote* (Crow), *winkte* (Lakota), *nádleeh* (Navajo), *agokwa* (Ojibwa), *ake'skassi* (Piegan), *keknatsa'nxwixw* (Quinault), and *tainna wa'ippe* or *tubasa* (Shoshone), to name a few (Garrett & Barret, 2003; Lang, 2011).

When colonial Europeans saw men who wore women's dress and performed women's duties in the tribe, they viewed it from a pathological lens and called them *berdaches* (Lang, 2011; Thomas & Jacobs, 1999). *Berdache* is a word of Arabic origin with a history prior to its application to Natives: It was associated with sodomy, someone who engaged in receptive anal intercourse, and male slaves used as prostitutes (Balestrery, 2012; Jacobs et al., 1997; Smithers, 2014). Europeans used the word *amazon* to describe female Natives who lived as males in the tribe (Balestrery, 2012; Jacobs et al., 1997). Berdaches were described as cross-dressers, sodomites, "hermaphrodites," and deviants by the European people (Balestrery, 2012; Smithers, 2014).

At its third annual spiritual gathering in 1990, a group of LGBT Natives sought to reclaim the positive nature of gender and affectional orientation variance in Native tradition as well as to unify all American Indian, Alaska Native, and Canadian First Nations tribes (Adams & Phillips, 2009; Anguksuar, 1997). The identity was selected from the Northern Algonquin term *niizh manitoag*, which translates to "two-spirited," which perfectly captured the traditional beliefs of the individual containing both feminine and masculine energy or spirits (Anguksuar, 1997).

It is not merely that two-spirited people have an affectional orientation difference but that their entire gender is different from that of heterosexuals: It can be a third gender, neither male nor female (Lang, 2011; Tafoya, 1996). Indigenous Americans are not alone in their identification of a third gender; as discussed in Chapter 14, the concept is found in Asian, Balkan, Polynesian, and Siberian cultures, to name a few (Lang, 2011). From a traditional Native viewpoint, the gender of the individual trumps the sex of the body (Thomas & Jacobs, 1999). The third-gender individual in these cultures experience both masculine and feminine qualities and is considered to be of a dual nature (Lang, 2011).

This identity also has an intense spiritual component. The two-spirited individual was seen as possessing both a male and a female spirit (Garrett & Barret, 2003; Tafoya, 1996). Those with this type of dual nature were seen as being blessed with a gift, touched by the supernatural (Lang, 2011). Some tribes (Navajo, Nuxalk) had two-spirits present in their origin stories (Lang, 2011). Because they have both male and female spirits, they are able to view the world from both masculine and feminine perspectives (Hall, 1994). As one two-spirited person stated, "Because you walk in both worlds. Because you are elements of both male and female—but you're neither. You don't fit in, you're a go-between. And consequently, it's easier for you to transcend from the physical to the spiritual realm" (Hall, 1994, p. 122).

Because of these unique abilities, in traditional societies and in some modern tribes and contexts, two-spirits had specific social identities and roles as well (Adams & Phillips, 2009; Garrett & Barret, 2003; Tafoya, 1996). They served as medicine men and women (traditional versions of shaman or priests); in highly respected ceremonial roles; as advisors and mediators; as caretakers and teachers of children; and in economic and supportive roles, such as cultivating, cooking, and weaving (Adams & Phillips, 2009; Evans-Campbell, Fredriksen-Goldsen, Walters, & Stately, 2007; Sheppard & Mayo, 2013). Two-spirits were known for their caregiving ability; they cared for the ill, the mentally unwell, and the elderly and raised children (Evans-Campbell et al., 2007). As part of the collective parenting network, they would either assist parents with children, support a family that was struggling by caring for or fostering its children, or mentor other two-spirited children (Evans-Campbell et al., 2007). Two-spirits could also instruct others in their journey to achieving balance; two-spirits are an asset to others and are considered to be of great value to their communities (Hall, 1994).

In these contexts, roles, and identities, two-spirited persons were not just accepted but valued (Garrett & Barret, 2003). To understand the true depth of this acceptance and the two-spirit identity, one must understand the spiritual values of indigenous American tribal cultures (Garrett & Myers, 1996). Although tribes have different regional cultures, languages, traditions, and celebrations, they share many core values, such as balance, harmony with people and nature, cooperation, collectivism, and sharing of wealth (Garrett & Myers, 1996). All of these values have to do with the overarching spiritual belief regarding what has been called the *circle of life* (Garrett & Myers, 1996).

The Western use of dichotomous or binary categories and linear thinking is quite foreign to Native traditional culture (Garrett, 1996). Native concepts are circular, in reflection of natural phenomena; all life and nature exist through cycles and circles (Garrett, 1996). The earth is round and experiences the seasons in cycles: Rain falls from the sky, only to evaporate and be drawn back up into the clouds. From life to death to rebirth of some kind, every living being or natural phenomenon follows a circular pattern (Garrett & Myers, 1996). In this circle, everything is interconnected and interdependent in an intricate web that is in constant motion and transformation (Garrett & Myers, 1996). From one perspective, it may look as if nature is independent and finite, as in gazing at the beginning or end of a river. But if one had the eyes of a bird, one would see that the river flows into another and into the ocean in an interconnected web (Garrett, 1996). "All things are connected like the blood, which unites a family" (Book Publishing Company, 1988, p. 14).

As humans are also part of nature, they follow the same spiral. Like all things, they are alive, have spiritual energy, and are essential to the circle (Garrett & Myers, 1996). "Circles of life surround us, exist within us, and comprise the many relationships of our existence" (Garrett & Myers, 1996, p. 91). Disharmony occurs when people are out of balance and lose sight of their truth and role (Garrett & Myers, 1996). Each person's role is to find deep meaning and that person's truth, walking in step with the circle and flow of life (Garrett & Myers, 1996). Well-being and harmony result from the full realization of the specific purpose that one was meant to fulfill; the Native cultural value of noninterference is key in respecting each person's divine right to live authentically (Garrett & Myers, 1996). All individuals also have their own circle, meaning, purpose, and role, in some tribes symbol-ized by medicine wheels (Garrett & Myers, 1996). The medicine wheel indicates the way in which people live their lives, their approach to life; it represents how they focus their time and energy in each direction (mind, body, spirit, and nature), which represents both their values and their priorities (Garrett & Myers, 1996).

This reverence and respect for the individual in the collective indicates that variation is also seen as natural and valuable (Garrett & Barret, 2003). The eagle feather contains both light and dark colors, dualities and opposites, yet neither is more valuable than the other (Garrett & Barret, 2003). Both are from the same feather; both are natural, authentic, and connected; and it takes both of them for the eagle to fly (Garrett & Barret, 2003). Gay and heterosexual and male and female are not seen as opposites; in Native philosophy, there are no opposites as there are in Western cultures (Garrett & Myers, 1996). They are elements of the same intricate system that fluctuate and influence each other (Garrett & Barret, 2003).

Two-spirited individuals are no different. They are integral and valuable people in society; they are connected to everyone and everything. The two-spirit grows and transforms, becoming an integral and important influence on the community (Garrett & Myers, 1996). The reverence for those who are two-spirited comes from the spiritual belief that they were born in balance and harmony, indicating that they carry a special gift in the way that they walk through this world (Adams & Phillips, 2006; Garrett & Barret, 2003). Part of this gift was also specific emotional characteristics: high levels of empathy, passion for helping people, a desire to care for others who are vulnerable or need help, and natural mentorship and teaching abilities (Evans-Campbell et al., 2007). Two-spirits are seen as being natural bridge makers, bringing harmony, balance, and peace to their tribe; thus, their social and spiritual roles are naturally selected based on this belief (Adams & Phillips, 2006; Garrett & Barret, 2003).

Modern two-spirits are not nearly as universally accepted; with the impact of colonization, indoctrination, years of generational oppression, genocide, and trauma, much of the traditional culture and many of its beliefs have been lost by modern Natives (Cameron, 2005). Current Native beliefs regarding two-spirits have similarly been distorted throughout time (Cameron, 2005; Robinson, 2014). In addition to experiencing forced colonization and the influence of missionaries in tribal lands, Native youth were often sent to boarding schools hundreds or thousands of miles away from their tribes (Evans-Campbell, Walters, Pearson, & Campbell, 2012; U.S. Department of Health and Human Services, 2001). From 1880 to 1930, half of all Native children attended these schools, which functionally committed cultural genocide: These children were forced to assimilate to Christian and European beliefs and experienced harsh punishment for speaking their tribal languages or practicing cultural traditions (Evans-Campbell et al., 2012; U.S. Department of Health and Human Services, 2001). Although these boarding schools still exist, they do not continue to seek forced acculturation; however, their distance from the tribe can still cause separation and isolation (Evans-Campbell et al., 2012; U.S. Department of Health and Human Services, 2001).

Both the colonization and indoctrination that occurred at the boarding schools and Victorian and compulsory Christian beliefs and values, which were profoundly homophobic and homonegative, influenced the psyches of Native tribes (Balestrery, 2012; Balsam, Huang, Fieland, Simoni, & Walters, 2004; Cameron, 2005). In addition, along with the forced acculturation in residential boarding schools were high rates of sexual abuse (Cameron, 2005). Because much of the sexual abuse was same-sex in nature, Natives began associating lesbian, gay, bisexual, transgender, queer, questioning, intersex, asexual, ally, pansexual/polysexual, and two-spirited (LGBTQI+) persons with sin and/or as seeing them as criminal sex abusers. This is a far cry from the valuable, spiritual, and caretaking members of the community that two-spirits were always embraced as prior to colonization (Balestrery, 2012; Cameron, 2005). This also caused many two-spirited individuals to struggle with their own identity and experience mental health problems (Evans-Campbell et al., 2012).

Some Native communities have embraced their traditional beliefs, including those surrounding two-spirited people (Adams & Phillips, 2009). The level of acceptance for the two-spirited depends on levels of European acculturation and the adoption of traditional cultural values (Walters, 1997). When tribes have readopted traditional Native values, two-spirits are able to thrive with a greater level of acceptance than other non-Native LGBTQI+ persons, as tribal messages trump outside culture (Adams & Phillips, 2009; Evans-Campbell et al., 2007). Rather than being seen as cut off from God, as Christian beliefs indicate, two-spirited individuals are told that they have a special connection with the spirit world and the spiritual (Adams & Phillips, 2009). They also learn their spiritual and social roles as well as their value throughout tribal history (Adams & Phillips, 2009). This differing viewpoint can be healing and restorative and facilitate an important identity shift (Adams & Phillips, 2006). LGBTQI+ persons no longer see themselves as broken, sinful, and condemned but rather as full of value and gifted (Adams & Phillips, 2006). Needless to say, this paradigm shift can be supportive, validating, and empowering. In these communities, two-spirited persons have begun to reclaim their social, caretaking, and spiritual roles as well (Evans-Campbell et al., 2007). One of the key roles being reclaimed is caring for children: "When we care for the children, we are a part of the heart of the community. Central to the whole Native community and that's helping us regain our traditional roles" (Evans-Campbell et al., 2007, p. 85).

Identity Development

These two antithetical acceptance levels create two potentially different pathways of identity development: one positive and one negative (Adams & Phillips, 2006, 2009). If two-spirited individuals grow up in a negative context, they experience rejection similar to other non-Native LGBTQI+ populations, which means growing up with high heterosexism and negative attitudes regarding their affectional orientation (Adams & Phillips, 2006, 2009). Two-spirits who grow up in the positive framework report that they always knew they were two-spirited, always felt comfortable with their identity, and always were fully out (Adams & Phillips, 2009). Thus, the environment of acceptance can either support and prevent adjustment problems or directly contribute to them.

Native persons today may identify with the label of being two-spirited or may not; they may identify with multiple identities or another area altogether under the LGBTQI+ umbrella (Balestrery, 2012). Identity differences may vary depending on whether one has grown up in a tribal environment or an urban area. Because half of indigenous people are in urban centers today, that would certainly impact their knowledge about and use of the two-spirited identity (Balestrery, 2012; Tafoya, 1996). Their chosen identity term also depends on socioeconomic, generational, and other political attitudes (Balestrery, 2012; Tafoya, 1996, 1997).

Knowledge of Issues and Problems

Experiences of Bias

Although little research has been done on two-spirited people's health and mental health, there are many studies on Natives in general and several on two-spirits in particular. Natives in general have high rates of physical and mental health problems (National Center for Health Statistics, 2006, 2016). The minority stress model predicts that like other "sexual minorities," two-spirited individuals will experience even higher levels of discrimination, prejudice, and marginalization compounded by their intersectional minority identities of being two-spirited, indigenous, and (for women) female (Balestrery, 2012; Meyer, 2003). Each of these minority statuses can lead to complex experiences of racism, heterosexism, sexism, and marginalization that can impact physical and mental health (Adams & Phillips, 2006; Meyer, 2003; Walters, Evans-Campbell, Simoni, Ronquillo, & Bhuyan, 2006).

Two-spirits are more likely than heterosexual Natives to be exposed to discrimination and victimization, which serves as a significant risk factor for later health issues (Chae & Walters, 2009; Simoni, Walters, Balsam, & Meyers, 2006). They experience high rates of exposure to homophobia in heteronormative contexts (Balsam et al., 2004; Fieland et al., 2007; Walters, Simoni, & Horwath, 2001). They are at risk for hate crimes (Norrell, 2001), which can be verbal, physical, or sexual in nature (Walters et al., 2001). Gay Native youth are twice as likely to be physically abused and 6 times more likely to experience sexual abuse than heterosexual Native youth (Barney, 2003). Native women have experienced increased violence since colonization: Two-spirit women have been found to experience disturbingly high levels of sexual (85%) and physical (78%) abuse (Lehavot, Walters, & Simoni, 2010). Much of this assault and abuse occurs in Native communities; however, even urban Natives who grow up outside of tribal lands experience higher levels of physical abuse, sexual abuse, and physical and sexual assault than heterosexuals (Balsam et al., 2004).

Because of these high rates of abuse, two-spirited individuals face a horrific choice: leave their families and communities to be true to themselves or stay with their community and drown their authentic feelings (Brotman, Ryan, Jalbert, & Rowe, 2002). As a result of postcolonization changes to Native beliefs and attitudes, the two-spirited person is now seen as an embarrassment and taboo among many Native community members and in families (Brotman et al., 2002). Many choose to leave their communities because they are unsafe and they fear being assaulted or killed (Brotman et al., 2002). Unfortunately, even when two-spirited people are welcomed in a non-Native gay community, they have been found to face racism due to their Native ethnicity (Balsam et al., 2004; Fieland et al., 2007; Walters et al., 2001).

Physical and Mental Health Challenges

The impact of these stressors takes its toll. More than one third of two-spirited individuals have been found to be in fair or poor health, with more than half having some kind of physical pain and impairment (Balsam et al., 2004; Chae & Walters, 2009). Two-spirited males have been found to have high rates of HIV (Burks, Robbins, & Durtschi, 2011; Simoni et al., 2006). Two-spirits are also more likely to have poor mental health (Balsam et al., 2004). They have incredibly high rates of suicidal ideation, suicide attempts, and completed suicides; two-spirit youth are twice as likely than heterosexual Native youth to have suicidal ideation or to attempt suicide (Barney, 2003; Wilson, 2007). They also have higher rates of alcoholism and other substance abuse (Balsam et al., 2004). Substance abuse as well as suicide in two-spirited persons has been directly linked to boarding school attendance: Having attended such a school was related to substance abuse as adults (Evans-Campbell et al., 2012; Yuan, Duran, Walters, Pearson, & Evans-Campbell, 2014). These problems are compounded by the fact that many Natives mistrust treatment and health care organizations as well as the government; therefore, they are less likely than Caucasians to seek medical or mental health care (Burks et al., 2011).

The research has also revealed some protective factors for two-spirited individuals. When two-spirits have more education and are gainfully employed, they are protected from some of the negative impacts of discrimination (Chae & Walters, 2009). Among two-spirited persons being raised in an urban setting, being adopted into another family was also found to be a protective factor, perhaps because of socioeconomic advantages (Yuan et al., 2014). Racial actualization, or embracing their identity as indigenous, serves as a moderator of physical and mental health problems (Chae & Walters, 2009). Similarly, coming out and fully accepting and incorporating the two-spirit meaning and beliefs into one's identity has been found to predict a high level of confidence and good health (Brotman et al., 2002).

Counseling Skills and Techniques

There has been very little research on counseling two-spirited persons. However, some literature can guide counselors toward developing a positive and healing experience for two-spirited clients. Counselors must first ensure that they are open to exploring their thinking and biases regarding affectional orientation, race, and spirituality (Garrett & Barret, 2003). Counselors must be culturally sensitive to the client's intersectional identity, which can include racial, affectional orientation, spiritual, gender, and social issues (Burks et al., 2011). Two-spirit-identified counselors should also be aware that they may have boundary crossings with other two-spirit clients because of the small size of the community (Everett, MacFarlane, Reynolds, & Anderson, 2013). Multiple relationships may be acceptable when culturally appropriate but call for the inclusion and consent of all parties, transparency, full disclosure, and a clear plan and rationale for the boundary crossing, as well as consultation and documentation (Everett et al., 2013).

The counselor should also be cognizant of the rich diversity in culture among tribes and not make assumptions about cultural experiences or identities (Evans-Campbell et al., 2012). Some clients may identify or will identify with being two-spirited; others will not (Garrett & Barret, 2003). Some persons may not identify or wish to identify with the spiritual component central to a two-spirit identity (Garrett & Barret, 2003). The key to learning about a Native client is authentic listening, patience, and respectful exploration (Garrett & Barret, 2003). On meeting clients, counselors should assess for intersectional identities and intercultural differences as well as internalized messages clients have made in regard to their gender and affectional orientation (Evans-Campbell et al., 2007). Counselors should also understand and supportively confront any fears about seeking support, particularly from an institution or organization (Evans-Campbell et al., 2007). The barriers to seeking help and treatment are typically related to a lack of cultural competence, discrimination, trauma, and a mismatch with identity (Walters et al., 2001).

The main goal for counseling should be to develop a positive LGBTQI+ and/or two-spirited identity in the client's indigenous identity; in either case, learning about or reconnecting with Native history surrounding gender, affectional orientation, spirituality, and social roles for two-spirited tribal members can be healing (Evans-Campbell et al., 2007; Walters, 1997; Walters, Simoni, & Evans-Campbell, 2002). In this identity exploration, counselors should be aware that clients' identity will evolve; it might not fit into a neat category (Garrett & Barret, 2003). Exploring all of the facets of clients' identity, how they felt about these aspects growing up, and the negative or positive messages they heard is important (Garrett & Barret, 2003). Other themes that may arise in counseling are issues of family, both the family of origin and becoming a parent. Native cultural beliefs include a strong obligation to become a parent (Garrett & Barret, 2003). Embracing the idea that parenting is an option for two-spirited persons and their historical roles as foster and adoptive parents can also be helpful (Garrett & Barret, 2003).

Counselors need to be aware of the unique issues that these clients have with substance abuse and addiction. There are predominantly social reasons why indigenous people are at risk for substance abuse (Garrett & Barret, 2003). Assessing the client for substance use and abuse and finding culturally sensitive ways to help the client understand and cope with the suffering that underlies the impulse to use are also important (Garrett & Barret, 2003). It is also important to note that some substance abuse programs may not be appropriate for LGBTQI+ individuals; likewise, some LGBTQI+ substance abuse programs may not be prepared for the unique needs that a two-spirited person has in terms of race and the impact of colonization (Garrett & Barret, 2003).

Counselors need to both provide and connect two-spirited clients to safe and supportive environments where they can explore the multiple facets of their identities and experiences (Garrett & Barret, 2003). Providing psychoeducation and guiding people to connect with supportive and affirmative family members, Native communities, and two-spirited organizations can help clients find a source of strength and further develop their identity (Walters et al., 2002, 2006).

Some two-spirited persons have called their coming out process a *becoming out*, in which they fully become who they were always intended to be as two-spirited; they have also referred to this process as *coming home* (Walters et al., 2006). Identifying with the indigenous worldview to see themselves on a deeper spiritual level can serve to provide a framework for their identity that is based not just on their affectional orientation and attractions (Walters et al., 2006). The other healing component of this framework is to embrace their role to the people: of being a caretaker, healer, and spiritual warrior (Walters et al., 2006). It is noteworthy that this Native framework may help non-Natives to understand a different way of viewing their own gender differences. However, an identity as two-spirited specifically means that a person has some Native heritage and identity. For a nonindigenous person to claim a two-spirited identity can be seen as cultural appropriation (Cameron, 2005).

Conclusion

Traditional Native views of LGBTQI+ persons were incredibly affirmative. With the advent of European and Christian colonization and the cultural and physical genocide all tribes experienced, the value of the two-spirit shifted to become negative. Embracing these traditional Native beliefs can bring an alternative viewpoint to these clients. Instead of subscribing to an oppressive belief system in which they are seen as less than, sinful, taboo, and unworthy, through psychoeducation and counseling work, two-spirit persons can replace this negative stigma with an understanding of their value and of their inherent importance to the community around them. Embracing the belief that because of this gender and affectional orientation difference, they are connected to their ancestors and future generations with a spiritual ability to find balance and harmony others do not naturally possess can promote healing and wellness (Walters et al., 2006). Counselors' work with clients will center around helping two-spirited or LGBTQI+ clients have courage in their *becoming*: considering who they were, who they are, who they are becoming, and who they were always meant to be in finding their way on their own circle of life (Garrett & Barret, 2003).

Questions for Further Discussion

1. What are Wilma's intersectional backgrounds and identities?
2. How has Wilma interpreted or made meaning of her gender and affectional orientation differences?
3. What unique aspects of her experience have impacted her meaning making?
4. What could she be at risk for in terms of physical and mental health difficulties?
5. What counseling techniques could be utilized to help Wilma develop a positive identity?

Resources

1. Learn more about the two-spirit identity at http://nativeout.com/.
2. Review resources on the two-spirit identity available through the Native Youth Sexual Health Network at http://www.nativeyouthsexualhealth.com/twospiritdirectory.html.
3. Read about two-spirit issues in schools at http://www.safeandcaring.ca/wp-content/uploads/2013/08/Two-Spirited-Web-Booklet.pdf.

References

Adams, H., & Phillips, L. (2006). Experiences of two-spirit lesbian and gay Native Americans: An argument for standpoint theory in identity research. *Identity, 6*(3), 273–291. doi:10.1207/s1532706xid0603_4

Adams, H., & Phillips, L. (2009). Ethnic related variations from the Cass model of homosexual identity formation: The experiences of two-spirit, lesbian and gay Native Americans. *Journal of Homosexuality, 56,* 959–976.

Anguksuar, R. L. (Yup'ik). (1997). A postcolonial perspective on Western [mis]conceptions of the cosmos and the restoration of indigenous taxonomies. In S. Jacobs, W. Thomas (Navajo), & S. Lang (Eds.), *Two-spirit people: Native American gender identity, sexuality and spirituality* (pp. 100–118). Chicago, IL: University of Illinois Press.

Balestrery, J. E. (2012). Intersecting discourses on race and sexuality: Compounded colonization among LGBTTQ American Indians/Alaska Natives. *Journal of Homosexuality, 59,* 633–655. doi:10.1080/00918369.2012.673901

Balsam, K. F., Huang, B., Fieland, K. C., Simoni, J. M., & Walters, K. L. (2004). Culture, trauma, and wellness: A comparison of heterosexual and lesbian, gay, bisexual, and two-spirit Native Americans. *Cultural Diversity and Ethnic Minority Psychology, 10*(3), 287–301. doi:10.1037/1099-9809.10.3.287

Barney, D. D. (2003). Health risk-factors for gay American Indian and Alaska Native adolescent males. *Journal of Homosexuality, 46*(1–2), 137–157. doi:10.1300/J082v46n01_04

Book Publishing Company. (1988). *How can one sell the air? A manifesto for the Earth.* Summertown, TN: Author.

Brotman, S., Ryan, B., Jalbert, Y., & Rowe, B. (2002). The impact of coming out on health and health care access: The experiences of gay, lesbian, bisexual and two-spirit people. *Journal of Health & Social Policy, 15*(1), 1–29.

Burks, D. J., Robbins, R., & Durtschi, J. P. (2011). American Indian gay, bisexual and two-spirit men: A rapid assessment of HIV/AIDS risk factors, barriers to prevention and culturally-sensitive intervention. *Culture, Health & Sexuality, 13*(3), 283–298. doi:10.108 0/13691058.2010.525666

Cameron, M. (2005). Two-spirited Aboriginal people: Continuing cultural appropriation by non-Aboriginal society. *Canadian Woman Studies, 24*(2/3), 123–127.

Chae, D. H., & Walters, K. L. (2009). Racial discrimination and racial identity attitudes in relation to self-rated health and physical pain and impairment among two-spirit American Indians/Alaska Natives. *American Journal of Public Health, 99,* S144–S151.

Evans-Campbell, T., Fredriksen-Goldsen, K. I., Walters, K. L., & Stately, A. (2007). Caregiving experiences among American Indian two-spirit men and women: Contemporary and historical roles. *Journal of Gay & Lesbian Social Services, 18*(3–4), 75–92. doi:10.1300/J041v18n03_05

Evans-Campbell, T., Walters, K. L., Pearson, C. R., & Campbell, C. D. (2012). Indian boarding school experience, substance use, and mental health among urban two-spirit American Indian/Alaska Natives. *American Journal of Drug & Alcohol Abuse, 38,* 421–427.

Everett, B., MacFarlane, D. A., Reynolds, V. A., & Anderson, H. D. (2013). Not on our backs: Supporting counsellors in navigating the ethics of multiple relationships within queer, two-spirit, and/or trans communities. *Canadian Journal of Counselling and Psychotherapy, 47*(1), 14–28.

Fieland, K. C., Walters, K. L., & Simoni, J. M. (2007). Determinants of health among two-spirit American Indians and Alaska Natives. In I. H. Meyer & M. E. Northridge (Eds.), *The health of sexual minorities: Public health perspectives on lesbian, gay, bisexual, transgender populations* (pp. 268–300). New York, NY: Springer.

Garrett, M. T. (1996). Reflection by the riverside: The traditional education of Native American children. *Journal of Humanistic Counseling, Education and Development, 35,* 12–28.

Garrett, M. T., & Barret, B. (2003). Two-spirit: Counseling Native American gay, lesbian, and bisexual people. *Journal of Multicultural Counseling and Development, 31,* 131–142.

Garrett, M. T., & Myers, J. E. (1996). The rule of opposites: A paradigm for counseling Native Americans. *Journal of Multicultural Counseling and Development, 24,* 89–104.

Hall, C. (1994). Great spirit. In M. Thompson (Ed.), *Gay soul: Finding the heart of gay spirit and nature* (pp. 116–130). San Francisco, CA: Harper.

Jacobs, S., Thomas, W. (Navajo), & Lang, S. (1997). Introduction. In S. Jacobs, W. Thomas (Navajo), & S. Lang (Eds.), *Two-spirit people: Native American gender identity, sexuality, and spirituality* (pp. 1–20). Chicago, IL: University of Illinois Press.

Lang, S. (2011). Transformations of gender in Native American cultures. *Litteraria Pragensia, 21*(42), 70–81.

Lehavot, K., Walters, K. L., & Simoni, J. M. (2010). Abuse, mastery, and health among lesbian, bisexual, and two-spirit American Indian and Alaska Native women. *Psychology of Violence, 1*(S), 53–67. doi:10.1037/2152-0828.1.S.53

Meyer, I. H. (2003). Prejudice, social stress, and mental health in lesbian, gay, and bisexual populations: Conceptual issues and research evidence. *Psychological Bulletin, 129,* 674–697. doi:10.1037/0033-2909.129.5.674

National Center for Health Statistics. (2006). *Health, United States, 2006 with chartbook on trends in the health of Americans.* Hyattsville, MD: U.S. Department of Health and Human Services.

National Center for Health Statistics. (2016). *Health of American Indian or Alaska Native population.* Retrieved from http://www.cdc.gov/nchs/fastats/american-indian-health.htm

Norrell, B. (2001, August 1). *Mother of murdered Navajo teen says it was a hate crime.* Retrieved from the *Indian Country Today* website: http://www.indiancountry.com

Robinson, M. (2014). "A hope to lift both my spirits": Preventing bisexual erasure in aboriginal schools. *Journal of Bisexuality, 14*(1), 18–35. doi:10.1080/15299716.2014.872457

Sheppard, M., & Mayo, J. B. (2013). The social construction of gender and sexuality: Learning from two-spirit traditions. *Social Studies, 104*(6), 259–270. doi:10.1080/00377996.2013.788472

Simoni, J., Walters, K., Balsam, K., & Meyers, S. (2006). Victimization, substance use, and HIV risk behaviors among gay/bisexual/two-spirit and heterosexual American Indian men in New York City. *American Journal of Public Health, 96,* 2240–2245. doi:10.2105/AJPH.2004.054056

Smithers, G. D. (2014). Cherokee "two-spirits": Gender, ritual, and spirituality in the Native South. *Early American Studies, 12,* 626–651. doi:10.1353/eam.2014.0023

Tafoya, T. (1996). Native two-spirit people. In R. P. Cabaj & T. S. Stein (Eds.), *Textbook of homosexuality and mental health* (pp. 603–617). Washington, DC: American Psychiatric Press.

Tafoya, T. (1997). Native gay and lesbian issues: The two-spirited. In B. Greene (Ed.), *Ethnic and cultural diversity among lesbians and gay men* (pp. 1–10). Thousand Oaks, CA: Sage.

Thomas, W., & Jacobs, S. (1999). ". . . And we are still here": From Berdache to two-spirit people. *American Indian Culture & Research Journal, 23*(2), 91–107.

U.S. Department of Health and Human Services. (2001). *Child maltreatment: 1999.* Washington, DC: U.S. Government Printing Office.

Walters, K. L. (1997). Urban lesbian and gay American Indian identity. *Journal of Gay & Lesbian Social Services, 6*(2), 43–65. doi:10.1300/J041v06n02_05

Walters, K. L., Evans-Campbell, T., Simoni, J. M., Ronquillo, T., & Bhuyan, R. (2006). "My spirit in my heart": Identity experiences and challenges among American Indian two-spirit women. *Journal of Lesbian Studies, 10*(1–2), 125–149. doi:10.1300/J155v10n01_07

Walters, K. L., Simoni, J. M., & Evans-Campbell, T. (2002). Substance use among American Indians and Alaska Natives: Incorporating culture in an "indigenist" stress-coping paradigm. *Public Health Report, 117*(Suppl. 1), S104–S117.

Walters, K. L., Simoni, J. M., & Horwath, P. F. (2001). Sexual orientation bias experiences and service needs of gay, lesbian, bisexual, transgendered, and two-spirited American Indians. *Journal of Gay & Lesbian Social Services: Issues in Practice, Policy & Research, 13*(1–2), 133–149. doi:10.1300/J041v13n01_10

Wilson, A. M. (2007). N'tacimowin inna nah': Coming into two-spirit identities. *Dissertation Abstracts International: Section A. Humanities and Social Sciences, 68*(6), 2341.

Yuan, N. P., Duran, B. M., Walters, K. L., Pearson, C. R., & Evans-Campbell, T. A. (2014). Alcohol misuse and associations with childhood maltreatment and out-of-home placement among urban two-spirit American Indian and Alaska Native people. *International Journal of Environmental Research and Public Health, 11,* 10461–10479. doi:10.3390/ijerph111010461

Section IV

EMERGING ISSUES

• • •

A few salient themes in the emerging research on lesbian, gay, bisexual, transgender, queer, questioning, intersex, asexual, ally, pansexual/polysexual, and two-spirited (LGBTQI+) issues reflect the current personal and political problems that the queer community faces. First, the role of ethnicity is explored for people of color as well as immigrant populations. Second, the role of religion as both a positive and negative influence for affectional orientation and gender minorities is explored. Finally, the role of counselors as advocates for LGBTQI+ people in multiple contexts is discussed.

THE ROLE OF ETHNICITY

Chapter 20

Counseling an LGBTQI+ Person of Color

Joel M. Filmore and Misty M. Ginicola

*Silence kills the soul; it diminishes its possibilities to rise
and fly and explore. Silence withers what makes you human.
The soul shrinks, until it's nothing.*

—Marlon Riggs

• • •

Awareness of Attitudes and Beliefs Self-Check

1. Close your eyes and picture a gay Black man. What do you see? How are your biases and stereotypes of both being gay and being Black present in your image? How does it change if you picture a woman?
2. What does your culture teach about gender roles? Who evidenced these gender roles as you grew up?
3. If you had to leave the family and culture of your origin, what would impact you the most?

Case Study

Eric, a 24-year-old Asian male, comes to counseling to get help in figuring out how to come out to his family. He reports that he knew he was gay at age 9. Even then, he knew how "unacceptable" it was for him to like other boys. He just knew that he was gay and that no one could ever find out. Eric's first suicide attempt was in his freshman year of high school. The message that he heard from his family, culture, friends, and classmates was that it was not okay to be gay. "Every time I looked in the mirror, that is what I saw—a gay boy. I hated myself." He reports that he attempted suicide again at 16 years old. After that attempt, he was sent to counseling. Slowly he began coming to terms with his affectional orientation. He reports that in college he was finally able to embrace being out at his university and was active in the queer campus community. However, he reports that he never felt fully comfortable. He often experienced microaggressions surrounding his ethnicity, even from other lesbian, gay, bisexual, transgender, queer, questioning, intersex, asexual, ally, pansexual/polysexual, and two-spirited (LGBTQI+) people. He also reports experiencing racism in terms of dating. He would connect with other men only to hear them say, "Sorry, I'm just not into Asian guys." After a few unsuccessful relationships, he began dating Turrell, an African American man who attended the same university; he is now in graduate school. Eric says that he and Turrell have been together for almost 2 years. They want to meet each other's families and move forward in their relationship. Turrell is currently out, but his relationship with his family is strained. Eric says he cannot imagine coming out to his family. He has recently had an increase in suicidal thoughts and depression.

• • •

Ethnicity and Affectional Orientation

Although all persons have multiple intersectional identities, such as race/ethnicity and affectional orientation, most LGBTQI+ developmental theories are based solely on a single identity of either race/ethnicity or affectional orientation (Fukuyama & Ferguson, 2000). Thus, these studies often leave out minorities. Of the research that focuses on identity development in terms of affectional orientation, the majority originates from research on White gay male populations. In that research, White gay males are used as the norm, and all other affectional racial populations are viewed from a perspective of similarity or dissimilarity (Parks, Hughes, & Matthews, 2004).

The developmental research on White gay and lesbian populations supports the notion of general sequential development of identity (Cass, 1979; McCarn & Fassinger, 1996). However, there is little research on the identity development of queer people of color (QPOC). This presents a difficult situation for clinical professionals as they attempt to navigate and understand the experiences of their queer clients of color. Anecdotally speaking, one could understand that many clinicians who work with QPOC might think that having intersectional identities means that their clients might experience multiple challenges, but the reality is that with multiple minority identities come exponential distress, problems, and challenges (Meyer, 2003).

QPOC are at a significantly higher risk than queer Caucasians for depression and suicide (Alegría et al., 2007). As they experience both discrimination and prejudice because of their race and LGBTQI+ minority status, they may experience multiple layers of oppression in addition to other marginalized identities, such as being of advanced age, being female, having a disability, and so on. They also experience unique cultural factors within their particular intersection that make them potentially unsafe in each individual context (Chu, Goldblum, Floyd, & Bongar, 2010; Ghabrial, 2016). For example, it may not be safe to come out as LGBTQI+ in their ethnic culture, but they may also experience race-based prejudice in the queer communities. These experiences of discrimination can lead to greater psychological distress, greater acculturative stress, and worse mental health (Araújo Dawson & Panchanadeswaran, 2010; Moyerman & Forman, 1992). Sutter and Perrin (2016) found that among QPOC, LGBTQI+-based discrimination impacted mental health directly, which led to suicidality. Similarly, when QPOC experienced race-based discrimination, it led to significantly worse mental health (Sutter & Perrin, 2016). In fact, QPOC have cited feeling disconnected with both communities, navigating the relationships between their ethnicity and LGBTQI+ identity, and coming out as causing intense stress and anxiety (Ghabrial, 2016). The stress of blending two identities whose communities do not accept each other as well as managing multiple marginalized statuses accounts for this distress (Crosby, 2007). This disturbance will depend on the level of identity integration that a client has been able to accomplish with each identity (Ohnishi, Ibrahim, & Grzegorek, 2006). In addition, differences in each ethnic culture may create diverse types of difficulties for LGBTQI+ people of color.

Despite the fact that QPOC have been largely ignored in research, there is evidence to suggest that cultural issues play a role in how their affectional orientation is expressed and emerges (Bieschke, 2008). The struggle between respecting one's cultural identity, norms, and traditions and having the desire and need to identify authentically can have a profound impact on the development of sexual identity as well as the coming out process (Chung, Szymanski, & Markle, 2012). Most QPOC will internalize some level of heterosexist and homophobic prejudice because stigmas surrounding LGBTQI+ identities are part of the cultural context in which they are raised (Chung et al., 2012). African Americans, Latin Americans, Asian Americans, and Native Americans experience difficulty navigating their ethnicity and LGBTQI+ identity. As Native Americans were discussed at great length in Chapter 19 because of their unique history of acceptance of the two-spirited, only African Americans, Latin Americans, and Asian Americans are discussed further here.

African Americans

Although we do not intend to present an exhaustive discussion surrounding African American culture, four areas intersect with LGBTQI+ issues in a significant manner: increased racism and heterosexism, masculinity and stigma, issues surrounding HIV, and the role of the Black church.

Racism and Heterosexism

Because African Americans experience significantly higher rates of racism in society than other ethnic minority groups, the experience of heterosexism and internalized homophobia, which is directly related to psychosocial distress, becomes significantly more impactful in Black LGBTQI+ persons. This is particularly salient for African American women, who face three minority statuses as LGBTQI+, Black, and female (Syzmanski & Meyer, 2008). The greater number of marginalized identities relates to increases in psychological distress, health issues, relational problems, and feelings of invisibility surrounding one or more of the intersectional identities (Brooks, Inman, Malouf, Klinger, & Kaduvettoor, 2008). Black women in particular can be impacted by messages of hierarchical and patriarchal culture, by which they are further oppressed (Hagen, Arczynski, Morrow, & Hawxhurst, 2011). As the number of one's multiple marginalized identities increases, so does the likelihood of experiencing microaggressions, which are incredibly detrimental to mental health (Sue, 2010).

Masculinity

The construct of modern Black masculinity is partially due to the impact of oppressive and discriminatory experiences toward the Black community. The dominant White culture defines masculinity in terms of behavior and power; however, Black men cannot always achieve these ideals because they are denied traditional opportunities of masculine affirmation such as education, employment, and property ownership (Malebranche, 2003). Therefore, often exaggerated behavioral standards for masculinity take the place of status indicators (Malebranche, 2003). These behavioral standards include how one holds oneself, hypersexuality and prowess, managing impressions of others, emotional constriction, and masculine posturing to show evidence of strength and power (Majors, 1992; Malebranche, 2003; Wolfe, 2003). This can inadvertently lead to the rejection of any semblance of femininity in that masculine context. Concordantly, in the Black culture, "homosexuality" is often seen as a deviant behavior that has infiltrated the culture from the White population (Harris, 2010).

All things that represent Whiteness, then, may inherently be rejected by the Black culture, particularly because of the history of slavery, oppression, and discrimination. African Americans who attend college or speak Standard English can be harassed for acting White. The image of a Black man's masculinity is also distorted through the limited images in the media of overtly sexual heterosexual athletes or criminals. Media images of the LGBTQI+ community are often seen as the opposite: as effeminate, affectionate, or celebratory, which all reflect cultural norms of a White LGBTQI+ community (Malebranche, Fields, Bryant, & Harper, 2009).

Because of these stereotypes, Black men who have sex with men (BMSM) are seen through this lens and victimized, stigmatized, and discriminated against in their own culture and community (E. L. Fields et al., 2015). When Black gay men exhibit gender and affectional orientation variance openly, it contradicts the way in which Black men experience their masculinity in both a sexual and racial context (Davis, 1999). These problematic messages lead to immense psychological distress and fear of being found out: BMSM report feeling great anxiety surrounding keeping their affectional orientation a secret (E. L. Fields et al., 2015). This can clearly impact Black gay men's willingness to disclose their LGBTQI+ identity (Malebranche et al., 2009). The social pressure to conform to Black norms of masculinity is such that it may impact compensatory sexual behaviors of BMSM in such a way that these men may engage in substance use, violence, fighting, and risky sexual behavior to maintain their manhood (E. L. Fields et al., 2015; McCoy, 2009). BMSM are also more likely than heterosexual African Americans to avoid preventive services and messages surrounding HIV for fear that they could be identified as gay, which is linked to exponentially increasing rates of HIV in BMSM (E. L. Fields et al., 2015).

HIV and the Black Gay Male

In the African American community, HIV infections have become an epidemic (Arnold & Marlon, 2009; S. D. Fields, Malebranche, & Feist-Price, 2008; Jones et al., 2008; Lemelle, 2004; Lichtenstein, 2000; Malebranche, 2003; Malebranche, Arriola, Jenkins, Dauria, & Patel, 2010; Malebranche et al., 2009; Mays, Cochran, & Zamudio, 2004; Williams, Wyatt, Resell, Peterson, & Asuan-O'Brien, 2004). African American gay and bisexual men are at the highest risk for the spread of HIV; they also represent the fastest growing new cases of HIV, with a 20% increase in new cases in just 2 years, from 2008 to 2010, although this increase has now stabilized (Centers for Disease Control and Prevention, 2016). Although scientists have been unable to pinpoint the cause of this disparity in the rapid acquisition of HIV infection in the African American community, theorists believe that masculine gender-role pressure and the lack of support from the family and the community at large may be to blame (Arnold & Marlon, 2009; Malebranche et al., 2010; Mays et al., 2004; Miller, 2005a). This lack of support may clearly affect the development of Black men who identify as gay as well as those who, although they do not own the label of gay, actively participate in sexual activity with other men. This serves to increase high-risk behaviors that directly increase the rates of HIV infection in this community (S. D. Fields et al., 2008; Lichtenstein, 2000; Malebranche, Peterson, Fullilove, & Stackhouse, 2004). Another cause of this increased acquisition of HIV could be the social phenomenon of being on the *down low*. A man on the down low refuses to claim the identity of gay but engages in sexual activity with other men, all the while maintaining a heterosexual masculine persona and role in society, even to the extent of having a girlfriend/wife and family (Lapinski, Braz, & Maloney, 2010). The experience of being on the down low is related to the social stigma associated with being gay in the African American community as well as to the influence and role of organized religion in the Black community (Lapinski et al., 2010).

The Black Church

The African American church has historically had a significant influence in the Black community, and even those individuals who do not necessarily actively participate in Black religious institutions are still significantly impacted by the views and beliefs of the church (Lemelle, 2004). Black faith-based organizations have their beginnings in historical discrimination and segregation (Lemelle, 2004). Because they were denied opportunities to worship in White churches in larger society, Black persons organized their own churches in Black religious denominations as a means of accessing spirituality and collective coping (Pinkney, 2000). Black churches have a historic role of providing education, spiritual formation, and shelter from the oppressive forces of the dominant social culture (Billingsley, 1992). As a result of historical experiences with slavery, the African American church has taken a more conservative stand when it comes to morality and worldly involvement. This has included the rejection of "homosexuality" as immoral. Unfortunately, this has had the unintended effect of hindering the Black church's response to the HIV epidemic (Miller, 2007).

The struggle for the Black church is among helping those in need (e.g., HIV-positive individuals who are sick), tackling sources of oppression for LGBTQI+ persons, and condoning sexual behavior that it strongly preaches against (Fullilove & Robert, 1999). Many churches are immobilized because of adherence to interpretations of biblical scriptures that endorse homophobia and heterosexism and limit the inclusion of programming to prevent HIV (Fullilove & Robert, 1999; Khosrovani, Poudeh, & Parks-Yancy, 2008). Unfortunately, these negative attitudes have been found to be directly linked to HIV in gay males. In a study of seropositive Black men, factors that impeded the successful resolution of HIV status included Black homophobia, issues coping with dual identities, and life histories that included severe trauma and rejection by Black churches (Rose, 1998).

When Black LGBTQI+ persons are not welcome in the church, it has the effect of decreasing their religious identity as well as threatening the historical and cultural resources that are unique to the African American church (Miller, 2005b). Because of their lower than average socioeconomic status, many African Americans rely on organizations such as the church to assist them in meeting many of their basic needs, including health care. Faith-based organizations' disaffirming attitudes toward LGBTQI+ persons may be possible deterrents to their seeking health services. Such attitudes create strained relationships in their social networks and environments where care is most needed, thereby creating unintentional distance between the provider and the client, which in turn reduces the capacity for social support (Lemelle, 2004). These negative experiences in the Black church have been found to negatively impact the African American LGBTQI+ population's mental health (Hagen et al., 2011).

In one qualitative study, a participant described his feelings as a child growing up in the Black church:

> I was repressed. I use to think I was abnormal. My brothers and mother [are] very religious. We would go to church all the time. The feelings, about liking another guy, I did not explore any of that stuff, I was too scared. It was the same but different in church. I was scared because the preacher would say stuff like, "we ain't hatching no faggots up in here." And the whole church, including my mother, would scream "Amen!" I knew what a faggot was because my brothers called me that. (Miller, 2007, p. 57)

The participants in Miller's (2007) study experienced homophobia as demeaning and painful, negatively impacting their humanity and dignity. The dominant view that "homosexuality" is a sin is an assault on the individual, requiring the development of coping skills in Black LGBTQI+ persons (Miller, 2005b). In order to diminish the negative feelings that are created, some Black LGBTQI+ persons feel that they must make a choice between their affectional orientation and their affiliation with the church, and sometimes the community. For Black LGBTQI+ persons who grew up in the church, the castigation of affectional orientation variance can be alienating, and these feelings have the potential to challenge their willingness to continue their connection to the church and, possibly, with God (Miller, 2005a, 2005b).

Latin Americans

Although most LGBTQI+ persons have enjoyed more accepting attitudes in mainstream culture, there still exists increased prejudice toward this population among Latin Americans (Toro-Alfonso & Varas-Díaz, 2004). Latin communities' dominant heterosexist biases continue to impede the ability of queer Latinos and Latinas to disclose their affectional orientation (Connally, Wedemeyer, & Smith, 2013). As with African Americans, several specific cultural elements may impact Latin Americans' experience of intersectionality when attempting to integrate their LGBTQI+ identity. These cultural experiences include, among others, machismo and *marianismo*, Catholicism, *familismo*, and *respeto.*

Machismo and Marianismo

The concept of *machismo,* or strong male pride evidenced in stereotypical masculine behavior, such as sexual virility and power, is a pervasive cultural value present in Latin American communities (Goicolea, Coe, & Ohman, 2014; Marcos & Cordero, 2009; Stevens, 1973). This focus on machismo is the opposite of *marianismo,* which represents the female value of feminine virtue, represented by piousness, purity, and passiveness. This set of values represents the rigidness of gender roles in the Latin community, which can be harmful to both heterosexual men and women but incredibly damaging to Latin American LGBTQI+ persons. The presence of gender and affectional orientation variance directly violates this binary gender differential, paving the way for oppression, discrimination, and violence focused toward the LGBTQI+ Latin community. It can also make it difficult for LGBTQI+ Latin Americans to develop a positive identity surrounding such gender and affectional orientation variance.

Catholicism

Another influence on LGBTQI+ acceptance in the Latin community, as well as the perpetuation of heteronormativity and homophobia, is related to the most commonly practiced religion of Latin Americans, Catholicism (García, Gray-Stanley, & Ramirez-Valles, 2008). Growing up in a Latin community, it is common to experience the immersion of the Catholic religion in family, schools, and the overarching culture. Although Catholicism and religion in general can serve as a protective factor against a variety of difficulties, for LGBTQI+ Latin Americans, the lack of acceptance in the church can cause further complications to their positive development of identity as LGBTQI+ persons. As adolescents, Latin Americans may experience incredible conflicts surrounding their faith, which represents a value set immersed in the larger culture. As adults, LGBTQI+ Latin Americans are likely to abandon their culture's primary religion. Among those who seek out other religions, many find another religion that is more welcoming of LGBTQI+ persons.

Familismo

In addition to machismo and general Catholic values, Latin Americans also have the influence of *familismo* (Falicov, 2010; Freeberg & Stein, 1996). *Familismo* is a construct that underscores the importance of the family unit. The family is seen as a single collectivist organism that sacrifices individuality for the betterment of the collective. It is not uncommon for traditional Latino families to live together or close by, even after marriage. There is a loyalty, reciprocity, and solidarity in the immediate family, but also with the extended family, that fosters interdependence. It is this interdependence that can hinder queer Latinos from coming out. If they are rejected based on their LGBTQI+ identity, Latin Americans may lose their family and community, which are absolutely essential components of their cultural identity.

Respeto

The construct of respect, or *respeto*, is a guiding principle in traditional Latin families (Connally et al., 2013; Freeberg & Stein, 1996). The notion of respect for authority as well as for elders is a traditional value ingrained in Latin children from birth. This conditioning and respect for authority not only is associated with prosocial behavior but helps to increase parental oversight, even in the absence of the parents. Many Latin families may be unsupportive of gender and affectional orientation variance, given other values in the Latin American culture. Therefore, when LGBTQI+ persons do disclose their gender or affectional orientation identity, it may be seen as a direct affront to the idea of *respeto*; the family may see them as disrespecting themselves, their roles, and their family, which can bring shame. In addition, acculturation to Western culture may also be seen as a factor in identifying as LGBTQI+, which can bring about further feelings of disloyalty and diminished family functioning (Connally et al., 2013).

Asian Americans

As minorities, Asian Americans also evidence increased minority stress. In Asian American cultures, several cultural values can come into direct conflict for LGBTQI+ persons: stigma, complementarity, collectivism and conformity, and shame.

Stigma

Being LGBTQI+ often carries with it an intense stigma in Asian cultures. Affectional orientation variance is still also widely seen as dysfunctional and abnormal in Asian cultures. Even in samples of Chinese psychiatrists, the majority believe that it is not normative (Cong & Gao, 1999). In some Asian cultures, it is still considered illegal to engage in sexual acts with someone of the same sex (Bhaskaran, 2002). Therefore, this view of LGBTQI+ persons as flawed, broken, or abnormal impacts the psyches of LGBTQI+ persons, who may internalize messages of homophobia as well as remain closeted and develop low self-esteem (Ohnishi et al., 2006).

Complementarity

Harmony and complementarity are reflected in Asian cultures (Bridges, Selvidge, & Matthews, 2003; Chung & Katayama, 1998). They are reflected in the concept of the yin and the yang as well as multiple notions throughout the cultures. Where it becomes problematic for LGBTQI+ Asian persons is that this concept additionally applies to gender and relationships: Males and females are seen as binary opposites that must merge to bring about balance. This then can be interpreted to mean that same-sex relationships are unnatural, disharmonious, and not in balance, violating essential components of Asian cultures.

Collectivism and Conformity

In some Asian populations there is a strong pressure to conform to traditional gender roles, norms, and collectivist values, much like in some Latino populations, with loyalty and obedience to family considered the expectation rather than a suggestion (Ohnishi & Ibrahim, 1999). The strong pull of conformity to group norms, along with obligation and duty, is a factor that can negatively impact an Asian affectional minority from coming out or living an authentic life that may violate gender roles. In many Asian families, daughters and sons serve specific familial roles, as do their future heterosexual partners. These roles will be different for an LGBTQI+ person who may not conform. There can also be great conflict between acculturating and honoring the family's traditional expectations.

Shame

Violating cultural values or family expectations can bring shame and embarrassment to the entire Asian family, going back several generations (Chan, 1989). Because an LGBTQI+ identity can violate multiple cultural values and roles, individuals may wait to disclose their identity for fear of shaming their family. If they do disclose, they potentially risk a pervasively negative and rejecting reaction, with an admonition regarding the shame they have brought to the family (Ohnishi et al., 2006). Ohnishi and colleagues (2006) cited a case in which an Asian American lesbian client, after coming out, was told by her mother "that she would rather that she (her daughter) gets cancer and dies than identify as a lesbian" (p. 83). Experiences like this can understandably lead to increases in suicidality and shame.

Culture-Centered Counseling

Wynn and West-Olatunji (2009) postulated that ethnic minorities (African Americans, Asian Americans, Latin Americans, and Native Americans) who were also LGBTQI+ were at risk for more psychological distress due to the current cultural stigma surrounding their ethnicity. In a counseling framework, counselors should avoid imposing their own schemas onto the client but rather should engage in viewing the world from their clients' point of view, with all of their intersectional identities. Considering ecosystemic factors and the impact of oppression, prejudice, heteronormativity, personal and cultural historical experiences, religion, racism, and family dynamics and beliefs, the counselor should conceptualize clients' way of viewing their LGBTQI+ identity and associated needs. Counselors should consider the client's social context as well as how multiple marginalized statuses may influence these needs. The culture-centered approach involves first engaging clients in a reflection surrounding the impact oppression, marginalization, and negative LGBTQI+ messages have had on them. The second stage involves dialoguing with clients to achieve insight into new solutions. This could involve challenging those cultural values as well as evaluating the benefits and challenges surrounding disclosure. Finding appropriate ethnic and LGBTQI+ social support is also crucial in this stage. Finally, the counselor helps move clients to action, encouraging them to actively confront barriers in their lives.

Conclusion

LGBTQI+ persons of color experience another level of difficulty in integrating their intersectional identities. Cultural values that are an integral part of their ethnic identity may conflict strongly with their identity as LGBTQI+ people. Often rigid gender roles and expectations are part of an overall collective belief system that is challenged by a nonbinary and/or a nonheterosexual persona. People may then be faced with an identity crisis: They may feel that they can be Black/Latin/Asian/Native *or* LGBTQI+ but not Black/Latin/Asian/Native *and* LGBTQI+. Although only ethnicity was discussed here, the intersectional identities of LGBTQI+ persons are vast: Their age and generation, disability status, religion and/or spirituality, socioeconomic status, and immigrant or indigenous status all interact with their ethnicity, affectional orientation, and sense of gender. A counselor needs to help clients unpack the multiple levels of marginalization that lead to increased minority stress in their multiple identities.

Questions for Further Discussion

1. What are the cultural messages that Eric has received regarding his affectional orientation?
2. What similarities does Eric's Asian culture have with African American cultural beliefs that impact the judgment of LGBTQI+ persons? What differences are there between the two cultures in terms of these values?
3. What similarities does Eric's Asian culture have with Latin American cultural beliefs that impact the judgment of LGBTQI+ persons? What differences are there between the two cultures in terms of these values?
4. What similarities does Eric's Asian culture have with Native cultural beliefs that impact the judgment of LGBTQI+ persons? What differences are there between the two cultures in terms of these values?
5. How could Eric's counselor approach his unique needs as an Asian American gay male about to come out to his family?

Resources

1. Visit the Queer People of Color Collective website at https://queerpoccollective.com/.
2. Read more about and hear people's stories regarding the experience of homophobia and racism at https://462thirdworldsolidarity.wordpress.com/the-unique-challenges-facing-queer-people-of-color/.
3. Surf resources for QPOC through the Association for Lesbian, Gay, Bisexual, and Transgender Issues in Counseling at http://www.algbtic.org/queer-people-of-color.html.

References

Alegría, M., Mulvaney-Day, N., Torres, M., Polo, A., Cao, Z., & Canino, G. (2007). Prevalence of psychiatric disorders across Latino subgroups in the United States. *American Journal of Public Health, 97,* 68–75. doi:10.2105/AJPH.2006.087205

Araújo Dawson, B., & Panchanadeswaran, S. (2010). Discrimination and acculturative stress among first generation Dominicans. *Hispanic Journal of Behavioral Sciences, 32,* 216–231. doi:10.1177/0739986310364750

Arnold, E. A. B., & Marlon, M. (2009). Constructing home and family: How the ballroom community supports African American GLBTQ youth in the face of HIV/AIDS. *Journal of Gay & Lesbian Social Services, 21,* 171–188.

Bhaskaran, S. (2002). The politics of penetration: Section 377 of the India Penal Code. In R. Vanita (Ed.), *Queering India* (pp. 15–29). New York, NY: Routledge.

Bieschke, K. J. (2008). We've come a long way, baby. *The Counseling Psychologist, 36,* 631–638. doi:10.1177/0011000008320077

Billingsley, A. (1992). *Climbing Jacob's ladder: The enduring legacy of African-American families.* New York, NY: Simon & Schuster.

Bridges, S. K., Selvidge, M. M. D., & Matthews, C. R. (2003). Lesbian women of color: Therapeutic issues and challenges. *Journal of Multicultural Counseling and Development, 31,* 113–130.

Brooks, L., Inman, A., Malouf, M., Klinger, R., & Kaduvettoor, A. (2008). Ethnic minority bisexual women: Understanding the invisible population. *Journal of LGBT Issues in Counseling, 2*(4), 260–284.

Cass, V. C. (1979). Homosexual identity formation: A theoretical model. *Journal of Homosexuality, 4*(3), 219–235.

Centers for Disease Control and Prevention. (2016). *HIV among African Americans.* Retrieved from http://www.cdc.gov/hiv/group/racialethnic/africanamericans/

Chan, C. S. (1989). Issues of identity development among Asian-American lesbians and gay men. *Journal of Counseling & Development, 68,* 16–20.

Chu, J. P., Goldblum, P., Floyd, R., & Bongar, B. (2010). The cultural theory and model of suicide. *Applied & Preventive Psychology, 14,* 25–40. doi:10.1016/j.appsy.2011.11.001

Chung, Y. B., & Katayama, M. (1998). Ethnic and sexual identity development of Asian-American lesbian and gay adolescents. *Professional School Counseling, 1,* 21–25.

Chung, Y. B., Szymanski, D. M., & Markle, E. (2012). Sexual orientation and sexual identity: Theory, research, and practice. In N. A. Fouad, J. A. Carter, & L. M. Subich (Eds.), *APA handbook of counseling psychology: Vol. 1. Theories, research, and methods* (pp. 423–451). Washington, DC: American Psychological Association. doi:10.1037/13754-016

Cong, Z., & Gao, W. (1999). Xinli yisheng jiezhen tongxinglian xianzhuang de chubu diaocha [A preliminary survey to the psychotherapists working with homosexual clients]. *Chinese Journal of Behavioral Medical Science, 3,* 225.

Connally, D., Wedemeyer, R., & Smith, S. (2013). Cultural practice considerations: The coming out process for Mexican Americans along the rural U.S.-Mexican border. *Contemporary Rural Social Work, 5,* 243–248.

Crosby, T. E. (2007). Marginalized identities and multiple oppressions: GLBTQ people of color negotiating everyday life. *Dissertation Abstracts International: Section A. Humanities and Social Sciences, 68*(3), 1114.

Davis, J. E. (1999). Forbidden fruit: Black males' constructions of transgressive sexualities in middle school. In W. J. Letts IV & J. T. Sears (Eds.), *Queering elementary education: Advancing the dialogue about sexualities and schooling* (pp. 49–59). Boulder, CO: Rowan & Littlefield.

Falicov, C. J. (2010). Changing constructions of machismo for Latino men in therapy: "The devil never sleeps." *Family Process, 49*(3), 309–329. doi:10.1111/j.1545-5300.2010.01325.x

Fields, E. L., Bogart, L. M., Smith, K. C., Malebranche, D. J., Ellen, J., & Schuster, M. A. (2015). "I always felt I had to prove my manhood": Homosexuality, masculinity, gender role strain, and HIV risk among young Black men who have sex with men. *American Journal of Public Health, 105*(1), 122–131. doi:10.2105/AJPH.2013.301866

Fields, S. D., Malebranche, D., & Feist-Price, S. (2008). Childhood sexual abuse in Black men who have sex with men: Results from three qualitative studies. *Cultural Diversity and Ethnic Minority Psychology, 14*(4), 385–390. doi:10.1037/1099-9809.14.4.385

Freeberg, A. L., & Stein, C. H. (1996). Felt obligations towards parents in Mexican-American and Anglo-American young adults. *Journal of Social and Personal Relationships, 13,* 457–471. doi:10.1177/0265407596133009

Fullilove, M. T. F., & Robert, E. (1999). Stigma as an obstacle to AIDS action. *American Behavioral Scientist, 42,* 1117–1129.

Fukuyama, M. A., & Ferguson, A. D. (2000). Lesbian, gay, and bisexual people of color: Understanding cultural complexity and managing multiple oppressions. In R. M. Perez, K. A. DeBord, & K. J. Bieschke (Eds.), *Handbook of counseling and psychotherapy with lesbian, gay, and bisexual clients* (pp. 81–105). Washington, DC: American Psychological Association. doi:10.1037/10339-004

García, D. I., Gray-Stanley, J., & Ramirez-Valles, J. (2008). "The priest obviously doesn't know that I'm gay": The religious and spiritual journeys of Latino gay men. *Journal of Homosexuality, 55*, 411–436. doi:10.1080/00918360802345149

Ghabrial, M. A. (2016). "Trying to figure out where we belong": Narratives of racialized sexual minorities on community, identity, discrimination, and health. *Sexuality Research & Social Policy*. Advance online publication. doi:10.1007/s13178-016-0229-x

Goicolea, I., Coe, A.-B., & Ohman, A. (2014). Easy to oppose, difficult to propose: Young activist men's framing of alternative masculinities under the hegemony of machismo in Ecuador. *Young, 22*, 399–419.

Hagen, W. B., Arczynski, A. V., Morrow, S. L., & Hawxhurst, D. M. (2011). Lesbian, bisexual, and queer women's spirituality in feminist multicultural counseling. *Journal of LGBT Issues in Counseling, 5*, 220–236. doi:10.1080/15538605.2011.633070

Harris, A. C. (2010). Sex, stigma, and the Holy Ghost: The Black church and the construction of AIDS in New York City. *Journal of African American Studies, 14*, 21–43.

Jones, K. T., Johnson, W. D., Wheeler, D. P., Gray, P., Foust, E., & Gaiter, J. (2008). Nonsupportive peer norms and incarceration as HIV risk correlates for young Black men who have sex with men. *AIDS and Behavior, 12*(1), 41–50.

Khosrovani, M., Poudeh, R., & Parks-Yancy, R. (2008). How African-American ministers communicate HIV/AIDS-related health information to their congregants: A survey of selected Black churches in Houston, TX. *Mental Health, Religion & Culture, 11*, 661–670.

Lapinski, M. K., Braz, M. E., & Maloney, E. K. (2010). The down low, social stigma, and risky sexual behaviors: Insights from African-American men who have sex with men. *Journal of Homosexuality, 57*, 610–633. doi:10.1080/00918361003712020

Lemelle, A. J., Jr. (2004). African American attitudes toward gay males: Faith-based initiatives and implications for HIV/AIDS services. *Journal of African American Studies, 7*(4), 59–74.

Lichtenstein, B. (2000). Secret encounters: Black men, bisexuality, and AIDS in Alabama. *Medical Anthropology Quarterly, 14*, 374–393.

Majors, R. B., J. (1992). *Cool pose: The dilemmas of Black manhood in America*. New York, NY: Simon & Schuster.

Malebranche, D., Arriola, K., Jenkins, T., Dauria, E., & Patel, S. (2010). Exploring the "bisexual bridge": A qualitative study of risk behavior and disclosure of same-sex behavior among Black bisexual men. *American Journal of Public Health, 100*(1), 159–164. doi:10.2105/AJPH.2008.158725

Malebranche, D. J. (2003). Black men who have sex with men and the HIV epidemic: Next steps for public health. *American Journal of Public Health, 93*, 862–865.

Malebranche, D. J., Fields, E. L., Bryant, L. O., & Harper, S. R. (2009). Masculine socialization and sexual risk behaviors among Black men who have sex with men. *Men and Masculinities, 12*(1), 90–112.

Malebranche, D. J., Peterson, J. L., Fullilove, R. E., & Stackhouse, R. W. (2004). Race and sexual identity: Perceptions about medical culture and healthcare among Black men who have sex with men. *Journal of the National Medical Association, 96*(1), 97–107.

Marcos, N., & Cordero, T. (2009). *Situation of lesbian and trans women in Ecuador: Shadow report—international covenant on civil and political rights*. Quito, Ecuador: Taller de Comunicación Mujer/ International Gay and Lesbian Human Rights Commission.

Mays, V. M., Cochran, S. D., & Zamudio, A. (2004). HIV prevention research: Are we meeting the needs of African American men who have sex with men? *Journal of Black Psychology, 30*(1), 78–105. doi:10.1177/0095798403260265

McCarn, S. R., & Fassinger, R. E. (1996). Revisiting sexual minority identity formation: A new model of lesbian identity and its implications for counseling and research. *The Counseling Psychologist, 24*, 508–534.

McCoy, R. (2009). Ain't I a man: Gender meanings among Black men who have sex with men. *Souls, 11*(3), 337–346. doi:10.1080/10999940903088952

Meyer, I. H. (2003). Prejudice, social stress, and mental health in lesbian, gay, and bisexual populations: Conceptual issues and research evidence. *Psychological Bulletin, 129,* 674–697. doi:10.1037/0033-2909.129.5.674

Miller, R. L., Jr. (2005a). An appointment with God: AIDS, place, and spirituality. *Journal of Sex Research, 42*(1), 35–45.

Miller, R. L., Jr. (2005b). Look what God can do: African American gay men, AIDS, and spirituality. *Journal of HIV/AIDS & Social Services, 4*(3), 25–46.

Miller, R. L., Jr. (2007). Legacy denied: African American gay men, AIDS, and the Black church. *Social Work, 52*(1), 51–61.

Moyerman, D. R., & Forman, B. D. (1992). Acculturation and adjustment: A meta-analytic study. *Hispanic Journal of Behavioral Sciences, 14,* 163–200. doi:10.1177/07399863920142001

Ohnishi, H., & Ibrahim, F. A. (1999). Culture-specific counseling strategies for Japanese nationals in the United States of America. *International Journal for the Advancement of Counseling, 21,* 189–206.

Ohnishi, H., Ibrahim, F., & Grzegorek, J. (2006). Intersections of identities: Counseling lesbian, gay, bisexual, and transgender Asian-Americans. *Journal of LGBT Issues in Counseling, 1*(3), 77–94.

Parks, C. A., Hughes, T. L., & Matthews, A. K. (2004). Race/ethnicity and sexual orientation: Intersecting identities. *Cultural Diversity and Ethnic Minority Psychology, 10*(3), 241–254. doi:10.1037/1099-9809.10.3.241

Pinkney, A. (2000). *Black American.* Upper Saddle River, NJ: Prentice Hall.

Rose, S. (1998). Searching for the meaning of AIDS: Issues affecting seropositive Black gay men. In V. J. Derlega & A. P. Barbee (Eds.), *HIV and social interaction* (pp. 56–82). Thousand Oaks, CA: Sage.

Stevens, E. P. (1973). Machismo and marianismo. *Society, 10*(6), 57–63.

Sue, D. W. (2010). *Microaggressions in everyday life: Race, gender, and sexual orientation.* Hoboken, NJ: Wiley.

Sutter, M., & Perrin, P. B. (2016). Discrimination, mental health, and suicidal ideation among LGBTQ people of color. *Journal of Counseling Psychology, 63*(1), 98–105. doi:10.1037/cou0000126

Szymanski, D. M., & Meyer, D. (2008). Racism and heterosexism as correlates of psychological distress in African American sexual minority women. *Journal of LGBT Issues in Counseling, 2*(2), 94–108. doi:10.1080/15538600802125423

Toro-Alfonso, J., & Varas-Díaz, N. (2004). Los otros: Prejuicio y distancia social hacia hombres gay y lesbianas en una muestra de estudiantes de nivel universitario. The others: Prejudice and social distance towards gays and lesbians in a sample of university students. *International Journal of Clinical and Health Psychology, 4,* 537–551.

Williams, J. K., Wyatt, G. E., Resell, J., Peterson, J., & Asuan-O'Brien, A. (2004). Psychosocial issues among gay- and non-gay-identifying HIV-seropositive African American and Latino MSM. *Cultural Diversity & Ethnic Minority Psychology, 10*(3), 268–286.

Wolfe, W. (2003). Overlooked role of African American males' hypermasculinity in the epidemic of unintended pregnancies and HIV/AIDS cases with young African American women. *Journal of the National Medical Association, 95,* 846–852.

Wynn, R., & West-Olatunji, C. (2009). Use of culture-centered counseling theory with ethnically diverse LGBT clients. *Journal of LGBT Issues in Counseling, 3,* 198–214. doi:10.1080/15538600903317218

Chapter 21

Counseling LGBTQI+ Immigrants

David Barreto, Amy Moore-Ramirez, Melanie Kautzman-East, and Ryan Liberati

I'm a gay, undocumented immigrant; I have to be optimistic.
—Jose Antonio Vargas

• • •

Awareness of Attitudes and Beliefs Self-Check

1. Close your eyes and picture a gay immigrant. What do you see? How are your biases and stereotypes present in your image?
2. What immigrants do you know who are out as lesbian, gay, bisexual, transgender, queer, questioning, intersex, asexual, ally, pansexual/polysexual, and two-spirited (LGBTQI+), including celebrities or characters in movies or on television? How might this underrepresentation impact the LGBTQI+ persons who are also immigrants?
3. What are the attitudes that you have toward immigrants? How about undocumented immigrants? What is your knowledge base regarding LGBTQI+ treatment in different global cultures?

Case Study

Bobby is an 8-year-old undocumented immigrant from Central America who self-identifies as bisexual and lives in an urban area of California. When Bobby's counselor, Jon, first meets Bobby at his school, he appears to be functioning well with the exception of some self-esteem and socialization issues. However, Bobby tells Jon about how he often has to take care of himself after school for several hours until his parents get home from work. It is overwhelming at times because he has to take care of the household chores in addition to caring for his younger siblings. In addition, Bobby is scared to tell his parents about his affectional orientation because of the conservative societal norms of his Central American culture. He is afraid that his parents may send him back to Central America to live with relatives if he tells them about his affectional orientation. Jon is unsure about how to best help Bobby. First, Bobby's parents seem to have developmentally inappropriate expectations of his ability to take care of himself and the household duties. Although Jon believes that Bobby's family could benefit from assistance from state and local social service agencies, he is apprehensive about the impact receiving those services may have on the family's immigration status. Second, Jon is struggling over how to best help Bobby with his affectional orientation. Although Jon believes that it is important to help foster the child's exploration of his identity, he is also aware of the possible implications Bobby's affectional orientation may have on his ability to stay in the country.

• • •

Issues for LGBTQI+ Immigrant Communities

LGBTQI+ immigrant issues have been overlooked in the counseling and related literatures. The intersection between LGBTQI+ rights and immigrant rights has been ignored; these matters have been treated as separate issues. It has been only recently that immigration reform has become a part of the national agenda (Nakamura & Pope, 2013). In 1990, the ban on affectional minorities looking to immigrate to the United States was lifted (Nakamura & Pope, 2013). Although there has been forward movement, many LGBTQI+ immigrants continue to deal with multiple forms of marginalization related to immigration status, ethnicity, affectional orientation, and/or gender identity. Individuals who are immigrants tend to rely on their ethnic immigrant communities as a safe retreat from their unfamiliar new environment (Nakamura & Pope, 2013). These communities, however, can be unreceptive to immigrants who identify as LGBTQI+ (Boulden, 2009).

Even though the literature on LGBTQI+ immigrant communities is sparse, three key areas have been identified as important to this population: health care, housing, and legal concerns. Although health care providers have been working to meet the unique needs of LGBTQI+ patients, these individuals continue to experience health disparities resulting from discrimination and ignorance. The effects of this discrimination range from LGBTQI+ patients deciding against disclosing their affectional orientation to avoiding seeking treatment. In addition, research has shown that the LGBTQI+ population generally receives a lower quality of care than do heterosexual patients. The needs of immigrants further contribute to LGBTQI+ individuals' struggle because of factors including issues related to documentation status and cultural misunderstandings (i.e., differing values, language barriers), limited access to health information, and limited access to health care (Chávez, 2011).

Housing is another concern for LGBTQI+ migrant individuals. Most research related to this issue centers around migrants' ability to integrate or assimilate into their new communities. In addition, immigrants face difficulties and discrimination regarding access to housing (Border Action Network, 2008). LGBTQI+ immigrant populations' largest concerns pertaining to housing are homeless youth and the elderly as they move into retirement communities. Not much is known about young adults or the middle-aged. Given this limited body of literature, more research is needed to understand the multifaceted needs of immigrants in their efforts to experience and maintain safe housing (Chávez, 2011).

Historically speaking, the association between sexuality and immigration law has been difficult. Affectional orientation has been used as justification for migration exclusion, and the lines between what is considered legal and illegal status seem to shift over time. Issues of HIV status, obtaining asylum on the basis of gender identity or affectional orientation, and the inability of U.S. citizens to sponsor their same-sex partners have all affected LGBTQI+ immigrants' ability to become permanent residents of the United States (Chávez, 2011).

Despite the lack of research in this area, it is clear that LGBTQI+ immigrants face many impediments and have needs that are not currently being met. Because of the either/or status that has long been held by these individuals (i.e., the fact that they must identify as either LGBTQI+ or immigrant), many report feeling invisible (Lewis, 2010). Although LGBTQI+ immigrant communities have grown in visibility, more research is needed to expand the understanding of the challenges faced by this population. Understanding the commonalities and differences among immigrants of varying ethnic backgrounds will help to inform clinicians who may encounter these individuals in mental health settings (Nakamura & Pope, 2013).

Varying Acceptance and Exposure

Intergroup marginalization, in which more influential group members oppress weaker members, adds pressure to individuals who are already experiencing marginalization by members of the dominant society (Harris, 2009). An example of intergroup marginalization appropriate for this topic is homophobia among immigrant communities (Battle & Harris, 2013). In a study by Chávez (2011), LGBTQI+ immigrants identified that they were most likely to seek help from friends and family. A confounding factor to individuals seeking help from their informal support systems is the homophobia that may lie in these immigrant communities.

Rust (2000) identified three coping mechanisms as common among migrant affectional and gender minorities. First, LGBTQI+ immigrants may conceal their affectional orientation to gain support from their ethnic community. Second, individuals may leave their ethnic community and immerse themselves in the LGBTQI+ community. The third coping skill involves advocacy: LGBTQI+ immigrants may choose to be a part of both communities and challenge homophobia. No matter the coping skill used, the intergroup marginalization experienced by LGBTQI+ immigrants can have a negative impact on their identity and perception of self-worth (Battle & Harris, 2013). Being accepted as a member of a social group positively affects an individual's well-being. Those individuals who are experiencing multiple forms of marginalization and isolation are especially vulnerable to mental health issues. This sense of belonging is especially important for recent immigrants as they seek support from their new community (Battle & Harris, 2013).

How National Attitudes Impact Understanding of Affectional Orientation and Gender

Many advocacy groups are working at the intersection of racial justice, affectional orientation, and gender identity, confronting falsehoods and prejudices that continue to impede the rights and opportunities of LGBTQI+ people, especially LGBTQI+ people of color. As discussed in Chapter 20, many LGBTQI+ people of color will experience marginalization from majority populations as a direct result of both their affectional orientation and their race. LGBTQI+ individuals of color will also experience intense marginalization in their own ethnic and racial groups due to their gender identity and affectional orientation (Siegel et al., 2012). In the 20th century, advocacy groups began advocating for many changes to take place that have led to an increase in positivity as it relates to national attitudes toward LGBTQI+ people. Society has seen a move toward inclusion and acceptance for gay people in both secular and religious institutions. According to Whitley (2001), it is clear that Americans' attitudes toward both lesbians and gay men have become increasingly less negative over the past 30 years; however, a significant number of Americans continue to view "homosexuality" as morally unacceptable. The negative attitude toward LGBTQI+ people that suggests that affectional orientation variance is morally unacceptable often leads to physical and verbal aggression or assault (Whitley, 2001). Often because of the overwhelmingly negative attitude of society as a whole, LGBTQI+ individuals will experience greater stress directly linked to concealing their affectional orientation because of the lack of safety and increased risk factors of being out (Meyer, 2003).

According to Siegel and colleagues (2012), religiosity and religious affiliation appear to be essential factors in public opinion of less support for lesbian and gay equality. There appears to be complete disparity across religious groups, as well as how often one attends religious services, in the level of support for full equality, particularly when it comes to marriage equality (Siegel et al., 2012). According to this study, only 24% of Americans who attend regular church services are in favor of marriage equality. Similarly, Norton and Herek (2013) found that higher levels of "psychological authoritarianism, political conservatism and anti-egalitarianism, and (for women) religiosity are consistent predictors of sexual discrimination" (p. 749). In addition, belief systems surrounding gender are excellent predictors of attitudes toward LGBTQI+ communities. In a study conducted by Whitley (2001), the best predictor of negative attitudes toward LGBTQI+ persons was the gender of the participant (more negative attitudes from males) accompanied by a hyper-gender-role orientation. A gender belief system would further support the theory that heterosexual individuals often harbor negative feelings or attitudes toward the LGBTQI+ community as a means of maintaining traditional gender-role distinctions (Whitley, 2001). Similarly, Rees-Turyn, Doyle, Holland, and Root (2008) found that persons applied a rigid gender-role orientation when considering LGBTQI+ persons: These rigid gender roles can cause people to assume that having any gender variance is equated with being gay or lesbian. Similarly, Rees-Turyn et al. found that people were also likely to espouse gender-role stereotypes of gay men and lesbians, believing that all gay men must be effeminate and lesbians masculine.

At the same time, Americans appear to be trending toward the belief that affectional orientation and gender variance is something a person is born with and not a choice (Siegel et al., 2012). More than 65% of Americans now believe that affectional orientation variance has biological causes and support civil rights for LGBTQI+ persons (Siegel et al., 2012). A study conducted by Siegel and colleagues (2012) also found that most Americans (89%) agree that transgender people merit the same rights and safeguards as other Americans. Most American people were willing to back a Congressional expansion of federal hate crime laws in order to increase safeguards for a person's gender, affectional orientation, or gender identity. Most Americans (75%) also erroneously believe that it is already illegal to discriminate based on gender identity or affectional orientation, even though those protections are missing from a significant number of states.

Creating Support and Advocacy for LGBTQI+ Immigrants

According to the U.S. Census Bureau (2003), 11.7% of the U.S. population is foreign born. In 2012, almost 41 million immigrants lived in the United States (Nwosu, Batalova, & Auclair, 2014). It has not yet been ascertained how many of these immigrants identify as LGBTQI+. However, based on research conducted for the Office of Refugee Resettlement of the U.S. Department of Health and Human Services (Heartland Alliance, 2012), it is estimated that between 3.8% and 4.6% of refugee and asylum seekers are LGBTQI+. In light of this figure, it can be estimated that current immigrant populations contain a significant LGBTQI+ presence.

LGBTQI+ immigrants experience great hardships over and above the typical struggles that are experienced by recent immigrants (Tiven & Neilson, 2009). These difficulties include both psychological and social problems that can lead to serious deleterious impairment. This immigrant population requires specific interventions and tailored support in order to flourish in their new living environment. Counseling efforts should focus on the unique strengths-based experiences and characteristics of LGBTQI+ immigrants and identify and explore assets to help them become successful.

Challenges of LGBTQI+ Immigrants

Family-Related Challenges

LGBTQI+ immigrants are less likely than heterosexual immigrants to have familial connections and may not be open about their affectional orientation to any family they might have in the United States (Tiven & Neilson, 2009). Coming out to family may lead to conflict and ostracism, resulting in even more survival stressors and ensuing serious mental health problems. Revealing their sexual identity can also put in jeopardy social resources that LGBTQI+ immigrants are receiving from their ethnic community and friends.

For some immigrants, there may be a high expectation of and commitment to family norms that can conflict with an individual's affectional orientation, resulting in a struggle between remaining dedicated to family values and living openly as an LGBTQI+ person (A. Morales, Corbin-Gutierrez, & Wang, 2013). This is especially the case with Latino immigrants, who come from cultures that place serious importance on family devotion. This conflict will be significantly pronounced for LGBTQI+ immigrants living in the United States, where there is more acceptance and opportunities for exploration of affectional orientation compared to Latin American countries.

Challenges Accessing Resources

Gay and lesbian organizations are more prevalent in large urban areas, which makes resources for LGBTQI+ immigrants more accessible to those living in bigger cities. However, those living in nonurban areas could have trouble accessing LGBTQI+ resources. Whether in urban or nonurban areas, gay and lesbian organizations may be structured in a Westernized manner, which may make them unfriendly or unwelcoming to foreigners (Tiven & Neilson, 2009). These organizations are designed to market and appeal to U.S. citizens, and the services provided are focused on meeting the needs of LGBTQI+ citizens. This approach may not work well with noncitizens who are not familiar with how social services are accessed and provided in the United States.

Challenges With Immigration and the Legal System

One of the most significant legal challenges for LGBTQI+ immigrants is the lack of recognition of same-sex immigrant families in the United States. This problem has been thoroughly detailed in the literature (e.g., Dunton, 2012). Particularly troubling is when a partner is left behind in the context of dangerous oppression in the country of origin. Even in these types of dire circumstances, the United States denies refugee status to individuals on the basis of their same-sex relationships. Gay immigrants who have left their same-sex partners for immediate safety reasons have no recourse in becoming reunited in the United States. This can cause substantial guilt and distress in gay immigrants as they cope with the notion that they have abandoned their loved one.

Challenges With Social Oppression and Discrimination

The experience of social oppression and discrimination is almost guaranteed for LGBTQI+ immigrants. Those who face prejudice and discrimination are at higher risk for HIV and substance abuse (Bianchi, Zea, Poppen, Reisen, & Echeverry, 2004; E. Morales, 2013). Facing stigma and oppression results in poor self-esteem, social estrangement, and mental stress that can in turn contribute to high-risk sexual behaviors such as unprotected sex. Racism and homophobia can also worsen internal and external barriers that a new LGBTQI+ immigrant is attempting to overcome.

A qualitative study conducted by A. Morales et al. (2013) showed that gay immigrant Latinos are commonly exposed to homophobic verbal aggressions. These types of experiences often happen in the workplace and have negative impacts on an individual's emotional state. The study found that despite these experiences of prejudice, the immigrants were able to default to a variety of coping strategies and access support systems to help them persevere through these types of adversities.

Challenges With Acculturation and Identity Development

Adjusting to a new sociocultural landscape can present many unique difficulties for LGBTQI+ immigrants. They are confronted with many new social domains, such as LGBTQI+ communities, their ethnic communities, work environments, and mainstream society (E. Morales, 2013). All of these domains have different standards, rules, and customs that may clash and elicit significant distress, requiring rapid adaptations and social supports that may not be available to newly arrived persons. Having to manage all of these different and often conflicting sociocultural dynamics with few psychosocial resources can result in problems with acculturation and identity development. Issues with acculturation and identity development can exacerbate the adversities an LGBTQI+ immigrant is confronting, triggering a cycle in which hardships are continuously experienced without any respite and result in worsened well-being.

LGBTQI+ immigrants face significant obstacles as they acculturate to American culture and simultaneously develop an affectional orientation identity. In particular, Mexican gay men are confronted with the concept of *machismo*, an active/passive model of sex roles and effeminate conceptions of affectional orientation variance (E. Morales, 2013). These models of gender and affectional orientation are imported from their Mexican culture, which can conflict with developing an identity as a gay individual and with acculturating into general Western society. In his ethnographic study of Mexican gay immigrants, Thing (2010) showed the dynamic interplay between gay social networks and a variety of sociocultural variables, such as geography, ethnicity, and social class, in shaping identity. One notable dynamic is an integration between models of affectional orientation variance from pre- and postmigration cultures. Immigrants from other international areas could experience similar intersectionality between various psychosocial domains.

Acculturation levels and well-being are significantly correlated in LGBTQI+ immigrants. A quantitative study by Bianchi and colleagues (2004) found a connection between acculturation and positive health behaviors in a sample of gay Latino immigrants. This study also found that active coping strategies mediated the connection between acculturation and well-being. It appears that acculturation increases engagement in active coping strategies, leading to increased accessing of resources that promote healthy living. For example, immigrants who know English and familiarize themselves with U.S. culture are less hesitant to seek out resources that support health behaviors.

From Macro to Micro Practices: Creating Supports and Advocacy

As can be gathered from the selective review of challenges that LGBTQI+ immigrants encounter, comprehensive interventions are required to fully address these challenges. In this section, support and advocacy recommendations are offered using Bronfenbrenner's (1989) ecological systems theory as an organizing paradigm. Bronfenbrenner's theory explores the bidirectional influences on the individual at different levels of the ecological system. The macro, exo-, meso-, and microsystem levels are used here to delineate supports and advocacy for LGBTQI+ immigrants.

Macrolevel Supports and Advocacy

The macrosystem involves cultural values, principles, and attitudes that have an impact on the individual or on a societal group. At this level, counseling and mental health organizations can engage in support and advocacy initiatives that are directly applicable to LGBTQI+ immigrants. Mental health organizations and counseling associations at the state and national levels can explicitly include LGBTQI+ immigrants in their mission statements and strategic objectives. Establishing affectional minority immigrants and refugees as a priority group for counselors can positively influence attitudes and perceptions in the counseling community. Furthermore, efforts can be made to educate counselors on the challenges faced by this population. Many counselors may be unfamiliar with the experiences of LGBTQI+ immigrants, requiring specialized training to help provide more tailored services. Through these education and advocacy efforts, the impact on values and attitudes can change favorably in support of affectional minority immigrants (Potocky-Tripodi, 2002).

Exolevel Supports and Advocacy

The exosystem houses social entities and settings, such as businesses, governmental institutions, and social agencies, whose actions and decisions have a significant bearing on the individual. At this level, counseling organizations can attempt to develop and support public awareness campaigns to help the general population become aware of the issues and needs of LGBTQI+ immigrants. Educating citizens could lead to more awareness of this population among other agencies and organizations, such as medical, legal, business, and governmental stakeholders, potentially fostering more resource availability and accessibility (Potocky-Tripodi, 2002).

Furthermore, counseling and mental health organizations should support lobbying efforts that increase policies designed to assist LGBTQI+ immigrants in transitioning into their new communities and to prevent mental health problems. Advocacy can also focus on policies that simplify the processes of obtaining entry and U.S. visas for LGBTQI+ refugees and asylum seekers (E. Morales, 2013). Sidhu (2009) provided general lobbying guidelines that can be used to advocate for policy change. Details were also provided on different types of advocacy. From election activities to legislative initiatives, counseling organizations have many opportunities to support LGBTQI+ immigrant issues.

One major legislative issue that would have a significant impact on LGBTQI+ immigrants and refugees is family equality. There is especially a great need for more advocacy for national legislation that would recognize same-sex families as legitimate and as equal to opposite-sex families in immigration contexts (Dunton, 2012). Political organizations at the national level are designing legislation intended to provide more benefits to same-sex couples and families. These political initiatives could gain more momentum if mental health advocates support them.

Mesolevel Supports and Advocacy

The mesosystem level is where the interrelationships and partnerships between institutions and groups significantly impact the individual. In this domain, counselors and counseling agencies have the opportunity to assume a leadership role to catalyze collaborations between relevant stakeholders and community institutions to provide supports for LGBTQI+ immigrants. For example, partnerships can be developed with medical clinics to secure proper health care resources for immigrants who are also affectional orientation and gender minorities. Collaborations can also be fostered with educational institutions, such as community colleges, to assist in the acculturation process by providing learning opportunities such as English language courses, social skills training, and job readiness training. In this scenario, counselors can support gay immigrants by building resilience through counseling while educational institutions provide learning experiences that will promote acculturation and occupational success.

One major area that needs attention is the accessibility of medical care for LGBTQI+ immigrants, especially those who are diagnosed with HIV (Chávez, 2011). Partnerships can focus on public information campaigns to dispel inaccurate biases and assumptions about HIV and gay immigrants that create barriers to providing community-based medical services. Such campaigns could potentially help reduce fears experienced by LGBTQI+ immigrants that prevent them from seeking out medical services by creating a more welcoming and accepting environment. Prevention efforts can also be made to reduce the spread of HIV and other sexually transmitted infections among the LGBTQI+ immigrant population. Some data suggest that some gay immigrants engage in more sexually risky behaviors than heterosexual immigrants, increasing their exposure to disease (Bianchi et al., 2004). HIV prevention initiatives may target LGBTQI+ urban communities where newly arrived immigrants settle.

The goal of these partnerships is to ensure equitable access to comprehensive services and care, eliminate any barriers to services, and adapt assistance to the individual challenges that are faced by LGBTQI+ immigrants (Potocky-Tripodi, 2002). Through collaborative partnerships, counselors can design prevention, education, and outreach programs that specifically serve and address the needs of this population. Furthermore, such collaborations can be created to welcome and embrace members of this population, many of whom come to the United States to escape homonegativity and to live more authentically (Bianchi et al., 2004).

Microlevel Supports and Advocacy

The microsystem contains individuals and groups that have an immediate and direct influence on the individual. Here the focus is on how counselors are advocates for gay immigrants and how they can use supportive interventions to help LGBTQI+ immigrants overcome their challenges. Counselors can function as advocates for their LGBTQI+ immigrant clients, verifying that immigrants have access to the proper resources and are being assisted by the professional helping community. In many respects, the counselor can be viewed as taking on the role of a case manager. It must be confirmed that the client is receiving the quality services that are necessary for a stable transition into a new culture and to encourage physical and mental health (Potocky-Tripodi, 2002). These services and resources include translation services, health care, sexual health information, educational opportunities, and job search assistance. Even when formal case management is being offered and used, counselors can still advocate for their clients by holding the system accountable and helping LGBTQI+ immigrants or refugees navigate through the complex array of social services.

Developing and maintaining a social support system is crucial for LGBTQI+ immigrants to thrive in their new environment. This is especially the case for LGBTQI+ immigrants, who typically are not open about their affectional orientation with their families and are likely to experience conflict with family members when they come out or are outed. Counselors can assist in this process by helping LGBTQI+ immigrants locate and establish connections with groups and individuals that can become part of their social support network. One tool that can be adapted and used to facilitate social network awareness and development is a sociogram (Green & Mitchell, 2008). Sociograms visually help the counselor and client identify a range of support systems that vary from close and supportive to less close and more distant.

As discussed previously, LGBTQI+ immigrants have major difficulties with acculturation, which can lead to serious mental health problems. Some of the supports already mentioned, such as social skills training, can help address issues with acculturation. Counselors can use additional interventions to encourage the acculturation process and to address any distress that an LGBTQI+ immigrant might be experiencing from acculturation difficulties. Some of these interventions include normalizing feelings of fear and frustration, deconstructing and learning from negative experiences, bringing attention to and building off of positive experiences, and developing existential meaning around the individual's immigration journey (Potocky-Tripodi, 2002). In addition, assertiveness training and the learning of problem-solving skills can be important interventions that assist LGBTQI+ immigrants in more confidently navigating new or intimidating situations. Both assertiveness and social skills training could also facilitate connections and immersion with LGBTQI+ social networks. Such connections have been shown to be important in sexual identity formation in gay Mexican immigrants (Thing, 2010). Ultimately, empowerment is the overarching aim of all of these interventions and in the counseling experience. Empowerment will allow LGBTQI+ immigrants to persevere through challenging circumstances, such as discrimination and oppression, and to thrive and succeed as LGBTQI+ individuals in their new country.

Counseling Strategies

When considering effective, evidence-based counseling strategies for working with LGBTQI+ immigrant clients, it is important to be aware of eight key issues surrounding affectional orientation and how they may be further complicated by one's immigration status: (a) misunderstanding and misinformation, (b) invisibility, (c) identity development, (d) lack of support systems, (e) family problems, (f) violence, (g) sexual abuse, and (h) sexually transmitted infections (Pollock, 2006).

Misunderstanding and Misinformation

The first issue, misunderstanding and misinformation, indicates that both counselor and client should have a mutual understanding of affectional orientation and cultural values. It is imperative that the counselor take the time to develop an understanding of clients' worldviews and their understanding of their affectional orientation and gender orientation. Some clients, particularly children, may have misguided beliefs about sexuality from other worldviews. These misunderstandings and misinformation can be further complicated if the counselor does not take the time to also understand the cultural norms of the client. These norms may be in conflict with the cultural norms of the host culture (Pollock, 2006).

Invisibility and Identity Development

Invisibility and identity development are two more important issues that will impact the development of an effective counseling strategy. A client's affectional orientation is often unknown by others unless the client chooses to disclose it. It is important to consider the relative impact that being an invisible minority may have on a client who may already be struggling to adjust to a host culture. An effective counseling strategy will help clients develop as LGBTQI+ persons while developing their own cultural identity (Pollock, 2006).

Lack of Support Systems and Family Problems

Many LGBTQI+ individuals experience a lack of support systems when first understanding their affectional orientation or gender orientation. Many individuals also experience strained or nonexistent relationships with family members. When developing an effective counseling strategy with this population, it is important to consider the needs of the client in relation to support and familial relationships. An effective counselor will assess clients' current level of support and their desire for increased support. It is important not to assume that all LGBTQI+ clients have a strained relationship with their family or are lacking in support systems. As with all clients, it is important to first gather all possible information before making conclusions (Pollock, 2006).

Violence, Sexual Abuse, and Sexually Transmitted Infections

Last, violence and sexually transmitted infections are also important factors to consider when developing an effective and evidence-based counseling strategy for use with LGBTQI+ immigrant clients. An assessment of the violence and abuse the client has experienced is imperative for effective treatment. Types of violence could include bullying, sexual abuse, physical abuse, emotional/psychological abuse, verbal abuse, or exclusion. It is important to assess for both individual incidents as well as patterns of violence. Immigrants can be at particular risk for abuse because of their immigration status and potential lack of knowledge of their rights and resources (Pollock, 2006).

Conclusion

This chapter has examined the issues immigrant and international LGBTQI+ communities face in the United States. Too often intersections among race, gender, class, affectional orientation, and immigrant status keep this population hidden from much of the research literature (Battle & Harris, 2013). The current literature points to the importance of these individuals being connected to a community as well as connected to a counselor who works to empower them. With this information, a counselor can develop and use counseling strategies that will effectively meet the needs of this population.

Questions for Further Discussion

1. What resources might Bobby need? How could Jon locate these services in Bobby's community?
2. What might be the obstacles to Bobby receiving the services he needs? How might Jon help Bobby overcome those obstacles?
3. What types of advocacy interventions could Jon be a part of to help improve the culture and resources for all LGBTQI+ immigrants?

4. How might Bobby's counseling and advocacy plan look different if he were in a rural area?
5. What counseling techniques can Jon use to assist Bobby in positive identity development as well as in meeting his needs as an immigrant?

Resources

1. Learn more about advocacy issues for LGBTQI+ immigrants at https://www.immigrantjustice.org/programs/lgbt-immigrant-rights-initiative.
2. Become familiar with Immigration Equality's free services for LGBTQI+ immigrants at http://www.immigrationequality.org/.
3. Read more about why comprehensive and inclusive immigration reform is important for LGBTQI+ persons at http://www.hrc.org/resources/comprehensive-inclusive-immigration-reform.

References

Battle, J., & Harris, A. (2013). Belonging and acceptance: Examining the correlates of sociopolitical involvement among bisexual and lesbian Latinas. *Journal of Gay & Lesbian Social Services, 25*(2), 141–157. doi:10.1080/10538720.2013.782520

Bianchi, F. T., Zea, M. C., Poppen, P. J., Reisen, C. A., & Echeverry, J. J. (2004). Coping as a mediator of the impact of sociocultural factors on health behavior among HIV-positive Latino gay men. *Psychology & Health, 19*(1), 89–101.

Border Action Network. (2008). *Human and civil rights violations uncovered: A report from the Arizona/Sonora border.* Tucson, AZ: Author.

Boulden, W. (2009). Gay Hmong: A multifaceted clash of cultures. *Journal of Gay & Lesbian Social Services, 21*, 134–150.

Bronfenbrenner, U. (1989). Ecological systems theory. *Annals of Child Development, 6*, 187–249.

Chávez, K. R. (2011). Identifying the needs of LGBTQI+Q immigrants and refugees in southern Arizona. *Journal of Homosexuality, 58*(2), 189–218.

Dunton, E. S. (2012). Same sex, different rights: Amending U.S. immigration law to recognize same-sex partners of refugees and asylees. *Family Court Review, 50*(2), 357–371.

Green, R., & Mitchell, V. (2008). Gay and lesbian couples in therapy: Minority stress, relational ambiguity, and families of choice. In A. S. Gurman (Ed.), *Clinical handbook of couple therapy* (4th ed., pp. 662–680). New York, NY: Guilford Press.

Harris, A. C. (2009). Marginalization by the marginalized: Race, homophobia, heterosexism, and "the problem of the 21st century." *Journal of Gay & Lesbian Social Services, 21*, 430–448.

Heartland Alliance. (2012). *Rainbow Welcome Initiative: An assessment and recommendations report on LGBT refugee resettlement in the United States.* Retrieved from http://rainbow-welcome.org/uploads/pdfs/ORR%20Report%20MASTER%20COPY_01.2012.pdf

Lewis, R. (2010). Lesbians under surveillance: Same-sex immigration reform, gay rights, and the problem of queer liberalism. *Social Justice, 1*(119), 90–106.

Meyer, I. H. (2003). Prejudice, social stress, and mental health in lesbian, gay, and bisexual populations: Conceptual issues and research evidence. *Psychological Bulletin, 129*, 674–697. doi:10.1037/0033-2909.129.5.674

Morales, A., Corbin-Gutierrez, E. E., & Wang, S. C. (2013). Latino, immigrant, and gay: A qualitative study about their adaptation and transitions. *Journal of LGBT Issues in Counseling, 7*(2), 125–142.

Morales, E. (2013). Latino lesbian, gay, bisexual, and transgender immigrants in the United States. *Journal of LGBT Issues in Counseling, 7*(2), 172–184.

Nakamura, N., & Pope, M. (2013). Borders and margins: Giving voice to lesbian, gay, bisexual, and transgender immigrant experiences. *Journal of LGBT Issues in Counseling, 7*(2), 122–124. doi:10.1080/15538605.2013.785235

Norton, A. T., & Herek, G. M. (2013). Heterosexuals' attitudes toward transgender people: Findings from a national probability sample of U.S. adults. *Sex Roles, 68*, 738–753. doi:10.1007/s11199-011-0110-6

Nwosu, C., Batalova, J., & Auclair, G. (2014, April 28). *Frequently requested statistics on immigrants and immigration in the United States.* Retrieved from the Migration Policy Institute website: http://www.migrationpolicy.org/article/frequently-requested-statistics-immigrants-and-immigration-united-states-3

Pollock, S. L. (2006). Counselor roles in dealing with bullies and their LGBT victims. *Middle School Journal, 38*(2), 29–36.

Potocky-Tripodi, M. P. (2002). *Best practices for social work with refugees and immigrants.* New York, NY: Columbia University Press.

Rees-Turyn, A., Doyle, C., Holland, A., & Root, S. (2008). Sexism and sexual prejudice (homophobia): The impact of the gender belief system and inversion theory on sexual orientation research and attitudes toward sexual minorities. *Journal of LGBT Issues in Counseling, 2*, 2–25. doi:10.1080/15538600802077467

Rust, P. C. (2000). The impact of multiple marginalization. In E. Disch (Ed.), *Reconstructing gender: A multicultural anthology* (pp. 248–254). Mountain View, CA: Mayfield.

Sidhu, J. K. (2009). Social workers and immigrant advocacy. In F. Chang-Muy & E. P. Congress (Eds.), *Social work with immigrants and refugees: Legal issues, clinical skills, and advocacy* (pp. 329–365). New York, NY: Springer.

Siegel, L., Shore, E., Contee, C., Levihn-Coon, A., Rand, K., Dakin, A., . . . Moore, C. (2012). *Public opinion and discourse on the intersection of LGBT issues and race.* Retrieved from https://opportunityagenda.org/files/field_file/lgbt_report_2012.pdf

Thing, J. (2010). Gay, Mexican and immigrant: Intersecting identities among gay men in Los Angeles. *Social Identities, 16*, 809–831.

Tiven, R. B., & Neilson, V. (2009). Working with lesbian gay, bisexual, and transgender immigrants. In F. Chang-Muy & E. P. Congress (Eds.), *Social work with immigrants and refugees: Legal issues, clinical skills, and advocacy* (pp. 257–272). New York, NY: Springer.

U.S. Census Bureau. (2003). *The foreign-born population in the United States, March 2002.* Retrieved from http://www.census.gov/prod/2003pubs/p20-539.pdf

Whitley, B., Jr. (2001). Gender-role variables and attitudes toward homosexuality. *Sex Roles, 45*, 691–721.

THE ROLE OF RELIGION

Chapter 22

The Role of Religion and Spirituality in Counseling the LGBTQI+ Client

Misty M. Ginicola, Brett H. Furth, and Cheri Smith

> *My choices, it seemed, were to be branded a sinner and*
> *live my life alone; to abandon my faith, the one thing I held most dear*
> *in the entire world; or to lie to everyone, pretend I was straight,*
> *and forget about it all.*
>
> —Justin Lee

• • •

Awareness of Attitudes and Beliefs Self-Check

1. Close your eyes and picture a religious person. What do you see? How are your biases and stereotypes present in your image? What images of sexuality, affectional orientation, and gender are present in or absent from the image?
2. What holy people or religious figures do you know who are out as lesbian, gay, bisexual, transgender, queer, questioning, intersex, asexual, ally, pansexual/polysexual, and two-spirited (LGBTQI+), including celebrities or characters in movies or on television? How might this underrepresentation impact LGBTQI+ persons who seek faith?
3. What are your own experiences with religion and spirituality? How might these shape your attitudes toward helping a religious LGBTQI+ client?

Case Study

In his late 40s, Singing Dragon,[1] a Caucasian Druid, just started embracing his gay identity. He had recently come out to his wife and was going through a divorce. He explained that his emerging gay identity, his draw to Celtic Druidry, and his Texan and Scottish heritages were all connected. He realized that he was gay *and* that he was Neo-Pagan at around the same time. When he spoke about his Druidry, Singing Dragon also touched on the severed relationship with his blood relatives, including his parents, the very family members through whom

---

[1]Based on an interview in Furth (2015).

he inherited his Pagan lineage. Singing Dragon said, "Well, because I am involved in a very dysfunctional family, and kind of grown up that way, I really didn't have any family to relate to. And now my family is my two kids that are grown. They're my family. They know I'm Druid Pagan. They know I'm gay. They seem to be doing okay with it. But my Paganism has been so important . . . They don't care that I'm gay, my Pagan brothers and my Gods. They are what I call my family. My parents, my blood family, I have no connection with them, they're gone." Singing Dragon explained how Druidry makes his resolution possible: "Well, I think because it's my way to connect, to find out what happened before the family became dysfunctional." He reported that reconnecting with his ancient Scottish ancestors gave him an anchoring connection to blood kin despite the disconnect he had with his immediate family of origin.

He talked about how important the historical deified Greek man Antinous, a young beautiful Greek lover of the Roman emperor Hadrian, was to him and how he was one of his primary deities: "He came to me. I was in one of those moods where I was just an absolute wreck. I was beginning to realize that I can't play the Jekyll and Hyde role of being married, gay, and trying to be Druid and Pagan, it ain't working. I think that was when I came to the realization of that. I felt like I was in a fog. The ritual just opened up all the gates. And I was just absolutely beside myself. And we were outside. It was a Full Moon ritual, 'cause we were outside burning the offerings for the Full Moon. And I was standing there after it was all over with talking to [a friend], and I was telling him about all of this, and all of a sudden, it's like he had a premonition. And he zoned out for a minute. About that same time, I heard somebody call my name. And I looked around and I didn't see anybody. And I heard it say it again, and it says, 'Take my hand'—'cause I saw this hand through the fog, and thought what the hell. [The voice said,] 'Take my hand, follow me and I will heal you, I will teach you, I will guide you where you want to be and where you need to be. My name is Antinous, and I'm here for you.' And I went, 'Oh my God, what?' I had never experienced anything like that, I didn't know what the hell that was, but it caught my undivided attention. And [my friend] zoned back in, and he mentions something about, 'Somebody just came to you.' I went, 'Dude, this is too weird, I'm getting chills all over me.'"

• • •

Religion and Spirituality

For many like Singing Dragon, a religious or spiritual experience can catch their undivided attention. Issues relevant to clients' religious and spiritual experiences can emerge in counseling and, for LGBTQI+ clients, religion could have had either a positive or negative influence. As both spirituality and religion are discussed in this chapter, the definitions of and differences between both are important to clarify. *Spirituality* has been defined as an animating force in human life, as well as a sensitivity to the spirit and soul, that may or may not be connected to a specific religious practice (Miller, 1999; VandenBos, 2015). The word *spirituality* comes from the Latin *spiritus*, which translates to "breath of life" (Elkins, Hedstrom, Hughes, Leaf, & Saunders, 1988). The Association for Spiritual, Ethical, and Religious Values in Counseling (2016) has called spirituality the "infusion and drawing out of spirit in one's life. It is experienced as an active and passive process" (para, 1, line 14). Spirituality is also described as an innate capacity that moves each person toward positive human outcomes, such as hope, knowledge, love, growth, and transcendence (Association for Spiritual, Ethical, and Religious Values in Counseling, 2016; Burke et al., 1999). *Religion* represents a systematic approach to achieving spirituality: It is organized and typically surrounds participation in specific rituals in the religious community (Burke et al., 1999; VandenBos, 2015). Religion also involves specific moral teachings on how to achieve spirituality with recognition of a definition of holy, sacred, and divine (VandenBos, 2015).

Religion and Identity Development

Although there is substantial literature on the intersection of religion and affectional orientation, only two models account for the influence of religion on affectional orientation identity development (Ginicola & Smith, 2016; Yarhouse, 2001). Yarhouse (2001) believed that individuals first experience identity confusion and crisis. Once these are resolved, they move to identity attribution, in which they start to explore their identity. They may begin to embrace an LGBQ identity or a modified identity based on their religious beliefs in the identity foreclosure versus expansion stage (Yarhouse, 2001). Individuals then experience identity reappraisal, in which they may embrace an LGBQ identity or identify other reasons for their attractions to people of the same sex (Yarhouse, 2001). Yarhouse believed that embracing either a gay identity or other reasons for their attractions meant that these individuals had reached identity synthesis. Although this was the first model to consider the role of religion in affectional orientation identity development, it was not supported by empirical research, and it also included denial of LGBTQI+ identity despite possessing "same-sex attractions" as equally authentic as acceptance of the LGBQ identity, which is not supported by research. Accepting one's identity has been associated with lower depression and anxiety, fewer conduct problems, increased hope and optimism, and higher self-esteem and life engagement (Moe, Dupuy, & Laux, 2008; Rosario, Schrimshaw, & Hunter, 2011).

Ginicola and Smith (2016) created the FAITH (foundation, attraction, internalizing/externalizing, transitioning, healing) model of affectional orientation identity development as part of an empirical qualitative study of individuals' identity development stories, including those of individuals who identified as ex-gay and those who had fully embraced their identity. Ginicola and Smith found that the first stage, or foundation, is important to consider because each individual has a unique background; the positive or negative attitudes of families, peers, religion, and the overall culture toward the LGBTQI+ community are crucial in setting the stage for ease or difficulty of identity development. The second stage is attraction variance, in which individuals first experience an attraction to someone of the same sex. The next stage is the internalizing/externalizing of meaning regarding this attraction. After experiencing such an attraction, individuals may most likely be confused and attempt to understand the nature of their experience. While they struggle to make comprehensive meaning, they are impacted by both their own perceptions and family and community perceptions of being non-heterosexual. In this process, people can fluctuate, go back and forth in interpretation, or continue to be unsure. They may also get stuck at this point, failing to accept a positive identity surrounding their experiences. This can be where counselors can have a significant impact on positive identity development. Although counselors cannot always impact family perceptions, they can help clients by helping challenge their own negative perceptions as well as providing psychoeducation and referrals to affirmative religious organizations. This can create a new social network that can enhance clients' feeling of acceptance by others, even if their family of origin does not accept their affectional orientation.

Once they have an accepted positive meaning associated with their LGBQ identity, individuals concurrently experience transitioning to acceptance and the healing stage

(Ginicola & Smith, 2016). They not only continue to work on accepting their affectional orientation identity but also accept their new religious beliefs or reality, whatever their experience may be. Finally, they may need to heal from religious and psychological trauma as well as the potential loss of their community or religion of origin. For most participants in Ginicola and Smith's (2016) study, this was not a static stage; rather, participants continued to shift back and forth between accepting their reality and healing from the damage that they had experienced in this process (see Figure 22.1 for a pictorial representation of this model).

Understanding the positive or negative nature of the impact of religion and spirituality on counseling clients is incredibly important. Whereas affirming spiritual beliefs and religious communities can protect individuals from harm and help facilitate a positive experience, rejecting beliefs and communities can severely traumatize individuals. These negative impacts can cause a delay in development or severe psychopathology, such as depression and anxiety disorders.

Religion and Spirituality in Counselors

One recent and major issue of contention in relation to religion in counseling has been the extent to which counselors' religious beliefs should impact their clients (American Counseling Association [ACA], 2011; *Ward v. Wilbanks*, 2010). All counselors are entitled and encouraged to have their own value systems, including a healthy and engaged spiritual life and/or sense of existentiality (ACA, n.d.). However, some counselors who belong to nonaffirming religions and/or who espouse nonaffirming religious beliefs have expressed discomfort in counseling clients who are from the LGBTQI+ community (ACA, 2011; *Ward v. Wilbanks*, 2010). As imposing their beliefs on clients is not allowed ethically, these counselors have argued that they should be able to refer LGBTQI+ clients to other counselors because (a) they are not competent to work with LGBTQI+ persons; (b) they feel that if they affirm LGBTQI+ persons, they are compromising their religious beliefs and responsibility to their god; and (c) if they are ethically required to affirm LGBTQI+ persons, then they are being discriminated against on the basis of religion (ACA, 2011; *Ward v. Wilbanks*, 2010).

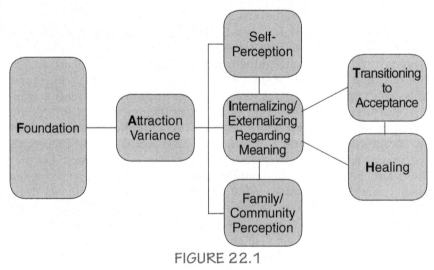

FIGURE 22.1

FAITH Model of
Affectional Orientation Identity Development

The first objection that nonaffirming counselors have is that they do not have compe-tence with LGBTQI+ communities (*Ward v. Wilbanks,* 2010). It is true that counselors can-not practice outside their competence: Standard A.11.a. in the *ACA Code of Ethics* reads, "If counselors lack the competence to be of professional assistance to clients, they avoid enter-ing or continuing counseling relationships" (ACA, 2014). However, this objection assumes that it is acceptable to remain without counseling competence. It also assumes that as pro-fessional counselors, they do not need to have professional competence with a population with which they have a value difference. Issues surrounding professional competence can be identified as having multiple components, including having appropriate counseling knowledge, having counseling skills based on empirical evidence, showing ethical and clinical judgment, and possessing appropriate interpersonal attributes (Herlihy & Corey, 2015; Locke, Myers, & Herr, 2001; Overholser & Fine, 1990). Competence is not a static or fixed concept, however; not every counselor will have professional competence all of the time with every client (Herlihy & Corey, 2015; Locke et al., 2001; Overholser & Fine, 1990). There is no question that all counselors may find themselves with a lack of competence when serving a specific client; however, all counselors are required to seek supervision and consultation, make ethical decisions, and build their competence (ACA, 2014). When it comes to cultural competence, counselors do not have the option to choose to not build their competence with different groups of clients; counselors must establish and build their multicultural competence (ACA, 2014). It would not be acceptable to say, "I have no com-petence with working with women, so I can't counsel them." Likewise, a counselor cannot claim incompetence as a reason to never work with African Americans, those with dis-abilities, persons from other countries, and those with various religious beliefs. Similarly, counselors cannot refuse to work with LGBTQI+ persons on the contention that they do not possess the competence to do so and do nothing to build that competence.

The second part of the opposition to working with LGBTQI+ clients is that asking a counselor with religious values to affirm an LGBTQI+ person compromises the counsel-or's own religious values. We also take issue with this belief. When one enters the field of counseling, one is agreeing to work with a variety of different types of people, treat them with dignity, and provide a space for them where they can experience acceptance and non-judgment (ACA, 2014). Does this mean that a counselor will agree with and support every decision a client makes? Or that a counselor would make those same decisions? Absolutely not. However, because the counseling relationship is one of the most important aspects in reaching counseling goals (Norcross & Wampold, 2011), counselors must display positive regard, warmth, empathy, and a nonjudgmental attitude. Even when a counselor believes that the client has a harmful thought pattern or behavior, the counseling method utilized is typically supportive confrontation. Professional counselors are required to maintain pro-fessional boundaries with their clients (ACA, 2014)—this also includes understanding that clients' lives and values are separate from their own. Counselors do not impose their own values on clients; rather, they expose clients' values and assist them in finding their own path (ACA, 2014). For example, clients may choose to have sexual relationships prior to marriage, and their counselor may believe that this is not an appropriate decision mor-ally speaking. Can the counselor refuse to counsel these individuals? Absolutely not—that would be very unethical. If a client's behavior could compromise a counselor's own spiri-tuality, then a religious counselor may see almost no clients.

Finally, some have claimed that to not be allowed to refer clients on the basis of a value difference is discriminatory. The nature of discrimination is often confusing, particularly to people who have privilege and have not commonly experienced discrimination. *Discrimina-tion* is defined as differential treatment of persons from different groups and involves over-whelmingly negative, injurious, and hostile treatment (VandenBos, 2015). Asking counselors who have religious beliefs to treat all clients the same, with dignity and empathy, as is required of nonreligious counselors, is *not* discrimination. Discrimination is referring a client or refusing services to a client based on a demographic factor, such as ethnicity/race, culture, age, ability status, sex, religion or spirituality, language, marital status, socioeconomic status, immigrant status, or affectional orientation and gender identity (ACA, 2014). Therefore, the counselor refusing to counsel a client based on a value conflict is openly practicing discrimination (ACA, 2014). Even the act of referring clients out when they are in crisis and incredibly vulnerable may harm clients, particularly if they are already suicidal or depressed (ACA, 2011, 2014). Just as in other helping professions, such as medicine and nursing, working in the counseling profession means serving all patients or clients who seek help and doing no harm. An ethical doctor would not turn down a patient for a life-saving procedure because the doctor does not like something about the patient's life; likewise, an ethical counselor seeks to help all clients with what may be life-saving interventions as well.

In essence, counselors must work to maintain and improve competence with diverse groups of clients through education, professional development, supervision, and consultation (ACA, 2014). When clients contact counselors, the counselors take responsibility for those clients' services. If the counselors cannot serve them for some ethical reason (e.g., their caseload is full), then they should provide competent referrals right away (ACA, 2011). If at any time counselors identify a value conflict that causes them to want to terminate or refer a client, they must do personal and professional work to gain insight into their reactions and not impose their values on the client (ACA, 2011, 2014). They also need to utilize an ethical decision-making process to identify what they should do in such an instance (ACA, 2014). They should work to gain competence while they are seeing a client, as they do with other issues (Herlihy & Corey, 2015; Locke et al., 2001; Overholser & Fine, 1990). If counselors truly believe that they will cause a client harm, they should not be seeing any clients until these issues are resolved.

Negative Religious and Spiritual Beliefs or Experiences

Many religions continue to be disaffirming, identifying same-sex relationships as either morally corrupt or a test from God to which the individual must respond with either conversion to heterosexuality or celibacy (Human Rights Campaign, 2016). Although there are references to "homosexuality" in religious scriptures, they are usually sparse or do not play a central role in the religion, other messages of love and acceptance often do (Bowens, 2011). Fundamentalists, or those associated with a conservative movement in Christianity that interprets the Bible in a literal manner, are the most vocally opposed to affectional orientation and gender variance in the United States (Maret, 1984). In Christianity specifically, these Bible verses surrounding affectional orientation variance can be seen as typical of the historical context, along with references to stoning someone for being a victim of rape or dishonoring that person's parents (Bowens, 2011). However, fundamentalist religions typically ignore undesired passages (e.g., those making it a sin to eat bacon) but demand compliance to the "homosexuality" passages as well as those regarding the lower status of women (Bendroth, 2016). This can lead LGBTQI+ persons of any disaffirming religion either to have a crisis surrounding integrating their faith and their affectional orientation and/or to experience religious trauma surrounding interactions with religious leaders (Bowens, 2011). Chapters 23 and 24 directly address these issues.

Existing Affirmative or Semi-Affirmative U.S. Religions

Not all religions are disaffirming. In fact, several organized religions are accepting and affirming of LGBTQI+ persons. Although some are not completely affirming, there are movements and organizations in them moving to increase their semi-affirmation to complete affirmation and acceptance of LGBTQI+ members and families. In order to gain competence in the area of religion, it is important to learn more about these faith organizations. Clients experiencing a crisis of faith surrounding their attempts to integrate their LGBTQI+ identity with their religion of origin may need counselors to refer them to affirmative religious organizations (Bozard & Sanders, 2011). There are a variety of existing affirmative religions to consider, and the following is not intended to be an exhaustive list of affirmative religions. Resources for identifying LGBTQI+ places of worship are included at the end of this chapter. In addition, by reviewing an organization's website or prescreening a referral, a counselor can identify more affirmative locations for a client. It would also behoove counselors to establish regular contacts with religious and spiritual organizations in the community and become familiar with religious organizations that are affirmative.

Buddhism

Attitudes toward LGBTQI+ persons among followers of the Buddhist religion vary; the religion itself allows for much more acceptance than Christian religions (Numrich, 2009). The level of acceptance among Buddhist followers will range from condemnation to tolerance to full advocacy (Numrich, 2009). However, it is important to note that even sects that condemn affectional orientation variance do not condone the oppression of same-sex couples (Numrich, 2009). This could be because core elements in Buddhism involve not exploiting or harming others (Human Rights Campaign, 2016). In some sects, such as Zen Buddhism, no difference is mentioned or understood between relationships with opposite-sex partners and those with same-sex partners. Although the Dalai Lama made negative comments surrounding same-sex relationships in 1997, he has now expressed more acceptance (Human Rights Campaign, 2016). Buddhist literature also reflects neither support for nor opposition against same-sex marriage, which indicates that it is not a religious issue (Human Rights Campaign, 2016). More information can be found with two American LGBTQI+ Buddhist organizations, the Gay Buddhist Fellowship (http://gaybuddhist.org) and the Lotus Sisters (http://www.lotussisters.org).

Christian Religions

Catholicism
In general the Roman Catholic Church is still mostly disaffirming of LGBTQI+ persons; however, it welcomes celibate gay and lesbian people into the church (Human Rights Campaign, 2016). This is a significant shift from earlier views that affectional orientation variance was inherently immoral (Westerfelhaus, 1998). However, numerous individual parishes go a step beyond and support marriage equality and LGBTQI+ relationships as equal to heterosexual ones (Human Rights Campaign, 2016). Pope Francis established more LGBTQI+-affirming attitudes in his recent encyclical *Amoris Laetitia*; he also has been quoted as saying, "If a homosexual person is of good will and is in search of God, I am no one to judge" (Human Rights Campaign, 2013, para. 1, line 1). New Ways Ministry (http://www.newwaysministry.org/index.html) and Dignity USA (https://www.dignityusa.org) are Catholic ministries and organizations that support Catholic persons who are also LGBTQI+.

Episcopal Church
Although the Worldwide Anglican Communion is opposed to LGBTQI+ acceptance in the church, several countries, including the Episcopal Church in America, are formally accepting of LGBTQI+ persons (Sherwood, 2016). The Episcopal Church in America includes the following statement on its website:

In 2003, the first openly gay bishop was consecrated; in 2009, General Convention resolved that God's call is open to all; in 2012, a provisional rite of blessing for same-gender relationships was authorized, and discrimination against transgender persons in the ordination process was officially prohibited; and in 2015, the canons of the church were changed to make the rite of marriage available to all people, regardless of gender. (The Episcopal Church, 2016, para. 2, line 3)

Not all Anglican members approved of this broad acceptance; however, the rule was passed with overwhelming support (Grundy & Winston, 2015). Integrity USA (http://www.integrityusa.org) is an organization in the Episcopal Church that continues to advocate and educate others in the faith.

Methodism

The Methodist Church has experienced disagreement surrounding this issue, with several clergy and churches being pro-LGBTQI+ and even performing marriage ceremonies for same-sex couples (Frykholm, 2014). The People of the United Methodist Church (n.d.) have stated that members and families should never reject or condemn lesbian or gay individuals; there should be no violence or abuse toward LGBTQI+ persons. However, they still maintain formal admonitions against same-sex relationships, which they believe are incompatible with Christianity (People of the United Methodist Church, n.d.). The Methodist Church is currently reviewing its stance on LGBTQI+ persons. The main advocacy group in the Methodist Church is called Affirmation (http://www.umaffirm.org/).

Presbyterian Church USA

The Presbyterian Church USA has been unable to reach consensus on formal acceptance of LGBTQI+ persons but does ordain self-identified LGBT clergy (Johnson, 2007). However, in 2015, it approved a marriage amendment that does not formally recognize same-sex marriages but does allow pastors to perform such ceremonies if they wish (M. K. Smith, 2015). Around the same time, the commissioner provided a resolution to provide resources and support for LGBT persons around the globe who are vulnerable to violence and to provide "safety, sanctuary, and support to LGBT refugees and asylum seekers" (Presbyterian Church USA, 2014, p. 1). The Human Rights Campaign (2016) reported that the Presbyterian Church USA continues to have no consensus surrounding the interpretation of scripture on same-sex practices; therefore, affirmation varies by denomination. The main LGBTQI+ advocacy group for Presbyterians is More Light Presbyterians (http://www.mlp.org).

United Church of Christ

The United Church of Christ is recognized as one of the most progressive, welcoming, and affirming denominations in the Christian faith when it comes to LGBTQI+ issues (Human Rights Campaign, 2016). In 1969, the United Church of Christ committed to fighting for civil rights for the LGBTQI+ community (Dart, 2013). In 1972, it ordained its first openly gay minister; in 1975, it created antidiscrimination policies protecting LGBTQI+ persons (Human Rights Campaign, 2016). The United Church of Christ published an affirmation of same-sex marriages in 2005 (Dart, 2013). Because it is such an affirming religion, the Church operates its own advocacy group called LGBT Same Gender Loving Ministries (http://www.ucc.org/lgbt).

Hinduism

Prior to colonialism in India, Hindu religions were affirming and accepting of a wide variety of sexual desires and behaviors (Vanita, 2004). Following colonialism, many Indian attitudes toward sex in general and same-sex relationships in particular became negative (Vanita, 2004). There is no central authority for the Hindu religion, so attitudes can vary depending on the temple or ashram. However, the Hindu religion has long accepted many forms of sexual desire and behavior (Vanita, 2004). The Hindu American Foundation (n.d.) created a policy brief that directly addressed this issue: They believe that all Hindus should affirm LGBTQI+ persons, fight for LGBTQI+ rights, and openly embrace marriage equality and same-sex relationships. The Gay and Lesbian Vaishnava Association (http://www.galva108.org) is an information and support network for LGBTQI+ Vaishnavas and Hindus.

Islam

Islam in any country tends to be particularly unsupportive of same-sex relations and condemns affectional orientation variance; in some countries, affectional orientation variance is still punishable by death (Human Rights Campaign, 2016; Ireland, 2006; Sanjakdar, 2013). In the United States, attitudes in mosques and community centers toward LGBTQI+ persons are relatively nonaffirmative. However, isolated communities from around the globe seek to affirm LGBTQI+ persons and do so in their mosques (Sanjakdar, 2013). Although affectional orientation variance is not affirmed, transgender persons are fully accepted according to interpretations of Islamic law in some countries, such as Iran, which also pays for sexual reassignment surgery (Hamedani, 2014). Because "homosexuality" is still punishable by death in Iran, many LGBT persons change their gender through "sex reassignment surgery" to avoid being prosecuted for having same-sex relationships (Hamedani, 2014). In the United States there are two main advocacy groups for LGBTQI+ Muslims: the Muslim Alliance for Sexual and Gender Diversity and (http://www.muslimalliance.org) and Muslims for Progressive Values (http://www.mpvusa.org).

Judaism

Reform Judaism is accepting and affirming of LGBTQI+ persons (Human Rights Campaign, 2016). Conservative Judaism has also called for full inclusion; however, not all Conservative Jewish institutions are accepting of LGBTQI+ persons (Human Rights Campaign, 2016). Orthodox Judaism, however, is not accepting of same-sex relationships (Itzhaky & Kissil, 2015; Kissil & Itzhaky, 2015). There is an incredible amount of hostility and homophobia in the Orthodox community toward lesbian and gay members (Shapiro Safran, 2013). JONAH, an Orthodox Jewish "homosexuality" conversion program, recently had to close after a judge found it guilty of making fraudulent claims about its conversion rates (Levine, 2015). Organizations serving LGBTQI+ Jewish persons include Keshet (http://www.keshetonline.org), Tirtzah (for Orthodox queer women; https://tirtzah.wordpress.com), and Eshel (http://www.eshelonline.org), to name a few.

Unitarian Universalism

The Unitarian Universalist Association is one of the most affirming churches in the United States (Human Rights Campaign, 2016). It has had female ministers since 1863, has had openly gay ministers since 1979, and welcomed a transgender minister in 1988 (Human Rights Campaign, 2016). Its stance on LGBT issues is not just to provide and affirm LGBTQI+ persons in their communities but also to actively advocate and work toward equality for LGBTQI+ persons (Unitarian Universalist Association, n.d.). The congregation celebrates Pride, Transgender Day of Remembrance, and National Coming Out Day, among others (Unitarian Universalist Association, n.d.). It also has created programs and education curricula surrounding LGBTQI+ persons and promoting acceptance (Unitarian Universalist Association, n.d.).

Wiccan/Neo-Pagan Religions

The American Neo-Pagan and Wiccan community is perhaps rare in how it as a religious community has by and large welcomed, supported, and affirmed its LGBTQI+ members. The American Neo-Pagan community at large, which has strong roots in the hippie movement and feminism, is generally supportive of individuals who fall into typically marginalized social categories, including LGBTQI+ individuals, and their affectional orientation and gender identities (Berger, Leach, & Shaffer, 2003; Kirner, 2014; Magliocco, 2004; Orion, 1995; Pike, 2001; Pizza, 2014; Saunders, 2012). Most American Neo-Pagans are White, working class or middle class, highly educated yet underpaid, politically progressive, and urban (Berger et al., 2003; Furth, 2015; Magliocco, 2004; Pizza, 2014). Magliocco (2004) found that "many lesbians, gay men, and bisexuals are drawn to Neo-Paganism because of its accepting attitude toward all affectional orientations, especially compared with the judgmental stance of most mainstream religions," and that the religion "attracts intelligent nonconformists critical of the dominant paradigms" (p. 62).

Furth (2015) found that the majority of Neo-Pagan participants in his study identified as men or women, one identified as a transgender woman, and another identified as intersex. Twelve of 52 individuals interviewed explicitly identified as some form of LGBTQI+, and several were or had been part of a polyamorous relationship. Polyamory—whether heterosexual, bisexual, or gay—is a practice not usually perceived as taboo in this religious community (Kaldera, 2005; Kraemer, 2012). Furthermore, several LGBTQI+-identified informants said that they at least in part were drawn to and identified with Neo-Paganism because it allowed them an affirming context for exploring and expressing alternative affectional orientations and gender identities that are—as exemplified by Singing Dragon's narrative—usually considered sacred in these religious traditions (Furth, 2015).

It is tragic that many Neo-Pagans report that their family relationships were injured *because* they claimed a Neo-Pagan identity (Furth, 2015). Rejection by one's family of origin for choosing Neo-Paganism has been explored by others, such as Wales (1994) and Wilson (2005). Ethnic Neo-Pagans (ones with a specific European ethnic focus) face a particular dilemma. When they become identified with an ethnoreligious tradition that strongly emphasizes blood ancestors and kin, they simultaneously experience or risk rejection by their own parents and other blood kin for choosing such a religious tradition (Furth, 2015).

The generally positive view of LGBTQI+ individuals in American Neo-Paganism is not surprising when one considers that for this religious community "the hallmark of their spirituality is its celebration of diversity in all its forms" and that "those who are homophobic within their community are particularly offensive because they go against Neo-Pagans' image of their community and its ideals" (Berger et al., 2003, p. 234). Although American Neo-Pagans often report and show acceptance, affirmation, and even celebration of LGBTQI+ sexualities and gender identities, this is not always the case. Some subgroups, such as the White-racist Ásatrú or Norse-centered Heathens described by Gardell (2003), may be less accepting of or even hostile to LGBTQI+ individuals, as may more nativistic Eastern and Central European Neo-Pagans, as they are especially focused on what could be called traditional family values, including homogenized notions of masculine and feminine gender roles (Blain, 2002; Furth, 2015; Gardell, 2003; Saunders, 2012). Some Wiccans also have problems with certain aspects of sexual or gender minority identities, as some traditional Wiccan traditions are theologically founded on a gender dichotomy. This polarized gender dichotomy—for both humans and deities—is epitomized by their notions of heteronormatively gendered deities ("the God" and "the Goddess") and the "Great Rite" (Adler, 1986, p. 110). The

Great Rite is a ritual wherein a High Priestess (typically a cisgender woman) and the High Priest (typically a cisgender man) ritually perform acts (that may or may not involve sex) that symbolize the God and the Goddess as part of their magical fertility practices (Lepage, 2013).

Another example of disagreement in the American Neo-Pagan community about gender is the recent—and sometimes heated—debate about "womyn-only" spaces and identities in the Dianic Wiccan and other women-only traditions (see Adler, 1986, pp. 121–125, for a traditional description of Dianic Wicca). Mirroring the debate Browne (2009) described over the womyn-born-womyn policy that excludes transgender women at the Michigan Womyn's Music Festival, this contention over who qualifies as a woman came to a head in the Neo-Pagan community at the 2011 and 2012 PantheaCon conventions (Pitzl-Waters, 2012; Schulz, 2012). PantheaCon, which is held annually in San Jose, California, is the largest Neo-Pagan convention in the world; these conferences attract academics and other speakers and attendees from the diverse Neo-Pagan community and offer talks, workshops, and several public rituals (Pitzl-Waters, 2012; Schulz, 2012). During the 2011 conference, a man and several transgender women were not allowed to participate in a Dianic ritual because they were not cisgender women or womyn, and similar problems arose at the 2012 conference (Pitzl-Waters, 2012; Schulz, 2012).

In response to this traditional focus on a heteronormative gender dichotomy in Wicca, groups like the Radical Faeries—a gay men's tradition—have emerged (Adler, 1986; Pike, 2001). Several practitioners also challenge this dichotomy, which they consider exclusionary of LGBTQI+ individuals and their affectional orientation and gender expressions, and suggest alternative ways to experience affectional orientation and gender in various forms of Wicca (Aburrow, 2014; Ford, 2005; Hedenborg-White & Tollefsen, 2013; Kaldera, 2002; Kraemer, 2012, 2013; Penczak, 2003). The American Neo-Pagan community is overwhelmingly accepting, reaffirming, and celebratory of LGBTQI+ individuals and their affectional orientation and gender identities and expressions, including theologically and in rituals. However, as the PantheaCon controversy highlights, this diverse religious community continues to renegotiate how it and its subcommunities perceive and relate to LGBTQI+ individuals in their religious community and in American society at large.

LGBTQI+ Safe Spaces in Nonaffirming Religions

Many nonaffirming religions still have organizations in them that work toward building acceptance in their faith communities. LGBTQI+ Mormons have Affirmation (http://affirmation.org), Baptists have the Association of Welcoming and Affirming Baptists (http://www.awab.org), and Lutherans have ReconcilingWorks (https://www.reconcilingworks.org). If a client reflects a certain preference for a religion in attempting to find an affirmative congregation, a counselor can do a brief Google search for LGBT and that denomination's name along with searching for any in the local community. Almost every religion has LGBTQI+ persons who decide to stay with their congregation to work toward inclusion; many have formed formal organizations that can benefit other LGBTQI+ persons of that faith. It is just a matter of finding those organizations and affirming congregations. As referenced previously, counselors should have established spiritual and religious connections and resources for referral in their community.

Additional Counseling Issues

Some congregations additionally have pastoral counselors. It is imperative for individuals seeking counseling from pastoral counselors to research the individual's credentials to gain an understanding of what type of training this religious leader might possess in the area of counseling. It can vary from no training, to a semester class, to training that may have led to formal counseling credentials for that individual. Beyond exploring training, it is also important to consider the values of the faith tradition the pastoral counselor reflects. Although the counseling profession's ethics code is against imposing values in a counseling setting, that same criterion may not be followed in a pastoral counseling setting. However, many pastoral counselors can also be quite affirming. Counselors should also prescreen individual counseling or support groups through faith-based organizations to determine that they will not further harm LGBTQI+ clients.

Similarly, some faith-based universities, even those housing Council for Accreditation of Counseling and Related Educational Programs (CACREP)–accredited programs, may also teach counselors to avoid serving LGBTQI+ clients as well as have policies that do not allow open LGBTQI+ students (Sells & Hagedorn, 2016; L. C. Smith & Okech, 2016a, 2016b). There has been a dialogue about whether these programs should be receiving CACREP accreditation at all (Sells & Hagedorn, 2016; L. C. Smith & Okech, 2016a, 2016b). This discourse highlights the intense issues in and conflicts surrounding this complex intersection of faith and LGBTQI+ communities (Sells & Hagedorn, 2016; L. C. Smith & Okech, 2016a, 2016b).

Conclusion

Issues surrounding religion and spirituality may arise for both the counselor and client in the counseling experience. Both spirituality and affectional identity will be important to many clients. By not imposing their own religious beliefs, by providing an affirming experience for clients, and by having knowledge of religions and congregations that are accepting of LGBTQI+ persons, counselors can provide help for clients who are attempting to successfully integrate their LGBTQI+ identity with their faith, religion, and/or spirituality. Although including religious and spiritual contexts in counseling can sometimes feel uncomfortable, counselors must be aware of how important this is for clients, particularly LGBTQI+ clients who may seek out therapy to assist with their integration. The GRACE (goals, renewal, action, connection, and empowerment) model, covered in Chapter 23, provides counselors with a specific framework to help these clients.

Questions for Further Discussion

1. If the counselor Singing Dragon is working with found that their own religious beliefs conflicted with Singing Dragon's Pagan beliefs and gay identity, what steps should the counselor take to ensure that they can still provide him with quality counseling services?
2. How might Singing Dragon experience his gay identity differently if he were in another affirmative religion? How about a safe space in a nonaffirming religion?
3. How did Singing Dragon's divine experience and reinterpretation of spirituality seemingly move him toward a better understanding of himself?
4. What experiences might Singing Dragon have in his family, friends, and religious community that might challenge his feeling of acceptance?
5. How could the FAITH identity model apply to Singing Dragon's experience?

Resources

1. Find affirmative religious supports at http://www.gaychurch.org/.
2. Review the Soulforce website at http://www.soulforce.org/.

3. Find out more about affirmative faiths at http://www.hrc.org/resources/faith-positions.
4. Read through the Unitarian Universalists' support of the LGBTQI+ community on their website at http://www.uua.org/lgbtq.
5. Read ratings of denominational policies on LGBT equality through Believe Out Loud at http://www.believeoutloud.com/background/christianity-and-lgbt-equality.

References

Aburrow, A. (2014). *All acts of love and pleasure: Inclusive Wicca.* London, UK: Avalonia.

Adler, M. (1986). *Drawing down the moon: Witches, Druids, goddess-worshippers, and other Pagans in America today* (2nd ed.). Boston, MA: Beacon Press.

American Counseling Association. (2011). *Brief for the American Counseling Association as amicus curiae in support of defendants-appellees and affirmance.* Retrieved from http://www.counseling.org/resources/pdfs/EMUamicusbrief.pdf

American Counseling Association. (2014). *ACA code of ethics.* Alexandria, VA: Author.

American Counseling Association. (n.d.). *American Counseling Association's Taskforce on Counselor Wellness and Impairment: Wellness strategies.* Retrieved from http://www.creating-joy.com/taskforce/tf_wellness_strategies.htm

Association for Spiritual, Ethical, and Religious Values in Counseling. (2016). *ASERVIC white paper.* Retrieved from http://www.aservic.org/resources/aservic-White-paper-2/

Bendroth, M. (2016). Time, history, and tradition in the fundamentalist imagination. *Church History, 85*(2), 328–342. doi:10.1017/S0009640716000020

Berger, H., Leach, E., & Shaffer, L. S. (2003). *Voices from the Pagan census: A national survey of witches and Neo-Pagans in the United States.* Columbia, SC: University of South Carolina Press.

Blain, J. (2002). *Nine worlds of weid-magic: Ecstasy and Neo-Shamanism in North European Paganism.* London, UK: Routledge.

Bowens, M. R. (2011). *Ready to answer: Why homophobic church is an oxymoron.* Bloomington, IN: Author House.

Bozard, R. L., & Sanders, C. J. (2011). Helping Christian lesbian, gay, and bisexual clients recover religion as a source of strength: Developing a model for assessment and integration of religious identity in counseling. *Journal of LGBT Issues in Counseling, 5*(1), 47–74. doi:10.1080/15538605.2011.554791

Browne, K. (2009). Naked and dirty: Rethinking (not) attending festivals. *Journal of Tourism and Cultural Change, 7,* 115–132. doi:10.1080/14766820903033666

Burke, M. T., Hackney, H., Hudson, P., Miranti, J., Watts, G. A., & Epp, L. (1999). Spirituality, religion, and CACREP curriculum standards. *Journal of Counseling & Development, 77,* 251–257.

Dart, J. (2013). UCC has been progressive pacesetter. *The Christian Century, 130*(16), 14–15.

Elkins, D. N., Hedstrom, L. J., Hughes, L. L., Leaf, J. A., & Saunders, C. (1988). Toward a humanistic-phenomenological spirituality. *Journal of Humanistic Psychology, 28,* 5–18.

Ford, M. T. (2005). *The path of the green man: Gay men, Wicca and living a magical life.* New York, NY: Citadel Press.

Frykholm, A. (2014). A time to split? *Christian Century, 131*(8), 22–25.

Furth, B. H. (2015). *Gimme that real old time religion: Re-embedding White identities through ethnic Neo-Pagan reconfigurations of European heritage in Texas* (Unpublished doctoral dissertation). Texas A&M University, College Station.

Gardell, M. (2003). *Gods of the blood: The Pagan revival and White separatism.* Durham, NC: Duke University Press.

Ginicola, M. M., & Smith, C. (2016). *Gay and religious: The development of the FAITH affectional orientation identity model.* Manuscript in preparation.

Grundy, T., & Winston, K. (2015). Episcopal Church adopts same-sex liturgy, causing "distress" for some Anglicans. *Christian Century, 132*(16), 15.

Hamedani, A. (2014, November 5). *The gay people pushed to change their gender.* Retrieved from the BBC News website: http://www.bbc.com/news/magazine-29832690

Hedenborg-White, M., & Tollefsen, I. B. (2013). Introduction: Gender in contemporary Paganism and esotericism. *Pomegranate, 15*(1/2), 7–11. doi:10.1558/pome.v15i1-2.7

Herlihy, B., & Corey, G. (2015). *ACA ethical standards casebook* (7th ed.). Alexandria, VA: American Counseling Association.

Hindu American Foundation. (n.d.). *HAF policy brief: Hinduism and homosexuality.* Retrieved from http://www.hafsite.org/media/pr/haf-policy-brief-hinduism-and-homosexuality

Human Rights Campaign. (2013). *Griffin: Pope Francis resets decades of hateful and hurtful anti-LGBT vitriol.* Retrieved from http://www.hrc.org/blog/griffin-pope-francis-presses-reset-button-on-lgbt-issues

Human Rights Campaign. (2016). *Explore: Religion and faith.* Retrieved from http://www.hrc.org/explore/topic/religion-faith

Ireland, D. (2006, September 11). Targeted by death squads. *Advocate,* pp. 28–30.

Itzhaky, H., & Kissil, K. (2015). "It's a horrible sin. If they find out, I will not be able to stay": Orthodox Jewish gay men's experiences living in secrecy. *Journal of Homosexuality, 62,* 621–643. doi:10.1080/00918369.2014.988532

Johnson, W. S. (2007). A way forward? *Christian Century, 124*(7), 28.

Kaldera, R. (2002). *Hermaphrodeities: The transgender spirituality workbook.* Bloomington, IN: Xlibris.

Kaldera, R. (2005). *Pagan polyamory: Becoming a tribe of hearts.* Woodbury, MN: Llewellyn.

Kirner, K. (2014). Healing community: Pagan cultural models and experiences in seeking well-being. *Pomegranate, 16*(1), 80–108. doi:10.1558/pome.vl6il.17934

Kissil, K., & Itzhaky, H. (2015). Experiences of the Orthodox community among Orthodox Jewish gay men. *Journal of Gay & Lesbian Social Services, 27*(3), 371–389. doi:10.1080/10538720.2015.1051686

Kraemer, C. H. (2012). Gender and sexuality in contemporary Paganism. *Religion Compass, 6,* 390–401. doi:10.1111/j.1749-8171.2012.00367.x

Kraemer, C. H. (2013). *Eros and touch from a Pagan perspective: Divided for love's sake.* London, UK: Routledge.

Lepage, M. (2013). A Lokian family: Queer and Pagan agency in Montreal. *Pomegranate, 15*(1/2), 79–101.

Levine, A. (2015, June 10). Jew v. Gay. *Village Voice,* pp. 8–16.

Locke, D., Myers, J. E., & Herr, E. L. (Eds.). (2001). *The handbook of counseling.* London, UK: Sage.

Magliocco, S. (2004). *Witching culture: Folklore and Neo-Paganism in American culture.* Philadelphia, PA: University of Pennsylvania.

Maret, S. M. (1984). Attitudes of fundamentalists toward homosexuality. *Psychological Reports, 55*(1), 205–206. doi:10.2466/pr0.1984.55.1.205

Miller, W. R. (1999). *Integrating spirituality into treatment: Resources for practitioners.* Washington, DC: American Psychological Association.

Moe, J. L., Dupuy, P. J., & Laux, J. M. (2008). The relationship between LGBQ identity development and hope, optimism, and life engagement. *Journal of LGBT Issues in Counseling, 2*(3), 199–215. doi:10.1080/15538600802120101

Norcross, J. C., & Wampold, B. E. (2011). Evidence-based therapy relationships: Research conclusions and clinical practices. *Psychotherapy, 48*(1), 98–102. doi:10.1037/a0022161

Numrich, P. D. (2009). The problem with sex according to Buddhism. *Dialog, 48*(1), 62–73.

Orion, L. (1995). *Never again the burning times: Paganism revived.* Prospect Heights, IL: Waveland Press.

Overholser, J. C., & Fine, M. A. (1990). Defining the boundaries of professional competence: Managing subtle cases of clinical incompetence. *Professional Psychology: Research and Practice, 21*, 462–469.

Penczak, C. (2003). *Gay witchcraft: Empowering the tribe.* Newburyport, MA: Red Wheel Weiser.

People of the United Methodist Church. (n.d.). *Human sexuality backgrounder.* Retrieved from http://www.umc.org/what-we-believe/human-sexuality-backgrounder

Pike, S. M. (2001). *Earthly bodies, magical selves: Contemporary Pagans and the search for community.* Berkeley, CA: University of California Press.

Pitzl-Waters, J. (2012, February 23). *The PantheaCon gender conversation continues.* Retrieved from the Patheos website: http://www.patheos.com/blogs/wildhunt/2012/02/the-pantheacon-gender-conversation-continues.html

Pizza, M. (2014). *Paganistan: Contemporary Pagan community in Minnesota's Twin Cities.* Farnham, UK: Ashgate.

Presbyterian Church USA. (2014). *Commissioner resolution. On the global crisis for LGBT people and their families: A Presbyterian Church (U.S.A.) response.* Retrieved from http://oga.pcusa.org/site_media/media/uploads/oga/pdf/2014_item_09-20_cr_02_commissioner_resolution_to_the_221st_general_assembly_of_the_presbyterian_church.pdf

Rosario, M., Schrimshaw, E. W., & Hunter, J. (2011). Different patterns of sexual identity development over time: Implications for the psychological adjustment of lesbian, gay, and bisexual youths. *Journal of Sex Research, 48*(1), 3–15. doi:10.1080/00224490903331067

Sanjakdar, F. (2013). Educating for sexual difference? Muslim teachers' conversations about homosexuality. *Sex Education, 13*(1), 16–29.

Saunders, R. A. (2012). Pagan places: Towards a religiogeography of neopaganism. *Progress in Human Geography, 37*, 786–810. doi:10.1177/0309132512473868

Schulz, C. (2012, February 22). *Overview of the PantheaCon gender debate.* Retrieved from the Patheos website: http://www.patheos.com/blogs/agora/2012/02/overview-of-the-pantheacon-gender-debate/

Sells, J. N., & Hagedorn, W. B. (2016). CACREP accreditation, ethics, and the affirmation of both religious and sexual identities: A response to Smith and Okech. *Journal of Counseling & Development, 94*, 265–279. doi:10.1002/jcad.12083

Shapiro Safran, R. (2013). *A multidimensional assessment of orthodox Jewish attitudes toward homosexuality.* Available from ProQuest Dissertations and Theses Global. (Order No. 3520925)

Sherwood, H. (2016, January 12). *Anglican church risks global schism over homosexuality.* Retrieved from *The Guardian* website: http://www.theguardian.com/world/2016/jan/12/anglican-church-england-global-schism-homosexuality-gay-rights

Smith, L. C., & Okech, J. A. (2016a). Ethical issues raised by CACREP accreditation of programs within institutions that disaffirm or disallow diverse sexual orientations. *Journal of Counseling & Development, 94*, 252–264. doi:10.1002/jcad.12082

Smith, L. C., & Okech, J. A. (2016b). Negotiating CACREP accreditation practices, religious diversity, and sexual orientation diversity: A rejoinder to Sells and Hagedorn. *Journal of Counseling & Development, 94*, 280–284. doi:10.1002/jcad.12084

Smith, M. K. (2015). *Presbyterian Church (U.S.A.) approves marriage amendment.* Retrieved from https://www.pcusa.org/news/2015/3/17/presbyterian-church-us-approves-marriage-amendment/

The Episcopal Church. (2016). *LGBTQ in the church.* Retrieved from http://www.episcopalchurch.org/page/lgbt-church

Unitarian Universalist Association. (n.d.). *Lesbian, gay, bisexual, transgender, and queer justice.* Retrieved from http://www.uua.org/lgbtq

VandenBos, G. R. (2015). *APA dictionary of psychology* (2nd ed.). Washington, DC: American Psychological Association.

Vanita, R. (2004). "Wedding of two souls": Same-sex marriage and Hindu traditions. *Journal of Feminist Studies in Religion, 20*(2), 119–135.

Wales, R. (1994). *Dancing the wheel: A study in Wicca and a psychological interpretation of an alternative religious practice* (Doctoral dissertation). Available from ProQuest Information & Learning. (Order No. AAM9511409)

Ward v. Wilbanks, *Case No. 09-CV-11237.* (2010). Retrieved from http://www.counseling.org/kaplan/EMU.pdf

Westerfelhaus, R. (1998). A significant shift: A pentadic analysis of the two rhetorics of the post-Vatican II Roman Catholic Church regarding homosexuality. *Journal of Gay, Lesbian, and Bisexual Identity, 3,* 269–294.

Wilson, A. M. (2005). Opening the broom closet: A Pagan perspective on parenting and religious discrimination. *Dissertation Abstracts International: Section B. Sciences and Engineering, 66,* 2884.

Yarhouse, M. A. (2001). Sexual identity development: The influence of valuative frameworks on identity synthesis. *Psychotherapy: Theory, Research, Practice, Training, 38*(3), 331–341. doi:10.1037/0033-3204.38.3.331

Chapter 23

The GRACE Model of Counseling: Navigating Intersections of Affectional Orientation and Christian Spirituality

R. Lewis Bozard, Jr. and the Rev. Cody J. Sanders

You are not sick, and you are not wrong.
And God Does Not Hate You.
—Sean Penn as Harvey Milk

• • •

Awareness of Attitudes and Beliefs Self-Check

1. Imagine that a client approaches you to help her change her affectional orientation. She grew up Orthodox Jewish and tells you that her faith is a huge piece of who she is. She cannot be gay and Orthodox. She tells you that she feels that she has to choose between her heart and her soul. As you hear her speak, what are your fears and anxieties about working with this client?
2. When have you felt in conflict with religion/spirituality at any point in your life? What did you choose to do about the conflict? How will this impact your attitudes toward someone who chooses differently?
3. What feelings would you have toward a family that asks you to change their son from gay to heterosexual because they do not want him to go to hell? Would you have negative feelings and attitudes? Would you have empathy? How might these attitudes impact your work with them in working from an affirmative perspective?

Case Study

William is a 35-year-old gay White male who lives in a medium-size city in the United States. William's formative childhood culture was not affirming of affectional orientation variance. Members of William's family sometimes made disparaging remarks about a man they knew who was gay, and William internalized these negative messages. William was somewhat active in the mainline

Protestant Christian church his family attended, and as a teenager he participated in the church's youth group. As William became aware that he felt attracted to other boys, he experienced confusion. Because of the negative messages he had received from his culture about affectional orientation variance, William developed deficits in self-esteem. He met with his church's youth pastor, Kate, to discuss his emerging affectional orientation.

William told Kate that he believed he might be gay and was afraid of what God and other people would think of him. Kate communicated to William the position of the church, which at the time was standard among many mainline Protestant groups. She told him that she cared about him and that God loved him but that, in the language of the church, "homosexuality" was "incompatible with Christian teaching." William then struggled within himself to make sense of this conflictual message that he could be accepted by God and his religious community as long as he denied his affectional orientation and lived a celibate life to retain good standing. Therefore, William attempted to suppress his sexual feelings for males and feigned interest in females. He prayed to God throughout his high school years that his sexual feelings would be reoriented toward females.

William moved to a larger city to attend college at a medium-size state university. Feeling the greater cultural freedom and acceptance in this more diverse context, and now living several hours away from his hometown, with its non-affirming influences, William began to date other men for the first time in his life. He joined the campus lesbian, gay, bisexual, transgender, queer, questioning, intersex, asexual, ally, pansexual/polysexual, and two-spirited (LGBTQI+) student group. During his second semester, William came out as a gay man. Because William associated religion with condemnation of his affectional orientation based on the church and culture in which he was raised, he discontinued all religious participation and changed his belief system to allow room for the possibility of God's existence; however, he made no attempt to define God or to practice any active spiritual connection with God. William could not believe that God would have created him to be a gay man and yet denied William the joy of a relationship and intimacy with another man. Yet he knew of no alternative Christian belief system, so he simply distanced himself from all things related to God and spirituality.

During the time between college and his mid-30s, William had a series of relationships with other men and solidified his gay identity both internally and outwardly through his social associations. William entered a committed relationship at age 32 with Javon, an African American man. Triggered by the legalization of same-sex marriage in their state, Javon and William decided to wed. As the two of them were married, William's thoughts returned to his childhood church, in which marriage—in that context between a man and a woman—was closely associated with spirituality. Having placed his faith on hold since college, William began to wish for spiritual connection again as a source of meaning in his life but felt unsure of where to find such connection. He decided to seek counseling to explore his feelings.

When Brenda, a licensed professional counselor, met William, she saw him as a young man of 35 in good health with a stable career and a family of origin that, although not fully accepting of his affectional orientation, remained on generally good terms with him. Yet William described a feeling of sadness that as he attempted to reengage spirituality, he felt disconnected from the faith of his childhood. Furthermore, he continued to believe that all Christian congregations would be rejecting of his affectional orientation, including his marriage to Javon. So he felt isolated and uncertain. William denied suicidal ideation but endorsed feeling that his life was missing meaning at a deep level.

• • •

Spirituality and Affectional Orientation

Susan, an ordained pastor in the Christian tradition, remembers being questioned at the age of 16 by her pastor about whether she was "homosexual." Susan knew that in her church context, the only acceptable answer would be no. So Susan lied. She said, "No." "That's good," Susan's pastor replied, "because God doesn't love homosexuals, and they can't be part of the church" (Parker, 2010, p. 3).

Many affectional minority persons who do—or once did—identify as religious people find the sentiment expressed by Susan's pastor painfully familiar. Religion is often associated with condemnation and rejection of affectional minority individuals. Churches sometimes command members whom they discover to be romantically involved with a member of their own sex to choose between church membership and their romantic attractions. Intense debates rage over conducting same-sex marriages. Religious organizations advocate unethical counseling practices that attempt to convert lesbian, gay, and bisexual people into heterosexual people to satisfy their own narrow interpretations of scripture. Meanwhile, affectional minority believers find themselves spiritually homeless, fearing that God rejects them—or worse, condemns them to eternal punishment for attractions they never chose—and living with the consequences potentially for years.

Fortunately, these destructive and abusive religious contexts do not represent the full range of spiritual options. As discussed in Chapter 22, many congregations and religiously oriented organizations exist that are explicitly or implicitly affirming and accepting of affectional minority members and participants. Mental health benefits of spirituality, such as relaxation, optimism, and social connectedness, can benefit affectional minority individuals who affiliate with affirming churches (Lease, Horne, & Noffsinger-Frazier, 2005).

When clients who have been rejected by religion present for counseling, counselors may be unsure of how to work with them. Neither counselor nor client may realize that successful, healthy, and meaningful integration of sexual and spiritual identities is possible. Therefore, we offer the GRACE (goals, renewal, action, connection, and empowerment) model as an outline for use in working with LGBTQI+ clients who have an interest in exploring possible engagement with spirituality, especially in Christian contexts (Bozard & Sanders, 2011).

Spirituality tends to be rather contextual given the specific belief systems and spiritual practices associated uniquely with various faith traditions. Although the model was developed with a focus on beliefs and practices of the Christian tradition, we believe that the GRACE model can be effectively adapted for application to clients of other spiritual identities (Bozard & Sanders, 2011). We are ordained in the Christian tradition, so navigation of the Christian faith, with both its positive and negative experiences, has constituted an integral part of our own personal life experiences. With Christianity being the largest religion in the United States, counselors in many areas are likely to encounter clients with a specific history or interest in Christianity (Newport, 2009). Furthermore, it is believed that the model may be adapted for use with gender minority (e.g., transgender) individuals, but as less attention has been given to gender diversity than to sexual diversity in most religious contexts to date, we currently limit the model's explicit application to sexual aspects of identity.

Ethical Dilemmas of Requests for Sexual Orientation Change Efforts (SOCE)

When a counselor who affirms and supports persons of diverse affectional orientations approaches work with affectional minority people, the request for assistance in affectional orientation change can be jarring. In an era of ever-increasing social acceptance of and political equality for affectional minority people, it is alarming that these efforts—referred to variously as *reparative therapy, conversion therapy,* or *ex-gay ministries*—remain so prevalent. As discussed in Chapter 8, counselors who practice reparative or conversion therapy view lesbian, gay, and bisexual orientations as abnormal, pathological, or morally/religiously reprehensible and thus requiring cure or repair. The goal of affectional orientation change, therefore, is to change one's orientation to heterosexual.

In contrast to this view, major mental health organizations, including the American Counseling Association (ACA), have stated clearly that these efforts are ideologically misguided and potentially dangerous to clients. Whitman, Glosoff, Kocet, and Tarvydas (2013) noted that in 1998 ACA passed a resolution opposing the continued portrayal of lesbian, gay, and bisexual people as mentally ill based on their affectional orientation, and in 1999 the ACA Governing Council adopted an additional statement opposing the promotion of reparative therapy. In addition, they noted that no existing therapeutic techniques approved by ACA or other major mental health organizations would train counselors in conversion therapy.

In 2013, the largest proponent of ex-gay ministry—the evangelical Christian organization Exodus International—closed its doors (Lovett, 2013). Nevertheless, the practice of reparative therapy by counselors and ex-gay ministries by religious professionals is still ongoing. What is more, the desire to access these practices persists, as religious and social prejudice against affectional minority people continues to influence individuals, families, and communities to view affectional minority people as pathological and/or sinful and in need of cure, healing, or repair. Although Sherry, Adelman, Whilde, and Quick (2010) noted that counselors should avoid assuming that affectional minority religious clients are necessarily dealing with identity conflicts between their religious beliefs and their affectional orientation, there are certainly many affectional minority clients who present with issues pertaining to just such conflict.

Dahl and Galliher (2009) found that in a study of 105 lesbian, gay, bisexual, queer, and questioning young adults 18 to 24 years old, 42% of the participants reported having grown up in a family that attended religious services weekly, and another 44% reported having grown up in families that attended services less frequently. Moreover, 46% of these participants reported having at least some experiences of being an open affectional minority and religious at the same time, whereas 54% reported never having experiences of being concurrently religious and open as an affectional minority (Dahl & Galliher, 2009). Assessing current perceptions of religious and sexual identity, 80% of the sample reported having either somewhat or not at all integrated their religious and sexual identities. Furthermore, Dahl and Galliher found that among those who disclosed their affectional orientation in religious settings, 60% reported experiences of conflict ranging from minor to extreme. Although some chose to dis-identify with their religious group as a result of this experience of conflict, others continued religious activity with the same religious group despite experiencing increased tension and conflict (Dahl & Galliher, 2009).

Responses to the intersection of religious faith and affectional orientation and gender identity vary. In a study of 422 affectional minority respondents, 29.3% reported converting from a nonaffirming to an affirming religion, 14.5% reported already holding affirming beliefs, 10.5% rejected God/religion altogether, and 12.4% reported continuing their beliefs but feeling shame and guilt (Sherry et al., 2010). In total, the largest group of participants experienced sexual identity as a catalyst for changing religious beliefs, the second largest group identified as spiritual and not religious, a third group indicated never experiencing conflict between religious and spiritual identity, and 43 respondents self-reported as still searching for religious or spiritual identities and beliefs that felt congruent with their affectional orientation.

As these studies suggest, for many affectional minority persons, successfully navigating conflicts in religious/sexual identity development will eventuate in drastically altering previously held religious identities or abandoning religious involvement altogether. For others, successful identity development will lead to a process in which the integration of both a minority sexual identity and a religious identity is of vital importance (Dahl & Galliher, 2009). For still others, their intention may be to change their affectional orientation or gender identity in order to live a life congruent with their deeply held religious beliefs concerning the pathological or sinful nature of their affectional or gender identity. For counselors, the presentation of a desire for affectional orientation change in therapy presents an ethical dilemma.

Bartoli and Gillem (2008) argued, "As therapists, we are called to foster a therapeutic process that will help clients find healthy expressions of all parts of themselves" (p. 206). Jenkins and Johnston (2004) noted that in an attempt to honor all parts of a client's sense of self (affectional orientation, gender identity, religious commitments, etc.), some counselors may believe that offering reparative therapy is a method of honoring the self-determination or choices of clients wishing to change their affectional orientation. Knowing, however, that the extant research suggests that reparative or conversion therapy is ineffective and can cause harm in the lives of LGBTQI+ people (Haldeman, 2002b), counselors wishing to address the ethical dilemma of client requests for affectional orientation change require a way forward beyond simply refusing to point clients toward practitioners of reparative or conversion therapy.

Affectual Orientation Minority *and* Religiously Affirmative Counseling: An Ethical Imperative

Although practicing, promoting, or encouraging orientation change efforts is unethical and contrary to professional standards set by organizations like ACA, the American Psychological Association, and other mental health organizations, the ethical dilemma raised by clients' requests for SOCE is not alleviated by simply dismissing the request or discouraging clients from seeking such therapeutic interventions. Whitman et al. (2013) advised counselors to educate clients requesting reparative or conversion therapy about the potential harm this type of therapy can induce. They suggested that, without imposing their own values, counselors must try to help clients make informed decisions while leaving the door open for the clients to return to them should conversion therapy prove ineffective or harmful.

Even this, however, does not address the real complexity of the ethical dilemma of the request. Counselors seeking to practice affirming counseling for affectional minority clients must also attend to the complexities and intersections between sexual and religious identifications and commitments. Thus, Haldeman (2002a) noted that the first task of counselors working with clients requesting SOCE should be a careful assessment of motive.

Given that the experience of religious or spiritual identity is often as deeply held and as highly valued as one's sexual identity, Haldeman (2002a) argued that the same respect accorded sexual identity should be displayed for clients' religion or spirituality. Indeed,

> In some circumstances, it is more conceivable, and less emotionally disruptive, for an individual to contemplate changing sexual orientation than to disengage from a religious way of life that is seen as completely central to the individual's sense of self and purpose. (p. 262)

The imposition of the primacy of sexual identity over a client's religious or spiritual identity can feel as invalidating as the imposition of religious views that discriminate against affectional minority individuals. Instead of this imposition of primacy of one aspect of a client's identity over any other, addressing the ethical dilemmas posed by these intersections aims toward an integrative approach.

Bartoli and Gillem (2008) suggested that when working with clients facing tensions and conflicts between sexual and religious identity development, counselors should view their work as aiding clients in finding points of connection between religious and sexual identities. This involves exploring attachments to each identity and the meaning that clients hold about those identities that may be contributing to inner conflict. Davidson (2000) argued, "We must begin to understand spirituality not simply as an issue or concern, but as a lived dimension and transformative worldview in the lives of some gay, lesbian, and bisexual persons" (p. 410).

What is typically called *identity* is a tapestry incorporating various threads woven into a seemingly integrated whole; individuals can see their religious backgrounds intersecting in various places with their current religious views and spiritual practices. These religious strands of the identity tapestry also intersect in various other places with the many identity threads making up racial identity, affectional orientation, gender identity, cultural heritage, and so on. The points of connection that Bartoli and Gillem (2008) noted—the places where threads overlap and become interwoven in many complex ways—become sites of curiosity for counselors aiming toward an affirming and integrative approach to clients' affectional orientation and spirituality. Undertaking these explorations ethically may require counselors to expand their repertory of knowledge and resources to aid clients in addressing identity conflicts that precipitated requests for SOCE.

There are, for example, many resources involved in the process of exploring and integrating the multiple strands of one's identity that are outside a counselor's purview of practice. In addressing the intersection of affectional orientation and faith, Dahl and Galliher (2009) found that two thirds of participants were aided by an increased knowledge of biblical and religious readings, whereas 27% were helped by becoming involved in a religious organization that affirmed affectional minority persons, 18% of whom changed religious affiliations to aid in the process of religious and sexual identity integration. Another 17% of participants were aided by the support of clergy in dealing with religious and sexual identity conflicts. Only 13% of participants reported either somewhat or completely integrating their sexual and religious identities with the support of a counselor.

In their study of 583 participants involved in organized faith groups, Lease et al. (2005) found that, for those affectional minority persons who joined affirming religious groups, overt accepting behaviors and attitudes of the group provided a helpful contrast to negative societal messages about their affectional orientation. They concluded, "Interaction with an affirming faith group is clearly beneficial" (p. 385), and they encouraged counselors to develop the ability to provide information to affectional minority clients regarding affirming faith groups. Although affectional minority clients often desire involvement in religious institutions, Kubicek and colleagues (2009) found that many study participants did not feel comfortable attending a church of predominantly affectional minority congregants. Particularly for those who had grown up in more conservative religious traditions, going to a predominantly LGBTQI+ church was experienced as jarring. Thus, it is helpful for counselors to become aware of other religious contexts that are not exclusively populated by affectional minority congregants but that hold a welcoming and affirming stance toward affectional minority persons.

Counselors may encounter the need to access a wider literature than exists in the field of mental health counseling and psychology to prepare for this work with LGBTQI+ religious clients. In the literature on pastoral counseling, early attempts to generate meaningful literature around affectional orientation–related issues (McNeill, 1976,

1988) spawned a slow but steady stream of scholarship from pastoral theologians and pastoral counselors wishing to address affectional minority issues with a greater degree of proficiency (Graham, 1997; Griffin, 2006; Kundtz & Schlager, 2007; Marshall, 1997; Switzer, 1999; Tigert, 2005). For counselors desiring greater skill in working with LGBQ clients around religious (particularly Christian) narratives and themes, these works will be invaluable sources.

Davidson (2000) reminded counselors of the importance of considering integration as a *process* because sudden abandonment of valued religious expression can result in extreme isolation. We offer here the GRACE model as a means of assessing and integrating religious identity with LGBTQI+ clients in the counseling process, taking seriously the complexities of lived human experiences and the need for a thoughtful and careful process that honors all parts of a client's multiply constituted human identity.

The GRACE Model

The GRACE model was developed to address conflicts between faith and affectional orientation, especially in Christian contexts (Bozard & Sanders, 2011). However, the GRACE model could be readily adapted for application with clients of other spiritual identities. The painful and isolating events and messages communicated to many affectional minority individuals from within some religious sectors are contradicted by the GRACE model's invocation of the theological concept of grace, with its uplifting connotations of acceptance and connection with God. Counselors can apply the model to assist their clients in moving toward a healthy integration of their affectional orientation and their spirituality. In this way, clients who have experienced faith and affectional orientation as sources of internal conflict and emotional pain may experience new hope and vitality as they come to experience both their affectional orientation and their spirituality as complementary strengths.

The GRACE model consists of five dimensions: goals, renewal, action, connection, and empowerment (Bozard & Sanders, 2011). The goals and renewal dimensions help to prepare clients. The connection and empowerment dimensions help clients to integrate positive changes into their lives toward spiritual connection. The action dimension serves as a bridge between preparation and integration by inviting clients to assume risks and move forward. The model may sometimes be applied in a linear fashion; however, in some cases the dimensions may be applied in varying sequences based on the needs of specific clients. The GRACE model may prove most relevant when spirituality emerges as a concern of a client, especially one who claims some form of Christian identity. The model may be useful in helping clients to clarify values, explore new possibilities for spiritual engagement, and ultimately be able to experience faith as a positive strength in their lives.

Goal Exploration

Goal exploration includes four potential foci: (a) the client's religious history, (b) affective considerations, (c) identification of client goals, and (d) assessment of client readiness (Bozard & Sanders, 2011). Affectional minority clients will likely describe qualitatively diverse encounters and engagements with religion. Some clients will currently identify as Christian; whereas others will have rejected the faith because of negative encounters; and still others will be uncertain about the nature of their faith identity, perhaps desiring to be Christian but having been told that they are sinners condemned to eternity in hell because of their natural sexual attractions. The counselor may find it useful to inquire about experiences related both to clients' understanding of and connection with God and to their experiences with Christian people and communities, as the nature of these experiences may differ. The counselor might assess aspects of spirituality that have been experienced as positives and aspects that have been experienced as negatives.

Affective considerations focus on feelings about faith. Are there emotional blocks preventing clients from progressing in spiritual development? Feelings related to themes such as condemnation, isolation, rejection, and shaming in spiritual contexts will require clinical attention in order to help clients move forward and be ready to embrace healthy spirituality. A grief approach may be necessary to process estrangement from Christian communities and loss of what were once foundational spiritual beliefs.

Identification of goals involves consideration of clients' desires for spiritual life. Do they desire a relationship with God, a relationship with a church community, or personal spiritual practices such as meditation and prayer? Spirituality contains both communal and individual elements, and clients will present along a continuum based on their personal histories and hopes.

Assessing client readiness is essential to ascertaining when and how quickly clients might be able to move toward spiritual engagement. Accurate assessment is critical for the production of successful outcomes, as clients who are encouraged to move forward with spiritual connection before they are ready may experience further frustration or trauma. Consideration of religious history, affective considerations, and goals will inform this assessment process.

Renewal of Hope

Many clients who have received negative messages about their affectional orientation from religious sources present for treatment with low levels of hope for faith connection. Spiritually induced guilt, shame, confusion, and rejection color client perceptions of spirituality. Clients with condemnatory and isolating experiences of religion may need a renewal of hope that faith can be for them an affirming and strengthening dimension of life. Clients who have believed the frequently disseminated messages that "same-sex attraction" and relationships are sinful—displeasing to God—may need to believe for the first time in their lives that religion can be fully accepting and affirming of them as lesbian, gay, or bisexual people. The number of Christian churches and organizations with explicitly supportive and welcoming stances toward sexual inclusivity is increasing. Even in contexts in which official institutional statements remain discriminatory, subgroups and individuals in those contexts may be sexually inclusive to varying degrees. Clients may discover hope in the fact that the few biblical passages used to justify rejection of same-sex relationships may actually be irrelevant to affectional orientation as it is understood in our current times (Brawley, 1996). Both counselor and client may access online resources, access print publications, and consult with affirming Christian clergy to expand their awareness of opportunities for full inclusion in Christian faith and contexts (e.g., Brownson, 2013; De La Torre, 2007; Human Rights Campaign, 2015; Michaelson, 2011; Sanders, 2013; Soulforce, 2015). Even without a full understanding of the details in the initial stages of counseling, general awareness that full spiritual acceptance is possible can help clients begin to renew hope that meaningful and supportive spirituality is possible.

Action

As clients begin to transition from preparation to integration, several aspects of action may be useful to consider. Do clients desire to remain, renew, or create (Bozard & Sanders,

2011)? That is, how might initial engagement with spirituality occur? Clients may have current relationships with God and church, allowing for the potential for change in an existing spiritual space. Clients who are currently disconnected may be able to reconnect with former relationships in healthier ways. Or clients may seek new opportunities, contexts, beliefs, or relationships as a means toward spiritual vitality. Each choice to remain, renew, or create implies specific opportunities and, perhaps, challenges.

In advance of participating in a spiritual congregation or other community, clients may want to consider whether they want to be *out* about their affectional orientation and, if so, when and how they might share that aspect of their identity. Some clients may feel more comfortable testing the waters—gaining a sense of the community context—before making a full disclosure. Others may feel fully comfortable sharing their sexual identity and their partner/spouse with the community. Although clients should be supported in either choice they make, motivations for hiding one's sexual identity may be worthwhile to explore.

Further considerations of the action dimension include the following:

- *Timing.* When will clients be ready to begin engaging spirituality? Does something more need to happen before clients are ready?
- *Priorities.* What do clients hope to accomplish through spiritual engagement? Which goal is most important?
- *Resources.* What resources will be necessary or helpful for action to occur? Counseling; bibliotherapy; social support from partners, family members, or friends; and awareness of the religious experiences of other affectional minority people could be important sources of strength.

Connection

As stated previously, clients may prefer connection with God or connection with people through spiritual community or both forms of connection simultaneously. For some affectional minority clients, connection with God will be the most concerning, especially for clients who have received messages, perhaps their whole lives, that God condemns same-sex activity and relationships. Helping clients to become open to new possibilities of joyful, affirming experiences of religion may be an important role for the counselor. Perhaps clients will need to let go of previous hateful images of God and embrace loving images of God. Clients may need to understand that although ideas and feelings associated with God's acceptance and rejection can be changed, doing so may require repeated reinforcement on their part over an extended period of time.

Clients may have believed or been told that scripture and church organizations condemn same-sex activity and relationships. This history of belief, sometimes reinforced with emotion-laden condemnation from members of faith communities, frequently constitutes a major barrier to connection with God. Although most counselors have no formal theological education, and in many cases no familiarity with practices and beliefs of specific churches and religious organizations, counselors can inform clients that many people of faith today interpret holy texts in affirming ways. Clients who desire to learn about biblical interpretations may be directed to online resources, books, or appropriate religious representatives. Clients may benefit from an acknowledgment of the distinction between God and those who profess to follow God. Critical statements of condemnation from some religious people can and should be understood as separate and distinct from God's acceptance. Exploration of possible motives behind such critical viewpoints might be beneficial. Motives might include homophobia, unquestioned social stereotypes, and simple ignorance. The counselor's empathy and support might serve as a meaningful bridge to envisioning God in a similarly caring and supportive light.

Clients seeking connection with a congregation or other religious community may feel intimidated by the process of locating affirming faith contexts. Clients living in rural and ideologically conservative areas may be at a disadvantage, with fewer opportunities for supportive face-to-face experiences of spiritual community than those available to LGBTQI+ people living in more populous and progressive contexts. Online links to spiritual communities may be especially valuable to the former. Counselors can remind clients that they may move slowly, at their own pace, in seeking spiritual community. Increasing numbers of churches are moving toward explicitly accepting and affirming stances, including conducting blessings of same-sex relationships and marriages. Even in churches in which no explicit statement of welcome has been proclaimed, subgroups and individuals in the congregation may be accepting. For example, one of us is acquainted with a local congregation in the southern United States that belongs to a denomination that continues to formally condemn same-sex activity. Yet in the local church, a Sunday school class has made formal public statements in support of full affectional minority acceptance and attracts a diverse class membership. Counselors will do well to learn about affirming spiritual communities in their local area. Furthermore, counselors may caution clients that even in formally affirming contexts, some individuals may be less progressive in their personal views so that clients will hold realistic expectations.

Empowerment

Empowerment—ongoing external and internal sources of strength and support—is important on a long-term basis. LGBTQI+ Christians continue to face persistent challenges from various sources in society. Intentional clinical processing of client experiences and feelings throughout the process is crucial. Clients with affectional orientation variance may even encounter social resistance to religious identity and connections from within the LGBTQI+ communities due to the distrust resulting from a long history of religious oppression. Simultaneously, clients can draw strength from allies they encounter in face-to-face and online contexts. Attention to self-esteem, sexual identity development, and spiritual identity development in the counseling context can be important empowering elements in the quest to connect with God and spiritual communities.

Application of the GRACE Model in the Case of William

In considering William's case, Brenda considered potential contributing factors to William's report of an underlying lack of meaning. Brenda surmised that based on his psychosocial history, including the value William had once placed on his Christian faith, his present condition might be exacerbated by the critical messages William had internalized about his affectional orientation from the church and the resulting social and spiritual alienation he experienced as he discontinued his attention to faith and the faith community. Brenda began to explore with William questions about meaning, identity, and spirituality. She invited William to imagine that his life had gone in a different direction, that, for example, he had been part of a church during his adolescent and college years that was accepting of his affectional orientation. William expressed his belief that he likely would still be active in his religious faith, as God and church had been important sources of meaning and direction and community for him as a young man.

In applying the GRACE model with William, Brenda reviewed William's religious history as he had shared it during the intake process. Following are ways in which Brenda addressed the dimensions of the GRACE model with William.

Goal Exploration

Brenda asked William to identify aspects of his religious experiences that he believed held special influence in his life in the past or present. William reiterated the highlights he had previously provided, naming his profession of faith, baptism, disappointment that his prayers to become heterosexual were not answered, and rejection of active spirituality because he believed God and the church regarded him as sinful because of his affectional orientation. Brenda discussed William's feelings about these experiences. William denied any presently strong feelings about the religious experiences other than a moderate sadness when he thought about his loss of faith. He recalled feeling anger in his earlier years toward God, the church, and others who condemned gay people like him in the name of religion.

Brenda reflected to William the losses he had associated with his religious history. She then asked him whether he could identify strengths he associated with religion in spite of the ways it had been hurtful for him. William pointed out the sense of purpose he had once found in his Christian faith. Brenda asked William whether he might be able to regain that sense of purpose if he could find a way to reengage his spirituality. William endorsed the possibility but stated his reticence about trying to connect with the church again. Together, Brenda and William identified a possible goal as healthy reconnection with faith in ways that William could find both desirable and meaningful. Brenda determined that William was ready to move forward with exploration of faith because he had an explicit goal, stated his desire to move forward in exploring that goal, and did not present any significant emotional barriers necessitating resolution.

Renewal of Hope

William's sense of optimism increased based on the possibility that he might be able to find positive ways to again connect with God and church. The counselor inquired with William about what kind of religious community he might see himself wanting to join. He stated that he would most readily identify with a congregation in the same Protestant denomination in which he had grown up. During one of their sessions, Brenda conducted some basic online research with William about local affirming congregations. They learned through a basic Internet search that William's denomination remained officially opposed to same-sex activity and relationships. William expressed disappointment. At Brenda's urging, they continued searching other sites and discovered a congregation about 10 miles from William's home that was affiliated with his former denomination yet at the local level had posted some statements of support of the LGBTQI+ community on the local church website. William felt hope intermingled with caution at this discovery.

Action

Brenda asked William whether he envisioned himself more as potentially renewing his former faith or as creating a new engagement with faith. William said he believed his desire was probably more in the vein of renewal. Brenda asked William how open he expected to be about his gay identity if he were to connect with a congregation. William had no doubt that his desire was to be fully out in whatever spiritual context he might engage in. William felt as though any form of secrecy about his affectional orientation would be like a return to the closet from which he had emerged years earlier. William did express some feelings of trepidation and discomfort at the thought of attending a church service for the first time in a matter of years. He felt unsure about how he would be accepted, especially if his partner attended with him. Brenda assured William that such feelings were not surprising to her. They discussed together step by step what William might be likely to encounter during his first visit to the church, processing feelings he might encounter at each point and how he might respond or rethink the circumstances.

Brenda and William discussed the timeline with which William expected to act on his religious exploration. William was clear that he wanted to move with caution, giving himself ample time to acclimate and assess, but he saw himself as being ready to act on his explorations in the near future, perhaps in a matter of weeks. William appreciated Brenda's assurance that she would support him and continue to process with him any disturbing feelings that might emerge as he acted. Finally, Brenda invited William to prioritize his hopes regarding spiritual exploration. Brenda inquired about whether William felt more of a desire to connect with God or to connect with a religious community. William replied that connection with a church where he could feel completely accepted as a gay man seemed most important but that he also desired a deeper connection with God.

Connection

Brenda and William next began to prepare for William's first visit to the church they had earlier discovered on the Internet. Brenda advised William that he might consider contacting the church pastor in advance of his visit to inquire about the church's position on acceptance of affectional orientation variance if that would be helpful to him. William opted just to show up for a regular church service and see what impressions he would gain through the experience. Brenda added that, like most Christian denominations, the denomination had an unofficial and independent LGBTQI+ advocacy organization called All Together that William might wish to investigate for possible membership or utilization of their online resources.

William reported in the next session that he had visited the church. The experience felt intimidating and provoked some anxiety in William, but he pushed through the rather mild discomfort and had a positive experience. Several of the church members greeted him and invited him to return. William noticed what appeared to be two gay and lesbian couples seated in the service, which felt reassuring. He planned to return. Brenda noted that William appeared to be more upbeat, demonstrating a level of energy and enthusiasm that she had not yet witnessed in their work together.

Empowerment

Empowerment is ideally an ongoing process that continues beyond the extent of the therapeutic relationship. In this case, Brenda offered empathic support to William through multiple means, including encouraging William to focus on the potential for positive outcomes through reengagement with his lost spirituality, providing practical information such as resources about affirming congregations in the area, and sensitively validating the painful feelings he associated with past experiences with religion. As William increased his participation in the church he chose, he became further empowered by the acceptance and support of friends he began to make there and church staff members.

William saw Brenda for counseling for a total span of around 1 year. As he slowly embraced religious involvement again, they continued to address episodes of anger and sadness that would emerge as the church context triggered memories of his previous negative interactions with the unaccepting church of his childhood. William reported that his presenting symptoms improved and mostly disappeared by the end of his work with Brenda. William reported an increase in his overall happiness with life. Spirituality provided a context for William to give explicit attention to developing a deeper level of meaning in his life. His reemerging faith in God furthermore provided an additional source of internal strength for his life. Brenda effectively worked with William in navigating his conflictual feelings about the Christian identity that had once been so meaningful for him and then helped to empower him in recovering and expanding his religious faith as a positive element in his life.

Conclusion

Counselors sometimes feel reticent about discussing spirituality in depth with clients. Counselors who work with clients with affectional orientation variance may be aware of the unethical practice of reparative therapy with its damaging effects and associate religion exclusively with such anti-LGBTQI+ stances. Yet many affectional minority people desire to engage in or reengage faith for a number of healthy motives, including the positive energy that belief in God can bring to life and the feelings of social acceptance offered in a welcoming community context. The GRACE model offers clinicians an outline to help LGBTQI+ clients—most explicitly those with a Christian identity or preference but perhaps others as well—to navigate the sometimes perilous intersection of affectional orientation and spirituality.

Questions for Further Discussion

1. What issues should Brenda consider in terms of William's previous attempts to reorient his orientation in terms of her conceptualization of his case? What if William described his experience with conversion or reparative therapy as "abusive"?
2. What resources outside of Brenda's counseling could be helpful in her work with William? How should she familiarize herself with these resources?
3. What specific counseling interventions, techniques, and theories might Brenda utilize to apply various dimensions of the GRACE model? For example, could techniques like art therapy, sandplay, or the Miracle Question (i.e., How will the future be different when the problem is no longer present?) be helpful with William?
4. If William were Jewish rather than Christian, how might Brenda adapt the GRACE model? What aspects of the model may not adequately address other traditions?
5. If William began presenting with strong feelings of anger toward organized religion because of his experiences, should Brenda introduce the possibility of reconnecting with spirituality? If so, how and when might she do it? If not, why not?

Resources

1. Visit the Believe Out Loud website at http://www.believeoutloud.com/.
2. Read Anthony Ashford's essay on why Christians should embrace same-sex relationships at http://www.religioustolerance.org/ashford00.htm#menu.
3. Read Reverend Patrick S. Cheng's blog on why coming out receives God's grace at http://www.huffingtonpost.com/rev-patrick-s-cheng-phd/sin-as-the-closet-grace-a_b_510437.html.
4. Listen to an alternative interpretation of Bible verses regarding "homosexuality" at http://www.upworthy.com/there-are-6-scriptures-about-homosexuality-in-the-bible-heres-what-they-really-say.
5. Find more resources through the Gay Christian Network at https://www.gaychristian.net.

References

Bartoli, E., & Gillem, A. R. (2008). Continuing to depolarize the debate on sexual orientation and religion: Identity and the therapeutic process. *Professional Psychology: Research and Practice, 39*(2), 202–209. doi:10.1037/0735-7028.39.2.202

Bozard, R. L., & Sanders, C. J. (2011). Helping Christian lesbian, gay, and bisexual clients recover religion as a source of strength: Developing a model for assessment and integration of religious identity in counseling. *Journal of LGBT Issues in Counseling, 5*(1), 47–74. doi:10.1080/15538605.2011.554791

Brawley, R. L. (Ed.). (1996). *Biblical ethics and homosexuality: Listening to scripture.* Louisville, KY: Westminster John Knox Press.

Brownson, J. V. (2013). *Bible, gender, sexuality: Reframing the church's debate on same-sex relationships.* Grand Rapids, MI: Eerdmans.

Dahl, A. L., & Galliher, R. V. (2009). LGBQQ young adult experiences of religious and sexual identity integration. *Journal of LGBT Issues in Counseling, 3*(2), 92–112. doi:10.1080/15538600903005268

Davidson, M. G. (2000). Religion and spirituality. In R. M. Perez, K. A. DeBord, & K. J. Bieschke (Eds.), *Handbook of counseling and psychotherapy with lesbian, gay, and bisexual clients* (pp. 409–433). Washington, DC: American Psychological Association.

De La Torre, M. (2007). *A lily among the thorns: Imagining a new Christian sexual ethic.* San Francisco, CA: Jossey-Bass.

Graham, L. K. (1997). *Discovering images of God: Narratives of care among lesbians and gays.* Louisville, KY: Westminster John Knox Press.

Griffin, H. L. (2006). *Their own receive them not: African American lesbians and gays in Black churches.* Cleveland, OH: Pilgrim Press.

Haldeman, D. C. (2002a). Gay rights, patient rights: The implications of sexual orientation conversion therapy. *Professional Psychology: Research and Practice, 33*(3), 260–264.

Haldeman, D. (2002b). Therapeutic antidotes: Helping gay and bisexual men recover from conversion therapies. *Journal of Gay and Lesbian Psychotherapy, 5,* 119–132. doi:10.1300/j236v05n03_08

Human Rights Campaign. (2015). *Explore: Religion and faith.* Retrieved from http://www.hrc.org/topics/religion-faith

Jenkins, D., & Johnston, L. B. (2004). Unethical treatment of gay and lesbian people with conversion therapy. *Families in Society, 85,* 557–561. doi:10.1606/1044-3894.1846

Kubicek, K., McDavitt, B., Carpineto, J., Weiss, G., Iverson, E. F., & Kipke, M. D. (2009). "God made me gay for a reason": Young men who have sex with men's resiliency in resolving internalized homophobia from religious sources. *Journal of Adolescent Research, 24,* 601–633. doi:10.1177/0743558409341078

Kundtz, D. J., & Schlager, B. S. (2007). *Ministry among God's queer folk: LGBT pastoral care.* Cleveland, OH: Pilgrim Press.

Lease, S. H., Horne, S. G., & Noffsinger-Frazier, N. (2005). Affirming faith experiences and psychological health for Caucasian lesbian, gay, and bisexual individuals. *Journal of Counseling Psychology, 52*(3), 378–388. doi:10.1037/0022-0167.52.3.378

Lovett, I. (2013, June 20). *After 37 years of trying to change people's sexual orientation, group is to disband.* Retrieved from the *New York Times* website: http://www.nytimes.com/2013/06/21/us/group-that-promoted-curing-gays-ceases-operations.html?_r=0

Marshall, J. L. (1997). *Counseling lesbian partners.* Louisville, KY: John Knox Press.

McNeill, J. J. (1976). *The church and the homosexual* (4th ed.). Boston, MA: Beacon Press.

McNeill, J. J. (1988). *Taking a chance on God: Liberating theology for gays, lesbians, and their lovers, families, and friends* (2nd ed.). Boston, MA: Beacon Press.

Michaelson, J. (2011). *God vs. gay? The religious case for gay equality.* Boston, MA: Beacon Press.

Newport, F. (2009, December 24). *This Christmas, 78% of Americans identify as Christian.* Retrieved from http://www.gallup.com/poll/124793/this-christmas-78-americans-identify-christian.aspx

Parker, S. (2010, Winter). A voice of inclusivity. *Voices,* p. 3.

Sanders, C. J. (2013). *Queer lessons for churches on the straight and narrow: What all Christians can learn from LGBTQ lives.* Macon, GA: FaithLab.

Sherry, A., Adelman, A., Whilde, M. R., & Quick, D. (2010). Competing selves: Negotiating the intersection of spiritual and sexual identities. *Professional Psychology: Research and Practice, 41*(2), 112–119. doi:10.1037/a0017471

Soulforce. (2015). *Soulforce.* Retrieved from http://www.soulforce.org

Switzer, D. K. (1999). *Pastoral care of gays, lesbians and their families.* Minneapolis, MN: Augsburg Fortress.

Tigert, L. M. (2005). *Coming out through fire: Surviving the trauma of homophobia.* Cleveland, OH: United Church Press.

Whitman, J. S., Glosoff, H. L., Kocet, M. M., & Tarvydas, V. (2013, January 16). *Ethical issues related to conversion or reparative therapy.* Retrieved from https://www.counseling.org/news/updates/2013/01/16/ethical-issues-related-to-conversion-or-reparative-therapy

Chapter 24

Working With LGBTQI+ Clients Who Have Experienced Religious and Spiritual Abuse Using a Trauma-Informed Approach

Misty M. Ginicola, Joel M. Filmore, and Michael Stokes

I've spent literally years injuring myself, cutting and burning my arms,
taking overdoses and starving myself,
to punish myself so that God doesn't have to punish me.
It's taken me years to feel deserving of anything good.
—Anonymous client of Dr. Marlene Winell

• • •

Awareness of Attitudes and Beliefs Self-Check

1. Close your eyes and picture someone being religiously abused. What do you see? How are your biases and stereotypes of what is abuse present in that image? What did your image leave out?
2. What people have gone public regarding religious abuse? What kind of abuse has been highlighted in the media? Are emotional and psychological trauma ever prominent?
3. How do you view religious leaders? How could this viewpoint present a bias when working with clients who have been victims of religious abuse?

Case Study

Marcus is a 34-year-old biracial, African American, self-identified gay male. He was recently released from prison after having served 18 months of a 3-year sentence for robbery, in which he stole a purse. Prior to the robbery conviction, Marcus had spent the previous 10 years living as a transgender prostitute in order to support his addiction to crack-cocaine and heroin. During his first session, Marcus shares with you that he was a victim of sex trafficking, whereby he was coerced into prostitution through intimidation and the use of narcotics as a tool of control. He discusses his early childhood, of being biracial in a White, racist, Christian family, and how experiences of physical, emotional, and sexual abuse were his earliest memories. As he also presents with some gender variance, he remembers hearing consistent negative beliefs surrounding his feminine traits, with family members telling him to be more masculine.

As a young adult, Marcus turned to religion as a means of "stopping being gay." He lived for a number of years in a religious commune that focused on the use of prayer, biblical reading, and abstinence to no longer give in to his sexual urges. He discusses how the shame of living "two lives" took its toll on him, as he was unable to be celibate. He would go through cycles of using drugs and having sex with men, only to return to the church to be forgiven. One of his prominent mentors, Jacob, worked with him on stopping the sexual thoughts he had, but when Marcus attempted to question theological philosophy about LGBTQI+ persons, Jacob would scold him to not ask so many questions and just take it on faith. Jacob would require Marcus to pray and at one point did not trust Marcus to leave the commune, as he felt Marcus "was fighting so many demons Satan was bound to win" if he went out on his own.

Marcus continued to feel guilt over not being able to stop having sexual thoughts about men, which led him to believe that he was evil, which in turn would drive him to relapse. He finally left the church when Jacob, about whom he cared very deeply, told him, "Maybe you're just not trying hard enough." This one event changed his view of religion and religious people to the present day. He shares how the friend who told him that he was not trying hard enough was someone who had watched him struggle to be a "strong man of God" over a number of years. He states that he realized, in that moment, that perhaps religious people were his problem. As he is now sober, he is looking for support to change his life in a better way, "without God or his people."

• • •

Religious Conflict

The church has historically had a significant influence in Western society. Even those individuals who do not actively participate in religious institutions are still impacted by the views and beliefs of the dominant Christian church in the United States. Although the notion of attempting to change someone's orientation from "homosexual" to heterosexual is not new, sexual orientation change efforts have become ever more common over the past two decades (Chaney, Filmore, & Goodrich, 2011; Drescher, 2003; Drescher & Zucker, 2006) and are almost exclusively performed by individuals with strong religious beliefs (Beckstead & Morrow, 2004; Jones & Yarhouse, 2007). The desire to be heterosexual reflects many ministries' multiple homophobic and heterosexist attitudes that impact not only their congregants but also all lesbian, gay, bisexual, transgender, queer, questioning, intersex, asexual, ally, pansexual/polysexual, and two-spirited (LGBTQI+) persons, as most evangelical religions seek to change legislation to reflect these values.

The connection between homophobia and oppression on the one hand and religious institutions on the other has a basis in history (see Chapter 1) as well as modern events. As discussed in Chapter 1, the more than 100 anti-LGBT so-called freedom laws have one thing in common: They are written from religious standpoints (Bendery & Signorile, 2016). These laws are most often based on Christian religious freedom to not provide goods and services to anyone who identifies as an affectional orientation or gender minority (Bendery & Signorile, 2016). These proposed (and some passed) laws stipulate that religious individuals should not have to provide goods or services to LGBTQI+ persons, as this could potentially violate their religious values. The authors of these laws are religious and openly espouse discrimination of LGBTQI+ persons. The authors and sponsors of these anti-LGBT bills deny that they are discriminatory. Christian conservatives believe that affectional orientation is something one chooses and reflects a lack of morals, and thus LGBTQI+ persons should not enjoy protections similar to ethnic minorities and those with disabilities (Chaney et al., 2011). These laws represent the message that is loud and clear in disaffirming religions: If you are an LGBTQI+ person, you are less than and not worthy of God's acceptance (Chaney et al., 2011).

Spiritual Abuse (SA)

The literature is replete with research on the benefits of religion and spirituality in terms of both treating mental health problems andachieving overall wellness (Stone, 2013). It may be difficult for some to imagine that such a positive influence could also be abusive; however, a mounting body of evidence indicates just that (Stone, 2013). Winell (n.d.) postulated that religious trauma would be more recognized in society and the mental health field were it not for taboos surrounding questioning mainstream religions. Winell (n.d.) pointed out that "toxic beliefs and abusive practices" are not isolated to small cults; mainstream, popular religions plagued with mind and behavior control, fundamentalist beliefs, and emotional abuse are just as likely to do harm to people.

Definition of SA

SA, sometimes also termed *religious abuse*, is not easily defined and evidences some disagreement in the literature. However, Oakley and Kinmond (2013a) defined *SA* as

> the coercion and control of one individual by another in a spiritual context. The target experiences SA as a deeply emotional personal attack. This abuse may include: manipulation and exploitation, enforced accountability, censorship of decision-making, requirements for secrecy and silence, pressure to conform, misuse of scripture or the pulpit to control behavior, requirement of obedience to the abuser, the suggestion that the abuser has a "divine" position, and isolation from others, especially those external to the abusive context. (p. 21)

Experience of SA

Oakley (2009) found that SA is situated in a cultural context, with a surrounding culture supporting power inequality between the offender and victim of SA, and in a community with permeable boundaries at the societal level. The perpetrators of SA may be religious leaders, but they also may be mentors or family members operating in a religious context (Oakley & Kinmond, 2013a). Blue (1993) identified the fact that unlike many other forms of abuse, the perpetrator of SA may be completely unaware of the impact of the abuse; perpetrators may instead believe that they are acting out of moral necessity and are being helpful to the victim. Also important to consider in terms of cultural context is that although religious cults are not supported by societal culture, mainstream religions are. Because this type of abuse can occur in mainstream religions, it can often further isolate victims because they receive cultural messages that these experiences are within the range of normal (Oakley & Kinmond, 2013a).

As LGBTQI+ youth who grow up in a disaffirming religion are engaging with developing an alternative identity (Cass, 1979), they encounter messages in the cultural context that are heteronormative, with potentially no positive LGBTQI+ role models. There are multiple cultural messages related to affectional orientation and gender variation that reflect such differences as unfavorable (Jackson, 2011). Without any known LGBTQI+ persons in their experience, these youth are left to problem-solve these identity issues themselves (Sue, 2010). In their religious community and family context, they receive and internalize messages that are profoundly homophobic in nature. One participant in a study by Ginicola and Smith (2016) of the influence of religion on identity development recounted the following:

> I grew up in Southern Mississippi, in a place where Baptist is the only religion. My parents were, and still are, ultra-conservative Evangelical Christians. We were in church every time the doors opened . . . I heard a sermon . . . concerning homosexuality. "If a man lie with a man as he lieth with a woman." . . . In that moment, I had two revelations: 1. I am a homosexual, and 2. I am going to burn in hell for all eternity.

Part of the cultural context for religious-based abuse has historical roots. Blue (1993) noted that in Baxter's *The Reformed Pastor,* which was published in the mid-1600s, elements of SA were actually included as instructions to Christian religious leaders. However, these methods are certainly not restricted to Christianity. The *shepherding* movement that began in the 1960s is still utilized in some Christian religions (Plowman, 1975). In opposition to the liberal, secular culture, the church became the small community hub where conservative values were still intact (Moore, 2004). In this surrogate family, the bonds within became stronger as the secular community's bonds became more diffuse (Moore, 2004). Shepherds were responsible for discipling and mentoring small groups of individuals. Many shepherds required members to take on the role of a disciple, in submission and obedience to the interpretations of the scripture with the shepherd's requests considered divine (Okeyan, 2000). Although this movement was formally abandoned, the principles have persisted in the consciousness of many religions (Okeyan, 2000). These strategies were revisited in the first book ever published on SA (Johnson & VanVonderen, 1991). Although SA can occur in any religion, it is widely documented in charismatic and evangelical churches (Enroth, 1992).

LGBTQI+ persons commonly experience shame and confusion attached to their understanding of their own attractions, which causes them to internalize much of their thoughts and feelings (Sue, 2010). The internalization process only perpetuates feelings of isolation, confusion, and embarrassment at discussing their affectional orientation (Omoto & Kurtzman, 2006). At some point, they may seek help from such a shepherd or mentor in the church. In a disaffirming context, the shepherd or mentor will embrace individuals while simultaneously rejecting their sin. This mentorship is likely to include ex-gay and faith-based reparative experiences designed to reorient their attractions or manage the addictive, sinful impulses of "same-sex attraction" (Wolkomir, 2006). The individuals receive a strong message that the only way to receive love and support as well as to achieve their spirituality is to change their affectional orientation.

Those who perpetrate SA have been found to have certain personality characteristics, including narcissistic elements (Ward, 2011). They also tend to be charming, with good interpersonal skills, which they often use to manipulate others (Ward, 2011). The literature also supports the fact that these spiritual leaders may experience insecurity in their beliefs but feel security in overcompensation and domination of others (Appleton, 2003; Blue, 1993). Some leaders feel that they have to portray a confident self-image of faith at all times; therefore, they may eschew questions or critiques (Blue, 1993). Needing to feel more significant and important is another factor in these abusers' personalities; thus, they respond poorly to personal and church-related criticism (Blue, 1993). Many leaders in ex-gay movements have identified as ex-gay themselves; some have later come out as not ex-gay but rather LGBTQI+ and admitted to sublimating their own attractions by attempting to change others (Ring, 2015; Truth Wins Out, n.d.). Others have left their posts because of scandals surrounding being outed for continuing to have same-sex relationships (Truth Wins Out, n.d.).

Winell (2006) postulated that the context of a church with fundamentalist beliefs can often draw vulnerable persons; these individuals so greatly desire what the church provides for them that they will tolerate abuse from their spiritual leaders. Using Maslow's (1968) hierarchy, Winell (2006) demonstrated that the church, which may also serve as an extended or replacement family, can provide a member with

> survival (food water, and shelter), safety (physical and psychological security), belonging (love and acceptance), self esteem (approval and recognition), intellectual achievement (understanding and exploring), aesthetic appreciation (order, structure, and beauty), and self actualization (full realization of one's potential, the process of becoming who you are). (loc. 992)

Fundamentalists possess such confidence in their isolated access to truth and God, eliminating any ambiguity, resolving all fears, and satisfying the core needs of safety (Winell, 2006). The themes of fulfillment found in a fundamentalist church are rescue from death (i.e., the promise of an afterlife), protection from self (i.e., humans' natural inclination is toward sin), and escape from freedom and responsibility (e.g., God's will is always done). The congregation provides an ethical and moral code, a sense of belonging, and connectedness with God (which represents ultimate intimacy) and the family of God (i.e., the congregation that will go to great lengths to care for its members). The parishioner can find meaning, stimulation and escapism (i.e., engaging in stimulating excitement or drama that also allows one to escape from the world—examples would be conversion stories, prophesying, and fighting for moral imperatives), self-acceptance, and self-importance in the church. In addition, parishioners gain access to the sense of spirit, take on social causes, feel personal power, and achieve victory over threats in the world. Although Winell (2006) acknowledged that meeting people's needs is a positive aspect of religion, linking all sources of fulfillment to one external source that can take these provisions away at any point if the parishioner fails to obey can be dangerous.

The advantages of being involved in a fundamentalist religion also apply to LGBTQI+ persons. However, what complicates issues for LGBTQI+ individuals is that they are under an immense amount of minority stress, experiencing internalized homophobia and external cultural messages of heterosexism, homophobia, and homoprejudice (Meyer, 2003; Wood & Conley, 2014). When the church community fulfills all of their needs and then is removed, it can be even more dangerous, as LGBTQI+ persons are at a significant risk for suicide (Wood & Conley, 2014).

SA also involves a process or cycle of abuse, as do other experiences of abuse (Oakley, 2009). Individuals have a positive experience in the community; they feel valued, included, and loved (Oakley, 2009). However, victims of SA also commonly report a feeling of indebtedness: They feel that they must repay this generosity and wish to keep that warm connection (Kinmond & Oakley, 2015). They also hold the perpetrator in a position of spiritual and/or religious power, which can be seen as a divine position (Kinmond & Oakley, 2015). Perpetrators may exercise this power in requiring the individuals to be accountable to them, including them in decision making and censoring thoughts and experiences contrary to the belief system of the perpetrators (Appleton, 2003; Kinmond & Oakley, 2015; Parsons, 2000). Censorship and silence is a key part of SA: "Individuals come to realize that if they raise an issue, they quickly become the issue" (Kinmond & Oakley, 2015, p. 153). Many individuals are encouraged to focus on relationships in the place of worship and become isolated from the outside world; they receive the message that *the world* is an atmosphere of great danger and that the only place where they are certain to be safe is in the confines of the religious organization and its relationships (Kinmond & Oakley, 2015). The abuser may then manipulate victims in many ways. For example, the abuser may counter an individual's experience of disbelief or distress over something that the perpetrator did by telling the victim that these events never happened or discredit the victim in other ways (Kinmond & Oakley, 2015). Victims may feel confused, powerless, and disconnected from reality and their own perceptions, leaving them with self-doubt (Oakley & Kinmond, 2013a). When the abuser is a religious leader or is complicit with the primary abuser, victims can sometimes find their current struggles directly addressed in the message of a sermon in order to further manipulate them (Oakley & Kinmond, 2013a). If sexual abuse is included in this process, the impact on the individual's emotional, psychological, and spiritual life is devastating (Doyle, 2009). One of the key components of SA is that the scriptures and sacred texts are used to induce shame in the victim, which is key in the process of oppression (Oakley, 2009; Parish-West, 2009). As a result, the SA victim will remain compliant and submissive (Skedgell, 2008). The final aspect of this process is the level of control and obedience required by the religious community and abuser: The church becomes God, and nothing but blind allegiance will suffice to receive the positive regard, companionship, and community that the congregation provides (Oakley & Kinmond, 2013a). Members of the congregation who are loyal are given special status with positive regard and praise as rewards (Oakley & Kinmond, 2013a). When members do not conform, they experience emotional and social ostracism (Kinmond & Oakley, 2015).

This process works similarly for LGBTQI+ persons (Wood & Conley, 2014); however, the control is exercised surrounding their internal attractions (Morrow, 2003; Wolkomir, 2006). They are encouraged to share their intimate emotions and thoughts surrounding their attractions with their abuser. Each thought or feeling related to the authentic experience of their identity is met with a critique of their morality and how they must fight against their own sinful nature. If LGBTQI+ persons question acceptance of their affectional orientation (e.g., "Why would God make me gay?"), they are promptly silenced with the abuser's interpretation of the scripture. The abuser could out them to the congregation; the abuser could also ensure that "homosexuality" is a regular sermon topic in the congregation. As long as LGBTQI+ persons fight their attractions and seek forgiveness, they are accepted, even when they make mistakes and have sex with someone of the same sex. As long as they are repentant, they are accepted back into the fold. However, if they do not conform in some manner, the abuse necessitates that they be ostracized and isolated.

The essence of this abusive relationship is that "it is about power . . . and it is done in the name of God" (Oakley & Kinmond, 2013a, p. 24). The other foundational aspect is fear, usually fear of damnation (Winell, 2008). Seeing the self as inherently bad and not thinking or feeling are also foundational messages that individuals internalize from the cycle of SA (Winell, 2008). LGBTQI+ parishioners enter into these power relationships in an attempt to experience acceptance and change their orientation (Wolkomir, 2006). They can also lose their intuitive sense and trust in their own judgment (Wehr, 2000). They begin to hate themselves, a feeling that is intensified if they fail to maintain a heterosexual life (Morrow, 2003; Wolkomir, 2006). Their overarching message is to absolutely not think or feel about their authenticity, their attractions, the depression they feel in attempting to be heterosexual, and the fact that the sexual orientation change efforts are not working (Morrow, 2003; Wolkomir, 2006; Wood & Conley, 2014).

If a parent is responsible for abuse to a child and that abuse is related to the parent's religious beliefs, the outcome for the LGBTQI+ client may be long-term negative impacts on the client's psychological well-being (Bottoms, Nielsen, Murray, & Filipas, 2003; Simonič, Mandelj, &

Novsak, 2013). In the case of SA and LGBTQI+ persons, the parent could be the abuser, physically, emotionally, and spiritually. These stressful experiences in childhood lead to increased psychiatric symptoms, negative coping factors, and revictimization in "sexual minorities" (Schneeberger, Dietl, Muenzenmaier, Huber, & Lang, 2014). This level of trauma would be intense and could result in a complex form of posttraumatic stress disorder (PTSD).

Leaving this cycle of abuse becomes difficult, as the religious institution has become the LGBTQI+ person's primary support as well as that person's primary abuser (Kinmond & Oakley, 2015). In addition, the victim has been repeatedly told that that particular place of worship is the *only* place where the victim can find spiritual fulfillment; this *truth* cannot be found in the frightening secular world or with other religions, which are misled and not following scripture in the intended manner (Kinmond & Oakley, 2015). A single church (or synagogue, mosque, etc.) may claim better alignment with scriptural texts than other similar churches even of the same denomination (Kinmond & Oakley, 2015). When individuals are finally ready to leave the abuse, they may have been prompted by several experiences, including developmental change (for children, getting older; for adults, this can be a change in thinking that is less rigid) or finding no resolution to a question surrounding fundamentalist doctrine (Winell, 2006). The person may have become disillusioned with fundamentalist attitudes and their intolerance, experienced sexism and patriarchy, and been disappointed with Christian life and/or the community (Winell, 2006). The person also may have reached out past the congregation and gained new information or other worldviews and found comfort in a secular setting and other fulfillments (Winell, 2006). LGBTQI+ persons may have additionally become tired of fighting themselves and getting nowhere with their affectional orientation.

The process of breaking away from the abuse may be abrupt or gradual (Winell, 2006). The majority of trauma symptoms may often begin after individuals leave. Although they have left the congregation, they realize the extent of the damage done in the church; they may also have internalized many of the negative beliefs, which they continue to struggle with on their own. Beyond the shift in belief systems, the loss of social support and connection with a community can also be traumatic (Winell, n.d.). The individual experiences disturbance at physical, psychological, social, emotional, and spiritual levels (Ward, 2011). Many LGBTQI+ persons report a complete loss of their faith and spiritual beliefs (Wood & Conley, 2014). Winell (n.d.) has termed this set of symptoms *religious trauma syndrome*, in which the person has several PTSD symptoms, depression, anxiety, and anger. Wehr (2000) also found posttraumatic symptoms in SA survivors. Winell (n.d.) identified the key symptoms as follows:

- *Cognitive:* confusion, difficulty with decision making and critical thinking, dissociation, identity confusion
- *Affective:* anxiety, panic attacks, depression, suicidal ideation, anger, grief, guilt, loneliness, lack of meaning
- *Functional:* sleep and eating disorders, nightmares, sexual dysfunction, substance abuse, somatization
- *Social/cultural:* rupture of family and social networks, employment issues, financial stress, problems acculturating into society, interpersonal dysfunction

Winell's (2006, n.d.) collection of client quotes speaks volumes regarding the impact of SA:

> My form of religion was very strongly entrenched and anchored deeply in my heart. It is hard to describe how fully my religion informed, infused, and influenced my entire worldview. My first steps out of fundamentalism were profoundly frightening and I had frequent thoughts of suicide. Now I'm way past that but I still haven't quite found my place in the universe.

My parents have stopped calling me. My dad told me I'm going to hell (he's done this my whole life!).

I lost all my friends. I lost my close ties to family . . . I've lost so much because of this malignant religion and I am angry and sad to my very core . . . I have tried hard to make new friends, but I have failed miserably . . . I am very lonely. (Winell, n.d.)

Winell (2008) postulated that individuals experience four major events that are traumatic: (a) the loss of a structure that was supporting all of their needs, (b) the shattering of many of their core beliefs and assumptions, (c) trauma surrounding betrayal, and (d) shattered or lost faith. Winell (n.d.) noted that the individuals who are most at risk for experiencing traumatic symptoms are those who grew up in religion, were part of a very controlling congregation resulting in a sheltering from experiences external to the community, and/or were very personally involved in their congregation. LGBTQI+ persons additionally may have no other community; after sexual orientation change efforts and years of indoctrination, some LGBTQI+ persons may have such internalized homophobia that being around open LGBTQI+ people is not an option at first.

Additional Counseling Challenges

Clients who exhibit symptoms of religious trauma may have issues in the counseling environment (Oakley & Kinmond, 2013a). Because of likely PTSD-like symptoms, they may experience issues surrounding connecting with and trusting the counselor; fearing for their safety; and feeling unworthy of love, positive regard, and support (Gilbert, 2013; Turell & Thomas, 2002). Conversely, they may also exhibit the survival behaviors that they did in the SA context by submitting fully to the counselor and subjugating themselves (Ward, 2011). In addition, even experiencing care and concern from the counselor may trigger PTSD symptoms and memories of their abuser, who also showed great care and concern but injured them severely (Kinmond & Oakley, 2015). Because of the experience of the trauma, it may be difficult to disclose and speak of experiences that they may have sought to repress (Kinmond & Oakley, 2015). They may also have had disclosures violated in the context of their SA, which would make it difficult for them to trust the confidentiality of counseling.

Counselors will need to develop expanded self-awareness with this population. Their understanding of religion and spirituality, as well as their own experiences, both positive and negative, could bias them when working with the client with SA (Oakley & Kinmond, 2013a, 2013b). Counselors should be very careful not to impose their own beliefs on any client, but particularly the client with SA, whom they could traumatize further. They should make no assumptions; be highly self-aware of their biases; and work to explore the client's own attitudes, values, and beliefs under these manipulated and traumatic experiences (Kinmond & Oakley, 2015). As religious trauma is not formally a diagnosis, clients may doubt the severity of their trauma experiences (Winell, 2006). When working with an LGBTQI+ client who has experienced religious trauma, counselors will need to be competent in LGBTQI+ issues, religious and spiritual issues, religious trauma, and how affectional orientation and gender variance is viewed in that particular religion; they will additionally need to be well versed in a trauma-informed approach.

Gubi and Jacobs (2009) also found that counselors who work with spiritually abused clients can experience vicarious traumatization and crises of faith themselves. Conversely, counselors also found a deep spiritual sense by working with these clients; however, they had to counter negative attitudes surrounding religious communities. This research suggests that counselors need to practice self-care when working with this population as well as seek appropriate supervision and consultation.

A Trauma-Informed Approach

Counselors should carefully assess LGBTQI+ clients for previous experiences of abuse; taking a full history surrounding religious experiences is also important (Super & Jacobson, 2011). When the client exposes the experience of SA, the counselor should name the abuse for the client and discuss the negative impacts of being "victimized and stigmatized by religion" (p. 191). The next step should be to define the client's affectional orientation and explore what role the client wishes spirituality to have in their life. Using a client-centered approach and setting goals consistent with the client's stated wishes are crucial (Super & Jacobson, 2011). Counselors should be very sensitive to power differentials in the counseling relationship; checking in with clients about how they are experiencing the counseling process can be empowering and allow the clients the opportunity to use their voice (Kinmond & Oakley, 2015). Finally, counselors should use specific techniques to assist clients in healing from the abuse as well as to resolve the internal conflicts they feel regarding their affectional orientation; in addition, if clients wish to rebuild their spirituality, counselors should assist in this regard (Super & Jacobson, 2011). In any approach, counselors should consider the client's experiences of trauma.

Trauma-informed care is a framework for counseling a trauma survivor that involves considering the impact of the trauma in every aspect of the counseling approach. The trauma-informed counselor creates contexts that are physically, emotionally, and psychologically safe (Hopper, Bassuk, & Olivet, 2010). The overarching goal of a trauma-informed approach is to build a sense of control and empowerment in trauma survivors. Trauma-informed cognitive behavior therapy has also been found to be helpful in situations in which abuse was connected to religion and spirituality; specifically, using psychoeducation, mindfulness and breathing techniques, regulation of emotion, and cognitive behavior therapy strategies can be helpful in reaching client goals (Walker, Reese, Hughes, & Troskie, 2010).

Many youth report feeling isolated, confused, and angry in regard to their affectional orientation and external rejecting messages (Jackson, 2011). With many of these feelings unresolved and the SA adding to their issues, individuals often report having some common themes around guilt, shame, and fear. Working toward increasing self-empowerment is a key goal for those who have experienced SA (Kinmond & Oakley, 2015) and will also facilitate a positive LGBTQI+ identity. Counselors should also help the client build a social network of authentic support (Oakley & Kinmond, 2013a).

In working through SA, counselors should also ensure that they are continuing to create a safe space (Oakley & Kinmond, 2013a); this is important in terms of clients' acceptance of their LGBTQI+ identity. Helping clients regain control of their thoughts and beliefs, reclaim their feelings and intuition, and heal from the trauma become the overarching goals when working with those who have survived SA (Rauch, 2009; Winell, 2006). One element that can be helpful in healing is assisting clients in recognizing manipulation and learning how to think for themselves; positing questions for self-discovery and self-evaluation can help in this regard (Winell, 2006). The client may explore themes related to a replacement of those experiences that led to the false sense of fulfillment when experiencing SA (Winell, 2006). Themes may include discovering choice and responsibility, accepting and receiving, choosing and creating, clarifying one's own values, and regaining control over one's life and beliefs (Winell, 2006). Super and Jacobson (2011) described the creation of a spiritual timeline as a strategy to reflect and process the impact of the trauma. The client in this case was able to tell their story and identify emotions that they were not conscious of prior to this experience (Super & Jacobson, 2011). This suggests that the use of narrative therapy strategies may be helpful for this population as well.

Counselors should also help guide clients to build their self-identity and sense of self-love. This will require rebuilding their assumptions by exploring them and testing them for validity (Winell, n.d.). For example, counselors may challenge the previous belief that "humans are essentially bad and weak" and dependent on God's salvation, for "humans are fundamentally good and precious, deserving of unconditional love as they are" (Winell, 2006, loc. 4646). As applied to LGBTQI+ issues, this exchange of beliefs could be from "being gay is inherently immoral" to "giving and experiencing authentic love is moral."

Oakley and Kinmond (2013b, 2014) developed the BADIS and ESSTA acronyms to represent the issues that present with a client who has experienced SA (BADIS) and the counselor responses that are needed (ESSTA). BADIS stands for blame, accountability, damage, inability to work with others, and scripture. ESSTA stands for empowerment, supervision, support, training, and awareness. Blame involves individuals internalizing the problem with their experiences as themselves; when they raised concerns in the SA relationship with their perpetrator, they were disempowered and their silence was reinforced. The appropriate therapeutic response is empowerment, helping clients to regain their voice. Accountability refers to the pressure to reveal personal details and the subsequent discomfort that victims of SA feel in doing so. The appropriate therapeutic response here is to maintain supervision, working with a supervisor to ensure that the counselor is building a relationship with the client in an appropriate, ethical, and safe manner. Damage addresses how the client has been traumatized by those who have used shame, fear, and manipulation. The counselor should respond with support, maintaining safety and client boundaries. Inability to work with others refers to a pattern of distrust and defensiveness, particularly when control or criticism is present. Counselors should use training or psychoeducation to help the client establish healthy relationship behaviors. Finally, becoming aware of how scripture (sacred texts) was used as part of the abuse is important; the counselor should respond by increasing client awareness, assisting clients with their spiritual journey and knowledge of scripture, if and when desired.

A component of the GRACE (goals, renewal, action, connection, and empowerment) model (Bozard & Sanders, 2011) is to reconnect clients to their spirituality and a community, if that is indeed the clients' goal, as well as to explore alternative translations of spiritual text. For SA survivors this could be traumatic and trigger flashbacks, memories, and immense emotional distress (Kinmond & Oakley, 2015). However, Kinmond and Oakley (2006) found that when a client is ready for such discourse, knowing that it is available and that the counselor understands such issues is reassuring. Even then, the counselor should not merely correct the interpretation; the counselor should attempt to empower clients to reflect and consider alternative interpretations themselves (Oakley & Kinmond, 2013a).

Conclusion

A client who has experienced SA is scarred at an existential level. LGBTQI+ persons are already fighting societal negative messages surrounding their gender and/or affectional orientation. The appeal of the church is understandable: There is physical, cognitive, and social-emotional support and positive regard. Messages surrounding the world being a dangerous place resonate deeply; indeed, the world can be quite dangerous for a minority. However, the attractiveness of the church is an illusion when it is being used to spiritually abuse congregants. All elements of support are withdrawn and hostility will be present in their place when LGBTQI+ persons question the leader or wish to be authentic to their LGBTQI+ identity. The impact of SA on LGBTQI+ persons is immense: It further increases their sense of self-hatred, represses their intuition and identity development, and creates a betrayal and mistrust of others. The counselor working with an LGBTQI+ person who has experienced SA requires additional skills as well as acceptance and patience.

Questions for Further Discussion

1. What types of abuse did Marcus survive? How does religion factor into these different types of abuse?
2. What elements of Marcus's experience with his church, and with Jacob in particular, match the description of the cycle of SA?
3. How might SA for an LGBTQI+ person like Marcus be more complex?
4. What counseling challenges are present in Marcus's case?
5. What types of strategies would help Marcus heal from the abuse? Why would reintroducing spirituality, at least at this point in Marcus's experience, not be appropriate?

Resources

1. Read Dr. Marlene Winell's beliefs regarding religious trauma as a syndrome at http://journeyfree.org/rts/.
2. Visit the website Recovering From Religion at http://www.recoveringfromreligion.org/#home.
3. Read the *Atlantic* article on the health effects of leaving religion at http://www.theatlantic.com/health/archive/2014/09/the-health-effects-of-leaving-religion/379651/.
4. Become familiar with the advocacy group Faith in America at http://www.faithinamerica.org/.
5. Read a survivor's story about religious trauma at http://www.patheos.com/blogs/excommunications/2014/12/religious-fundamentalism-a-survivors-story/.

References

Appleton, J. (2003, June). Spiritual abuse. *Christianity and Renewal*, pp. 22–25.

Beckstead, A. L., & Morrow, S. L. (2004). Mormon clients' experiences of conversion therapy: The need for a new treatment approach. *The Counseling Psychologist, 32,* 651–690.

Bendery, J., & Signorile, M. (2016, April 16). *Everything you need to know about the wave of 100+ anti-LGBT bills pending in states.* Retrieved from the Huffington Post website: http://www.huffingtonpost.com/entry/lgbt-state-bills-discrimination_us_570ff4f2e4b0060ccda2a7a9

Blue, K. (1993). *Healing spiritual abuse: How to break free from bad church experiences.* Downers Grove, IL: Intervarsity Press.

Bottoms, B. L., Nielsen, M., Murray, R., & Filipas, H. (2003). Religion-related child physical abuse: Characteristics and psychological outcomes. *Journal of Aggression, Maltreatment & Trauma, 8*(1–2), 87–114. doi:10.1300/J146v08n01_04

Bozard, R. L., & Sanders, C. J. (2011). Helping Christian lesbian, gay, and bisexual clients recover religion as a source of strength: Developing a model for assessment and integration of religious identity in counseling. *Journal of LGBT Issues in Counseling, 5*(1), 47–74. doi:10.1080/15538605.2011.554791

Cass, V. C. (1979). Homosexual identity formation: A theoretical model. *Journal of Homosexuality, 4*(3), 219–235.

Chaney, M. P., Filmore, J. M., & Goodrich, K. M. (2011). No more sitting on the sidelines. *Counseling Today, 53*(11), 34–37.

Doyle, T. P. (2009). The spiritual trauma experienced by victims of sexual abuse by Catholic clergy. *Pastoral Psychology, 58*(3), 239–260. doi:10.1007/s11089-008-0187-1

Drescher, J. (2003). The Spitzer study and the culture wars. *Archives of Sexual Behavior, 32,* 431–432.

Drescher, J., & Zucker, K. J. (Eds.). (2006). *Ex-gay research: Analyzing the Spitzer study and its relation to science, religion, politics, and culture.* New York, NY: Harrington Park Press.

Enroth, R. (1992). *Churches that abuse.* Grand Rapids, MI: Zondervan.

Gilbert, P. (2013). *The compassionate mind.* London, UK: Constable.

Ginicola, M. M., & Smith, C. (2016). *Gay and religious: The development of the FAITH affectional orientation identity model.* Manuscript in preparation.

Gubi, P. M., & Jacobs, R. (2009). Exploring the impact on counsellors of working with spiritually abused clients. *Mental Health, Religion & Culture, 12*(2), 191–204. doi:10.1080/13674670802441509

Hopper, E., Bassuk, E., & Olivet, J. (2010). Shelter from the storm: Trauma-informed care in homelessness services settings. *The Open Health Services and Policy Journal, 3,* 80–100. doi:1874-9240/10

Jackson, L. (2011). *The psychology of prejudice: From attitudes to social action.* Washington, DC: American Psychological Association.

Johnson, D., & VanVonderen, J. (1991). *The subtle power of spiritual abuse: Recognizing and escaping spiritual manipulation and false spiritual authority within the church.* Bloomington, MI: Bethany House.

Jones, S. L., & Yarhouse, M. A. (2007). *Ex-gay? A longitudinal study of religiously mediated change in sexual orientation.* Downers Grove, IL: Intervarsity Press.

Kinmond, K., & Oakley, L. (2006, May). *This is abuse and people need to know that: Counselling for spiritual abuse.* Presentation at the British Association for Counseling and Psychotherapy Research Conference, Glasgow, United Kingdom.

Kinmond, K., & Oakley, L. (2015). Working safely with spiritual abuse. In P. M. Gubi (Ed.), *Spiritual accompaniment and counselling: Journeying with psyche and soul* (pp. 145–162). London, UK: Jessica Kingsley.

Maslow, A. H. (1968). *Toward a psychology of being* (2nd ed.). Princeton, NJ: Van Nostrand.

Meyer, I. H. (2003). Prejudice, social stress, and mental health in lesbian, gay, and bisexual status: Conceptual issues and research evidence. *Psychological Bulletin, 129,* 674–697. doi:10.1037/0033-2909.129.5.674

Moore, D. S. (2004). *The shepherding movement: Controversy and charismatic ecclesiology.* London, UK: Bloomsbury Academic.

Morrow, D. F. (2003). Cast into the wilderness: The impact of institutionalized religion on lesbians. *Journal of Lesbian Studies, 7*(4), 109–123. doi:10.1300/J155v07n04_07

Oakley, L. (2009). *The experience of spiritual abuse in the UK Christian church* (Unpublished doctoral dissertation). Manchester Metropolitan University, Manchester, UK.

Oakley, L., & Kinmond, K. (2013a). *Breaking the silence on spiritual abuse.* New York, NY: Palgrave Macmillan. doi:10.1057/9781137282873

Oakley, L., & Kinmond, K. (2013b, April). Spiritual abuse: A challenge for safeguarding practice in church. *Caring,* pp. 87–95.

Oakley, L., & Kinmond, K. (2014). Developing safeguarding policy and practice for spiritual abuse. *Journal of Adult Protection, 16*(2), 87–95.

Okeyan, P. Y. (2000). *Manipulation, domination and control.* London, UK: Kingsway.

Omoto, A., & Kurtzman, H. (2006). *Sexual orientation and mental health: Examining identity and development in lesbian, gay, and bisexual people.* Washington, DC: American Psychological Association.

Parish-West, P. (2009). *Spiritual abuse within the Judaeo Christian tradition: Implications for practice* (Unpublished master's thesis). University of Derby, United Kingdom.

Parsons, K. (2000). *Ungodly fear.* Oxford, UK: Lion Hudson.

Plowman, E. E. (1975, October). The deepening rift in the Charismatic movement. *Christianity Today*, pp. 65–66.

Rauch, M. (2009). *Healing the soul after religious abuse: The dark heaven of recovery.* Westport, CT: Praeger.

Ring, T. (2015, January 12). *Former "ex-gay" leader comes out.* Retrieved from *The Advocate* website: http://www.advocate.com/ex-gay-therapy/2015/01/12/former-ex-gay-leader-comes-out

Schneeberger, A. R., Dietl, M. F., Muenzenmaier, K. H., Huber, C. G., & Lang, U. E. (2014). Stressful childhood experiences and health outcomes in sexual minority populations: A systematic review. *Social Psychiatry and Psychiatric Epidemiology, 49,* 1427–1445. doi:10.1007/s00127-014-0854-8

Simonič, B., Mandelj, T. R., & Novsak, R. (2013). Religious-related abuse in the family. *Journal of Family Violence, 28*(4), 339–349. doi:10.1007/s10896-013-9508-y

Skedgell, K. (2008). *Losing the way.* Richmond, CA: Bay Tree.

Stone, A. M. (2013). Thou shalt not: Treating religious trauma and spiritual harm with combined therapy. *Group, 37*(4), 323–337.

Sue, D. W. (2010). *Microaggressions in everyday life: Race, gender, and sexual orientation.* Hoboken, NJ: Wiley.

Super, J. T., & Jacobson, L. (2011). Religious abuse: Implications for counseling lesbian, gay, bisexual, and transgender individuals. *Journal of LGBT Issues in Counseling, 5*(3–4), 180–196. doi:10.1080/15538605.2011.632739

Truth Wins Out. (n.d.). *Ex-gay scandals and defection.* Retrieved from https://www.truthwinsout.org/scandals-defections/

Turell, S. C., & Thomas, C. R. (2002). Where was God? *Women and Therapy, 24*(3–4), 133–147.

Walker, D. F., Reese, J. B., Hughes, J. P., & Troskie, M. J. (2010). Addressing religious and spiritual issues in trauma-focused cognitive behavior therapy for children and adolescents. *Professional Psychology: Research and Practice, 41*(2), 174–180. doi:10.1037/a0017782

Ward, D. J. (2011). The lived experience of spiritual abuse. *Mental Health, Religion & Culture, 14,* 899–915. doi:10.1080/13674676.2010.536206

Wehr, D. S. (2000). Spiritual abuse: When good people do bad things. In P. Young-Eisendrath & M. E. Miller (Eds.), *The psychology of mature spirituality: Integrity, wisdom, transcendence* (pp. 47–61). New York, NY: Brunner-Routledge.

Winell, M. (n.d.). *Part 1: RTS—It's time to recognize it.* Retrieved from http://journeyfree.org/rts/rts-its-time-to-recognize-it/

Winell, M. (2006). *Leaving the fold.* Oakland, CA: Apocryphile Press.

Winell, M. (2008). *Religious trauma syndrome.* Retrieved from the British Association for Behavioural & Cognitive Psychotherapies website: http://www.babcp.com/Review/RTS-Trauma-from-Religion.aspx

Wolkomir, M. (2006). *Be not deceived: The sacred and sexual struggles of gay and ex-gay Christian men.* Brunswick, NJ: Rutgers University Press.

Wood, A. W., & Conley, A. H. (2014). Loss of religious or spiritual identities among the LGBT population. *Counseling and Values, 59,* 95–111. doi:10.1002/j.2161-007X.2014.00044.x

COUNSELOR ADVOCACY

Chapter 25

Becoming an Ally: Personal, Clinical, and School-Based Social Justice Interventions

Diane Estrada, Anneliese A. Singh, and Amney J. Harper

> *Activists are cultural artists.*
> *They envision a world that does not yet exist,*
> *and then take action to create that world.*
>
> —Robyn Ochs

• • •

Awareness of Attitudes and Beliefs Self-Check

1. Have you ever identified yourself as an ally, whether you are lesbian, gay, bisexual, transgender, queer, questioning, intersex, asexual, ally, pansexual/polysexual, and two-spirited (LGBTQI+) or not? Why or why not?
2. Have you ever participated in advocacy and social justice work for a marginalized group? Why or why not?
3. What uncomfortable emotions, fear, or anxieties might you experience being an advocate and social justice activist for the LGBTQI+ communities? Why?

Case Study

Sara is a 28-year-old heterosexual Latina. She is a doctoral candidate in a counseling program in the southeastern United States. Her identity as a woman of color has given her some experience with issues of discrimination, racism, and sexism. Some of her graduate school training addresses issues of race, ethnicity, and gender. However, no course has addressed issues of affectional orientation or gender identity/expression. During her adolescent years, Sara became aware that many of her family and friends identified as lesbian, gay, bisexual, or transgender. Her ally voice was born in her late adolescent years as she advocated for equal rights in her peer group and addressed the use of derogatory language in her peer group and with family members. Some of her peers responded by cutting off relationships; others by becoming more distant; and others by making changes, thus continuing to be an inspiration for her further advocacy. In her family, she faced assumptions regarding her own affectional orientation when she began to speak out for just language in family conversations. Several family elders also reminded her that the Catholic Church does not support "those lifestyles."

In college, Sara found herself leaving church services after a priest stated that HIV and AIDS were "God's punishment to gays." This was particularly painful because Sara views herself as a very spiritual person and had found a place of belonging in the church. However, the god she believes in does not match the description of judgment that the priest had associated with God's wrath. This was particularly hard for her to hear, especially because her godfather (an ally in her own life) had recently died from AIDS. She had looked up to the priest in the past, and even though she knew that what he said was not acceptable to her, there was a small part that also questioned what God really did think about her as an ally.

In graduate school she became an advocate attending equal rights protests and Pride events. It was during Pride that she encountered the Ku Klux Klan for the first time. Although she was terrified by the amount of hatred in many Klan members' eyes, her resolve was strengthened when she realized that affectional orientation and gender identity/expression was a place where she could use her privilege to stand up for the rights of others. Her connections with many friends in the LGBTQI+ community strengthened her commitment to speak out and not let the fear of hatred silence her. She wanted to be an active advocate and found herself providing advocacy education to her friends and family members. Sara began to share her viewpoint regarding LGBTQI+ issues in society among those on whom she most relied for support: her Hispanic family and friends. She was genuinely shocked to find that her own support community experienced homophobia and heterosexism that reflected the majority culture. Once again, she found herself frustrated, indignant, and confused. How could people who knew the hurt of being classified as an "other" classify others in such hurtful ways? Her mother began to interrogate her in an "accusatory tone" about being "a lesbian." Her friends talked in a derogatory tone about "those former high school friends who are queer." Her Catholic friends would constantly quote the Bible as a defense for why they were following "God's law" when ostracizing members of the LGBTQI+ community. Sara struggled to make sense of what was "right and wrong" and internalized this question as she reflected on who she is and in what she believes.

• • •

What Is an Ally?

Becoming an ally to LGBTQI+ people is a critical component of being an effective and affirming counselor and entails lifelong learning and commitments. The Association for Lesbian, Gay, Bisexual, and Transgender Issues in Counseling (ALGBTIC) competencies (Harper et al., 2013) specifically outline an entire section on ally competencies and working with allies as clients, reflecting the importance of not only becoming a strong LGBTQI+ ally but also understanding what it means to be an ally to LGBTQI+ people and communities (see http://www.algbtic.org/competencies.html). We acknowledge the important role of all allies, including those who identify as LGBTQI+ (e.g., a queer-identified person can serve as a transgender ally); however, for the purpose of this chapter, we use the word *ally* to mean heterosexual and cisgender persons. The focus of this chapter is on the nature of privilege for heterosexual, cisgender allies and how that privilege can be used to promote the rights of LGBTQI+ people.

Becoming an LGBTQI+ Ally

In order to understand the role of LGBTQI+ allyship, counselors should understand what the term *ally* refers to and entails. Scholars have defined an *ally* as a person who has commitments to members of historically marginalized populations and communities and takes action to address and reduce injustice toward these people and communities (Fabiano, Perkins, Berkowitz, Linkenbach, & Stark, 2003). Becoming an ally of a person or community is a journey and process of educating oneself and others, so there are naturally various stages of ally identity development.

A Model of Ally Identity Development

Edwards (2006) articulated three stages of ally identity development. The first stage involves being *allies for self-interest*. The motivation behind this type of allyship is typically to advocate for people that allies personally know who are experiencing oppression. Allies for self-interest may view acts of injustice as exceptions to what commonly occurs and may not be interested in addressing larger systems of oppression, instead focusing on the individuals who commit unjust acts. These allies also may not be able to identify their own privilege and may separate themselves from perpetrators of injustice. In the second stage, *allies for altruism,* the motivation behind allyship is to take action and help other people. Allies for altruism express dismay with systems of oppression; however, they also separate themselves as exceptions to these systems of injustice. These allies may be able to identify their own privilege, yet they may experience guilt and attempt to avoid discussions of privilege. Individuals in the third stage, *allies for social justice,* are motivated to be allies not only for themselves or for others but for everyone. Allies for social justice focus on changing systems of injustice and aim to empower historically marginalized people and communities. In doing so, allies for social justice welcome examinations of their own privilege and critique themselves and others in order to help identify injustices they themselves or others may commit.

Applying the Edwards (2006) model of ally identity development to LGBTQI+ allyship, one can see that counselor LGBTQI+ allies for self-interest may express dismay when seeing one of their lesbian friends experience employment discrimination but may not be able to identify the systemic laws, policies, and other oppressions that influence the lives of LGBTQI+ people and communities. These allies would also not examine their own perpetration of heterosexism in their personal and professional values, behaviors, and interactions. LGBTQI+ allies for altruism would be more motivated by wanting to do the *right thing* for LGBTQI+ people and communities; however, they may not be able to fully critique systems of heterosexism and identify their role in perpetrating homophobia and transphobia. In contrast, LGBTQI+ allies for social justice would be motivated to end the systemic injustice of heterosexism for LGBTQI+ people and communities as well as for themselves. LGBTQI+ allies for social justice would be able to identify how they themselves are hurt by heterosexism as well as identify ways in which they may have internalized and perpetrated heterosexism with the aim of addressing and reducing societal heterosexism.

General and Specific LGBTQI+ Experiences of Oppression

Once one understands the different types of allyship as they relate to LGBTQI+ people and communities, it is then important to identify one's strengths and limitations related to identifying one's own privilege, as well as the common experiences of oppression people under the LGBTQI+ umbrella face. As described throughout this book, LGBTQI+ people may face general experiences of oppression, such as discrimination in employment (e.g., being fired for being LGBTQI+) and family building (e.g., adoption, custody rights); however, they also face more specific experiences of discrimination. Transgender people, for instance, face specific challenges related to changing their assigned sex at birth on their driver's licenses and Social Security cards. LGBTQI+ allies also should know the common mental health impacts of various oppressions LGBTQI+ people and communities face. LGBTQI+ youth report higher rates of suicide attempts, alcohol and drug abuse, depression, and anxiety related to experiences of heterosexism (Hatzenbuehler, 2011; Russell & Joyner, 2001). Bisexual people report feeling misunderstood by both heterosexual and LGBTQI+ communities, thus often feeling isolation and alienation (Persson & Pfaus, 2015).

Resilience and Stress Coping

LGBTQI+ allies should also be aware of the resilience and stress coping that LGBTQI+ people develop and that LGBTQI+ communities support to buffer themselves from discrimination. For instance, research shows that transgender people's resilience to oppression may include nurturing a sense of hope, developing an evolving sense of gender identity, connecting with a transgender activist community, and engaging in self-care (Singh, Hays, & Watson, 2011). An important factor in resilience and stress coping can be protective factors like supportive people in one's life.

Intersectionality

In addition to understanding the different stages of ally development, types of general and group-specific oppression, and resilience experiences, LGBTQI+ allies need to have an understanding of intersectionality. As highlighted throughout this book, there is immense diversity in the LGBTQI+ community in terms of race/ethnicity, gender, religion, disability, citizenship status, class, and so on. LGBTQI+ allies strive to be intentional in their learning about the diverse LGBTQI+ groups. In safe schools work, it can be common for people to say, "If this was a racist comment, it would not be tolerated in schools." However, not only is this not true, because racism exists in schools and LGBTQI+ students of color experience heterosexism and racism, but these types of statements position oppressions one against another in a hierarchy. LGBTQI+ allies use intersectionality to challenge this type of thinking systemically and in their own values, actions, and behaviors. Strong LGBTQI+ allies work on reducing monosexism and heterosexism but also work simultaneously on reducing all other oppressions (e.g., classism, racism, ableism). Ultimately, the process of developing into an LGBTQI+ ally is one of striving for social justice while consistently engaging in self-reflection and action for social change.

The Need for Allies

With the foundations of LGBTQI+ allyship understood, it becomes important to identify the need for LGBTQI+ allies. LGBTQI+ allies for social justice can challenge systemic injustices in a way that LGBTQI+ people cannot. LGBTQI+ activists and community organizers have long worked to changed societal values and behaviors regarding LGBTQI+ oppression. However, as much progress as has been made in LGBTQI+ civil rights, there remains much work to be done. LGBTQI+ allies are often quite effective in calling for and proactively making systemic change regarding heterosexism. Therefore, the need for LGBTQI+ allies remains at the micro-, meso-, and macrolevels of society.

Ally Behaviors and Actions

There are many ways that allies can involve themselves in the struggle for LGBTQI+ rights (Rostosky, Black, Riggle, & Rozenkrantz, 2015). They are important contributors to the rights of those they speak up for because of their privileged position (Munin & Speight, 2010). They are in unique positions to build coalitions with other members of the privileged group because of their own membership in that group (Munin & Speight, 2010). Often when LGBTQI+ voices have been silenced or ignored, allies are able to use the privilege they hold to get those same ideas heard. By creating bridges, they are able to create a space for the voices of LGBTQI+ individuals where none was previously available. There are many ways in which allies can do their work. Thus, as allies begin their developmental process, it can be useful for them to spend some time reflecting not only on their position of privilege in society relative to their ally status but on how they personally can be effective and at what level(s) they will intervene. Not every ally will feel comfortable protesting in the center of a national movement. Some allies are better at enacting change behind the scenes. Others find their gifts in providing emotional support to LGBTQI+ individuals or confronting bias when they encounter it.

A new trend in the popular discourse on ally identity is the idea that allies must move beyond thinking of *ally* as an identity to thinking of *ally* as a verb (Utt, 2013). Similarly, Utt (2013) would argue that one does not assume the label of ally but should earn the label by acting as an ally and then being acknowledged as such. In this line of thinking, instead of saying, "I am an ally," one might instead say, "This is how I ally." This idea has come to light in the wake of some of the criticisms of allies who may like to be seen as allies but who do not do much in the way of actual advocacy or activism on behalf of or with the LGBTQI+ community (Utt, 2013). Here the term *ally* is used as both a noun and a verb.

Although it has been argued that emotional support and simple agreement with the spirit of the LGBTQI+ movement are important in and of themselves (Reason & Broido, 2005), LGBTQI+ people have begun to call on their allies to step up to the plate and do more. To be an ally today, one must do more than passively wait for opportunities to ally. There is much to be done, and allies are encouraged to seek out the places where their voices and their work are most needed.

So what does it look like to intentionally consider one's ally behaviors? Many individuals have a personal connection to a member of the community, such as a family member or friend (Asta & Vacha-Haase, 2013; Rostosky et al., 2015). Although personal connections are important, it is also crucial that allies have a vested interest in social justice (Asta & Vacha-Haase, 2013; Rostosky et al., 2015). Most of the research on allies has focused on families of LGBTQI+ individuals, and it is proposed that this special connection creates a unique ability to build bridges between LGBTQI+ populations and cisgender heterosexuals (Ryan, Broad, Walsh, & Nutter, 2013). Thus, necessity may often dictate initially that allies who are connected through an individual member or members answer the call when their loved one is in need (e.g., of help navigating barriers; of help addressing institutional forms of homo/bi/transgender prejudice; of emotional, mental, or physical support). However, without a greater connection to the LGBTQI+ rights movement, that ally behavior does not hold much meaning.

Asta and Vacha-Haase (2013) argued that sustaining one's role as an ally tends to require viewing the LGBTQI+ rights movement as part of an individual's larger sense of the need for social justice or that person's personal social justice mission. So an important aspect of becoming an ally is gaining knowledge and awareness of the greater struggle and the many forms of institutionalized oppressions. In order for one's ally behaviors to become a useful part of the larger movement, the first step is to build knowledge and awareness of both the LGBTQI+ community and the LGBTQI+ rights movement and also the ally's relative position of privilege in it (Reason & Broido, 2005). This is true not only for heterosexual, cisgender allies but for allies who identify as LGBTQI+ as well. Just because one understands the issues surrounding one's own identity (e.g., LGBTQI+) does not mean that this person understands the community for which the person is becoming an ally (e.g., transgender people). When allies enter into ally work without this context and background, they can often detract from the larger movement (as it takes energy and time for members of the community to educate them); often missteps can cause harm to people or the community when one acts without knowledge. For example, an ally might provide misinformation about transgender populations by assuming their issues are the same as those of LGBTQI+ individuals.

Just as one may need to gain a greater awareness of larger LGBTQI+ movements and communities, it is also important to engage in the reflective process of examining one's own relationship with privilege. Reason and Broido (2005) argued that although good can be done by allies who are not self-aware, any sustained efforts at allying must be accompanied by self-reflection, especially as it relates to one's personal identities and the privilege one experiences as a result of those identities. For example, in the case study for this chapter, as an ally, Sara might choose to contextualize the relationships she has lost along the way as she has allied with an understanding of her own privilege so that her experiences are not positioned at the expense of misunderstanding the ways in which members of the LGBTQI+ communities may have lost relationships in their lives because of their identities. Although both experienced losses, and those losses cannot be compared, there is an institutional difference in the source of that loss that is an important thread in the stories and lived experiences of LGBTQI+ individuals. Sara, by being willing to step up, has been personally impacted by those relationships that did not stand by her. Her losses were a byproduct of a cis/heterosexist system; however, she still holds a position of privilege in that system as a heterosexual, cisgender person. It is also important for Sara to evaluate how other identities she holds, such as Latina or female, although also oppressed, do not nullify her heterosexual or cisgender privilege. Similarly, a White gay man still holds White racial privilege and cannot directly relate his experiences as gay to those of a Latina woman. These are important distinctions because of the invisibility of privilege and the nuanced ways in which heterosexual and cisgender privilege are present. An important role of allies is being a source of support and validation for members of the LGBTQI+ community, because that support and validation is often absent outside of the community (and often inside it also). Reason and Broido stated, "Accurately witnessing and listening can be a powerful mechanism of support" (p. 86). Therefore, by being able to reflect on their own personal relationship with privilege, allies will be better able to provide this support and validation to LGBTQI+ people.

In addition to developing knowledge and awareness, it is also useful for allies to identify and understand different levels of intervention. Not every ally will get involved in large national movements or protests. There is an importance and place for all allies. It is important, however, for allies to reflect on what level they would like to intervene at in order to either match their current skill set or develop the skills that are necessary at that level. Reason and Broido (2005) argued that there are three areas in which allies can intervene: supporting members of the oppressed group, working with members of the privileged group to help inspire and educate them, and promoting changes at the institutional or cultural level. These three levels fit closely with the levels identified here (micro/individual, meso/group/community, macro/systemic/institutional).

Micro- or Individual-Level Interventions

Most allies will begin their work at the microlevel or individual level. Much of the ally literature to date has focused on families of LGBTQI+ individuals as allies (Ryan et al., 2013). Highlighted in that context is the idea that families have an immediate rationale for becoming allies, as they seek to support and often protect their loved ones. Thus, many of their initial efforts are geared toward impacting their loved one directly. There are different levels at which one can intervene and similarly different levels on which the effect is seen (see Figure 25.1). Figure 25.1 describes the interplay between the level of intervention and subsequent possible levels of effects of the intervention.

In the case example of Sara, Sara intervened in her peer group when derogatory language was used. At the microlevel, individuals intervene in a one-on-one setting or in small groups (or with a family). This type of intervention targets a particular concern or issue as it is seen on a personal level. When a change is made at this level, the system that fosters and promotes heterosexism and cissexism is not directly challenged. It takes many individual or microlevel efforts to begin to change the culture of a particular community and many more to make any sort of an impact at the macrolevel. Although it is possible that a one-on-one intervention may have a larger impact (perhaps this might be seen if an individual act somehow attracts national attention), it typically is not the intention of the intervention. The impact at this level is usually directly on an individual or a small number of individuals. By addressing the culture in her personal peer group, Sara is creating a small safe place where her friends who are LGBTQI+ know that they will be supported. Her friends may join in and become a part of this supportive culture, or if they reject it, either they will keep the environment unsafe or the other members of the peer group will eventually not support them in their actions. It is possible that the members of this small

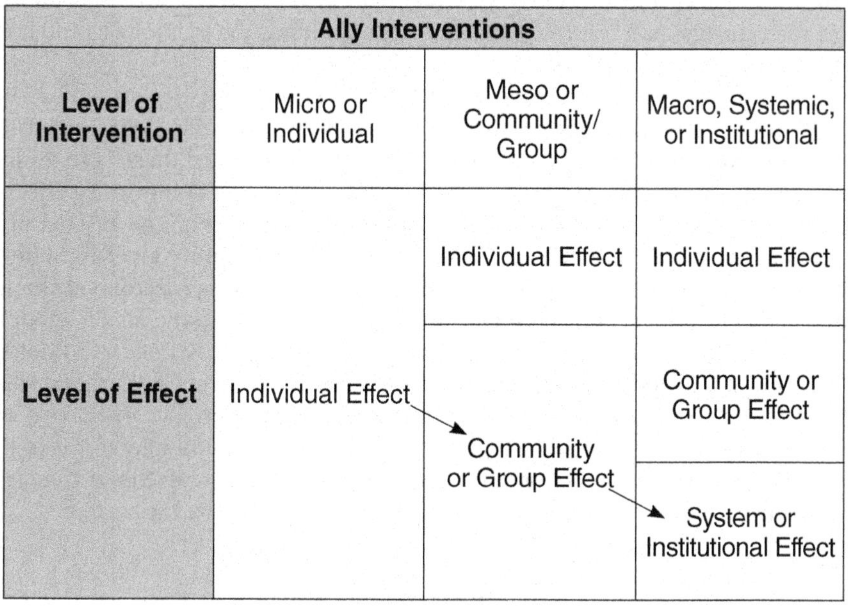

Ally Interventions			
Level of Intervention	Micro or Individual	Meso or Community/ Group	Macro, Systemic, or Institutional
Level of Effect	Individual Effect	Individual Effect	Individual Effect
		Community or Group Effect	Community or Group Effect
			System or Institutional Effect

FIGURE 25.1

Ally Intervention Levels

peer group will impact other groups around them if they have some influence in their environment. Then this intervention on the individual level or microlevel would have an impact at the next level up, the mesolevel or group/community level.

An important aspect that needs to be understood is that even when an individual intervenes on the individual level and has an individual impact, it is not necessarily small. For the person who benefits from the impact, it can be lifesaving. This type of support is incredibly important for individuals who without it may have no safe place to go. To exemplify this, it can be helpful to look to the next level of intervention where this same level of effect is sought. At a mesolevel or community level, interventions can include creating safe spaces through ally trainings (e.g., Safe, Safe Zone, Safe Space, Ally Safe Zone) that can be found in various iterations across the nation (often in schools and other institutions). Allies are educated with the intent that they will take what they have learned and use it to create safe spaces for LGBTQI+ individuals in their own respective areas (Ryan et al., 2013). It is important to note that different levels of intervention can result in achieving the same goal, as indicated in Figure 25.1. In this example, safe space training may also result in an individual-level impact, just as Sara's effort with her friends may also result in a similar individual-level impact.

Meso- or Community-Level Interventions

As discussed in the example of safe space trainings, interventions at the mesolevel or community level can also have different levels of impact. In safe space trainings, typically there is a broad-scale effort, usually housed in a single institution or group, to educate a larger group of individuals than is seen at the individual level or microlevel. For example, a university may have a regular training in which allies from various units or departments across the campus and surrounding communities are trained. Such trainings are geared toward having an impact on the community in which they are enacted. Through such trainings, individuals will find that they have more and more safe spaces than they did previously. Although this effort is broad, it does not directly address the systemic barriers in place that create the need for a safe space. It does not change systems or institutions. However, the allies who are trained in the program may go on to make or support such changes as a result of those trainings (and thus the trainings would have a macrolevel impact).

For example, an area Sara noted that was particularly problematic was her spiritual community. Although Sara has not done this yet, she could intervene in her church or with her spiritual community in order to foster change. This change could then have an individual effect (on members of the congregation who are LGBTQI+) or a community effect (by then becoming a supportive group or institution that has power in the community to impact those around it), or at the systems level it could begin with the community level and later result in a shift in the church's position on the national level (thus enacting macrolevel change).

For many allies, this level of intervention is more accessible than the next level up. Because many allies will find themselves in communities where they already have a foothold or voice, it can be easier to access and subsequently address issues at this level. Similarly, these individuals often already have a working knowledge of a community, group, or institution and therefore can more readily assess what needs to happen and what it will take to make it happen. It also can hold more personal meaning for some as they interact with the system as a way to make a difference for those they know who are directly impacted by the system.

Macro, Systemic, or Institutional Interventions

At the macrolevel, individuals typically intervene by working to shift policy, law, or the broader climate or culture. These interventions target systems that operate at the state, regional, national, or international levels. People most often associate macrolevel work with large marches or protests. We see Sara getting involved in this way as she attends marches and Pride events. However, there are many ways to engage at the national level. Many national organizations seek to influence policy and law by lobbying for LGBTQI+ rights. There are many ways to support such movements. Also, individuals can interact with their government by doing their own lobbying. There are also avenues, such as in one's professional organizations, where national interventions can occur.

This level of intervention requires allies to have a broader knowledge and awareness base as well. Often this knowledge is not readily accessible, and allies will have to do research to find out what types of policies and legislation exist and what groups are fighting them. This level also demonstrates the greatest need for coalition building. National efforts are most effective when they have a large base of support. At each level, being reflective of one's privilege is important in order to center the voices and needs of the individuals who are LGBTQI+. Ally privilege can be used to grant access, but often the most important thing an ally can do is to step aside once the door is open so that LGBTQI+ people can use their voices.

At the national level, the impact can reach through all three levels. This is why it can be so important to have allies who are willing to step up at this level of intervention. Successful interventions typically have an impact on individuals and communities as well as systems. Sometimes national efforts might target one more than the other as their goal. For example, an issue of great concern to the transgender community is the many different iterations of "papers to pee" bills. These are legislative efforts to restrict access to public restrooms for transgender individuals by enforcing strict assigned sex segregation in restrooms. Although making communities safer and more inclusive and shifting national policy are certainly goals, the heart of these movements is really the impact that these changes will make on the lives and safety of transgender individuals.

Challenges and Barriers

There are many benefits to being an ally and engaging in ally behaviors (Asta & Vacha-Haase, 2013; Rostosky et al., 2015). Some of these benefits include the ability to engage in personal growth through gaining knowledge, skills, and awareness; positive interpersonal relationships; a sense of belonging and community; a sense of purpose or meaning; opportunities to live according to one's values; and so on (Rostosky et al., 2015). Yet despite the many positives of allying, allies can also face many challenges and barriers themselves just from being allies (Asta & Vacha-Haase, 2013).

In the Competencies for Counseling LGBQQIA Individuals is a section specifically on counseling allies (Harper et al., 2013; see http://www.algbtic.org/competencies.html). An important competency noted is acknowledgment that as a result of advocating for LGBTQI+ individuals, allies will often encounter challenges or barriers from those in both the heterosexual/cisgender communities and the LGBTQI+ community. This can be seen in derogatory terms used in the LGBTQI+ community, such as *breeders, fruit flies,* or *fag hags.*

Outside of the LGBTQI+ community, when allies ally, they risk being perceived as LGBTQI+ and therefore are at times subject to the same oppression that LGBTQI+ individuals face. Similarly, sometimes just being seen as sympathetic to LGBTQI+ individuals can result in the same. We see how Sara experiences this as her family makes assumptions about her affectional orientation. These kinds of assumptions are often made as a way to discredit the person's perspective. Although it is true that allies can be discriminated against or receive some of the same oppressive treatment, they still enjoy many heterosexual or cisgender privileges that are not accessible to LGBTQI+ individuals.

An important part of allies' power lies in their position of privilege, in their being a part of the privileged group, because they are able to utilize that position to foster support (Munin & Speight, 2010). It is precisely this group membership, however, that also makes it difficult for them to be accepted as a true part of the LGBTQI+ community. Although some communities embrace their allies, recognizing the importance of their contributions over their position of privilege, other communities keep them at a distance because they are members of the group with privilege. It is a complex position they hold, as they are essentially fighting the very privilege that they themselves enjoy (Munin & Speight, 2010). In the LGBTQI+ community, there can be a lot of pressure on allies. At times allies can find themselves held to a high standard in terms of knowledge and awareness and their involvement. For developing allies, this can be intimidating. Some allies will question whether they have the knowledge or skills to be effective allies (Asta & Vacha-Haase, 2013). Some allies also experience a sense of not being a true part of the LGBTQI+ community. They may question their right to be included or to use their voices to speak up (Asta & Vacha-Haase, 2013). Reason and Broido (2005) stated,

> Allies must find a precarious balance between knowing when to take a seat at the table . . . when to speak up; when to be silent in order to listen to the experiences of others; and when to leave the table altogether, so as not to infringe on or usurp the role of target group members in advocating for their own liberation. (p. 88)

Because of their position as it relates to their privilege, in the community, allies are expected to promote the needs of LGBTQI+ individuals, which also means at times putting their own needs aside. Sometimes allies experience negative attitudes and perceptions from members of the LGBTQI+ community because the latter are slow to trust those who are not LGBTQI+, and there may be a sense among allies that they need to pay their dues or that they can never really understand the experiences of LGBTQI+ individuals. Some communities embrace and celebrate their allies, whereas others hold them at a distance. It is important to acknowledge that being an ally is a complex and difficult thing to do; allies should be understood for the many things they contribute to the greater movement.

Using a Framework for Advocacy

> Advocacy is an important aspect of every counselor's role. Regardless of the particular setting in which she or he works, each counselor is confronted again and again with issues that cannot be resolved simply through change in the individual. All too often, negative aspects of the environment impinge on a [student's] well-being, intensifying personal problems or creating obstacles to growth. When such situations arise, effective counselors speak up! (Lewis & Bradley, 2000, p. 3)

Advocacy: Awareness of Self and Other

Many competencies (e.g., the Multicultural Counseling Competencies, Counselors for Social Justice Advocacy Competencies, Association for Specialists in Group Work Multicultural and Social Justice Advocacy Competencies, ALGBTIC competencies) addressing advocacy and social justice highlight the need for an awareness of self that is inclusive of multicultural identities (e.g., gender identity and expression, race, ethnicity, affectional orientation, ability, social class, age, religion, nationality), privilege and oppression statuses, and systems of oppression. This awareness of self is aimed at creating an active self-reflective practice that recognizes the impact of biases based on each person's human experiences influenced by the person's own social identity locations.

Collison et al. (1998) invited the following reflections to assess six personal activism dimensions:

1. *System:* Am I inside or outside of the affected system?
2. *Social group:* Am I a part of the privileged or the oppressed group?
3. *Style:* Will I intervene indirectly or confront directly?
4. *Self-view:* Do I see myself as personally effective or ineffective?
5. *Information:* Do I know a lot or a little? How accurate is what I know?
6. *Consequence:* Will the personal and organizational consequence of the action be major or minor?

These self-reflection questions provide a platform for readiness for taking action and advocating for marginalized communities. Roysircar (2009) cautioned many in the mental health fields not to fall into the perfection trap that basically immobilizes activism on the basis of not knowing things perfectly. We acknowledge that the culture of perfectionism often works against activism, and counselors also embrace the basis of competency guidelines in the mental health fields for advocacy work. In this framework, we acknowledge that developing as an advocate and advocating are part of a lifelong reflective process with no set expectation of arriving at the nirvana of human perfection in social justice and advocacy work.

Sara is a work in progress as an ally. She has engaged in the ally developmental process as an ally for self-interest, as evidenced by her own experience of oppression as a Latina, and may not be able to address her own privilege in a heterosexist system. She has also experienced parts of being an ally for altruism, as she has become dismayed about socially unjust institutions and organizations such as religion and the Ku Klux Klan. And yet she separates herself as an exception to a system of injustice. Her process focuses on the injustice of the other without reflection on automatic benefits she possesses because of her privileged identification as heterosexual. She experiences guilt and walks away from the institutional conversation of privilege. Although her perspective may be one in which she is protesting an injustice, she inadvertently continues to silence a social justice stance for change by not engaging in a macrosystem oppression dialogue, a mesosystem discussion, and a microsystem reflection. In order for Sara to engage in the third stage of allying, she needs to reflect on the aforementioned points regarding her own privilege and begin to ally for everyone, herself included. In this stage she would need to invite an analysis of macrosystem privilege and marginalization and support a true social justice advocacy.

Social Justice and Advocacy

The social justice frame provides a natural fit for advocacy by addressing the impact of environmental factors on human development. Indeed, as allies embrace issues of multiculturalism (e.g., ethnicity, race, gender and gender expression, affectional orientation, social class), the need to take into account individuals' contextual and cultural values as core to who they are as human beings (Sue, Arredondo, & McDavis, 1994) becomes an essential part of advocacy work. The American Counseling Association (ACA) has endorsed multicultural competencies (Sue et al., 1994) as an important factor in the provision of competent counseling services. These competencies have been operationalized to facilitate counselors' ability to intervene at the individual, familial, and larger systemic levels (Sue et al., 1994). In doing so, the multicultural competencies call for counselors to be knowledgeable about ways in which social systems may harm clients' well-being through oppression and discrimination. Furthermore, counselors are encouraged to advocate for their clients' rights at multiple systems levels.

The call to advocacy spurred the development of advocacy competencies (Lewis, Arnold, House, & Toporek, 2002). ACA has endorsed these competencies asking counselors "to recognize the impact of social, political, economic, and cultural factors on human development," and as a result of this recognition, "when counselors become aware of external factors that act as barriers to an individual's development, they may choose to respond through advocacy" (Crethar, Bradley, Lewis, Toporek, & Tripp, 2006, p. 5).

Advocacy Competencies

The ACA Advocacy Competencies provide a framework for creating interventions to support the rights of LGBTQI+ individuals in various contexts. Competencies (e.g., the Multicultural Counseling Competencies, ALGBTIC competencies, transgender competencies, ACA Advocacy Competencies) aim to help create a safer environment for members of a target or oppressed community and to empower individuals and groups to eliminate barriers to access and equity (Burnes et al., 2010; Harper et al., 2013; Lewis et al., 2002). Many of these competency frameworks are based on feminist, multicultural, and social justice theoretical foundations (Burnes et al., 2010).

The framework for the ACA Advocacy Competencies (Lewis et al., 2002) is described along two dimensions (extent of client involvement and level of intervention/advocacy). The extent of student/client involvement refers to acting with or acting on behalf of the student/client. The level of intervention/advocacy is divided into three levels: (a) the student/client (microlevel), (b) school/community advocacy (macrolevel), and (c) the public arena (mesolevel). The intersection of the two student/client involvement domains and three levels of interventions creates six domains of advocacy: (a) client/student empowerment, (b) client/student advocacy, (c) community collaboration, (d) systems advocacy, (e) public information, (f) social/political advocacy.

The ACA Advocacy Competencies and Social Justice in Schools

Advocacy can happen in multiple settings. Ratts, DeKruyf, and Chen-Hayes (2007) provided examples of how to enact the ACA Advocacy Competencies in the school setting. They suggested that at the student/client level, school counselors advocate with and for students through empowerment and advocacy. They suggested that school counselors can empower students by delivering different trainings on tools for self-empowerment, such as making class presentations on communication skills, facilitating groups on bullying, and so on. Advocacy for the student may be enacted by the school counselor participating as a moderator in conversations between teachers and students in a way that maintains the safety of the individuals given the differential power dynamic. Ratts et al. suggested that at the school community level, the school counselor's role is that of an ally seeking systemic change in response to environmental barriers. The school counselor is called to take on a leadership role in disrupting the status quo that inhibits equal access to a quality education; these can be environmental and resource factors, such as harassment of LGBTQI+ youth. The public arena advocacy level involves education of the public and/or social/political systems. This level requires that school counselors educate the public on problems of access and inequities in the education system. Ratts et al. stated that this level of advocacy requires knowledge of systems and an ability to develop relationships with various constituents.

Advocacy in the LGBTQI+ Communities

In order to address advocacy issues in the LGBTQI+ community, advocates need to be well informed about the social justice issues impacting the community. According to Burnes et al. (2010), an understanding of the minority stress model (Meyer, 2003) is a good foundation for such understanding. The minority stress model explains the daily stressors that minorities face stemming from the systemic oppression that assaults these individuals through micro- and macroaggressions. With awareness and knowledge of these systemic stressors, the LGBTQI+ advocate works through the appropriate level of response based on the ACA Advocacy Competencies to address empowerment and advocacy for LGBTQI+ individuals and communities at the micro-, meso-, and macrosystem levels (Toporek, Lewis, & Crethar, 2009).

The latest version of the ALGBTIC competencies in counseling underscores the need to be informed about the issues faced by LGBTQI+ communities. Counselors need to have a comprehensive understanding of the nuances of developmental issues faced by individuals and families in these communities. They must be cognizant of the various intersections of identities and the impact of oppressive and marginalizing systems on human development, cultural viewpoints, career and lifestyle development, group interactions, professional ethical guidelines, mental health assessments, and research and program evaluations (Harper et al., 2013). These revised competencies add guidelines for working with ally individuals and intersex individuals. For guidelines on counseling and advocacy for intersex individuals, please refer to the ALGBTIC competency guidelines (Harper et al., 2013).

The ally competency guidelines address the counselor as ally and counseling of individuals who identify as allies. The guidelines for counselor as ally center on counselors' awareness and knowledge of issues faced by LGBTQI+ individuals and communities, such as the sociocultural, political, and economic climate that leads to institutional policies impacting LGBTQI+ individuals. Counselors are also encouraged to increase their awareness of their own similarities with and differences from LGBTQI+ individuals and communities by talking with others in the communities, reading histories of the communities, and reading personal narratives from members of the communities. These guidelines (Harper et al., 2013) also include recommendations for "supporting individuals' decisions about coming out" (p. 23). They also encourage a context for self-reflection, when to take action, and when to refrain from action. They provide a reminder that the process centers on the LGBTQI+ individual's experiences and needs and reminds well-meaning potential allies to reflect on their own sociopolitical context and the possible seductions and unintended impact of privileged actions.

Advocacy and Group Work

The Association for Specialists in Group Work has endorsed a set of competencies for multicultural and social justice principles in group work (Singh, Merchant, Skudrzyk, & Ingene, 2012) that addresses awareness of self and others, strategies and skills, and social justice advocacy. Some of the suggestions made for moving into social advocacy work include becoming aware of possibilities for community organizing and activism at the local, state, and national levels as well as identifying potential ways to provide group worker expertise. Group work counselors also participate in consciousness-raising groups related to issues of social justice; they should also initiate discussions and training opportunities that identify how personal statuses of privilege and oppression influence the group community (Singh et al., 2012).

In Sara's case, these guidelines would be helpful for her to implement. For example, she could use her privilege as a member of the dominant group at church to voice concerns and raise questions about the ways she (as a woman) and others are being marginalized in the church setting. She could also form an activist group of church members who want to address privilege and marginalization in the system of the church. She can also participate in social consciousness groups that will invite constant self-reflection on how incessant systems of privilege and oppression can intrude on her life and other people's lives.

Conclusion

The role of the counselor as ally of the LGBTQI+ community is an ethical obligation. However, it may be intimidating to understand how and when a counselor should serve as an advocate. By providing specific models, theories, and strategies, this chapter highlights multiple ways emerging allies can impact their clients, their local communities, the LGBTQI+ communities, and the larger society. New allies may be fearful of what their advocacy may cost; understanding where one fits as an ally in a group of oppressed people can also be intimidating. However, to stand back and do nothing in the face of inequality is to condone it. Inequality, homophobia, heterosexism, and monosexism impact all people—heterosexuals as well as affectional orientation and gender minorities. These attitudes restrict each person's expression while overtly damaging and oppressing those who do not fit the rigid gender and sexual roles prescribed by society. Martin Luther King, Jr., said it best: "Injustice anywhere is a threat to justice everywhere."

Questions for Further Discussion

1. What barriers does Sara face in developing as an ally?
2. What stage of ally development is Sara currently in? How would you support her further development in allying?
3. How does her own identity as a marginalized person (woman of color) help and hinder her ability to understand the LGBTQI+ experience?
4. How do the professional competencies (Multicultural Counseling Competencies, Counselors for Social Justice competencies, Association for Specialists in Group Work competencies) guide Sara in challenging and supporting her multidimensional identities as a person of color; cisgender, heterosexual female; developing ally; and counselor/counselor-in-training?
5. What is something great that an ally has done that had a real-world impact on LGBTQI+ people?

Resources

1. Read GLAAD's guide on how to be an ally at http://www.glaad.org/resources/ally.
2. Read the Human Rights Campaign's guide on how to be an ally at http://www.hrc.org/blog/how-to-be-an-lgbt-ally.
3. Read about the essential components of allyship at http://geneq.berkeley.edu/ally-ship.
4. Become familiar with the work of the Ally Coalition at http://theallycoalition.org/.
5. Surf the GSA Network website at https://gsanetwork.org/resources/creating-inclusive-gsas/straight-allies.

References

Asta, E. L., & Vacha-Haase, T. (2013). Heterosexual ally development in counseling psychologists: Experiences, training and advocacy. *The Counseling Psychologist, 41*, 493–529.

Burnes, T. R., Singh, A. A., Harper, A. J., Harper, B., Maxon-Kann, W., Pickering, D. L., . . . Hosea, J. (2010). American Counseling Association competencies for counseling with transgendered clients. *Journal of LGBT Issues in Counseling, 4*, 135–159. doi:10.1080/15538605.2010.524839

Collison, B. B., Osborne, J. L., Gray, L. A., House, R. M., Firth, J., & Lou, M. (1998). Preparing counselors for social action. In C. C. Lee & G. R. Walz (Eds.), *Social action: A mandate for counselors* (pp. 263–277). Alexandria, VA: American Counseling Association and ERIC Counseling and Student Services Clearinghouse.

Crethar, H. C., Bradley, L. J., Lewis, J., Toporek, R., & Tripp, F. (2006, April). *Promoting systemic change through advocacy competence.* Presentation at the American Counseling Association Conference & Expo, Montreal, Canada.

Edwards, K. E. (2006). Aspiring social justice ally identity development: A conceptual model. *NASPA Journal, 43*(4), 39–60. doi:10.2202/1949-6605.1722

Fabiano, P. M., Perkins, H. W., Berkowitz, A. D., Linkenbach, J., & Stark, C. (2003). Engaging men as social justice allies in ending violence against women: Evidence for a social norms approach. *Journal of American College Health, 52,* 105–112.

Harper, A., Finnerty, P., Martinez, M., Brace, A., Crethar, H. C., Loos, B., . . . Lambert, S. (2013). Association for Lesbian, Gay, Bisexual, and Transgender Issues in Counseling (ALGBTIC) competencies for counseling with lesbian, gay, bisexual, queer, questioning, intersex, and ally individuals. *Journal of LGBT Issues in Counseling, 7,* 2–43. doi:10.1080/15538605.2013.755444

Hatzenbuehler, M. L. (2011). The social environment and suicide attempts in lesbian, gay, and bisexual youth. *Pediatrics, 127,* 896–903.

Lewis, J., & Bradley, L. (Eds.). (2000). *Advocacy in counseling: Counselors, clients, and community.* Greensboro, NC: ERIC Clearinghouse on Counseling and Student Services.

Lewis, J. A., Arnold, M. S., House, R., & Toporek, R. L. (2002). *ACA advocacy competencies.* Retrieved from http://www.counseling.org/Resources/Competencies/Advocacy_Competencies.pdf

Meyer, I. H. (2003). Prejudice, social stress, and mental health in lesbian, gay, and bisexual status: Conceptual issues and research evidence. *Psychological Bulletin, 129,* 674–697. doi:10.1037/0033-2909.129.5.674

Munin, A., & Speight, S. L. (2010). Factors influencing the ally development of college students. *Equity and Excellence in Education, 43*(2), 249–264.

Persson, T. J., & Pfaus, J. G. (2015). Bisexuality and mental health: Future research directions. *Journal of Bisexuality, 15*(1), 82–98. doi:10.1080/15299716.2014.994694

Ratts, M. J., DeKruyf, L., & Chen-Hayes, S. F. (2007). The ACA advocacy competencies: A social justice advocacy framework for professional school counselors. *Professional School Counseling, 11*(2), 90–97. doi:10.53330/PSC.n.2010-11.90

Reason, R. D., & Broido, E. M. (2005). Issues and strategies for social justice allies (and the student affairs professionals who wish to encourage them). *New Directions for Student Services, 110,* 81–89.

Rostosky, S. S., Black, W. W., Riggle, E. D. B., & Rozenkrantz, D. (2015). Positive aspects of being a heterosexual ally to lesbian, gay, bisexual, and transgender (LGBT) people. *Journal of Orthopsychiatry.* Advance online publication. doi:10.1037/ort0000056

Roysircar, G. (2009). The big picture of advocacy. *Journal of Counseling & Development, 87,* 288–294.

Russell, S. T., & Joyner, K. (2001). Adolescent sexual orientation and suicide risk: Evidence from a national study. *American Journal of Public Health, 91,* 1276–1281.

Ryan, M., Broad, K. L., Walsh, C. F., & Nutter, K. L. (2013). Professional allies: The storying of allies to LGBTQ students on a college campus. *Journal of Homosexuality, 60,* 83–104.

Singh, A. A., Hays, D. G., & Watson, L. (2011). Strategies in the face of adversity: Resilience strategies of transgender individuals. *Journal of Counseling & Development, 89,* 20–27. doi:10.1002/j.1556-6678.2011.tb00057.x

Singh, A., Merchant, N., Skudrzyk, B., & Ingene, D. (2012). *Association for Specialists in Group Work: Multicultural and social justice competence principles for group workers.* Retrieved from https://static1.squarespace.com/static/55cea634e4b083e448c3dd50/t/55d3f911e4b0ac4433ebd4cd/1439955217809/ASGW_MC_SJ_Priniciples_Final_ASGW.pdf

Sue, D. W., Arredondo, P., & McDavis, R. J. (1994). Multicultural counseling competencies and standards: A call to the profession. *Journal of Counseling & Development, 70,* 477–486.

Toporek, R., Lewis, J., & Crethar, H. (2009). Promoting systemic change through ACA advocacy competencies. *Journal of Counseling & Development, 87,* 260–268. doi:10.1002/j.1556-6678.2009.tb00105.x

Utt, J. (2013, November 8). *So you call yourself an ally: 10 things allies need to know.* Retrieved from the *Everyday Feminism* website: http://everydayfeminism.com/2013/11/things-allies-need-to-know/

Glossary of Terms

Advocate (noun) a person who, on behalf of a marginalized group, works to educate others, confronts intolerance, and promotes social equity. (verb) to actively promote a specific cause; to work to educate others, confront intolerance, and promote social equity.

Affectional minority (noun) a person whose affectional orientation differs from that of the majority of other members of the surrounding society and its corresponding culture. This term also indicates a sense of marginalization experienced by the person who is not heterosexual. Sometimes referred to as **sexual minority,** although that can be a problematic term (see "Problematic Terms to Avoid").

Affectional orientation (noun) the direction in which one is predisposed to bond emotionally, physically, sexually, psychologically, and spiritually with others. This alternative term is meant to replace **sexual orientation** (see "Problematic Terms to Avoid"), which can overemphasize sexuality in the bonding and relationship process.

Affectional orientation variance (noun) an affectional orientation that differs from that of the majority of other members of the surrounding society and its corresponding culture.

Agender (adjective) describing a person who identifies as being without gender. This term reflects having a nonbinary gender identity (not male or female) or being gender neutral. A synonym of **neutrois.**

Allosexism (noun) behavior that permits preferential treatment of allosexual persons and discrimination and prejudice against asexual people, with the implicit assumption that allosexuality is the preferred or correct way of being.

Allosexual (adjective) describing a person who experiences sexual attraction to other persons. This term is an alternative to using *sexual* to describe people who are not asexual.

Ally (noun) a person who (a) has empathy for LGBTQI+ people, (b) provides support to a person or people who are LGBTQI+, and (c) identifies with a privileged category compared to the individuals or groups the person is supporting or advocating for. (verb) to act as a member of a privileged category in relation to those for whom one is advocating by (a) actively confronting bias and privilege both personally and in others; (b) believing that bias, prejudice, and discrimination against the LGBTQI+ population are issues that require social justice advocacy; and (c) participating in active advocacy for individuals and/or groups who identify as LGBTQI+. For example, a heterosexual or gay male could be an ally for a transgender person.

Androgyne (noun) a person who does not ascribe to culturally assigned gender roles in terms of gender expression and nonbinary identity.

Androgynous (adjective) see **androgyny**

Androgyny (noun) a form of gender expression that includes both or indeterminate culturally defined masculine or feminine traits.

Androsexual (adjective) describing a person who is attracted to males and/or masculinity. This term is typically used by persons who identify as genderqueer, as categories such as heterosexual or gay indicate bonding with someone of the opposite or same sex, which does not apply to genderqueer persons.

Aromantic (adjective) describing a person who feels little to no romantic desire and/or attraction to other people and lacks interest in being part of romantic relationships.

Asexual (adjective) describing a person who feels little or no sexual desire and/or attraction to other people and lacks interest in having a sexual relationship. Asexuality is recognized as an affectional orientation. Also known as "ace" in the asexual community.

Assigned sex (noun) see **assigned sex at birth**

Assigned sex at birth (noun) the sex that a person was interpreted to be at birth, typically by a medical professional, based on external physical sex characteristics (e.g., genitalia) that represent cultural concepts of male and female sex as well as a potential chromosomal analysis. Used most often to describe intersex persons.

Bi (adjective) see **bisexual**

Bias incident (noun) any act intended to harm and/or harass a person based on that person's demographic background and/or identity. In relation to LGBTQI+ persons, such incidents are typically due to affectional orientation and gender variance but can also be experienced due to another demographic (e.g., race/ethnicity, nationality, religion, or ability) or intersectional identity.

Bigender (adjective) describing people who experience two distinct genders within their identity, typically culturally assigned feminine and masculine.

Binary (noun) the classification of gender and/or affectional orientation into only two separate categories (e.g., masculine/feminine and heterosexual/gay), indicating that these are distinct and opposite ways of being.

Biphobia (noun) negative attitudes regarding bisexual individuals expressed through fear, aversion, anger, intolerance, and/or discomfort. Biphobia can result from a belief in bisexual stereotypes and/or discomfort with a nonbinary identity.

Bisexual (adjective) describing a person who is predisposed to bond emotionally, physically, sexually, psychologically, and spiritually with more than one sex or gender. Some use this identity to indicate bonding with both males and females, whereas others use this identity to indicate bonding with other gender identities beyond a male/female binary, including third-gender, genderqueer, and transgender persons. The attraction or interest is not necessarily equally split among these sexes or genders.

BlaQ (adjective) see **BlaQueer**

BlaQueer (adjective) describing a Black person who identifies intersectionally as a queer person.

Bottom surgery (noun) surgical intervention on one's genitals for the purposes of aligning one's body with one's gender identity and expression.

Butch (noun) a person who identifies with masculine cultural traits at a physical, sexual, mental, and/or emotional level. Although this term has been used in a derogatory manner, it has also been reclaimed as an affirmative identity. (adjective) describing someone who is butch.

Cisgender (adjective) describing a person whose gender identification matches that person's designated sex at birth. This term is meant to describe a non-transgender person.

Cisnormativity (noun) an assumption that all persons are cisgender, with an implicit assumption that the cisgender identity and cisgender people are superior to the transgender identity and transgender people.

Cissexism (noun) behavior that permits preferential treatment of cisgender persons and discrimination and prejudice against transgender, third-gender, and genderqueer people, with the implicit assumption that cisgender is the preferred or correct way of being. A synonym of **genderism.**

Closeted (adjective) describing a person who does not disclose their affectional orientation or gender identity to others. This lack of disclosure could be due to fear regarding the reaction of others, which could include rejection, loss of family and peer relationships, and/or loss of housing/employment.

Coming out (verb) a process in which a person identifies and accepts their own affectional orientation and/or gender variance and shares this identity with others. Coming out can be a partial, gradual, or lifelong process.

Constellation (noun) the structure of a polyamorous relationship (e.g., a couple with an additional partner, a person with two separate partners, or a group of four persons who partner with one another).

Cross-dresser (noun) a person who wears clothes and accessories that represent cultural concepts of another gender as a practice of gender expression. This alternative term is meant to replace **transvestite** (see "Problematic Terms to Avoid"), which has become associated with a sexual fetish and paraphilia identified by the *Diagnostic and Statistical Manual of Mental Disorders* as transvestic disorder.

Demisexual (adjective) describing a person who feels no sexual desire and/or attraction to other people unless the person experiences a strong emotional connection with that other person. This term is meant to indicate an identity along a continuum between asexual and allosexual.

Designated sex at birth (noun) the sex that a person was interpreted to be at birth, typically by a medical or birthing professional, based on a cursory inspection of external physical sex characteristics (e.g., genitalia) that represent cultural concepts of male and female sex. The designation of sex occurs prior to one's own self-identification of gender identity.

Differences of sex development (noun) a medical term used to describe individuals who are born intersex.

Disorders of sex development (noun) see **differences of sex development**

Diverse sexualities and genders (noun) a term referring to LGBTQI+ people as a group representing both affectional orientation and gender identity. A synonym of **gender and affectional minority; LGBTQI+;** and **marginalized orientations, gender identity, and intersex.**

Down low (adjective) describing a person, typically from within the African American community, who does not disclose their affectional orientation to others. This person may also live a heterosexual life in public, with heterosexual romantic and sexual relationships.

Drag (noun) the wearing of clothes and accessories that represent cultural concepts of another gender as a form of entertainment and performance.

Drag king (noun) see **drag queen**

Drag queen (noun) a person who wears clothes and accessories that represent cultural concepts of another gender as a form of entertainment and performance. A drag queen dresses in traditional female attire, whereas a drag king dresses in traditional male attire.

Ey/eir (pronouns) see **hir/ze**

Feminine of center (adjective) describing gender expression (as in feminine presenting) and gender identity as represented by one's own understanding of oneself, one's behavior, and how one relates to others in a culturally assigned feminine manner. Feminine of center is consistent with femme, transfeminine, submissive, and so on.

Feminine presenting (adjective) describing gender expression, evidenced by demeanor, body language, behavior, interests, activities, hairstyle, clothing, and accessories, that represents culturally defined feminine concepts.

Femme (noun) a person who identifies with feminine cultural traits at a physical, sexual, mental, and/or emotional level. (adjective) describing someone who is femme.

Fluid (adjective) an aspect of an identity, either affectional orientation, gender, or sexual behavior, that may shift and change over time within or between multiple options.

Fluidity (noun) see **fluid**

FtM/F2M (adjective) see **MtF/M2F**

Gay (adjective) describing a person who is predisposed to bond emotionally, physically, sexually, psychologically, and spiritually with someone of the same sex and/or gender. The term is most often used to refer to males who are predisposed to bond emotionally, physically, sexually, psychologically, and spiritually with other males, as in "gay men."

Gender (noun) the feelings, attitudes, and behavior associated with a person's sex, which typically represent cultural concepts of male and female sex. In many cultures, a third option is also recognized.

Gender affirming surgery (noun) see **gender confirmation surgery**

Gender and affectional minority (noun) LGBTQI+ people as a group, both representing affectional orientation and gender identity. A synonym of **diverse sexualities and genders; LGBTQI+;** and **marginalized orientations, gender identity, and intersex.**

Gender binary (noun) the classification of gender and sex into only two separate categories, masculine and feminine, indicating that these are distinct and opposite ways of being.

Gender confirmation surgery (noun) a set of surgical procedures that modify a person's body to reflect that person's gender identity. This term most often refers to top and/or bottom surgery but may also include surgery to modify secondary sex characteristics, such as face shape. The term is more affirming than **sex reassignment surgery** (see "Problematic Terms to Avoid").

Gender dysphoria (noun) a mental disorder as defined by the American Psychiatric Association's *Diagnostic and Statistical Manual of Mental Disorders, Fifth Edition.* The symptoms included are meant to encompass a transgender person's experiences in which intense distress is experienced over the mismatch between one's designated sex and gender identity. This is a controversial diagnosis, as it pathologizes gender variance and being transgender as a psychiatric illness. Some argue that the transgender experience would be better represented as a medical issue; others argue that its inclusion in the *Diagnostic and Statistical Manual of Mental Disorders* helps legitimize treatment in terms of gender confirmation surgery.

Gender expansive (adjective) describing a person who expands conventional notions of gender identity and expression beyond the binary of masculine and feminine. A synonym of **gender variant.**

Gender expression (noun) the external representation of one's gender identity, evidenced by demeanor, body language, behavior, interests, activities, hairstyle, clothing, and accessories. A synonym of **gender presentation.**

Gender fluid (adjective) describing how gender identity may shift and change over time within or among multiple options.

Gender identity (noun) a person's own feelings and sense surrounding being male, female, or transgender. Gender identity is expressed through how people label themselves and is typically reflected in their expression and presentation, which may reflect cultural concepts of male and female sex or a blending, as may be the case for androgynous or genderqueer persons.

Gender minority (noun) a person whose gender identity, in relation to their designated sex at birth, differs from that of the majority of other members of the surrounding society and its corresponding culture. This term also indicates a sense of marginalization experienced by the person who is gender nonconforming.

Gender-neutral (adjective) denoting unisex or all-inclusive gender quality (e.g., a gender-neutral bathroom or gender-neutral pronouns).

Gender-nonconforming (adjective) describing a person whose gender identity and gender presentation are not aligned with cultural expectations of masculine and feminine.

Gender-normative (adjective) describing a person whose gender identity and gender presentation are aligned with cultural expectations of masculine and feminine.

Gender orientation (noun) a person's own feelings and sense surrounding being male, female, or transgender. Gender orientation is expressed through how people label themselves and is typically reflected in their expression and presentation, which may reflect cultural concepts of male and female sex or a blending, as may be the case for androgynous or genderqueer persons. A synonym of **gender identity.**

Gender presentation (noun) the external representation of one's gender identity, evidenced by demeanor, body language, behavior, interests, activities, hairstyle, clothing, and accessories. A synonym of **gender expression.**

Gender role (noun) the set of societal and cultural norms that identify acceptable and desired behaviors associated with someone's sex, typically represented as male or female.

Gender variance (noun) see **gender variant**

Gender-variant (adjective) describing a person whose gender identity and expression differ beyond the binary of conventional notions of masculine and feminine. A synonym of **gender expansive.**

Genderism (noun) behavior that permits preferential treatment of cisgender persons and discrimination and prejudice against transgender, third-gender, and genderqueer people, with the implicit assumption that cisgender is the preferred or correct way of being. A synonym of **cissexism.**

Genderqueer (adjective) describing a person whose gender identity is not reflected by the binary of male or female. This is also used as an umbrella term, similar to *third gender* and *transgender,* to reflect people who are gender nonconforming and/or nonbinary. Genderqueer persons may think of themselves as a combination of male and female (e.g., bigender), no gender (e.g., agender), multiple genders (e.g., pangender, omnigender), genderfluid, or third gender. Similar to *queer,* this term reclaims a once derogatory term as an affirmative identity. Be aware, however, that some persons still find the term *queer* offensive.

Gynephilic (adjective) see **gynesexual**

Gynesexual (adjective) describing a person who is attracted to females and/or femininity. This term is typically used by persons who identify as genderqueer, as categories such as heterosexual or gay indicate bonding with someone of the opposite or same sex, which does not apply to genderqueer persons.

He/his (pronouns) terms used to describe association with a male gender–identified person. These are based on a person's preference. Always ask gender-nonconforming persons what pronouns they utilize.

Heteronormativity (noun) an assumption that all persons are heterosexual, with an implicit assumption that the heterosexual identity and heterosexual people are superior to the LGBTQI+ identity and LGBTQI+ people.

Heterosexism (noun) behavior that permits preferential treatment of heterosexual persons and discrimination and prejudice toward affectional minorities or queer people, with the implicit assumption that heterosexuality is the preferred or correct way of being.

Heterosexual (adjective) describing a person who is predisposed to bond emotionally, physically, sexually, psychologically, and spiritually with someone of the opposite sex or gender.

Hir/ze (pronouns) terms used to describe association with a third-gender-identified person. These are based on a person's preference. Always ask gender-nonconforming persons what pronouns they utilize.

Homophobia (noun) an umbrella term for negative attitudes regarding sexual minorities or queer individuals expressed through fear, aversion, anger, intolerance, and/or discomfort. Homophobia can result from a belief in gay stereotypes and/or discomfort with same-sex relationships and sexuality. The term is sometimes used to describe negative attitudes toward any member of the LGBTQI+ community, although *biphobia* and *transphobia* specifically address these other populations. In the past, homophobia has been overly associated with extreme cases of fear and hate crimes, despite its definition encompassing a range of negative attitudes. A synonym of **homoprejudice.**

Homoprejudice (noun) negative attitudes regarding sexual minorities or queer individuals expressed through fear, aversion, anger, intolerance, and/or discomfort. Homoprejudice can result from a belief in gay stereotypes and/or discomfort with same-sex relationships and sexuality. A synonym of **homophobia.**

Hormone replacement therapy (noun) a medical process, typically for transgender or gender variant persons, in which sex hormones are administered and carefully monitored to help transition persons from their designated sex at birth to a gender expression and presentation that is more congruent, authentic, and in harmony with their gender identity. This can involve the administration of hormone blockers and sex hormones in order to feminize or masculinize one's body.

In drag (adjective) see **drag**

In the closet (adjective) see **closeted**

Intersectionality (noun) interdependent and overlapping demographic social categories (e.g., affectional orientation, age, disability, ethnicity/race, gender/gender orientation, immigration status, indigenous identity, religion/spirituality, socioeconomic status). These overlapping categories can carry varying and more complex experiences of marginalization and/or privilege.

Intersex (adjective) describing a person whose sex development in utero differs from the expected sex presentation at birth, resulting in ambiguous or both male and female chromosomes, hormones, internal/external sexual organs, and/or secondary sex characteristics. A synonym of **disorders of sex development/differences of sex development.**

Latinx (adjective) a gender-neutral descriptor for a person who identifies as Latin American. This term is a replacement for *Latina* and *Latino*, which carry connotations of female and male sex, respectively.

Lesbian (noun) a female-identified person who is predisposed to bond emotionally, physically, sexually, psychologically, and spiritually with other women. (adjective) describing someone who is lesbian.

LGBTQI+ (adjective) an acronym used to describe those with affectional orientation and gender variance. It represents lesbian, gay, bisexual, transgender, queer, intersex, plus other identities, including but not limited to questioning, asexual, allied, pansexual/polysexual, and two-spirited. A synonym of **diverse sexualities and genders; gender and affectional minority;** and **marginalized orientations, gender identity, and intersex.**

Marginalized orientations, gender identity, and intersex (noun) LGBTQI+ people as a group, representing both affectional orientation and gender identity. A synonym of **diverse sexualities and genders, LGBTQI+,** and **gender and affectional minority.**

Masculine of center (adjective) describing gender expression (as in masculine present-ing) and gender identity as represented by one's own understanding of oneself, one's behavior, and how one relates to others in a culturally assigned masculine manner. Masculine of center is consistent with butch, transmasculine, aggressive, boi, and so on.

Masculine presenting (adjective) describing gender expression, evidenced by demeanor, body language, behavior, interests, activities, hairstyle, clothing, and accessories, that represents culturally defined masculine concepts.

Men who have sex with men (noun) males who participate in sexual behavior with other males. This term differentiates between affectional identity and sexual behavior. It is most frequently used in the field of medicine and HIV/AIDS education and prevention.

Misgender (verb) to refer to a person by pronouns and other gendered words that do not align with that person's gender identity. Most often utilized in the context of transgen-der identity.

Monogamous (adjective) see **monogamy**

Monogamy (noun) a relationship practice of committing to one person at a time for pur-poses of bonding.

Monosexism (noun) behavior that permits preferential treatment of monosexual persons and discrimination and prejudice against nonbinary people, with the implicit assump-tion that monosexual is the preferred or correct way of being.

Monosexual (adjective) describing a person who is predisposed to bond emotionally, phys-ically, sexually, psychologically, and spiritually with people of only one sex or gender.

MtF/M2F (adjective) an abbreviation describing a transition for a transgender person, where the first letter indicates the designated sex at birth and the second letter indicates the individual's gender identity and expression. FtM/F2M indicates a female transition to male, whereas MtF/M2F indicates a male transition to female.

Mx. (noun) a gender-neutral descriptor for use with a surname. This term replaces *Mr.*, *Mrs.*, and *Ms.*, which carry connotations of male or female sex.

Ne/nir (pronouns) see **hir/ze**

Neutrois (adjective) describing a person who identifies as being of a neutral gender. This term reflects having a nonbinary gender identity (not male or female) or being gender neutral. A synonym of **agender.**

Nonbinary (adjective) describing the classification of gender and/or affectional orienta-tion into more than two categories that are conceptualized as not separate and distinct.

Non-monosexual (noun) a person who is predisposed to bond emotionally, physi-cally, sexually, psychologically, and spiritually with people of more than one sex or gender. This term describes persons who identify as bisexual, pansexual, and polysexual.

Omnigender (adjective) describing a person whose gender identity reflects multiple gender identities, expressions, and presentations. A synonym of **pangender** and **polygender.**

Omnisexual (adjective) describing a person who is predisposed to bond emotionally, physically, sexually, psychologically, and spiritually with others regardless of sex or gender. A synonym of **pansexual.**

Open (adjective) see **out**

Out (adjective) describing a person who has disclosed their affectional orientation or gen-der identity to others. This could be a partial or gradual process and may not occur in certain contexts out of fear of rejection and discrimination. See **coming out.**

Out of the closet (adjective) see **out**

Outing (noun) unwanted and/or involuntary disclosure of a person's affectional orienta-tion or gender identity.

Pangender (adjective) describing a person whose gender identity reflects multiple gender identities, expressions, and presentations. A synonym of **omnigender** and **polygender.**

Pansexual (adjective) describing a person who is predisposed to bond emotionally, physically, sexually, psychologically, and spiritually with others regardless of sex or gender. A synonym of **omnisexual.**

Pass (verb) see **passing**

Passing (adjective) describing (a) a transgender person who is perceived and/or accepted as their gender of identity or (b) an affectional minority who is perceived and/or accepted as heterosexual.

Polyamorous (adjective) see **polyamory**

Polyamory (noun) a relationship practice of being romantically involved with and/or committing to more than one person at a time for purposes of bonding.

Polygender (adjective) describing a person whose gender identity reflects multiple gender identities, expressions, and presentations. A synonym of **omnigender, pangender,** and **polygender.**

Polysexual (adjective) describing a person who is predisposed to bond emotionally, physically, psychologically, and spiritually with many different sexes or genders. The attraction and interest are not necessarily equally split among these sexes or genders.

Pomosexual (adjective) describing a person who challenges, avoids, or denies alignment with any affectional orientation label.

Queer (adjective) (a) describing a person whose gender identity and affectional orientation are not reflected in traditional heterosexual or gay labels and categories; or (b) an umbrella term used to describe the entire community of LGBTQI+ persons, as in the "queer community." This term reclaims a once derogatory term as an affirmative identity. Be aware, however, that some persons still find the term *queer* offensive.

Queer community (noun) an umbrella term used to describe the entire community of LGBTQI+ persons, reflecting a rejection of conventional gender identity and affectional orientation. This term reclaims a once derogatory term as an affirmative identity. Be aware, however, that some persons still find the term *queer* offensive.

Questioning (adjective) describing a person who is not sure about or is actively exploring their affectional orientation and/or gender identity. (verb) to be unsure about or actively exploring one's affectional orientation and/or gender identity.

Relationship systems (noun) a desire for and consensual practice of intimate relationships in a particular context, either monogamous or polyamorous, with or without sexual intimacy (as may be the case for some asexuals).

Romantic attraction (noun) an experience of affinity for another person that directs the wish to participate in intimate behavior (e.g., flirting, dating, commitment). Romantic attraction is often conflated with other types of attraction, including sexual, physical, emotional, and spiritual attraction.

Same-gender-loving (adjective) a term used most often in the African American community to reflect a person who is predisposed to bond emotionally, physically, psychologically, and spiritually with people of the same sex or gender.

Sex (noun) a classification of a person as male or female, typically assigned at birth based on a cursory examination by a medical or birthing professional.

Sexism (noun) behavior that permits preferential treatment of one sex (typically male) and discrimination and prejudice against another sex (typically female), with the implicit assumption that one sex (typically male) is the preferred or correct way of being.

Sexual assignment surgery (noun) a set of surgical procedures that modify a person's body to assign a gender in the case of a person being intersex, having ambiguous or both male and female genitalia. Although doctors often recommend that it occur shortly after birth and throughout childhood, this is controversial, as it does not require the consent of the child (just the guardian). Current recommendations by intersex advocacy organizations and the American Counseling Association are that sexual assignment surgery wait until the child is old enough to consent.

Sexual attraction (noun) an experience of affinity for another person that directs the wish to participate in physical intimate behavior (e.g., kissing, touching, intercourse). Sexual attraction is often conflated with other types of attraction, including romantic, emotional, and spiritual attraction.

Sexual behavior (noun) a person's sexual practices that usually involve kissing, touching, stimulation of genitalia, and intercourse, as well as other erotic behaviors designed to increase sexual arousal and satisfaction. This term is often used in medical and HIV/ AIDS education and prevention, as in "risky sexual behavior," which involves having unprotected sex, having multiple sexual partners, having sex while under the influence of alcohol or drugs, and so on.

Sexual orientation change efforts (noun) methods utilized by faith-based and secular organizations in an attempt to convert a lesbian, gay, bisexual, or queer (LGBQ) person to heterosexual.

Sexuality (noun) broad feelings, thoughts, experiences, and expressions surrounding sex, attraction, sensuality, sexual behavior, and preferred activities.

She/her (pronouns) terms used to describe association with a female gender–identified person. These are based on a person's preference. Always ask gender-nonconforming persons what pronouns they utilize.

Social transition (noun) the process of moving from a designated sex at birth to a gender expression and presentation congruent, authentic, and in harmony with one's gender identity. This coming out process may be gradual or planned for one specific time. A social transition involves gender presentation and expression, which involves demeanor, body language, behavior, interests, activities, hairstyle, clothing, and accessories. It also may involve a name change, with gender and name changes on legal documents.

Third gender (noun) a gender identity not reflected by the binary of male or female. (adjective) (a) describing a person whose gender identity is not reflected by the binary of male or female; (b) describing the societies, both historic and modern, that have three or more recognized gender identities; or (c) an umbrella term, similar to *genderqueer* and *transgender,* that reflects people who are gender nonconforming and/or have nonbinary identities.

Top surgery (noun) surgical intervention on one's chest or breasts for the purposes of aligning one's body with one's gender identity and expression.

Trans (noun) a person whose gender identity does not match their designated sex at birth. This term is inclusive of binary (male/female) and nonbinary (genderqueer) identities. The term was sometimes expressed in the past as *trans**, as some persons use *trans* as an abbreviation for *transman* and *transwoman.* As a result, this term may be used in a confusing manner. (adjective) describing a person whose gender identity does not match their designated sex at birth.

Transgender (adjective) (a) describing a person whose gender identity does not match their designated sex at birth or (b) an umbrella term for both binary (male/female) and nonbinary (genderqueer) identities whose gender identity and designated sex at birth are incongruent. Some transgender persons will identify as genderqueer, whereas some may identify as transmen or transwomen. Some others will identify simply as male or female.

Transgender man (noun) a transgender person who wishes to identify as male while recognizing and/or honoring his transgender identity. A transgender man's gender identity is male, but he was designated as female at birth.

Transgender woman (noun) a transgender person who wishes to identify as female while recognizing and/or honoring her transgender identity. A transgender woman's gender identity is female, but she was designated as male at birth.

Transition (noun) the process of moving from a designated sex at birth to a gender expression and presentation congruent, authentic, and in harmony with one's gender identity. This coming out process may be gradual or planned for one specific time. It may involve a social transition (e.g., involving demeanor, body language, behavior, interests, activities, hairstyle, clothing, and accessories, name change, legal documents) and/or a physical transition (e.g., involving hormones, gender confirmation/affirming surgery). (verb) to undergo such a transition.

Transman (noun) see **transgender man**

Transphobia (noun) negative attitudes regarding transgender individuals expressed through fear, aversion, anger, intolerance, and/or discomfort. Transphobia can result from a belief in transgender stereotypes and/or discomfort with nonbinary gender identification and affectional orientation.

Transwoman (noun) see **transgender woman**

Two-spirit(ed) (noun) an indigenous/Native person to the Americas who embraces a third gender, which represents both masculine and feminine spirits in one person. This person's identity can involve both affectional orientation and gender variance. Two-spirited persons were historically valued, respected, and honored for their spiritual and social roles in a tribe. (adjective) describing someone who is two-spirit(ed).

Ve/vis (pronouns) see **hir/ze**

Women who have sex with women (noun) females who participate in sexual behavior with other females. This term differentiates between affectional identity and sexual behavior. It is most frequently used in the field of medicine and HIV/AIDS education and prevention.

Problematic Terms to Avoid

Biological sex (noun) a medicalized term indicating classification as female or male based on hormonal, chromosomal, and anatomical indicators. This term is problematic, as biology and genetics do not always result in a concordant and clear sex presentation, as in the case of intersex persons. It is also problematic because it undermines the role of the gendered brain and/or gender identity, which may not match these physiological indicators. It also suggests that transgender persons wish to move against their biology, when it is very likely that something biological or physiological is causing their gender variation.

Biologically female (adjective) see **biological sex**

Biologically male (adjective) see **biological sex**

Born a man/woman (adverb) a phrase used to indicate someone's designated sex at birth. This term is problematic for the same reason *biological sex* is. In addition, people are born as babies, not as men or women.

Genetic sex (noun) see **biological sex**

Genetically female (adjective) see **biological sex**

Genetically male (adjective) see **biological sex**

Hermaphrodite (noun) an outdated term describing an intersex person, or a person whose sex development in utero differs from the expected sex presentation at birth, resulting in ambiguous or both male and female chromosomes, hormones, internal/external sexual organs, and/or secondary sex characteristics. This term is medically problematic, as the word was originally meant to indicate two complete sets of genitalia, which intersex persons do not have. Historically the term was used to describe intersex people as oddities or freaks and used to stigmatize.

Homosexual (adjective) an outdated term describing a person who is predisposed to bond emotionally, physically, psychologically, and spiritually with someone of the same sex and/or gender. This term is problematic because it has been used in numerous historical, medical, and religious contexts to denote a marginalizing, pathological, immoral, and negative identity.

Lifestyle (noun) a derogatory term when used to describe affectional orientation or gender identity, reflecting it as a choice. For example, heterosexual persons are described as having lives, but LGBTQI+ people are described as having lifestyles.

Post-op (adjective) see **pre-op**

Pre-op (adjective) an outdated term previously used to describe the status of a transgender person's surgical transition. This term is problematic because many transgender persons may not wish to transition surgically. Use of this term suggests that a transgender person must have surgery to have a valid transgender identity.

Same-sex attraction (noun) an outdated term previously used to describe sexual attraction to someone of the same sex. This term is problematic because it is used in a context to represent only sexual attraction rather than bonding and relationships. It has also been used in numerous historical, medical, and religious contexts in a marginalizing, pathological, immoral, and negative manner.

Sex change (noun) an outdated term previously used to describe gender confirmation, gender affirming, or sex reassignment surgery. This term is problematic because it suggests that a person is changing their sex rather than aligning it with an already-existing gender identity. Use of this term suggests that a transgender person must have surgery to transition to the sex of their gender identity.

Sex reassignment surgery (noun) a medical term describing a set of surgical procedures that modify a person's body to reflect that person's gender identity. The term most often refers to top and/or bottom surgery but may also include surgery to modify secondary sex characteristics, such as face shape. A synonym of **gender confirmation surgery/gender affirming surgery,** which are more affirming terms.

Sexual minority (noun) a person whose affectional orientation differs from that of the majority of other members of the surrounding society and its corresponding culture. This term also indicates a sense of marginalization experienced by the person who is not heterosexual. This can be a problematic term because it puts all of the focus on a person's sexual life, similar to the term **sexual orientation.**

Sexual orientation (noun) the direction in which one is predisposed to bond emotionally, physically, sexually, psychologically, and spiritually with others. This term is problematic because it focuses solely on the sexual aspect of a person's relationship.

Sexual preference (noun) a derogatory term when used to describe affectional orientation or gender identity, reflecting it as a choice.

Sexuality variance (noun) an affectional orientation that differs from that of the majority of other members of the surrounding society and its corresponding culture. This term also indicates a sense of marginalization experienced by the person who is not heterosexual. This can be a problematic term because it puts all of the focus on the person's sexual life, similar to the term **sexual orientation.**

Straight (adjective) describing a person whose affectional orientation is heterosexual. This term is problematic because it suggests that non-heterosexuals are the opposite of straight, which is crooked, twisted, or wrong in some manner.

Transgender (noun) a term that has been incorrectly used to describe a transgender person, such as, "Mark is a transgender." This is not an accurate use of the term. It is similar to saying "Mark is a gay."

Transgendered (adjective) a term that has been incorrectly used to describe a transgender person, such as, "Sue is transgendered." This is not an accurate term or accurate usage. It is similar to saying "Sue is gayed."

Transsexual (noun) an older medical and psychological term for *transgender*. It was used to describe a person who desired to transition socially, medically, and/or surgically. Although this term is not utilized as a synonym of *transgender* or as a modern term in the community, some persons still use this as an identity. Never use this term unless a person directly reports identifying with it. A transsexual man's gender identity is male but was designated female at birth. A transsexual woman's gender identity is female but was designated male at birth.

Transvestite (noun) an outdated term used to describe a person who wears clothes and accessories that represent cultural concepts of another gender in order to derive pleasure. This term has now been replaced by the term *cross-dresser*, which reflects someone who dresses in another gender's clothing as a form of gender expression. In the past, *transvestite* as a term was confused with *transgender* and *transsexual*. It has also become stigmatized, as it has become associated with a sexual fetish. It is also highly pathologized as a paraphilia identified by the *Diagnostic and Statistical Manual of Mental Disorders* as transvestic disorder.

Index

Figures are indicated by "f" following the page number.

(Continued)

Androgyny, 360
Androsexual person, 360
Anjaree, 135
Anxiety
    Black gay men and, 276
    Caucasian asexual individuals and, 255
    experiences of, 202–203, 220
    fear of affectional orientation-based violence and, 178
    gay males throughout life span and, 158–159
    with intimacy, 154
    minority stressors and. *See* Minority stressors
    parents of intersex child and, 245
    queer people of color and, 274
    religion and, 299–300, 335
    stigma and, 78–79
    surgical transition and, 195
    therapies for, 103, 133
    transgender persons seeking mental health services for, 193
APA Task Force, 89, 90–91
Argentina, gender identity in, 188
Aromantic persons, 253, 360
Arseneau, J. R., 110
Art therapies, 103
Asexual persons, 251–258
    bias experiences of, 253–255
    case study, 251–252
    counseling of, 255–256
    counselor attitudes and belief awareness on, 251
    defined, 8, 252, 360
    differences, awareness of, 252–253, 256
    mental health challenges of, 255, 257
    physical health challenges of, 255
    prevalence, 254
Asexual Visibility Education Network (AVEN), 252, 256
Asian Americans
    collectivism and conformity of, 279–280
    coming out process for, 66
    complementarity and, 279
    shame and, 280
    stigma, impact on, 279
Assertiveness training, 293
ASSET (Affirmative Supportive Safe and Empowering Talk), 44
Assigned sex at birth, 8–9, 194, 217, 246, 346, 351, 360
Association for Lesbian, Gay, Bisexual, and Transgender Issues in Counseling (ALGBTIC)
    Competencies Taskforce, 117
    on competency standards, 4, 104, 117, 344–345, 351, 355
    on empowerment, 114
    on internalized heterosexism, 235
    on intersex counseling, 245–246
    on transgender counseling, 197
Association for Multicultural Counseling and Development, 4–5, 5*f*
Association for Specialists in Group Work, 6–7, 355
Association for Spiritual, Ethical, and Religious Values in Counseling, 298–299

Association of Welcoming and Affirming Baptists, 307
Asta, E. L., 347–348
Attachment-based therapies, 103
Attitude and beliefs awareness of counselors
    of adulthood experiences, 49
    for affirmative counseling competency, 109, 113–114, 235–236
    on allyship, 117–118, 343, 347–348, 352–353
    of asexual persons, 251
    of bi/pan/poly persons, 171, 179
    competency self-check, 3, 7–9
    of developmental conceptualizations, 31
    of disaffirming therapy, 87
    of evidence-based practices, 97, 103–104
    of gay men, 151
    of heternormativity, 53–54
    of identity development, 61
    of immigrant LGBTQI+, 285
    of intersex persons, 241
    of lesbians, 129
    multicultural competency and, 7–9
    of physical and mental health challenges, 75
    of queer-identified persons, 213, 222
    of queer people of color, 273
    of questioning orientation, 227, 231–232, 237
    on religion and spirituality, 297, 300–302, 313, 329, 336
    of science of orientation, 21
    self-awareness, 159–161
    of transgender persons, 183
    of two-spirits, 259
    of youth LGBTQI+ development, 41
Attraction
    asexual experience of, 253
    biological basis for, 22–23
    continuum of, 216
    defined, 366, 367, 369
Austin, A., 201
Authenticity
    of counselors, 115, 200–201, 219, 222, 265
    empowerment and, 65–66, 80
    identity development and, 50, 57, 159, 163, 216, 275, 334
    Native Americans on, 261–263, 264
    for queer persons, 221
    transitioning and, 185–186
AVEN (Asexual Visibility Education Network), 252, 256
Aversion therapies, 90–91

B

Baltrinic, Eric R., 227
Baptist religion, 307
Barreto, David, 285
Bartlett, P., 155
Bartoli, E., 317, 318
Baxter, R., 332
Becoming out, 265–266

C

(Continued)

F

G

H

I

N

Y

Z